MASTERPLOTS II

POETRY SERIES
REVISED EDITION

MASTERPLOTS II

POETRY SERIES
REVISED EDITION

5

Listening to the Music of Arsenio Rodriguez–
On My First Son

Editor, Revised Edition
PHILIP K. JASON

Project Editor, Revised Edition
TRACY IRONS-GEORGES

Editors, Supplement
JOHN WILSON   **PHILIP K. JASON**

Editor, First Edition
FRANK N. MAGILL

SALEM PRESS

Pasadena, California   Hackensack, New Jersey

Editor in Chief: Dawn P. Dawson

Project Editor: Tracy Irons-Georges	*Research Supervisor:* Jeffry Jensen
Production Editor: Cynthia Beres	*Research Assistant:* Jeff Stephens
Copy Editor: Lauren Mitchell	*Acquisitions Editor:* Mark Rehn

Some of the essays in this work originally appeared in *Masterplots II, Poetry Series*, edited by Frank N. Magill (Pasadena, Calif.: Salem Press, Inc., 1992), and in *Masterplots II, Poetry Series Supplement*, edited by John Wilson and Philip K. Jason (Pasadena, Calif.: Salem Press, Inc., 1998).

∞ The paper used in these volumes conforms to the American National Standard for Permanence of Paper for Printed Library Materials, Z39.48-1992 (R1997).

Library of Congress Cataloging-in-Publication Data
Masterplots II. Poetry series.— Rev. ed. / editor, Philip K. Jason ; project editor, Tracy Irons-Georges
    p. ; cm.
    Rev. ed.: Masterplots two / Frank Northen Magill, 1992-1998.
    Includes bibliographical references and indexes.
    ISBN 1-58765-037-1 (set : alk. paper) — ISBN 1-58765-042-8 (vol. 5 : alk. paper) —
    1. Poetry — Themes, motives. I. Title: Masterplots two. II. Title: Masterplots 2. III. Jason, Philip K., 1941-   . IV. Irons-Georges, Tracy.

PN1110.5 .M37 2002
809.1—dc21

            2001055059

First Printing

TABLE OF CONTENTS

TABLE OF CONTENTS

TABLE OF CONTENTS

MASTERPLOTS II

POETRY SERIES
REVISED EDITION

LISTENING TO THE MUSIC OF ARSENIO RODRIGUEZ IS MOVING CLOSER TO KNOWLEDGE

Author: Victor Hernandez Cruz (1949-   )
Type of poem: Narrative
First published: 1982, in *By Lingual Wholes*

The Poem

Victor Hernandez Cruz, who was born in Puerto Rico, grew up in New York City and remains in the forefront of the "Nuyorican" poetry scene that began developing in the late 1960's. "Listening to the Music of Arsenio Rodriguez Is Moving Closer to Knowledge" salutes Afro-Cuban music and the great musician in its title, as well as those who love this music. Rodriguez was a blind percussionist, player of the *tres* (a small nine-stringed guitar), composer, and bandleader. His impact on the mambo style in Cuba in the 1930's was immeasurable, and he was responsible for the mambo craze that took the Northeastern United States by storm in the early 1950's. In New York City, the Caribbean Hispanic community enjoys Afro-Cuban music under the general rubric of salsa. Nuyorican poets such as Hernandez Cruz, Sandra María Esteves, and Pedro Pietri are close to their musical culture; the study *The Latin Tinge* (1979) by John Storm Roberts offers valuable insights into the character and popularity of salsa.

Hernandez Cruz has written a free-verse poem of five stanzas that dispenses with nearly all punctuation. His speaker raves about the influence of Arsenio Rodriguez's music and ridicules those "researchers" who would attempt to study the results of its impact. The stuff of knowledge is in the music; to study its aftereffects—the "puddles of water" that the listeners have become—is inane.

The speaker shares a humorous moment with a friend who also deeply loves listening and dancing to Arsenio Rodriguez; they seem to laugh at those who can only focus on "the puddles of water/ that we have turned into/ all over your room." Rodriguez's music causes the people to melt; even Doña Flores comes to the room from a neighboring apartment to enjoy the experience. All are so strongly affected by the rhythms and sounds that liquefying is the only possible response. The water they become is warm and "good." The music from the hi-fi could be said to wipe them out.

The imagery of stanza 4 has a surreal quality. The air opens, curtainlike, and "whistles/ in the thousands of afternoons/ that everybody is/ nervously plucking." The people undergo a metamorphosis as music propels them toward a safe haven for expressing the freedom that dancing provides. Ultimately, everything in them rises to meet the *son*, a dance rhythm that predated the rumba of the mid-1920's.

In stanza 5, "explorers" and researchers are one: They are incapable of understanding the magical power of the musical spirit and drive of Arsenio Rodriguez. They ask feebly at the close of the poem if it has rained and whether the windows are open, because they can find no one to explain the water on the floor.

Forms and Devices

Hernandez Cruz writes poems that mingle allusions and direct references to salsa and Latino culture, using speech patterns and idioms that are popular among Puerto Ricans in New York. He uses metaphor conventionally to illustrate that music allows one to attain knowledge and self-esteem. Arsenio Rodriguez's music is as magical, mystical, and vital as life-sustaining water. Its damage is constructive, not negative; here Hernandez Cruz reverses the usual meaning of the word "damage" in keeping with common practice in African American and Northeastern Latino jargon, in which "bad" means very good.

When Rodriguez plays the tres, the listeners absorb the music by allowing his playing of their sensibilities to be the creative force of the music itself. That they are all "nervously plucking" means that they are approaching wisdom. The adverbial adjective "transformationally" is mock-intellectual slang.

The predominant figurative device used by Hernandez Cruz in this poem is little known to non-Hispanic people. It is "Spanglish," a deliberate form of slang that blends Spanish and English words or phrases, resulting in a colorful idiom. The poem contains three phrases that could be considered Spanglish: "to *liquidarse*," or liquefy; "flowers in the wind/ who know no *bossordomos*"; and "to *dance el son*," to dance the *son* rhythm. Hernandez Cruz himself may have coined *bossordomos* as a slanglike expression centered on the word *sordo*, meaning deaf.

Note that the first and third phrases use the English infinitive "to" in order to make the phrase. For the third phrase, one would say *danzon el son* or *bailar el son* in formal Spanish. The effect achieved by Spanglish is a tongue-in-cheek reconciliation of the two languages. It is a product of improvisation, and the improvisation that distinguishes music and language throughout the Americas is a creative force that ensures and sustains a culture's survival.

Hernandez Cruz uses a figure of speech known as metonymy when he says "Listen to the box." The box is the hi-fi set or radio transmitting the music, which is what Hernandez Cruz actually wants the reader to hear; it is the immediate source of the "damage" that Rodriguez's music creates for the benefit of the mind, body, and soul. Magical and surrealistic images characterize stanza 4, beginning with the air that whistles as it opens. The poet uses hyberbole when he speaks of "the thousands of afternoons" of listening, dancing, and living with the music. The wordplay of "transformationally swimming" reaffirms that the listeners are moved "to where it is safe to dance/ like flowers in the wind."

Themes and Meanings

The central feature of "Listening to the Music of Arsenio Rodriguez Is Moving Closer to Knowledge," from the title to the final line ("Has it rained?"), is its light-heartedness and sense of whimsy. Some things, it says, such as sensuous music, cannot by analyzed; they should simply be experienced. If one is not capable of experiencing the music directly, one is simply not going to understand it.

One moves closer to awareness, self-worth, and knowledge through Arsenio Rodriguez's music because its power to liquefy makes one feel a union of water and knowledge. The intrinsic qualities of warmth and passion in the music have a special appeal to the Caribbean Latino sensibility.

The poem's vivid irony lies in the comparison of the researchers' scrutiny of the pools of water with the knowledge the speaker and his friends gain from directly experiencing the music. The poem satirizes the academicians' preoccupation with the puddles, since they are unaware of the water's essence and intangible qualities. Theirs is the kind of intellect that cannot rise to "*dance el son.*" The neighbors, represented by Doña Flores, love the music and willingly liquefy under its spell. *Flores* means flowers, and, as Mrs. Flores is affected, so are the flowers in stanza 4 that "dance/ . . . in the wind." The poem's organic spontaneity creates a bridge in stanza 3 between Flores and flowers—the people, who are lively and beautiful, and the metaphorical essence and spirit of the people. The water is warm because it is those who are alive in their exultation who are transformed.

The ending of the poem leaves the explorer-researchers seeking answers and understanding to absurd questions. They have missed the beauty and truth of the music of Arsenio Rodriguez: They will never be wise.

Ron Welburn

A LITANY FOR SURVIVAL

Author: Audre Lorde (1934-1992)
Type of poem: Lyric
First published: 1978, in *The Black Unicorn*

The Poem

"A Litany for Survival" is a short poem in free verse containing three dense stanzas and a concluding three-line stanza. The title refers to a type of communal prayer involving alternating speakers, usually a leader and a congregation of petitioners. The form of the poem enacts the title's scene: The lead speaker begins the prayer, directly addressing the other petitioners yet speaking as if also one of the petitioners. The first two stanzas could be delivered by the leader's solitary voice, as both stanzas give prolonged descriptions of the petitioners' needs and circumstances. The petitioners' multiple voices then deliver the third stanza, which proceeds in parallel phrases with succinct repetition similar to the rhythmic verses that a congregation would chant in unison. The leader's and the petitioners' voices blend together in the concluding stanza in which a resolution is given for the grave situation that has prompted the ceremony.

As in most ceremonies in which prayer is offered, the petitioners recognize their own insignificance and their defenselessness in relation to powers greater than themselves. They know that those with greater power desire to terrorize them into deathly silence—a silence that will erase their memories and extinguish their children's dreams for the future. Although the petitioners face their own obliteration, their prayer does not, as prayers normally do, request divine intervention. Engaging in the communal ceremony represented by the poem is itself a means of resisting the will of the powerful. The act of self-expression and the communal sharing of their own desires, all of which are embedded in their meditation, enable the petitioners to resist those who desire their defeat.

The vocality of the poem derives from the oral literary traditions of Africa. Audre Lorde lures the reader into a ceremony that promises to be a common prayer. After joining the ceremony, however, the readers find themselves in unfamiliar supernatural territory where the power being summoned is not the distant, omnipotent Father of Christian faith. The readers discover and the petitioners remember that the power being summoned lies within themselves in their own communal voice.

Forms and Devices

The prayer ritual is immediately signaled in the poem's opening line with the words "For those of us who . . . ." This phrase, which also appears at the beginning of stanza 2, creates a solemn mood, alerting the reader that a hallowed ritual is being performed. Reverence is required of the reader as alternating voices utter a precise array of images that evoke intense emotional reactions. Stanzas 1 and 2 follow the same form and describe the petitioners' situation; therefore, these two stanzas might be uttered by the same voice, which functions as the celebrant who leads the ritual but does not assume a position of superiority over the other petitioners. The celebrant speaks not for but with the other petitioners and is clearly included in the dedication "For those of us who. . . ." The celebrant intimately describes the grave situation of the petitioners' lives in images that evoke feelings of insecurity, instability, and precariousness.

Life, for the petitioners, takes place "at the shoreline," a place of constant change where they face momentous decisions with apprehension. The celebrant envisions another time unlike the unbearable present. In the "now" of the present time, their desires must be squeezed into confined spaces "in doorways coming and going." These spaces were designed for more impersonal pursuits. In the present, they are forced to express love cautiously at inopportune times—"in the hours between dawns/ looking inward and outward/ at once before and after"—because security is not possible. The first stanza ends with a fusion of metaphor, simile, and personification, making the present animate—a living thing that must be nourished so that it can propagate the future: "seeking a now that can breed/ futures/ like bread in our children's mouths."

Stanza 2 begins by repeating the dedication "For those of us/ who. . . ." This reminds the readers that they are witnessing a ritual. The first voice then amplifies the imagery of nourishment begun in stanza 1 by superimposing maternal imagery. However, these are not the entirely soothing maternal scenes that the reader expects them to be. The customary repose one anticipates in a maternal image is subverted because the suckling ones are being fed fear along with their "mothers' milk." Because the nourishment is coming from a maternal source, the deception is nearly perfect. The mother cannot be rejected even though the nourishment she provides has been contaminated with fear, which will ultimately be lethal. The fear fed to the petitioners at their mothers' breasts is the perfect weapon designed by the "heavy-footed" people in power. Their ingenious design gives the "illusion of . . . safety" while it also engenders a paralyzing fear that results in a lifetime of terrified silence.

In the third stanza, the other voices speak, chanting phrase after phrase in unison, naming their painful life experiences in pulsating cycles. The collective voice emanating from each phrase crescendos into a mystical incantation that finally breaks through to the realization that fear has caused them to be silent—but their silence never eliminated their fear. The incantation concludes with all voices uttering the final stanza. All have summoned the courage to speak, for speech is the antidote to the censure that has proved so detrimental to self and survival: "So it is better to speak," the voices chant, "remembering/ we were never meant to survive."

Themes and Meanings

The ultimate anxiety of the petitioners is based on their awareness that the condition of their lives offers no provision for a better future for their children. The petitioners know that the future already exists in the present and that the future must be nourished in the present so that their children's existence will not be similarly distressed.

Reviewing their own situation as a group and contemplating what the future holds for their children has brought the petitioners to discover the elaborate scheme perpetrated by the powerful. They realize and articulate in their prayer how daily events (the sun rising and setting, eating, indigestion) have become unexpected sites of stifling silence and unrelieved insecurity, a legacy of ruin for their children. As the ceremony continues, the petitioners recognize and echo the leader's belief that they "were never meant to survive." Through their collective ceremonial recitation, they are emerging from their silence, speaking their new understanding, dispelling the deception that has silenced them for so long, and restoring and empowering themselves.

In "A Litany for Survival" as in many of her other works, Lorde is concerned with the politics of marginalization. Knowing the devastating effects of being devalued and discarded, Lorde asks bold questions about who is chosen for such treatment and why. As an African American, feminist, and lesbian thinker, Lorde often experienced life from the position of the outsider. Much of her work is an exploration of the alienation one feels as an outsider, but Lorde does not stop there. She is also concerned with the process of reversing marginalization and restoring self-worth and belonging. To unmake systematic marginalization, Lorde concentrates on understanding how the system was made. In "A Litany for Survival," she carefully exposes the elaborate scheme that powerful and esteemed members of society use so successfully to subdue and disempower those they designate as "other." Lorde does not, in this poem, name the "others," and this opening allows all marginalized people and groups to join the ceremony and identify with the poem's petitioners. With a masterstroke, Lorde identifies the fulcrum of the devious scheme. This scheme does not rest solely on what the powerful do but on the way they enlist the "others" to carry it out: The scheme requires the complicity of the marginalized members of society; therefore, the "others" are implicated in their own marginalization. The consequences of all this for the marginalized are self-reproach and silence. Such silence seals their destiny, but it also conceals the culpability of the powerful. For the marginalized, silence leads to social death. However, Lorde's message to the marginalized is always one of hope and life. She points the way in the poem: To invigorate and preserve life, one must speak, share one's experience, name one's fear, and seek communion.

Veta Smith Tucker

THE LITTLE CAR

Author: Guillaume Apollinaire (Guillaume Albert Wladimir Alexandre Apollinaire de Kostrowitzky, 1880-1918)
Type of poem: Lyric
First published: 1918, as "La Petite Auto," in *Calligrammes*; English translation collected in *Calligrams*, 1970

The Poem

"The Little Car" is written in free verse, its forty lines divided into six stanzas, excluding the calligram inserted in the middle of the poem. It is autobiographical, relating the feelings and impressions of Guillaume Apollinaire as he thinks back on his journey with friends from Deauville across the French countryside to Paris, where they enlisted to fight in World War I.

By providing the date, hour, and location of their departure, Apollinaire establishes a specific setting and moment in time. The mention of the "little car" in the third line, and in the title, gives a sense of significance to a usually trivial detail. The following one-line stanza tells that the men in the car numbered three, a number that appears two more times in the poem.

In the next stanza, the poem shifts to a more profound level as the speaker suggests that their seemingly innocuous journey actually symbolizes the end of an entire "era." War is described in apocalyptic and prophetic metaphors as a wave of mysterious and otherworldly forces unleashed around the frail, helpless little car. Armies become "furious giants"; planes are "eagles" flying from their nests; submarines seem like "fish" ascending from the sea.

The poem shifts back to a more intimate focus in the fourth stanza. The "dogs" can be seen in two ways: literally, as dogs the speaker hears barking in the distance, or figuratively, as the dogs of war beckoning their destructive forces. The speaker expresses empathy with the battling armies in that he carries them within himself. The landscape on which the armies "meandered" suddenly transforms into the pleasant little villages and locales of the French countryside. The poem then expands its focus to encompass universal concepts. Contrasting sensations of beauty and horror are combined as the speaker again envisions war: those facing death hail "brightly colored life"; men fight at heights "higher than the eagles glide"; a fighting man "falls like a shooting star."

In the next stanza, the speaker expresses his feelings that the war will somehow transform the world. The mysterious dreamlike image of the "merchant" arranging a "showcase" and the giant shepherds leading "silent flocks" can be read metaphorically as rich and powerful men staging the war, leading people moved by the tyrants' rhetoric, feeding on their violent words. The poem then shifts back to a more intimate force, the dogs on the road.

Next, Apollinaire inserts a calligram, a device he used in many poems. A calligram is designed to appeal literally to the sense of vision by arranging the words in a picture that in some way deals with the poem. This calligram resembles two people riding in a little car down a winding road, as a chauffeur clutches a steering wheel. The text of the calligram describes more details of the quiet little journey.

The final stanza is a very direct telling of their arrival in Paris as the draft is being posted. Here, the speaker again expresses his sense of inevitable change the war will effect on both personal and worldly levels.

Forms and Devices

The most significant aspect of the poetic form of "The Little Car" is its freedom. Apollinaire wanted to divorce himself from the traditional poetic forms of the past, feeling they did not allow enough freedom for him to express himself in a spontaneous manner. The stanzas are not uniform in either line length or line number; he even offers a one-line stanza.

To further distance himself from the rigid forms of the past, Apollinaire removed all punctuation from the poem. One can see how lack of punctuation serves his purposes for the poem: Without punctuation, words and meaning become ambiguous; ideas and images flow and shift with more ease, just as images and impressions change and transform as they swirl through the speaker's mind during an emotional moment.

The most dramatic resistance against traditional poetic form is the inclusion of the calligram. Just as a poet uses imagery to help the reader form a vision in his or her mind, Apollinaire provides the vision by literally forming words into a picture. This concept stretches the poem's appeal to different senses. The effectiveness of the calligram is debatable, though, because the words seem subordinated to the image, their meaning obscured and impact weakened by the more powerful visual effect of the picture.

The frequent shifts in focus, the sense that the speaker is moving in and out of reality and dream, sometimes functioning in both at the same time, and the coupling of contrasts and incongruities all stem from Apollinaire's use of a technique dubbed "simultanism." This technique is similar to a painting style known as cubism. Cubism sought to expand conventional ways of seeing by showing every surface from all possible perspectives at the same time. For example, a cubist painting of a table would show the top, bottom, and all four sides of the table at once. Likewise, Apollinaire's poetry does not follow any conventional or logical approach of relating experience. The poem expresses contrasting perspectives and types of consciousness simultaneously. It subverts our conventional associations of death and war by combining contrasting sensations of beauty and horror in such images as a dying man falling like "a shooting star." Apollinaire believed that the simultaneous experience of both the splendid and the hideous, the refined and the vulgar, or the joyful and the sorrowful would expand one's perception in such a way as to reveal some truth of life, to help one better understand life.

Similarly, the poem exists in both a dream world and in reality simultaneously— two different types of consciousness. For example, following the elaborate and prophetic metaphor of the merchant and the shepherds, the "dogs on the road" bark at both the "silent flocks" of the dreamlike image that inhabits the speaker's imagination and at the actual tangible flocks on the French countryside, which the speaker is watching from the little car. Simultaneous experience also can be seen in the way the poem shifts focus back and forth from the trivial (happy forests, the little car, changing a tire) to the more profound (heading into a new era, horrifying prophecies of war).

Themes and Meanings

The dominant theme of "The Little Car" is war. At that time in history, the world was facing a war of such proportions and involvement as never experienced before. With hindsight, one sees that Apollinaire's predictions about the effects of World War I were correct. The world was embarking upon a new era. World War I not only significantly altered the geography of Europe, but technology made war less personal. Armies could hide in their trenches or fly high in their planes dropping bombs and shooting at nameless, faceless enemies who were hundreds, if not thousands, of feet away.

The contrast of this little car traveling along the French roads helpless against the overwhelming forces unleashed around it speaks to the powerlessness that many felt once war broke out. War, itself, seems to be a hideous, living force operating independently of the people who first provided the spark to let it live. Though people begin war, it eventually takes on a life of its own. People lose complete control of the entity. Apollinaire offers a vision of a demonic entity summoning his "furious giants" from the other world. All the world is victim to this apocalyptic chaos.

The nature of war reverberates throughout the poem. To many, war signals the approaching of judgment day, the end of the world. Almost every war in history has caused people to question the ability of humankind to sustain itself, to ask whether self-destruction is inevitable. Apollinaire's poem, however, envisions not destruction, but otherworldly transformation on a universal scale. The poem envisions great and mysterious powers encircling the earth, causing even the dead to tremble "fearfully in their dark dwellings." It speaks of "skillful new beings" arranging a "new universe" and "giant shepherds" leading "silent flocks."

"The Little Car" also deals with individual perception and involvement with war. The poem's tendency to shift between a narrow personal perspective and a broad focus encompassing all of humankind suggests the way an individual reacts to a momentous event. The speaker's life before the advent of war was centered around trivial details, such as the little car, but now he is thrust into concerns of universal consequence. Thus, at times the speaker mentions the gigantic supernatural forces of war encircling the world, but then mentions matters of more intimate concern, such as the travelers needing to change three tires during their journey.

There are also contrasts between specific immediate time and the timeless nature of war. The poem offers such specific references as "August 31, 1914/ A little before midnight I left Deauville" and "Farriers summoned/ Between midnight and one in the morning." "Furious giants" who rise "over Europe" or "dead" who "trembled fear-fully in their dark dwellings" suggest eternal beings and timelessness itself. This contrasting perspective, however, is inherent in the title. That a poem entitled "The Little Car" actually is about the encroaching horror of war comments on the role trivial elements play in significant events. This irony inherent in the contrasting focus is embodied in the line " . . . the little car had driven us into a New era."

Heidi Kelchner

LIVE ACTS

Author: Charles Bernstein (1950-   )
Type of poem: Lyric
First published: 1980, in *Controlling Interests*

The Poem

"Live Acts" is a twenty-line poem in free verse. The title suggests a sign on a marquee outside a strip joint, one that would read in full, "Live Sex Acts." There is little in the poem, however, to bear out that legend; rather, the title resonates with the suggestions of something simulated—either the act itself or the passion of those engaged in it, as in a staged sex show. This resonance is often encountered in Charles Bernstein's poetry, in which the poet examines the question of sincerity and falseness in language and poetry.

Although the pronoun "I" is twice employed, it would not be accurate to characterize this poem as a first-person poem. The issue of the credibility of a poem (or of any statement) involves for Bernstein a questioning also of what it means to be a person. Bernstein tends to view the person as a social construct rather than as a natural fact, and whatever has been put together by human agency can be dismantled by that same agency. Bernstein's poetry operates from multiple viewpoints in order to demonstrate his thesis and to embody it for a reader.

While personal experience is involved at one level in "Live Acts" (the experience of a number of persons), the reader is never allowed to forget that a poem's meanings are primarily generated by its language rather than by the experience to which that language points. Hence, no "scene" is offered—the sentences and phrases do not even lead from one to another in any usual sense of logical progression, but instead juxtapose in sudden and puzzling ways. Puzzling over these, the reader is to be made aware of the role he or she has in generating the meaning of the poem. Sometimes the poem emerges from its own fog to afford a glimpse of a figure who might be the author, uttering something profound: "The closer we look, the greater the distance from which/ we look back." Here, surely, is a clue to the procedures and to their aims. Faced with such a riddling work, the reader examines closely its abrupt changes, its startling juxtapositions, only to be thrust back, repulsed from any closeness to the text.

As with the "live acts" of a sex show, where the viewer, longing for closeness and intimacy, finds neither of these so easily achievable, so the promise of the poem—the promise that convention holds out for the poem, that it will be an understanding hand laid on the reader's shoulder, a kind ear, a sympathetic voice—is not kept, and the reader may well feel cheated. If one has the patience to reflect upon the experience of the poem, however, one may find that it makes considerable sense and is indeed a salutary parallel to and preparation for the real difficulties of a real life.

Forms and Devices

Bernstein's beliefs find adequate embodiment in the forms and devices of this poem. "What I want to call attention to is that there is no natural writing style," Bernstein explains in his essay "Stray Straws and Straw Men" (in his collected essays, *Contents Dream*, 1986). "Live Acts," with its various tones and dictions, bears this out, sounding more like something written by a committee than the self-expressive utterance of a single individual's "native wood-notes wild." The poem sounds learned, low-class, and smart-alecky by turns, a little like a George S. Kaufman script for the Marx Brothers rendered by an aphasiac professor of literature.

Yet Bernstein is "crazy like a fox," simulating all this and more in the interests of making the reader aware—even painfully aware—of the unexamined assumptions lurking in uniformities of diction, attitude, and interpretation. As the poem declares in its final sentence, "These projects alone contain/ the person, binding up in an unlimited way what/ otherwise goes unexpressed." One sense of "projects" is surely that they are the brief essays into varieties of tone and diction of which the poem is composed. These bind up—present in poetic form—what otherwise would go unexpressed, and they do it in an unlimited way—that is, in a manner that hints at its own illimitability, at the potential of this particular procedure to go on virtually forever. The range of dictions available for the poet to appropriate is wide indeed, and it is mimetic of the world itself—large, thronged, and spherical, not at all to be contained in any discrete organization of words.

Themes and Meanings

Bernstein's poems have the awkwardness of the new, an unassimilability struggled for and wholly deliberate. Bernstein, who has written extensively on ideas of poetry, has admitted that such work as his and his associates' might prove a "discomfort" to customary expectations—expectations that would include transparency of language and intention, "personal communication," and the appearance of words "flowing freely" from poet to reader, a sort of "lisping in numbers" which sanctifies the notion of poet as Nature-inspired genius. To Bernstein, those and other devices are too easy, thus too glib, a means to emit poetic signals. It tends to reduce the poem to nothing more than the poet's personality. He wants the attention on the text, not on the character of the person who assembles the text. Even better, emphasis should be placed on the person who is immediately assembling the text: the reader. Bernstein wants to make texts that challenge readers to put the meanings together for themselves. He wants active engagement, not passive consumerism. Bernstein writes: "The cant of 'make it personal' & 'let it flow' are avoidances—by mystification—of some very compelling problems that swirl around truth-telling, confession, bad faith, false self, authenticity, [and] virtue."

These, then, are some of Bernstein's themes—in this poem as in his work generally—and the reader needs to see that they are implicit and tacit rather than spelled out and obvious. Bernstein does not believe in handing to the reader a poem precooked on a plastic platter; the meaning of a poem lies in the effort required to decode it. This much is clear: Bernstein's is a poetry of demystification, one that foregrounds language and not personality, and his poems are not to be "plugged into" "indiscriminately"; they must rather be wrestled with until their particular qualities become apparent to the reader-agonist.

To all of this, there is a political dimension, indicated by the poet in his interview with Tom Beckett. Bernstein speaks of his own poetry as concerned with the constituting power of language, as seeing language itself as the medium, which it foregrounds. He says that he is committed to changing society and that, since language controls how people think, he believes that people must be brought to examine their own words, phrases, and assumptions. This cannot be done through a perpetuation of past poetries, but through a poetry that calls the reader's attention to the ways in which it makes meanings. He notes that "objects are constituted by social values encoded in language." He also notes that reading and writing "can partake of non-instrumental values and thus be utopian formations." In other words, as "Live Acts" puts it,

> Impossible outside you want always the other. A continual
> recapitulation, & capture all that, against which our redaction
> of sundry, promise, another person, fills all the
> conversion of that into, which intersects a continual
> revulsion of, against, concepts, encounter,
> in which I hold you, a passion made of cups, amidst
> frowns.

David Bromige

LIVING ALONE

Author: Hayden Carruth (1921-   )
Type of poem: Lyric
First published: 1992, in *Collected Shorter Poems, 1946-1991*

The Poem

"Living Alone" is a fairly long poem (165 lines); it might appear at first to be in free verse, but actually it employs several types of rhyme, rhythm, and formal lineation. Excluding the epigraph and dedication, the poem is divided into seventeen sections, several of which are further divided into stanzas. The poem is dedicated to John Cheever, an American prose writer, and begins with an epigraph taken from one of Cheever's works. In this epigraph an observer on a ship sees a Ping-Pong table washed off the ship's deck because the helmsman made a miscalculation. Watching the table bobbing in the ship's wake, the observer is reminded of the plight of someone washed overboard.

The first section of the poem is a single stanza that acts as a backdrop for the melodrama that follows. The narrator of the poem sees, through the insulated window of his apartment, a solitary chrysanthemum, the last one of the season. As wind and ice tear at its head, a gull cries and hovers above it. In the second section the narrator compares his pain to that of a "snake run over." It is not until the third section that the reader learns the source of his pain and shock: He has been expelled "from her house" by his "successor" and is now living alone—thus the title of the poem. Although the reader learns that her name is Rachel and that the speaker probably knows her grandmother, he never identifies her as wife or lover. He simply states that he was "Jettisoned in one night" and that he felt as if he were "falling as a parachutist might/ in vacant air, shocked/ in the silence, nowhere."

In subsequent stanzas readers learn that, in addition to his emotional misery, the speaker is physically ill. He compares the way he feels with having a bad cold— possibly pneumonia, flu, bronchitis—while in a strange town with no one he can call and a fever that, along with the winter sunset, brings thoughts of mortality. At one point he talks about both fearing and seeking death as other men have done. He adds that women must have felt this way too, but then expresses doubt about his ability to make any judgment regarding women: "I disclaim/ whatever knowledge I thought once/ to have of them."

In the first of the two tercets that make up the fifth section of the poem the narrator expresses his belief that "Experience is unique" and implies that he will not compare his plight with others who may have suffered similar fates. In the second tercet he makes an immediate turn by crying out to François Villon, Spartacus, and others who have suffered similar indignities. As the poem progresses he sarcastically complains of the "endless joy" of housekeeping; complains of thin apartment walls that inundate him with a mother's cruelty to her child, the ubiquitous flushing of toilets, and children screaming; complains of pins, tacks, and glass in the wall-to-wall carpeting; and in general complains of the squalor and boredom of living alone in an apartment.

In the end the narrator turns his troubles and his energies toward the blues—that art form that seems specifically created as a refuge for the lonely and the spurned. Readers who know of the music of Charles Ellsworth "Pee Wee" Russell may have a special insight into the last two sections of the poem, but Carruth's faith in the power of jazz shines through regardless.

Forms and Devices

The first obvious device used in this poem is the epigraph from an unnamed work by John Cheever. It sets the tone for the entire poem. The "I" of Cheever's piece feels powerless in the face of the sea. Even the ship is out of his control, in the hands of an erring helmsman. He identifies with an inanimate object washed overboard and lost from everything that could give it meaning. The "I" of Carruth's poem exhibits similar feelings about being at the mercy of a wrong-thinking person who throws him into a veritable sea of troubles where he is at the mercy of forces he cannot understand.

Carruth uses alliteration, assonance, and a dizzying array of rhyme schemes and patterns of lineation. The single nine-line stanza of the first section uses one of the most complex mixtures of alliterations and end rhymes in the whole poem:

> Mystery. Seeds of every motion.
> See out there beyond the thermal-
> pane that last chrysanthemum
> in the frozen bed by the concrete wall
> winging wildly its lavender
> and shattered head. How fast
> the wind rises. How the mud
> elaborates in patterns of ice.
> A gull, hovering, shudders and cries.

The reader should notice that at the end of the second line the poet forces a line break in the middle of a word. The break not only provides an end rhyme with the fourth line but also enhances the alliterative effect of all the *m* sounds in the first three lines and the final "mud" of the seventh line. Carruth uses a similar and more complex effect in the first two lines with "Mystery. Seed . . . motion./ See" and in the fourth, fifth, and seventh lines with "wall/ winging wildly . . ./ . . . wind."

The second section is divided into two stanzas of four lines each with a very conventional rhyme pattern: *aabb ccdd*. The third and fourth lines of each stanza are indented, giving these two quatrains the feeling of four rhyming couplets. The second quatrain opens with an inversion that appears to have no greater purpose than to generate an end rhyme with the next line: "comfort me who will then?/ Or otherwise that time soon when." Throughout the poem, Carruth continues to use inversions like this one to gain end rhymes.

The poem's rhyming patterns change with each new section, and no two sections use the same pattern. One of the more interesting rhyme schemes comes in the tenth section. This section has only one strophe of four lines. The final word of the second line rhymes with the final word of the third line (there is nothing unusual in that). The final word of the final line rhymes, not with the final word of the first line, as one might expect, but with the first word of the first line. There is also a wonderfully playful irony in this section. This is the only place where the "I" of the poem provides the name (Rachel) of the woman who has abandoned him. He exposes himself as an unreliable narrator by saying, "Rachel, your name won't rhyme, the language itself/ has given up on you. Zilch." Then, at the end of the next sentence, the very last word of the stanza, he gives her name a rhyme, "satchel."

The variety of stanza choices is as wide as that of rhyme schemes. Carruth runs the gamut from free form to couplet, tercet, quatrain, quintain, sestet, septet, and upward. By the time the reader reaches the end of the poem the constant and rapid changing of rhyme schemes and stanza types has left little doubt that the poet is a master craftsman and that his narrator is somewhat—but not hopelessly—paranoid.

Themes and Meanings

As the title suggests, the first and most pronounced theme of "Living Alone" is isolation. It is not, however, the only major theme and is probably not the most important. That distinction falls to survival.

The "I" of the poem starts as an outcast, a person who has been suddenly and permanently ejected from what he thought of as his home, the one place where he felt safe and had some sense of security about his identity. At first he falls victim to self-pity, wallowing in his own dirge about all the different ways he was wronged. Then the ordinariness of life starts nibbling at the fabric of his lament. The voices and vulgar noises that seep through the thin walls of his apartment, the boredom and occasional drudgery of housework done alone, and the simple process of growing older each day begin to reshape his complaints until he declares, "All one can do is to achieve nakedness."

His solitude appears to have brought him down to a point at which he is able to start up again. He questions whether he will return to the same place, be the same person or type of person. On the road to rebuilding (surviving), he turns to the art of music, specifically the blues. This move to the blues would suggest to a person already familiar with the work of Carruth that the poem is, at least in some part or fashion, autobiographical: Carruth has, over several decades, written extensively about jazz and the blues.

Edmund August

LIVING IN SIN

Author: Adrienne Rich (1929-　　)
Type of poem: Lyric
First published: 1955, in *The Diamond Cutters and Other Poems*

The Poem

Adrienne Rich's "Living in Sin" is a twenty-six-line single-stanza poem that effectively captures the stark contrast between a young woman's romantic notions and the bitter taste of daily realities once she acts on those notions.

Told entirely from the woman's point of view, the poem begins in the past, with the vision of how she thought her life would be living with the man she loved. The first two lines effectively convey her naïveté, her simple acceptance of a fairy tale version of her future once she has accepted his offer to come and live with him. The last two lines picture her waking up both literally and figuratively to the painful awareness of what the future holds.

The intervening twenty-two lines present a graphic account of her transition from daydreams to nightmares. Through devotion to her romantic fantasies, the young woman fails to anticipate the trials and disillusionments of daily life. Because she is in love, she imagines that commonplace cares and chores such as cleaning and cooking would not be part of her world. Her small apartment "would keep itself;/ no dust upon the furniture of love." Her vision of a studio with "a plate of pears,/ a piano with a Persian shawl" seems taken from a painting or a scene in a romance novel rather than from real life. Even once there in her new life, it seems a betrayal of her fantasy to wish things were different, "half heresy" to resent the dripping faucet and the filthy windows. However, the harsh "morning light" dissipates her illusions; the reality of her situation becomes apparent. The light "coldly would delineate" the unpleasant particulars of a morning after: the cheese scraps, the "sepulchral bottles," and the insects in her cupboards.

Rich makes it clear that the young woman's unpleasant physical surroundings are not her only problem as she emerges from her fantasy into a colder world. The relationship, too, looks different in the morning light of daily life than it did in her romantic imagination. In lines 15-18, readers get a glimpse of her boyfriend, whose "urging" is partly responsible for her living in sin. He is no longer seen as a figure in a painting, a romanticized musician or artist in his studio. The brief glimpse of him is not very promising. In these four lines he yawns, plays a few notes on the keyboard, shrugs, looks in the mirror, rubs his beard, and goes to buy cigarettes. The impression is of a man who is preoccupied, uninterested, and self-absorbed. There is no mention of an affectionate word or romantic gesture. The piano, it seems, is not the only thing out of tune.

The discordant notes continue as the young woman makes the bed and dusts the table, an attempt, perhaps, to restore some harmony to her small cramped space. While doing so she is "jeered by the minor demons" and neglects the coffee pot, which "boil[s] over on the stove." The last four lines effectively present her new awareness and her fears for the future. She is not completely disillusioned: "By evening she was back in love again," but she awakens "throughout the night," dreading the new reality that the daylight will bring.

Forms and Devices

The power of "Living in Sin," an unrhymed free-verse poem, comes from the way it builds in emotional intensity as it progresses. The woman's early unrealistic fantasy, filled with pears, a piano, and a Persian shawl, makes the present seem even more acrid than it might otherwise. Such imagery is in sharp contrast with the "scraps/ of last night's cheese" and the empty bottles revealed by the morning light.

Her image of "a cat/ stalking the picturesque amusing mouse" is no preparation for confronting the animal life that does infest her studio or seeing the "beetle-eyes" that would fix her own in the kitchen. Indeed, part of the sin in the title may be the sin of living too long with the illusions of romantic fantasy. The unreality of this view is captured in the first seven lines, both through specific images such as the Persian shawl and the mouse, and through the slightly grandiose phrasing, such as "no dust upon the furniture of love."

The diction shifts dramatically in the next seven lines. The negative connotations of "writhe," "tramp," "coldly," and "sepulchral" snap the woman, and the reader, out of romantic reverie and place her squarely in her present life. When the insect's eyes "fix her own" they not only stare back at her, they also fix (correct) her romantic vision, and they fix her firmly in the present moment.

Rich also varies the diction and the context in this section just enough to reinforce her theme. The piano with an exotic shawl in line 5 becomes a keyboard "out of tune" in line 15. The stairs become personified and "writhe" under the weight of the milkman. The daylight, which at first simply reveals the contents of the studio, becomes personified as "relentless" as it approaches inexorably to remind her of her situation.

Rich's achievement in "Living in Sin" is her ability to keep focused on the specific details of the young woman's fantasies and her present situation. Most of the poem describes in vivid sensory detail a single day in the life of the woman living in sin. The "minor demons" that jeer at her are conveyed in very concrete images set against the grandiose language and imagery of her earlier romantic notions.

Themes and Meanings

"Living in Sin" is an early poem by one of America's leading poets of the second half of the twentieth century. It foreshadows several of the themes and techniques of the more than twenty books of poetry that followed. Its concern with male/female relationships and the societal judgment suggested by the title are a major aspect of her many books of poetry, as well as her collections of essays and talks. The poem represents just one sketch in a large portfolio of works concerned with the proper role of both men and women in a society that seldom questions the status quo or the confining limits that it unthinkingly imposes on both sexes, especially women.

Contrary to what readers may expect, the sin mentioned in the title refers not so much to social condemnation of living together out of wedlock—even though the word "tramp" is rich with suggestions of social disapproval—as it does to a way of life: the young woman's sordid living conditions, her strained relationship with her man, and her unrealistic expectations. A less proficient writer may have held up the woman as a victim of antiquated social mores and prejudice. However, "Living in Sin" is a richer, more powerful poem because it refuses to engage in facile criticism of social attitudes. Rather, the poet keeps attention focused on the disillusionment of a single individual, one who is more a victim of her own illusions than of social prejudice. Society is at fault only inasmuch as it encourages young people to buy into romantic concepts that have little basis in the daily lives of men and women.

Rich moves the reader smoothly from past fantasy to present reality to a dramatic sense of foreboding as the woman contemplates the future. The last few lines convey a sense of panic, almost as if she is trapped and cannot extricate herself. She is in a new reality, one at least partly of her own making. (The word "in" appears in all the words of the title, "Living in Sin.") Words change significance over the course of the poem. The word "love" as used in line 23, "back in love again," has quite a different feel from the much earlier "furniture of love," in line 2. Rich moves effortlessly from the literal to the symbolic. The milkman's tramp and the morning light, a simple description in line 9, become fused into an ominous symbol in the last two lines, as she feels "the daylight coming/ like a relentless milkman up the stairs." It is an effective ending that leaves the woman, and the reader, anxious and uncertain as the future approaches.

Danny Robinson

LOBSTERS

Author: Howard Nemerov (1920-1991)
Type of poem: Meditation
First published: November, 1962; collected in *The Blue Swallows*, 1967

The Poem

Howard Nemerov's "Lobsters" is a philosophical meditation on the inevitability of death occasioned by the narrator's pausing to observe lobsters kept, awaiting purchase, in a supermarket fish tank. Told in loose blank verse, the poem consists of two verse paragraphs, one a single continuously running sentence of nine lines and the second a more developed unit of twenty-two lines. The meditation then ends with a single line that functions much like the punchline of a joke, giving the poem's meditation its unexpected ironic close.

The poem begins within the reassuringly familiar confines of a contemporary supermarket, mockingly dubbed the Super Duper, and focuses immediately on the tankful of marine curiosities. The lines tidily recount the familiar practice of a shopper selecting a living lobster and then returning home to kill the creature before serving it with a "sauce of melted butter." The poem reviews the process in an efficient deadpan tone despite the shocking singularity of the transaction, largely unexamined by those who participate in it—certainly nowhere else in the market are shoppers expected to select and then kill their dinners. Indeed the grim act of killing is itself rendered euphemistically: the shopper will go home and "drop [the lobster] into boiling water." The stanza is a single unbroken sentence. Such lexical tidiness reinforces both the neatness of the ghastly transaction and the swiftness of the approaching execution. That process essentially empowers the shopper by permitting a happy sense of superiority to the helpless animals in the tank. It is that comfortable distancing that the poem will eventually discount.

If such a singular transaction appears to be routine, Nemerov cautions, it is only because shoppers seldom pause to contemplate the creatures. Thus in the lengthy second verse paragraph, the poet first lovingly lingers to observe what the rest so easily ignore. In a generous section (fifteen lines) largely free of distracting figurative language, the poet details the "beauty of strangeness" that marks these mysterious creatures so absurdly out of place in the market. The loving eye of the narrator records the lobsters' slow, dreamlike underwater movements and then inventories their rich dark colorations. He observes sympathetically their helplessness, their "imperial claws" held shut by pegs, and how they sleep away their final hours in evident ignorance of the depth of their precariousness.

In a brutal intrusion of otherness and an abrupt shift of focus the poet suddenly introduces the harsh pronoun "we" to indicate the casual shopper who without reflection simply selects dinner. The "we" implicates the reader. After the generous description of the creatures, however, it is difficult for any reader to participate in the shopping transaction without some hesitation. Indeed the poet suggests that occasionally there will be a shopper (like the poet himself) alert enough to pause sufficiently to identify with these helpless creatures, a mind that "sinks down" into the sandy tank bottom and who feels metaphorically the lobster's chilly shell. At that moment of close identification the poet realizes that despite the casual assumption of superiority by the other shoppers, there is an uneasy correspondence between these magnificent creatures awaiting a death they cannot begin to understand and the shoppers themselves. The store lobsters are suddenly not merely dinner but rather an occasion to ponder mortality. The existential dilemma that faces the shopper—is there anything beyond the material world, "something underneath the world"—is answered in a devastatingly ironic closing one-liner: only the "flame beneath the pot that boils the water." Death lurks beneath the calm world of the tanked lobsters and beneath the well-appointed Super Duper world of the shoppers as well.

Forms and Devices

"Lobsters" is an example of symbolist poetry, specifically, a poem that validates the argument, made a generation earlier most prominently by poets such as William Butler Yeats and Wallace Stevens, that the most familiar objects in the natural world are packed with an unsuspected significance that is detected only by the open, interactive eye in moments of unexpected insight. Such poems detach a familiar object from its surroundings to consider its implications, to read its meaning. That poetic process is suggested metaphorically here by the harsh overhead store lighting that makes the lobsters conspicuous despite their natural camouflage colorings. Natural objects, if thus observed, possess dense metaphoric value, and the phenomenal world can instruct those willing to observe and reflect. Nemerov, in describing his role as a poet, has said, "I not so much look at nature as I listen to what it says." The poem, as a meditation, begins without the distraction of a dramatic situation or any complex narrative line and thus is compelled not by action but rather by observation. Specifically the "plot" here is the evolution of a thought, the process in which the loving description of the lobsters moves inexorably (and paradoxically) toward a wholly unexpected conclusion.

As in the nature poetry of Robert Frost, that reflection is rendered in a low-pitched unadorned blank verse (largely iambic pentameter) that mimics the casual rhythms of everyday speech. That use of conversational diction and familiar sentence constructions, so flexible and so handy, creates the sense of the ordinary that is essential to the poem's argument. The poem, however, heightens the poet's deep feeling for the lobsters by frequently deploying rich liquidy long vowels that slow down the recitation of the lines and thus create a lingering, sensual feel to the poetic lines.

Importantly, given the compact and meticulous detailing of the lobsters that the narrator provides, the poem uses figurative language only twice and each time for thematic effect. First the tanked lobsters are compared to somnambulists, or sleepwalkers, to suggest the creatures' unenviable existence dumbly unaware of their approaching fate, a philosophy that the poem will ultimately reject. And later when the shopper actually selects a lobster, the animals are described as "slow, gigantic spiders," the implicit metaphor functioning as a distancing device. The metaphor creates a comforting insulation—they are not really lobsters but rather mythical, hence unreal creatures—against the unpalatable reality that the strange, beautiful sea animals must be killed to become "our needful food." Ultimately, that strategy of distancing will also be rejected by the poem.

Tone is critical here because any casual summary of the poem might make it sound brutally pessimistic. This brief poem, despite its startling closing line and its apparently grim reflection of the death that awaits every living creature, maintains a gentle, wry tone. Surely, in linking the shoppers and the lobsters Nemerov recognizes that as living creatures they share a strikingly similar fate in the face of death. To suggest the larger natural world itself, Nemerov uses as metaphor the great glass fish tank, which, he notes, is supplied by a continuously renewing source of cold, fresh water. Against the obvious temporariness of its endangered occupants, the tank symbolizes the "[p]erpetually renewed" and, hence, permanent natural world itself that surrounds even the shopper. In this Nemerov is not some existential philosopher negotiating, with anxious fears, the terrifying implications of his thinking. Rather he is a naturalist, detached yet sympathetic, an amused observer, like Frost before him, of the simplest, most evident realities of the natural world. Thus the poem closes in a bemused sense of comic irony.

Themes and Meanings

The poem works to overcome what any reader would resist: the uncomfortable identification with the helpless, hapless creatures in the store's tank. These trapped creatures, at once at home and yet decidedly out of place, exist absurdly unaware of their approaching fate, indeed exist in a sort of suspended animation, a dream state, to await an entirely and wholly meaningless death that lurks all about the natural world. That description of the lobsters, "[p]hilosophers and at the same time victims," tallies uncomfortably close to the situation of the shoppers themselves. The poem then provides the reader the unexpected (and perhaps) unwanted gift of generous humility. There is no protection from that final jolting line. In the penultimate line the poet lingers over four ellipsis dots that trail off into a pause and offer the hope of an affirmation of something, anything, beyond the material world. The ellipsis pause, however, only makes the closing line that much more startling. Yes, there is something bigger than the world: death, as slow and gradual and inevitable as the fire beneath the lobster pot.

But the poem itself counters any pull of anxiety over such a conclusion. Death here is not malevolent or profound or even personal. The poem offers three strategies for engaging the world, two unworkable extremes and a satisfying alternative. That every living thing dwells metaphorically in a pot under which slow-boils a fire does not negate that world's richness, evidenced by the poet's loving detailing of the lobsters themselves in the opening stanza. If the poem then asks that the reader accept the absurdity and inevitability of death, it rejects living like the lobsters, too-content in the apparent firmness of the sand, existing in an uncomplicated sort of dream state, unaware of the world, and slowly moving to death. But the poem also dismisses living like the unthinking shoppers, casually insulated from their own world, distancing themselves from that world and never pausing to investigate the beauty and strangeness of the most familiar objects whose unsuspected complexity would stun them. Rather the reader is challenged to live like the narrator himself, stoic, alert, open-eyed, and willing to accept with bemusement the rich ironies of the magnificent living world shadowed, paradoxically, by death.

Joseph Dewey

LOCKS

Author: Kenneth Koch (1925-   )
Type of poem: Lyric
First published: 1962, in *Thank You and Other Poems*

The Poem

"Locks," a love poem, is an extended list of locks that have brought the narrator "happiness." The twenty-eight-line poem, written in free verse, is actually one sentence long; the sixteen different locks mentioned in this catalog are separated by semicolons. The lines are lengthy, nearly half of them spilling over to a second or third line of indented text.

The single-stanza poem's first line is "These locks on doors have brought me happiness," and the list commences. The variety of locks suggests the narrator's full, vigorous life—a life replete with experience. The first happily remembered lock, for instance, is "The lock on the door of the sewing machine in the living room/ Of a tiny hut in which I was living with a mad seamstress." The next is "The lock on the filling station one night when I was drunk/ And had the idea of enjoying a nip of petroleum."

It quickly becomes clear that these locks are not only literal—although some do seem more literal than others—but also metaphoric or symbolic. "The lock inside the nose of the contemporary composer who was playing the piano and would have ruined his concert by sneezing, while I was turning pages," for instance, cannot be a hardware-store variety lock any more than "The lock in my hat when I saw her and which kept me from tipping it,/ Which she would not have liked, because she believed that naturalness was the most friendly" can.

The narrator, fully alive and alert to physical sensations, has lived in the world and enjoyed its pleasures. He has lived in a hut, ridden a camel in the desert, witnessed a "lipstick parade," and felt alert to the physical thrill of "gales of sweetness blow[ing] through me till I shuddered and shook."

The narrator presents himself as a man of the world, a man not easily shocked, a man fairly unruffled by physical danger or discomfort. This pose, however, is touchingly undermined at the end of the poem. The "locks" with which the poem concludes, presumably the locks that have brought the narrator the greatest happiness of all, are "the lock on the sailboat/ That keeps it from taking me away from you when I am asleep with you,/ And, when I am not, the lock on my sleep, that keeps me from waking and finding you are not there." The narrator's bravado comes to seem a pose, or at the least a less significant element than the reader might have supposed, of a much deeper and more rounded character. The narrator is, in fact, utterly dependent on a lover, so much so that he expresses special gratitude for the ability to sleep when they must be apart. To awaken without her by his side would be too great a horror.

Forms and Devices

Perhaps the central irony in this poem is that it is written in free verse, an open poetic form that does not rely upon traditional rhyme schemes or regular metrical patterns. It is ironic considering the title and the subject of the poem: "Locks." A lock is a kind of limiting device, something that bars the access to something else, such as a room. Similarly, strict adherence to form can be a kind of limitation for a poet, and early experimenters with free verse, such as Walt Whitman in America and Charles Baudelaire in France, consciously rebelled against the kinds of fixed forms and a slavish devotion to rhyme and meter that they viewed as limiting to the possibilities of poetic expression. There is, then, a kind of humor in the fact that Koch should write a hymn of praise to locks and use the least "locked" form, free verse, in which to do it.

To say that the poem is written in free verse, however, is not to say that Koch ignores the question of meter altogether. Koch employs the most traditional metrical line in English poetry in the poem's first line: "These locks on doors have brought me happiness" is written in iambic pentameter. The first line, however, is the only one written in such a formal, regular meter. It is almost as if, having expressed his "happiness," the narrator feels the kind of freedom from restraint that allows him to experiment more boldly with meter.

The meter of the remainder of the poem is not fixed, yet there remains a kind of music and rhythm. "Locks" benefits a good deal from being read aloud. To read the poem orally or to listen to it being read is to hear how Koch builds its momentum. The first two feet (a foot is a poetic unit of two or three syllables), for twenty-one of the twenty-eight lines, for instance, consist of an iamb followed by an anapest—or at least a close variation of that pattern. (An anapest contains three syllables, the first two unstressed, the final one stressed.) Not every line approximates the iamb/anapest pattern in its first two feet, but enough of them do to help give the poem a loose kind of structure. "Locks" sounds like a poem rather than straight prose.

Readers who believe that free verse is no different from prose or that free verse is inherently disorganized or unmusical will have their ideas challenged elsewhere with "Locks." Koch uses sound devices such as assonance, or the repetition of vowel sounds, throughout the poem. Koch plays with long *o* sounds, for example, in the fragment "The nose of the contemporary composer who was playing the piano." Koch almost always writes in free verse, but it would be a mistake to assume that he has therefore forgotten that poetry has its roots in the musical tradition.

Themes and Meanings

"Unscrew the locks from the doors!/ Unscrew the doors themselves from their jambs!" wrote Walt Whitman, the American poet whose impact on the American poetic tradition has been greatest, in "Song of Myself." Whitman's sensibilities were essentially Romantic, and in these lines he is calling for a radical "unlocking" of old hierarchical political structures and old strictures governing interpersonal relations. Whitman is the great poet of democracy, hearkening back, in his thinking and writing, to the ideas of the French philosopher Jean-Jacques Rousseau, who wrote, "Man is born free, but is everywhere in chains." For Rousseau, as for Whitman, humankind is essentially free but has been corrupted by institutions of society, such as governments and churches, that create limitations to that freedom. If people are to return to their free and natural state, they must revolt against the tyranny of kings, the dogma of churches, and the conventions of social intercourse that prevent them from being free and natural with one another.

Koch is clearly the beneficiary of this Romantic tradition. Were it not for Whitman, writing approximately one hundred years earlier, free verse would probably not have developed to the point where a poem such as "Locks" would have been possible. Much of the humor in this poem lies in the fact that Koch builds upon Whitman's techniques—in his use of free verse, in his cataloging, in his lengthy lines—to sing the glories of something as "un-Whitmanic" as locks. Koch is perhaps parodying a deeply admired predecessor, much as he does in "Variations on a Theme by William Carlos Williams," a poem that appears in the same volume as "Locks."

Yet the poem is by no means pure parody with no underlying seriousness. Koch summed up some of his thoughts about his own poetics in an interview with Elizabeth Farnsworth: "I don't intend for my poetry to be mainly funny or satirical, but it seems to me that high spirits and a sort of comic view are part of being serious." In "Locks," Koch uses humor to ask his readers to consider a serious question: What kind of freedom would be possible without some kinds of limitations? Locks have given the narrator possibilities for privacy that allowed sexuality to thrive (the lock on the door of the tiny hut), have prevented him from possible bodily harm ("The lock on the family of seals, which, released, would have bitten"), and, most important, have kept him from "waking and finding you are not there" when separated from his loved one. Without the lock of blissful sleep, the narrator would be forced to confront a deep loneliness potentially more harmful than anything else an unpredictable, treacherous world might offer.

Douglas Branch

LOCKSLEY HALL

Author: Alfred, Lord Tennyson (1809-1892)
Type of poem: Dramatic monologue
First published: 1842, in *Poems*

The Poem

"Locksley Hall" is a dramatic monologue in which the youthful speaker, revisiting the site of an earlier love affair, comes to terms with his rejection by the woman he once loved. Through the course of the poem he seeks consolation first in imagining his beloved's future misery with her new husband; next in foreseeing a brighter future for humankind, based on his own childhood visions of the future; and finally in dreaming of escape from the restrictive society that played a role in ending the lovers' relationship.

The poem begins with the speaker's arrival at Locksley Hall, the stately home of his wealthy uncle, where, after his own father's death, he came to nourish "a youth sublime" with "the fairy tales of science" and nights of gazing at the stars. He then recalls the youthful romance that blossomed between himself and his cousin, Amy. Unfortunately, however, their relationship ended unhappily, for the speaker cries, "Oh my cousin, shallow-hearted! O my Amy, mine no more!" His cousin, "Puppet to a father's threat," has married another, presumably wealthier, suitor.

The poem then turns to an exploration of the jilted speaker's mingled feelings of jealousy, resentment, and lingering affection toward his former lover. He asks "Is it well to wish thee happy?" in spite of his lover's decision to settle on "a range of lower feelings and a narrower heart than mine!" He continues to wrestle with this issue, asking, "Can I think of her as dead, and love her for the love she bore?" Yet he must answer himself, "No—she never loved me truly: love is love for evermore."

Dejected, the speaker tries to hide from his own "deep emotion" by recalling an earlier time in his life, when he yearned for the "large excitement that the coming years would yield." Seeking "the wild pulsation that I felt before the strife," he imagines a fantastic future of flying machines, aerial combat, and one-world government. However, the plodding pace of progress forces him to ask, "What is that to him that reaps not harvest of his youthful joys?"

After entertaining notions of retreating to a simpler life, however, the speaker rejects this option in favor of continuing to serve the cause of progress that he sees as his own society's chief purpose in the world. At the conclusion of the poem the speaker bids a final farewell to Locksley Hall with a claim to have renewed the "ancient founts of inspiration" that had previously been emptied by his own bitterness and frustration.

Forms and Devices

"Locksley Hall" takes the form of a dramatic monologue, in which a fictional character assumes the speaking role, rather than the poet himself, as in the case of a lyric poem. The thoughts expressed by this character cannot, therefore, be directly attributed to Tennyson himself, but must be understood as those of a fictional persona who may or may not reflect the poet's own attitudes. Tennyson said of the poem that it "represents young life, its good side, its deficiencies, and its yearnings."

Nevertheless, it is clear that the poem does largely reflect Tennyson's attitudes about the inhibiting social and economic restrictions imposed upon his generation, as well as his earnest hopes for the possibilities of scientific, as well as social, progress.

The occasion upon which this dramatic monologue takes place is the speaker's return to Locksley Hall after a prolonged absence. This event acts as a frame for the retelling of his sad tale, as well as for his bitter reflections about the past and his hopes for the future. The frame also serves as a transition from one section of the poem to another, as when the speaker emerges from his reverie to hear his "merry comrades . . . sounding on the bugle-horn."

The poem consists of 194 lines, arranged into ninety-seven rhymed couplets. The simplicity of the rhyme scheme is offset, however, by the complex meter—trochaic octameter—as well as the unusual length of the lines, which allows Tennyson to make full use of his familiar rolling cadence. This distinctive pattern is perhaps one reason why "Locksley Hall" has produced a large number of quotable slogans for every cause from scientific advancement to British imperialism. At the poem's inspiring conclusion Tennyson coins this oft-quoted cheer for technological progress: "Forward, forward let us range,/ Let the great world spin for ever down the ringing grooves of change." (It is interesting to note that Tennyson based this line on his mistaken belief that the newly developed steam locomotive ran in grooves, rather than on rails.)

In rejecting the temptation to run off to an exotic island in the East, Tennyson's speaker also utters the declaration, "Better fifty years of Europe than a cycle of Cathay." This became a catch phrase for the superiority of the progressive West over what was then considered to be the static East.

Perhaps the most famous line from "Locksley Hall," however, is the perhaps all-too-familiar "In the Spring a young man's fancy lightly turns to thoughts of love." While it is quite distant in tone from the poem as a whole, the phrase has taken on a life of its own.

One of the more effective devices used in "Locksley Hall" is that of apostrophe, in which the speaker addresses a listener who is not actually present. In this case the absent auditor is Amy herself, who is bluntly told by the speaker, "thou art mated with a clown,/ And the grossness of his nature will have weight to drag thee down."

When she eventually comes to regret her choice of a husband, as the rejected suitor predicts she will, Amy is told simply to "Turn thee, turn thee on thy pillow: get thee to thy rest again." Tennyson's repeated use of apostrophe is far more effective than a third-person description of the same events.

Themes and Meanings

"Locksley Hall" begins as the personal expression of one young man's feelings of anger and betrayal after a failed romance. He proclaims to his former love: "Better thou and I were lying, hidden from the heart's disgrace,/ Roll'd in one another's arms, and silent in a last embrace."

Tennyson soon turns the focus of the poem from personal frustration to wider—and more universally relevant—social criticism. Blaming her family's ambitious expectations for his cousin's rejection of him, he complains: "Cursed be the social wants that sin against the strength of youth!/ Cursed be the social lies that warp us from the living truth!" Tennyson thus condemns the demands of society that impose artificial limitations upon the otherwise limitless possibilities of youth.

Feeling the need of some worthy pursuit to distract him from his broken-hearted state, the speaker declares, "I myself must mix with action, lest I wither by despair." However, the "warped" world in which he finds himself offers opportunity only to the wealthy: "What is that which I should turn to, lighting upon days like these?/ Every door is barr'd with gold, and opens but to golden keys."

Faced with an apparently empty future himself, the speaker seeks solace in his dreams of the future of humankind. Here Tennyson's poetry reads like a science-fiction novel in verse: "For I dipt into the future, far as human eye could see,/ Saw the Vision of the world, and all the wonder that would be;// Saw the heavens fill with commerce, argosies of magic sails,/ Pilots of the purple twilight, dropping down with costly bales."

Tennyson offers a vision not only of scientific progress but also of social and political progress, predicting a kind of United Nations a century before its time: "Till the war-drum throbb'd no longer, and the battle-flags were furl'd/ In the Parliament of man, the Federation of the world.// There the common sense of most shall hold a fretful realm in awe,/ And the kindly earth shall slumber, lapt in universal law."

While the speaker laments the plodding pace of scientific progress, which moves "but slowly, slowly, creeping on from point to point," he nevertheless embraces the theme of progress in general, declaring: "Yet I doubt not thro' the ages one increasing purpose runs,/ And the thoughts of men are widen'd with the process of the suns."

The personal satisfactions of being a participant in this abstract historical progression pale in comparison to those imagined by the speaker in the exotic lands he describes as "Summer isles of Eden lying in dark-purple spheres of sea." There, he thinks, "would be enjoyment more than in this march of mind,/ In the steamship, in the railway, in the thoughts that shake mankind."

Ultimately, however, he rejects the temptation to retreat "Deep in yonder shining Orient" and "take some savage woman" to "rear [his] dusky race." After contemplating this escape from the pressures and limitations of his own society, he condemns the notion with a healthy dose of imperialism, uttering: "Fool, again the dream, the fancy! but I *know* my words are wild,/ But I count the gray barbarian lower than the Christian child." Despite the obstacles of Victorian society, he nevertheless sees himself as "the heir of all the ages, in the foremost files of time."

The poem is a dynamic mixture of bitterness and optimism. It concludes with the approach of a storm and the speaker's pronouncement: "Let it fall on Locksley Hall, with rain or hail, or fire or snow." While he abandons his former home to the approaching storm clouds, however, he does not completely abandon his flickering hope for a brighter future.

Edgar V. McKnight, Jr.

LONDON

Author: William Blake (1757-1827)
Type of poem: Lyric
First published: 1794, in *Songs of Innocence and of Experience*

The Poem

"London" is a sixteen-line poem composed of four stanzas of alternatively rhyming short lines. "London" is included in the "Songs of Experience" section of William Blake's larger work, *Songs of Innocence and of Experience* (1794) and contributes to Blake's portrait of fallen human nature.

Blake focuses his attention on the condition of London, England, the capital not only of the country but also of "culture," yet, as the four stanzas make abundantly clear, Blake does not share the opinion that this city sets a positive example. Each stanza of "London" points out ways in which the British monarchy and English laws cause human suffering.

The poem is written in the first person and reports the narrator's observations as he walks through the streets of London. Stanza 1 opens near the River Thames, the heartline of the British Empire; it connects the capital city with the rest of the world. Here Blake observes that everything he sees is "charter'd"—owned by and bound to someone—including the river, which ironically should flow freely to the ocean. The narrator comments that everywhere he looks he sees unhappiness and people suffering.

The second stanza reports what the narrator hears as he walks these imprisoning avenues: human cries of anguish and fear. Not only does he find this suffering in individual misery, but Blake also says that the legal dictates he hears carry with them threats to human freedom. He concludes the second stanza by equating laws with "mind-forg'd manacles"—strictures that limit the human imagination, the human heart, and the human soul.

The third stanza maintains the focus on the sounds that Blake hears as he walks the London streets. He gives examples of persons who are enslaved by the British system of law, by economic boundaries, by the church, and by the monarchy. He says that each chimney sweep's cry is an affront to the Church of England, the state religion. The irony is that the Christianity Blake criticizes is founded on the principle of doing good to others, in particular the less fortunate; Blake says that the sweep's pitiful cry is a reminder to and a black smudge on the very institution that should be helping the child. Blake then lists a second victim of the British government and church: the "hapless Soldier" who fights to preserve the monarchy and whose death sigh bloodies the royal palace walls.

The final stanza of the poem is set in darkness—Blake is listening in the midnight streets to the cries of young prostitutes as they curse the men who victimize them, the wives who are equally victims, and the religion that forces people to think that they must marry and stay married no matter what. "London" ends on a pessimistic note in which Blake reviles the one sacrament that should offer hope to present and future generations: marriage. Instead of being predicated on love and mutual respect, Blake sees it as something that enslaves the body and soul in much the same way that stanzas 2 and 3 point out that English laws victimize the less fortunate.

Forms and Devices

"London" is a deceptively "simple" poem, in part because the language is plain, the lines are short, and the imagery is seemingly everyday. Yet the impact of this poem depends on the multiple layers of meaning that Blake expects readers to see in his choice of words and in the associations that readers will make. Furthermore, "London" is included as a part of a larger work: *Songs of Innocence and of Experience*, a collection of poems that examine and criticize the fallen world.

Because "London" is a "Song of Experience," it is set in contrast to the images that Blake presented in the first half of the work: "Songs of Innocence," poems that showed children frolicking, nature in bloom, people happy and loving, a world before Adam and Eve fell—an event that, according to Blake, brought law, government, monarchy, religion, and other "evils" into the world. "London" represents the antithesis to the world Blake showed readers in "Songs of Innocence"; "London" shows readers an urban landscape consisting of buildings. Nowhere in the poem does Blake include a reference to the natural world except to the River Thames, which he characterizes as "charter'd"—owned and bound by British law. In this fallen world nothing is free, not even the minds and souls of the people. Throughout the poem, Blake makes use of layered meanings and references, as he does in the word "charter'd," which not only means "given liberty," but also refers to ownership and landholding.

Thus "London" depends for its impact on ironic contrasts. In the second stanza, Blake repeats this device by using the word "ban," which not only refers to an announcement of marriage—what should be an occasion for joy—but also implies bonds and enslavement rather than liberty. So when Blake, in this stanza, describes the pitiful cries of people enslaved by law and custom, he implicitly heightens the impact of his criticism by contrasting the antithetical meanings of the word "ban": political and legal prohibition and proclamation of a forthcoming marriage. Blake demands that readers make this type of connection; to miss these layers of meaning is to miss the harsh criticisms that Blake directs at the English monarchy, church, and legal system.

Finally, Blake uses appeals to the senses to heighten the poem's impact. By having the narrator walk through this sordid scene and report what is heard and seen, Blake forces the reader into an immediate confrontation with the human suffering the poet sees all around him. The speaker hears children crying in the person of the chimney sweep and in the diseased prostitute's blinded newborn; he hears despair in the dying sigh of the soldier; he sees death and suffering on every street.

Themes and Meanings

Blake's purpose in creating the *Songs of Innocence and of Experience* was to level criticism at late eighteenth century English society. In these poems, Blake contrasts the unfallen innocence of children with the sordid, repressed attitudes of the adult world—a world ruled by the church, the monarchy, and English common law. Blake viewed himself as a prophet whose task it was to shake people out of their complacent acceptance of their fallen circumstances. In "London," he turns his attack on the capital city, thus pointing out that the very heart of the English Empire is diseased and corrupt. By choosing syphilis as the symbol for all that is wrong with England, Blake is able to condemn institutions and emotions that are sacred to most people: love and marriage. He seems more antagonistic toward the civil and religious laws that sexually repress people than he does toward the husband who cheats on his wife by visiting a prostitute. Nor does he condemn the prostitute for her behavior.

He sees the prostitutes as physically, emotionally, and morally imprisoned by a system that makes them depend on their wealthy customers for their income. He also makes it clear that such victimization works both ways: The venereal disease that the men pass on to and contract from these young women also poisons innocent wives at home and the unborn children of both wives and prostitutes.

The poem concludes with the "youthful Harlot's curse": disease for the straying husband and his unsuspecting wife, syphilitic blindness for children of both women, and a condemnation of marriage as the institution that drives people to form loveless unions, that enslaves people instead of teaching them to love—emotionally and physically. There is angry irony in Blake's choice of words in the concluding line of the poem when he refers to the carriage carrying the young bride and groom from the church as the "Marriage hearse."

It is not only the church that draws Blake's anger in "London": The monarchy is also blamed for the people's woes. In part, the English government and the church are inseparable because the Church of England is the official state church. Of equal importance is the fact that, as the most powerful force in England, the government should protect rather than victimize its citizens. "London" shows that this is not the case. Soldiers who willingly lay down their lives to defend their ruler stand as testimony to their leaders' greed. This was especially pertinent in light of the recent bloody American Revolution, which Blake saw as a reaction against the greedy tyranny of the British monarchy. In poems such as "London," Blake hoped to shock his readers into demanding reform by pointing out the corruption and suffering that existed all around them.

Melissa E. Barth

LONDON

Author: Samuel Johnson (1709-1784)
Type of poem: Satire
First published: 1738

The Poem

   London (the full title is *London: A Poem in Imitation of the Third Satire of Juvenal*) is a long poem of 263 lines written in heroic couplets. Samuel Johnson's first important writing and his second-greatest poem (after "The Vanity of Human Wishes"), this literary imitation of Juvenal's Satire III (part of Juvenal's *Satires*, from the second century C.E.) is neither a translation nor a paraphrase of the original. It is a genuinely new and vigorous composition about corrupt eighteenth century London, "part of the beauty of the performance," Johnson himself wrote in 1738, " . . . consisting in adapting Juvenals Sentiments to modern facts and Persons." As such, the poem was a direct challenge to Alexander Pope, the supreme contemporary imitator of Horace, who supposedly welcomed the publication of *London* with the prophecy that its anonymous author "will soon be deterré." Johnson's satire against an urban wasteland did help to unearth him from literary obscurity and appropriately earned the praise of the great poet-critic T. S. Eliot two centuries later.

   The poem opens with an unnamed narrator expressing mixed emotions about the pending departure of his friend, "Thales," from Greenwich, England, by boat to some rural retreat of primitive innocence in Wales. The narrator may regret losing Thales to "Cambria's solitary shore" but fully sympathizes with his friend's abhorrence of a physically and morally dangerous London.

   From line 35 to the end of the poem, Thales utters a powerful diatribe against the city and, as Donald Greene notes in *The Politics of Samuel Johnson* (2d ed., 1990), makes use of all the commonplaces of contemporary opposition propaganda against the administration of the prime minister, Sir Robert Walpole. Bemoaning a city preoccupied with "vice and gain," in which learning goes unrewarded, Thales prays for his escape to an Edenic "happier place" far from pensioned politicians in the pay of Walpole's regime. Parliament itself is a major wellspring of national corruption, tainting the already "poison'd youth" of the land, spreading lies as truths, seeking a coward's peace with Spanish marauders of English trade who dared to cut off an ear of Captain Robert Jenkins, and enriching itself by controlling the populace through the government newspaper *The Daily Gazetteer* and the recent Stage Licensing Act, which was causing liberty-loving English drama to be displaced by depraved Italian opera.

   By contrast, Thales is the truth-telling good man (*vir bonus*) found in classical satire, a true-blue Protestant Englishman who despises the corrupting invasion of foreigners—especially slavish Frenchmen, who win preferment by flattery, deceit, and an unprincipled readiness to do anything for the ruling class. In a money-hungry metropolis of topsy-turvy values, poverty is the only crime that provokes universal ridicule and neglect, whereas wealth causes an admiring nation to help rebuild rich Orgilio's mansion, gutted by fire. So widespread is urban violence from drunkards, street gangs, and murdering burglars that the amount of rope needed to hang this growing horde of criminals would use up all the reserves of hemp needed to rig the ships for King George II's annual visits to his royal mistress in Hanover, Germany. Consequently, Thales must bid farewell to London, and he promises that if his narrator-friend should ever retire to rural innocence in Kent, then Thales will leave Wales and join him there to help inspire the creation of satires against the vices of the age.

Forms and Devices

At the heart of Johnson's moral artistry is a moral realism that has roots in Juvenal's Satire III but that, influenced by a Christian-Renaissance vision of right and reasonable conduct, bears comparison with other eighteenth century works: Scribler satires, William Hogarth's prints, and Henry Fielding's novels. Claiming later to have had all sixteen of Juvenal's satires stored and poetically transformed in his mind, Johnson may well have composed *London* rapidly, mostly in his head, before he committed the verses to paper.

The poem was his first major bid for literary fame. It is much more of a poetical transformation of the Juvenalian satire than some previous commentators have recognized. The changes are an early indication of Johnson's distinctive moral vision and poetic voice. For example, in keeping with his Christian sense of moral decorum, he deleted Juvenalian references to sexual debauchery, homosexuality, slop basins, and wayward gods, and substituted sanitized generalizations and reverential references to a "kind heaven" protecting poor mortals.

Even more original was Johnson's creation of a political poem, replete with stock opposition propaganda and allusions to a glorious libertarian past, from a Latin satire relatively silent about Roman politics. Despite considerable restrictions on the eighteenth century press, Johnson enjoyed more freedom of political expression than Juvenal could assume under an imperial dictatorship. Even though Johnson acknowledged the irrelevance of his adaptation (lines 182-209) of Juvenalian verses on rebuilding burnt mansions to English manners, the rest of *London* was of immediate topical relevance to the current political scene and to his own bitter sense of being an outcast in the city.

Finally, Johnson's poem is far more compressed, more elegant, and more aphoristic than those of Juvenal, the angry but casual satirist of Rome. *London* is almost sixty lines shorter than Satire III, not only because of Johnson's omission of Juvenalian digressions and an entire section on crowded Roman streets, but also because of his remarkable rhetorical conciseness, which engenders summary moral generalizations. Thus, a single pithy and beautifully alliterated line, "And ev'ry moment leaves my little less," condenses almost two flaccid lines of Latin verse literally translated as "my means are less today than they were yesterday, and tomorrow will rub off something from what remains." Again, the well-known Johnsonian maxim "Slow rises worth,/ by poverty depress'd" ennobles, with its antithetical verbs, this homely literal translation of the Latin equivalent: "It is no easy matter, anywhere, for a man to rise when poverty stands in the way of his merits."

Young Samuel Johnson in *London* proved himself a master of the closed pentameter couplet—better known as the heroic couplet—that John Dryden had refined and Pope perfected. In Johnson's hands, the closed couplet lines were at the magnificent service of his insistent search for moral order and rational control in a poem describing urban anarchy in vivid detail and striking generalizations that sometimes border on allegorical abstractions ("Behold rebellious virtue quite o'erthrown"). The intellectual density of some of his severely compressed lines can surpass the virtuoso poetic wit of even Pope. For example, Thales states a compulsion "To pluck a titled poet's borrow'd wing"—more prosaically, to expose an aristocratic poetaster's unoriginal literary productions under the metaphorically second-hand inspiration of a winged Pegasus, the mythological flying horse beloved of the Muses and all first-rate poets. Symmetry, balance, antithesis, and paradox provide a rhetorical harmony for the discordant subject matter: "Here malice, rapine, accident conspire,/ And now a rabble rages, now a fire."

Themes and Meanings

London is an idealistic outsider's view of England's depraved capital city, summed up in the poem's Juvenalian epigraph, "Quis ineptae/ Tam patiens urbis, tam ferreus ut teneat se" ("For who can be so tolerant of the city, who so iron-willed as to contain himself"). The theme of an idealistic or innocent youth's exposure to a corrupt city, in a journey to or from the country, surfaces repeatedly in Johnson's fiction—for example, in *Rasselas* (1759)—and in the works of fellow eighteenth century Englishmen: in William Hogarth's engravings of the 1730's of a rake's or harlot's progress to ruin, and in Henry Fielding's great novel *Tom Jones* (1749). The theme has classical roots in Greco-Roman myths of poetic escape to bucolic simplicity but also registers the genuinely bittersweet reactions of contemporary authors, so often born in the provinces, to the stunning realities of a fast-growing and fast-paced London.

Although Johnson later became famous for his love of London, this early poem strikes a note of repulsion. A thirty-year-old newcomer to the city born and reared in the provincial town of Lichfield, he surely felt neglect and endured poverty as a journalist-editor for Edward Cave's *The Gentleman's Magazine*. Fame and fortune must have seemed elusive to him as he struggled in the callous and crowded center of British culture, crime, commerce, and councils of state. Even though he interlards his satire with stock opposition propaganda against Walpole's regime, he also gives vent to heartfelt abhorrence of urban excesses and grinding poverty. Part of the poem's bitterness stemmed from the encouragement of his natural rebelliousness by his friendship with the charismatic and unstable minor poet Richard Savage, who is sometimes, perhaps erroneously, equated with Thales. Savage, too, was an erudite, hypersensitive, and poverty-stricken author who, like Thales, had to escape to Wales, and who, unlike Johnson, died in 1743 without achieving enduring fame and fortune in the big city.

Allied with the central theme of exposing the moral and physical horrors of the modern metropolis through ridicule for the reader's satiric instruction are two motifs of escape. The first is the classical myth of rural retirement from the city, adapted from Juvenal's Satire III to embrace British geography, including remote places such as Wales, Scotland, Ireland, Kent, and the banks of the rivers Severn and Trent. There is even a probable allusion to the new pauper colony of Georgia (lines 170-175), founded by James Oglethorpe in the early 1730's as a philanthropic and religious-oriented settlement in North America.

The poem's geographical escapism extends to an escapism in time. Juvenal's fleeting hints of an ancient golden age are nothing compared to Johnson's insistent and periodic appeals to visions of former English greatness as a foil to the stark national decline visible everywhere in the city. Radically innovating from Juvenal's original hints, Johnson created a new, more political poem of opposition propaganda that contrasts Robert Walpole's supposedly cowardly policies toward Spain and France during a looming "War of Jenkin's Ear" against the Spanish (1739) with the greatness of Queen Elizabeth I (lines 19-30), Edward III (lines 99-105), Henry V (lines 117-122), and Alfred the Great (lines 248-253). Indeed, Thales's very retirement to Wales is a re-creation of the flight of ancient Celtic Britons from foreign Saxon invaders (lines 7-8, 43-48). The pursuit and preservation of English liberty and Christian rectitude require an escape from the economic enslavement and ethical chaos generated in the capital city.

Thomas M. Curley

THE LOOM

Author: Robert Kelly (1935-   )
Type of poem: Poetic sequence
First published: 1975

The Poem

    The Loom is a long poem of more than four hundred pages by one of America's most prolific and versatile poets. It takes up a thorny issue of contemporary poetry, the divided self, which is presented in many forms as the speaker ventures over the earth in search of a way to dissolve his own internal oppositions to become whole and imaginative in a new life. Robert Kelly's voluminous output as a writer is characterized by a lush and vivid imagination and a supple writing style that is clear, crisp, flexible in its command of a wide variety of experiences and topics, ranging from love stories to allegories, fables, romantic adventures, comic absurdity, myth, and occult lore. Hardly anyone compares with him for breadth of interest or facility with language or volubility. His canon comprises over fifty volumes of fiction and poetry, and his output even includes a series of short-story collections that have commanded high praise from critics.

    The Loom is an early work that establishes some of the major themes of his subsequent poetry, in particular the complex relation between the sexes, which represents for Kelly not only the dynamics of love, but the terms of conflict between soul and self, ego and world. *The Loom* is an exploration of the identity of man and woman, self and soul, as these terms undergo a transformation through a loosely jointed quest narrative.

    The poem, divided into thirty-six segments of narrative and commentary, is written in a fluid discourse of short lines, on a border between dramatic monologue and private revery. One is never quite sure where one mode of delivery ends and the other begins. The language is sinuous and moves effortlessly between direct address and dreamy introspection as one is drawn into the life of an intelligent, humorously candid man who shares his efforts to satisfy his sexual and emotional cravings.

    The loom of the title is the imagination itself, which weaves into the design of its story the various myths by which a man slowly transforms himself from embattled opposites to serene lover of several women, each of whom represents an aspect of soul, his own and the world's. Though the quest has a long history in poetry, Kelly's version of it is modern and original. He begins the narrative by seating himself before a table, as medieval bards would do before reciting a long heroic epic. The reader learns immediately that there are "two rhythms" to harmonize, two realms of awareness to bring into phase, which Kelly identifies as "City & Language," "place & talk," or world and self. The table is parsed into its psychological root as *tabula*, the blank slate of mind on which experience makes its marks. It is also the table of seances, where spirits are summoned and made to talk across the border of death and sleep.

Finally, the table is an altar where one partakes of communion with a holy spirit, and shares the ritual with others, his readers.

Kelly appropriates many of the conventions of epic narrative, including invocations to the muse and a ritual descent into the underworld of memory, from which heroes have traditionally set forth on their mythic voyages. Having deployed this classic machinery for his own narrative, one learns the essential purpose of the tale (the argument), that the sexes have been falsely polarized and separated from one another, and that wholeness resides in transposing sexual differences back into one human sensibility. Only then can *"we move/ naked at last/ beyond the garments/ male & female one/ & none."*

Each of the thirty-six sections of *The Loom* features a woman as the object of the quest. Her presence in the poem is a focal point of each tale or meditation; she figures as the lover, as goddess, muse, or as a dimension of the narrator's own self which he cannot bring into phase with the rest of his awareness. Woman here is both real and figurative, an actual woman, such as the wife he addresses as Helen, and the echo of mythic females whose historic or psychological significance reverberates behind the name of Helen. Sometimes, as in the case of Isabella, who appears twice in the sequence, in sections 3 and 16, she is like an Ariadne figure who helps Theseus, her lover, find his way out of the labyrinth at Minos. Lady Isabella is also a guide of sorts, a counselor to the ironic narrator as he plunges into the early stages of his journey toward rebirth.

The journey starts the moment the narrator is seated at his table and settled into his memory trance. Readers find him on the deck of an ocean liner, speaking to Lady Isabella, who is traveling with her father back to the island of Mallorca from Naples. Lady Isabella's father is founder of the Cabeza Foundation, an institute that studies the relation between the mind and the brain (*cabeza* is Spanish for head.) Readers see her through the ironic perspective of the narrator, who makes everything she says seem absurd, especially when she informs him that the motto of the institute is "To free the mind/ from the circuitry/ of the brain."

The Mediterranean, where the ship sails, is the locus of ancient mythology, and Homer's *Odyssey* (c. 800 B.C.E.) is the principal narrative from which Western journey and quest literature springs. The ocean liner fades into another, smaller, ship where the narrator meets Odysseus, who prefers his Roman name, Ulysses, and who introduces him to a new lover, Korinna. The narrator's brief relation with Korinna parallels the episode in the *Odyssey* where Odysseus falls in love with Calypso and lives with her on an island for ten years. Korinna is "much earlier than Odysseus," she tells the narrator, and she confides that she is one of the "blonde witches" of the Dordogne, the cave region of western France. "I had an odd feeling/ I wanted to worship her," he says, as he perceives in her the powers of a goddess. She, too, is a counselor and repeats the message of Lady Isabella that the "mind belongs to itself," and not merely to the logic of one's senses, the world of the brain.

Other episodes take a reader to California, to the mountains where he meets a young woman whose loyalty to an older man, a kind of Sisyphus who spends his life trying to climb a mountain, prevents her from becoming the narrator's lover. Her restraint is also a lesson in reserve, the soul's continence. The most striking of these early adventures occurs in section 11, where a hired hand on a ranch leads the cattle out into a field, slaughters a bullock, and throws a spell over the bewildered rancher and his family. The narrator behaves with godlike austerity as he makes his sacrifice. Already he is partly transformed into a mythological figure, a Dionysus.

Section 16 returns to the ship carrying Lady Isabella to Mallorca, where the narrator is her aggressive lover. At the point of seduction, however, they quarrel and he swims back to Los Angeles and returns home. In section 21, he is the "lame God," the figure of Pan or Eros, whose realm is a fertile garden, the pagan world of love and innocence. In other episodes, he meets Isis, the Egyptian goddess and sister/lover of Osiris whom she has restored to life. The narrator has traveled through his cultural memory to relive the experience of many heroes, and has undergone harrowing ordeals, such as his kidnapping and torture recorded in section 23, where he is buried and figuratively reborn. Finally, he returns home as Adam, first man, the link between the "creature world" of apes and the human world of anxiety and death. His skull looks back at him as the reminder of his mortality, but his mind has leaped free, as Lady Isabella said it should. The rains pour down into the desert as the sign of his renewal.

Forms and Devices

Although it is a complex work involving many references and allusions, the technical devices in *The Loom* are relatively simple. To allow for a quick flow of discourse in the poem, the lines are kept short and are enjambed in a loose, conversational rhythm of varying meters. Stanzas are irregular and can run for several pages. There is no set length of line but, on average, the lines do not exceed eight or nine syllables and are rarely fewer than two or three syllables. Sometimes a paragraph of prose will intervene. Kelly occasionally indents a line to mark a shift in tone or to separate units of thought or action in a stanza. These indentations vary and, perhaps, suggest the length of certain pauses in the flow of narrative. Otherwise, the poem is a graceful discourse, textured by occasional passages of verse from Greek, Spanish, and Provençal poetry and by the sheer exuberance of figures and place-names sprinkled throughout.

The discourse itself is a playful mixture of literal reminiscence, humorous commentary, hyperbole, and allegorical episodes. Literal and figurative events merge subtly in the language as the story unfolds; the characters are drawn realistically only to be elevated in the next phrase to their allegorical identities as gods, psychological functions, or as elements of human sensibility. Often the same figures are demoted back to their literal selves once more, as with Lady Isabella, Helen, and the protagonist himself.

The role of metaphor and symbol in the text is like the Double Axe of section 4, which has "Two blades, separate, wielded by one haft." They signal the double lives of events and objects in the narrator's memories, and thus bridge the separate worlds of fact and ideas, sense and imagination. Metaphors abound in the discourse as the vehicle of ambiguous reality, the double nature of things as phenomena in the sphere of mortality and death, and as ideas that live forever in the mind. Hence, gardens, flowers, women, adventures are all metaphorical in their capacity to mirror both sides of human existence.

Themes and Meanings

The Loom is a postmodern retelling of myth and fables; it does not pretend to serious intent or formality in its method of narration and argument, but recognizes its tradition through a complex allusiveness to epics by Homer, Vergil, and Ovid. The classical world of epic literature is a realm of mythical imagination which the narrator longs to repossess in his own words. The flight of mind from the world of mere sense and reason is achieved through the narrator's figurative descent into his cultural memory, where he merges tales of his own actual experience with those of epic narrative—hence, the figure of the loom as the metaphor of imagination, with its capacity to join the threads of different sources into the same woven fabric.

Kelly does not labor the familiar metaphor of the loom as imagination, but we see it constantly in the narrow strip of language that forms his poem. Its continuous presence, page by page, throughout the work is the woven tapestry created by the collaborative energies of mind and brain. One frequently returns to the speaker at his table in California to be reminded of the weaver at his work—that he draws the threads of narrative partly from his own store of facts about the world and partly from what he fabricates out of pure fantasy.

The modern character of this retelling of myth lies in its self-conscious attitude toward the narration; Kelly knows he is telling an epic journey and draws attention to the act of telling often throughout the poem. The emphasis is not on the adventures or the heroes involved but on the artist who conceives and propels his figures forward by means of other texts and his own ingenuity. Like other ambitious long poems by postmodern writers, Kelly's poem is as much about the effort to write as it is about what is written. Yet even as the writer draws attention to himself as the maker of his tale, the humor, vividness, compelling interest of the tales he tells lure one from disbelief into the spell of the work; this, too, is part of the humor and complexity of the poem. Magic has its ways, its will over the skeptical modern mind, despite the obvious artificiality of writing a poem and of reading it in a book.

The power of the tale lies chiefly in the myth it invokes. All stories have at their core some immutable and universal moment of truth about human nature contained in the myth or paradigm around which the story revolves. Each of Kelly's episodes in the poem is anchored by a myth in which all the literalness of the event dissolves into allegorical generality. The kidnapping that occurs in section 23 begins realistically and relates the details of his seizure and imprisonment. Gradually one sees the tale give way to a parable about the soul's powers to communicate with nature. The body in the muddy pit is isolated and helpless, until "a dream-guardian" stood over it and "taught me a song to sing," which gave it the power to call down the rain. In terms of the poem's own epistemological scheme, the brain is that part of us that only reckons with the phenomena of daily life and does not perceive the mythical moment transforming events. The mind (or soul) is that function of memory and spiritual perception that transforms information into great truths. Kelly would have readers believe that the women he presents are various embodiments of the mind and that his male persona is the commonsense brain longing to transcend its practical realm through love.

The Loom also presents certain ideas that Kelly first formulated in the early 1960's as a member of the group of "deep image" poets in New York, writers who had introduced the theories of the Swiss psychiatrist Carl Gustav Jung into American poetry. Language itself has its own memory, according to Kelly, and some of its terms are the descendants of a long line of antecedent terms composed of some of the same vowels and consonants. When used in poetry, such terms as "moon" and "ocean" reverberate with their long history as human sounds and signs, and confer mystery when placed in the modern sentence. Poetic language possesses incantatory powers to awaken the listener's or reader's unconscious; its terms derive from sacred liturgy and chant, spells and other magical rites, where repetition of vowels and certain repeating rhythms produced ecstasy or other religious states in the participants. The luxurious vowelness of the word "loom" itself promises, by its own dark sound, to draw one into an incantatory recitation of other rich images by which to escape from the mere quotidian world.

"Clean song," Kelly writes admiringly in section 24; "A light voice/ accurately lifted up,/ proclaiming the note/ dead on pitch." This is the ideal of poetry, the perfect execution of voice and idea together. The opposite is the merely adequate, the realm of information and dead act. "What will kill me/ is the adequate." The triumph of *The Loom* lies in its own magical intensity as fable, in its power to convey its readers to mythical worlds on the strength of its syllables and brief rhythmic phrases. The poem may, in fact, be a celebration of those powers by the poet, who, at the first writing of the poem, had turned thirty-six, the number of sections he gave to the poem. Readers leave him in the poem, back at his table where he began his work. Not only is the table the place of food, an altar, but it is also the desk where art is made. Outside, the quotidian world is glazed with newly fallen rain, where the desert has suddenly "crashed into flower."

Paul Christensen

THE LOST BABY POEM

Author: Lucille Clifton (1936-   )
Type of poem: Lyric
First published: 1972, in *Good News About the Earth*

The Poem

Lucille Clifton's "the lost baby poem" is an elegy—a poem written in mourning for one who has died—yet it is also a lyric of hope and a promise made to an absent presence: the lost baby.

The speaker is a woman who has been forced by her poverty to abort her baby. The "almost body" was swept out to sea with the sewage, she says—an observation both powerfully repulsive and grief-ridden. The questioning refrain, "what did I know about waters rushing back . . ." refers to her inexperience at the time. Could she have found some way to avoid her final choice? The line hints at her subsequent suffering: the terrible realization of what she has done, rushing back to her.

One recognizes that the waters are those "under the city," but they also represent female waters. The author alludes to the ageless link between the female spirit and reproductive cycle and to the cycles of the moon and tides. Thus "the waters" are also the waters of the womb, or life-giving waters. Apart from the the obvious, the "waters rushing back" may refer to her sorrow: "what did I know about drowning/ or being drowned." In stanza 1, however, the speaker wishes most simply to state what happened.

The second stanza explains further the circumstances that influenced the speaker's actions. The images are cold and bleak; the memory is difficult for her to confront. Yet in stanza 2, the woman refuses guilt, blame, and self-pity. Whereas the first stanza ends with a tone hovering near self-reproach and remorse, this section calmly explains the necessity of her decision: "you would have been born into winter/ in the year of the disconnected gas/ and no car."

The speaker goes on to imagine, if the baby had been born, the "thin walk" (the only walk) she and her baby might have made together on a day of bitter weather. The baby that would have been is imagined as "ice" and "naked as snow"—the coldness of death and the crystalline beauty and purity of snow combine in this image to suggest the persistence of a mother's love even after her acceptance of the loss.

The lines serve as a reminder that to lose the baby at birth would have been to endure another kind of death, still a terrible loss. The hard times "and some other things" weighed heavily enough to convince her that abortion was necessary, but her yearning for it to have been otherwise still exists.

The third stanza shifts in tone and perspective. The speaker looks forward to the unfolding of her life and the lives of her family. The lost baby's "definite brothers and sisters" will be fully nurtured; their mother vows never to be "less than a mountain" for them. For the "never named sake" of the baby, the speaker promises to be the mother now that she could not be in the past.

Her incantation—"let the rivers pour over my head/ let the sea take me for a spiller/ of seas" (should she fail her children)—underscores the gravity of her oath. Having been forced to go against the natural order of things once, and having suffered the consequences, she has no intention of invoking the waters' wrath again. Nor does she intend at any cost to allow the pressures of the world to induce her to take such an action again. The poem ends not in helpless sadness but with strength and with the conviction that she can now choose her sacrifices.

Forms and Devices

Because Lucille Clifton's work is rooted in the African American experience, many of her poems have celebrated black music and paid homage to jazz and blues; "the lost baby poem," too, uses the sounds of the blues. Repetition of words and phrases suggests a percussive blues rhythm, as in the lines "I dropped your almost body down/ down to meet the waters" and the repeated phrases in "what did I know about waters rushing back/ what did I know about drowning."

The poem is also structured like a blues song, beginning with a statement in stanza 1, continuing in stanza 2 with an expansion of that statement—and a subtle adjustment in tone—and ending with a resolution or rebuttal. In the narrative line of the poem, the first part introduces the situation (with regret); the second provides details that sharpen that feeling of regret into proud indignation, even outrage perhaps; and the final part delivers the speaker from dejection—cures her blues—with an incantatory vow not to let life treat her (or her children) that way again. The wonderful paradox found in most blues lyrics is present here: Wrenching sadness and even despair are coupled with spirited and determined optimism.

Longer than many of Clifton's other poems, "the lost baby poem" is able to sustain unifying images through the three stanzas. The sewage/sea waters of the first stanza (which turn to desolate ice in the middle stanza) return in the third stanza as rivers—signifying revival or baptism. The monuments of the natural world are invoked throughout the poem—the sea, the north wind, winter snow, a mountain—to suggest the strength of the natural world and its order, of which human beings partake. Its specific place, however, is an urban landscape, reflecting as do many of Clifton's poems the experiences shared by people in many African American communities in the United States.

The poem seems to begin in the middle of a conversation. This technique, and the use of the first person, allow the reader to share more easily the intimacy of the "conversation." In addition, the use of everyday language—black language—gives the poem a directness that engages one, comfortably or not. Thus, to witness and comprehend this very private self-confrontation is made possible by Clifton's choice of language. Its simplicity reflects the clear convictions of the speaker—her intention to cope, simply, without self-pity or bitterness.

Clifton has said of her style, "I have never believed that for anything to be valid or true or intellectual or 'deep' it had to first be complex. I deliberately use the language that I use." Her language is outwardly—and deceptively—simple. Seldom are her words longer than three syllables. The free, open verse is written in short lines, succinct and direct. Yet the compactness renders a great complexity of emotions. The very restrained ending of stanza 2 is an example: "if you were here I could tell you these/ and some other things." Its understatement is moving.

Themes and Meanings

Lucille Clifton's work is rooted in the black experience, in Christian idealism, and in her feminine sensibilities. "Femaleness" is the energy that informs many of her poems: she often writes about children, family, and keeping a household. She is interested in revealing personal joys and sadnesses in order to suggest the experiences people share—what makes human experience a continuous and collective experience.

Clifton is a self-proclaimed poet of black culture, and she clearly wishes to transmit values. As in her many children's stories, she wishes to convey the "good news" that despite dark days there can be and should be joy to look forward to, that ultimately the world is defined by possibility. This vision is strongly embraced in "the lost baby poem." The pledge of the third stanza clearly indicates that the speaker aims for better days. Also evident is the conviction that people *do* have choices.

The poem also resonates with communal and historic tidings: It re-announces and reminds readers of the plight that affects many women—many of them black and all of them poor. Not really a political poem (except in the sense that personal problems often lead to political action), it nevertheless takes on a topic that has become highly political. Clifton understands the complexity of the issue of abortion, and she offers no direct comment on the difficult maze of arguments surrounding it. She does offer her view, via the poem, that people must be allowed to nurture life—their own and their children's—for the good of the community and humanity.

The last cathartic stanza suggests that the mother's blues for the lost baby have somehow made a bright future possible for her other children. In that way the poem has served its purpose as a blues elegy—it has exorcised the speaker's sorrow and has validated, without devaluing the lost baby's life, her sacrifice. It is one of Clifton's most complex and lyrical poems.

The poem celebrates a reverence for life and the sacred will to continue life in the face of great hardships. One should note that no judgment of the speaker's choice to have aborted her baby is made. The poem cuts to the heart of this woman's dilemma and searches for understanding, forgiveness, dignity, and hope rather than passing judgments of right or wrong or voicing all-too-easily espoused solutions to the problems of poverty and the loss of self-esteem. As in blues music, the solitary personal journey is most important, and the individual voice that sings of its experience offers the most vivid, the most valuable, and the most comforting wisdom.

JoAnn Balingit

THE LOST CITIES

Author: Ernesto Cardenal (1925-   )
Type of poem: Meditation
First published: 1967, as "Las ciudades perdidas"; collected in *Homenaje a los indios americanos*, 1969; English translation collected in *Apocalypse, and Other Poems*, 1977

The Poem

Ernesto Cardenal's "The Lost Cities" consists of nine sections of irregular stanzas, ranging from six to twenty-six lines. The meditative poem arises from a visit to the Guatemalan ruins of Tikal, vestiges of the Mayan civilization at its apex. It pays homage to the great achievement of the classical Mayan civilization, laments its disappearance, and envisions its return to its former grandeur. The poem opens and closes with multisensory descriptions of nocturnal creatures inhabiting the abandoned ruins of the Mesoamerican city. They represent nature's return to their home displaced by temples carved out of the jungle's rock. The body of the work deals with the cyclical nature of time and the rise and fall of civilizations. The poet wonders whether the stone temples will again emerge from beneath the vines and thickets.

The Mayan concept of time is the dominant recurrent theme. Secondary themes of religion and the changing faces of civilization are intertwined with its primary focus. The poet as visitor to Tikal meditates upon the ruins, envisions its past splendor, contrasts it with present-day Central American society, and hypothesizes the return of its former greatness. The juxtaposition of temporal descriptions from different eras leads the reader backward and forward through time. Abrupt contrasts with Nicaragua's harsh dictatorship and the brutality of the military regime temporarily break the harmonious and mystical aura of the acropolis. Even as it is overrun with jungle flora and fauna, its majesty is awe-inspiring and thought-provoking. While the poet wonders whether the Maya can reclaim mastery over their temples, stelae, towers, chronicles, and genius, nocturnal creatures claim Tikal as their domain as his question remains unresolved.

Forms and Devices

The structure is a loose arrangement of irregular verse lines. Each verse describes a particular aspect of the ancient Mayan civilization and its historical context. Each stanza serves as a descriptive passage that may be rearranged to form a panoramic composite. Generally, lines alternate between three and four stressed syllables. The stanzas do not adhere to a consistent metric pattern. They vary in length, and some contain lines with more or less than four stressed syllables.

The poem's content is more consistent than its structure. Symbols found in nature and antiquity convey the poet's temporal message. Nocturnal scenes open and close the poem. Among the plentitude of flora and fauna, only the jaguar that "roars in towers" reappears. In the third stanza, this sacred creature returns in the form of a high priest's cape, an evocation of ritual ceremony that revives Mayan past splendor. The revered jaguar's endurance links nature's strength to human aspirations and their search for divine union.

The second stanza distinguishes between the present-day wildlife and their stylized depiction in frescoes. The poet contrasts their endurance and integrity with the lives of descendants of the ancient inhabitants. He wonders how the contemporary Maya can record their greatness in hieroglyph, painting, and dethroning "tyrants." In closing, he questions how they can rebuild their civilization.

The third stanza provides a visual explanation for these questions. As the acropolis lies buried beneath the jungle, only wild animals inhabit the abandoned city. The sacred quetzal shares Tikal with the lowly tapir. The poet evokes the past deification of the bird through personification of the present-day bird as the poem describes the jungle, where the anteater, tapir, and "the *quetzal* (still garbed like a Maya) go." As a recurring image linking this sacred creature with its former role as deity, quetzal feathers reappear on fans with jaguar capes worn by the high priests. The religious ceremony seeks to transcend human limitations through shouts and drumbeats, copal incense, and smoke rising from pinewood torches.

This montage of synesthetic images acutely portrays the abandoned city at its apex. The former greatness of Tikal's high priests is vividly envisioned, accentuated by ceremonial scents and sounds. The poem juxtaposes this scene with the description of present-day Tikal, where only howling monkeys in zapote trees replace the city's former splendor.

The fifth stanza is a one-line statement interrupting the pastoral reverie: "There are no names of generals on the stelae." This shocks the reader back to the present and prepares the context of the remaining stanzas. The poet contrasts the ancient Maya with the modern-day inhabitants of the Petén region and Central American society. He lists characteristics of the ancient Maya deemed superior to those of contemporary society and emphasizes that the Mayan language, records, and art do not acknowledge leadership. No names of rulers or high priests were immortalized. The seventh stanza continues this observation, as the poet relates that the Mayan language lacks words for "master" and "city wall." This stanza's major emphasis is on the democracy of religion. While Tikal was a city of temples honoring the gods, priests did not enslave or colonize peasants in order to create and fortify their capital.

The eighth stanza develops the concept of unifying the disparate elements of Mesoamerican culture past and present. The stanza's axis, religion, links past and present icons. It begins by identifying "Jesus as the God of the Maize." The ancients again counterpoint modernity by linking disparate symbols of modern civilization: "They had no wars, nor knew the wheel/ but they had calculated the synodic path of Venus." While the stanza characterizes the civilization as utopian, unadorned nature simplifies this astronomical achievement by incorporating a ceiba tree on the horizon and parrots returning to their nest. The second half of the stanza links religion to the Mayan concept of time. "Time was holy. Days were gods." The stanza ends by refraining the cyclical pattern of time and religion.

The final stanza returns to nightfall and the wildlife that rules present-day Tikal. It links the poem to the opening scene of nocturnal creatures inhabiting the ruins. The poet again wonders if the measure of time will return to mark the civilization's passing.

Themes and Meanings

Cardenal was influenced by Amerindian themes. Ancient civilizations of Mesoamerica arise from the text. The Mayan perspective of time as cyclical is evident throughout the poem. Each verse creates a passage to the following verse in a continuous thread that reinforces the thematic interplay between past and present. He repeats the temporal unit of *katún* several times as a multifaceted link that connects the stanzas thematically as well as structurally. The brilliance of the most accurate calendar ever calculated is linked to other accomplishments of the Mayan civilization throughout the seventh stanza.

The term *katún* appears in the first, eighth, and ninth stanzas. *Katún* is the final day of the Mayan twenty-year cycle, which consists of 7,200 days. When the Spaniards confronted the Maya in 1541, their arrival coincided with the first year of *Katún* 11. This date was an omen of the impending demise of the Mayan civilization, and it continues to serve as a symbol of recurring misfortune. The eighth stanza encapsulates this temporal vision: "They adored time: the mysterious/ effluxion of time." This concept is concretized in the examples that follow. Each day was assigned a deity. The past and future were intermingled in their oral history and glyphs. "They used the same *katúns* for past and future,/ in the belief that time was re-enacted/ like the motions of the heavenly bodies they observed."

Other symbols reinforce the poem's temporal theme. The cycles of night and day, dark and light, life and death, and Jesus as the "God of the Maize" and the string of dictators and generals. The staff of Mayan life, corn, recurs in the second, third, and seventh stanzas as the *milpa*, or cornfields that domesticate the jungle and reinforce the alternating cycles of taming the earth and letting it run wild. Jesus is also equated with the God of Corn as the image contrasts the hierarchy of a destructive and deadly military regime that replaces a supreme being in contemporary Petén as well as in Central America.

The eighth stanza reinforces the advancement of the Maya at the height of their civilization, in juxtaposition with the concept of advancement in modern society: "they never left the Stone Age, technologically speaking." The stanza lists elements that the Maya lacked, though their absence did not detract from their accomplishments. "They had no applied sciences. They were not practical." The stanza enumerates achievements in religion, astronomy, mathematics, and art. The ancients lacked the tools that drive contemporary societies: metallurgy, the wheel, a system of weights, and war.

The last days of Tikal are shrouded in mystery. Their grandeur is frozen in poignant images: "Stelae remain unfinished,/ blocks half cut in quarries." These rocks are crystallized in time as wildlife buries the human masterpiece. Tikal serves to inspire, to herald the emergence of another great civilization in the infinite cycle of time.

Carole A. Champagne

THE LOST PILOT

Author: James Tate (1943-   )
Type of poem: Elegy
First published: 1966; collected in *The Lost Pilot,* 1967

The Poem

"The Lost Pilot" is a poem in free verse, its forty-eight lines divided into sixteen stanzas, each of which is three lines in length. The title, along with the dedication to the poet's father (emphasizing the fact that the father died at the extremely young age of twenty-two), establishes a mood of loss both violent and tragic. The loss of a pilot suggests the loss of direction and control. The loss of a pilot/father foreshadows the great personal grief and bewilderment with which the poet will struggle throughout the length of the poem.

Appropriately, the poem is written in the first person, which allows great immediacy of emotion and brings the reader close to the intense and complex relationship of the poet to his lost father. The complexity of grief is at the very heart of the elegiac tradition in poetry, a tradition which seeks to reconcile the living to the reality of death. It is fitting, then, that this poem is addressed directly to the lost father, as only he can know the answers to those questions generated by his son's feelings and bewilderment.

The poem begins with a startling declaration: "Your face did not rot/ like the others." The sudden and shocking physical nature of this statement re-creates for the reader the emotional tenor of the pilot's death and the son's bereavement. It also characterizes the desperate tone of the elegy as the son seeks some consolation, however unlikely or grotesque. As the pilot died young and, presumably, in flames, his body did not suffer the deterioration either of age or of interment, fates which people in general and, as the poem goes on to explain, the lost pilot's surviving crewmen in particular, must eventually confront. Surely, this is a meager consolation, but then the unique circumstances of the poet's loss are bitterly deprived of ordinary comfort.

The poem continues as the poet gives voice to the injustice of his father's death, comparing the wrong he suffered to the sufferings of Job. Yet it is his own bereft situation to which the poet must somehow become reconciled, so in the body of the poem, he gives specific voice to his own doubts, hopes, and despair. He tries to talk his father down, out of the sky from which he never returned, hoping to receive from him the information and guidance every son desires from his father. In his desperation, he even bargains with the lost pilot, promising to keep their proposed reunion a secret from his father's widow and surviving crewmen. He receives no word in reply. In the closing stanzas, the poet is left alone with his grief, feeling that his eternally young, romantic father is somehow more alive in his mysteriousness than is he himself in his all-too-real bereavement. In the end, he accepts the silence of his misfortune only because he has no other choice.

Forms and Devices

The major encompassing form of "The Lost Pilot" is James Tate's unique version of the traditional elegy. It is this form which the poem fulfills through its general tones (anger and grief), its rhetorical methods (sorrowful exclamation and the interrogation of the lost pilot and of the facts of death itself), and final resignation. Ironically, it is the relationship of this poem to its elegiac forebears—works such as John Milton's "Lycidas" and Walt Whitman's "When Lilacs Last in the Dooryard Bloom'd"—that must substitute for the more intimate yet now impossible relationship between the poet and his father.

Presiding over the entire elegy is the metaphor of the lost pilot himself; it is into this metaphor that the poet's father has disappeared, never having had the time or life to be anything but a metaphor to his son. His lostness has many significant qualities which contribute to his mysteriousness: Being lost, he can only be presumed dead, thus leaving his son in a state of perpetual uncertainty; being lost, he represents a continual challenge to his son to find him, as Telemachus was challenged to find his father Odysseus in Homer's *Odyssey* (c. 800 B.C.E.); being a lost pilot, he represents an eternal contradiction as someone who is responsible for leading others and yet is lost himself. Toward the end of the poem, this metaphor finds its final shape in that of "a tiny, African god" forever orbiting the earth, eternally inscrutable, exotic, and out of reach.

The imagery of the poem serves to emphasize the distinctions between the mystery of the father's fate and the grim reality of the fates of those who survived him. His copilot's face has turned to "corn-/ mush," a bland and featureless foodstuff, while the lost pilot's is gemlike, having grown "dark,/ and hard like ebony." His blinded gunner's face is disfigured by "blistered eyes," while the lost pilot's face retains the smoothness of "an original page." Such contrasting images make the status of the living seem much poorer than the status of the lost.

While "The Lost Pilot" adheres to no formal pattern of rhyme or meter beyond its being divided into stanzas of equal length, it does make striking, if irregular, use of various musical devices. The proliferation of imperfect rhymes (such as "rot" with "co-pilot" and "life" with "sky") throughout the poem underscores the imperfect connections between the lost father and his son, connections the son is ultimately powerless to improve, much less to perfect. Finally, the fact that the end-stopped lines in the poem (such as "He was more wronged than Job.") are so overwhelmingly outnumbered by enjambed lines (that is, lines in which the thought runs over into the lines that immediately follow them) seems to maintain a continuous sense of imbalance, urgency, and precariousness, all of which are appropriate to the poet's emotional and psychological situation.

Themes and Meanings

"The Lost Pilot" is a poem about bereavement and the many improvisations that the heart performs as it seeks a way to hope and to live again after a shattering loss. The poet confronts a literal and figurative void as he mourns the disappearance of a father he never knew. Denied, by the unique and violent circumstances of his pilot-father's wartime death (1944 was the most terrible year of World War II), the consolations of a conventional funeral ritual, he is also denied the consolations of fond memory, as he has virtually no memories of his father at all. (The poet was less than one year old when his father was lost.) Without memories, the poet is forced to the abstract extreme of grief, an extreme at which his actions become the most vivid imaginable representations of the uncertainties and anxieties of human grief. One wonders in what ways every individual is an orphan. To what extent is every human being diminished by the universal and individual reality of death? The bargaining into which the poet enters with his orbiting father could be seen as emblematic of the ways in which all religions and philosophies seek to question and to cajole the unknown. Because his father cannot step down from the sky, the poet can only continue to state his case to the silence. In this, the poet suggests to the reader that everyone must find means to accept limitations to their individual lives and happiness which, though inevitable, are not necessarily endurable.

Losing a father means losing a point of origin, and Tate demonstrates how life can be suspended ("I feel dead") by a failure to devise a means to root one's life in personal and historical origins. Society can offer funeral rituals and time-worn platitudes to the bereft, but loss is finally a very personal, singular experience. An individual gifted with any sort of imagination is eventually compelled to use that imagination to express his or her own grief in all its singular intensity, and by so doing to root himself, if not in the irrevocably lost point of origin, at least in the total reality of his actual circumstances.

While the speaker of "The Lost Pilot" appears to conclude on a resignation to despair, the poem may not be entirely a hymn to hopelessness. The very fact that the poem is made at all and made so well, so intensely, represents a kind of victory. Grief has not destroyed the poet. Rather, it has made him eloquent and led him to a profound, if painful, self-knowledge and to the making of an urgent gesture of community with other living human beings.

Donald Revell

THE LOTOS-EATERS

Author: Alfred, Lord Tennyson (1809-1892)
Type of poem: Lyric
First published: 1832, in *Poems*; revised in *Poems*, 1842

The Poem

"The Lotos-Eaters" in its final form is 173 lines long. The first forty-five lines, the proem, are an imitation of the Spenserian stanza, a form used in Edmund Spenser's gigantic Christian allegorical epic, *The Faerie Queene* (1590, 1596). It is made up of eight even lines of iambic pentameter, plus a ninth line an extra iamb long. The rhyme pattern is *abab, bcbc, c.*

The proem describes a scene from the *Odyssey* (c. 800 B.C.E.) in which Odysseus and his men, after a terrible storm, arrive on the shores of the land of the lotos-eaters. His men are returning home to Ithaca after participating in the sack of Troy. It is known from Homer that in the end Odysseus actually will reach Ithaca and the others will die in the course of various adventures on the sea. Their difficult journey, however, almost ends on this island, because of the drugging effect of the lotos plant, a staple of the inhabitants.

In Homer's epic, Odysseus tells the story in a first-person narrative, saying, "My men went on and presently met the lotos-Eaters,/ . . . But any of them who ate the honey-sweet fruit of lotos/ was unwilling to take any message back, or to go/ away, but they wanted to stay there with the lotos-eating/ people . . . and forget the way home." Alfred, Lord Tennyson's version, on the other hand, is in the third person until line 46. The word "Courage" is spoken by Odysseus himself, as he directs his men to land their ship. Tennyson proceeds to describe in lyrical elaboration of the Homeric text the dreamy country of the lotos-eaters. His description is a frank imitation of several famous poems about magical lands. In these lands, sleep, reverie, inaction, and all that is the opposite of industry are the rule. Several places in *The Faerie Queene* come to mind, such as the cave of Morpheus, god of sleep, and the house of Despair, a personification who destroys men by sapping their will to live.

Another important influence is James Thomson's short epic *The Castle of Indolence* (1748), which is also based on Spenser. The Greek sailors, drugged by the lotos, lose their will to continue the struggle against the sea and decide to abandon their efforts to return home. Home, their families, and their domestic lives become bittersweet memories, sentimentally moving, but pale and powerless to motivate further heroic exertions. They sing a "Choric song" that evokes the gentle, aesthetic sense of indolence and restfulness, their drugged state of perpetual reverie and laziness.

The land of the lotos-eaters is not simply idyllic and pastoral. It is so restful that men become tired without working: "There is sweet music here that softer falls/ Than petals from blown roses on the grass." There is "Music that gentlier on the spirit lies,/ Than tired eyelids upon tired eyes." Under the effects of the lotos, the men of Ithaca find no reason to return to the sea. Their duty as sailors now seems too great a demand, and they complain of life's harshness, as if it were unjust that they should work so hard and continually struggle against the elements: "Why are we weighed upon with heaviness,/ And utterly consumed with sharp distress./ While all things else have rest from weariness?"

Stanza 3 of the choric song sounds like a pastoral appreciation of woodland beauties, but it is actually an aspect of the sailors' case against heroic adventure and industry: Why should they struggle on the sea, when the natural way of life is surrender to the cycles of nature? Great struggles are unnatural, for nature itself is free from effort: "The flower ripens in its place,/ Ripens and fades, and falls, and hath no toil, fast-footed in the fruitful soil."

Stanza 4 carries this argument further, pointing to the ultimate fruitlessness of great endeavors. Although when a flower falls, it leaves a seed to grow "in the fruitful soil," their human efforts are in vain. The sailors argue that the struggles of people only end in death, and so they turn away from the sea, a challenge to human courage and ingenuity and, thus, a symbol of ambition and goals: "Hateful is the dark blue sky,/ Vaulted o'er the dark blue sea." The effort to sail across the ocean to wage war is pointless. It is better to surrender, like the falling flower, to the cyclic laws of nature: "All things have rest, and ripen toward the grave/ In silence—ripen, fall, and cease:/ Give us long rest or death, dark death, or dreamful ease." So stanza 5 describes the restful alternative: It is better to dream and, in this dream, transcend the present to live in sweet memories of the past.

In stanza 6, they foresee the evil outcomes of the final return to families that are now in disorder—families that have changed beyond recognition after the men's ten-year absence at Troy. As is known from the *Odyssey* and Greek tragedies, they are right. Only doom awaits them.

The sailors swear to remain indolently in the magical land and live like gods in stanza 8. Verses 155 to the end evoke the luxurious and carefree life of the Greek gods as described by the Roman poet Lucretius (circa 96-55 B.C.E.) in his famous philosophical poem *De rerum natura* (c. 60 B.C.E.; *On the Nature of Things*). This passage presents Tennyson's version of the Lucretian epicurean cosmology and moral system, a system in which humankind is freed by philosophy from superstitious fear and in which an enlightened self-interest and acceptance of pleasure provide the thinker with spiritual peace.

The last lines summarize the poem, which turns out to have been one long argument against industry. The sailors imagine they are gods looking down on the life of humans. The Greek view of death does not give meaning to life; thus, one's actions, whether heroic or not, do not count in the long run. The sailors conclude by saying they will not return to the sea.

Forms and Devices

"The Lotos-Eaters" could be seen as a stitching together of imitations of several other epic poems Tennyson admired. The proem imitates those moments in Spenser's

The Faerie Queene that describe reverie as an evil temptation to the Christian state, scenes that suggest a state of drowsiness and a sense of will-less dreaming. This effect is heightened by Tennyson's use of the Spenserian rhyme scheme to communicate languor and lassitude. The Spenserian stanza allows only three rhymes, *abab, bcbc, c.* Tennyson heightens this effect by simplifying the pattern further, rhyming, for example, "land" with "land" in the first quatrain. The other rhymes are also purposefully weak and unadventurous: "soon," "afternoon," "swoon," and "moon."

The streams, rolling hills, fields, and valleys of the lotos land give a sense of illusion because they are constantly connected with the verb "seem," connoting mere appearance. They are lit by a paradoxical dream light from the sun and moon, which appear in the sky at the same time. The similes also promote a sense of illusion by comparing the elements of this pastoral scene to vague and half-seen things. The descending stream is like smoke moving downward. It seems to pause in the air as it descends and is like "thinnest lawn." Lawn in this case is a kind of cloth used to represent waterfalls in the theater. There are numerous images of falling, slow descent, and settling.

"A land where all things always seemed the same!" is an allusion to a line from Lucretius in which nature argues with man that death and sleep are not so different from one another, and therefore death should not be feared even as life should not be clung to. The references to Thomson's imitation of Spenser have the same effect: "And up the hills, on either side, a wood/ Of blackening pines, ay waving to and fro,/ Sent forth a sleepy horror through the blood,/ And where this valley winded out, below,/ The murmuring main was heard, and scarcely heard, to flow."

The "Choric Song" is in theory a balladic genre. In contrast to the epic mode of the proem, its rhythms and rhyme scheme are shifting and melodic. This combination of epic and pseudoballadic verse is found elsewhere in Tennyson, particularly in "The Lady of Shallot" (another story that opposes an unreal, poetically beautiful world to a deadly daily reality).

The song, however, involves a sort of contradiction, for although its imagery and style suggest release, surrender, and passivity, its rhetorical structure argues initiative and careful thought. The sailors may be drugged, but they go to great trouble to make a strong argument for inaction. The rhetorical qualities of the "Choric Song" thus may foreshadow the sailors' leaving the island, abandoning their paradise of effortless living.

Themes and Meanings

Tennyson wrote several poems that, like "The Lotos-Eaters," were drawn from Greek epic materials. "Ulysses"—a monologue by the hero of the *Odyssey* in which he contemplates life after his return to Ithaca—is the most famous. There is also *Œnone* (1832, 1842), a lengthy poem about Paris's lamenting lover, abandoned by him for Helen; "The Sea Fairies," about mythic sea nymphs, the nereids; and "The Hesperides," from which material was taken for "The Lotos-Eaters."

These lyric poems drawn from epic narrative aimed to be "modernizations" of classical themes, updating traditional sentiments into the Victorian context. In "The

Lotos-Eaters," the central theme is: Should a person live in a world of romantic vision and aesthetic reverie or turn from this dreamy life of art to the stable world of facts and hard work? For Spenser and Thomson, the moral is clearly drawn. The Cave of Morpheus and the Idle Lake are fascinating inventions, but they are places that a vigorous individual, filled with the Protestant ethic, should shun.

With Tennyson, one senses an ambivalence about the dream land, as if suspended between the Victorian love of the romantic and the insistent intrusion of scientific fact. In Spenser and Thomson, knights representing the virtue of hard work and stringent religious principles defeat the forces of indolence, but here the abandonment of the magical land is only implied. Although one knows that Odysseus's sailors finally left those shores to be destroyed in their further adventures, such heroism is not represented directly in the poem.

Robin Kornman

LOT'S WIFE

Author: Wisława Szymborska (1923-   )
Type of poem: Dramatic monologue
First published: 1976, as "Żona Lota," in *Wielka liczba*; English translation collected
in *Sounds, Feelings, Thoughts: Seventy Poems by Wisława Szymborska*, 1981

The Poem

The story of the death of Lot's wife in the biblical book of Genesis has both intrigued and disturbed many readers. Angels command Lot to take his family and flee the evil cities of Sodom and Gomorrah, telling them not to look back. For disobeying this warning, Lot's wife is turned into a pillar of salt.

"Lot's Wife" features forty-three unrhymed lines of varied lengths. Its unnamed title character apparently is speaking to the reader after her death. The paradox implied by having her do this is compounded by other unusual circumstances as the poem unfolds. Although the speaker discusses her possible reasons for turning back toward Sodom and therefore perishing, she seems either unable or unwilling to reveal her true reasons for doing so. She begins noncommittally, "They say I looked back from curiosity./ But I could have had reasons other than curiosity." Nowhere does she state exactly what *did* happen; rather, she presents a variety of possibilities. She suggests reasons such as longing for a silver bowl she left behind, distraction while adjusting her sandal, and even weariness of looking at the back of her husband's neck. Mentioning that Lot would not have stopped even had she died, she adds that she may have looked back in resentment of him.

The wife also alleges fearing that someone was following them and hoping that God had decided not to destroy the cities. She states that she may have felt fatigued, lonely, or frightened at going into the wilderness. After mentioning these feelings, she suggests glancing back while setting down her bundle, or turning away in revulsion at the vermin she saw on her path. At yet another point, she claims that the crackling of the flames made her think the Sodomites were laughing at her for running, causing her to look around in anger.

After describing possible mental states, the speaker goes on to blame the difficult mountain path for her turning, claiming first that she slipped while stepping on a loose stone, then that she drew back from a chasm in her way, and finally that she slipped off a cliff and saw the burning city as she rolled down. She not only fails to state what prompted her to look back but also pictures increasingly severe events, as if repeating a bad dream that keeps getting more threatening, until the story has unraveled in absurd and contradictory claims.

Forms and Devices

Although no translation can fully communicate the sounds of the original, translators Magnus J. Krynski and Robert A. Maguire captured much of Wisława Szymborska's technique. The lines are similar in length and, as far as grammar permits, usually display the same phrasing and word order as the Polish, although minor exceptions occur. For example, where the original sixth line reads "m òża mojego, Lota," the translation has "of Lot my husband," putting Lot's name before his relationship to the speaker. The translation stresses the rhythmic nature of the line, with the stressed syllable "Lot" between the unstressed "of" and "my," allowing the line to be read more fluidly than "of my husband, Lot," its literal rendering. This subtle change preserves Szymborska's original rhythm.

"Lot's Wife" uses conversational language, which, combined with the uneven lines and lack of rhyme, gives a strong impression of everyday communication. However, the apparent simplicity is deceptive. The language itself is carefully chosen. For instance, seven of the lines in English, or almost one-sixth of the poem, begin repetitively with "I looked back." (There is an eighth in the Polish.) Almost half the poem's repetition is lost in translation generally—as in lines which in Polish, but not English, begin with the same preposition. Still, the translation has rhythm and repetition enough to create a pattern in which the woman who died because she looked back at Sodom returns to her death again and again. Adding to this perception of recurrence are echoes of sound between words, as in the statement that wild animals "crept and leapt" to escape destruction. The language also suggests a confused or out-of-breath quality on the part of the narrator. For instance, some "sentences" are single words, such as "Remoteness." Such isolated words help emphasize the meaning expressed with great economy of language; they also make it seem as if Lot's wife is trying to recollect jumbled or confusing memories.

Besides the patterns of language, the images suggest imprecise thought, being organized by association of ideas. After stating that she looked back "from fear" of the animals on the path, the wife reflects that "By now it was neither the righteous nor the wicked" who fled, but "simply all living creatures/ . . . in common panic." Immediately after this, she wonders if she looked back from loneliness, as if the "living creatures" which shared nothing but fear made her realize her isolation. Many ideas contradict previous ones; the speaker's shame at "stealing away" from Sodom as if betraying it is followed immediately by her anger at the illusory Sodomites jeering at her from the walls. This stream of possible motives gives an impression of complex mental processes, helping make the speaker of the poem more than a two-dimensional icon while also rendering her puzzling.

The narrative confusion is amplified when the speaker asserts that she did not turn back by choice, as previously suggested, but rather because of a physical mishap. Moreover, she abruptly contradicts one accident story—that she slipped—with another, that she continued running and fell off the cliff. Further reminding the reader of how hard interpreting events can be, she adds that anyone watching her tumble would have thought she was dancing. Finally, underlining the absolute lack of certainty in her story, she states, "It is not ruled out that my eyes were open" as she fell, and "It could be that I fell, my face turned toward the city." The reader wonders which reconstructions, if any, are accurate and which are fantasies or falsehoods. Lot's wife may have looked back while rolling down a cliff, while fixing her sandal, or while dropping her burden to the ground, but she could not have done all three simultaneously. The monologue therefore becomes a paradox.

Themes and Meanings

Like the scriptural narrative upon which it draws, "Lot's Wife" offers much opportunity for speculation. The fate of Lot's wife is known, but neither her reasons for looking back nor her name are given in the Bible. Both her singular doom and the paucity of other information have prompted many reactions, from simple pity to elaborate speculation about her reasons for turning. Commentators have alleged motives ranging from desire for the corrupt pleasures of the doomed cities to rebellion against authority, although Genesis makes no such statement.

Szymborska's character discusses most of the less lurid motives traditionally ascribed to Lot's wife, including materialism (her desire for the silver bowl), resentment of her husband's orders, regret for the doom of Sodom, and fear. However, she confesses to no truly evil motive. If she longs for her bowl, she seems more to miss a prized keepsake than to display greed. In her shame at "stealing away" from Sodom, she displays a possibly misplaced devotion, but she does not seem the sensualist imagined by some readers of the Bible. Indeed, many of the reasons she suggests imply no fault of her own, but only misfortune. She sounds neither especially noble nor ignoble if she is attempting to be truthful, although her trustworthiness itself is questionable.

The colloquial language reinforces the impression of Lot's wife as an everyday person, probably in late middle age (she complains about having "felt old age" in her bones as she fell behind her husband and daughters). Her evident confusion about her own motives reflects not only the varied reasons ascribed to her by biblical commentators but also the confusion most people have about their own impulses, especially the soul searching they are likely to do after their actions lead to some catastrophe. The mystifying uncertainty as to whether the wife cannot remember or will not divulge what she does remember also recalls the often contradictory interpretations placed upon the scriptural story. Almost at the midpoint, as if mulling the issue over repeatedly has led her to some insight, she adds, impossibly, that she looked back for all the reasons she has considered, and probably a few of which she has not thought.

Lot's wife demonstrates how difficult motives often are to analyze. She also suggests how unsure anyone's knowledge of others is, for one cannot know fully what happened, just as the hypothetical observer would not have known whether the speaker was falling or dancing as she spun down the cliff. Lot's wife does not seem particularly wicked to the reader of this poem, although the reader depends on her for this impression and cannot be certain whether she is confused, lying, or simply playing games in offering the multiple possibilities.

Paul James Buczkowski

LOVE (III)

Author: George Herbert (1593-1633)
Type of poem: Lyric
First published: 1633, in *The Temple*

The Poem

"Love" (III), a relatively brief poem of three six-line stanzas, concludes the central section of George Herbert's *The Temple*, entitled "The Church." This collection of devotional lyrics is structured as a sequence that covers the inevitable fluctuations of religious experience as a person strives to lead a faithful life. "Love" (III) is the third poem by that name in "The Church." The first two, appearing early in the sequence, lament the fact that earthly love tends to attract more attention than the much more deserving holy love. By the end of "The Church," however, the persona created by Herbert is able to concentrate on sacred love, and "Love" (III) dramatizes a climactic meeting between a worshiper and God, imagined not as a remote figure of vengeance or stern judgment but as an inviting lover.

The speaker narrates an action that has evidently already taken place, but despite the past tense of the verbs, the experience described is powerful and immediate, in part because the poem is structured as a dialogue. Herbert is often thought of as a person of a secure and lasting faith, but many of his poems reveal that beneath such a faith is a large amount of tension and worry. In "Love" (III), the persona's nervous uneasiness is gradually overcome by the gentle words of a kind lover who has an answer for every question.

Herbert seems to be saying that divine love compensates for all human weaknesses. Instead of instantly accepting Love's invitation, the persona is hesitant, painfully aware that he is "Guilty of dust and sin," and is therefore unworthy to be in the presence of such a perfect host. As Herbert imagines it, however, divine love is not conditional: It does not deny the fact of human inadequacy, but renders it inconsequential. Humankind is indeed "unkind" and "ungrateful," but the resulting sense of shame serves no useful purpose. In fact, it reinforces one's turn from God: "Ah my dear," says the shameful man, "I cannot look on thee." Distance from God, not human weakness or guilt, is the real spiritual problem, and Love tries to remedy this by drawing closer and closer through the course of the poem.

One of the deepest ironies here is that the persona clings so resolutely to his sense of guilt and unworthiness. Despite every gentle assurance from Love, man seems to revel in confessing his own wickedness and yearns for punishment: "let my shame/ Go where it doth deserve," he says, even after Love takes him by the hand and smiles. Herbert shows much psychological insight in dramatizing how deeply embedded is the human resistance to love, a resistance that—at least in Christian terms—may only be overcome by the exemplary and loving sacrifice of Christ. Only when Love reminds the persona that he "bore the blame" for all human guilt by taking human form and suffering the Crucifixion is he properly humbled and prepared to accept the love he so desperately needs. The poem ends not on the painful spectacle of the Crucifixion, though, but on the joy of Communion, a celebration of God's love. After being exhausted by relentless, self-doubting questioning and gently overwhelmed by a divine figure who will not be outsmarted in debate or denied in love, the persona announces his capitulation and assent in a simple, monosyllabic assertion—"So I did sit and eat"—that is characteristic of Herbert's dramatic art of understatement. To say the least, this is no ordinary meal. In fact, it marks the intersection of the ordinary and the extraordinary, the human and the divine, desire and fulfillment.

Forms and Devices

Herbert is rightly regarded as a master of poetic form and language, and "Love" (III) is one of the best examples of how deceptively simple his lyrics are. Here Herbert reduces extremely complicated theological and psychological themes—the potentially devastating consequences of human sin and the avoidance of love—to a dramatic dialogue that is both a realistic debate and an allegory. One could call this a "love" poem, because in many ways it is deeply indebted to secular love lyrics, one of the most widely known and influential genres of Renaissance poetry. As in so many of his other poems, Herbert draws from this tradition basically to parody or reinterpret it.

The typical secular love lyric tells a tale of frustrated love, of a desiring man courting a mistress unable or, in most cases, unwilling to give in to his desires. Consummation of any sort is rarely achieved, and if it is, it prompts continuing worry rather than lasting satisfaction. Herbert's poem turns this pattern around: The personified Love is no flighty or indisposed mistress but an attentive, generous, and gentle divine being whose existence erases rather than intensifies human incapacity. Much like the illustrated religious emblem books of the time, Herbert pictures an allegory of the wooing of Amor (Love) and Anima (the human soul), and the key issue is not whether one can seduce or win someone's love but whether one can accept divine love that, unlike the love of a Petrarchan mistress, is freely given.

The language of "Love" (III) is, at least on the surface, remarkably transparent and direct. Herbert uses a relatively high proportion of monosyllables throughout the poem, increasing dramatically toward the end: About three-quarters of the words in each of the first two stanzas are monosyllables, and in the last stanza, only one of forty-seven words has more than one syllable. This heightens the colloquial sound of the poem and makes it read like an overheard conversation. Beneath this colloquial simplicity, however, is a subtle design. For example, Herbert structures the poem using alternating line lengths, and this formal technique helps convey the persona's evolving mood. One of the problems of the persona is that he tends to say too much: Instead of accepting, he argues with Love. His protests, however, gradually become quieter and briefer. In the first part of the poem, his voice dominates, at least insofar as he speaks at length while Love's brief statements fill only the short lines of the stanza. This is reversed in the final stanza, where Love speaks the long lines and the persona speaks the short ones, underscoring his move toward satisfaction and silence.

Unlike many other poems by Herbert and the so-called Metaphysical poets with whom he is usually linked, "Love" (III) does not rely heavily on elaborate or ingenious metaphors, but the poem gains resonance by his use of sacramental and biblical allusions which confirm that "Love" (III) is about no simple invitation to love or dinner. If the persona is a "guest," Love is implicitly the "host," not only a kindly benefactor but the substance of the Communion ceremony. The entire scene recalls Luke 12, where a guest is gently urged to sit and be served by Christ. Finally, especially in its place at the close of "The Church" and directly following a poem entitled "Heaven," "Love" (III) may also call to mind one's final entrance into heaven, described as a feast in Revelation 19:9.

Themes and Meanings

The problem of love is central to Herbert. Throughout the poems of "The Church" he repeatedly analyzes and dramatizes various aspects of this problem, particularly the recurrent failure of humankind to love God properly. Many poems catalog human evasiveness ("The Agonie"), attachment to earthly rather than heavenly ideals ("Frailty"), unwillingness to serve God ("Miserie"), and habitual (to use the titles of some other poems) "Unkindness," "Ungratefulness," "Vanity," "Giddiness," and "Affliction." To be sure, humankind has positive strengths and moods as well, and there are poems of "Assurance," "Grace," "Praise," and "Prayer," but the impression one may have after reading through "The Church" in its entirety is that the devotional life is a gradual ascent, often interrupted, to a precarious peak. Nothing seems to be accomplished "once and for all" in Herbert, including love—perhaps especially love.

This pattern puts much weight on the final poem of the sequence, which is in some respects both a triumphant ending and a conclusion in which nothing is concluded. The persona in "Love" (III) is chastened by a sense of his own sin. On the one hand, this is a lesson constantly reinforced by the poems of "The Church," and perhaps it is meant to be a good sign that the speaker at last apparently has no illusions about the limits of human power. Yet even at this late stage in the sequence, knowledge has not yet become wisdom. He has learned only half of the lesson: He is indeed "Guilty of dust and sin," but in the last analysis—and in the last moment of time—this does not matter. Human perfection or worthiness is not required by God, who simply smiles at the thought that anyone could actually deserve heaven on merit alone. The persona is so convinced that sin cancels love that he is blind to the basic Christian belief that love cancels sin. This should be a comforting doctrine, but Herbert suggests that it is nevertheless difficult to accept. Almost to the very end, the persona tries to assert his power and play a role in the ceremony. His offer, "My dear, then I will serve," is a touching confession of obedience but also a willful resistance to acknowledging that his primary role in the affair is to be loved, not to love, to be served by a figure of divine love that far overshadows any possible human love. One suspects that this is a lesson that needs to be learned again and again.

As uneasy and challenging as the poem is, it is still a triumphant conclusion to "The Church." The sequence of lyrics ends not on a fine point of theology but with what is simultaneously a subtle and commonplace observation about emotional and spiritual life: Love is difficult, chastening, and critical—"quick-eyed," in short— but all-embracing, redemptive, and the ground of humankind's being, if one can accept it.

Sidney Gottlieb

LOVE AMONG THE RUINS

Author: Robert Browning (1812-1889)
Type of poem: Lyric
First published: 1855, in *Men and Women*

The Poem

The design of this poem is similar to that of Robert Browning's powerful dramatic romance, *"Childe Roland to the Dark Tower Came"* (1855). In each poem a solitary youth, absorbed in his own reflections, is walking through a desolate landscape late in the day and eventually comes to a tower. In *"Childe Roland to the Dark Tower Came,"* however, a sense of ominous foreboding is relentlessly intensified until the very last line, whereas in "Love Among the Ruins" the scene is one of pastoral serenity with no sound but the tinkling of bells as drowsy sheep browse on lush green hills. As the title of the poem suggests, there are some traces of the ruins of a former civilization to be seen; nature is gradually reclaiming and healing the desecrated land.

According to the speaker, there had once been an awe-inspiring city on this site, dominated by an imposing palace, which was the residence of a king who could command an army of a million soldiers. No specific locale is named, but the repeated references to charioteers suggest that this was the site of an ancient civilization such as Troy, Babylon, or Persia. All of this was so long ago that the whole enormous complex with its palace and its hundred-gated marble wall is only a legend among the pastoral people who now inhabit the region.

The shepherd finally comes in sight of a little turret which is gradually being undermined and covered over by wild vegetation. This is all that is left of the great tower from which the monarch and his retainers used to view the chariot races and other war games. Here the shepherd has a rendevous with a girl with "eager eyes and yellow hair." His description of her youthful beauty and animation is in striking contrast to the futility of human aspirations suggested by the solitary turret and buried ruins surrounding it. As he begins to think about his beloved, the mental picture of the glorious city he had been reconstructing in his imagination seems to flicker and fade. Visualizing the woman he loves, who is awaiting him so eagerly, he reflects that her love and devotion are far more valuable to him than all the material possessions that might be obtained by men motivated by lust for gold and glory. The shepherd concludes with the three simple words that contain the moral of the entire poem: "Love is best."

Forms and Devices

The most striking thing about this work is the unusual juxtaposition of long and short lines. Browning wrote many of his most famous poems, such as the frequently anthologized "My Last Duchess," in blank verse; however, he was also a tireless experimenter with rhymes and meters. He seemed anxious to demonstrate his technical versatility and perhaps to compete in this respect with his famous contemporary Alfred, Lord Tennyson, who was better educated than the autodidactic Browning and was a master of all aspects of poetic composition.

The combination of one long line, which could be construed as trochaic pentameter with an extra syllable, or feminine ending, with a line of only three syllables, has several functions. The short line, which always rhymes with the preceding long line, is intended to suggest the sound of the sheep's bells as they "tinkle homeward thro' the twilight." The alternation of the long and short lines suggests the rolling hills that are an essential feature of the landscape. Since the long line is deliberately made to seem too long, the short line by contrast also suggests the remnant of a structure that has toppled because it became too lofty, like the Tower of Babel. The mismatched couplets suggest a contrast between the proud and overbearing ruler of the vanished empire and the rustic simplicity of the present inhabitants.

Some critics have complained that the ongoing contrast between such long and short lines is ungainly and that the continuous suggestion of tinkling sheep bells begins to seem annoying after a few stanzas. This is a matter of individual taste. Nevertheless, the radical innovation of contrasting such dissimilar lines in a couplet does help to evoke the scene and mood the author intended.

Browning was an ardent admirer of the great English Romantic poet Percy Bysshe Shelley. It can readily be seen that "Love Among the Ruins" is written in the same spirit as was Shelley's "Ozymandias." In that famous sonnet, Shelley depicts a ruined civilization, which the vainglorious ruler Ozymandias had thought he was establishing to last a thousand years. In both "Love Among the Ruins" and "Ozymandias," the moral is conveyed by using the verbal picture of a ruined civilization as a metaphor for the vanity of human aspirations.

Both Shelley and Browning frequently visited Greek, Roman, and other ruins, and the poets could not help but absorb the lesson those silent ruins convey. Centuries ago, ambitious, bustling populations had believed that their civilizations would last forever; eventually there was nothing but broken columns, crumbling walls, and silence. Shelley described a barren desert, while Browning's picture of a ruined civilization is softened with glimpses of fluffy sheep on rolling green hills and a beautiful young woman passionately in love with a young man. Just so, the poem of the pious and sentimental Browning poem reflects a more optimistic mood and suggests a more positive philosophy than that of the atheistic and suicidal Shelley.

Themes and Meanings

On the surface, "Love Among the Ruins" appears to have a very simple message. It is the same message that would be voiced a century later by antiwar activists during the late 1960's, whose slogan was "Make love, not war." When Browning wrote his poem, Great Britain under Queen Victoria was nearing its zenith as a military and mercantile power. In the words of the jingoistic English poet Rudyard Kipling in his poem "Recessional," his nation had established "dominion over palm and pine." The British Empire included huge portions of Asia, Africa, North America, and Australia. The British boasted that "Britannia rules the waves" and "The sun never sets on British soil." In geographical area, it was by far the largest empire the world had ever seen.

There were Englishmen, however, who were questioning the wisdom of such extensive conquest and exploitation. Browning's poem can be read as a warning that Great Britain could go the way of Egypt, Persia, Greece, and Rome and end up losing all her territorial possessions. This was what actually began to happen a hundred years later in the aftermath of World War II.

"Love Among the Ruins" can also be read as a self-revealing rationalization on the part of the poet. Browning's love affair with Elizabeth Barrett, who became his wife in 1846, is perhaps the most famous love relationship that has ever existed between two such prominent literary personalities. The marriage seems to have had an inhibiting influence on Browning. Elizabeth was a more successful poet at the time of their marriage and continued to enjoy greater popularity than her husband for the rest of her life. During that period, Browning lived in her shadow.

Browning produced little poetry during the years of his marriage; he did not become lionized as a poet and as a public personality until after her death in 1861. "Love Among the Ruins" could be interpreted as a confession that Browning was willing to sacrifice fame and financial success for the love of his wife. One might conjecture that he may have felt that he would jeopardize their idyllic relationship if he were to compete with her too openly. Elizabeth Barrett Browning was a frail and sickly woman, but she evidently had a domineering personality. Her influence over her husband had both positive and negative aspects. Without her love and inspiration, Browning might never have become the great poet that he was; during their years of marriage, however, he seems to have been content to play a passive role. The ruined tower in "Love Among the Ruins" may even symbolize his own disappointed ambitions.

Bill Delaney

LOVE CALLS US TO THE THINGS OF THIS WORLD

Author: Richard Wilbur (1921-   )
Type of poem: Lyric
First published: 1953; collected in *Things of This World*, 1956

The Poem

"Love Calls Us to the Things of This World" is a lyric poem written in blank verse. The title is taken from Saint Augustine and gives theological support to the particular mood of acceptance significant to the poem.

The poem is set in the first awakening of consciousness after sleep in the morning. The time of initial dislocation between sleep and waking is often portrayed negatively in literature; at first waking, one can often feel alien to the world, even to one's own life. Indeed, even in this poem it is a "cry of pulleys" from clothes being hung out early in the morning that wakes the "astounded soul," hardly a pleasant way of being roused from sleep. Yet immediately the laundry is identified with angels in the awake but still-dreaming mind.

The poem next plays with the observer's imaginings of angels dressed in the bedsheets, blouses, and smocks hanging on the line. As if on cue, the breeze begins and the laundry comes to life with "halcyon feeling" that fills the scene with a "deep joy of their impersonal breathing."

The waving laundry is next compared to white-water rapids in their rippled dancing until the breeze stops and the garments "swoon down into so rapt a quiet/ That nobody seems to be there." This sudden stillness brings the consciousness in the poem back to a realization that the "punctual rape" of the day is waiting, the day lived without the magic and delight of the angels that the half-awakened mind imagines. With this realization, the speaker in the poem wishes that he could remain in this pleasant waking fantasy.

Yet he knows he cannot. He does realize, however, that the daily round of common events has its own beauty, a beauty that contains the playful epiphany of the first moments of his morning. The soul of the man "descends once more in bitter love/ To accept the waking body"; the emotion may have bitterness in it, but it is also an emotion of love. As the soul must descend and accept the waking body, so the laundry must be taken down and worn, though it will be dirtied by doing so.

This "clean linen" will be worn by thieves, by lovers who are (like the laundry) "fresh and sweet to be undone," and by nuns. By choosing nuns to complete this earthly trinity, Richard Wilbur makes a particularly apposite choice. Just as the thieves and lovers contrast with each other, so do the nuns and angels. Nuns are creatures of this world as angels assuredly are not, but their existence speaks of the world of the spirit to which the man in the poem awakes. The nuns are termed "heaviest," but they walk in a "pure floating/ Of dark habits." They live in a world of wakened fact but also of the bodiless joy of the opening of the poem; so, by inference, do all humans.

Forms and Devices

On the page, "Love Calls Us to the Things of This World" appears at first to be semi-free verse, the lines metered but of indeterminate lengths. On close reading, however, one sees that the poem is actually written in blank verse. Typographically, the lines are scattered, and there are many dropped lines, much as one sees in William Shakespeare's plays when two characters share one line of iambic pentameter. Thus there is only one line—"Yet, as the sun acknowledges"—that is not a pentameter line, and this line is lacking only one foot. The effect is that a leisurely, seemingly loosely constructed poem does take a definite shape, much the same as the consciousness in the poem itself does accept a form. In both cases, the shape is one of discovery of meaning and correspondence.

The poem is about a joyous acceptance, and the poet indeed takes a delight in language. "Love Calls Us to the Things of This World" is full of playful language, perhaps most notably in its use of puns. The awakened soul fancifully seeing angels is described as "spirited from sleep." The laundry causes the morning air to be "awash with angels." When consciousness wins the upper hand and insists that these objects are not angels but laundry, the "soul shrinks." When the speaker rails against the "punctual rape of every blessèd day," there are two puns involved. The first is "blessèd," used as both an epithet and an affirmation of the sanctity of the commonplace. Second, the entire phrase is about the killing nature of habit. Yet the nuns "walk in a pure floating/ Of dark habits," which are reminders that one's daily actions are meaningful, that the things of this world are not only of this world.

The voice in the poem is another carefully considered construct of the poem. Only once is anything specific said about who it is who awakens in the poem; Wilbur writes in one line that "the man yawns and rises." In all other instances, nothing as particular is noted. Usually, the being in the poem is simply referred to as the "soul." There are two major reasons for this. The poem is about disembodied dreams that take a shape in common objects as the awakened consciousness ceases to dream. Therefore, as the consciousness in the poem gets out of bed, Wilbur refers to "the man" where he had twice previously used "soul." He has become once more of this world. Also, the poet wants the situation he describes to apply to all humankind, and too much particularization would be inconsistent with this goal.

Themes and Meanings

"Love Calls Us to the Things of This World" is a key poem in Wilbur's body of work and is typical of a vital concern of the poet. Wilbur has felt the appeal of philosophic speculation—indeed, there is much reference to philosophical texts throughout his work—but he has always insisted on the primacy of the objects of this world, "the world's hunks and colors," as he puts it in this poem. Meaning and beauty can be apprehended by the sense that is carefully attuned to observation. This poem is central to the poet himself—he chose to take part of its title for the volume in which it was collected, *Things of This World* (1956), which won a Pulitzer Prize.

Essentially, the poem is about the creative process, the relation of imagination to reality. The newly awakened soul at the beginning of the poem playfully makes the laundry into angels. This is emblematic of metaphor, seeing one thing in terms of another.

The soul takes such delight in the exercise, however, that the world itself seems a dull and uninspiring place where mundane actions seem a "punctual rape of every blessèd day." It is love, which is the central creative principle in Wilbur's work, that calls the soul back to "accept the waking body." The agent for this action may be a "bitter love," but it is love nevertheless.

The acceptance of this world by the soul does not imply a rejection of metaphor. Metaphor must be seen as the tool it is and not a displacement of reality. The speaker playfully sees the laundry as angels, then puts the notion aside and dresses. Yet once he has seen in this metaphoric fashion, the clothes will never feel the same on his back. Thus the mind can construct new metaphors from experience, so "the heaviest nuns walk in a pure floating/ Of dark habits." The soul called back to the world from sleep by love can bring with it a greater ability to see that each day is "blessèd."

In another poem, "Praise in Summer," Wilbur wonders why the poet so likes "wrenching things awry," why there is such delight in metaphor. He wonders if people have become so accustomed to everyday life that they do not really know it: "Does sense so stale that it must needs derange/ The world to know it?" "Love Calls Us to the Things of This World" may answer this question, one of Wilbur's central concerns.

Because one loves, one lives in and loves the world, but because of the imagination one is able to appreciate this world, to which one might otherwise become inured. Certainly the morning vision of seeing bedsheets as angels is a "wrenching things awry," but it is a metaphor that, once accepted as metaphor and not reality, allows one to view the world afresh. This is the central role for metaphor in Wilbur's work, and nowhere is it better developed than in "Love Calls Us to the Things of This World."

Robert Darling

LOVE IS NOT ALL: IT IS NOT MEAT NOR DRINK

Author: Edna St. Vincent Millay (1892-1950)
Type of poem: Sonnet
First published: 1931, in *Fatal Interview*

The Poem

"Love is not all: it is not meat nor drink" is a sonnet with a traditional structure of octave and sestet in its fourteen lines. Its focus is a personal message addressing the question of the depth, importance, and transitory nature of love. The reader may assume that the poet speaks directly to him or her concerning a message that is both emotionally and intellectually "suffered"—as traditionally expressed in a sonnet. Akin to much sonneteering, this poem bears no title except a number in both its original publication and in its collected version. Thus it is referred to by its first line, a practice dating back to Renaissance times.

The "love" discussed in this sonnet is not dramatically different from that in many Millay works, nor is the love unique in the long tradition of sonnet-making. It is partly the technique used that makes this poem singular and oft-repeated. The stark language and bold metaphors create an ambivalent tone and an uneasy resolution to the sonnet.

In the first six lines, the poet provides a negative definition of what love is not, ending with a transition that is somewhat startling: Without love, one "is making friends with death." The change causes the reader to stop suddenly to contemplate the clipped irony of the close of the octave. The lines seem almost final, as though the poet has abandoned the traditional format and divulged the sonnet's solution before the proper moment.

The sestet, or last six lines, reflects a new line of thought. The poet begins to wonder whether, in spite of the fact that lack of love can be related to death, she might trade love for life's necessities. If her situation became bad enough, she wonders if she would sell love for mental peace or trade love's memory for food. The sonnet ends on a surprisingly ambiguous note expressing deep doubts; the poet can say, "I do not think I would," but she cannot say with certainty that she would not.

Forms and Devices

"Love is not all: it is not meat nor drink" is tied closely to the revitalization of the sonnet observed in the work of nineteenth century English poet Elizabeth Barrett Browning. Browning and Millay share the limelight in returning the form to its traditional content—love. This focus is reflected in Browning's *Sonnets from the Portuguese* (1850). She not only revitalizes the intimate, personal direction of the love sonnet but also experiments with format, taking new liberties with old devices. "How do I love thee?" introduces a sonnet (Sonnet 43) by stating the problem quickly, in half a line, with the solution occupying most of the sonnet's remaining lines.

"Love is not all: it is not meat nor drink" opens in the anticipation that its format will conform to the traditional sonnet schematic, fourteen lines of iambic pentameter having a rhyme pattern suggesting compliance with the traditional Petrarchan scheme (that is, octave and sestet) or relying upon the English (Shakespearean) use of three quatrains and a couplet.

Millay, however, chooses pieces of both traditions. She employs an octave and sestet in content, wherein the problem (statement) occurs in the first eight lines and the solution (resolution) occurs in the last six lines. Her innovation is seen in the rhyme pattern, wherein Millay uses the Shakespearean pattern (*abab, cdcd*) instead of the rigorous *abba, abba* of the Petrarchan form. Flexibility in sound is gained by creating a fresh approach to the older Italian form.

In content, Millay strikes out rapidly (as sonneteers must) to make her point. Her negative metaphors ("not meat nor drink") create the illusion that she is suggesting that love is unimportant or not vital to life. She elongates the negative by forging more metaphors and encompassing essentials of life—food, shelter, and slumber.

In line 3, she begins a metaphor whose repetition strongly suggests the boredom of a life in which men "sink and rise and sink and rise again." Lines 5 and 6 continue the metaphor along the lines of illness and accident. Here too the author suggests that love is useless in any healing process.

It is line 7 that introduces the juxtaposition of an irony that negates all previous statements. Indeed, Millay clearly admonishes the reader that love may fail to feed, shelter, or heal; nevertheless, unless one attempts to love, one is flirting with death. The insertion of "even as I speak" emphasizes the urgency toward which she tries to persuade her reader. The octave closes with a seeming solution: love or die.

Opening the sestet, line 9 plods slowly and rhythmically to set up a dichotomy typical of much of Millay's work. The use of the expletive "It may well be" (a grammatical device delaying the real subject of the sentence) is an intentional delay tactic used by the poet to suggest the doubt that exists somewhere deep in her thought. The repetition of this phrase in line 14 reinforces the delay, the doubt, and the possibility that one may have to trade the best of love for another way of life, another kind of peace.

This technique, the use of a surprise ending that capitalizes on irony, exists in many of Millay's sonnets, especially the earlier offerings in *The Harp-Weaver and Other Poems* (1923). This trait is one reason her sonnets remain interesting and fresh through the years.

Themes and Meanings

That love poems, including sonnets, delve deeply into the poet's personal and intimate thoughts is an inherent aspect of the form. Indeed, lyric poetry in general has traditionally been an avenue for expressing a subjective thought or feeling. The Italian poet Petrarch, in the fourteenth century, developed the sonnet style now called the Italian sonnet; English poets, including Sir Thomas Wyatt and William Shakespeare, later adapted and altered the form. Within this long tradition, Edna St. Vincent Millay relies upon some very traditional heritage while creating her own particular use of the form.

As a sonneteer, Millay dramatizes love in fresh and personal ways. Millay's candle "burns at both ends" (as she once wrote), and this light brings myriad reactions to love in her sonnets. Her first publication in 1917, *Renascence and Other Poems*, featured sonnets as well as the primary lyrics. This tendency continued, as Millay included sonnets in most of her major works.

"Love is not all: it is not meat nor drink" was a part of *Fatal Interview* (1931) and it may be an expression to one of her lovers. Edmund Wilson and Elizabeth Atkins maintain that, although this may be the case, the poem seems to be "the perfect expression of Millay's sentiments to her husband, Eugen Boissevain."

Some critics suggest that the octave represents sexual love, perhaps since the metaphors are so physical and the repetition of sinking and rising may allude to erection. The second portion of the octave may refer to Eugen's care of Millay during her various illnesses. The contrast of love with physical problems ("thickened lung," "fractured bone") is a departure from the metaphor of the first four lines, if one accepts Wilson's and Atkins's position, and could be construed as literal in meaning.

On the other hand, one might take the position that the second part of the octave is simply an extension of the earlier metaphors. This explication seems in keeping with the original problem that "Love is not all" and the idea that Millay wishes to extend her statement to a host of physical possibilities. This wide range builds intensity toward the irony to be delivered in the close of the octave.

To clarify the meaning of the sestet, one might conclude that Millay has reached a maturity in her life and writing. Many critics comment upon Millay's gradual growth toward more general themes and her departure from highly personal and intimate comments as she approaches universals; this may be endlessly argued. The literal meaning, if one assumes this posture, is a caustic, realistic view of life; one may be forced to give up "valued love" in search of either mental peace or a physical need, such as food. The mature Millay often writes in a similar surrendering fashion in her poetry. Life, she has discovered, is rife with the uncertainty of commitment. This position is supported by other sonnets in *Fatal Interview*; particularly noteworthy in this respect are the sonnets from this period that appear in the *Collected Sonnets* (1941). It is this understanding of the uncertainties of love and life that enriches the later poems of Millay.

Jeanette A. Ritzenthaler

LOVE POEM

Author: John Frederick Nims (1913-1999)
Type of poem: Lyric
First published: 1947, in *The Iron Pastoral*

The Poem

"Love Poem" is a twenty-four-line poem in six stanzas of four lines each; the second and fourth lines of each stanza rhyme. Although the oddly generic title is an accurate description of the poem, its very generality also provides the reader with a subtle clue that this may not be a traditional example of love poetry.

Indeed, in the poem's first three words, the speaker directly addresses his beloved as "My clumsiest dear." The woman he loves, as the reader quickly learns, breaks nearly everything that encounters her "quick touch." Her hands wreak disasters—they "shipwreck vases"—and chip glasses. They are like proverbial bulls in a china shop, he says, and they catch in fine cloth like the burrs of weeds. The poem's first four stanzas follow an alternating pattern in which stanzas 1 and 3 depict the woman's clumsiness and stanzas 2 and 4 describe the qualities that make the speaker love her in spite of it.

In stanza 2, the tone suddenly becomes gentler as he states that her clumsiness disappears where "ill-at-ease" people with troubles are concerned. She can make a refugee, standing uncomfortably in the doorway, feel at home. She "deftly" steadies the drunkard for whom the very floor seems to be moving. Stanza 3 returns to her awkwardness in the physical world, humorously explaining that she has no depth perception—a dangerous situation when traffic is involved. She is "the taxi driver's terror." Having no idea how close anything is, she shrinks from distant approaching headlights but tries to dash across the street in front of streetcars that are practically upon her.

Yet in "traffic of wit," the poet says in stanza 4, she is an expert. When it comes to words and, more important, to "people and love," she can move with complete comfort and control. In the stanza's final line, he quietly states that this quality makes him love her, makes him devoted to her. Stanza 5 returns to the humorous tone, but now her clumsiness and his love for her come together in the same lines. Never mind the spilt coffee and lipstick stains on his clothes, he says; love creates a heaven that is unbreakable. Moreover, the bourbon that she spills will even provide the "glory" to buoy up their souls to that heaven.

In the final stanza, the breaking of glasses seems almost celebratory, like glasses purposely broken after a toast or during a marriage ceremony. The sound is music to the poet's ears because he realizes that the clumsiness is an inseparable part of the unique person whom he loves. The poem's final two lines provide the same sort of summation that the last two lines of a sonnet, that most traditional form of love poetry, often do: "For should your hands drop white and empty/ All the toys of the world would break." The poet drops the humorous tone that has recurred throughout the poem, admitting the seriousness of his love for the woman and confessing that without her, clumsiness and all, life would be silent and joyless.

Forms and Devices

One of the most notable features of "Love Poem" is its balance between humor and tenderness. John Frederick Nims uses the technique of hyperbole (extreme exaggeration) skillfully to help create that balance. Hyperbolic overstatement was once a common technique of traditional love poetry; the poet would declaim his lover's (or would-be lover's) overwhelming beauty and state that without her he would surely waste away and die. Nims, however, turns the use of hyperbole within the context of love poetry upside down: He exaggerates his beloved's faults.

The woman he is addressing does not merely accidentally break vases; her hands "shipwreck" them. Not a glass or two, but "all glasses" are chipped by her touch. Her reactions to traffic in the street are almost cartoonish; she "shrinks" in terror from distant headlights or "leaps" directly in front of streetcars. Nims expands her confusion to cosmic proportions, encompassing all time and space. Misjudging time (she is always late) and distance, she is "A wrench in clocks and the solar system." She has spilled enough bourbon to float their very souls. By the last stanza, she seems to be smashing glasses constantly, "early and late."

Yet Nims does balance those descriptions with the more traditional uses of overstatement. She may chip "all" glasses, but she is also adept at helping "all ill-at-ease fidgeting people." The poet himself is "all devotion." The final two lines provide the last hyperbolic statement and possess a seriousness that perfectly balances the poem's sense of whimsy; her death would break "All the toys of the world."

Nims is generally a traditionalist when it comes to poetic form, writing with careful attention to structure. "Love Poem" is written in four-line stanzas, the most traditional of forms in English lyric poetry. The second and fourth lines of each stanza rhyme; the rhymes are simple and unstartling. Within this framework, however, one finds effective use of imagery that is both precise and surprising. The word "apoplectic," for example, in "red apoplectic streetcars," personifies the inanimate streetcar while reiterating its red color and describing the panic of the driver hitting the brake at the instant the woman leaps in front of him. Similarly, in the image of her "lipstick grinning on our coat," the "grinning" both personifies the lipstick mark and implies the joy of their love.

Themes and Meanings

Although the poem puts a twist on the traditional love poem, there are precedents for a poem in which a poet takes pains to describe imperfect aspects of a lover. In Sonnet 130, William Shakespeare runs through a whole catalog of traditional praises while humorously stating that none of them applies to his love. Her eyes are "nothing like the sun," her hair is like "black wires," and her breath "reeks." Her cheeks are not rosy; she does not move like a goddess. Yet in the last two lines, he states that she is as wonderful as any to whom those comparisons are applied.

Similarly, eighteenth century English poet and dramatist William Whitehead wrote in "The 'Je Ne Sais Quoi'" that his lover (whom he gives the traditional name Celia) has neither a graceful face, shape, nor air. He, too, expresses his love for the woman he describes: He loves the "provoking charm/ Of Celia altogether." (The French phrase *Je ne sais quoi*, meaning "I know not what," refers to an unexplainable quality.)

At the center of "Love Poem" is the idea that no person is perfect and that love accepts and overcomes that fact. Whatever faults the person one loves may have are made up for by the qualities in him or her that one loves and respects. One has no doubt that the poet addresses a real person here rather than the unrealistic, idealized image found in some love poetry. He praises her talent for helping others and her quick mind even as he gently takes her to task for her "quick touch." Reversing the cliché that "love is blind," the poet states that sometimes love can see, accept, and thereby grow stronger. Also implied is the necessity of separating the important from the trivial: Wit and love for people are important; clumsiness is not.

Moreover, as Whitehead's poem does in referring to Celia "altogether," "Love Poem" recognizes that all aspects of a person are inextricably intertwined. It therefore does not begrudgingly accept the clumsiness, but finally, praises it joyfully. The last two stanzas express this paradoxically. First, it is the very bourbon that she spills that lifts them to "love's unbreakable heaven." Second, if she should die (therefore, one would think, making breakable objects safe), all toys everywhere would break at that moment. Ironically, those realizations bring the poet to the sort of devotion toward his beloved that would be perfectly at home in an Elizabethan sonnet. In stanzas 4 and 5, Nims uses the royal "we" to refer to himself, indicating that her love makes him feel like a king. He worships her at her knees, he says—thereby transforming her into a goddess. When he vows to "study wry music" for her sake, she even becomes his muse, inspiring him with the sound of breaking glasses.

H. McCrea Adams

THE LOVE SONG OF J. ALFRED PRUFROCK

Author: T. S. Eliot (1888-1965)
Type of poem: Dramatic monologue
First published: 1915; collected in *Prufrock and Other Observations*, 1917

The Poem

"The Love Song of J. Alfred Prufrock" struck readers as an astonishingly original poem when it appeared in Harriet Monroe's *Poetry* magazine in 1915. Although it belongs to an established genre—the dramatic monologue—the tone, the language, and the character of Prufrock are highly original.

The ironies of the poem begin with a title promising a "love song" from the lips of a person with a decidedly unromantic name. Still, a lover's name should not be held against him, and the first two lines of the poem do seem to promise a graceful lyric: "Let us go then, you and I,/ When the evening is spread out against the sky." In the third line, however, the reader is jolted by an unexpected and decidedly unromantic simile. The evening is spread out "like a patient etherised upon a table."

After arousing, then abruptly defying, expectations, T. S. Eliot intimates that the "you" of the poem is not Prufrock's ladylove but a confidante—in effect, the reader—who will accompany him on a visit to some sort of evening party or soiree. The reader is led on a route through a shabby urban neighborhood on a foggy October evening to a place where "women come and go/ Talking of Michelangelo." Prufrock, who has "an overwhelming question" to ask, is fearful. He suspects that he will not be acceptable. If he starts up the stair to the party and then turns back, "they" will have a perfect view of his balding head. Clearly, Prufrock is a middle-aged bachelor—thin, fussy, and self-conscious. How can he "presume" to ask his question?

Although he shrinks from the inevitable scrutiny of the women in general, his question is for "one" who may refuse to respond favorably to it. The question is, it appears, a marriage proposal, or at least a declaration of love. He agonizes over the possibility of rejection and rehearses all the likely reasons for it. He is an insignificant man who has "measured out [his] life with coffee spoons." He is timid, ineffectual, and inarticulate, but he is driven by a desperate wish to escape the ranks of the men he has seen leaning out of windows along his route to the party.

Prufrock briefly fancies himself a heroic character: a beheaded John the Baptist, a Lazarus returned from the dead, a Hamlet who can assert himself and win the admiration of the woman and her friends. He quickly realizes, however, that he can never be "Prince Hamlet," only "the Fool." He makes a last effort to compensate for his failings. Perhaps he can comb his hair in such a way as to disguise his bald spot. Can he walk on the beach and attract the attention of mermaids in the surf? No, he concludes, and he wakens from his reverie with a sinking sense of drowning in reality. The question will never be asked, and Prufrock will remain a lonely and unhappy man.

Forms and Devices

Eliot's monologue differs markedly from those of nineteenth century poets such as Robert Browning and Alfred, Lord Tennyson. Unlike the protagonists of Browning's "My Last Duchess" and Tennyson's "Ulysses," Prufrock cannot control his situation, and he does not speak logically or coherently. Listening to him is more like overhearing one musing to oneself. The "you" of the poem disappears early; after line 12 ("Let us go and make our visit"), Prufrock is entirely self-absorbed.

The poem comprises 131 lines of various lengths with flexible rhythm and rhymes. Eliot uses couplets, cross rhymes, and unrhymed lines. The result is a blend of traditional poetic sound effects and free verse. The unpatterned nature mirrors the distracted state of Prufrock, who would like to produce a true love song but can manage only a confidential confession of his own ineptitude.

Prufrock's repetitions reveal his anxieties: "Do I dare?"; "how should I presume?"; "I have known them all." He also repeats the answer he expects from the woman if he ever does succeed in making his declaration to her: "That is not what I meant at all." Like other features of the poem, these iterations come at irregular intervals.

The poem's imagery is antiromantic: Like a "patient etherised upon a table." The city streets are tawdry and depressing; the women Prufrock will meet chatter meaninglessly of "Michelangelo"; he feels himself "pinned and wriggling on the wall." He contrasts "the cups, the marmalade, the tea" with the more momentous matters he would like to broach, but his grand visions always give way to bric-a-brac and bored tea drinkers. He sees himself as going down, descending a stair in defeat or drowning in the sea.

Eliot introduces in this poem a technique he would make famous in *The Waste Land* (1922): the ironic interjection of quotations from earlier poets. This poem commences with a six-line epigraph from Dante in which one of the denizens of his Inferno confides in his visitor because he cannot conceive of the latter ever escaping from hell, but whereas Dante will return to write his poem, Prufrock cannot escape his private hell. There are also references to or scraps from such varied sources as Hesiod's *Works and Days* (c. 700 B.C.E.), William Shakespeare's *Hamlet* (c. 1600-1601), Andrew Marvell's "To His Coy Mistress" (1681), and the Gospels.

When spoken by Prufrock, however, all sublimity drains from these passages. The comparison with Hamlet is particularly ironic. Hamlet, too, is an indecisive man who muses and delays, but he ultimately acts when sufficiently pressured. Prufrock has no prospect of such pressure: no ghostly father, no enormous wrong to rectify, not even an Ophelia—only a languid lady friend who will not take him seriously. He feels impelled to an antiheroic stance and compares himself to literary and biblical figures for the sake of denying any resemblance.

Themes and Meanings

Unlike the principal characters of most previous poets and storytellers, Prufrock is neither hero nor villain—he is simply a failure. Even heroes destined to fail normally begin with hopes and possibilities, but not far into "The Love Song of J. Alfred

Prufrock," one senses the impossibility of this man fulfilling his aspirations. He is already middle-aged, set in his ways, and hopelessly irresolute; he is more like someone resigned to reading about heroes than someone who will ever take action.

Thus Eliot permits the reader no vicarious successful experience. Prufrock is a figure to be pitied, but he is also a disturbing presence because his weaknesses, his mediocrity, and his sense of isolation are all too common in the modern world. When an optimist such as Walt Whitman insisted that all people are potential heroes, he meant that they chiefly lacked recognition. The stuff of heroism abounds, Whitman would say, especially in a democratic society that permits the individual to develop a sense of personal worth. For the most part, these heroes remain anonymous; collectively, they constitute the strength of society.

Prufrock has something that Whitman's heroes lacked—a name—but he has precious little else. He has done nothing constructive with his freedom, and his keen awareness of his shortcomings destroys the self-esteem that theoretically ought to flourish in a free society. If Prufrock could compose a real love song, or any valid song, he would be achieving a victory of sorts, but he lacks the capacity to express his situation. "It is impossible to say just what I mean!" he exclaims at one point. The meaning emerges not from what he says but from what Eliot, through the images, the ironic quotations, and the obsessive repetitions, shows. The eloquence is Eliot's.

Prufrock lives in a world that is no better than he is. It is happier than he is, however, because of its capacity to avoid reflection—especially self-reflection—by busying itself superficially with culture (the chatter about Michelangelo), gossip, and social amenities. Lacking the talent for such unself-conscious distractions, he attempts to take refuge in literature and dreams, but they solace him only fitfully, and he must awaken to the oppressive reality of his life.

Prufrock's failure engages sympathy for him as a human being who must live with a residual sense of inadequacy. In his mediocrity, he is a more representative figure than Hamlet. Although he understands the mediocrity of his surroundings and of the society he frequents, he cannot rise above them. His plight raises the question of whether it is better to be a Prufrock than one of the presumably more well-adjusted people whom he so dreads confronting: Is disillusionment better than illusion?

To be a reader of Eliot's poem is not exactly to be a Prufrock or, for that matter, to become disillusioned. It is, however, to be greeted with what Herman Melville called a "shock of recognition" that forcefully counters the temptation to exist in a condition of complacent insensibility. It is difficult afterward to slip into the guise of one of those women "Talking of Michelangelo."

Robert P. Ellis

LOVELIEST OF TREES, THE CHERRY NOW

Author: A. E. Housman (1859-1936)
Type of poem: Pastoral
First published: 1896, in *A Shropshire Lad*

The Poem

A. E. Housman's "Loveliest of Trees, the Cherry Now" consists of three four-line, essentially iambic stanzas, or quatrains, in which the poet, through his observation of the beauty of the natural world, is reminded of the brevity of his own life and resolves, henceforth, to experience life with intensity. The poem begins with an image from nature, a cherry tree in bloom, which suggests the beauty of life at its prime, and then focuses throughout on the poet's response to it. As the poet beholds the cherry, the "Loveliest of trees," in its springtime finery, "Wearing white for Eastertide," he experiences a sense of oneness with the natural world and assumes, simply, that he is part of it.

The second stanza continues an elaboration of the effect of this glorious sight upon the poet. While he considers the perpetual rebirth of nature, he is reminded sharply that of his biblical "threescore years and ten,/ Twenty will not come again," and further calculation of his mortality, following the biblical allotment, ironically confirms that he has "only" fifty years left. He becomes aware of his own transience in the midst of nature's splendor.

The change in the poet's perception of the natural scene, but not of the scene itself, is charted by the succeeding descriptions of the cherry tree. The second mention of the tree, in the third stanza, as one of many "things in bloom," though a conventional representation of trees, nonetheless suggests the speaker's consciousness has moved beyond the growth associated with springtime into the blooms of maturity and, therefore, to a consideration of his own limited existence. The poet's harmony with the natural world is weakened as he ponders his own certain death.

While literally referring to the whiteness of the cherry blooms, the image of the "cherry hung with snow" continues the progression of the symbolistic patterns from birth to growth to death. The "snow" on the trees, a matter of much discussion among critics and scholars, suggests connections between the notions of Easter and rebirth in addition to winter and death. The tree itself, in effect, has guided the poet from a view of a springtime world of rebirth to one "hung with snow." The young poet's perception that the blooms will melt and disappear reflects his realization that even the "loveliest" aspects of nature reveal a world in decay. He does not, however, in the face of such knowledge, succumb to pessimism or despair, but rather determines to renew his passion for living.

Forms and Devices

Housman is indebted to the pastoral tradition, an ancient poetic form in which shepherds and rustics sing and converse or occasionally occupy themselves with farming. Early in the evolution of the pastoral, it became an artificial and unnatural form, with the "shepherds" often discussing life at court, but more modern use of the pastoral mode includes any poem of rural people and setting. In "Loveliest of Trees, the Cherry Now," Housman employs a more sophisticated concept of the pastoral, which conveys complex ideas through simplistic personages. The complexities of life have been reduced to a level that can be communicated by a rustic youth who expresses the truths of his own insights. The poetic voice of a simple country lad enables Housman, an erudite scholar, to avoid sentimentality or the betrayal of his own voice in the poem.

Housman's use of the rustic setting and the pastoral persona that evokes a more primitive world of shepherds and simple folk is part of the same impulse that led nineteenth century Romantic poet William Wordsworth, whom Housman admired, to the simple character in the bucolic setting. Housman's changing responses to the external world that are reflected through the "ages" of man invite comparison with Wordsworth, who follows the same pattern in his "Ode on the Intimations of Mortality from Recollections of Early Childhood." Despite the fact that Housman's intimations of nature, however, are not of nature's divinity, but of his own mortality, both poets suggest a process inspired by the loss of a harmonious relationship with nature, which takes the persona from innocence to knowledge to resignation.

Other technical patterns that contribute to a sense of growth and development appear in Housman's manipulation of images of sunrise, dawn, and spring—all of which suggest invitations to the young lad to revel in a world at its prime—to end with images of death, graveyards, and darkness. The clear images of death that end the cycle indicate the intimations of mortality discovered in the innocent's view of the world, which becomes forever colored by those intimations.

The simplicity in "Loveliest of Trees, the Cherry Now" that is more apparent than real is further substantiated to a large extent by the use of irony and paradox—both qualities that modern criticism has come to view as marks of complexity in poetry. The persona's ironic realization that he has "only" fifty more years to live and that is "little room" to enjoy all that life has to offer reflects his complex response to his own mortality. Also, the striking use of paradox, wherein the persona's acknowledgment of certain death renews his zest for living, permits Housman to avoid pessimism and despair and to provide some benefit to the persona from his woeful predicament.

Themes and Meanings

"Loveliest of Trees, the Cherry Now" is the second of sixty-three poems in *A Shropshire Lad*, Housman's work that represents a concern with the problem of the change that characterizes existence. The poem depicts the poet's first awareness of mutability and death in his world of youth and beauty, in that his perception of the facts of his existence indicate that the "loveliest" things in nature contain the seeds of decay and death. Yet, at the poem's end, the poet, conscious of his own mortality, retains some sympathy with nature.

In *A Shropshire Lad*, the theme of change is explored relentlessly, proceeding from the first consciousness of mortality to a complete state of alienation from youthful harmony and innocence. Terence, the rustic lad, endures various revelations of change and death and eventually removes himself from Shropshire and the naïveté of his youth to exile in London and the resignation of manhood.

The journey, represented in terms of a progression from innocence to experience, is highlighted by Housman's subtle allusions to *Paradise Lost* (1667, 1674), the epic poem by the seventeenth century English poet John Milton, who depicts Adam's innocence in Eden and his subsequent recognition of human evil and death. Echoing Milton's narration of fallen angels in a universe of death, Housman illumines his theme of lost innocence as he attempts to come to terms with the human condition. For Housman, the cherry, the "loveliest of trees," serves as the Tree of Knowledge, as it sparks the recognition of death and decay that ultimately blights the pastoral Eden. Shropshire becomes Eden after the Fall, from which Terence, the innocent country lad, is eventually expelled.

It was in his reliance upon the pastoral tradition that Housman achieved the most felicitous treatment of an extraordinarily persistent theme in literature. In his poetic mode, Shropshire is, in effect, a pastoral Arcadia, an ancient region in Greece incorporated into early pastorals and suggesting idealized rural simplicity and contentment. This idealization provides a symbolic environment through which the innocent persona's discovery, initially contained within himself, broadens thematically to include estrangement and ultimate departure from the lost land of the imagination.

The transition from innocence to experience is relayed not in terms of time, but in widely differing geographical areas, and it follows the pastoral's original distinction. Terence's expulsion from the peace and contentment of Shropshire and the sympathy of humanity and nature takes him to a life of loneliness, anxiety, nostalgia, and loss in alien, hostile London. The fact that Shropshire and London are seen symbolically as two different poles of existence emphasizes the loss sustained by the knowledge of death but is offset by a vision of maturity required to adjust to life without the security of youth. Paradoxically, the search for permanence in a world of change can only be achieved through the loss of the essence of existence.

"Loveliest of Trees, the Cherry Now" records a discovery each individual makes about the nature of his or her world and presents this commonplace event with all the complexities and contradictions that accompany this discovery. The development of Housman's theme corresponds to the evolution of a feeling in the persona and, consequently, encourages in the reader a shock of recognition of universal experience. Each individual reader may participate in an emotional and imaginative response to the elemental facts of his or her own existence.

Mary Hurd

LUCIFER IN STARLIGHT

Author: George Meredith (1828-1909)
Type of poem: Sonnet
First published: 1883, in *Poems and Lyrics of the Joy of Earth*

The Poem

George Meredith's "Lucifer in Starlight" explores a motif introduced in the Christian Old Testament and examines the stymied ambitions of an angel fallen from Heaven who was the embodiment of pride and temptation. Meredith's poem achieves distinction in approaching the theme from a rationalist, possibly Deist-influenced, point of view.

In the poem, the fallen angel Prince Lucifer rises out of his "dark dominion," the region beneath the earth to which he had been consigned after his rebellion against Heaven. His flight above the world is marked by his rising higher than the birds or any other natural beings, until, as the sun might be, he is "in cloud part screened." He catches glimpses of the "rolling ball" of Earth below, including views of "Afric's sands" and "Arctic snows." He rises into a region closer to Heaven, which brings renewed pain to scars left from his embattled rebellion, apparently still not completely healed. He has reached a "middle height," where he regards the stars. These stars, however, represent not Heaven but natural law. They are the "brain of Heaven." The fallen angel, who still nursed hopes for ascension to the highest places, is chastened by the sight and falls again.

The poem plays upon a famous passage from the Old Testament book of Isaiah, 14:12-21, in which the "bright morning star" is depicted as having once nursed the highest ambitions, for he had hoped to set a throne above the stars of heaven: "I will rise high above the cloud-banks/ and make myself like the Most High." The subsequent passages in Isaiah make clear that these were the thoughts supposed to have been held by a fallen "oppressor" and "ruler" who once "shook the earth, who made kingdoms quake, who turned the world into a desert," and who now lay dead: "maggots are the pallet beneath you,/ and worms your coverlet." The subject of the passage is "a corpse trampled underfoot," an image that may be taken, and has been taken, either literally or figuratively.

In Meredith's imaginative transformation of the story, Lucifer is not a fallen, earthly ruler, but instead an angel who defied and rebelled against Heaven, and who was scarred and sent to the Christian underworld, Hell. The ambitions that are projected on the fallen ruler in Isaiah are the exact ambitions upon which Meredith's Lucifer acts.

In "Lucifer in Starlight," the events unfold as literal and actual. Lucifer rises from a world that, at the time Meredith was writing, was geographically well delineated and scientifically well understood. Lucifer then reaches a "middle height," which is the traditional Middle Kingdom, or the land that resides halfway between the human and divine worlds. Yet the divine is no longer divine: The stars are not Heaven, but the "army of unalterable law." They are the signs of a clockwork universe. Below him, on the "rolling ball," Lucifer has seen "sinners . . ./ Poor prey to his hot fit of pride." In regarding the sinners, and in then regarding the stars, Lucifer confronts the fact that mortals have free will, while he, as a supernatural being, does not. The sinners are not doomed to fail against temptation, as he is doomed to fail against natural law.

Forms and Devices

Although sonnets are more typically meditative or lyric, "Lucifer in Starlight" is predominantly narrative in nature. It introduces a character, gives the character inward thoughts and outward actions, and details a series of events that reach a striking climax. Meredith relates his narrative without digression, making no obvious authorial observations or reflections. The details of the narrative itself carry the message of the poem, with those details enhanced by Meredith's choice of terms.

The traditional sonnet is comprised of an octave, or eight-line stanza, followed by a sextet, or six-line stanza. The usual rhyme scheme for the octave in the sonnet is *abba abba*, the scheme Meredith used in this poem. For his two rhymes, he chooses two extremely distinctive sounds, represented by "uprose" and "fiend." While several different terminal rhyme schemes are common for the subsequent sextet, Meredith chose an unusual one: *cdc eed*. These rhymes are closer in nature, which may help reinforce the finality of this stanza. The *c* and *d* rhymes are especially similar, represented by "scars" and "Awe." The rhyming of the latter with the final line, "The army of unalterable law," serves a more than musical purpose. "Awe," which is a biblical-style metonymic name for "God," becomes linked with the concept of natural or physical law, suggesting similarity or identity.

Meredith's choice of terms determines the reader's understanding of the poem. Writing for a contemporary audience likely familiar with the passages from Isaiah, and undoubtedly familiar with Christian biblical tales of the revolt among the angels, the poet could suggest character and setting with great economy. His readers recognized the "fiend" who was "tired of his dark dominion." Lucifer's flight above the "rolling ball" announces his supernatural character, since Meredith was writing his poem at a time when few scientists were contemplating the possibility of flight by using physical law to human advantage.

Even while tapping his biblical source, Meredith carefully established a nineteenth century worldview. Lucifer's world was not the geographically limited one of Isaiah, but rather a "rolling ball," and the "far recesses of the north" mentioned in Isaiah were now "Arctic snows." The Christian God is not named as such, but described in terms having nothing to do with supernatural power and everything to do with human response to sublime experience: "Awe."

Stars are the most prevalent image in the poem, occurring explicity in the title, first line, and eleventh line, and implicitly elsewhere, especially in the final two lines. The Christian Heaven is depicted only in terms of these stars. They are "the brain of heaven." In the last lines, they represent a Heaven firmly transformed into universe, which could be encompassed by human understanding without resort to supernatural explanation: "Around the ancient track marched, rank on rank,/ The army of unalterable law." Meredith underlines his attitude by calling the Milky Way the "ancient track," which resonates with the notion that he is retelling a tale that is itself ancient, but in human terms only.

Themes and Meanings

Meredith's remarkable poem arose at a time when arguments were reaching a fever pitch between advocates of the church and advocates of rationalism, many of whom were influenced by the English Deism movement of the seventeenth and eighteenth centuries. The Deists had advocated a worldview that embraced the concept of a Creator but that rejected the idea of an interceding deity. Once the mechanical universe of the Deists was set in motion, the Creator's role was done. The work of such pioneering rationalists as Sir Isaac Newton and James Hutton supported this mechanistic view of the universe. In Meredith's time, the greatest proponent of rationalism was Charles Darwin, whose evolutionary theory renewed and deepened the debate, often acrimonious, between representatives of the church and the halls of science.

Throughout these centuries, despite the debates and acrimony, many within the rationalist camp never divorced themselves entirely from the church or religious thought. The language, terms, and ideas of Christianity remained important at all levels of discourse. Meredith's "Lucifer in Starlight" embodies this in dramatic form. By demonstrating its continued interest to contemporary readers, Meredith asserted the power of the biblical story and biblical perspective in the most direct manner. That the poem continued to attract readers through the succeeding century indicates that not only the issues but also Meredith's rhetorical approach are of enduring interest.

The overwhelming impact of the poem arrives from its critique of the traditional Christian outlook, however. The language, themes, and story of the poem are derived from that outlook, yet the narrative of "Lucifer in Starlight," line by line, moves inexorably toward its rationalist conclusion, in which Lucifer, a uniquely Christian being, is defeated. Even though supernatural in nature, he is not defeated by the swords of Heaven, nor by the thunderbolts of a higher supernatural deity. He is defeated by a simple sight. He sees the stars, which represent the eternal laws of the physical universe. In a real sense, he sees reason.

With the lines, "Soaring through wider zones that pricked his scars/ With memory of the old revolt from Awe," Lucifer is revealed as a kind of Sisyphus. He is engaging in a struggle he has lost before, but which he feels compelled to engage in again. His proper place, as a supernatural being, is a "dark dominion." Yet he grows tired of that place and rises to fight once more against "the army of unalterable law." Just as Sisyphus is doomed to forever push a boulder to the top of an unscalable hill, Meredith's Lucifer is doomed to repeat his futile effort.

The strength of its message makes "Lucifer in Starlight" compelling as an artistic expression of one of the great intellectual debates of Western society. Meredith's skill with words, sure command of his poetic form, and dramatic flair give the work lasting value as a literary work.

Mark Rich

LUKE HAVERGAL

Author: Edwin Arlington Robinson (1869-1935)
Type of poem: Lyric
First published: 1897, in *The Children of the Night*

The Poem

"Luke Havergal" is a haunting poem of thirty-two lines about a desperately be-reaved man being tempted by a voice from the grave to commit suicide in order to re-unite with a beloved woman who is dead.

One of Edwin Arlington Robinson's finest performances, "Luke Havergal" was a favorite of President Theodore Roosevelt, who, even though he promoted the poem and the poet's career, found the contents of the poem to be obscure in meaning. Al-though Robinson by his own admission aimed "to put a little mysticism" in his verses, the morbid death-prone mysticism of "Luke Havergal" is not all that difficult to deci-pher. The poem conveys, through sound and image, a compelling emotion of a half-crazed longing for love that entices a man grieving over the death of his beloved woman to take his own life.

Reared in Gardiner, Maine, Edwin Arlington Robinson created a mythical "Tilbury Town" out of his New England birthplace and populated the fictional place with eccen-trics, such as this desolate lover, who lead wasted, blighted, or impoverished lives. The poet was an American exemplar of the realism permeating European literature, especially novels and short stories, in the second half of the nineteenth century. Appropriately, "Luke Havergal" reads like a revealing and realistic short story in verse, providing readers with a snapshot portrait of a lonely main character; its "plot" is a sad case of grief-stricken abandonment of the desire to live, and the pursuit of a beloved woman in death.

The first stanza is an exhortation by a voice from the grave tempting Luke Havergal to reunite with a departed woman through a journey into death in a place of falling leaves, twilight, and setting sun.

The second and third stanzas repeat the call for Luke Havergal to seek darkness and death in the gloomy west on a bitter, suicidal walk lit, not by the dawn of the rising sun in the east, but by the fire of his unrequited, desperate passion flashing from his eyes and reflecting on his forehead. The falling leaves are but a reminder of a dying nature and a dying Creator of nature (lines 13-14) that seem in sympathy with Luke Hav-ergal's suicidal thoughts. Death is good, and to be in hell beside the departed woman will almost be a heaven for Luke Havergal.

The final stanza practically repeats the first stanza as it presents the voice's climac-tic, and possibly successful, effort to seduce lonely and love-stricken Luke Havergal to trade his wretched life for a promise of romance in the grave.

Forms and Devices

"Luke Havergal" is a lyric poem consisting of four stanzas whose prevailing meter is iambic pentameter with variations. The eighth line of each stanza is an iambic dimeter beat echoing the sound and sense of the previous line in its closing words ("In eastern skies," "To tell you this," "Luke Havergal").

Of particular interest in each eight-line stanza is the unusual and intricate rhyme scheme (*aabbaaaa*), which repeats final sounds so as to convey a powerfully cumulative insistence in the voice's seduction of poor Luke Havergal. This repetition of final sounds combines with the repetitious last two lines of each stanza to provide Luke with an almost unavoidable compulsion to commit a romantic suicide.

The images and allusions all stress darkness and death—the destination and terrible outcome of Luke Havergal's romantic desolation and desperation. In contrast to the rising sun of "eastern skies" is Luke's wild "twilight" time for a walk to the gloomy "western gate" of the setting sun, under which vines bloom to a terminal blood-red ripeness and where leaves fall like fleeting and fading words that are ultimately indecipherable. Luke's eyes are fiery red, and his forehead is flushed crimson. It provides him with an unnatural light for his way into the dark on his topsy-turvy pilgrimage into hell, activated by his misplaced fidelity to the memory of his beloved dead lady. Like a God who slays Himself—possibly like a Christ-Creator who allows Himself to be crucified—Luke finds himself tempted to harrow hell, through suicide, in an attempt to recover the object of his desire.

Most important, this suicidal pilgrimage may well be Robinson's modern version of the classical journey into Hades by a Roman hero such as Aeneas. Aeneas was similarly drawn into a dark rendezvous with his dead lover, Queen Dido, under the guidance of the Sibyl, the Roman prophetess at Cumae in Vergil's great epic poem, the *Aeneid* (c. 29-19 B.C.E.). In fact, the ruling motif of Robinson's entire poem seems to be this classical allusion to the Sibyl at Cumae by the gates of Hades. The motif of the Vergilian journey into Hades acts as an implicit underlying contrast for the desperate romantic plight of a modern antihero, Luke Havergal.

Themes and Meanings

"Luke Havergal" is an address to a lovelorn man, spoken by a seductive voice from beyond the grave to encourage him to rejoin a dead lover by taking his own life. He is told that he may find her through suicide. Although the poem might appear to display a faith in life after death, the intense desolation of his experience points, rather, to an expression of longing for death and an inability to endure more life in such grief-stricken loneliness.

Readers coming to terms with the poem should have in mind the famous classical tale of Aeneas's walk into Hades, led by the Sibyl at Cumae (who communicated prophecies on torn leaves blown into the wind). They were on their way to meet his former lover, the dead Queen Dido, who had committed suicide; the story appears in book 2 of Vergil's *Aeneid*. If Luke Havergal is reminded that sacrifice is necessary for his descent into the dark and his reunion with his beloved ("God slays Himself with every leaf that flies,/ And hell is more than half of paradise"), analogously the Roman hero Aeneas must wait until the Sibyl sacrifices to the goddess of the night for his entrance into the underworld where his suicidal lover Dido passes her melancholy existence.

What follows is a paraphrase of pertinent passages from book 2 of the *Aeneid* for comparison with "Luke Havergal." Aeneas had been told by the prophet Helenus to seek, upon his arrival at Italy, the cave of the Sibyl at Cumae, a woman of deep wisdom, who could foretell the future and give Aeneas proper advice for founding the great Roman empire. Aeneas found her, and she warned him that the descent to the underworld was easy but that the return was perilous. Aenas and the Sibyl found themselves in the Fields of Mourning, where unhappy lovers dwelled who had been driven to suicide. There Aeneas caught sight of Dido and, weeping, addressed her: "Was I the cause of your death? I left you against my will." She, like a piece of marble, was silent and averted her gaze. He was shaken and wept long after he lost sight of her.

Thomas M. Curley

LULLABY

Author: W. H. Auden (1907-1973)
Type of poem: Lyric
First published: 1937; collected in *Another Time*, 1940

The Poem

W. H. Auden's "Lullaby," his most famous love lyric, perhaps is better known by its famous first line, "Lay your sleeping head, my love." In musical and rhetorical lines of mostly trochaic tetrameter verse, the narrator watches his sleeping lover through the night and, in four ten-line stanzas, reflects upon the value and necessity of both passionate love and beauty and their brevity.

The speaker gazes upon his lover beside him and sings this philosophical "lullaby" about love, beauty, and time's ruthless pull. The speaker realizes that time eventually will erode his lover's beauty, as it some day will suck children down into their graves. He prays to be allowed to hold his beloved in his admittedly "faithless arm" until dawn, because at this enchanted moment the beloved seems to him to be "entirely beautiful." The speaker asks for a temporary reprieve from time for this one exquisite night to prolong the beauty of the moment and of his lover.

In the next stanza, the narrator reflects on the timeless and boundless feelings people experience when they are ardently in love and feel united in body and soul. Lovers seem to "swoon" into an enchanted union in which their bodies and spirits merge—it is as if Venus, the goddess of love, suffused them with feelings of sympathy, "universal love," and "hope" so that the mortals feel unity and timelessness. Into this idyllic feeling of timeless passion, Auden inserts another form of intense "carnal ecstasy," which is experienced through the mind. Ascetic hermits through abstract thought find a mystical passion that also leads to feelings of unity and timelessness. Auden equates these two different modes of finding passionate and timeless unity—one through the body with a mortal lover, and one through the mind with a spiritual entity.

As in many Auden poems, there is a sudden reversal in the third stanza. The speaker makes an ironic shift in attitude away from the timeless feelings of ecstasy associated with passionate love to the more realistic view that this moment of tenderness and ecstasy may vanish at the stroke of midnight. Even though he realizes that nothing is certain and his lover's faithfulness may evaporate, even though this moment of passion may be as short-lived as the latest fashionable madman's ranting, and even though this night may cost him dearly, the speaker is ready to pay the costs and to suffer whatever pains the cards of fortune may heap upon him. At any cost, he wants nothing to be lost from this one magical, fleeting night—"Not a whisper, not a thought,/ Not a kiss nor look." He wants to seize this night of passionate ecstasy from time and make it eternal.

In the last stanza, the magical night ends, the vision of beauty and love fades, but the speaker prays for a benevolent day that will bless his still dreaming lover. Apparently, the speaker has been contemplating the beauty of his lover and their passion the entire night. The speaker hopes that the dawn brings his beloved a day so beautiful that this lovely mortal world will obliterate the need for supernatural worlds—the day should be a veritable heaven on earth. He invokes the "involuntary powers" of love, beauty, and poetry, and hopes they will feed the lover so that he may survive all the times of dryness and times of insults that life may bring. The speaker wishes his lover will be blessed and soothed by this lullaby and will be watched over by a benevolent godlike human love.

Forms and Devices

Auden was fond of rhetorical patterns of repetition, especially complex forms of parallelism leading to paradoxes. He also juxtaposed surprising ideas to create unique metaphors. For example, grammatically parallel phrases begin two of the last four lines of the poem. Line 37 begins with "noons of dryness," and line 39 with "nights of insult," which are ways Auden metaphorically depicts difficult time periods in life. "Noons of dryness" metaphorically links the hottest time of day to the tactile image of "dryness" to imply a kind of sterile desert. "Noons" and "nights" are linked by parallelism, which implies that the speaker wants his beloved not only to wake up that day to joy and beauty, but also to be protected by his human love every day for his whole life. It is paradoxical that Auden uses specific times, noon and night, metaphorically to imply a wish for timeless love and joy.

The meditations on love, beauty, and passion in "Lullaby" take place over a single night which the speaker wishes to preserve. Auden makes this one night partially appear "timeless" by using present-tense verb forms in all stanzas of the poem: He uses "lay" and "let" in stanza 1; tries "have," "lie," and "wakes" in stanza 2; employs "pass," "raise," and foretell in stanza 3; and ends with "let," "bless," and "find" in the final stanza. He makes this magical night consistently "present" so that subliminally one may participate in the speaker's meditation.

Auden favors speakers who seemingly are present, but also to some degree are detached from the action, contemplating it. His speaker in "Lullaby" has a complex vision of human love and sees the contradictory impulses and feelings implied. By asking a sleeping beloved, who cannot answer, to rest on his "faithless arm," the speaker implies that he wants love (but not necessarily undying fidelity) and that all human love is transient. Auden's speaker seems to be conscious of his own contrary impulses; he wants passion and wants it never to end, but knows it must end. He seems to observe himself thinking; the poem's readers look over his shoulder.

Themes and Meanings

Auden, who wrote many different forms of poetry, here blends two traditions—the nursery-rhyme lullaby and the *carpe diem* motif. Since the poem begins by addressing an adult lover, not a child as is usual in a lullaby, it is a nontraditional form of the lullaby. Yet the poem is also very musical; it ends by being soothing and wishing eternal love for the lover just as a parent might wish for eternal happiness for an innocent child in a traditional lullaby.

Auden also includes variations of the *carpe diem* theme in this lyric. In a traditional *carpe diem* poem, such as Andrew Marvell's "To His Coy Mistress," a male speaker, usually promising undying devotion and love, tries to persuade a reluctant or coy female beloved to make love to him now while they are still young and passionate rather than old and gray. He claims if they love each other they are, in a way, "married" and should consummate their passion. In "Lullaby," the gender of the beloved is ambiguous; since Auden was homosexual, both lover and beloved could be males. The speaker in "Lullaby," instead of promising eternal love, says that his arm is "faithless" and questions the whole notion of fidelity. Most *carpe diem* poems are attempts to establish a carnal affair, but Auden's poem seems to be set after the lovers have made love—a kind of post-coitus meditation. In both traditional *carpe diem* poems and Auden's "Lullaby," passionate love is primary and necessary. The goal of this poem and of more traditional *carpe diem* poems is to preserve a fleeting moment of carnal ecstasy and intense beauty and thereby temporarily to defeat time. In "Lullaby," therefore, Auden playfully and artistically weaves together nontraditional elements from both the *carpe diem* and lullaby traditions to create his own new hybrid form of poetry.

"Lullaby" also is about the power of poetry to accomplish the impossible—to freeze time temporarily. To make a magical night of love immortal and timeless, the poet writes a poem about it that captures the contrary pulls between passion, beauty, time, and human awareness of all three and relays it to readers in the present tense. By writing the poem, Auden attempts to preserve the feelings and attitudes evoked by one of the most powerful emotions humans ever experience: passionate love.

David J. Amante

LYCIDAS

Author: John Milton (1608-1674)
Type of poem: Elegy
First published: 1638, in *Justa Edouardo King*; collected in *Poems of Mr. John Milton*, 1645

The Poem

"Lycidas" is a pastoral elegy in which John Milton laments the drowning of his friend and schoolmate, Edward King, at the University of Cambridge. Mainly iambic pentameter, with irregularly appearing short lines of six syllables, the poem's 193 lines are divided into verse paragraphs of irregular length and changing rhyme schemes. In the convention of the pastoral poem, the first-person persona of the poem is a shepherd, who speaks of King as the lost shepherd Lycidas; in the convention of the elegy, "Lycidas" progresses through sadness over an individual's death and reflection on human mortality to a final consolation—not only in the redemptive message of Christianity, but in recognition of the social value of the poet's art. Milton uses these two forms not primarily to express personal grief over King's death, but to engage the dominant political and religious issues of his age.

"Lycidas" opens by addressing the laurels and myrtles, symbols of poetic fame; as their berries are not yet ripe, the poet is not yet ready to take up his pen. Yet the untimely death of young Lycidas requires equally untimely verses from the poet. Invoking the muses of poetic inspiration, the shepherd-poet takes up the task, partly, he says, in hope that his own death will not go unlamented.

The poet recalls his and Lycidas's life together in the "pastures" of Cambridge, and notes the "heavy change" suffered by nature now that Lycidas is gone—a "pathetic fallacy" in which the willows, hazel groves, woods, and caves lament Lycidas's death. Milton concludes this passage, however, by suggesting that nature's apparent sympathy is, in fact, the subjective perception of the mourning shepherds: "Such, Lycidas, thy loss to shepherd's ear" (line 49).

The shepherd-poet reflects in the following verse paragraph that thoughts of how Lycidas might have been saved are futile. The poet turns from lamenting Lycidas's death to lamenting the futility of all human labor: What meaning can work have when all life comes to this? Why not give oneself over to physical pleasures, the poet asks, when life may be cut short before one can attain the rewards of a moral life?

At this point, another voice asserts itself in response to the poet's questions; Phoebus, the sun-god, an image drawn out of the mythology of classical Roman poetry, replies that fame is not mortal but eternal, witnessed by Jove (God) himself on judgment day.

Milton then turns "Lycidas" to one of pastoral poetry's chief functions in the Renaissance, as commentary on ecclesiastical abuses. Following a procession of mythical nautical figures, "the pilot of the Galilean lake" (either Saint Peter or Christ) derides those shepherds (clergymen) who, unlike Lycidas, care more for their own well-being than for their sheep. Such shepherds neglect their flocks, "rot inwardly," and spread only disease. In a couplet that is clearly apocalyptic, the poet stresses the fate of such clergymen at the hands of God's avenging angel: "But that two-handed engine"—apparently a double-edged sword—"at the door,/ Stands ready to smite once, and smite no more" (lines 129-130).

The poem's pastoral landscape and elegiac tone then reassert themselves. The poet calls for flowers to deck the hearse of Lycidas but then recognizes that this is a foolish and simply rhetorical plea: Lycidas has no hearse since his body remains adrift in the sea. Such expressions are merely "false surmise" to comfort frail minds reticent to confront the awfulness of Lycidas's death and the dispiriting reflections to which it gives rise. The poet then invokes an explicitly Christian angel rather than a pagan, pastoral deity to "look homeward" (line 163) and pity those who grieve over the loss of Lycidas.

The last two verse paragraphs establish the elegy's Christian consolation and the poet's readiness now to embark on his poetic career. Lycidas is not dead but resurrected in Christ (lines 172-73). Shifting into third-person narrative, the poem concludes with the "uncouth swain," the shepherd-poet himself, rising and, in a gesture of hope, preparing to leave the pastures he shared with Lycidas for "fresh woods, and pastures new" (line 193).

Forms and Devices

The first function of the language of the poem is to create a sense of the pastoral environment, and Milton does this by continual reference to the natural elements of the countryside and to the pagan deities that haunt the pastoral landscapes of classical Greek and Roman poetry. The poet also needs to establish the allegorical reference of this pastoral to an English setting and to the issues that concerned King and himself as divinity students at Cambridge. Milton thus adds some specifically English and Christian figures to his cast of mythological characters: for example, Camus, the god of the River Cam that runs past Cambridge, and "the pilot of the Galilean lake."

The shifting rhyme scheme of the poem (and some lines have no rhymes at all) suggests the disorder created by Lycidas's death and, perhaps, the shepherd-poet's admitted inadequacies as a poet, although one recognizes it as the creation of Milton's own exceptional poetic talent. The irregular lengths of the verse paragraphs, ranging from eight to thirty-three lines long, also contribute to this atmosphere of disorder. The shepherds' sense of disorder in nature is reflected in the rhythm (the sound) of the poem: "Such, Lycidas, thy loss to shepherd's ear" (line 49).

The upset emotions that are themselves the true source of disorder are expressed also through the expletive repetition of key words and phrases: "once more" in line 1, "dead" in line 8, the name of Lycidas used three times in the first verse paragraph and continually throughout the poem, and "now thou art gone" in lines 38-39. Repetition also serves to introduce the final consolation of the poem, with "weep no more" repeated twice in line 165; here, however, the repetition is not an emotional expletive but a forceful imperative. This closing sense of consolation must then, in some way, dispel the psychological disorder of the shepherds and reestablish harmony in the poem. Indeed, the final verse paragraph, the shortest and most concise in the poem, contains the simplest rhyme scheme—*abababcc*—rhyming words that refer again to the beauties of the pastoral setting. Order can once again be found in nature and heard in the ears of the poem's readers.

Themes and Meanings

John Milton was an intensely religious writer, which is to say, a political writer, since in the seventeenth century, politics and religion were inseparable elements of English society. Milton's greatest work, *Paradise Lost* (1667), retells the story of Genesis in the form of an epic in order to "justify the ways of God to men" (*Paradise Lost*, line 26). The great political conflicts of the age, that led ultimately to the English Civil War in the 1640's, involved questions about the doctrinal and administrative nature of the Church of England. In the eyes of many of Milton's contemporaries, episcopacy (church administration by a hierarchy of bishoprics) left control of church doctrine in the hands of a few when people needed to be free to encounter scripture in light of their own rational understanding. Such a hierarchy of clergy also opened the church to abuse by individual clergymen whose motives were personal gain and political ambition, rather than the moral and spiritual instruction of their parishioners, their "flocks." Milton did not separate these political and religious concerns from his poetic interests. In fact, as one can judge from "Lycidas," these concerns constitute the motivation and foundation for his career as a poet.

Although the occasion of "Lycidas" is the death of Edward King, Milton's reflections on this loss lead to the central moral and political questions of the poem and of his own life: What is the meaning of a moral life when death can cut it off at any time? The rewards of the greedy and self-indulgent are evident in the physical pleasure they take from life; but what are the rewards of the good? What is the good of a religion administered by a corrupt clergy? What help is it to be a good man and, for Milton, a good poet?

Pastoral poetry was thought of by Renaissance writers as the poet's apprenticeship; poets must hone their skills in this form before attempting the greater achievement of epic. Milton's two chief models for this conception of the poet's career were Vergil (70-19 B.C.E.), the classical Roman poet who composed his pastoral *Eclogues* (43-37 B.C.E.) before writing his great epic, the *Aeneid* (c. 29-19 B.C.E.); and in English poetry, Edmund Spenser (c. 1552-1599), who began his career with the pastoral *Shepheardes Calender* (1579) before writing his greatest work, the epic *The Faerie Queene* (1590, 1596). In this pastoral, Milton gives this progression from pastoral to epic, from apprenticeship to full acceptance of the poet's task in mature society, a psychological dimension. As the poem moves from allegorical pastoral deities to more explicit references to the figures of Christianity itself, without the mask of the pastoral, so the pleasures of youth, including indulgence in "false surmise," give way to recognition of the truth, however awesome it may be, and to mature acceptance of life's responsibilities. For Milton, that maturity required the responsibility of the poet to confront the imperative political issues of his age. Milton did not, as Edward King had done before his untimely death, choose a career in the clergy. Instead, he chose to find a wider audience as a poet. The restoration of order at the end of the poem announces Milton's control over his craft and his acceptance of responsibility for a literary career committed to an unflinching engagement with the political and religious conflicts that shaped English society in the mid-seventeenth century.

James Hale

LYING IN A HAMMOCK AT WILLIAM DUFFY'S FARM IN PINE ISLAND, MINNESOTA

Author: James Wright (1927-1980)
Type of poem: Lyric
First published: 1962, in *The Lion's Tail and Eyes: Poems Written out of Laziness and Silence*

The Poem

James Wright's "Lying in a Hammock at William Duffy's Farm in Pine Island, Minnesota" is a free-verse lyric of only thirteen lines, yet it manages to encapsulate many of the concerns and tactics of much longer poems in both the British and American traditions. On one hand, the poem has a commonplace matter-of-factness that can be taken at face value with no further exploration necessary. On the other hand, the poem moves with the sparse intensity of a haiku through a subtle but limited accumulation of imagery.

As he unfolds the poem, the poet positions himself in a hammock, not at a desk, which might seem more conducive for writing, lazing away a late summer afternoon. The utterance of the poem is one with the moment in the hammock. Many poets have used the device of positioning themselves in the natural world as if to suggest that the poet is "writing to the moment," that is, that the poet in this case is writing the poem in the hammock at William Duffy's farm in Minnesota. Thomas Gray, the eighteenth century British poet, used the same device, as suggested by his title "Elegy Written in a Country Churchyard." Other poems by Wright that suggest a particular positioning of the poet are "As I Step over a Puddle at the End of Winter, I Think of an Ancient Chinese Governor" and "Depressed by a Book of Bad Poetry, I Walk Toward an Unused Pasture and Invite the Insects to Join Me." To heighten the effect of positioning, there are rarely past participles or past-tense verbs in such titles.

It was William Wordsworth's famous definition of poetry in the preface to *Lyrical Ballads, with Other Poems* (1800) that moved the whole notion of poetry away from product, as words written on paper, to process, as "spontaneous overflow of powerful emotions . . . recollected in tranquility." Wright's tranquil moment in a hammock, however, requires no recollection. Unlike William Wordsworth's "Lines Written a Few Miles Above Tintern Abbey," this poem appears to be a moment experienced more than a moment remembered. The poem unfolds a series of epiphanies as the poet observes the world from his hammock on a summer day.

Forms and Devices

Just as Thomas Gray chose the close of day for his "Elegy Written in a Country Churchyard," Wright chooses a moment "as the evening darkens and comes on." Whereas Gray met a droning beetle as he was walking in the Stoke Poges churchyard,

Wright, suspended in a hammock between heaven and earth, says, "Over my head, I see the bronze butterfly,/ Asleep on the black trunk." The assumption that butterflies can sleep is a bit of poetic license, even a bit of personification.

The alliteration of "bronze butterfly . . . black branch" serves to tie the opening imagery together in a very pleasant way. Just as Gray's droning beetle has been overanalyzed into a portent of death, a deathwatch beetle, so Wright's butterfly is likely to be overanalyzed for its symbolism of metamorphosis and immortality. It is enough to accept the butterfly for exactly what it is, nothing more, and to take delight in its "Blowing like a leaf in green shadow." Initially, what the poet sees is significant. Wordsworth called sight "the most despotic of the senses" because it controls so much of poetry. Indeed, for someone to say "I see" is to say "I comprehend."

Very quickly, Wright varies his imagery, his deep sensory experiences. Next, through his sense of hearing, the poet becomes aware that "Down the ravine behind the empty house,/ The cowbells follow one another/ Into the distances of the afternoon." Wright lets the metonymy of "cowbells" stand for the cattle plodding in a line; he knows cows habitually "follow one another." Comfortable in his hammock, the poet can hear and imaginatively see without even turning his head.

When the poet does choose to look, "To [his] right,/ In a field of sunlight between two pines,/ The droppings of last year's horses/ Blaze up into golden stones." Through a certain slant of light, framed by "two pines," piles of dried dung become precious and valuable. The poet suggests that such metaphors lie all around. If people would just look, or wait patiently for the propitious angle of light, or just be lucky to be in a hammock at the right time and place, they would see them. Wordsworth declared that it is the poet's job to direct readers so that they discover the extraordinary in the ordinary. Line by line, Wright fulfills his role as seer, one who understands.

Because the poem is so bound up in imagery of the natural world, the reader may forget that a poem is a "made thing," in itself quite unnatural. Wright may be telling a lie, for in a sense every poem is a lie. After all, he says he is "lying in a hammock." The poet is totally in control of what is made. If he says the butterfly sleeps, it sleeps. If he says cowbells ring in the distance, they ring. If he says horse dung becomes golden stones, then it must be so. Whatever world the poet, the maker, sings into being is the only world there is for the space of a few lines.

Themes and Meanings

Although a hammock is made for relaxing, it is confining. When the poet says, "I lean back," there is not much more he can do. Like rocking chairs, hammocks are very specific pieces of furniture. While it is true sailors slept in hammocks in the confinement of cramped ships, and were even buried at sea in them, when they are transferred to land, hammocks are a novelty, not a necessity. They are an afternoon indulgence of a lazy person, in which the burdens of the workaday world may pleasantly be buried.

Leaning back carefully so he does not fall out, the poet experiences another fortunate moment when he catches sight of "A chicken hawk [floating] over, looking for home." This is another bit of personification, like the sleeping butterfly. There could be any number of reasons for the chicken hawk to be flying above him. It might be looking for a meal, but the poet decides otherwise. Birds abound in poems, and often they carry symbolic weight.

Almost abruptly the poet concludes, "I have wasted my life." From butterfly to cowbells, from horse droppings to chicken hawk, how does he arrive at this conclusion? And in what tone are these words spoken? The reader can read the line five ways, emphasizing a different word each time and evoking five different tones of voice. The reader can imagine the words spoken with disgust, with sadness and longing, or with abject resignation, or the reader can hear the five words spoken with a smile of satisfaction, as if to say, "Would that we all could waste our lives so profitably."

If the poet has wasted his life, then the reader has wasted time poring over thirteen lines. It is for the reader to decide. The surprising announcement "I have wasted my life" is as galvanizing and as challenging as the famous closing line of Rainer Maria Rilke's "Archaic Torso of Apollo," which commands, "You must revise your life." Like Rilke, Wright invites the reader to be co-conspirator in "wasting" life with him, this time in a hammock on a Minnesota farm on a late summer evening with nothing more extraordinary than a butterfly, cowbells, horse dung, and a chicken hawk for company.

R. Parks Lanier, Jr.

LYRICS OF LOWLY LIFE

Author: Paul Laurence Dunbar (1872-1906)
Type of poem: Book of poems
First published: 1896

The Poems

Lyrics of Lowly Life is a collection of 115 lyric poems by African American poet Paul Laurence Dunbar. The collection contains poems written in both standard English and African American dialect. The meter of the poems follows standard iambic and trochaic patterns. Dunbar employs a variety of traditional stanza and rhyme patterns.

The first poem in *Lyrics of Lowly Life* is "Ere Sleep Comes Down to Soothe the Weary Eyes," written in standard English, on the subject of death. In the opening stanza, Dunbar describes the persona's deep weariness after a day of searching unsuccessfully for "magic gold," the goal of his waking dreams, probably material goods. He resists sleep because it brings dreams that deceive by making the world appear better than it is. This conflict between sleeping dreams and waking frustrations tortures the subject, making him desire and dread both sleep and wakefulness. In the second stanza the subject's drowsy state causes harsh memories to become "poisonous vapors." In the third stanza phantoms continue to invade the narrator's consciousness until depression deepens into "teeming gloom" and "inexplicable pain."

The poem's second half begins with lighter images about a place "Where ranges forth the spirit far and free." This hope for escape into imagined "lands unspeakable— beyond surmise" ends abruptly, when "Fancy fails and dies" of weariness. The next stanza depicts self-scrutiny, a sort of judgment time, hinting to the reader that when sleep does come it might be accompanied by death. The poet's soul moves into a state beyond the "sad world's cries," into "the last dear sleep whose soft embrace is balm," sealing forever the narrator's eyes.

In addition to standard English lyrics Dunbar wrote dialect poems. The purpose of the majority of dialect poems at this time period was to entertain readers with charming characters and a combination of lively rhythm, hyperbole, and humorous images. However, another purpose of dialect poetry was to portray African Americans as carefree and childlike. That is, dialect poetry was popular in nineteenth century America because it reflected the stereotypes of black Americans favored by prejudiced white minds. The language in these poems contains deliberate errors in usage and spelling. An example of Dunbar's dialect poetry from *Lyrics of Lowly Life* is "When Malindy Sings." The poem begins,

> G'way an quit dat noise, Miss Lucy—
> Put dat music book away;
> What's de use to keep on tryin?
> Ef you practises twell you're gray.

The poem consists of nine eight-line stanzas in which the narrator relates to "Miss Lucy" the superior singing talents of "Malindy." The tone is gay and humorous, and the poem easy to understand. In the second stanza Miss Lucy learns that she "ain't got de tu'ns an' twistin's/ Fu' to make it sweet and light." Regarding Malindy, however, the poem's speaker has nothing but praise: Malindy's warbling outdoes "Robins, la'ks, an' all dem things"; her singing silences the fiddler, converts sinners, and indeed travels to the "very gates of God," at the poem's end.

In a small number of his standard English and dialect poems Dunbar expresses the reality of the racism that shackled him as man and artist. For example, "We Wear the Mask" (a standard-English poem) reveals that the outward cheerfulness of his African American subjects in his dialect poems is a mask of cheerfulness that hides their "torn and bleeding hearts." In writing this poem Dunbar momentarily removes the mask and says bluntly that in both slavery and the oppression that came after, black people have hated wearing a mask that belies both their suffering and their human dignity. In the third stanza the poet allows the "tortured souls," now unmasked, to cry out to God the pain they suffer because of racism's power in society and art. The repetition of "We wear the mask" as the poem's last line acknowledges that the mask is still demanded of the black race living in a racist and predominantly white society.

In two other standard English lyrics Dunbar looks behind the mask another way: He portrays the humanity and nobility of two African Americans. In "The Colored Soldiers" he honors the black soldiers who fought for their own freedom as members of the Union Army during the Civil War. In "Frederick Douglass" he elegizes the great African American ex-slave and abolitionist.

Dunbar also escapes racist rules for the portrayal of black subjects in at least one dialect poem. At first "An Ante-Bellum Sermon" seems to be another portrayal of happy slaves, this time listening to a preacher's words. However, in a manner similar to the composers of spirituals, the preacher transforms a call for heavenly freedom into a call for freedom from slavery on this earth.

Forms and Devices

Certainly the most obvious device Dunbar employed was, as noted previously, the use of African American dialect in many of his poems. Although these poems were popular, they have generally not stood the test of time well. The stereotypical nature of this use of dialect seems, to put it mildly, off-putting to many modern readers. Also, as critics have pointed out, the stylized "Negro dialect," as it was called, of the nineteenth century did not even reproduce the sounds of folk speech accurately; it had evolved its own set of conventions independent of the speech patterns and pronunciation of real African Americans.

Influential literary critic William Dean Howells, a champion of Dunbar's poetry, arranged for the publication of *Lyrics of Lowly Life*. In his introduction to the volume, Howells wrote that Dunbar's dialect poems are superior to his standard English poems and that they communicate African American life "aesthetically," "lyrically," and with humor. Howells was expressing a view of the time; today readers would agree with Dunbar himself that the dialect poems are not his best work. Yet Dunbar did combine the dialect sound with iambic and trochaic meters to great effect, a fact that can be best appreciated when the poetry is read aloud. The following stanza from "A Negro Love Song" is meant to entertain the reader, and entertain it does:

> Seen my lady home las' night,
> Jump back, honey, jump back.
> Hel' huh han' an' sque'z it tight,
> Jump back, honey, jump back.
> Hyeahd huh sigh a little sigh,
> Seen a light gleam f'om huh eye,
> An' a smile go flittin' by—
> Jump back, honey, jump back.

Dunbar himself was educated and well-read and spoke standard English, as did white writers who chose to write in dialect, such as Chandler Harris. Dunbar, as he says in "The Poet," from his *Lyrics of the Hearthside* (1899), wrote in dialect because publishers and the public wanted this kind of verse from any writer who portrayed African Americans: "the world, it turned to praise/ A jingle in a broken tongue." He wore this "mask" unwillingly, unhappy that it hid his real voice, demeaned his people, and enabled white Americans to ignore racial injustice.

Throughout *Lyrics of Lowly Life* Dunbar uses sound to great effect. In "Ere Sleep Comes Down to Soothe the Weary Eye," the title is repeated as the first and last line of each of the poem's six stanzas. The result reminds one of a lullaby, but it also sounds melancholy, with a heavy, sad beat created when the predominantly monosyllabic first line is read. The long vowel sounds in "sleep," "soothe," and "weary" add to this feeling.

Dunbar uses metaphor throughout his poetry. In "Ere Sleep Comes Down to Soothe the Weary Eye," the poet expresses the narrator's waking hope as finding the "magic gold" of material success. The poet personifies life as full of "aches," and griefs that haunt are the product of a "witch's caldron." In Dunbar's metaphors there is almost always a comforting familiarity, a clear meaning, rather than extraordinary invention and subtlety. This approach was in keeping with what readers of popular poetry in his time expected, whether the writer was Dunbar or Henry Wadsworth Longfellow, a popular European American poet of the period.

Dunbar's strongest use of metaphor occurs when he protests the need of African Americans to hide their humanity behind dialect and other subterfuges in order to survive in a racist environment. In "We Wear the Mask," the mask represents this duplicity. The line "We wear the mask" is used three times: to begin the poem, to end the second stanza, and to end the third and last stanza. The poet begins the poem wearing the mask, then in the second stanza removes the mask and faces the reader without it, and finally replaces it at the poem's end. While the mask is off, the poet reveals the pain it hides, crying out even to God for an end to this "guile" and all the injustice it implies. Only in his pain does Dunbar find this powerful metaphor. "We Wear the Mask" is the finest poem in *Lyrics of Lowly Life*, containing in its metaphor the history of a people wrapped in racism and the dilemma of an artist who must wear a mask.

Many of Dunbar's poems use images from nature or are about nature itself. In "Rising of the Storm," for example, the lake heaves with "a sob and a sigh." "Ballad" explains how a lover's loyalty brings a bright day and joy while a lover's deceit brings a dark day and sadness. In "The Lover and the Moon" a lover faces the dilemma of keeping his love faithful while he is on a journey. He prays to the moon that it keep an eye on the lover from whom he is parted. After the moon fails in its task and the lover loses his mate, he asks the sea to punish the moon, which is why in stormy weather "waves strain their awful hands on high/ To tear the false moon from the sky."

Themes and Meanings

The poems written in standard English in *Lyrics of Lowly Life* cover conventional topics, including the poet, nature in all its moods, love requited and unrequited, youth, aging, birth, and death. Dunbar's lyrics have a Romantic poet's emphasis on extremes of emotion—exhilarating joy and deep sorrow. A poem such as "Ere Sleep Comes Down to Soothe the Weary Eye" expresses a sadness that verges on the melodramatic. Other lyrics are more lighthearted. For example, in "Retort" the poet has a traditional head-versus-heart dialogue; he first doubts his love for "Phyllis" but then affirms it lest he be "worse than a fool." In "Passion and Love" a teary young girl is wooed by a passionate suitor whom she rejects and then by a more "aloof" one she accepts. Dunbar's lyric poems in standard English generally have simple themes, in keeping with the late nineteenth century American popular poetry tradition. Since "Ere Sleep Comes Down on Weary Eyes," the most complex lyric in this volume, is also first in the volume, Dunbar may well have believed that this was his most successful attempt to go beyond the conventions of the day.

Dunbar did not live long enough to witness and participate in the Harlem Renaissance of the 1920's. If he had, he would have heard his poetic descendants announce their independence from white influence and their determination to express the African American experience according to their own choice of language and form. In the achievement of these later poets the reader hears echoes of Dunbar's earlier voice.

Langston Hughes's poem "The Weary Blues," for example, is similar to Dunbar's "Ere Sleep Comes Down to Soothe the Weary Eyes" in content, but unlike Dunbar, Hughes particularizes the experience using the language and rhythms of the African American vernacular—in this case, of blues music. Hughes tells the reader about someone who (like the persona in Dunbar's poem) is near exhaustion but still awake. Hughes pictures his subject as a blues player "Droning a drowsy, syncopated tune." Though the musician is not actually dead at the poem's end, as Dunbar's subject seems to be, Hughes does picture him as one who sleeps "like a rock or a man that's dead." Significantly, Hughes affirms that the blues expresses a black man's soul, whereas Dunbar's poem does not specify the race of the poem's subject.

Likewise, Dunbar's poem "Sympathy," from the collection *Lyrics of the Hearthside*, is quite similar to Countée Cullen's later sonnet "Yet Do I Marvel." As Dunbar compared the poet—implicitly an African American poet—to a "caged bird," wondering why the bird keeps singing through his bars, Cullen asks the universe the reason God would "make a poet black, and bid him sing." Again, Dunbar does not explicitly identify the "caged bird" as a black poet, while Cullen does, but it is entirely reasonable to assume that Dunbar's own difficulties as an artist in a racist world formed the core of the poem.

Francine Dempsey

MAGIC FOX

Author: James Welch (1940-   )
Type of poem: Lyric
First published: 1971, in *Riding the Earthboy 40*

The Poem

"Magic Fox" pictures the destruction of the traditional life of American Indians, especially the northern plains tribes, resulting from corruption by the European American culture. It is the opening poem in *Riding the Earthboy 40* by James Welch, an American Indian of Blackfeet and Gros Ventre descent—his first book and only collection of poems.

Welch's family leased forty acres of land from their neighbors, the Earthboy family, where James rode his horse when he was a boy. Riding the leased land may be symbolic of the American Indians' traditional relationship to the land—they were stewards, not owners. That the lease was limited to forty acres may represent the nineteenth century restriction of the American Indians to reservations. "Magic Fox" and the other poems in the collection can be best understood in terms of the reality to which the title *Riding the Earthboy 40* points.

In "Magic Fox," truth by which American Indians once lived has slipped into the unreality of nightmare. In the first stanza, the speaker in the poem describes men "that rattled/ in their sleep," having snored so loudly that they shook down leaves. Kenneth Lincoln in *Three American Literatures* (1982) suggested that "the death chant, to meet the rattling darkness, has been transformed into the sounds of elderly men snoring leaves off the sun dance tree of life." In this state of affairs "Truth became/ a nightmare to their fox"—the sleepers' magic or spirit animal—and the fox transformed their horses into fish. The dreamlike character of the transformation is emphasized by the speaker following the statement "He turned their horses into fish" with a series of questions: "or was it horses strung/ like fish, or fish like fish/ hung naked in the wind?"

The second stanza begins with an image of stars falling on their catch—the fish, presumably, since "catch" usually refers to fish. Yet, abruptly in the second line, the speaker introduces a blond girl whose dancing drew the men around her skirts, and whose magic turned "fox and grief" into nightmare in their sleep. The poem ends with a declaration that the fish are stars "that fell into their dreams."

Forms and Devices

"Magic Fox" consists of two eight-line stanzas and a final couplet. Each stanza has its own unity. The first describes the nightmarish transformation of horses into fish—the failure of the fox's magic. The second describes the new magic of the blond girl, transforming both fox and grief into nightmare. The elements of fish from the first stanza and stars from the second combine in the couplet.

Although the sense of "Magic Fox" is elegiac—it is about the passing of a culture—the scene and sound are not funereal. The poem is alive with images of the natural world: green leaves, wind, dawn, dust, stars, and animals (fox, horse, fish, and birds). These natural elements act as both setting and symbol; they are repeated in the other poems in the collection, accumulating significance on which the reader can draw to interpret "Magic Fox."

The poems in *Riding the Earthboy 40* contain the referents of traditional or oral poems and stories—magic animals, the four directions, the seasons, songs, and dances—but Welch treats them all, if not ironically, in an unpredictable post-traditional way. Traditionally, American Indians felt a kinship with animal tribes, had faith in their instincts, were grateful for the sacrifices of their bodies for the sustaining of human life. They admired the special power or magic of animals and elevated some, such as Coyote the Trickster, to special status. In Native American stories Coyote's cousin, Fox, had special cunning.

Welch appropriates animals in these poems but does not always treat them in the traditional ways. Spider, for example, originally the troublemaker, is depicted in his poem "Snow Country Weavers" as a healer "weaving threads/ to bandage up the day." In the poem "Two for the Festival" Fox is not a cunning trickster, but rather an awkward dancer. In "Magic Fox," Coyote's cunning cousin has lost his magic, or, more accurately, when he tries his magic, it goes awry—changing horses into fish.

The poem is unrhymed and lacks a mechanical pattern; however, it is alive with assonance and internal rhyme, which make it sing. "Green leaves" and "sleep" ring in the opening lines, along with "grief," "sleep," and "dream," at the end of the poem. The combination of "into fish," "like fish," and "in the wind," at the end of the first stanza, provides a satisfying sound correspondence. These sounds are also onomatopoeic (sounding distinctly fishy), as are the sounds of "magic jangled memories" in the second stanza. The alliteration of "blonde as morning birds, began" contributes to the hypnotic effect of the blond girl's dance. Because it is somewhat irregular, the meter of the poem cannot be easily scanned; however, the balladlike cadence of the poem reveals itself when "Magic Fox" is read aloud. The pattern consists of approximately three stresses ending in an *o* vowel rhyme, followed by approximately four stresses and a breath pause.

Themes and Meanings

What is the reader to make of this dream scene in which truth changes into nightmare, a fox changes horses into fish, fish become stars, and a girl changes fox and grief into nightmare? As a successful poem should, "Magic Fox," to paraphrase Robert Frost, says one thing in terms of another, says one things and means another. Its meaning is layered: It can be interpreted in its present or immediate past, as well as in its historic past. Similarly, it operates at the personal or at the tribal level. It can be located in reservations or western expanses.

There is a slippery uncertainty to the "present" of the poem: Roles change, objects transmogrify. There is no stability—everything is falling. The leaves that fall are not dead but green, suggesting the destruction of life. Stars fall; the men fall in the dust around the skirts of the blond girl. Though the speaker states that "her magic jangled memories/ of dawn," the sleepers are too far gone to remember; they feel no grief and, perhaps, no regret. This is a picture of life in free fall, the individual results of which can be seen in the drunk Doris Horseman and her raving son in "Going to Remake this World" and other poems in the collection.

The blond girl is perhaps a too-obvious symbol of the European American influence so foreign to and destructive of the American Indians' way of life. The destruction is not so much the result of military conquest as of the kind of seduction imaged in the girl's dance, resulting in confusion, dependency, and loss of control.

The poem is about more than a present nightmare life, but about communal, reservation experience—where, in "The Only Bar in Dixon," Welch writes, "These Indians once imitated life." They no longer lived the actual life of the western expanses, but an imitation. Moreover, the subject of "Magic Fox" is plural: The magic fox was their fox; stars fell into their dreams.

The image of the blond girl is echoed in other poems in *Riding the Earthboy 40*, the repetition suggesting the importance of the motif. The girl in "Blue Like Death," Welch writes, "prized/ your going the way some people/ help a drunk to fall." Obviously, she is the downfall of the "you" in the poem. A woman addressed in the poem "In My First Hard Springtime," who offends the speaker's friends and mocks him, is described as "white and common." In "Gesture Down to Guatemala" the "blonde from Montana" is linked with drinking too much.

In these poems as well as in "Magic Fox," the blond-girl motif represents non-Native seduction and corruption, which results in the destruction of tradition and community as well as individuals. Blondeness or whiteness symbolizes death. In the title poem, Earthboy's cabin is described as bleached "white as bone" and the poem concludes: "Dirt [burial] is where the dreams must end."

The beginning of the end occurred in the 1830's. Falling stars announced the end of the traditional lifestyle of the Blackfeet. In 1837, following the Leonid meteor showers earlier in the decade, smallpox killed two-thirds of the Blackfeet population. Successive outbreaks killed even more. War and forced treaties completed the decimation, and the once free and independent tribe must have assumed a causal relationship between falling stars and end of life as they knew it. One historian described the U.S. Cavalry leading away the horses of the conquered Blackfeet like so many bagged fish on a stringer. This then is the probable inspiration for the image of horses turned into fish and magic turned into nightmare.

Gaymon L. Bennett

A MAGUS

Author: John Ciardi (1916-1986)
Type of poem: Lyric
First published: 1966, in *This Strangest Everything*

The Poem

John Ciardi's "A Magus" is composed of forty-seven lines forming four stanzas of unequal length. The title, which can mean a wise man, an astrologer, a magician, or a priest, apparently refers to the "missionary from the Mau Mau" mentioned in the first line. As the narrator relates in the opening stanza, this missionary has come to testify to "an amazing botany" apparently caused by "spores blowing from space." This metamorphosis of plants into incredible hybrids provokes the cryptic observation, "The Jungle has come loose,/ is changing purpose."

The latter part of the first stanza is in italics to indicate the missionary's own words. The strange new qualities of transformed "Jungle" are apparently only part of a larger event, for the missionary declares, "Nor are the vegetations/ of the new continuum the only sign." He then claims that "New eyes" now regard the world and note its change, spreading the propaganda to form "new verbs" from its seed. "Set watches on your gardens," he ambiguously advises.

The second stanza opens with the narrator's cautious reaction to this incredible communication: "I repeat it as he spoke it. I do not interpret/ what I do not understand." Although claiming no comprehension of the message, he nevertheless intuits the nature of the messenger, for the religious overtones of his words—especially, "But he does come,/ signs do appear"—clearly link the missionary-magus to the supernatural events he describes.

In the following division of the stanza, the narrator goes on to relate other, equally strange phenomena, such as "poisoned islands," fish that "glow in the dark," and "unknown air." All of these contrast with the signs of the new organic "continuum," for they are the inorganic marvels of modern technology, as the references "lectern," "radar," "phone," and "planes" indicate.

As the preceding stanza did, the third begins with the narrator's own reactions. His opening question—"How many megatons of idea is a man?"—links humanity and technology, metaphysics and physics. His words are the same as before, with one significant exception: "I have heard, and say/ what I heard said and believe." His belief, although clearly centered on the natural world and its odd new order, is focused on the magus himself. Twice, the narrator asserts that he has witnessed miracles and portents—such as the transmutation of "water to blood" and the curiously faithful "cloud" formed by the birds—that surround the magus. Although the narrator sees these things with his own eyes, he remains mystified: "these things I believe whose meaning I cannot say."

Consisting only of a one-line statement ("Then he closes his fist and there is nothing there"), the final stanza abruptly ends both the poem and its miraculous vision. Both the unsettling question at the end of stanza 2 ("Is a fact true?"), and the sudden nothing in the magus' hand provoke readers to pose their own questions and make their own judgments.

Forms and Devices

"A Magus" contains many elements that are associated with clearly defined religious traditions. The poem's cryptic language, its references to the four elements (earth, air, fire, and water) and symbolic colors (black, white, and red), its presentation of inexplicable signs and occurrences, and its focus on a messianic herald of a new order all indicate that it belongs to the time-honored form of mystic revelation. The poet updates this tradition, however, by inserting concrete, quintessentially modern issues and attitudes into this framework.

Ciardi creates a complex, often suggestive, and mystifying poem by using such devices as eclectic imagery, unusual juxtapositions, and an almost regular rhyme scheme. Images of conflict and change are especially abundant throughout the poem. For example, the first stanza is dominated by images of strange, nightmarish transformations in the vegetable kingdom, such as fruit "with a bearded face that howls" and "Mushrooms that bleed." Through the common theme of change, colonialism and racism also provide images that become curiously linked to this "amazing botany." For example, the reference to the Mau Mau (a secret terrorist organization in Kenya) alludes to Kenya's transformation from colonial docility to militant independence, a new order that is surreally mirrored in the organic world's "new continuum." This implicit analogy is made more explicit by the missionary's metaphor "A root is a tongue," in which the idea of native land and native tongue become firmly united.

Images of technological conflict predominate in the second stanza. Certain scientific images—"radar," "[Geiger] counters," "red phone"—contribute global ecological and political associations to the poem's millenarianist vision. Yet others present modern technology within a context of violence, as when the planes "howl to the edge of sound" and "crash through" the world.

Ciardi even uses science's chronic interrogation of the universe as a symbolic image, for questions embody the insatiable, inquisitive hunger of the scientific method itself. For example, by asking, "Is a fact true?" the poet uses the assumptions and logic of scientific inquiry to highlight the values science implicitly asserts. When "Israeli teams" allegedly find "the body" of Christ, the question arises whether Christianity and Easter automatically are "false," or "not true." By posing the important question closing stanza 2, the narrator reminds the reader that the "fact" of science does not preserve an accurate, integrated picture of truth, although it may believe it does; actually, it only presents particular fragments of that truth.

This observation provides the context for the third stanza, in which the poet brings together many of the eclectically gathered images so as to convey a series of significant juxtapositions. Science and humanism, faith and reason, African and European, black and white—all converge in the irrational scene the narrator witnesses. Incredible, inexplicable "facts"—the British "Lion" who renounces his "Empire," the magus' spontaneously combustible hand, the supernatural "ray" that shoots "to the top of the air" from the magus' head—intermingle in the incomprehensible realms of magic and miracles.

The last stanza presents a final, critical, juxtaposition: When the magus "closes his fist and there is nothing there," illusion and reality, truth and lie, confront each other. Using the ultimate device of an open-ended ending, the poet deftly completes the poem's form and meaning by obscuring its own mystical vision and devices.

Themes and Meanings

It is no coincidence that "A Magus" first appeared in a poetry collection entitled *This Strangest Everything* (1966). A remarkable hodgepodge that contains abundant evidence of the social, political, and ecological crises of the Cold War years in which it was written, the poem encompasses a wide variety of themes. By employing unnatural images and irrational shifts of subject, however, the poet draws attention to the fact that its meaning cannot easily be reduced to some simple moral, religious, or sociopolitical statement.

By confronting readers with vivid devices, provocative questions, and a mystifyingly abrupt and not very satisfying ending, the poet forces them to acknowledge the fact that they are indeed reading a poem and not a history book or a newspaper. Poetry, acutely aware of its forms and devices, is the form that traditionally conveys in a highly memorable manner the bewildering complexity of the world.

At the center of this world is the mystery of life, "this strangest everything," which poets since time immemorial have been praising and celebrating in their poems. Ciardi's poetry is no exception, a fact emphasized both by this particular poem and by the poet's own advice to his readers: "To read a poem, come prepared for delight."

Ciardi provokes delight in a variety of ways throughout "A Magus," as its own unique surprises, mystifications, and evocations attest. Reveling in the myriad wonders of the real world, the poet also revels in the strange wonders of his own creation—of space-spores giving rise to howling fruit and upside-down trees, of planes that crash through time and space, of missionaries to Kenya who command birds to enter the fire of their hand, where they "glow like metal."

According to Ciardi, true poetry "insists on battering at life, and on making the poem capture the thing seen and felt in its own unique complex. It does not repeat; it creates." The rhyme and rhythm of the language in "A Magus," its strange premise and skewed vision, and its unsettling images and juxtapositions all combine to form a memorable experience, something "seen and felt," not merely read and summarized.

The multilayered complexity and dynamic depths of imagination displayed by the poem echo the richness of human experience itself. For significant human experience, as poet and narrator alike urge the reader to remember, is not rooted exclusively in the rational and explicable; as the narrator so insistently points out, the world is full of "things I believe whose meaning I cannot say."

The inability to formulate and express the meaning of experience, especially poetic experience, or even to understand fully what one hears and sees, is a central concept of the poem. It is also, as Ciardi would no doubt point out, one of the most common aspects of the indescribable, ever-changing reality of being human.

Terri Frongia

MALCOLM SPOKE / WHO LISTENED?

Author: Haki R. Madhubuti (Don Luther Lee; 1942-   )
Type of poem: Lyric
First published: 1969, in *Don't Cry, Scream*

The Poem

Haki R. Madhubuti's "Malcolm Spoke / who listened?" is written in the black poetry style of the 1960's, a free-verse, conversational form containing altered spelling,
short, explosive lines, and the rhythms of black street-corner speech. The title implies
that the social and political messages of Malcolm X were not heeded by African
Americans, who, for various reasons articulated in the poem, either were deceived by
other spokespersons or simply adopted superficial attributes of black consciousness.
The poem is a warning and somewhat of a diatribe chastising African Americans by
using Malcolm X as a symbol of political integrity and identity. The poet admits that
the messages are also for his own edification, suggested in the subtitle "*this poem is
for my consciousness too.*"

The first stanza describes outer trappings of black culture such as "garments" and
"slogans" and contrasts them with a genuine commitment to certain ideals. In the second stanza, Malcolm X is portrayed as a man who discarded the negative acts of hus-
tling and pimping to evolve from the life of a street hustler (whose physical identity
was also a distortion) to a revolutionary. His odyssey is juxtaposed to the dilemmas of
color identity within the black community and the transformation in the 1960's to
identities that valorized natural hairstyles and dark complexions. The poet is concerned with the way light skin has been associated with class pretensions among African Americans. The poem identifies historical signifiers of color identity, inverting
the "blackface" stereotype of minstrelsy to signify status in the 1960's based on
darker skin color. Aware that privileging lighter skin and other aspects of bourgeois
identity might be disingenuous, the poet emphasizes the new appearances (such as
"nappy-black" hair) but also warns of false alliances with intellectual whites who
might be insincere in their motives even though they are perceived as "authorities
on" militant'/ knee/ grows." Most important, however, is the deception by black
spokespersons through rhetoric that is overused and implicitly empty of true meaning.

The third stanza contrasts the pre-1960's image of the "hipster" with the black consciousness identity of the 1960's, evident in symbols of apparel. Attitudes of the
1960's are equated with African designs as opposed to Western clothing: The
"doublebreasted" suit is supplanted by the "dashiki," although the change in physical
garb does not necessarily mean a genuine projection of black consciousness. Furthermore, there are references to higher education as a credential of 1960's activists, but
the intellectual association with university training is undercut by the suggestion that
the would-be black leader has majored in "physical education," an obvious criticism
of academic depth. The fourth stanza uses the metaphors of "animals" and "colors" to

imply that exterior signs of black identity may not necessarily be sincere. The poem projects a genocidal ending for blacks, a black holocaust in the "unitedstates ofamerica's/ new/ self-cleaning ovens." The title of the poem is reprised in the ending along with the warning that African Americans need to listen to the message of Malcolm X.

Forms and Devices

The principal poetic device is the juxtaposition of pre-1960's identity symbols with those of the 1960's. These symbols are especially related to appearance versus reality, not only in physical style but also in the veracity of statements made on behalf of black identity. Because Malcolm X did not wear obvious African apparel, he is used as a measure of integrity without the possibility of deceit through physical representation. The notion of wearing "blackness" as opposed to actually living it is developed throughout. To "wear yr/ blackness" connotes a superficial identity that belies one's actual political consciousness, which may be anything but black. However, the first stanza also emphasizes the hypocrisy of language if one voices "slogans" that are also indications of insincerity, mimicry, and popular positions. The popularization of black rhetoric is reflected in the metaphor of musical notoriety symbolized by the music charts. Like popular music, rhetoric can also generate a "top 10" list of statements, which suggests widespread appeal but not necessarily depth of content.

The characterization of Malcolm X is achieved through the use of language drawn from street-corner black vernacular used throughout the poem. The phrases "supercools" and "doo-rag lovers," referring to Malcolm X's earlier life as a hustler and his conked or processed hairstyle, are linked to the image of the counterfeit black spokesman, the "revolutionary pimp," which combines both a progressive and retrogressive identity. Black vernacular is also used to describe color: "high-yellow" is used as a signifier of class prejudice within the black community, and the term "blackface," drawn from minstrelsy, is used as a parallel to disguise and deception. These images of color are historical markers in that they are derivatives of plantation and post-emancipation labels and terminology. Manipulation of language is another key device, particularly the respelling of certain words to achieve emphasis: "negroes" as "knee/ grows," "your" as "yr," "black" as "blk," and "from" as "fr." The collapsing of the spelling of "United States of America" to "unitedstatesofamerica" is another example of word manipulation used to achieve the effect of seeing the word or phrase in a different linguistic configuration.

The juxtaposition of physical symbols is found in the third stanza, where the "double-breasted" suit is paralleled to the "dashiki." Both items can be used to manipulate one's identity and also to deceive, the Western attire indicating the establishment and black bourgeois sophistication, the African clothing implying black nationalism. These images suggest that transitions in attire from European to African may not represent a true development of black identity. The imagery in the fourth stanza is also based on juxtaposition, repeating notions of color used earlier. The implication is that "dark meat"—people of color—and "whi-te meat" (the spelling of "white" is altered to approximate the pronunciation of "whitey")—people of European descent—can both be subject to deception. The final image of the "new/ self-cleaning ovens," directly evoking the Holocaust of World War II, uses the modern appliance to further the irony of genocide.

Themes and Meanings

The primary themes of the poem involve the potential for hypocrisy and deceit within the black consciousness/black nationalist movement of the 1960's because of deceptive leaders who appear to represent the black movement but who are not genuine representatives such as the icon Malcolm X. The idea of being sold out by black leadership is the ultimate message. However, the poem also operates on a psychological level, urging the reader to question identity through appearance and language. The prevailing theme of appearance versus reality is developed not only through the mockery of black nationalist clothing but also through the criticism of black rhetoric that becomes a cliché. The use of Malcolm X as the icon of trust and integrity is supported by Malcolm X's own transition from hustler to revolutionary. Malcolm X is portrayed as having shed the outer appearances of the hustler, emerging as a conscious representation of incorruptibility; he is juxtaposed to leaders who are visibly nationalist but who maintain intraracial hierarchies that reflect color distinctions of past eras. The irony is that Malcolm X also sought certain false physical attributes inasmuch as he was known to have straightened his hair during his years as a street hustler.

Though black consciousness can be corrupted through disingenuous leadership, there is also the possibility of infiltration by Caucasians and the undermining of militancy from within. Though the poem is not completely antinationalist, its projection of the physical trappings of the black nationalist as a disguise, its mockery of the dashiki and the natural hairstyle, is a warning against being seduced by language and style rather than adhering to the teachings of Malcolm X, who did not wear the apparel of the black nationalist but who was, nevertheless, an advocate of nationalism. The transformations of the 1960's that praised natural appearance, African clothing, and black imagery might themselves be contemporary versions of prior emblems of deception such as "blackface." Distinctions based on skin color are symbols of retrogressive political consciousness as well as the historical roots of intraracial color distinctions. Preference for a certain physical appearance is viewed as a game, a manipulation of appearance for reasons of status. The physical image of African Americans through hairstyles is also used to characterize pre-1960's identity in which emulation of white appearance ("straighthair") was associated with achieving bourgeois status. Certain artifacts of 1960's popular culture are used symbolically: "air conditioned volkswagens" are associated with intellectuals, and the study of "faulkner at/ smith" ironically indicates white liberalism and a trendy connection to the black struggle.

"Malcolm Spoke / who listened?" questions whether transitions in physical style and appearance are also representative of valuable political and social transformations. Essentially pessimistic about those who have overtly made the physical transition, the poet recognizes the possibilities of the "rip-off" in cultural terms, the replacement of color and class distinctions with measures of "blackness" represented in clothing and rhetoric. Though the poem is concerned with deception, it also articulates the outcome of failing to listen to the message of Malcolm X; that is, the possibility of the annihilation of African Americans through acts of genocide that rival the Holocaust.

Joseph McLaren

THE MAN-MOTH

Author: Elizabeth Bishop (1911-1979)
Type of poem: Lyric
First published: 1936; collected in *North and South*, 1946

The Poem

"The Man-Moth," by Pulitzer Prize-winning poet Elizabeth Bishop, is an early work; it was written when she first lived in New York City in 1935. The idea for this poem came to her from a misprinting of the word "mammoth" as "manmoth" in a newspaper. She was inspired to imagine what sort of creature this might be. The Man-Moth of the poem is a mysterious nocturnal inhabitant of the city—half man, half moth—whose fearful, obsessive actions represent the city's interior, imaginative life. The poem is a dreamlike fantasy that works as a fable or allegory of modern city life. It is interesting to put this poem into its historical context and to imagine the world in which the young Elizabeth Bishop, recently graduated from Vassar College, was writing, for this was during the Depression; moreover, events in Europe were already leading to World War II. Both the hopes and the darkness of the time seem reflected in the poem, which is tragic in tone.

"The Man-Moth" is a free-verse poem divided into six stanzas of eight lines each, with the short first line of each stanza indented. Each of these indented lines announces a different stage in the Man-Moth's story. In the first stanza, Bishop depicts not the Man-Moth but a man, seen from above, "battered moonlight" shining on the worn surfaces of city buildings and on the self-engrossed man himself. Images of light and shadow, the man as "an inverted pin," and the palpable sensation of moonlight, "neither warm nor cold," create a strange, lonely setting for events to follow.

The man pays little attention to the moon, in comparison to the Man-Moth, who emerges unseen in the second stanza, crawling from under the city sidewalk and beginning his climb toward the moon that he imagines "is a small hole" in the night sky. The Man-Moth is fearful and nervous but determined to "investigate."

His brave but naïve effort to crawl through the moon is doomed, however; there is no hole in the sky, and he cannot escape the city. He falls back down to it, where he must try to cope with the frightening apparatus of city life, particularly embodied in the subway train and the dangerous electrified third rail.

Images of the Man-Moth struggling to deal with the subway doors, riding backward so that he cannot see where he is going, and worrying that if he does not sit still and keep his hands in his pockets he will do something to hurt himself are easily recognized by anyone who has tried to get around in a large, modern city and has not found it easy. The Man-Moth is almost childlike in his vulnerability. These are all images of a loss of control, and like a sensitive child who must navigate the world of adults, the Man-Moth fears losing that control.

At this point in the poem when the Man-Moth seems most human, Bishop slightly adjusts the viewpoint by speaking to "you," distancing the Man-Moth from the reader. Casually, as a naturalist telling someone where to find bird's eggs or edible mushrooms, she describes the process for using a flashlight to get the Man-Moth to surrender his "only possession." The eye of the Man-Moth is mysterious, dark, and nonhuman—the eye of an insect. Fixed by the light, it closes and secretes a tear. Like a magician or street performer, he will try to palm or hide it, but Bishop tells the reader to pay close attention and "he'll hand it over"—a prize of cool water "pure enough to drink."

Forms and Devices

Bishop uses a regular number of lines in each stanza so that the poem has a formal appearance on the page, though it is in free verse. She does make use of irregularly placed consonant rhymes for emphasis and musical effect, such as the *t* sound at the end of "moonlight" and "hat," and the *s* sound at the end of "properties" and "thermometers" in the first stanza. She also uses consonant sounds within lines for musical resonance, such as "on," "pin," "moon," and "Man," also in the first stanza. Reading the poem aloud, one becomes aware of the musical interweaving of repeated vowel and consonant sounds throughout the poem. Although the sound patterns in the poem are irregular, these sounds give a fullness to the language and help pace the reading of the poem, which is slow and sonorous.

Strong visual imagery is extremely important in this poem. Images of light and dark create a sense of heightened drama and suggest the gritty realism of early black-and-white films set in city landscapes or black-and-white photography of the period. She describes the Man-Moth's shadow at one point as being like "a photographer's cloth," referring to the cloth photographers use to shut out light when using old-style view cameras. The photographer, with his head under a black cloth, looking through the round lens of the camera, is somewhat like the Man-Moth under the black sky looking at the round moon overhead or like the person who catches the Man-Moth and stares into his black eye with a flashlight to see the elusive tear.

Bishop also uses irony as a dramatic device. The first example is the title itself, which is customarily printed with an asterisk, leading the reader to a footnote explaining that the title was based on a mistake in a newspaper. The powerful original word "mammoth" provides ironic contrast with the trembling vulnerability of the Man-Moth. There is also dramatic irony in the lack of awareness in the man presented in the first stanza. Though he stands in his own small shadow, a shadow cast by the moon, he is only slightly aware of the moon's mystery and its effect on him, and he is not at all aware of the mysterious Man-Moth whose life parallels his own. Finally, the Man-Moth's attempt to escape through the hole in the sky, which is the moon, is ironic because it is both brave and foolish, an act doomed to failure. Elizabeth Bishop's view of the individual in the modern world clearly seems ironic.

The poet also uses Surrealist imagery for strong emotional impact. The Man-Moth is an irrational dreamlike figure acting out an existential dilemma that is difficult to express. Bishop mentions "recurrent dreams" in the poem, making a connection with Surrealist and Symbolist work that incorporate dreamlike images and evoke the subconscious.

Themes and Meanings

At one level, Elizabeth Bishop's poem is simply a strange and wonderful story, a fairy-tale fantasy about a character caught between two worlds like the Beast in "Beauty and the Beast" or some other transformation tale. There is no Beauty, however, to save the Man-Moth, who is the epitome of alienation in a modern, urban setting.

Like a moth, the Man-Moth spends his life in two opposite states, one as an obsessed creature pursuing the moon as a moth flies toward a street lamp, and the other as the subterranean larval being who lives in the earth-tunnels of the subway. Like a human, the Man-Moth strives for something better than what he knows, but all too often he falls back into fear and confusion and lives a life of unfulfillment.

The meaning of the moon is ambiguous, but clearly it is something lofty and impossible to reach. Typically, the moon is an emblem of madness and obsession, but it is also a romantic image of lovers and artists—a feminine power—reflective, cool, attractive, mysterious. Visually, the moon can look like a hole in the sky. Probably the young Bishop projected her own efforts to deal with the artist's life in the city into the poem. If the poem depicts the loneliness and frustration of the artist's struggle to create, however, it also has broader meaning: It seems to present the human struggle to escape earthly trials into some higher state of enlightenment. Some readers see the Man-Moth's struggle as a religious quest, but others are more likely to see it as an existential drama in which it is impossible to answer the universal "why?"

In any case, the quest is a lonely one. Although the poem is set in a city landscape, that landscape is almost empty of life. Even when the Man-Moth rides the subway, there is no feeling of crowdedness. The trains are "silent" and start moving at "full, terrible speed" as if no one were at the controls. When the Man-Moth thinks of the dangerous "third rail" of the train, it is his own impulse to touch it that he fears, not some outside threat.

Finally, the poet tells the reader, if the Man-Moth is forced to surrender his tear, like the bee losing its stinger, he will die. The tear, representing emotion, is "his only possession." Read literally, the poem tells the reader that it is death to give up feeling, however uncomfortable feeling can be. In strange and beautiful images, the poem depicts mysteries of human life.

Barbara Drake

THE MAN WITH NIGHT SWEATS

Author: Thom Gunn (1929-   )
Type of poem: Dramatic monologue
First published: 1987; collected in *The Man with Night Sweats*, 1992

The Poem

"The Man with Night Sweats" is one of a series of poems Thom Gunn has written about the acquired immunodeficiency syndrome (AIDS) epidemic in general and friends of his who either have the disease or have already died of it. The title refers to the night sweats that are one of the symptoms frequently experienced by victims of the disease. This poem is the dramatic monologue of a persona afflicted with AIDS remembering and pondering his past life and the way in which he became ill. In the first stanza, the speaker awakens in the night, sweating; the sheet has become wet and he feels cold even though he has been having erotic and passionate "dreams of heat." Now, the only residue of these dreams is the night sweat that has left his sheets wet and his body chilled. He rises from the bed to change the sheets, but he is immobilized by the remembrance and contemplation of his past sexual adventures and by a growing sense of helplessness. The second through the fifth stanzas involve his memories of these past experiences, which have resulted in his present condition. The final three stanzas return to the present as he contemplates that condition.

There are two basic tensions in the poem. The primary one is built on the contrast between the strong, masculine flesh of the speaker's body in the past and its weakened physical state in the present. When he was sexually active, he believed that he could "trust" his body, and he relished the sexual risks he took. At that time, it was as if he were shielded by his skin from harm, and when "it was gashed, it healed." In the present, however, the ill man, his protection gone, faces the pains of future physical deterioration. Because the shield that once protected him—explicitly his skin but also, by implication, a condom—has cracked at some point, his mind has been reduced "to hurry" and his flesh to a "wrecked" state.

Another element of tension is the contrast between heat and cold, in terms of both the man's physical temperature and the heat that is generated by sexual passion and erotic dreams. Ironically, although he is sweating, the speaker wakes up from his "dreams of heat" to cold, which is a marked contrast to the sexually active past, when he "Prospered through dreams of heat." The "residue" of that heat is sweat, and the need to change wet sheets is a contrast to the gratification of desire that followed sexual activity in the past.

He stands, hugging himself as though, thereby, he might be able "to shield" his body from the pains that await, as though "hands were enough" to stave off the approaching "avalanche," that is, the inevitable and overpowering progress of the disease that will sweep over him and, ultimately, destroy him. Now, his only protection is his hands, but they are incapable of performing such a task.

Forms and Devices

Despite the contemporary and even controversial concerns to which he turns his attention, Gunn has always been something of a formalist in an age in which free verse abounds. He frequently employs long-established forms of verse as well as traditional patterns of meter and rhyme, achieving, through the juxtaposition of avant-garde subject matter and classical forms, an effectively startling tone. In "The Man with Night Sweats," he alternates four quatrains with four couplets to produce a unique pattern of juxtaposition. This pattern represents a combination of traditional form and innovative alterations by the poet. The lines of both the quatrains and the couplets are iambic trimeter with several effective variations in the beats.

The rhyme scheme in the quatrains is *abab*; in the couplets it is *aa*. Many of the rhymes are full ("heat" and "sheet," "trust" and "robust," "in" and "skin"), although Gunn also employs slant rhymes, as in the third quatrain when he links "sorry" and "hurry," in the fourth quatrain in which he links "am" and "from," and in the concluding couplet, where "enough" is rhymed with "off."

The imagery of the poem centers on the sheets made wet by the night sweat and on the flesh of the speaker, which was once invulnerable but now suffers the effects of the illness. He can change the wet sheets, but he is unable to alter the condition that produced them. Among the metaphors is his comparison of his skin to a shield that once protected him but now has been pierced, resulting in flesh that is "reduced and wrecked." The "skin" is also clearly an allusion to and a metaphor for a condom, whose breaking may have resulted in the disease. In addition, the sheet might be considered, metaphorically, a kind of skin that was once dry and protective but now makes the speaker cold. The "dreams of heat" from which the persona awakens are a metaphor for the sexual passions of the past, experiences that he enjoyed and through which he "prospered" but which have now become emblematic of his physical decline. He compares the further physical deterioration that awaits him to an "avalanche" that he is not strong enough to stave off.

Themes and Meanings

"The Man with Night Sweats" is a poem about facing one's inevitable death. In this instance, the individual happens to be suffering from AIDS, but the universality of death and its effect on human beings are, nevertheless, present in the poem. As the speaker remembers the past, when he was full of life and unafraid to take sexual risks, he grieves for the good health that he will never again enjoy and for the fact that he might have been able to prevent the illness that is now racking his body. Another thematic element of the poem centers on this man's—and any human being's—helplessness in the face of physical decay.

The subject of death has always been prevalent in poetry of all ages and countries. Often, the contemplation of death is eased by the hope and consolation of eternal life, as in Alfred, Lord Tennyson's "In Memoriam" and John Milton's "Lycidas," or by the deceased person's return to and absorption by nature, as in Walt Whitman's "When Lilacs Last in the Dooryard Bloomed" and Percy Shelley's "Adonais." There is, however, no such consolation offered in "The Man with Night Sweats," only grief and a sort of quiet despair for the passion of the past that will not come again, the passion that was responsible for the wasting illness the speaker experiences. While dealing with the same theme—death and its effects on the human consciousness—Dylan Thomas urged a struggle against the impending end to life in his poem "Do Not Go Gentle into That Good Night," and something of the same notion is employed here by Gunn. His speaker hugs his own body in defiance of the illness, endeavoring to shield it from the "pains that will go through me." However, the body, now weakened by the disease, is no longer the shield that it was in the past, and the concluding couplet makes it clear that there is no hope: Hands are not powerful enough to "hold an avalanche off."

Another theme emanates from the contrast between the sexual companionship that was available in the past, when the "robust" body and the mind of the persona relished the heat of passion, and the loneliness with which he must now face his own death. The memories and dreams are insufficient consolation as he imagines the further deterioration of his body from a disease of which the night sweats are only a symptom.

W. Kenneth Holditch

THE MAN WITH THE BLUE GUITAR

Author: Wallace Stevens (1879-1955)
Type of poem: Lyric
First published: 1937, in *The Man with the Blue Guitar and Other Poems*

The Poem

"The Man with the Blue Guitar" is a long poem consisting of thirty-three rather short sections in four-beat couplets, most of them unrhymed. The title, which reminds the reader of a Pablo Picasso painting by the same title, suggests a musical piece, though more in the sense of an improvisation than a formal musical composition (something that Wallace Stevens imitates effectively in "Peter Quince at the Clavier").

The poem starts out in the third person but switches to the first person, so the piece becomes a dialogue between the guitarist and his audience, which acts as a kind of chorus. The chorus seems to pose certain idealized questions about its own place in poetry. Rejecting those overtures, the guitarist says that he plays things "as they are," although things "Are changed upon the blue guitar." He then goes on to improvise in various ways about how this might be done—in essence, about how poetry is related to the audience or to the world in general.

Stevens himself was an insurance executive, so he knew the world in a practical sense; yet he was also a poet, a creator. Though he did not confuse the two worlds, he saw them as coextensive. In "The Man with the Blue Guitar" he takes the reader into the world of the poet and asks the reader to see, feel, or improvise about the world from the poet's perspective.

Sections I-VI set the stage for the musical drama. Stevens tests out various interrelationships between the blue of the guitar, or the poet's imagination, and the green world, "things exactly as they are." The poet/guitarist depends upon the world he changes— shears, patches, tries to "bring . . . round"—but is never able to remake perfectly.

In section VII, the improvisation changes; the guitarist becomes more metaphysical. He begins to play with various ideas about reality and what the fictive person can do with it. Thinking becomes a metaphor or stage for the guitarist's, or poet's, activity as creator. It is as if the poet takes over the role of the godhead and in the process, now wholly secular, tests out the possibilities as well as the limits of a poet's abilities relative to the world.

The guitarist also sets himself a task: to "evolve a man" (section XXX). He speaks of the poet as singing "a hero's head,/ large eye," or creating man in a mythic or symbolic sense. He hopes to do more than this, and he uses certain metaphors for man, such as the clown on the stage (XXV) or the notion of "the old fantoche" (XXX), reminiscent of the "walking shadow" in William Shakespeare's *Macbeth* (1606).

In the final sections of the poem, however, the poet returns to the original thesis— the relationship between poet and audience. In the closing couplet, which is rhymed, suggesting a certain finality, the "imagined pine, the imagined jay"—the world and the imagination—are still in juxtaposition, as if to say the guitarist still needs to balance outer and inner worlds in the ever-changing drama called life.

Forms and Devices

As the title suggests, "The Man with the Blue Guitar" is similar to a musical piece, specifically an improvisation. There is no poetic precedent for this form, so the poet employs a loosely knit structure to fit his theme. The use of thirty-three (an odd number) parts suggests that there is nothing set about the overall composition. Similarly, in each part the number of couplets, usually five or six, varies from as few as four to as many as seven. Nor is the rhyming consistent, though certain sections do rhyme, giving the illusion of finality.

The poem is filled with musical terms to reinforce the aesthetic nature of the exercise; it is "a tune," a "serenade." At the same time, the musician is a creator, so Stevens employs images more appropriate to a carpenter. The guitarist's "bang" suggests violent action, where things may be "destroyed," but at the same time the guitarist (or builder) is "a mould" to shape things—ultimately "to evolve," or recreate, man himself. This is a mammoth task, involving "mountainous music," but it is still music and, therefore, temporary—always "passing away." While the "leaden twang" continues, however, it is like "reason in a storm," suggesting that all reality, including the listener, is caught up in the rhythms of the improvisation.

In addition to being musical, the poet is an artist. Like Pablo Picasso, the guitarist becomes an abstract expressionist, rearranging fragments of reality into a unified whole. One way the artist works is through color, changing the world so that what one sees is the "sun's green" and "cloud's red"—unnatural but imaginative realities. Sometimes colors are used to dismiss transcendent realities, the "gold self aloft," or to show the limits of the imagination, "enraged by gold antagonists in air." Stevens always returns to the blue imagination in balance with the green world; in fact, they are so close that occasionally the artist speaks of the "overcast blue of the air," as though mind and object often intermingle in the process of imagining, or creating.

The artist is a master of imagery—he works in visual representations; Stevens uses animals, for example, to fill in his canvas. Many might see the poet as "angelic," but for Stevens he is always of this world, "a worm composing on a straw." Sometimes he must deal with fluctuating subjects in the world, such as "liquid cats," but he never resorts to romantic or idealized visions, "the lark fixed . . . in the museum of the sky." He rather tries to maintain a balance between the guitarist, "the lion in the lute," and external reality, "the lion lock in stone."

Finally, the guitarist is also part dramatist. Sections I-VI are a virtual stage, after which the poem moves toward a climax in section XXII, where Stevens tells the reader directly: "Poetry is the subject of the poem." In XXV, the poet-dramatist imagines the mind itself as a stage, where the poet is a clown, and his "nose" and "fat thumb" are properties that help one to experience the dramatic and comic process of re-creating reality through imagination. Here the clown's nose is primary, for it enables the poet to give a center of gravity, or stability, to the poet vis-à-vis the world as he educates, entertains, indeed re-creates the world for his audience.

Themes and Meanings

Wallace Stevens was not a particularly philosophical poet, but he was an idea poet, for ideas always lurk behind his aesthetics. Unlike E. E. Cummings, who in poems such as "a man who had fallen among thieves" often centers on relationships, community, and love, thereby challenging Christians to live up to their biblical roots, Stevens is more concerned with immediate reality and how one perceives it. He dismisses belief systems in order to focus on the present as a poet. His challenge is to people in their immediate context, to their imaginative capability, and to this end he takes the reader inside the man with the blue guitar.

In the background of Stevens's poem are key thinkers of all times and places, notes Joseph Riddle in *The Clairvoyant Eye* (1965). Stevens assumes with Heraclitus that the world is in flux, and as a student of Georg Hegel he sees reality as moving forward creatively. Stevens also must have admired James Joyce's young Steven Dedalus as Steven pursues new worlds as poet and thinker in *A Portrait of the Artist as a Young Man* (1916). At the same time, he rejects the idea of God or the divinity of Christ, even undercutting Ralph Waldo Emerson's notion of transcendence, as he does T. S. Eliot's "still point," in favor of an immediate and changing world.

Where Stevens is most original is in his creative images, according to William York Tindall, through which he makes his reader ponder important subjects. He takes Paul Verlaine's marionette, for example, and puts him in the brutal world, "Oxidia"— violent and toxic, unlike the mythological Olympia. Here the marionette figure sees three crosses: Christ on the cross, a telephone pole, and the cross stick of the marionette. Rejecting transcendent answers, and located in the real world (the world of the telephone pole), the artist is able to entertain his audience, something that metaphysically may be both comic and tragic. That is the poet's (Stevens') idea of what is real.

Perhaps one of the strongest statements about the potential value of the imagination comes in section XIV, in which Stevens compares the imagination to a candle, which he says is "enough to light the world." In contrast to the German chandelier (which represents scientific knowledge, reason), the candle provides clear insight at any time of day:

> At night, it lights the fruit and wine,
> The book and bread, things as they are.

The fruit and wine and book and bread have no symbolic or sacramental value, but are simply "things as they are." Here, Thomas J. Hines has said, the blue guitar, which has been used throughout the poem, defines itself and its potential (the candle), and so proves that it can generate a definition of itself within its own constructs.

Hines also notes that philosophically, in the mid 1930's, Stevens was closest to Edmund Husserl's phenomenological method; in "The Man with the Blue Guitar," the poet organizes his world around a single intuition, with which he then works in a fictive or imaginative manner. He did not evolve a new notion of man's essence or being, but his improvisions on the blue guitar present a wide variety of options for looking at reality and at humankind's place in it.

Thomas Matchie

THE MAN WITH THE HOE

Author: Edwin Markham (1852-1940)
Type of poem: Ode
First published: 1899, in *The Man with the Hoe and Other Poems*

The Poem

Edwin Markham, who has been called "the dean of American poets," received national fame, and later worldwide fame, when he published "The Man with the Hoe." It changed his career immediately. The poem consists of forty-nine lines divided into five stanzas of social commentary that focus on America's working class and their sufferings. It is a striking poem of protest against exploited labor.

After viewing French artist Jean-François Millet's world-famous painting of a peasant leaning on his hoe, *The Man with the Hoe* (1862), Markham was inspired to write his poem in 1898. He is reported to have seen the original painting, which had a profound effect on him, in San Francisco. Markham was at a New Year's Eve celebration when he read the poem to an editor of the San Francisco *Examiner.* Shortly thereafter, the poem was published in that paper.

Because of its popularity, the poem was translated into many languages and reprinted in magazines, newspapers, and books numerous times. The poem's success allowed Markham to spend more time writing and lecturing. In regard to the reform movements concerning labor struggles of the time, the poem generated much controversy. The newspapers received many letters regarding "The Man with the Hoe." The poem was open to different interpretations. Some readers said that the poem was advocating socialism: Some were in support of the concept; others were against it. Others said the poem contained a prophetic message that could incite unessential reforms. Still others considered the poem a medium for expressing farmers' and workers' grievances.

For Markham, Millet's peasant symbolized the exploited classes worldwide. Markham said that he viewed it as "a poem of hope . . . . a cry for justice." In the fourth stanza, Markham addresses the "masters, lords, and rulers in all lands." He interrogates them with an implied sense of optimism:

Is this the handiwork you give to God,
This monstrous thing distorted and soul-quenched?
How will you ever straighten up this shape,
Touch it again with immortality;
Give back the upward looking and the light;
Rebuild in it the music and the dream;
Make right the immemorial infamies,
Perfidious wrongs, immedicable woes?

Forms and Devices

Selecting the best way to express his poetic ideas about social and spiritual beliefs, Markham chose blank verse, for it provided the flexibility he needed. As Markham employed language, he made use of several poetic devices, including vivid descriptions, extended metaphors, rhetorical questions, literary allusions, and symbolism.

In the first stanza, the reader is given a vivid description of a laborer who has been crushed by years of toil, struggles, and injustices, to the extent that one can visualize the negative effects: "Bowed by the weight of centuries," "The emptiness of ages in his face," "on his back the burden of the world." Markham asks, "Whose breath blew out the light within this brain?" Some other poets have also shown interest in the treatment of humankind. Among them is eighteenth century Robert Burns, who also was a farmer and a poet. In his poem "Man's Inhumanity to Man," he writes of the many ills that have befallen humankind: "Man's inhumanity to man,/ Makes countless thousands mourn."

The second stanza of "The Man with the Hoe" opens with an allusion to the Genesis creation story; Markham refers to humanity as the "Thing the Lord God made and gave/ To have dominion over sea and land." Markham suggests that humans have lost their position and are no longer held in high esteem, as God intended. Human dignity has been taken away. The "Thing" is the antithesis of the man whom David describes in Psalm 8:4-5: "What is man, that thou art mindful of him, and the son of man that thou dost care for him?/ Yet thou hast made him little less than God, and dost crown him with glory and honor./ Thou hast given him dominion over the works of thy hands...."

Markham continues to focus on some of the negative effects of the "Slaves of the wheel of labor." He clearly condemns the exploitation of labor. Such conditions have caused the laborer to have an "aching stoop" and to become devoid of mind and heart. Markham also challenges "the Judges of the World." In the last stanza, he alludes to changes in the future that may come about as a result of protests and rebellions. Consequently, Markham wants to know how the world will react "When this dumb Terror shall reply to God,/ After the silence of the centuries?"

Themes and Meanings

Markham has been called "the first real poet of Labor." This poem called attention to social problems and served as the topic of discussion for a wide range of audiences, including ministers, politicians, professors, students, debaters, and orators.

In order to understand why Markham wrote as he did, it is necessary to have some knowledge of his background. Markham was born in Oregon City, Oregon, the youngest child of pioneer parents who divorced soon after his birth. He moved with his mother, who was very demanding, to Lagoon Valley, California, and was put to lonely and difficult work on her farm and ranch before he was ten years old. He was constantly aware of the grind of toil. He wrote about his experience of hoeing the garden for long periods of time, as he encountered pain in his back. Markham was especially interested in the trials and tribulations of poor working people. He was concerned about the external forces and circumstances that affected them.

Markham experienced some hardships as he attempted to accomplish a number of his goals. Getting an education was not easy. Initially, Markham's mother did not financially assist him with his educational goals. Markham even ran away from home for a short period of time in 1867, and he did not return until his mother decided to help finance his studies. After matriculating at California College in Vacaville, he received his teacher's certificate. Later he studied at San Jose Normal School and Christian College in Santa Rosa. In 1872, Markham began his teaching career in Los Berros, California. Subsequently, he held an administrative position as superintendent of schools at Placerville, California. Additionally, Markham experienced three bad marriages.

Continuously developing his social and spiritual beliefs, Markham left the Methodist faith in 1876 and began to follow Thomas Lake Harris, a spiritualist and utopian socialist. Markham, like Harris, placed emphasis on universal charity and social harmony. He was interested in socialist utopian reform. Markham believed that spiritual faith could help to unify humankind.

"The Man with the Hoe" was a result of Markham's personal experiences and all the reading and thinking he had been doing for many years. Millet's painting was the stimulus to Markham's imagination; it was a picture in words for Markham's mind. The poet transformed the images into words and put them on paper. If it had not been for Millet's visual artistic expression, perhaps Markham would not have received the inspiration he needed to express his ideas in "The Man with the Hoe." Markham's poem is still timely and appropriate because it focuses on relevant social problems, which are still unsolved.

Nila M. Bowden

MANHATTAN, 1975

Author: Carl Rakosi (1903-   )
Type of poem: Narrative
First published: 1983, as "Manhattan"; collected as "Manhattan, 1975," in *The Collected Poems of Carl Rakosi*, 1986

The Poem

"Manhattan, 1975," a narrative poem in free verse, deals with various aspects of city life. The nature of New York life is reflected in the form of the poem; half-lines that begin at the left margin alternate with headless lines that begin where the half-lines that precede them end, giving the poem a broken, fragmented appearance. The traditional stanza form is replaced by five syntactical and semantic units. The title refers to Manhattan in particular, but in its criticism "Manhattan, 1975" describes any city experience.

The poem alternates between the description of street scenes and reflective passages. The first of the five units begins with a hypothetical dialogue, indicated by the conjunction "if" in the first line, between an imaginary female "you" and a male "I." The topic of the conversation is sexual. The youth of the woman is implied by the freshness of the earth and the upcoming buds, symbolizing the breasts of the young woman. Once fully matured, she will lose her virginity in the city. This thought is expressed by mentioning her hymen and by associating purity, which is her presexual but also pre-Manhattan stage, with the whiteness of buds. While the female "you" is introduced by the mention of her hymen, the first unit of the poem ends with the male "I," stating his sex in the double entendre of the line "P. S. Nuts to reason."

Summer is coming, and nature is awakening; so is the girl's sexuality. The male "I" is excited by her sexual awakening, as is indicated in the line "the tiniest nerve-endings trembling." At the same time, his feeling is repressed because it is "within its chest-walls"—a comparison of his feelings to people living within city walls. Dodo, the man's nickname, both suggests his puckish spirit and alludes to the dodo bird, or a fool, making fun of his feelings.

Beginning with the question "Who's that in the light/ cotton dress," the second unit deals with a grown-up woman who, driven by the desire for sex, follows a call from the earth, waiting for a lover. This idea is expressed by her dress, her behavior, and the biblical quotation from the book of Ruth (1:16). The part ends with a promise that the man reads in a smile and with his "down to earth" sexual failure.

The third unit is introduced by a song praising summer and implying opportunities for men to have sex. Suddenly, the poem shifts, and the joyful, lusty tone of the sexual allusions in the first unit is now replaced by references to death. Whereas the male repressed his emotions in the first part of the poem, now his feelings seem to be dead, "close, mortal musk," and intercourse becomes a mechanical act without love— "sexual, befuddling . . ./ a whiff of dead breaths/ intermittently crossing."

The lyrical "I" at the beginning of the fourth unit is a reflection of Carl Rakosi himself: "I could imagine lion cubs." The male-female relationship, expressed by the pronoun pair "I-you" in the first part of the poem, is connected to the fourth part by the word "progenitor"; both words suggest reproduction. The "progenitor" can also be associated with God through the references to the Old Testament in this passage, such as "And irrelevance, where was its sting" (a revision of 1 Corinthians 15:55-56). The anonymity of the city leads to a disillusioned confession by the poet: "O my radical past,/ I am not embarrassed,/ but is this all that remains?"

The poem closes with street scenes, expressing the negative influence of the city by means of the fading colors of the parrot's feathers. The anonymity of the city leads to a reduction of the human being to particular parts. Thus all one sees or hears from the woman at the opening of this fifth unit is her voice; furthermore, making love becomes a lucrative business, and the hustler is "cast in sandstone" like the saints of European cathedrals. The city experience has created a new species, the "hominid Americanus." The poem ends on a note of hope—"Lady, be comforted!"—despite all the misunderstandings and disputes.

Forms and Devices

"Manhattan, 1975" is written in the tradition of a group of poets, including Carl Rakosi, who called themselves "Objectivists." Objectivism claims that the poem is an object and has to be dealt with as such, apart from its meaning. Therefore, special consideration is given to form.

The form of the poem is eye-catching, because the lines are broken up. Each half-line, beginning at the left margin, is continued in the following line by a headless line that is set off from the left margin. "Manhattan, 1975" is a dialogue in which voices are separated by the half-lines and headless lines.

The form of this poem is a new, American one, appropriate for depicting American life. The traditional poetic devices of European literatures—such as rhyme, meter, even line and stanza—have been abandoned and replaced by dialogues. The poem has become narrative.

The dialogues that take place in this poem include the imaginary dialogue between a man and a woman in the first part of the poem, the actual dialogue between a woman and the parrot man, and the failure of dialogue between the two senators from North and South Carolina.

A further device of this poetic form is the use of quotations and intertextuality; that is, different parts of other texts are interwoven into the poem, such as references to the Old Testament. Rakosi uses biblical imagery, direct quotations from the Old Testament, and allusions to the Bible, in which a biblical quotation is changed: "And irrelevance,/ where was its sting?" Furthermore, he chooses biblical names, such as Ruth and Noah, reflecting his own Jewish heritage.

Themes and Meanings

Isolation and anonymity, as part of the city experience, are the central issues in

"Manhattan, 1975." Rakosi, who was a dedicated social worker, shows a great concern for the well-being of others, and at one point in the poem he questions his own personal accomplishments. As Diane Wakoski has said, Rakosi reminds the reader "that to live intelligently is never to relax or to leave unnoticed any slightly foolish thing."

"Manhattan, 1975" contrasts the American reality, of which Manhattan is the quintessential experience, with medieval and Renaissance England. The language of the poem and its form, reminiscent of Ezra Pound's headless lines, are American. Rakosi undoubtedly stands in the American tradition, as he points out in the poem himself: "I among them/ (impossible to keep Whitman out of this)." Walt Whitman (1819-1892) is the American poet par excellence, and he also lived in New York. Therefore, the poem portrays an American experience in an American narrative style.

In addition, Rakosi pays tribute to the American novelist Ernest Hemingway. The quotation "(I could imagine lion cubs at play/ bumping awkwardly against each other)" comes from Hemingway's novel *The Old Man and the Sea* (1952).

An allusion to T. S. Eliot, an American who became a British subject, bridging British and American elements, is given by the parrot that speaks Sanskrit, a language used in T. S. Eliot's poem *The Waste Land* (1922). The line "And irrelevance,/ where was its sting," which is essentially a Biblical quotation, also alludes to the poetry of John Donne.

The sensual character of "Manhattan, 1975," combined with its fondness for rituals, reminds one of the poet Robert Herrick. While in Herrick's May poems the Queen of May is in the center of the fertility rites, "insouciance is King/ of the May" in the city experience of America, where intercourse, as an expression of love leading to fertility, has become a mechanical act to be purchased on any corner.

The message of Puck, a spirit in English folklore, along with images from nature, becomes a paradox in Manhattan. Reality and ideal are separated like Ireland and Britain, as indicated by the line "From outside the pale," which is the dividing line between Catholic Ireland and Protestant Northern Ireland.

Rakosi's frustration with the city is also illustrated in the anonymous English "Cuckoo Song" (c. 1250). Rakosi adds to the Middle English "sumer is i-cumin in/ lhude sing cuckoo" an American "Yay." Furthermore, he changes the word "cuckoo," with which spring is associated, to the word "city." The city has replaced nature, as the alliteration of city and cuckoo indicates. Yet the poem offers comfort, implying that there is salvation after death, "He is safe with Noah now"; and the ending of the poem moves away from the anonymous, impersonal treatment of people living in New York to a more respectful and hopeful "Lady, be comforted!"

Hartmut Heep

THE MAP

Author: Elizabeth Bishop (1911-1979)
Type of poem: Lyric
First published: 1935; collected in *North and South*, 1946

The Poem

"The Map" is a descriptive poem divided into three stanzas. The first and last are eight-line stanzas with repeated Petrarchan rhyme schemes (*abbacddc*), while the longer central stanza is written in free verse.

In "The Map," Elizabeth Bishop records her thoughts on the nature of a map's relationship to the real world. Implicitly, the poem asks why maps fascinate people so much. The poet suggests that the human fascination with small-scale representations of land and water has to do with the imagined worlds maps can offer, the images of far-off people and places that maps can bring to mind. More precisely, maps excite the viewer's imagination. "The Map" celebrates the mapmaker's (or poet's) power to create illusion and fantasy as well as new ways of looking at what is real.

The poem begins with shapes and colors—what most people first notice about maps. For example, land is "shadowed green," and it "lies in water," which is blue. Here, however, all certainty ends, and a series of provocative but unanswered questions begins. The poet sees "Shadows," not sure if they are "shallows." Also uncertain is whether the line on the paper indicates the land's edges or "long sea-weeded ledges."

On first looking at the map, the poet sees water surrounding and supporting land. The second half of the first stanza, however, suggests a relationship between the land and the sea that is mysterious and unexpected. The land is active—it seems to lean, lift, and draw the water around itself. The poet asks, "is the land tugging at the sea from under?" Because these questions go unanswered, the reader begins to understand that not everyone interprets a map the same way.

In the long central stanza, the map receives the close inspection for which Bishop's poetry is well known. Newfoundland (perhaps "new found land") suggests that the imagination can create new territory, new realities. In Labrador, "yellow, where the moony Eskimo/ has oiled it," the dreamer, the "moony" imaginer, paints the land to suit her vision of it. Stroking the lovely bays "under a glass as if they were expected to blossom" suggests the map's magical quality as well as its aesthetic beauty. Perhaps "blossom" suggests how one's expectations grow while studying a map.

The poet also inspects the carefully printed names, which "run out to sea" and "cross the neighboring mountains." The juxtaposition of the artificial (printed names) with the "real" (sea and mountains) reminds the reader that the map is a man-made object. For the poet, it is a representation by which to compare reality with perception. Stanza 2 ends with a playful image: The peninsulas are "thumb and finger/ . . . feeling for the smoothness of yard-goods." The poet seems to prefer her fanciful perception to the real places the map represents. This image also looks again at the relationship of land to water.

Examining that relationship further, the poet suggests in stanza 3 that the "waves' own conformation" is what determines the shape of the land, rather than the land's outlines determining how far the water lies. The poet sees Norway running south in the shape of a hare, and then, getting back to the art of cartography, casually wonders, "Are they assigned, or can the countries pick their colors?" These three observations suggest questions of perspective. For example, how one sees an object—such as this map—is a very personal experience. The poet's (unrevealed) conclusions are her own; there are no definitive answers, no "favorites."

That is why the cartographer's representations and use of tools, records, and perceptions are "More delicate than the historians'." The historian attempts to deal with facts, and chronologies of events, objectively. Although she dares not distort truth, the mapmaker, unlike the historian, deals with possibilities imaginatively, for the artist celebrates the notion that to be completely objective is impossible.

Forms and Devices

Like many of Bishop's poems, "The Map" exemplifies her mastery of organic form. The poem's structure grows out of and also contributes to its expression. The rhymed stanzas (1 and 3) reflect precision, balance, and elegance—they have a life of their own, exactly as the map lives its life "unperturbed," existing "under a glass," independent of the viewer's scrutiny. The controlled pace of these stanzas helps to create the tone of careful exploration and tentative suggestion that the poet's observations convey, especially in the first stanza.

The map is, furthermore, an inanimate object made animate by the personification of land and sea. For example, "the land lean[s] down" and lifts and tugs, the waters "lend," and the profiles of land investigate. The rhymed stanzas are also the question stanzas, in which the poet asks (and never answers) questions about what she sees and imagines in the map. These unanswered questions shape the poem, propel it forward, and frame it with a tone of uncertain yet determined speculation.

The long, unrhymed stanza is a close description that seems to start at the top and move southward, as if the poet were running her fingers down along the map's colored lines. A running commentary of metaphors animates and finally personifies the peninsulas as women. Bishop uses a very natural word order, the same order of words one would use in a good sentence. This technique welcomes the reader into the poem, which reads as if the narrator were wondering aloud. The long, central stanza also uses first-person plural ("we"), as if to draw the reader further and more intimately into the poet's speculation on what a map really is and on its ultimate purpose.

In the first stanza, the verbs are very active; the land leans, lifts, and tugs. In contrast, stanza 2 begins with land that "lies flat and still." The following verbs in the same stanza reflect determined, if cautious, motion: "oiled," "blossom," "run," "cross," and "take." These verbs indicate that the poet's exploration in this stanza is painstaking and precise; she is well aware that details risk being overlooked "when emotion too far exceeds its cause."

Stanza 3 gathers together what the poet has learned about the map. She looks once more at the relationship of land to water (a recurring puzzle), and she notes other details: hare-shaped Norway and the "profiles" of land that investigate the sea. Yet this final stanza's main effect is to turn the viewer's attention away from the map and inward, for reflection. The final question—"can the countries pick their colors?"—accomplishes this shift in perspective because it reminds the reader that whoever drew the map made artistic (imaginative) decisions in its execution. It also introduces the final thematic statement, the poem's puzzling last line.

Themes and Meanings

The simplicity of the title promises a straightforward description of an object—a real map—which the poet delivers with fine-tuned and surprising nuances. One is soon aware, however, that the description is both objective and emblematic. That is, a real map is very carefully and faithfully described, but the map is also a symbol capable of suggesting meanings or connections beyond itself.

For one thing, the map is an emblem of imaginative promise. It might show its reader how to get to a specific place, or it might lead to hidden treasure. Because the images on maps are by definition constructions of the mind, perhaps the map represents the mind attempting to plot a landscape so that it can find its way.

By placing "The Map" first in both *North and South* (1946) and *The Complete Poems* (1969), Bishop also suggested that "The Map" may lead to a way of understanding her work, especially her sense of how an "objective" work of art may embody an artist's subjective experience. As early as the second line of the poem, for example, Bishop's subjective kind of seeing becomes apparent. Her fanciful images—the "clean cage for invisible fish" and "Norway's hare"—suggest that what one sees depends on how one looks or uses her imagination.

As with the ever-changing relationship between land and water, the concept of subjective perception arises often. The poet's unique and often whimsical account of the map reveals her uniqueness of vision—her way of experiencing the world and of expressing that experience. While the questions in stanza 1 first introduce the idea that individual perspectives can differ, the lines in stanza 2 suggest that individual perspectives—and not the external world itself—may in fact determine what is real.

In "The Map," Bishop is in fact exploring the imagination rather than the landscape. The poem might even be read as a rumination on the value or status of poetry. "The Map" is not about actual geography but about refusing to standardize the images each person projects onto a place. Bishop is trying to revive and renew sight, to make images new.

Expressing the imagination's own way of seeing, while retaining one's sense of the real world, is the challenge the artist accepts and struggles with. The question of whether empirical truth or imaginative truth is more valuable in humankind's efforts to chart the world around it is unanswerable. Probably, both perceptions are required.

The poet, however, uses more delicate, more powerful colors to paint the facts with a sharper and subtler stroke; they give reality a beauty and form that the historians' literal black-and-white representations cannot approach. The map-maker's images are fragile, yet keen and subtle, the results of a particular imagination shaping the real. That expression—the delicate "map-makers' colors"—comprises the poet's varied, rich, and peculiar ways of seeing.

JoAnn Balingit

A MAP OF MONTANA IN ITALY

Author: Richard Hugo (1923-1982)
Type of poem: Lyric
First published: 1973, in *The Lady in Kicking Horse Reservoir*

The Poem

"A Map of Montana in Italy" is a lyric poem in free verse, arranged into a single stanza of thirty-four lines. It is the opening poem in Richard Hugo's fourth book of poems, *The Lady in Kicking Horse Reservoir,* and it is dedicated to Marjorie Carrier.

The poem is written in the first person, in the present tense, the voice distinctively Hugo's. It is rather flat in tone, with subdued emotions. Although the syntax is simple and rather prosaic, the poem's style is tight, direct, and without extraneous words. The situation of the poem is that Hugo (who lived in Missoula, where he taught at the University of Montana from 1963 until his death in 1982) has come upon a map of Montana while he is touring in Italy. Perhaps the map has been tacked up on a wall, or maybe it is in an atlas open upon Hugo's lap.

The poem begins with two descriptive, though incomplete, sentences: "On this map white. A state thick as a fist/ or blunt instrument." The third sentence is complete but brief, straightforward, metaphoric, and declarative: "Long roads weave and cross/ red veins full of rage." The long and often undeveloped gravel or dirt roads of Montana are printed in red, symbolizing to Hugo that anger is a statewide characteristic. The introductory style of these sentences suggests that the speaker wishes to impress the reader with tough talk, as though he is in a pugnacious mood. Not until the poem's fourth sentence does the speaker identify himself as a Montanan. "Big Canada," he says, "map maker's/ pink, squats on our backs."

Next Hugo recalls the imagery of two of Montana's unique animals. He makes a witty connection between one of the map's colors, "Glacier Park's green," and his "envy" of the reclusive grizzly bears that live there, then he describes how "antelope sail/ between strands of barbed wire and never/ get hurt" on the eastern Montana prairie. Subsequently, over the next fifteen lines, he turns his attention to the people who live within the state's borders.

First, Hugo alludes to Billings and Great Falls, the state's "two biggest towns," describing them as "dull deposits/ of men getting along," who never miss church and censor "movies and books." Second, he calls Helena and Butte the state's "two most interesting towns," claiming they "have the good sense to fail." Then he turns to charging Montana's population with alcoholic immaturity ("There's too much/ schoolboy in bars") and with greed ("too much talk about money.)" There follows an oblique comparison of Montana with a Kafkaesque Poland, and suggestion that with "so few Negroes and Jews," the usual scapegoats of urban America, Montanans have been "reduced/ to hating each other, dumping our crud/ in our rivers, mistreating the Indians."

Returning to the map, Hugo notes how its color, white, aptly connotes "winter, ice." The description is used as a transition to Italy, where the snow is more distant and less threatening ("It's white here too/ but back of me, up in the mountains") and the wild animals of Italy, "obsequious wolves," are not as ferocious as Montana's grizzly bears.

Finally, as if pining for Montana's roughneck violence, Hugo tweaks the Italians, saying, "No one fights/ in the bars filled with pastry." Then he concludes with a general quizzical observation on the romance of the West: how, on the night before, "the Italians/ cheered the violence in one of our westerns."

Forms and Devices

The style of "A Map of Montana in Italy" is in many ways typical of the whole body of Hugo's poetry. Although Hugo studied with Theodore Roethke at the University of Washington in Seattle, the younger poet never adopted Roethke's broad interests in rhymed, formal verse, such as the villanelle, kyriel, and limerick, each of which Roethke employed quite successfully. Instead, Hugo seems to have discovered his own voice early and stayed with that voice throughout his life.

Hugo's voice is one of little modulation and tightly controlled pitch, a uniquely characteristic drone. Writing in "Richard Hugo: Getting Right," from a book-length collection of essays entitled *Local Assays: On Contemporary Poetry* (1985), Dave Smith says that Hugo's "music has always been insistent and derived from Anglo-Saxon sonic practices. He loves a strongly stressed line, usually three to five stresses, whose density and intensity is always willing to risk overwhelming the ear."

"A Map of Montana in Italy" aptly fits Smith's description. The poem's rhythm is irregular, a good example of free verse; however, while the lines seem to be measured in length predominantly by the eye, the poem still generally scans into five hard stresses per line, or an irregular pentameter.

Also typical of Hugo's style is this poem's use of alliteration, the repetition of consonant sounds at the beginning of words, and assonance, the repetition of vowel sounds. In his excellent collection of lectures and essays on poetry and writing, *The Triggering Town* (1979), Hugo writes of his interest in repetitive sounds. "When I was a young poet," he says, "I set an arbitrary rule that when I made a sound I felt was strong, a sound I liked specially, I'd make a similar sound three to eight syllables later. Of course it would often be a slant rhyme. Why three to eight? Don't ask. You have to be silly to write poems at all."

Note how in the following lines Hugo adheres to his rule of sound, stitching words together based in large part upon the repetition of the consonants *b, m, p,* and *g,* and the vowel sounds short *i,* short *a,* and long *e*:

> Big Canada, map maker's
> pink, squats on our backs, planning bad winters
> for years, and Glacier Park's green with my envy
> of Grizzly Bears.

Later in the poem, Hugo gets away from sweet-sounding lines and speaks in a voice that is more matter-of-fact and prosaic. Lines 24 and 25 read: "Each year, 4000 move, most to the west/ where ocean currents keep winter in check." There is much less music in that line. And the concluding three-and-a-half lines of the poem read:

> No one fights
> in the bars filled with pastry. There's no
> prison for miles. But last night the Italians
> cheered the violence in one of our westerns.

Except for a repetition of the *f* in fights and filled, and the *p* in pastry and prison, this section of the poem is much less alliterative. It is also less condensed; in those last three sentences Hugo uses the definite article (the) three times, when he only needed it once. The sentences are short, declarative, and rather dry. The poet's voice seems to have fallen completely away from its beginning high lyrical tone to a flatter, prosaic depression.

Themes and Meanings

Maps and references to towns on maps appear in many of Richard Hugo's poems. Hugo uses maps as anyone may use them: to dream about, move toward, and discover new territory. Thus, many of his poems become word maps for places themselves. Hugo's poems display psychological and social landscapes, as this poem does for Montana. It is the feel of Montana's size and natural beauty, its isolation from the rest of the world, its sense of abandonment, and its frontier violence and restlessness that Hugo hopes to survey in "A Map of Montana in Italy," especially as these are seen from a perspective of relative serenity in the Old World.

Hugo made three important trips to Italy. The first came during World War II, when he served as a bombadier in the Air Force. On the second, in 1963, he obsessively returned to the places he had known during the war. In an essay entitled "Ci Vediamo," Hugo relates how, centering on the war and the places he had known during the war, he meets an Italian soul mate named Vincenzo, who tells him, "Of all the Americans here during the war, you're the only one who ever returned." First Vincenzo bursts into tears, sobbing. Then Hugo responds, matching Vincenzo "sob for strangulated sob." On his third trip to Italy, from 1967-1968, funded by a Rockefeller Foundation Creative Writing Fellowship, Hugo wrote "A Map of Montana in Italy" and many other poems that went into *The Lady in Kicking Horse Reservoir*. As a result, Hugo wrote of Montana in this poem from the perspective of a returning American serviceman, scholar-poet, and tourist.

The poet's tone seems to be colored by several conflicting emotions: nostalgia for home; pride in Montana's physical beauty, wildness, and vigor; disgust for its juvenile bluster; anger over its restrictive behavior; and an underlying cynicism about the modern frontier state and the way its history is viewed by Hollywood. The poem's theme hinges not only on how Hugo views the wild, cold, tough, isolated, and depopulated map of Montana, but also on how it contrasts with Italy.

Hugo portrays Italy as a nonviolent place, entertained nevertheless by Hollywood's myth of violence in the West. He claims that Italy's "most ferocious animals" are "obsequious wolves," meaning that they are submissive, obedient, or servile. Italians themselves are not merely peaceful and civilized; saying that their bars are "filled with pastry" is like calling them cream puffs. Hugo's statement that "There's no/ prison for miles" seems ironic, as though he were disappointed that Italians are law-abiding citizens.

The final sentence of the poem serves to focus the double edge of Hugo's sentiment. He is as saddened by the reality of Western life as he is by those gullible enough to enjoy a romanticized version of its violence. Furthermore, the safety of civilized life in Italy strangely mirrors the pathos Hugo sees in contemporary Western life, where crimes, such as polluting rivers and mistreating Indians, are not at all like the bold outlines of good and evil pictured in Hollywood Westerns. Hugo's poetic persona is often one of the tough guy, reminiscent, as Hugo himself noted, of Humphrey Bogart's film image. In "A Map of Montana in Italy," Hugo's tough persona never flinches from exposing Montana's nihilism and abuse, characteristics that create a parallel toughness in the poet's voice.

William Hoagland

MARIANA

Author: Alfred, Lord Tennyson (1809-1892)
Type of poem: Lyric
First published: 1830, in *Poems, Chiefly Lyrical*

The Poem

"Mariana" is a lyric poem of seven twelve-line stanzas, each ending in a refrain. The epigraph, "Mariana in the moated grange," is from William Shakespeare's *Measure for Measure* (1604), in which Mariana has been deserted by her lover, Angelo. The poem is also indebted to John Keats's *Isabella* (1820).

"Mariana" begins with a vivid depiction of setting and mood. The grange and its garden have fallen into disrepair. The flower plots are clogged with "blackest moss." Like Mariana, they are fertile but bereft of human care; they remain fallow. The house, too, is neglected. The roof's "ancient thatch" is worn and full of weeds; "rusted nails" allow the pear tree to fall from the gable wall; the gate's "clinking latch," moved only by the wind, remains "unlifted." This description of physical decay is emphasized by the obsessive lament of Mariana's refrain. Her life is "dreary"; she is "aweary, aweary" because "He cometh not," and she wishes that she were dead. Hers is the only human voice to break the silence.

The still-life effect of stanza 1 is followed by the slow passage of time in the remaining stanzas. She weeps morning and evening, so preoccupied with her earthly longing for Angelo (the unnamed "he" who haunts the poem) that she cannot "look on the sweet heaven." She hears only the sinister "flitting of the bats." When she does look out her window, all she sees are "the glooming flats." When she is able to sleep, "she seemed to walk forlorn," but whether sleepwalking or dreaming, she is "without hope of change."

Natural elements only emphasize her isolation. She hears "the night-fowl crow" and "the oxen's low," but not Angelo, whose name echoes these rhymes. The vegetation surrounding the grange, where "blackened waters slept" and "clustered marish-mosses crept," is lushly cloying, the claustrophobia heightened by the tongue-tying syntax.

The poplar tree is symbolic of Mariana herself, its shadow falling "Upon her bed, across her brow." Standing alone in the landscape, it trembles in the wind, and its "gnarled bark" shows signs of age, while "the wooing wind aloof" plays on its limbs. The wind is symbolic of Angelo, invisible yet felt in the desire of Mariana's limbs.

In stanza 6, Mariana reaches her emotional crisis. Each sensory detail in "the dreamy house" is magnified and amplified, her senses reaching a hallucinatory lucidity. Doors creak, flies buzz, and mice shriek with maddening volume. The house seems haunted with "Old faces," "Old footsteps," and "Old voices."

In the final stanza, the poem's imagery comes together to "confound her sense" in both meanings of sense. Both perception and sanity are overthrown. She dreads the setting of the sun when "the day/ Was sloping toward his western bower." The use of the masculine "his" is important. Just as Mariana's name rhymes with that of the virgin goddess of the moon, Diana, so Angelo's name rhymes with that of the sun god, Apollo. (Ironically, Apollo pursued Daphne, the nymph who was metamorphosed into a tree.) Both the sun and Angelo have passed Mariana by. Since Apollo is also the god of rationality and order, his disappearance over the horizon also foreshadows the beginning of yet another haunting night.

Forms and Devices

"Mariana" appeared to universal critical acclaim for its pictorial qualities. It has been said that Alfred, Lord Tennyson's poem prefigured the practices of the Pre-Raphaelite painters and poets, for whom an accumulation of vivid detail and an emphasis on feeling over idea were major tenets. John Everett Millais's *Mariana* is one of the centerpieces of Pre-Raphaelite painting.

John Stuart Mill praised Tennyson's excellence in "scene-painting, in the higher sense"—that is, in "the power of *creating* scenery, in keeping with some state of human feeling; so fitted to it as to be the embodied symbol of it." The emotions in the poem are suggested by the accumulation of precise details, the layering of which acquire symbolic force, before being stated directly in the refrain.

The poem's point of view encourages the reader to identify with Mariana's state of mind. In *Tennyson: The Unquiet Heart* (1983), Robert Martin has said that the poem "foreshadows Tennyson's success in later works that were in all but name dramatic monologues." Mariana's perceptions and emotions become those of the reader's.

Distorted imagery reflects Mariana's hypersensitivity, a result of being deprived of human companionship. At the height of her crisis, she animates her environment with hallucinations. Her vision is magnified ("The blue fly sung in the pane"); her hearing is amplified ("the mouse/ Behind the wainscot shrieked"). Tennyson's own myopia may account for his tightly focused, close-up imagery, but the effect creates almost cinematic distortions of space and time, as in the slow-motion or time-lapse vision of the rusted nails falling from the knots.

Personification is another way Tennyson lends human emotion to inanimate objects. Used tritely, it can result in what John Ruskin called "the pathetic fallacy." Used properly and with purpose, however, personification can be a powerful projection of psychological reality. Nature is so embued with Mariana's psychological state as to become a projection of her own emotion. Mariana has only the inanimate world with which to converse, so it is no wonder that she sees the broken sheds as "sad," the grange as "lonely," or the morning as "gray-eyed" at the end of a sleepless night. The morning reflects her own lusterless eyes because she needs the empathy of her surroundings.

Several devices of repetition mimic the monotony that Mariana feels. Rhyme, assonance, and alliteration heighten the static quality of her vigil. Chief among these devices is the refrain itself, with its feminine rhymes of "dreary/aweary." Tennyson well knew, however, that the depiction of monotony should not itself become monotonous, so he takes care to vary the end of the refrain slightly in each stanza.

No analysis of a Tennyson poem would be complete without noting its musicality. The importance of sound in evoking Mariana's mood cannot be overemphasized. Soft vowels and consonants dominate, especially those of her and Angelo's names, to express the oh's and ah's of languishing desire. That Angelo's name is never uttered, only evoked in echo-like rhymes and in the implied comparison to Apollo, shows a deft psychological touch: Mariana is unable to speak her obsession.

Themes and Meanings

"Mariana" is a good poem with which to begin the study of Tennyson. It shows his technical strengths of pictorial and musical qualities, as well as his greatest weakness: a lack of philosophical depth. What Tennyson lacks in ideas, he makes up for in psychological acuity and emotional accuracy. Still, "Mariana" is more than a lyrical portrait of monotony in the manner of Keats, with its sensuous evocation of melancholy; it also reflects the Victorian search—or wait—for a subject and style of its own. Published in 1830 at the end of the Romantic period, "Mariana" begins to show the problem with the Romantic lyric stance in the face of emerging Victorian concerns.

A major Victorian concern was the crisis of doubt brought on by apocalyptic social and intellectual changes. While the Industrial Revolution was laying waste to a way of life close to nature, the explosion of scientific discoveries was similarly laying waste to traditional ideas about religion. The result was a general feeling of abandonment. In "Dover Beach," Matthew Arnold proposed that even in the absence of worldly or religious hope, couples could at least "be true to one another." Yet Mariana is deprived of even this consolation. Seen in this light, her abandonment by Angelo reflects this larger crisis in faith, and her inability to act is analogous to stalled Victorian energies.

In later poems, such as "Lucretius" and "Despair," Tennyson explores what happens when, in the absence of a transcendent faith, the material world is a person's only reality. He concludes that such a view can end only in despair. Under the weight of her desire for Angelo, Mariana cannot "look on the sweet heaven," and she sinks into the sensuous experience of her surroundings. Desire turns to despair. Only in the final refrain does Mariana invoke a higher power for the first time: "Oh God, that I were dead!" (In the poem's sequel, "Mariana in the South," Mariana joins a convent, forsaking worldly desire in order to focus her attention on the otherworldly.)

"Mariana" is the first of several early Tennyson poems, such as "The Lady of Shallot" and "The Palace of Art," to employ an isolated feminine alter ego to express Tennyson's conflict between passive escape and active engagement. "The Lotos-Eaters" choose reverie and sensation over worldly duties. Not until "Ulysses" does Tennyson resolve the conflict by opting for active engagement in the world. Significantly for the reading of "Mariana," "Ulysses" was Tennyson's way of dealing with his grief over the death of his friend Arthur Henry Hallam. Like Mariana, he felt abandoned by the friend he loved, and he wanted to die—if only to be able to join Hallam in death. In his elegy to Hallam, *In Memoriam* (1850), Tennyson's acknowledged masterpiece and a poem that has been called the single most representative work of the Victorian period, Tennyson compares himself to a widow awaiting her lover's return—a situation very similar to the one that he first explored in "Mariana."

Richard Collins

MARRIAGE

Author: Gregory Corso (1930-2001)
Type of poem: Meditation
First published: 1960, in *The Happy Birthday of Death*

The Poem

"Marriage" is a lengthy comic meditation in free verse on the topic announced by the poem's title. More specifically, the opening line poses two questions: "Should I get married? Should I be good?" The male speaker considers these questions, though he has no intended companion in mind. Rather, the meditation considers the various social archetypes of married life and whether they suit the speaker, who seems to see himself as a subversive of sorts. The poem is divided into seven verse paragraphs of varying length, and it is organized by a variety of scenarios the speaker imagines.

The longest of these scenarios imagines a conventional marriage to "the girl next door." This fantasy envisions a courtship that mixes the odd ("Don't take her to movies but to cemeteries") with the romantically orthodox ("she going just so far and I understanding why"). A familiarly comic scene of meeting the fiancée's parents follows, as does a description of the wedding and the honeymoon. At the imagined Niagara Falls honeymoon, the speaker is so horrified by the corny lasciviousness of the honeymoon ritual that he chooses not to consummate the marriage. He will, he imagines, stay up all night staring at the hotel clerk and "Screaming: I deny honeymoon! I deny honeymoon!" Eventually, he will abandon his marriage and live beneath Niagara Falls itself as "a saint of divorce," a crazed spirit bent on disrupting the marriage consummations in the thousands of "almost climactic suites."

All the scenarios similarly end in rejections of marriage. He next imagines a more blissful domestic scene with his wife "aproned young and lovely and wanting my baby." Here, his subversive tendencies play out as practical jokes aimed at suburban orthodoxy: He will cover the neighbor's golf clubs with old Norwegian books; he will speak insanely to local canvassers for charities; he will order "penguin dust" from the milkman. This fantasy gives way to a more serious scenario in which, motivated by love for his wife, he strives to be the ideal cultivated father, giving the child a rattle made from "broken Bach records" and sewing "the Greek alphabet on its bib."

Reality intrudes, however, and the speaker imagines that he is more likely to live in a rat- and roach-infested walk-up apartment in New York City than in such a blissful Connecticut farmhouse. There his wife will be yelling at him to get a job while his "five nose running brats in love with Batman" charge about the overcrowded apartment. As that fantasy ends in a rejection of marriage, he imagines one more scenario: a sophisticated Manhattan penthouse with an elegant wife in evening dress sipping a cocktail. Even that idyll is rejected: "No, can't imagine myself married to that pleasant prison dream."

Having concluded that marriage is impossible for him, the speaker muses briefly about love, but dismisses it as being "as odd as wearing shoes." Finally, he sees a fearful vision of himself alone and unmarried: "all alone in a furnished room with pee stains on my underwear/ and everybody else is married!" The knowledge that loneliness may well await those who reject the conventions of matrimony influences the melancholy tone of the concluding lines. He imagines that just as his own sensibility exists, so must it be possible for a woman whom he could marry to exist. She could exist anywhere, however—even in ancient Egypt—and both the speaker and the idealized lover wait alone.

Forms and Devices

Tone is a central issue in interpreting this monologue. By invoking and exaggerating orthodox images of matrimony, Gregory Corso comically burlesques the social order. The use of hyperbole and stereotypical images interspersed with absurdist proclamations ("yelling Radio belly! Cat shovel!") creates a humorous incongruity. Indeed, ironic or surprising juxtaposition accounts for much of the poem's originality and comedy. The image of hanging a picture of Arthur Rimbaud on the lawn mower juxtaposes the romantic decadence of the youthful French poet with the most conventional tool of suburban lawn maintenance. Such an incongruity, Corso implies, parallels the incongruity of the speaker's free spirit entering into orthodox matrimony. That Rimbaud abandoned his poetic vocation at a very young age and became a conventional businessman heightens the irony of the juxtaposition.

The poem progresses through a series of such tensions in which idyllic visions of marriage are quickly countered by nightmarish ones. Similarly, the conventional is repeatedly subverted by the unorthodox. The alternations of this poetic dialectic are reflected in the use of "but" and "yet" to mark the shifts in thought that lead to the rejection of traditional marriage and "goodness" in response to the questions of the opening line. The comic exaggeration and manic intensity of the frequent exclamations—the poem has thirty-five exclamation points—is balanced by certain seriousness. That human companionship must take the form of a surrender to social orthodoxy is a serious problem that Corso wishes to expose.

Both Corso's theme and technique are typical of the Beat movement in literature with which he is associated. The combination of deliberate anticonventionality with language charged with intensity and free association characterizes the work of Corso's contemporaries—Jack Kerouac, Allen Ginsberg, and William Burroughs. Like these writers, Corso reached his maturity in the highly conventional decade of the 1950's and reacted vehemently against the American Dream. The reader sees some of the stylistic consequences of this reaction in the speaker's penchant for disruptive absurdism. Saying "Pie Glue" instead of "I do" at the wedding ceremony, thinking "Flash Gordon soap" in the midst of his interview with his lover's parents, trying to dream of "Telephone snow"—all these forms of linguistic disruption of the expected reflect the Beat desire to shock the reader out of complacency.

The use of free verse and prosaic syntax (even while the content reaches for the bizarre) is also characteristic of Beat poetry. Similarly, the heavy use of allusion and proper nouns works to put the stuff of contemporary culture into the poem. This culture is itself a hodgepodge of old and new: Thus Ingrid Bergman can appear beside Tacitus, Blue Cross beside Bach, the Knights of Columbus beside the Parthenon. Weaving the items of a cultural mishmash into an extended diatribe, Corso taps the energy of his position as a self-appointed subversive in a highly conventional society.

Themes and Meanings

The poem's title and opening questions leave little doubt about the issues central to the work. Corso's approach, though, of considering a social institution in light of competing stereotypes is provocative. The poem implicitly argues that marriage can be more effectively understood through cultural images of it than through abstract considerations of love: "O but what about love! I forget love."

Corso deliberately focuses on rituals and the clichés that surround them, such as meeting the parents ("we're losing a daughter/ but we're gaining a son"), the wedding itself ("And the priest! he looking at me as if I masturbated/ asking me Do you take this woman for your lawful wedded wife?"), and the honeymoon ("all those corny men slapping me on the back/ She's all yours, boy! Ha-ha-ha!"). One may be tempted to dismiss these rituals and cultural clichés as formalities that are finally unimportant to the real issue of two individuals forming a lifelong bond. In "Marriage," however, Corso insists that the clichés reveal much about this culture. The form of the poem argues that clichés and stereotypes shape the actual life choices available to people.

One cannot help but notice how minor a role the wife plays in these imagined scenarios. Indeed, the poem has an egotistical and male bias that is not uncommon in Beat literature and American literature as a whole. The tendency in classic American literature for the male hero to flee from women and marital domesticity into the heroic wilderness runs from Mark Twain's *The Adventures of Huckleberry Finn* (1884) and Herman Melville's *Moby Dick* (1851) to Kerouac's *On the Road* (1957). While "Marriage" is hardly a quest romance as those novels are, it participates in the male rejection of home and marriage as imprisoning. Corso even uses the phrase "pleasant prison dream" to dismiss his final marriage fantasy. The surprising absence of feminist sensibility in a literary movement that celebrates the outsider and values difference is one of the characteristics that makes much of Beat literature seem dated.

Though one may find Corso's comic dismissal of marriage as oppressive conventionality to be a little glib, the poem nevertheless bespeaks a significant anxiety of modern society—that growing up involves a continual sacrifice of individuality and freedom, and that the price of insisting on those qualities is isolation and alienation. As a young man, Corso spent time in prison and (like Ginsberg) in the psychiatric wards of Bellevue Hospital. As "Marriage" shows in its concluding lines, Corso has a keen awareness of the price of not participating in social conventions. "All the universe married but me!" the poet hyperbolically exclaims, and the reader senses the seriousness of human aloneness lurking beneath the lively comic images: "so I wait— bereft of 2,000 years and the bath of life."

Christopher Ames

MARRIAGE

Author: Marianne Moore (1887-1972)
Type of poem: Satire
First published: 1923; collected in *The Complete Poems of Mariane Moore*, 1967

The Poem

   Marriage is relatively long for a non-narrative poem, nearly three hundred lines. The unidentified speaker retains distance from the subject, offering comments as a neutral "one" and as a more personal "I," but depending throughout on a technique characteristic of Marianne Moore: the interpolation of quotations as part of the poem's statement. The general tone is of detached, wry observation.

   The poem opens with a characterization of marriage as either an institution or an enterprise, followed by a query as to what Adam and Eve would think about it. The speaker then extends the Adam and Eve allusion to describe a generic bride and groom. The Eve-bride is characterized by beauty, accomplishment, and contradiction; she upsets the careful rationality of ordered creation with the disturbance of passion. The story of the snake in the garden of paradise is referred to as a convenient exoneration of Adam. The lengthy description of the Adam-groom begins with a vision of Adam in paradise as if depicted in a highly detailed Persian miniature. The speaker goes on to enumerate the man's assertive qualities, which can lead him to overlook the potential dangers of women as he maintains a formal pose, speaking with a specious sense of ownership of public accomplishments and external qualities; eventually, he foolishly begins to believe in his own image, satisfied that he has become an "idol." In the next several lines, he is described as being overcome with passion, against which his rational qualities are helpless, eventually "stumbling" over marriage, which will prove his (literal) downfall.

   At this point, the speaker intervenes with a commentary on "Unhelpfuwl Hymen," the classical god of marriage, characterizing the social institution as a lavish, artificial attempt to re-create lost paradisiacal bliss. The following fifty lines of the poem offer comments on the superficial outward forms of marriage in polite society, with teas, banquets, and social rituals, contrasted with the passionate and even violent reality underneath, in which assault may be called affection and male power may be asserted arbitrarily and destructively.

   The next fifty lines offer alternating commentary from the two partners. The man criticizes women for disappointing men by not always being beautiful; the woman accuses men of being obsessed with trivia. He retorts with a characterization of woman as nothing but a deceptive vessel (a coffin at that), and she replies that men's affections are shallow and inconstant. She accuses him of knowing "so many artists who are fools"; he shoots back that she surrounds herself with "so many fools/ who are not artists." Both individuals are absorbed in self-love: He is oblivious to the existence of other people, and she focuses narcissistically on her appearance. The speaker of the poem then intervenes with another question, asking what can be done for these "savages," and continues the commentary on the mystery of love and commitment, so impenetrable as to seem unreal. A successful marriage as a true union of opposites is rare, the speaker goes on to say; it is a matter of deceptive simplicity and a profound enigma. In the closing lines of the poem, the speaker tries to sum up the essential paradox of a successful marriage in the lines of Daniel Webster, "Liberty and union, now and forever," and offers an emblem of this union in a cryptic allusion to the cliché of the wedding portrait.

Forms and Devices

Marianne Moore's most characteristic poetic device was quotation of passages taken from her wide reading. *Marriage* makes liberal use of this device, drawing upon many sources for its far-flung allusions. An article in *Scientific American*, for example, provides an account of a young woman who writes simultaneously in three languages; *Marriage* incorporates the description into a characterization of the ideal bride as formidably and aggressively accomplished. Anthony Trollope's *Barchester Towers* (1857) provides the quotation commending the age of forty-five to seventy as the best time for a man to marry, sentiments ascribed to the fatuous groom in Moore's poem.

While the sources for her citations are disparate, ranging from scientific reports to women's magazines to the classics, a significant few recur in this poem. Richard Baxter's treatise on Christian doctrine and piety, *The Saints Everlasting Rest* (1649), is the source for four of the passages in *Marriage*. Baxter was an eighteenth century Puritan, and although she respected him as an authoritative spiritual voice, Moore's displacement of his words to an alien context might be seen as satirizing her sources. Thus, she makes Baxter's enumeration of the comprehensiveness of God's interest in humans ("past states, the present state," and so forth) into the pompous speech of her self-absorbed, immature Adam-groom. Along with Baxter, the Bible is quoted more than once (Ecclesiastes and Amos), which with the pervasive allusion to the biblical myth of Adam and Eve sets the poet's meditation on marriage firmly within the western Judeo-Christian tradition. The tradition itself, however, forms an object of satire as the poem's speaker pokes fun at this central institution. Also, Moore draws on more varied and secular sources, which counterpoint the religious sources: William Godwin (agnostic philosopher) and M. Carey Thomas (feminist educator) also provide citations, as do William Hazlitt and Francis Bacon.

Moore's method of developing her argument in *Marriage* is highly allusive and associational. The reader is expected to absorb allusions to Adam and Eve, Hymen, Ahasuerus (the so-called Wandering Jew of European folklore), the garden of the Hesperides (where the golden apples of Greek myth grew), William Shakespeare and a quotation from his play *The Tempest* (1611), and the nineteenth century American senator Daniel Webster. The associations surrounding these allusions, like the focus on a wedding masque in *The Tempest* in which the goddess Hymen appears, are expected to become part of the radiating meanings of the poem. The method also combines extremely abstract and analytic language with an intense pictorial sense. The narcissistic bride, for example, sees herself as "a statuette of ivory on ivory," a highly vivid image conveying the illusive fragility, purity, subtlety, and value of the art object. The icon of bride-as-statuette is followed by a sententiously precise abstract motto: "one is not rich but poor/ when one can always seem so right."

Themes and Meanings

While *Marriage* is a satirical poem, the object of its satire is elusive and ambiguous. At some points, marriage itself seems to be satirized as a romantic delusion. Given the author's orthodox and conservative Christian belief, however, such an interpretation has limited persuasiveness. Rather, her witty barbs seem aimed more at the incrustations of artificial forms and manners that have obscured the elemental passionate union, and equally at the deceptions and misrepresentations made in the name of marriage. When love comes into the discussion, it is either as infatuate fixation, as in the passage from Trollope on "love that will gaze an eagle blind," or the mutual narcissism of the self-absorbed couple. Finally, the speaker admits to an inadequacy of rational explanation in, characteristically, another cited passage, this one from French fabulist Jean de La Fontaine: "Everything to do with love is a mystery." The true paradox is the institution of marriage as a combination of public contractual obligation and intimate, emotional experience.

The contrast between the public, social façade of marriage and the internal emotional dynamics of a love relationship emerges most forcefully in the dialogue between man and woman that the speaker reports in the last half of the poem. This exchange is actually a series of alternating pronouncements rather than a true dialogue, as the two principals actually speak to each other only at one point. The promiscuity ascribed to males is imagined in the butterfly proposing, in a pun within a pun, to "settle on the hand" of the young woman. The natural freedom of the insect is associated with the libertinism of artists and contrasted with the boring philistinism of so-called polite society, which was earlier defined in the religious dedication to the superficial social ritual of afternoon tea (in a quotation from an aristocratic Frenchwoman writing in a women's magazine).

As with most social satire, *Marriage* is in many respects a topical poem. Besides understanding the literary, historical, and mythological allusions, the reader should have some acquaintance with the customs and forms of the society being depicted, and even with the personal lives of some of the sources cited. The butterfly quotation alludes to the marriage proposal made by Ezra Pound to Hilda Doolittle (better known as H. D.), which was reportedly opposed by her father in the words quoted. Similarly, the milieu of the drawing room and the afternoon "at home," no less than the formal studio portrait of the wedding couple, are integral to the poem's statement. Understanding these elements, like those of the poem's social context, enriches the reader's experience of the poem's philosophical statement.

Helen Jaskoski

THE MARSHES OF GLYNN

Author: Sidney Lanier (1842-1881)
Type of poem: Lyric
First published: 1878, in *A Mask of Poets* (edited by George Parsons Lathrop); collected in *Poems of Sidney Lanier,* 1884

The Poem

"The Marshes of Glynn," consisting of 105 lines, is considered Sidney Lanier's best long poem. In this poem, he experiments with new rhythms in opposition to the old, established meters of the poetry of his time. Using a form of logaoedic verse, Lanier freely employs iambs, anapests, and dactyls as well as a wide range of patterns from rhyming couplets to single-syllable lines to achieve the desired effect. Because of his interest in both poetry and music, Lanier explores the relationship between these two disciplines in this poem. Consequently, "The Marshes of Glynn" is arranged almost orchestrally, with the elements introduced and arranged much as instruments in a symphony perform together for maximum effect.

"The Marshes of Glynn" follows its first-person narrator from the edge of the marsh into its lush and mysterious depths. Lanier's use of long, flowing sentences filled with alliteration and assonance gives a sense of lushness to the setting his narrator inhabits. As the narrator contemplates life on the outskirts of the marshes, he is inexplicably drawn "To the edge of the wood// to the forest-dark." However, the edge of the marsh, though attractive during the "noon-day sun," is not enough to satisfy the seeking narrator. He has been content to spend the daylight hours on the edge of the wood, but, as twilight approaches, he recognizes the beauty of the "sand-beach" to the east and finally acknowledges his desire to enter the marshes.

As he enters the heart of the marshes, the narrator notes the features of life near the sea and considers their beauty. Any fear he has felt about approaching the depths of the marshes disappears when he enters the wood and sees that it has been touched with the "reverent hand" of the "Lord of the land." When he sees "what is abroad in the marsh and the terminal sea," he realizes that his "soul seems suddenly free." It is while contemplating this simplicity and the freedom of the marshes that he first sees the marshhen and decides that, like her, he will build his "nest on the greatness of God."

As the narrator contemplates the meaning of life in the marshes, night falls and the tide rushes in. With lush and descriptive language, Lanier describes the swamp at night—the fullness and the quiet—as a place of both ecstasy and uncertainty. While the sea overwhelms the land of the marshes with the "waters of sleep," the narrator reflects on what is going on underneath the surface. Envisioning the "souls of men" under these powerful, enveloping waters, he wishes that he could understand all that is under the tide that now covers the beautiful marshland he has discovered. However, all he can do is acknowledge that though he has come into the heart of the marsh and experienced it directly, it is not possible to completely understand it.

Forms and Devices

Lanier's interest in music is effectively illustrated in "The Marshes of Glynn" through the use of alliteration and assonance as well as through the use of long and flowing sentences to describe the marshlands. In contrast, Lanier also uses short phrases to illustrate the musical aspect of his poetry (for example, the double rhyme and flowing rhythm of the lines "Emerald twilights,—/ Virginal shy lights"). The use of strong, repeated stresses to illustrate the importance of what is being said has the effect of slowing the pace of the poem, while other lines move it forward using shorter, fast-paced dactyls. Throughout the poem, these rhythms work with the poem's internal rhymes and easy flow of words and phrases to create a sense of ebb and flow that emphasizes the musical quality of the work.

Another important aspect of "The Marshes of Glynn" is Lanier's rich use of metaphor and imagery. For Lanier, the woods symbolize the kind of paradise inhabited by God. As the narrator nears the woods, he feels a sense of fear and awe common when approaching God. In addition, Lanier describes this paradise by using language suggesting religious imagery: "Closets of lone desire" and "cells for the passionate pleasure of prayer" suggest cloisters or monasteries and thus the kind of reverence and holiness reserved for God and His holy places. When Lanier writes, "I will fly in the greatness of God as the marsh-hen flies," he equates the marsh-hen with the superiority of God and nature. However, the hen also represents the narrator and his intentions—"As the marsh-hen secretly builds on the watery sod,/ Behold I will build me a nest on the greatness of God." The narrator sees in the marsh-hen a way to live life in relation to God's greatness. Similarly, Lanier uses the sea as a dual image. Again, the sea symbolizes God, who is "Here and there,/ Everywhere." At the same time, the waters of the sea eventually flood the marshland with the "waters of sleep," the tide and its flooding symbolizing both God, who overcomes humanity with His nature, and death, which covers everyone with its "sleep."

Themes and Meanings

"The Marshes of Glynn" is dense with religious imagery and meaning. By entering the woods, the narrator is cleansed from his former world outside the marsh and acquires faith, which leads him to a union with the marsh and thus God's greatness. In observing and considering the marsh and all that is in it, he reaches that point where he can begin to understand—though not fully—the true meaning of this newfound faith. "The Marshes of Glynn" is also a poem about journeys. It examines both the narrator's search to understand self and his spiritual progress toward a union with God and nature. First, Lanier explores humankind's journey into the dark depths of self. The poem follows its narrator from the very edge of self-knowledge—the woods—to the depths of the narrator's questioning soul—the marsh—to discover that self-knowledge is not really possible. The poem also illustrates another kind of journey—the universal search for God and the ultimate truth of life through nature. The narrator desires to "fly in the greatness of God." By the poem's end, he has discovered that "from the Vast of the Lord will the waters of sleep/ Roll in on the souls of men." In this case, the sea represents God, whose tide envelops the marshes or the human soul. As in the narrator's search for self, he discovers that true knowledge of God and nature is impossible. In both cases, it is during the night in the marshes that the narrator comes to terms with the unknowable and, though it is unknowable, nevertheless gains peace.

The narrator's journey begins at "noon-day." At first, it is a journey of fear and hesitancy. This person does not want to leave the warmth of the comfortable world outside the "dim sweet woods." By twilight, however, he has left behind the comfort he has felt during the day and is drawn by these "dear dark woods" into the midst of all he fears. The unknown presents him with a land beyond his expectations, and he soon comes to prefer the freedom he discovers within the "world of marsh that borders a world of sea." Ultimately, he must face the night and the tide. Once again, faced with the unknown and unknowable, he must come to terms with the meaning of human existence: "But who will reveal to our waking ken/ The forms that swim and the shapes that creep/ Under the waters of sleep?" Though the narrator never finds the answer to this question, he accepts both this lack of knowledge and, ultimately, the inevitability of death. Like Lanier, the narrator searches for God's ultimate truth through nature and finds a peace that, though couched in uncertainty, is an answer he can accept.

Kimberley H. Kidd

THE MASK OF ANARCHY

Author: Percy Bysshe Shelley (1792-1822)
Type of poem: Ballad
First published: 1832

The Poem

The Mask of Anarchy, a ballad of ninety-one stanzas, was inspired by the "Peterloo Massacre" in Manchester, England. On August 16, 1819, several thousand people gathered in St. Peter's Fields to hear the orator Henry Hunt speak in favor of reform in the English government. The assembly was broken up violently by militia and cavalry, who attempted to arrest Hunt. At least ten people were killed and hundreds injured.

The first stanza tells how news of the massacre led the sleeping Percy Bysshe Shelley "To walk in the visions of Poesy"; the images he envisions within his poetic imagination are essentially a reenactment of "Peterloo," with a happy ending. The first twenty stanzas offer a hideous parade in which the sins of government hide behind the likenesses of individual politicians of the day. The poem's title is therefore a pun both on "mask," to conceal one's identity, and on "masque," a dramatic form of entertainment based on an allegorical theme. Murder "had a mask like Castlereagh," Robert Stewart Castlereagh, the Foreign Secretary who often introduced unpopular repressive measures in Parliament. Fraud bears the mask of Lord Chancellor John Scott Eldon, the judge who took two of Shelley's children away from him. Hypocrisy bears the likeness of Lord Sidmouth (Henry Addington), Home Secretary in the Tory Government. Other horrible beings follow, "All disguised, . . ./ Like Bishops, lawyers, peers, and spies."

Last in the procession is Anarchy himself, a symbol for the English government. He claims: "I am God, and King, and Law!" Anarchy's "white horse" is "splashed with blood," reminiscent of the Death that rode a pale horse in Revelation. He is followed by "hired murderers," loyal bloodthirsty soldiers whom Shelley associates with those who took part in the killings at "Peterloo."

The macabre masquerade spells doom for the oppressed. Thus, Hope is described as a "maniac maid" resembling "Despair." She rushes by the procession, proclaims her "Misery, oh, Misery!" and lies on the ground before Anarchy, resigned to a dismal fate. Then an ambiguous "Shape" emerges, causing Anarchy to flee and to trample his followers to death. This entity brings with it "A sense awakening and yet tender" that brings the people hope. A mysterious voice is heard, like the cry of the "indignant Earth," nature itself.

The impassioned speech made by this voice takes up the final stanzas of the poem. The speech is a cry from freedom, urging the oppressed to "Rise like Lions . . ." and to "Shake your chains to earth like dew." The first part of the speech paints a poignant picture of the dismal plight of the working class caused by despotism. Next the concept of freedom is discussed. To the common laborer, freedom means simply the food and shelter that are denied under tyranny. Freedom is synonymous with justice, wisdom, peace, and love. In the name of freedom, the oppressed from all across the country are urged to unite in a great "Assembly" to demand reform. Shelley suggests a nonviolent struggle: "Stand ye calm and resolute." The great potential within the united numbers of the oppressed is expressed in the final words of the speech: "Ye are many—they are few."

Forms and Devices

Shelley wrote *The Mask of Anarchy* to appeal to the working class. He avoided any overly sophisticated or difficult poetic techniques that might have made the poem inaccessible to an uneducated audience. This lack of sophisticated technique should not be viewed as a weakness. The poem's relatively simple language, structure, rhythm, and metaphors enhance its direct and vigorous message of liberty.

Structurally, the poem follows standard convention in the use and arrangement of stanzas. Each of the ninety-one stanzas has four lines, except for eight five-line stanzas scattered throughout, used in times of particular emphasis (for example, when the voice calls for those assembled to "Rise like Lions . . ." in stanza 38). The stanzas are arranged in an uncomplicated plot structure. The first twenty-one stanzas describe the procession. The next fifteen stanzas include Hope's desperate act, which provides the conflict and makes way for the entrance of the "Shape" and the voice. The remaining fifty-five stanzas make up the speech of freedom. Within this plot structure, the tendency is toward symmetry. After the introductory stanza establishing Shelley's dream, the descriptions of Murder, Fraud, Hypocrisy, and Anarchy receive two stanzas each. The following twelve stanzas that describe the horrible masquerade are balanced by the twelve stanzas (excluding the two on Hope) devoted to the mysterious, yet hopeful, "Shape." Within the final speech, thirteen stanzas portraying the slave-like conditions of the working class are balanced by thirteen stanzas describing freedom.

The poem's rhythm and rhyme are that of street balladry, a form accessible and familiar to the working class. The poem's prosody makes various stanzas easy to remember, like a well-worn song. Most of the stanzas consist of seven syllables per line of trochaic rhythm, a heavy stress followed by a light stress: "*I* met *Mur*der *on* the *way*—" (stressed syllables in italics). At times this meter varies to include lines of eight or ten syllables, but this rarely jars the rhythmic ease of the poem.

The simple rhyme scheme facilitates the rhythm's smooth beat. The four-line stanzas usually follow an *aabb* pattern, while the five-line stanzas follow *aabbb*. Frequently the scheme is even simpler in that all line-ending words within the stanza rhyme (for example, stanza 42 with "weak," "peak," "bleak," "speak"). Most of the rhymes are one syllable ("fly," "sky") with an occasional two-syllable rhyming couplet ("waken," "shaken") to make the poem even more musical.

Shelley is known for his elaborate metaphors and obscure allusions, but in *The Mask of Anarchy* he rejects such complex artifice and offers simpler, more familiar images and references to suit his poor, uneducated audience. Most of Shelley's readers would have recognized the allusion to Revelation in describing Anarchy as "Like Death in the Apocalypse." Similarly, the "Shape" who is "Brighter than the viper's scale" alludes to the snake, a well-known symbol of resistance to oppression. Throughout the poem, Shelley uses symbols and metaphors of oppression and liberty familiar to the common people of the day.

Themes and Meanings

Shelley's emotionally polemic poem is intended to further the cause of governmental reform, an issue that was dividing England at the time. Some of the reform efforts Shelley advocated were expanded suffrage and greater freedom of speech, press, and assembly. The poem supports these causes by metaphorically elaborating on the concepts of tyranny and liberty, describing the effects of each in concrete, poignant images. In simple yet searing language the poem vehemently denounces tyranny as exploitative and as going against the very laws of nature. Liberty, however, is a God-given right of every person. Living by the precepts of liberty will ensure a happier, more fruitful existence.

Liberty is seen in concrete and practical terms. The poem avoids any abstraction that would make freedom seem unrealistic and overly idealistic, a "superstition" doomed "soon to pass away." On the contrary, freedom is ". . . bread,/ and a comely table spread." It provides for the very necessities of life, clothing and food, things denied under tyranny.

Freedom is also associated with justice, providing for "righteous laws" that would forbid the kind of exploitation allowed by tyranny. Here one can see that Shelley did not advocate lawless revolution. Liberty does not mean the freedom to ignore law, but the establishment of equitable law. Lawlessness would be no improvement over tyranny. In fact, the masquerade of tyrants and the poem's title itself show that Shelley equates tyranny with anarchy. Tyranny creates gross inequities that will inevitably cause revolution and anarchy. Shelley warns of this by reminding the reader of France ("Gaul" in stanza 59), where injustice led to bloody revolution and to a more malevolent tyranny under Napoleon. Thus, as the poem states, liberty "Thou art Peace . . ." Blood would never be shed if governments functioned based on the true precepts of liberty.

This adherence to law is seen in Shelley's concept of the assembly and what they should do. This assembly, made up of the oppressed throughout England, is symbolic of the power of numbers against a lesser foe: "Ye are many—they are few." Shelley advocates a kind of passive resistance. The members of the assembly are to stand strong and resolute, "With folded arms and steady eyes," in the face of the enemy. They should allow the tyrants to "Slash, and stab, and maim, and hew,—" without retaliating or making any attempt to defend themselves. This should shame the enemy into defeat; some ("true warriors") will even join the protesters in their resistance. This is not a call for violent revolution or bloody revenge, but a plea for "righteous law" as suits the wisdom and reason of liberty.

In contrast, the consequences of tyranny are violence and suffering. This is seen in the bloodthirsty characters of the masquerade who knock out the brains of children and trample their subjects into a "mire of blood." The effect of tyranny on the working class is slavery, poignantly described in the first section of liberty's speech. Shelley created such a horrifying vision of tyranny that its antithesis—liberty—seems society's only legitimate haven.

Heidi Kelchner

MASKS

Author: Sonia Sanchez (Wilsonia Driver, 1934-   )
Type of poem: Lyric
First published: 1984, in *Homegirls and Handgrenades*

The Poem

"Masks" is a poem of forty mostly short, free-verse lines about the struggle African Americans face in defining themselves. The masks to which the title refers are not only those that blacks in America have adopted to protect themselves but also those that have been forced upon them.

The critic Houston Baker, Jr., sees two primary voices present in Sonia Sanchez's poetry. She has what he calls a "Greenwich Village/E. E. Cummings" voice, marked by a personal tone and a loud, confrontational voice that seems to explore the revolutionary edges of what a black aesthetic might be. "Masks" integrates these two sides of the poet and comes up with something new: It has the reflective nature of some of Sanchez's quieter poetry, but it also has a directly confrontational stance. Further, its images have an almost mystical quality distinct from the very direct quality of the images of many of her earlier poems.

The poem shows a willingness to be confrontational in its epigraph: "Blacks don't have the intellectual capacity to succeed," Sanchez quotes William Coors, chairman of Coors Brewing Company, which, in the early 1980's, when the poem was written, had been accused of unfair hiring and labor practices by the American Federation of Labor-Congress of Industrial Organizations. The implication is that such racist beliefs are both the cause and effect of living behind socially stereotyped masks.

The first stanza begins with images of rivers and lakes, imagery which by itself might suggest life and renewal. The lakes, however, are patrolled "by one-eyed pimps/ who wash their feet in our blue whoredom." This line suggests the images of African Americans as pimps and hookers that were popular in action films and television shows when Sanchez wrote this poem. Following the epigraph, the "pimps" in question might also be industrialists who are willing to hire blacks only for low-paying jobs, in effect making black people who work for them into "whores."

The second stanza talks about black people waiting for the right season "to change our masks"—not to take off masks, but simply to change them. Later in the poem, the narrator mentions hearing an "unhurried speaker" in a temple talk of "unveiled eyes." The need to "unveil" eyes speaks of the need to take the masks off completely. That the speaker is "unhurried" may suggest a lack of urgency. The message makes the narrator of the poem sit up straight and tall, but this spirit of rejoicing slowly sinks into a "twilight of/ distant smells," perhaps the smell of the drying blood on the masks mentioned in the unrhyming couplet which follows.

The "fee, fie, fo, fum" quote from the story "Jack the Giant Killer" has at least a double meaning. On one hand, the poetic narrator identifies with the trickster, Jack, whose blood is threatened by a ruling giant and who, in some versions of the story, hides from the giant in a cloak of darkness. On the other hand, Jack eventually defeats the giant. As quoted in this poem, these lines seem to offer a possible hope that those who consider themselves ruling "giants" will one day be toppled. Within the context of the poem, however, this hope might be read by some as having a hollow ring to it, and the implied threat may be seen as simply another mask.

The next stanza returns to pessimism. "O my people/ wear the white masks," the poem says, meaning that blacks live out roles defined by white society. The reference to speaking "without speaking" indicates the impotence of language spoken from behind such masks, and the "words of forgetfulness" blacks hear are the words that do not acknowledge the damages caused by the ongoing history of racial oppression. The final line, "o my people," is a statement of love and connection, but also of lament and sorrow.

Forms and Devices

The imagery that begins the poem—of water running, of a river flooding, of days growing short (as in the autumn), and of waiting for days to grow warm again—are images of natural life in motion. Sanchez uses this imagery to call attention to the stasis of waiting for the right season "to change our masks" and never finding the right one to abandon the masks.

"Our days are edifice," she says, conjuring a powerful metaphor of days that are like imposing, unchanging buildings. The poem goes inside such a building, a temple, where the narrator hears hopeful words of the possibility of change—specifically of the possibility of taking off the masks that blacks have to wear to adapt to white society. The spirit of change sinks, however, as if into a twilight.

The appearance of the story of "Jack the Giant Killer" has a certain connection to the "one-eyed pimps" mentioned near the beginning. The "one-eye" suggests a Cyclops, perhaps the Cyclops who patrolled an island on which Odysseus and his crew landed in Homer's *Odyssey* (c. 800 B.C.E.). The story is relevant in that the Cyclops spills the blood of, and eats, many members of Odysseus's crew. Odysseus and his remaining crew escape by disguising (or masking) themselves as sheep, after having bloodied and blinded, but not killed, the giant Cyclops. Like the story of Jack and the beanstalk, this poem contains the possibility that a tricky, less powerful person can overcome a larger, more powerful one.

This poem, however, has a pessimistic view of the ultimate consequences of relying on such masking. The danger, the poem warns, is that it is hard to take off a mask that one has used for protection. This comes through especially in the three short, unrhyming couplets. The calls in each case to bring the mask have an almost ritualistic feel, as if donning this mask, which is associated with whiteness and blood, is part of a regularly recurring rite. That these three couplets are set aside on the page, interrupting several stanzas about a speaker in a temple, also contributes to the impression that donning this mask is a distorted and unfortunate ritual.

Themes and Meanings

The story of Odysseus and the Cyclops bears an interesting relationship to this poem. What Sanchez sees happening to African Americans is analogous to the plight of Odysseus and his men, who are never able to take off their sheep's clothing.

"Masks" invites direct comparison to Paul Laurence Dunbar's "We Wear the Mask," written eighty-eight years earlier. Dunbar's poem talks of wearing the mask "that grins and lies" and "hides our cheeks and shades our eyes." Dunbar sees wearing a mask as an essentially effective defensive strategy, but one with a cost.

Sanchez's poem focuses on the cost. Once masks are worn, they stay on. As she implies at the beginning of the poem, seasons change, but the time for taking off the masks never arrives. The need to look at the world directly is understood, but still the masks are donned. The mask changes not only the way one is seen but also the way one sees.

Such masks are ultimately ways for people who are black to live in a white society. As such, they are "white" masks, "chalk" masks, masks that draw the blood of the wearer because they do not let even the wearer of the mask see himself or herself clearly. The result is that people "speak without speaking," meaning that they let the mask do the speaking for them.

The final cost is seen in statements such as the racist statement made by William Coors that Sanchez uses to begin the poem. Masks are used as Dunbar's poem makes clear, to hide one's true thoughts from such a potentially antagonistic person. It is easy for such a person to see only what he or she wants to see or is willing to see of the people behind the masks.

It would not have been out of character for Sonia Sanchez to write an angry and compelling diatribe in response to the statement by William Coors. What she wrote instead is a meditative, and to an extent mournful, account of the pain of living behind masks and the need, but also the difficulty, of removing such masks.

Thomas J. Cassidy

MEDITATION ON A MEMOIR

Author: J. V. Cunningham (1911-1985)
Type of poem: Meditation
First published: 1945; collected in *The Judge Is Fury,* 1947

The Poem

"Meditation on a Memoir" is a brief poem of sixteen lines that are arranged in four stanzas of four lines each. The meter is iambic dimeter, a very short and unusual metrical line. The first stanza contains three questions, the next two stanzas respond to those questions, and the final stanza resolves the poem with another question. The title announces both the approach (meditation) and the subject (memoir). To meditate is to think deeply on the significance of a subject, and it is not the usual poetic mode in J. V. Cunningham's work. "Memoir" is a word that Cunningham uses a number of times in his poetry, and it requires some commentary. For Cunningham, a memoir is the revelation of all of the intimate details in a person's life. Another poem by Cunningham, "Memoir," makes clear what type of revelations are involved: "Now that he's famous fame will not elude me:/ For $14.95 read how he screwed me." The first line of "Meditation on a Memoir" immediately calls such revelations into question: "Who knows his will?" Does anyone truly know himself or herself well enough to reveal all in a memoir?

The second stanza continues to undermine the claim that anyone can know his or her "will" well enough to confess all in a memoir. People's lives consist of the "Surf of illusion," and they can find peace in sleep only by "skilled delusion." This is framed syntactically as an answer to the questions of the first stanza. "Illusion" and "delusion" seem closely related to each other, but they make up two very different worlds: awareness and sleep. Both of these are guided or determined by the error of illusion or willed delusion. Therefore, one cannot truly know one's own will; any pretense to knowledge is mere illusion.

The third stanza shifts the perspective from the questioning speaker to an observer of the inner life of the memoir writer. At that moment, "silence hears/ In its delight/ The tide of tears/ In the salt night." One reveals one's inner self not in the words of a memoir but in the "silence" where "the tide of tears" is released. This is in direct opposition to the illusion and delusion of stanza 2. Silence is delighted by the breaking of illusion into the inevitable tears. Silence is also the opposite of the audience that is hungry for the truth of a person's life that a memoir represents.

The last stanza completes the poem by coming back to the questions with which it began. The questions are the appropriate answer to the pretense of self-knowledge that a memoir assumes. Now, after piercing the "skilled delusion" that protects such false knowledge and having heard the tears, the speaker announces the final estimation: "Who knows what themes,/ What lunar senses,/ Compel his dreams?" The dreams and themes that make up a memoir are controlled not by the self but by a tidal and lunar force. The dreams that are supposed to be the most personal part of an individual are not one's own; rather, they are compelled and controlled. The poem attacks the Romantic assurance of self-revelation and calls self-knowledge into question.

Forms and Devices

The poem is unusual in its use of very regular iambic dimeter. The effects of such a short poetic line are significant. The short and regular lines are gnomic and epigrammatic as they sort out large and general principles in human affairs. In addition, the lines in the first and last stanzas are end-stopped, while those of the second and third stanzas are run on. This follows the syntactic form of question and answer. The rhymes of the poem are also of interest. The rhymes of the first stanza promise certainty, as "will" is related to "fulfill" and "mood" to "conclude." The rhymes of the second stanza undo any claim to completion in the conjunction of "illusion" and "delusion." In addition, the subjects of a memoir are paired in the rhyme of "themes" and "dreams."

Cunningham often uses personification in his poems. Here "silence" is portrayed as a human figure who listens with "delight" to the tears that are released. Cunningham tends to use personification rather than images, since the poems deal with general principles instead of particular occurrences. However, there are a few images in the poem. For example, in the second stanza, the image of surf suggests a swirling of illusion that destroys any stability. However, surf that "Spins from the deep" is connected to a sustained metaphor that controls the structure of the poem: the moon that controls the tides of all of the oceans and seas. The movement of the moon controls the "tide of tears" and the surf of the second stanza. Humankind is tossed about by some unknown, greater power just as the seas are tossed about by the moon. The question of the first line of the poem is answered by the metaphor that concludes the poem: "What lunar senses,/ Compel his dreams?" People do not control or know their wills; their themes are only dreams and they are compelled by something other than human will. The pride of people in both knowing and revealing their wills is reduced at the end to a creature who is moved back and forth at the will or whim of another uncontrollable force.

Themes and Meanings

There are a number of significant themes in "Meditation on a Memoir." First, the memoir is a common theme for Cunningham. In "To a Student," he distinguishes memoirs from fiction: "Fiction is fiction: its one theme/ Is its allegiance to its scheme./ Memoir is memoir: there your heart/ Awaits the judgment of your heart." Fiction is an imaginative creation that is true to its "scheme" or art. Memoirs subordinate art and design to one's "heart." Fiction is a classical form, while a memoir is a Romantic form.

Will is another important theme. Cunningham uses will in the Shakespearean sense: It represents people's untrammeled desires that must be controlled by reason and conscience. Cunningham wrote a critical essay on a phrase by Hamlet to his mother: "Reason panders wills." In this example, reason should guide but instead gives license to the will to act. It is clearly an important theme to Cunningham as a Shakespearean scholar and a poet. The average reader may not realize what is at stake with the seemingly innocent first line: "Who knows his will?" Cunningham has a classical perspective on art and morality; the will should be controlled rather than exercised or revealed.

The controlling metaphor of the poem is also directly related to the theme. The poem begins by questioning people's abilities to know and then reveal their wills and moves to an obliteration of any control by them. They are tossed around at the will of a greater power that they are not even aware of, the "lunar senses" that "compel" their dreams. Cunningham seems to use "senses" in this passage in a very precise way. Once again it is a personification: The lunar force acts out of its own instinctual senses and, therefore, negates the will of humankind. The use of silence in the third stanza is another thematic reversal. Silence is filled with "delight" to hear people break down and reveal their tears. This contrasts to the earlier claim to will and fulfillment. There is none of that now, only frustrated tears that are heard by silence rather than published in the revealing words of memoirs.

Humankind's dreams and themes also have thematic implications. One's dreams are not one's own but are determined and controlled by the "lunar senses." The themes expected in a memoir are not one's own but are compelled by an outside force. The end result is a mockery of any pretense to a true memoir. Most of the poems of J. V. Cunningham are very brief, and "Meditation on a Memoir" is a more detailed and expansive poem than Cunningham's usual epigrams. It is a poem that deals with philosophical as well as aesthetic issues. People's claims to be transcendent beings who are in control of their destinies or even their concepts of themselves and their wills are undermined, and a memoir is seen as either an illegitimate or impossible form or art.

James Sullivan

MEETING AT NIGHT

Author: Robert Browning (1812-1889)
Type of poem: Lyric
First published: 1845, as "Night and Morning," in *Bells and Pomegranates, No. VII: Dramatic Romances and Lyrics*; as "Meeting at Night," in *Poems*, 1849

The Poem

"Meeting at Night" is a short poem divided into two parts, each consisting of a single six-line stanza. The poem was originally entitled "Night and Morning" and included a third stanza that described the speaker's departure; Browning later separated the concluding stanza and retitled the two poems "Meeting at Night" and "Parting at Morning." Although "Meeting at Night" is written in the first person, Browning rarely directly identified himself with his speakers. When asked about this poem and "Parting at Morning," Browning indicated that the poems' speaker was male.

As the title suggests, "Meeting at Night" describes the speaker's nighttime journey to meet his lover. The poem focuses on the speaker's anticipation of the meeting and the stages of his journey. Although by the poem's end the purpose of the journey is made clear to the reader, the speaker does not explain where he is going or why and never gives any details about his relationship with the person he is meeting. Given that the meeting takes place at night and at a remote location, it may be an illicit rendezvous.

In the first stanza, Browning takes advantage of the nighttime setting to create a contrast between the energetic speaker and the inert and featureless landscape. The reader is not provided with a narrative but is offered a series of images and details that suggest the speaker's state of mind. The speaker, who is traveling by boat, begins by presenting a spare, camera-like representation of the sea, sky, and land. In the first two lines the speaker's minimalist descriptions of the "grey sea," "long black land," and "yellow half-moon" emphasize the darkness of the night, which makes it difficult for the speaker to see what is around him. At the same time, the speaker's response indicates that he is not interested in his surroundings but is instead focused on arriving at his destination. The remainder of the stanza emphasizes the speaker's eagerness to reach land. The effect of the speaker's vigorous rowing on the water is conveyed through a vivid metaphor in which "startled little waves" form "fiery ringlets" as they are awakened from "sleep." Browning allows the speaker's personification of the waves to parallel and foreshadow the end of the second part of the poem, in which the speaker is reunited with (and perhaps awakens) his lover. The speaker's lover is thus identified with nature (the waves). The link between the speaker's lover and the natural world is also important in the last lines of the poem, in which the image of the boat's "pushing prow" coming to rest in the "slushy sand" takes on sexual overtones. By the end of the first stanza, the male speaker is identified as active and dominant over nature, which is identified as passive and female.

In the second stanza, readers learn that the speaker's journey is by no means over: He must still walk a mile on the beach and cross three fields before he will arrive at his lover's farm. The first stanza's pattern of moving toward and finally arriving at a destination is thus repeated. Since the speaker is still traveling in darkness, his description of his reunion with his lover is related almost entirely through his sense of sound: his tap at the window, the sound of his lover striking a match, the sound of a voice, and in the last line, the sound of their two hearts beating. The sounds the speaker relates are in themselves commonplace, but here they take on intense meaning and enhance the mystery and excitement of the speaker's reunion. When the speaker's lover lights the match, one realizes that the darkness of the speaker's journey is finally over, both in the literal and the figurative sense. The poem ends with the speaker's implied claim that the lovers' reunion is a kind of epiphany that blots out the "joys and fears" of everyday life.

Forms and Devices

The poem is written in iambic tetrameter, but many of the lines include anapestic feet that hurry its pace. Browning's use of a traditional yet somewhat irregular meter seems appropriate for this speaker, who is both in control and in a hurry. Browning uses the rhyme scheme to insert a subtle contradiction of the poem's implicit assertion that love is the speaker's ultimate goal. Each stanza follows the same pattern: *abccba*. In this rhyme scheme, the last three lines (*cba*) reverse the sequence of the first three (*abc*), and the last line rhymes with the first. Thus, while each stanza moves forward toward a goal (the beach, the lover), the rhyme scheme moves backward, signalling that the speaker cannot remain with his lover indefinitely.

As indicated above, Browning also uses imagery and figurative language to convey the speaker's situation and attitude. The poem's opening lines present the bleak and almost colorless setting of the speaker's journey: "grey" sea, "black" land, and a "yellow" half-moon. The poem's tone seems to shift when the speaker personifies the waves, which "leap" to form "fiery ringlets": Suddenly the water is full of motion and color, but only in response to the speaker's actions and preoccupations. The speaker's first use of "I" takes place in the fifth line—"I gain the cove"—as if to reinforce the notion that he is in control of his environment. Browning uses personification not to enhance the role of nature in the poem but to emphasize the speaker's sense of dominance.

In the second part of the poem, Browning's images shift as the speaker reaches land and nears his goal. Although a mile of beach still separates him from his lover, the beach, unlike the bleak and cold water, is "warm" and "sea-scented." As discussed earlier, the imagery from this point on is predominantly aural, with the exception of the "blue spurt" of the match. The flash of light recalls the "fiery" appearance of the waves in the first stanza and strengthens the connection between the waves and the speaker's lover.

At the end of the poem, the speaker uses figurative language again, this time hyperbole, when he claims that the lovers' hearts are louder than a human voice; at the same time he downplays the importance of the "voice" and its "joys and fears" by not telling readers whose voice it is (it could be his or his lover's). The speaker's hyperbole attempts to bestow permanence upon the ecstatic moment, in which the heart, emotion, and union take precedence over the head, reason, and separation.

Themes and Meanings

The poem both asserts and questions the idea that passionate emotion, especially love, is not only powerful but also enduring and vital. The speaker argues for the power of love by insisting upon his ability to conquer all that separates him from his lover. Time, distance, and even the lovers' "joys and fears" cannot stand in his way and are not important once the two are together. Displaying characteristic Victorian optimism, the speaker believes firmly in his ability to achieve his goals and ends the poem at the precise moment when he has done so.

At the same time, the speaker's own words amply demonstrate the difficulty of attaining the kind of experience that he exalts. Most of the poem's few lines are devoted to recounting the distance that the speaker must travel and the obstacles he must overcome. The fact that the speaker must travel a considerable distance to reach his lover's farm is especially important. The speaker says nothing about his day-to-day life, but he obviously lives far from the rural setting that his lover inhabits. The physical distance between the lovers points to other ways in which they, as a man and a woman, are different and irrevocably separate. Both before and after marriage, Victorian men and women lived within separate social spheres; men were increasingly called upon to identify themselves with work and with the world outside the home, while women were encouraged to participate primarily in domestic activities and to nurture the emotional and spiritual life of the family. It is therefore significant that the meeting takes place within the female lover's home, because the experience itself is nonrational and belongs within the domestic and private women's sphere.

The speaker must eventually leave the farm, along with the realm of female experience and emotion, to return to the male world (which he does in the four-line "Parting at Morning"). The journey depicted in "Meeting at Night" is thus in part a journey from the male world to the female; this accounts for the long distance that the speaker must travel and for his need to separate himself from the passivity he associates with nature and the female realm. Although the speaker's intense emotion causes him to represent the moment of reunion as all-powerful, the distance between the speaker and his lover remains, like the distance between the social worlds of men and women, and this distance marks the reunion as a rare and transitory event.

Maura Ives

MEETING-HOUSE HILL

Author: Amy Lowell (1874-1925)
Type of poem: Lyric
First published: 1920; collected in *What's O'Clock*, 1925

The Poem

A short poem in free verse, "Meeting-House Hill" contains a single stanza composed of twenty-five lines. Although the title may be taken literally because Amy Lowell is describing the scene of an actual meeting house at the top of a hill, it also serves as a metaphor for the convergence of two cultures. The poem is written in the first person. As the speaker of the poem, Lowell addresses the reader directly, sharing her experience of observing the beauty of two vividly described scenes, one real and one imagined.

The first fifteen lines focus on the scene immediately before Lowell: the blue bay, the church in the city square, the spire reaching toward the sky. In line 16 this perspective changes as Lowell imagines seeing a clipper ship in the distance. The final nine lines describe the imaginary ship in as much detail as the actual scene that lies before her.

Lowell shows that the simple charm of an ordinary New England church matches the more exotic beauty of a "tea-clipper" returning from China. In so doing she moves the reader from the familiar reality of the meeting house to the imagined enchantment of the ship with its cargo of "green and blue porcelain." Focusing her attention on the ship and the "Chinese coolie" on its deck, she seems to wonder how the church would appear to him as he gazes at it from the ship. As Lowell reflects on the beauty of the two scenes, she shares with the reader the intense emotion she experiences when she perceives the blending of the two cultures into one image of spiritual beauty.

Coming from the wealthy and distinguished Lowell family of New England, Lowell traveled extensively in foreign countries. In contrasting the familiar loveliness of the church with the beauty of a tea-clipper just back from Canton, China, she reveals her fascination with ships and ocean travel and her appreciation for the beauty of foreign scenes. The poem reflects her lifelong interest in the Far East. In collaboration with Florence Ayscough, she published a collection of translations of ancient Chinese poetry, *Fir Flower Tablets*, in 1921. Her work was also influenced by her study of the concise haiku form of Japanese poetry, which is devoted to some aspect of nature. With its visual images, concern with shapes and moods of nature, and suggestion of a divine presence, "Meeting-House Hill" reflects the major qualities of the haiku.

Forms and Devices

In "Meeting-House Hill" Lowell employs a technique that became her trademark: word painting. The visual images provide an impression of reality that approximates the style used by Impressionist painters of the nineteenth century. Impressionist painting was characterized by short brush strokes, bright colors, and the play of light on objects. Lowell provides a word picture of the church through direct observation of the natural elements. Through her powers of intuition she extends the emotional experience to include the depiction of the ship that exists only in her mind.

Alliteration is the poem's most obvious poetic device. Lowell employs a variety of alliterative techniques to achieve a harmonious effect. In the phrases "blue bay beyond" and "shrill and sweet to me like the sudden springing of a tune," repetition of the initial consonant sound occurs in words within the same line. A more subtle form of alliteration occurs in the poem's first three lines, each of which ends with a word beginning with the letter *t:* "I must be mad, or very tired,/ When the curve of a blue bay beyond a railroad track/ Is shrill and sweet to me like the sudden springing of a tune."

In other instances alliteration comes from repetition of initial consonant sounds from previous lines. The following passage, for example, compares the church to the ancient Parthenon of Greece and later refers to the "pillars of its portico": "Amazes my eyes as though it were the Parthenon./ Clear, reticent, superbly final,/ With the pillars of its portico refined to a cautious elegance." Lowell enhances the alliterative effect by repeating the initial *r* sound of "rising" in the second syllable of "unresisting" in "Rising into an unresisting sky." These variations imbue the words with a melodious quality and create a sense of balance in the form of the poem.

Lowell is known as an Imagist, one who stresses clarity and succinctness in presenting poetic images. Sensuous imagery and precise economy of words characterize her poem. In describing the scenes she uses images of color. The whiteness of the church that "amazes" her eyes suggests purity. The green and blue colors of the porcelain in the hold of the imagined ship represent the sea and sky, as well as the beauty of East Asian art. In the phrase "curve of a blue bay," color combines with shape to create a vivid image.

In addition to the sight images, Lowell includes sounds engaging the aural sense and atmospheric images that appeal to the thermal sense. The light, high sounds coming "shrill and sweet" like the "sudden springing of a tune" capture her attention even before she sees the church. Atmospheric images add to the sensory impression. The church spire is "cool," and the ship's sails are "straining before a two-reef breeze."

The poem does not follow a set metrical pattern; instead it intertwines lines as long as sixteen to eighteen syllables with lines of only five to six syllables. Like the brush strokes of an Impressionist painting, short lines containing only one- or two-syllable words strengthen Lowell's imagery.

Themes and Meanings

Lowell was a dominant force in the Imagist movement founded by Ezra Pound. Imagists advocated the use of free verse, concrete images, and concise language. With its realistic sense impressions, simple language, and free-verse form, Lowell's "Meeting-House Hill" typifies Imagist poetry. *What's O'Clock* (1925), a collection of Lowell's best later work and the first volume of her poems published posthumously, was awarded the Pulitzer Prize in poetry in 1926. This volume included "Meeting-House Hill" along with poems about landscapes and seasons, including one of her most famous poems, "Lilacs." The central theme of both poems is the discovery of the unity that lies beneath the surface of diverse forms.

Lowell lived in two worlds. The first included the room from which she wrote and the familiar landmarks and gardens of her New England heritage. The other embraced the culture and poetry of the Far East, with its exotic beauty and serenity. "Meeting-House Hill" expresses the sense of oneness she experienced when images of both worlds met on that hill in New England. By juxtaposing the gritty reality of railroad tracks, a city square, and thin trees with the "clear, reticent, superbly final" Parthenon, Lowell's poem helps the reader see beyond the immediate, everyday world to catch a glimpse of something higher. The contrast is even more obvious when she compares the "pillars of its [the Parthenon's] portico refined to a cautious elegance" with "weak trees" and "a squalid hilltop." Vivid images convey a clear impression of the beauty of a familiar scene, as it suddenly stands out against the sky. Lowell describes the imagined scene in equally brilliant images as she explores the sense of unity represented by two diverse settings.

As Lowell perceives the harmony existing in the beauty of a New England church as well as in the face of a Chinese man on a ship, she describes her physical reactions to show the impact of her vision. She "must be," she writes, "mad, or very tired" when the sight of a church "amazes" her eyes. She feels "dizzy with the movement of the sky." Whether a church in New England, the Parthenon in Greece, or a ship returning from China, a sense of unity transcends the physical limits of one particular place. Her poem is her attempt to share the feeling of harmony she experiences when the diverse images blend.

Judith Barton Williamson

MEETING THE BRITISH

Author: Paul Muldoon (1951-   )
Type of poem: Lyric
First published: 1987, in *Meeting the British*

The Poem

The nine slant-rhymed couplets of "Meeting the British" tell a brief and simple story that encapsulates many elements in the history of the discovery and conquest of America by Europeans. The title sets up the situation of the poem, an encounter between Native Americans and British explorers in the eighteenth century. It is not until the last couplet, however, that one is entirely sure who is speaking and thus who is "meeting the British." This openness requires readers to complete the implications of the poem's details, implications not explicitly discussed in the text.

The speaker of the poem first notes the season and weather when he and his group "met the British": the "dead of winter," with snow-covered earth and sky the same "lavender" color. He remembers being able to hear the convergence of two frozen-over streams and recalls his own surprise at himself "calling out in French" to the European strangers. He then notes not a dramatic confrontation or the details of a high-level encounter but the fact that neither of the two British officers could "stomach" the tobacco used by the speaker's group. The speaker also, however, experienced a new sensation: the "unusual scent" from the handkerchief of the colonel, who explains (in French) that *"C'est la lavande,/ une fleur mauve comme le ciel"* (it is lavender, a flower purple as the sky). The last couplet notes the gifts of the British to the speaker and his people: "six fishhooks/ and two blankets embroidered with smallpox."

Forms and Devices

"Meeting the British" uses motifs and imagery carefully chosen to appeal to several senses to establish the complex web of relationship and difference, communication and missed communication, that the poem asserts is the essence of the encounter between the three cultures (British, French, and Native American) represented in the story. Even the form—couplets, but without regular meter and with only slant rhymes—suggests an order at best tentative, relationships at best problematic. The reader of the poem must supply much of what is not said directly, however, to complete the text.

The unusual word "lavender"—the color of the snow-covered earth and the sky, and the scent from the colonel's handkerchief—in itself carries one such motif. When it first appears in couplets 1 and 2, it emphasizes the speaker's sensitive appreciation of the natural world and the unity among earth, sky, and speaker. When it reappears, not in its English form but in the colonel's French, that reappearance emphasizes the distance between the main speaker, who knows "lavender" as a color in nature and an emblem of unity, and the colonel, whose "*lavande*" is first of all a perfume and only secondarily derived from the "flower purple as the sky." The mere image of the English gentleman-explorer carrying a perfumed handkerchief in the wilds of the new world further distances him from the speaker.

Just as "lavender" encompasses the complex relationships between British and Native American in appeals to the senses of sight and smell, so the "two streams coming together" which the speaker can hear despite their being frozen appeals to the sense of hearing and reminds readers of the incompatibility of the cultures. The speaker's own voice is "no less strange" to him than those muted water sounds when he remembers himself "calling out in French," not his own language; when the colonel is directly quoted in French, not English, readers are invited to hear strange and unexpected sounds incompatible with their habitual ways of communicating.

Even the sense of taste proves to be a point of difference: When the speaker recalls that neither British explorer "could stomach our willow-tobacco," the "our" places the Europeans' tastes outside the normal range for the speaker. The gifts offered to the speaker are similarly problematic: The fishhooks can only invite greater exploitation of the natural world, and the attractive blankets whose embroidery in reality is smallpox spell doom for the speaker and his people, doom much more profound than differing tastes in tobacco.

The speaker emphasizes that this encounter is with the incompatible by characterizing three elements in the story as "strange" or "unusual": first, his being able to hear the natural phenomenon of the two streams converging beneath the ice; second, his own use of French to hail the explorers; third, the aroma of the colonel's perfume. This progression, from the relatively familiar natural world through the speaker's own self-consciousness of linguistic alienation to a wholly different world of behavior and value, demonstrates the speaker's ultimate loss of control over his fate.

Themes and Meanings

"Meeting the British" above all concerns conflicts between cultures, especially those occurring when Europeans first conquered North America. The poem asks the reader, an English-speaker more than two hundred years after the encounter presented, to step inside the consciousness of the conquered culture. It lets a reader experience what it might have been like to have met the British for the first time.

Because the events in the poem happened long ago and the horrendous effects of European conquest on Native American populations are part of history, Paul Muldoon can give the imagined memories of the speaker melancholy resonance. Even the simple, almost hackneyed phrase "the dead of winter" in the first line implies, by the end of the poem, the deaths of many individuals and of an entire culture. The image of the "frozen" streams suggests not only the rigid, encrusted cultural elements that will prevent an amicable relationship but also death itself in the encounter of their "coming together." European influences had alienated the speaker from his language even before the events of this poem—he is able to speak French and knows enough to "call out" to the English officers in French.

The deepest and subtlest effect of the meeting between Native American and European here is the automatic assumption of the Englishmen that their culture is superior, and the ways in which the Native Americans acquiesce in this view. That the explorers do not speak a native language, but instead rely on the speaker's previous knowledge of French, demonstrates their desire to dominate and exploit, not to understand. Similarly, the movement from lavender in nature to lavender as an artificial perfume, part of a hyper-civilized affectation of one of the explorers, demonstrates in miniature the shift in values experienced by the speaker. Furthermore, since the speaker is remembering the encounter as an event in the past, and since the only words he quotes directly from the explorers is the description of the scent, his use of "lavender" to describe snow and sky may signify that he has adopted the colonel's very vocabulary, taking the linguistic infection as if it were a case of European-borne smallpox. Muldoon here gives a voice to the forgotten natives who bore the brunt of European expansion into the Americas.

Julia Whitsitt

MEMORIAL FOR THE CITY

Author: W. H. Auden (1907-1973)
Type of poem: Elegy/meditation
First published: 1949; collected in *Nones*, 1951

The Poem

"Memorial for the City" is a four-part meditation of 147 lines dedicated to the memory of Charles Williams, the English Christian theologian who died in 1945. The "City" of the title is all cities as they aspire to become "the City of God," as in the epigram quoted from Juliana of Norwich (c. 1342-1420).

Part 1 takes the view of a crow alternating with the lens of a camera; neither the animal nor the machine recognizes a spiritual dimension. Their view is that of Homer (c. eighth century B.C.E.), who narrated a world without the "meaning" of history since Christ. A crow can sit atop a crematorium and not care what is burning, in the same way that a camera can cover a battle without passion. Events of destruction and despair simply happen, from burning towns to weeping town officials. Natural beauty is the continuing, indifferent landscape for human suffering—the result is a deceptive picture of reality.

The Roman poet Vergil (70-19 B.C.E.) marked the period of transition from pre-Christian to Christian Rome. That city is in ruins after the devastation of World War II, but its destruction does not produce in us the grief of ancient Greeks. Pagan and Classical culture is history as "a chaos of graves"; the present state of postwar Europe suggests a future of "barbed-wire" stretching ahead without end. In concentration camps for prisoners of war and displaced persons, we bury the dead and bear misfortunes with a fortitude that we do not understand.

The second part catalogs Christian history to explain the present refusal to despair. Emperors and popes struggled with one another and produced a new kind of city: a center of civilization, a city-state in which people lived without fear of one another. Religious and spiritual values replaced secular and carnal ones; merchants and scholars helped to build "the Sane City," which welcomed learning and spiritual love, which placed public order before private desires. Then Martin Luther attacked the Roman Church as corrupted by material wealth, so Rome became "the Sinful City" during Europe's Protestant Reformation.

Then people began to look into the workings of nature and politics. What they found, to begin the Renaissance, was a nature without a soul, and those princes who took nature as their guide became ruthlessly ironic and efficient as machines. One consequence was the French Revolution, when Mirabeau (Honoré-Gabriel Riqueti) "attacked mystery" in Paris. He and his followers aimed to build "a Rational City," but Paris turned against the Revolution, "used up Napoleon and threw him away." "Heroes" of Reason inspired searches for perfection, for noble savages uncorrupted by civilization: "the prelapsarian man." Europeans searched for "the Glittering City," braving danger and despair. They found, instead of unfallen humanity in a golden city, a New World as a place for "the Conscious City."

Part 3 examines the ruins of a city bombed during the war. Barbed wire runs through the city, into the countryside. Images of the barbed wire run through one's dreams. It is the symbol of the human predicament, the inhumanity and corruption over which people trip and make fools of themselves. If the wire is a mirror of our spiritual condition, however, there is something behind the mirror: an "Image" which does not change as people change. It is an image of indifference. This "Image" is the "flesh" of "Adam waiting for His City." It is also "our weakness," which speaks the words of Part 4.

The poem ends with a dramatic monologue by "Our Weakness"—the voice of Adam, our human flesh. In human weakness is divine strength, for weakness is the fracture of pride. Therefore Adam did not become Lucifer and fall into absolute evil, because Adam was too "weak." Even classical gods and heroes were used by human weakness. Saints and lovers were fulfilled by weakness, and characters of great literary and musical imagination were products of saving weakness. These are the figures of mistakes and errors, vices and illusions, but they are the evidence of limitation and need; weakness causes people to discover their sinful selves, and that may rescue people from pride.

Forms and Devices

Each part of "Memorial for the City" is composed of a different verse form: first is an irregular, measured verse in three stanzas rhyming only on concluding couplets; second are nine regular, unrhymed stanzas of seven lines each; third are five regular, rhymed stanzas of six lines each; fourth are eighteen long, unrhymed lines, each line a completed sentence, most beginning with "I."

This variety of verse forms reinforces the variation of history, a main subject of the poem. Yet the primary device for developing the poem is an ironic use of metaphorical images of sight: from the balancing of crow and camera, with their cold, two-dimensional views of a static nature, to the mocking mirror between viewer and the Image of Adam, to the mirrors and photographers of Metropolis. One must break through the animal view, the mechanical vision; one must look past the mirror that reflects, to find the constant Image of impersonal Adam shared by all humanity.

The central symbolic image examined through the eyes of the crow, the lens of the camera, and in the reflection of history's mirror is the City. The poem marks the changing character of cities by abstracting a representative feature of the city at each significant phase of its development, turning that feature into an epithet, and capitalizing both epithet and city to suggest a personified entity: thus, European history is a movement of changing characters, from the "Post-Vergilian City," to the "Sinful City," "Rational City," "abolished City," and, beckoning all, the city Adam awaits, "the City of God."

An effective way to identify each city with its special historical era is to cite a person whose life contributed a particular quality to mark the city. Pope Gregory identifies the city in the sixth century; Martin Luther names it in the sixteenth century; and Mirabeau transforms it in the eighteenth century. Persons of history, however, become mixed with characters of myth, legend, and literature in the last section of the poem: from Prometheus to Captain Ahab. Such devices shape a poem of dense allusion to a history more product than producer of imagination.

Themes and Meanings

There are two dominant themes in "Memorial for the City": History can be flat and meaningless fact, or it can be substantial and meaningful fiction. The first theme is introduced in the first part of the poem, to mark the unchanging nature of a classical world before the advent of Christianity, but that theme does not disappear in the time of the "Post-Vergilian City." Flat and meaningless history as "eternal fact" always threatens to return, to emerge from the domain of substantial, meaningful history, because the foundation of human reality is a nature which is always the same. As a hard exterior, seen with crow's eyes or camera's lens, that nature knows no time and has an unchanging history. It returns to threaten repossession of modern humanity, but it never can, because there too much has been added by the Christian era.

Even when people "know without knowing," when people cannot see where the "barbed-wire" ends, they still know that they "are not to despair" because of history as substantial and meaningful fiction. The point about the fiction, made largely in the last section of the poem, is that it is what imagination makes of the raw material of nature and experience; cities are as much fictions as are the myths about Prometheus or the novels of Herman Melville. Cities express human character, in spirit as well as in body. Since Adam is the constant image behind the mirror, Adam is also the image of the continuing City. Until the heavenly City is reached, Adam's image, in all mankind, builds and rebuilds its city, waiting to be made perfect.

Finally, the "memorial" made here is a looking back into history to find a source of explanation for present circumstances, in which people suffer from miseries of war; but the "memorial" is also a sign of hope for the future, which may beckon with its promise of another city still to be built. Pride of accomplishment, of monumental buildings, and glittering glass skyscrapers will be undermined by essential human weakness, as all such cities have been in history. The "memorial" is for the death of pride and for the power of frailty to keep human history from becoming "a meaningless moment" of "eternal fact."

Richard D. McGhee

MEMORY

Author: Arthur Rimbaud (1854-1891)
Type of poem: Lyric
First published: 1895, as "Mémoire," in *Poésies complètes*; English translation collected in *Complete Works, Selected Letters*, 1966

The Poem

"Memory" is a poem of ten quatrains, divided into five sections. The lines in French are twelve syllables, cut with pauses and run on at unpredictable intervals. The stanzas rhyme in a regular *abba* pattern. "Memory" does not capitalize the initial letter of each line. Most probably composed in the spring of 1872, it remained unpublished until the posthumous *Poésies complètes*.

Formed around a riverside scene, perhaps drawn from memory of the August day in 1870 when Arthur Rimbaud first ran away to Paris, "Memory" is precise in its reference yet vague and fluidly suggestive in its language and imagery. The first line invokes "Clear water," an opening followed by two distinct sets of images. The first set gathers around concepts of purity, as in children's tears, white flesh, silk, and exalted emotion, with references to the old French monarchy and angels. An abrupt "No" cuts this thread and introduces a series of less abstract images: impressions of the river, moving gold, with cool, heavy plant arms; and a bed canopy of blue sky and bed curtains of shadow.

In the second section, the river frames little girls in green, who act the part of willow trees from which birds spring. A marsh marigold, qualified as a coin, an eyelid, and a mirror, rivals the heat-hazy sun. The exclamation—"Your conjugal vow, o Spouse!"—is tied to the next quatrain and the figure of Madame. It compromises the glowing flower image.

Section 3 presents Madame as well as He, the man. Madame was prefigured in the "Spouse" of the fourth stanza. She is rigid; threads of handwork fall about her like snow. She holds a parasol and proudly crushes a flower underfoot. Nearby, children are reading, red books set on flowery green, but this scene is cut by "Alas!" It is a background for the man's escape. "He" joins earlier images of purity, since his flight is "like a thousand white angels." "She" is "all cold and black." She runs after Him, leaving the riverside scene.

The poem plunges into the emotions of Section 4, regret for the arms of pure plants and April's moons in the river bed, joy in riverside wanderings on August evenings with their seeds of decay. "She" weeps under the city walls; poplars breathe from above. The poem returns to water, a dull, gray sheet with an old man dredging in an immobile boat.

A first-person narrator in the last section speaks of himself as a toy, with arms too short to reach flowers. Like the dredger, he is in an unmoving boat on dark water. As the poem ends, the voice laments willows and roses of the past and his own impotence, fixed as he is in place on a boundless eye of water. The last phrase, ". . . to what mud?" sounds a note of seeming hopelessness. The poet stresses emotional immediacy; the poem is written in the present tense.

Forms and Devices

"Memory" came late in Rimbaud's poetic career as one of the last of his verse poems. One of the usual identifying marks of verse is missing, as Rimbaud uses lowercase initial letters in all but sixteen of the poem's forty lines, contrary to his usual practice. Another suggestive point is that all of the rhyming words of the poem end in a mute *e*, what the French call "feminine" rhymes. Standard French verse form decreed the alternation of "feminine" with "masculine" rhymes. Rimbaud's "Drunken Boat" (1871) follows this rule scrupulously. This distinction is lost in translation, but it is unlikely to be a random variation in verse form. These are examples of deliberate formal experiment.

By far the most interesting formal variation in "Memory" is Rimbaud's off-beat use of the twelve-syllable verse line. An Alexandrine contains twelve syllables and pauses between the sixth and seventh syllables (the caesura). In orthodox French poetry, Alexandrine verse is chosen for serious and exalted subjects. Use of enjambment, the running on of a sentence from one line to the next without a pause, was a striking variation in form. In "Memory," the verses flow one into another with no respect for syntactical unities. They are broken by exclamations and interjections. The measured flow of classic Alexandrines is absent. In its place is a seemingly random ripple of language. The images of "Memory" also run one into another with the same disregard for formal structures.

Not only do the original French verses use end rhymes, they use interior rhymes, for example in stanza 2, "sombre—ombre," and in stanza 5, "ombrelle—ombelle." Assonances are used, as in stanza 3, "saules—sautent—oiseaux"; stanza 5, "prairie prochaine"; and stanza 10, "roses des roseaux." In their close sound relation, these words knit a structure within the compromised formal framework of "Memory," a doubled system of end and internal rhymes and assonance uniting the whole text.

The rapid succession of images and their juxtaposition in clear pictures are also distinctive. In the first stanza, clear water evokes a set of ideas tied with purity, and follows them to the Maid of Orleans and angels at play. The associations are linked through silk, which is like women's skin and lilies, and is also the stuff of the oriflamme, the red silk banner symbol of French kings. The pure lily is also a symbol of the Virgin Mary and of the French monarchy. Joan of Arc, who led an army to relieve Orleans in defense of the French monarchy, is a virgin and an exalted figure of religious nationalism. These links do not exhaust the images, but rather may be expanded until the river running through sun and shadow is the nucleus of a starburst of connections. "Memory" is formally dense; its many images, its complex pattern of rhyme and rhythm, and its breaking of traditional rules all contribute to its final richness.

Themes and Meanings

"Memory" paints an idyllic river landscape and then abandons it, glorifies escape, and ends in regret. It may refer specifically to the August afternoon of Rimbaud's first escape from his stern mother and younger sisters, left behind in their riverside city as he went to Paris; there were, however, many abandonments in Rimbaud's life. His father left when the poet was a young child. When Rimbaud wrote "Memory," he believed his father to be dead. (The older man died in 1878.) His older brother ran away shortly before Arthur did. When Rimbaud wrote "Memory," he had left Paris and poet Paul Verlaine to return home. He was contemplating another escape, both from France and from verse. (His flight to Belgium with Verlaine took place in July, 1872.) The composition of prose poems, later entitled *Les Illuminations* (1886; *Illuminations*, 1932), soon consumed his attention. *Une Saison en enfer* (1873; *A Season in Hell*, 1932), also prose, was his last literary composition and the only book he ever saw into print.

If abandonment and loss, abundant in the poet's life, are central in "Memory," so are the themes of joy and liberation. There is joy in the elaboration of the riverside scene, all purity, golden light, and flowers, with flashes of mythical, angelic figures. Rivers have their tutelary nymphs; Rimbaud's river has the brilliant, white flesh of women in the first stanza and the young girls, who are almost willow trees by the water, in the second section. The revels of angels, the gaily flashing banners of the warrior maiden, are positive, powerful images. The willow-girls allow birds to spring from them. The last stanza laments the dust shaken from willows by a wing; escape has a price, regret for the "April moons." Yet the escape, in a flurry of white wings, a bound over the mountain, is also part of the same energy and joy. The birds were already unbridled.

The cold, black, rigid figure of Madame, not only the poet's mother but also the force of structure, of rules of initials, of Alexandrine rhythm, of alternating rhymes, intrudes in the idyll, standing between the sun and the marsh marigold, crushing flowers, and scattering snowy threads over the prairie. On one side of her there is innocence, motion, warmth, children reading red books in green grass. On the other there are tears, a sheet of dark water, and an old man dredging from an unmoving boat. It is "her" rigidity that forces abandonment and loss, rather than the joy-filled flight for freedom.

The identification between "he," the man who escapes, and the first person of the last section centers around this old man. He is both the father whom Rimbaud believed dead and the poet himself, returning to dredge the dark waters of memory, repeating a pattern of loss. For Rimbaud, to speak of boats and water must recall his earlier "Le Bateau ivre" ("The Drunken Boat"), a wild journey of discovery ending in yearning for "a black, cold puddle where . . . a stooping child full of sorrows releases a boat frail as a May butterfly." Longer and more regular in verse form than "Memory," the "Drunken Boat" sketches the same pattern of intoxicating escape and eventual regret. The boat of "Memory," anchored to a boundless gray eye, is not identical to the waterlogged "Drunken Boat." The speaker in the last stanzas of "Memory" laments the past, yet he questions the chain which holds him to the mud beneath those boundless waters. At the heart of "Memory," in spite of its regrets of lost delight, lies the germ of another attempt at escape.

Anne W. Sienkewicz

MEMORY

Author: Christina Rossetti (1830-1894)
Type of poem: Lyric
First published: 1866, in *The Prince's Progress and Other Poems*

The Poem

"Memory" is a poem of thirty-six lines expressing a woman's voluntary renunciation of love, which, remembered with wrenching self-abnegation in life, will be consummated with her beloved in an afterlife of perfect fulfillment.

Part 1 of the poem was written in 1857, and part 2 came into being in 1865, when Christina Rossetti was at the height of her creative powers. The sister of the two Pre-Raphaelite writer-artists, Dante Gabriel and William Michael Rossetti, Christina gave expression to some of the escapist Pre-Raphaelite tendencies in her own poetry. She had, however, a uniquely religious sensibility, influenced by her intense involvement with the Anglo-Catholic movement within the Victorian Church of England. One of the greatest English religious poets of the nineteenth century, she strove for a disciplined purity in her daily life, giving up not only theater, opera, and chess, but even two suitors for her hand in marriage because of her scruples about the beliefs of one man and the lukewarm piety of the other.

"Memory" is a striking testimony to a woman's conscious rejection of love in her life, a courageous choice alleviated only by remembrance of her love and by the hope that the relationship will be renewed in paradise. The five stanzas of part 1 stress the woman's loneliness and courage in her choice to renounce love and yet to hide it in her hollow heart where it once gave joy. She has always kept her love a secret, and its renunciation required a stoically cool objectivity in the wrenching process of her rigorous self-examination and exorcism of love in this life. Nevertheless, her chilling choice to forgo romance in life has broken her heart, which gradually dies within her and causes her to age prematurely.

The four stanzas of part 2 examine the aftermath of her choice and elaborate on the single optimistic note of part 1—that love survived in the woman's memory despite the decision to reject romance: "I hid it within my heart when it was dead" (line 2). Part 2 affirms the enduring vitality of her supposedly dead love in the hiding place of her heart, where romantic memories reign over her existence through cold winters and splendid summers. Although she no longer worships a love that is "buried yet not dead" to her (line 30), in the autumn of her life, she indulges in romantic memories and dreams of a consummation of her love-longing in a paradise of love.

Forms and Devices

"Memory," a lyric poem consisting of nine four-line stanzas termed quatrains, has a rhyme scheme of *abab* in part 1 and *abba* in part 2. It is noteworthy that in part 2 the initial and final lines of each stanza end with the same feminine (or weak) rhyme, in keeping with the sense of the poem's conclusion that the woman's stoic renunciation of love has softened into tender remembrance and a fond hope of eventual reunion beyond the grave.

In part 1, the prevailing meter is iambic pentameter ("ĭ nŭr̆sed ĭt ĭn m̆y bŏsŏm whĭle ĭt lĭved"), although the last line of each stanza employs iambic trimeter ("ălóne ănd nŏthĭng săid"). In part 2, the metrical system in each stanza alternates between iambic pentameter (with an extra short sound on the feminine end rhyme in the first line of each stanza) and iambic dimeter (with an extra short sound on the feminine end rhyme in the last line of each stanza):

> I have a room whereinto no one enters
> Save I myself alone:
> There sits a blessed memory on a throne,
> There my life centres.

Cooperating with this appropriately controlled but fluctuating sound system is an abundance of assonance and consonance in the poem ("I nursed it in my bosom while it lived").

To underscore the contrast between experienced love and deferred love, the poem employs the earthier metaphor of having formerly "nursed" a vital love in the "bosom" in contrast to the chaster, more literal equivalent of having now "hid" a dead love in the "heart" (line 2). There are other metaphors, such as "the perfect balances" to convey the cold objectivity of the woman's judgment in renouncing earthly love (lines 9-12), such as "the bloodless lily and warm rose" to suggest the seasons and her lingering love (lines 27-28), or such as "life's autumn weather" to indicate her aging process (line 33).

The poem verges on allegory, a literary form that tells a story strong on meaning rather than on narrative, capitalizing on personified abstractions rather than on concrete symbols, characters, and events. Thus, the woman must contend with the personified abstractions of "truth" (lines 5-6), the "idol" love (lines 15, 17), and "a blessed memory on a throne" in her heart (line 23), where her life centers—without sinful idolatry—and where her buried love still lives (lines 24, 29-32). All this is a semiallegorical dramatization of the woman's inner psychology of love deferred through self-discipline.

The poem is terse and elliptically understated in its severe language. The diction is monosyllabic and bare-boned in its simplicity to convey the stoic determination to withhold love in life for a perfect consummation of romance in the hereafter.

Themes and Meanings

"Memory" is a poem about a woman's voluntary renunciation of love, although still cherished in memory in this life, with the hope for a perfect consummation of romance in a paradise of eros beyond the grave. What William Rossetti noted about his sister is relevant to the theme of self-abnegation in "Memory": "She was replete with the spirit of self-postponement." She created a poetry of deferral, deflection, and negation in which these denials and constraints gave her a powerful way to articulate a poetic self in critical relationship to the little that the world offers and to help her become one of the most moving religious poets of the Victorian era.

Antony H. Harrison, in *Christina Rossetti in Context* (1988), asserts a direct relationship between her strong religious sense of the emptiness of all worldly things and her portrayal of self-abnegation in a passionate romance: "As is clear to any student of Christina Rossetti's poetry, *vanitas mundi* is her most frequent theme, and . . . this theme is as pervasive in her secular love poetry, as it is in her devotional poems, where a wholesale rejection of worldly values and experiences would be expected."

Particularly arresting in "Memory" is the unusually honest and graphic description in part 1 of the woman's courageous decision that leads her to relinquish and yet cherish in memory her deferred love of another. The arduous psychological process of delaying the consummation of romantic passion as a matter of coolly deliberate, even ascetic, choice is an uncommon theme for love poetry, and Christina Rossetti handles her unusual subject matter with a compelling excellence.

Although this is not really a Pre-Raphaelite poem, "Memory" does exhibit some traits of her brothers' artistic preoccupations, such as an interest in a lover's passionate devotion for a departed lover, as in Dante Gabriel Rossetti's "The Blessed Damozel," where an escapist hope of reunion in an afterlife also cheers a disconsolate female speaker overcome with a comparable longing for love.

Thomas M. Curley

MEN AT FORTY

Author: Donald Justice (1925-   )
Type of poem: Lyric
First published: 1966; collected in *Night Light*, 1967

The Poem

"Men at Forty" is a short poem in free verse, its twenty lines divided into five stanzas. The meditative lyric both expresses how it can feel to be at the midstage of one's life and reflects on the condition of being middle-aged. Although Donald Justice was himself in his forties when he wrote it, the poem is in the third person, the poet wanting to convey an impression not so much of his personal experience as of the way things are. This is characteristic of Justice, although it is not characteristic of the dominant American poetry of the 1960's, which came to be called "confessional." As Justice said, in an interview collected in his book *Platonic Scripts* (1984), he "conscientiously effaced" his self in his poetry.

The poem's five declarative sentences affirm different facts about the situation of men at forty, all of which have to do with a sense of time passing. The men, one reads, "Learn to close softly/ The doors to rooms they will not be/ Coming back to." The rooms are metaphoric; they are the rooms of one's past which adults learn to leave behind—not with a boisterously youthful slam of the door, but with a quiet, perhaps wistful, close. In the poem's second sentence the men feel the landing of a stair moving beneath them "like the deck of a ship." Again the image seems not literal but rather to be a way of referring to the impression one has in middle age of being carried along on a voyage. Common human experience is that children take little note of time, whereas it seems to pass more and more swiftly as one ages. Thus, Justice's poem implies both that one does not have the impression in youth of being carried along (the men at forty feel the movement "now") and that the gentle swell one feels in middle age may become rougher later on.

The sense of time passing is again suggested in the poem's third sentence, which notes that men at forty see in mirrors a blend of the present and the remembered past: Deep in his own features the middle-aged man detects the face of the boy he was as well as that of his own father as a middle-aged man. In the only sentence which takes a single line, the speaker states that men at forty "are more fathers than sons." In this condition, belonging more to the world of the adult than to that of the child, men at forty are being filled, the poem's fifth sentence mysteriously declares. What fills the men is never made explicit, but the fifth sentence provides a powerful simile which describes it as being like the sound of "the crickets, immense,/ Filling the woods at the foot of the slope."

Forms and Devices

Many of Justice's poems are gracefully expressed within the constraints of traditional forms, but "Men at Forty" proves that he could skillfully write free verse as well. When asked what determines a line in unmetered verse, Justice observed (in *Platonic Scripts*) that it seems to be whim but that the poet should enforce the whim so that it comes close to being a perceptible principle. In "Men at Forty" meaning becomes the principle governing when lines are end-stopped and when they are enjambed. The enjambment in stanza 2, for example ("They feel it moving/ Beneath them now like the deck of a ship"), mimics the gentle swell being described, and the enjambment between stanzas 4 and 5, and between the first two lines of stanza 5 ("something// That is like the twilight sound/ Of the crickets"), creates a sense of flow appropriate to the pouring into and filling of the men which is being discussed.

Another principle seems at work when one notices that most lines end on an unstressed syllable. In part this fits the poem's quiet tone, which mentions doors closing "softly," a "gentle" swell, and such intimate moments as a boy secretly practicing "tying/ His father's tie" and the father's face being "warm with the mystery of lather." Such a tone is consistent with the elegantly restrained and self-effacing voice of the poet who once said he "would prefer quiet to loud any day" (*Chattahoochie Review*, Summer, 1989). The poem's quietness also provides a contrast to the last stanza's dramatic aural image of crickets, its three lines ending on stressed syllables. The understatement of the poem's next and final line ("Behind their mortgaged houses"), achieved by its ending on another unstressed syllable, and by its being an offhand prepositional phrase, makes the line all the more piercing.

Justice's skill with language lies not only in his ability to fashion a well-shaped verbal construct and to create a distinctive and dignified voice, but also in the beauty, clarity, and power of his images. They involve not only sight, but also perceived motion (the stair landing), remembered warmth (the father's face), and sound (the crickets). Cannily, Justice tightens his poem's unity by tying its elements together—by the rhyming of "father" with "lather," for example—and by establishing a list of activities in the poem's first half: closing doors, standing on a stair landing, looking into mirrors. The poem's second half is tied together by the motif of secrets running through the stages of childhood, adulthood, and old age. The boy wishes to be like his father and so "practices tying/ His father's tie . . . in secret"; the father is privy to adult rituals such as shaving, with its "mystery of lather"; and, later in life, men will arrive at the ultimate enigma, symbolized in the poem by the sound of crickets.

Themes and Meanings

Mutability and loss are recurrent themes in Justice's poetry, and "Men at Forty" is no exception. Doors closing, a stair landing in motion, a father's features becoming discernible in his son's face, and men being filled with something like the sound of crickets all become intimations of mortality.

Subtly and with originality Justice touches on traditional ways of imagining the human life span: the journey metaphor, for example, was invoked by Dante Alighieri in the opening words of *The Divine Comedy* (c. 1320), which translate as "in the middle of the journey of our life." It is also implicit in poems by Robert Frost ("The Road Not Taken," 1916, "Stopping by Woods on a Snowy Evening," 1923) and many others. In

"Men at Forty," as has been noted, it is as if men first notice they have embarked on a voyage after they have passed the midpoint of the biblical life span of three score years and ten. The trope of a stage of life being expressed as a time of day, found in Shakespeare's Sonnet 73 (1609) when the aging speaker says, "In me thou seest the twilight of such day," becomes, in "Men at Forty," the aural metaphor of the "twilight sound" of crickets. The commonplace conception of human life as an arc, rising and falling, which is part of a double entendre in the title of Gerard Manley Hopkins's poem "Spring and Fall: To a Young Child" (1918), is in Justice's poem suggested by the men at midlife being situated in houses at the top of a slope.

What destination awaits people at the end of their journey through life? The last stanza of "Men at Forty" presents a mystery followed by a certainty. The sound of the crickets is "immense," as will be the change from life to death, but the poem is ambiguous as to whether that immensity represents something positive or negative. The chirping of crickets can strike one as festive; many people in Japan keep crickets in cages as pets. It could, however, be experienced as frightening—the insect world taking over, as one imagines it does after the body decays. Perhaps to some the chirping simply sounds eerie. One cannot say, on the basis of this enigmatic aural image, that the poem either suggests an afterlife or rules it out.

Yet whatever lies beyond, if anything, the fact of death is certain, and its certainty is symbolized in the poem's last image—"mortgaged houses." People have their bodies, as it were, only on loan: They must be given up at death. When questioned about the last line of "Men at Forty," Justice replied, "the houses become, I'd like to think, almost an image for their bodies, the men themselves, extensions" (*Platonic Scripts*). Verbal technician that he is, Justice chose the precise adjective, for "mortgage" is, etymologically, "dead pledge."

Jack V. Barbera

MENDING WALL

Author: Robert Frost (1874-1963)
Type of poem: Narrative
First published: 1914, in *North of Boston*

The Poem

"Mending Wall" is a dramatic narrative poem cast in forty-five lines of blank verse. Its title is revealingly ambiguous, in that "mending" can be taken either as a verb or an adjective. Considered with "mending" as a verb, the title refers to the activity that the poem's speaker and his neighbor perform in repairing the wall between their two farms. With "mending" considered as an adjective, the title suggests that the wall serves a more subtle function: as a "mending" wall, it keeps the relationship between the two neighbors in good condition.

In a number of ways, the first-person speaker of the poem seems to resemble the author, Robert Frost. Both the speaker and Frost own New England farms, and both show a penchant for humor, mischief, and philosophical speculation about nature, relationships, and language. Nevertheless, as analysis of the poem will show, Frost maintains an ironic distance between himself and the speaker, for the poem conveys a wider understanding of the issues involved than the speaker seems to comprehend.

As is the case with most of his poems, Frost writes "Mending Wall" in the idiom of New England speech: a laconic, sometimes clipped vernacular that can seem awkward and slightly puzzling until the reader gets the knack of mentally adding or substituting words to aid understanding. For example, Frost's lines "they have left not one stone on a stone,/ But they would have the rabbit out of hiding" could be clarified as "they would not leave a single stone on top of another if they were trying to drive a rabbit out of hiding."

In addition to using New England idiom, Frost enhances the informal, conversational manner of "Mending Wall" by casting it in continuous form. That is, rather than dividing the poem into stanzas or other formal sections, Frost presents an unbroken sequence of lines. Nevertheless, Frost's shifts of focus and tone reveal five main sections in the poem.

In the first section (lines 1-4), the speaker expresses wonder at a phenomenon he has observed in nature: Each spring, the thawing ground swells and topples sections of a stone wall on the boundary of his property. In the second section (lines 5-11), he contrasts this natural destruction with the human destruction wrought on the wall by careless hunters.

The last sections of the poem focus on the speaker's relationship with his neighbor. In the third section (lines 12-24), the speaker describes how he and his neighbor mend the wall; he portrays this activity humorously as an "outdoor game." The fourth section (lines 25-38) introduces a contrast between the two men: The speaker wants to discuss whether there is actually a need for the wall, while the neighbor will only say,

"Good fences make good neighbors." The fifth section (lines 38-45) concludes the poem in a mood of mild frustration: The speaker sees his uncommunicative neighbor as "an old-stone savage" who "moves in darkness" and seems incapable of thinking beyond the clichéd maxim, which the neighbor repeats, "Good fences make good neighbors."

Forms and Devices

In his essay "Education by Poetry" (1931), Robert Frost offers a definition of poetry as "the one permissible way of saying one thing and meaning another." "Mending Wall" is a vivid example of how Frost carries out this definition in two ways—one familiar, one more subtle. As is often the case in poetry, the speaker in "Mending Wall" uses metaphors and similes (tropes which say one thing in terms of another) to animate the perceptions and feelings that he wants to communicate to the reader. A more subtle dimension of the poem is that Frost uses these tropes ironically, "saying one thing and meaning another" to reveal more about the speaker's character than the speaker seems to understand about himself.

When the speaker uses metaphor in the first four sections of "Mending Wall," he does it to convey excitement and humor—the sense of wonder, energy, and "mischief" that spring inspires in him. Through metaphor, he turns the natural process of the spring thaw into a mysterious "something" that is cognitive and active: "something . . . that doesn't love a wall," that "sends" ground swells, that "spills" boulders, and that "makes gaps." He playfully characterizes some of the boulders as "loaves" and others as "balls," and he facetiously tries to place the latter under a magical "spell" so that they will not roll off the wall. He also uses metaphor to joke with his neighbor, claiming that "My apple trees will never get across/ And eat the cones under his pines."

In the last section of the poem, however, the speaker's use of simile and metaphor turns more serious. When he is unable to draw his neighbor into a discussion, the speaker begins to see him as threatening and sinister—as carrying boulders by the top "like an old-stone savage armed," as "mov[ing] in darkness" of ignorance and evil. Through this shift in the tone of the speaker's tropes, Frost is ironically saying as much about the speaker as the speaker is saying about the neighbor. The eagerness of the speaker's imagination, which before was vivacious and humorous, now seems defensive and distrustful. By the end of the poem, the speaker's over-responsiveness to the activity of mending the wall seems ironically to have backfired. His imagination seems ultimately to contribute as much to the emotional barriers between the speaker and his neighbor as does the latter's under-responsiveness.

Themes and Meanings

"Mending Wall" is about two kinds of barriers—physical and emotional. More subtly, the poem explores an ironic underlying question: Is the speaker's attitude toward those two kinds of walls any more enlightened than the neighbor's?

Each character has a line summing up his philosophy about walls that is repeated in the poem. The speaker proclaims, "Something there is that doesn't love a wall." He wants to believe that there is a "something," a conscious force or entity in nature, that deliberately breaks down the stone wall on his property. He also wants to believe that a similar "something" exists in human nature, and he sees the spring season both as the source of the ground swells that unsettle the stone wall and as the justification for "the mischief in me" that he hopes will enable him to unsettle his neighbor's stolid, stonelike personality. From the speaker's perspective, however, when the neighbor shies away from discussing whether they need the wall, the speaker then sees him as a menacing "savage," moving in moral "darkness," who mindlessly repeats the cliché "Good fences make good neighbors."

The speaker does not seem to realize that he is just as ominously territorial and walled in as his neighbor, if not more so. The speaker scorns the neighbor for repeating his maxim about "good fences" and for being unwilling to "go behind" and question it, yet the speaker also clings to a formulation that he repeats ("Something there is that doesn't love a wall") and seems unwilling to think clearly about his belief in it. For example, the speaker celebrates the way that spring ground swells topple sections of the stone wall. Why, then, does he resent the destruction that the hunters bring to it, and why does he bother to repair those man-made gaps? Similarly, if the speaker truly believes that there is no need for the wall, why is it he who contacts his neighbor and initiates the joint rebuilding effort each spring? Finally, if the speaker is sincerely committed to the "something" in human nature that "doesn't love" emotional barriers (and that, by implication, does love human connectedness), why does he allow his imagination to intensify the menacing otherness of his neighbor to the point of seeing him as "an old-stone savage armed" who "moves in darkness"? To consider these questions, the speaker would have to realize that there is something in him that *does* love walls, but the walls within him seem to block understanding of his own contradictory nature.

Frost ends the poem with the neighbor's line, "Good fences make good neighbors," perhaps because this cliché actually suggests a wiser perspective on the boundary wall than the speaker realizes. This stone "fence" seems "good" partly because it sets a clear boundary between two very different neighbors—one laconic and seemingly unsociable, the other excitable, fanciful, and self-contradictory. On the other hand, this fence is also good in that it binds the two men together, providing them with at least one annual social event in which they can both participate with some comfort and amiability. To recall the two meanings of the title, the activity of mending the wall enables it to be a "mending wall" that keeps the relationship of these two neighbors stable and peaceful.

Terry L. Andrews

THE MENTAL TRAVELLER

Author: William Blake (1757-1827)
Type of poem: Lyric
First published: 1863, in *Life of William Blake*, by William Gilchrist

The Poem

"The Mental Traveller," written in 1803 but not published until 1863, consists of twenty-six long-measure quatrains, a stanza form commonly used in ballads. Since each line has four beats, the measure is considered longer than that found in more traditional ballad stanzas, in which every other line has only three beats. The poem's title refers to its narrator, a traveler from another mental realm who observes and describes the cycle of suffering in the "Land of Men & Women."

Perspective is an important element in William Blake's poetry, and it is important to realize that the traveler's perspective on human experience differs from the experience of the men and women themselves: The "dreadful things" the traveler hears and sees are things that "cold Earth wanderers never knew." Thus, rather than narrating the life stories of individuals, the mental traveler describes male and female archetypes that exemplify, in general terms, the nature of existence in the material world.

The narrator begins his description of the cyle of life with a grim recounting of the birth of a baby, "begotten in dire woe," who, if it is a boy, is nailed to a rock, crucified, and cut open by an old woman. As the boy becomes older, however, the woman grows younger, and their violent relationship is reversed: The male tears off his chains and "binds her down for his delight." Even at this early stage in the poem, the narrator makes it clear that the male-female relationship in the land of men and women is characterized by inequality and struggle rather than by harmony. Moreover, since the female is associated with nature (she is the male's "Garden fruitful Seventy fold"), this discord also exists between man and nature.

As the man grows older, he piles up wealth in a vampirelike way, feeding on "The martyrs groan & the lovers sigh." The female, however, becomes a baby, and in time she and her lover drive the man from his house. As a beggar, the male character wanders until he can find a maiden to embrace "to Allay his freezing Age." His embrace of the maiden leads to the contraction of his senses ("For the Eye altering alters all"), and he begins to grow younger. "By various arts of Love beguild," he pursues the maiden into a wasteland. Ultimately, he becomes the "wayward Babe" and she turns into the "Woman Old" described in the beginning of the poem. This frowning baby strikes terror into shepherds and wild animals, and none can touch him until the old woman nails him to a rock and begins the cycle all over again.

From the mental traveler's point of view, then, human life is an endless cycle of conflict between male and female, man and nature, rich and poor. Because men and women are not aware of this cycle, they are condemned to repeat all of the "dreadful things" the poem describes.

Forms and Devices

The structure of "The Mental Traveller" can be represented by a circle, and since the poem ends as it begins, the circle can be seen as constantly revolving. Among other things, this circle reflects the cycle of the seasons, the periods of life, and recurrent myths. Since the circle is never broken, no permanent change can take place in the land of men and women—everything must be repeated. Not even death interrupts the cycle. After growing old, the male character embraces a maiden and reverses the aging process.

Nature is symbolized by the female figure in the poem, and the male character uses nature both as a garden and as a source of rejuvenation. When the female is "a Virgin bright," he "plants himself" in her—a phrase that suggests both sexual intercourse and agriculture—and gains riches from her. Then, however, the female figure disappears and the male loses his vitality—his connection with nature and life seems to be severed as he grows older. While she reappears as fire, he experiences winter, and his "freezing Age" is reversed only when he can embrace a maiden. Thus, while the female archetype in the poem represents nature, vitality, and life, the male tends to fade, freeze, and create, through his altering vision, a vast desert. Toward the end of the poem, the male character takes the form of a baby who has the power to wither arms, drive animals off the land, and make fruit fall off trees. Thus the poem moves through the planting of spring, the harvesting of summer and fall (stanzas 8-9), and the freezing of winter (stanza 15), and then retraces the natural cycle so that the process is repeated. Throughout this process, the male lives off the female like a parasite; she, in her turn, beguiles and then nails down the male. In "The Mental Traveller," the natural cycle is seen as a battleground between the male and female archetypes: No progression is possible, since progression cannot exist without some kind of cooperation.

In keeping with the "dreadful" nature of the cycle in "The Mental Traveller," Blake uses sadomasochistic imagery to describe the relationship between the male and female archetypes in the poem. The baby boy is given to an old woman who commits a series of violent acts against him: She nails him on a rock, "binds iron thorns around his head," "pierces both his hands & feet," and "cuts his heart out at his side/ To make it feel both cold & heat." She lives, sadistically, for his shrieks. When the boy grows older, however, the violence is reversed, and he binds her down. As the fingers of the old woman "number every Nerve" of the male character, so the male character "plants himself in all [the] nerves" of the female figure. Human relationships, the poem suggests, are predicated on bondage and torture, and one of the most important cycles of "The Mental Traveller" is the tragic cycle of violence begetting violence.

Themes and Meanings

In any analysis of "The Mental Traveller," the narrator is one of the main puzzles. He tells the reader next to nothing about himself, yet the poem cannot be fully understood unless the speaker's perspective is somehow identified. There is a clue to his viewpoint, however, in the first two lines, in which the mental traveler says he has traveled through "a Land of Men/ A Land of Men & Women too." These lines are not redundant: The narrator suggests by the clarification in the second line that he is from a world in which the sexes are not separated, an androgynous realm that in Blake's myth is called Eternity. Thus he sees this land of men and women from the perspective of an eternal and presents it, not as some "cold Earth wanderer" might, but in his own visionary terms. According to Blake's myth, in Eternity or Eden the male and female principles are combined: There is none of the discord described in "The Mental Traveller" because men and women are united in a harmonious whole. From the point of view of the mental traveler, then, the idea of separate men and women is very troubling—it can only lead to conflict and suffering.

If the mental traveler is an eternal, the land he describes is Earth, shaped in the poem by the narrator's eternal perspective. In Blake's myth, this land would most likely be identified as generation, or the state of experience, a vision of life that is described in his *Songs of Innocence and of Experience* (1794). As several of Blake's other works make clear, in experience men and women are trapped in cycles. In some of these cycles, a revolutionary youth (often called Orc) rises up against the tyrant lawgiver (named Urizen) and defeats him, only to turn into a tyrant himself. Ultimately, another revolutionary youth appears, and the cycle is repeated. Violence begets violence, with no end in sight.

In terms of male versus female, the same process can be observed. Love turns into competition, and wiles and manipulation replace sincerity and innocence. The male and female archetypes in "The Mental Traveller" can never meet each other as equals: One is either older or younger than the other, and the relationship as a whole is characterized by bondage and submission, not cooperation and progress. The visionary presentation of the human condition presented in the poem is thus a fearful judgment on human life, which the traveler views as an endless cycle of violence and futility. The only way out of this cycle is for the men and women trapped in it to see themselves as the traveler sees them, to expand their mental vision and achieve a state of enlightenment in which separation would be replaced by unity, repetition by progress. In other words, the people of this fallen world need to know the nature of their existence and their power to transform it, for, as the narrator says, "the Eye altering alters all."

William D. Brewer

THE MERCHANT'S TALE

Author: Geoffrey Chaucer (c. 1343-1400)
Type of poem: Narrative
First transcribed: 1387-1400, in *The Canterbury Tales*

The Poem

"The Merchant's Tale" is the second of two poems in what is most commonly identified as fragment 4 of *The Canterbury Tales*. Each story-poem in the *Tales* is told by a different character in a group of pilgrims traveling to visit the shrine of Saint Thomas Becket in Canterbury. The tales range from high romance to low comedy. "The Merchant's Tale" is primarily among the latter, though it contains elements of poetry in the genres of courtly romance and homily as well.

Like most of *The Canterbury Tales*, "The Merchant's Tale" is preceded by a prologue that links it to the outer frame of the story of the pilgrims on their journey. The Merchant—in response the Clerk's tale of Griselda, the ultimately submissive wife—announces to the group that he and other married men have suffered much at the hands of their wives. He offers to tell a tale to illustrate a wife's unfaithfulness.

The story is of an old knight, January, who has lived a life of sexual promiscuity but at age sixty decides to settle down and get married. He claims to desire marriage because of the many virtues of a wife and the beauty of the "blisful ordre of wedlok precious." However, he insists on marrying a beautiful woman of no more than twenty years, and his motives are soon revealed as desiring a regular and lawful place to satisfy his sexual appetite. Prior to choosing a mate, January solicits his friends and brothers for advice but listens only to the advice from Placebo (whose name is Latin for "I will please"), which concurs with January's own desires to marry.

January chooses a young, attractive woman named May. In the tradition of courtly romance, May promptly becomes the object of affection of January's squire Damian, who becomes sick with love. May visits him—at the instructions of her husband—to comfort him. Damian gives her a letter professing his love; she reciprocates in a letter. A love triangle is formed, setting the circumstances for the primary action of the story.

In a cruel turn of fortune, January becomes blind and, as a result, jealous of his wife's activities. The old knight has a beautiful garden built for only himself and May for summertime lovemaking. May enables Damian to make a copy of the only key to the garden, however, and she arranges for him to be there when January brings her one day. Damian hides in a pear tree, and May, feigning a craving brought on by pregnancy, asks January to let her climb on his back into the tree. She climbs up to Damian, and they immediately consummate their love sexually.

Meanwhile, the gods Pluto and Proserpina, themselves a thematic echo of January and May, have been watching. In January's defense, Pluto gives the old man back his sight the instant May cheats on him, enabling January to see the lovers together in the tree. However, in defense of the feminine sex, Proserpina gives May a good answer for her actions; she explains to January that the cure for his blindness was for her to "struggle with a man upon a tree." If she appeared to be doing anything else, she says, then was it because January's sight had not fully returned at that moment. He accepts this explanation gladly, she and Damian are not found out, and the tale ends happily for all.

Forms and Devices

"The Merchant's Tale" conforms to a genre of narrative common to medieval French literature called "fabliau." Such stories are usually short, comic, bawdy accounts of characters of the middle or lower classes, involving one man stealing another's wife. The basic plot of "The Merchant's Tale" fits this genre, particularly with the stock feature of the lustful elderly husband cuckolded by a younger man. Part of the comedy of a fabliau of this type is the folly of an old man to think he can sexually satisfy his young, attractive wife and keep her faithful to him. January may seem the victim of an unfaithful wife, but his foolishness and inappropriate lust would have aroused no sympathy from Chaucer's medieval audience.

The tale is not pure fabliau, however. It also contains elements of courtly romance and sermon. The love triangle of January, May, and Damian in which the squire falls in love with his knight's wife is patterned after the tradition of courtly love. Here, however, that noble tradition is mocked by January's folly and sexual vanity, by May's easy capitulation of Damian's love, and by the absence of any tragic consequences for their sins.

The poem also contains elements of a homily or speech praising marriage. After introducing January and his intent to marry, the Merchant as narrator, for 125 lines, expounds on the virtues of taking a wife. However, January's actions and the Merchant's stated purpose of telling the story to criticize marriage tell the audience that all this high praise of marriage is not to be taken seriously. The sermonlike extolling of the virtues of marriage actually introduces great comic irony into the tale. The audience would have been amused to hear the narrator who at the beginning introduced the subject of marriage with "Wepyng and waylyng, care and oother sorwe/ I knowe ynogh," later saying with mock seriousness, "How myghte a man han any adversitee/ That hath a wyf?" and that a man "Upon his bare knees oughte al his lyf/ Thanken his God that hym hath sent a wyf."

In addition to this mock-homiletic style, the story employs a number of biblical allusions and examples, as a homily would. When January takes May to the garden, he invites her in with language from the biblical Song of Solomon. Earlier, the narrator cites Rebecca, Abigail, and Esther from Scripture as models of wifely virtue. Not surprisingly, however, what he says of them emphasizes what they did for others at the expense of their husbands.

Themes and Meanings

The purported theme of "The Merchant's Tale" is the unfaithfulness of a wife, but the story centers more on the foolishness of January, the old man who presumes to be sexually virile but only succeeds in being cuckolded. Much of the comedy comes from the ridiculous—to Chaucer's audience, at least—vision of an old man trying to hold on to his young wife's faithfulness. The names of the Merchant's main characters, January and May, reflect their physical and thematic contrast. January is unattractive and old, in the winter of life, and May is beautiful, young, and "fresshe," an epithet used frequently (and with ever-increasing irony) to describe her.

Although sex with May becomes permissible in God's eyes when they marry, January's obsession with it even within wedlock would be inappropriate by medieval standards, especially for a man of his age. As he anticipates the wedding night, the old man is arrogantly (and comically) concerned that she may not endure his sexual passion, his "corage . . . so sharp and keene." The Merchant provides a ghastly and comic description of the old man on the wedding night. His skin is rough "Lyk to the skyn of houndfyssh, sharp as brere" and "He rubbeth here about hir tendre face." The next morning he appears even more foolish when he begins to talk and sing like a young boy, except that "The slakke skyn aboute his nekke shaketh/ Whil that he sang, so chaunteth he and craketh." May, however, is not as enamored with him as he is with himself, as revealed in the marvelously comic line, "She preyseth nat his pleyying worth a bene."

January's blindness establishes another thematic pattern in the tale. When seeking advice from friends about whether to marry, January is blind to all but the advice he wants to follow. After he marries, his own self-flattery about his sexual prowess blinds him to the possibility of May's unfaithfulness; he never suspects she will choose to love Damian when he sends her to comfort him. When fortune turns against him and he becomes physically blind, the narrator even articulates the connection between his moral and physical blindness in one of the poem's several apostrophes:

> O Januarie,
>
> . . . .
> For as good is blynd deceyved be
> As to be deceyved whan a man may se.

When he regains his sight, it is only to the grief of seeing May's adultery, but he regains his bliss when he returns to moral blindness through her deceptive explanation of her actions.

Ultimately, despite its stated purpose, the tale is more critical of the old knight and his folly than of his wife. May, though unfaithful, outwits her husband—albeit with the help of a goddess—setting the precedent for all wives after her, the narrator says. None of the characters suffers for his or her actions in this comic tale. "This Januarie, who is glad but he?" the narrator asks in the closing stanza. He has regained his physical sight, and he trusts his wife's faithfulness and believes she is pregnant with his heir.

In the end, this foolish, immoral old man is only happy when he is blind to his wife's unfaithfulness and his own folly. As noted above, all the praises of marriage and the scriptural allusions are filled with irony. Though May is not as strongly condemned as the prologue would lead the audience to expect, the tale does present the ideal of marital joy as either an unattainable fantasy or a bliss gained (and maintained) only through ignorance.

Christopher E. Crane

THE MERCY

Author: Philip Levine (1928-   )
Type of poem: Narrative/elegy
First published: 1999, in *The Mercy*

The Poem

Philip Levine's "The Mercy" consists of one thirty-eight-line stanza written in primarily five-beat free-verse lines. The poem takes its title from the ship that brought the poet's mother to Ellis Island in the 1910's. As in many of Levine's poems, the grandeur and splendor of mercy is found in small and everyday events that offer only glimpses of the sublime, of redemption, and of joy. Such is the case in "The Mercy," a narrative elegy that depicts the journey of his mother, at the age of nine, from one home to another. "The Mercy" is the ship she travels on, where she encounters a Scottish sailor who offers her a slice of an orange, the first she has ever seen. The sailor attempts to teach her the word "orange" in English, "saying it patiently over and over." Thus, by line 8 readers learn that "The Mercy" is concerned not merely with journeying from Europe to America but also with metaphorical journeys, such as from innocence to experience, from confusion to clarity, and from isolation to acclimation.

This idea of journeying, of "A long autumn voyage," travels from its immediate context of the poet's mother's journey into the turbulent realm of language, as readers learn that "She prayed in Russian and Yiddish/ to find her family in New York." The Scottish sailor, too, supports this dimension of the poem, as he is at once intimately isolated from, yet ineffably in communion with, the poet's mother. Her prayers, speculates the speaker of the poem, go "unheard or misunderstood or perhaps ignored/ by all the powers that swept the waves of darkness." The considerable barriers of language, and by extension experience, are nullified by the literal and symbolic sweetness of the orange. The orange embodies a physical form of mercy by the poem's conclusion, as

> She learns that mercy is something you can eat
> again and again while the juice spills over
> your chin, you can wipe it away with the back
> of your hands and you can never get enough.

This is a lesson also learned by the speaker of the poem. He, too, travels into his imagination, researching the voyage of the ship that brought his mother to America and, in turn, afforded the speaker the opportunity for a better life. He learns of the hardships endured by his mother and others on board:

> 'The Mercy,' I read on the yellowing pages of a book
> I located in a windowless room of the library
> on 42nd Street, sat thirty-one days
> offshore in quarantine before the passengers
> disembarked. There a story ends.

The hardships found in this story, of traveling across the dark waves of the North Atlantic in late autumn/early winter, enduring an epidemic of smallpox, only to arrive and be refused to go ashore for a month longer, paradoxically reinforce the degree of mercy the poet, the poet's mother, and reader feel by the poem's conclusion. Ultimately, this is the telling moment of a life's transformation.

Forms and Devices

The straightforward declarative tone of "The Mercy" serves to simultaneously underscore and reinforce the import of the poem's story, as Levine writes in the poem that this, by all accounts, is a "true" story based on substantiated historical fact. The opening two lines set the tonal stage for the poem; "The Mercy" is a poem to be understood as one borne not only from truth but also from fact: "The ship that took my mother to Ellis Island/ eighty-three years ago was named 'The Mercy.'" This is a strategy Levine employs to preserve the people he holds dear, not only in the realm of art but also in the realm of indisputable, objective fact.

The tone also possesses a certain almost Frostian conversational ease as it moves from one moment or aspect of the story to the next. It is a voice intended to be heard by the common person. It is a voice one can trust; therefore, when the story begins to digress, readers are willing to follow it on its many tangential, but ultimately crucial, excursions. In line 9, Levine begins to journey toward what is at the heart of this poem:

> A long autumn voyage, the days darkening
> with the black waters calming as night came on,
> then nothing as far as her eyes could see and space
> without limit rushing off to the corners
> of creation.

This lyrical flourish breathes new life into Levine's deceased mother, recapturing her in a form when the Wordsworthian youth has just been lost. The glory and the dreams of such youth are overshadowed by the fear of the initial witnessing of the indifferent violence of nature, which in this poem is analogous with the unknown.

Perhaps the greatest technical achievement of "The Mercy," however, is how Levine vacillates between past and present tense and between first-, second-, and third-person pronouns. "The Mercy" begins in the past tense, and in line 3 it shifts to the present: "She remembers trying to eat a banana." A sense of immediacy reinforces the necessity of memory; in order to experience mercy, Levine says, people must exercise their memories so they might remember themselves and those for whom they care.

The poem's concluding fourteen lines contain another similar shift in time: "There a story ends. Other ships/ arrived, ... the list goes on for pages, November gives/ way to winter, the sea pounds this alien shore." The story of other immigrants continues until Levine reintroduces his mother, showing her eating the orange. It is a scene from a memory so acute that it has the facade of existing in the present: "She learns that mercy is something you can eat/. . . . you can wipe it away with the back/ of your hands and you can never get enough."

Throughout the poem, Levine addresses his mother, his audience, and himself. Hence, the point of "The Mercy" possesses a universal application. Levine avoids solipsism and egocentrism; instead, "The Mercy" works on the level of symbol, and is reluctant, in fact, to function on that level as well, as the insertion of historical facts in the poem testify. "The Mercy" is a poem with a utilitarian purpose. It is meant, through its techniques and strategies, to illuminate the consciousness of the reader, to urge the reader to examine memory in order to receive mercy from whatever higher powers that be.

Themes and Meanings

"The Mercy" contains a hopeful movement in the quest for uncovering an elementary metaphysics. This vision is founded on small, everyday things, such as an orange, the symbol of mercy and the vehicle of the metaphor for a deeper communication with the sublime. Still, this vision cannot possess the hope it does without first acknowledging the perceived terror humanity creates. While "The Mercy" is not quick to proclaim a resolution to the temporal or the spiritual, Levine forges ahead for as much joy and celebration as he can wrestle from experience.

The key elements of the poem, the ship, the poet's mother, and the orange, serve simultaneously as symbols and as facts. The ship, despite its title, is the vehicle toward mercy, while the orange embodies mercy, but only if Levine's mother chooses to peel and eat it. The story of his mother's journey, then, is the story of the millions of immigrants that came to America at the turn of the twentieth century. In a larger sense, it is the story of humanity striving to come to terms with living in the physical universe. Levine's willingness to undertake the sometimes oppressive and ungenerous powers of nature and society finally makes tenderness and empathy stand up against disenfranchisement. The poem—its characters and its elements, which readers are reminded exist as historical fact—attempts to defy the conditions of the world and survive with essential serenity.

Alexander Long

METAMORPHOSIS

Author: Louise Glück (1943-   )
Type of poem: Poetic sequence
First published: 1985, in *The Triumph of Achilles*

The Poem

"Metamorphosis" is a forty-nine-line lyric sequence divided into three numbered sections: "Night," "Metamorphosis," and "For My Father." It is written in free verse. Louise Glück has written a number of poems about her father; in this one, like the others, she seems to identify closely with her first-person narrator. She describes the metamorphosis of her powerful father into a childlike, dying man and her own development from fearful daughter into resilient adult.

"Night," the first section of the sequence, is a double portrait of the poet's parents. It begins by envisioning the couple at night in the father's sickroom. The father will die soon—as evidenced by the "angel of death" hovering over the scene—but only the mother perceives that death is in the room. The second stanza describes the mother ministering to the father. Gently touching his hand and forehead, she treats him as if he were a child instead of her husband. The poet says that her mother touches the sick man's body "as she would the other children's,/ first gently, then/ inured to suffering." While the dying man is portrayed as a vulnerable child, his wife is seen as a full-time mother who is used to suffering along with those in her care.

In the last stanza, the poet announces ambiguously, "Nothing is any different," possibly implying that her parents have always had a child-mother relationship. Then she identifies the cause of the father's dying: "Even the spot on the lung/ was always there." These lines end the first section on a despairing note; death is an omnipresent force in everyone's life.

The second section, "Metamorphosis," focuses on the relationship between the poet and her dying father. Again she describes him as childlike: "Like a child who will not eat,/ he takes no notice of anything." The poet, unlike her depiction of her mother in the first section, does not envision herself as a benevolent figure tending to his needs.

In the section's opening lines, she feels neglected by him, and then she compares his unseeing gaze at her to a blind man staring at the sun. Now that he is dying, he is beyond her power to affect him. In the last stanza, the sick father turns his face away from his daughter. She sees that his metamorphosis is complete: He is physically incapable of making any responsible, meaningful connection—or "contract"—with her.

The third section, "For My Father," shows the poet undergoing a metamorphosis of her own. Instead of describing her father in the third person, as she does in the poem's first two sections, she addresses him directly. She tells him that she will be able to live without him and that she is no longer afraid of death—his or her own. She also tells him, indirectly, that she loves him and will miss him after he dies: "I know/ intense love always leads to mourning."

The poet concludes by saying that she is no longer afraid of her father's body, thus hinting that he was a threatening figure in her childhood. Like her mother in the first section, she can now touch her father's face. She can acknowledge feelings of rejection and fear ("I feel/ no coldness that can't be explained") and treat her father with benevolence. She has metamorphosed into a kind parent figure, while he has metamorphosed into the helpless child she once was.

Forms and Devices

The poem exemplifies Louise Glück's penchant for combining the personal with the abstract. As in most of her poems, the language is stark, the ideas are briefly stated, and the overall effect resonates with significance far greater than the actual scene described. In "Metamorphosis," a relatively short poem, she mentions or alludes to the following: death, dying, excitement, suffering, solitude, love, mourning, fear, shock, and tenderness. These abstract words heighten the emotional impact of the sequence's three brief scenes: the mother tending to the father, the daughter observing the sick father, and the daughter tending to the father.

The abstractions occur in lines that are otherwise understated and conversational, such as the beginning of the second section: "My father has forgotten me/ in the excitement of dying." Glück's poems often reflect this overlapping of the ordinary with the extraordinary. A line that begins with a seemingly simple declaration suddenly evolves into a powerful observation or epiphany. This pattern is also seen in whole poems. In each section of "Metamorphosis," the concluding lines cast a new light on the images and emotions sketched in the preceding lines.

The first section's abrupt conclusion has a pained, almost hostile feeling to it. The poet refuses to sentimentalize the mutually dependent relationship between her parents. In the second section, the ending succinctly portrays a lifelong communication gap between father and daughter. Again, the last lines suggest that Glück refuses to soften her perceptions of her father even as he is dying. The last section ends on a more forgiving note. The poet seems to be moving toward an understanding of her father and his significance in her life. The concluding image of her hand against his cheek contrasts surprisingly with the blunt, aggressive statements she makes earlier in the section.

"For My Father" reverses the surprising course of the first two sections. Instead of moving away from potential sentimentality toward startling objectivity, the last section moves from objectivity toward a subtle expression of love. The poem's division into three parts contributes to the overall effect of a metamorphosis. Each section functions as a freeze-frame, portraying the poet's attitude toward her father.

In the first, she seems to feel removed from both of her parents; she is even not present in the scene she imagines. In the second, she is actively involved in the scene, but she is still unable to make contact with her father. In the third, she is finally able to address him directly—at least directly within the poem—and express a gentleness which seems meant as much for herself as for him.

Themes and Meanings

"Metamorphosis" is both a dry-eyed look at a dying man and a tightly controlled expression of self-preservation. The poet is trying to resolve her feelings toward her father, understand her family's past, and plan for her own future. Her terse, often oblique statements suggest that these related processes are difficult for her and not easily put into words.

Characteristically, Glück relies as much on the absence of detail as on specific information to convey the import of her message. Even the space between the separate sections has a weight to it; the poem moves stoically toward its resolution. "Metamorphosis" precedes by five years Glück's fifth collection of poems, *Ararat* (1990), which is a sequence of thirty-two poems about her family. In the later collection, Glück's father has died, and many of the poems deal with her continuing efforts to resolve her feelings for him.

The last poem in *Ararat* suggests that Glück has gone beyond the conflicting emotions and tentative reconciliation of "Metamorphosis." In "First Memory," she writes: "I lived/ to revenge myself/ against my father, not/ for what he was—/ for what I was." She concludes that the emotional pain she felt while growing up did not mean that she was unloved, but rather, "It meant I loved." The ending of "Metamorphosis" hints at such a resolution but does not state it outright. It is a poem about the process of overcoming pain and grief and moving on toward a new life; it is not about the fulfillment of that process.

"Metamorphosis" and the autobiographical poems in *Ararat* represent Glück's obsessive desire to plumb the depths of personal relationships. Many of her other poems (such as the nine-part sequence "Marathon" in *The Triumph of Achilles*) deal with romantic love relationships. In those poems, as in those about her family, Glück wields tight control over the emotions she displays in print. She refuses to give in to the obvious, the sentimental, or the overly ornamental figure of speech.

Glück is often an unsettling poet to read, because she is so willing to grapple with conflicting emotions that many people would rather not recognize in themselves. Although her poems are often rooted in her own life, the sketchy details, the reliance on abstractions, and frequent allusions to mythology give them broader application. Despite her seeming coldness at times, Glück's poems often return to the theme of love. In "Metamorphosis," a complex psychological portrait, she recognizes implicitly at the poem's end that the seemingly inappropriate emotions she has felt—hostility, neglect, and fear—may coexist with, and even heighten, her strong feelings of love for her father.

"Metamorphosis" is an example of Glück's continuing effort to look at herself and the world with a clear, unstinting gaze. Never one to sugarcoat a scene or ignore the drama of a small gesture, she captures in "Metamorphosis" the story of her own growth, which ironically, but perhaps inevitably, parallels the story of her father's decline.

Hilary Holladay

MICHAEL

Author: William Wordsworth (1770-1850)
Type of poem: Pastoral
First published: 1800, in *Lyrical Ballads, with Other Poems*

The Poem

    Michael is a long poem in blank verse, its 490 lines divided into sixteen stanzas. The Michael of the title is the poem's protagonist. The subtitle, "A Pastoral Poem," seems to challenge the traditional conception of pastoral poetry as a form for the idyllic and the bucolic, and to prepare the reader to accept the "low and rustic life" as the ideal pastoral.

    The poem is written in the third person. The poet himself assumes the role of narrator, guiding the reader to a tragic scene. There, he relates the tale of Michael with intense love and pure passions. In spite of some homely conversations, the poet speaks in his own character. From the viewer of a tragic scene to the listener of a tragic tale, the narrator emerges as the creator of a tragic poem in new style and new spirit.

    The poem begins with a two-stanza prelude. The poet, almost like a tour guide, introduces to the reader a hidden valley in pastoral mountains and advises the reader to struggle courageously in order to reach it. There, through "a straggling heap of unhewn stones," the poet thinks "On man, the heart of man, and human life." He decides to dignify the aged Michael for the delight of men with natural hearts and for the sake of youthful poets.

    The main body of the poem can be divided into three parts. Part one (stanzas 3 to 5) extolls the unusual qualities of Michael, an eighty-year-old shepherd—his gains from nature and his love for nature. Together with his wife Isabel and son Luke, Michael's household presents a picture of endless industry. Through the images of an ancient lamp and the evening star, the poet depicts that archetypal family as "a public symbol."

    The second part (stanzas 6-12) reveals the conflict between Michael's love for his inherited property and his love for his son. It vividly portrays Michael's care and love for his son from cradle to the age of eighteen. When he is summoned to discharge a forfeiture, however, Michael eventually chooses to send Luke to the city to earn money rather than sell a portion of his patrimonial land. Before Luke leaves, Michael takes him to the deep valley where he has gathered up a heap of stone for building a sheepfold. He not only educates Luke with two histories—the history of Luke's upbringing and the history of their land—but also asks Luke to lay the cornerstone of the sheepfold as a covenant between the father and the son.

    The last part contains only three short stanzas. It briefly recounts Luke's good beginning and eventual corruption in the city. Luke is driven overseas by ignominy and shame. Despite his grief over the loss of his son, the strength of love enables old Michael to perform all kinds of labor and to work at building the sheepfold from time to time as before. He lives another seven years, then dies with the sheepfold unfinished.

Three years later, at his wife's death, their estate goes into a stranger's hand. All is gone except the oak tree, which embodies both nature and Michael's indestructible spirit.

Forms and Devices

In September, 1800, William Wordsworth put forth his new poetics in his "Preface to *Lyrical Ballads*." Wordsworth opposed sentimentalism that resorted to violent stimulants and gaudy and inane phraseology to gratify certain stereotypes of imaginative association. *Michael* is one of the experimental poems Wordsworth wrote to demonstrate the strength of his new poetics. The success of *Michael* is characterized by the freshness of its subject, the naturalness of its diction, and the vividness of its rural picturesque imagery. Along with *The Ruined Cottage* (wr. 1797-1798) and *The Brothers* (1800), *Michael* establishes the common and rural life as a legitimate subject matter for Romantic poetry. By exploring elemental affections in a domestic world, the poem displays the beauty and dignity of lowly life and extracts cathartic pleasure from the pathos of humanity.

Wordsworth's efforts at experimenting with a new poetic language in *Michael* are obvious. For example, in lines 178-179, one reads "Thence in our rustic dialect was called/ The Clipping Tree—a name which it bears," and in lines 91-92, "To deem that he was old—in shepherd's phrase,/ With one foot in the grave." Apart from such declarative lines, in many places the reader can feel the poet's imitation of the language of the common people. For example, "Well, Isabel, this scheme/ These two days has been meat and drink to me" (283-284); "else I think that thou/ Hadst been brought up upon thy father's knee" (360-361). It is not the simple adoption of the language of ordinary men but Wordsworth's skillful metrical arrangement of the plain, simple diction that makes a new poetic language. The resilient, vigorous musical cadences of lines 40-52 are set in a basic iambic pentameter, which is pleasing to the English ear. The rhythm of the phrase "stout of heart and strong of limb" resembles the beating pulse of rustic people. The phrase "the meaning of all winds,/ Of blasts of every tone" gives symmetrical beauty to its syntactical visual form. The lines "he heard the South/ Make subterraneous music, like the noise/ Of bagpipers on distant Highland hills" link the inaudible subterranean sound to the sound of the noise. Yet because of the vastness of the pastoral landscape, the distance turns the noise into a music so subtle that it almost fades into the inaudible. Such peculiar aural sensitivity enables Wordsworth to convey the rustic people's intimacy with nature.

Wordsworth emphasizes that the story of Michael is "a history/ Homely and rude." The phrase "Homely and rude" expresses the peculiar beauty of the poem; in its tone, the poem is affectionate and homely. As shown in the lines "he to himself would say, 'The winds are now devising work for me!'" and "why should I relate/ That objects which the shepherd loved before/ Were dearer now?" the conversational style is exactly right for a tale to be told by "the fireside" or in "the summer shade."

This "homely and rude" beauty is effectively conveyed by the rustic symbols and images. By using the never-ceasing spinning wheels to represent "endless industry" and the humble lamp to stand for a modest but inextinguishable spirit as well as for frugality, Wordsworth gives the poem a rare freshness, simplicity, and profundity. Wordsworth typically employs a common rustic object such as a cottage to convey his extraordinary thematic ideas. In *The Ruined Cottage*, he uses the decaying of the cottage into a hut to depict the decline of Margaret's mind; in *Michael*, he uses the cottage on a rising ground with a large prospect and the lofty name "The Evening Star" to elevate Michael to a public symbol. The images in the second part of the poem are centered on the themes of education and protection. The old oak, the Clipping Tree (Michael), is opposed to a fettered sheep and a hooped sapling (Luke). As the central symbol of the poem, the sheepfold, an image of protection, evokes multiple meanings: It is the covenant between the father and son, the link of love, the anchor and the shield. At the end of the poem, the unfinished sheepfold, eternally fragmentary and incomplete, suggests the hope for human continuity. The oak, which carries the "inherent and indestructible qualities of the human mind" represented by Michael is permanent, while all human gains and losses are mere passing shows of being.

Themes and Meanings

Coming to terms with human loss and the power of love to support an otherwise unbearable situation are the poem's basic themes. The rich meanings of the poem, however, depend on how one interprets the character of Michael.

Michael, as an archetype, represents the collective entity of humanity. He is the shepherd or patriarch for humankind and the mother who rocks the cradle. He manages material loss with a cheerful hope, and he remedies and accepts the loss of his son in silent grief and stubborn perseverance. Throughout his life, he functions as the guide for a public life, the educator of youth, and the guardian of nature. Under Wordsworth's Romantic exaltation, Michael, an archetypal hero of unusual strength at an incredibly great age, embodies a natural paradigm, an inextinguishable spirit crystallized out of the good qualities bequeathed from generation to generation.

Michael can also be seen as a man of his time. As social history, *Michael* is relatively accurate; it records the infiltration of new capitalism into rural areas and the encroachment of trade upon the land. The prototype of Michael is that small independent proprietor of land called a "statesman." If one regards *Michael* as a lamentation over the rapid disappearance of this class of men, one may find Wordsworth politically quite conservative. In fact, Wordsworth does instill the spirit of his age into his imaginary character. To some extent, Michael is a rustic version of a self-made man; through his own efforts, he doubles his inheritance and wins the freedom of the land. He cherishes the freedom of the land as a sign of his individualist independence. Yet he is also tempted by the rags-to-riches story and by the opportunities of getting rich in the cities. Michael's pragmatic judgment of gain and loss eventually leads to his choice of property over his son. Michael's tragedy reveals the demoralization of domestic affections in the face of commercial realities. Luke's corruption is very much an extensive projection of Michael's inner corruption. At the loss of Luke, the individualist Michael, purged of the contamination of the material age, merges into the collective entity of the archetypal Michael.

Michael, above all, is Wordsworth's vision of Natural Man. Being a shepherd of nature, he merges his whole life with nature. Nature is the test of his courage, the fruit of his labor, and his ever-faithful companion. His blood and sweat nourish nature, and nature repays him with pleasure (lines 65-79). The covenant between him and nature is stronger than the covenant between him and his son, because nature is the anchor of human integrity and purity.

In his creation of Michael as a man of nature, Wordsworth not only expresses the "passions that were not my own" and his concern with the bond between nature and man, but also identifies himself with Michael to explore the bond between the rustic life and the poet. He shares Michael's sensitivity to nature, his experience and wisdom gained from nature, his singularity, and his solitude. Wordsworth's description of Michael as having breathed "the common air" and "learned the meaning of all winds,/ Of blasts of every tone" pictures an ideal natural poet who has gained freedom in the poetic representation of nature and human life. To create a new poetic path, Wordsworth needs Michael's indestructible spirit and must refuse to cater to the depravity of the age. Michael's stubbornness in not giving an inch of the free land expresses Wordsworth's determination to strike ahead, by himself, even when other poets fail to follow.

Although Wordsworth was only thirty when he wrote *Michael*, he seemed to imagine himself as an old poet of natural heart, using the tale to show "youthful Poets" his experience in composing poems. He notices what others might "see and notice not." From "a straggling heap of unhewn stones," the shapeless material of nature, he spins endlessly, as with Isabel's two wheels of "antique form." The natural objects, like "dumb animals," and the characters, like restless "summer flies," come and go in his murmuring imagination until his senses are blurred. Then he recollects the eternal truth in tranquil solitude. With this heap of rough stones, he hews and builds a sheepfold—a tombstone for Michael and an eternal monument for the poet. It is unfinished, for the old poet expects continuity. It turns back into its original material, "a straggling heap of unhewn stones," for the old poet hopes that the youthful poets can start anew.

Qingyun Wu

MIDDLE PASSAGE

Author: Robert Hayden (1913-1980)
Type of poem: Narrative
First published: 1945; revised in *Collected Poems*, 1985

The Poem

"Middle Passage" is a three-part narrative poem that uses various personae to depict in the Symbolist style—using suggestion rather than direct statement—the trans-Atlantic slave trade. Resembling T. S. Eliot's *The Waste Land* (1922), the poem is a synthesis of historical voices, an assemblage of brief dramas unified by both a poetic consciousness—"Middle Passage: voyage through death/ to life upon these shores"—and an invisible, ethereal consciousness in the guise of a spiritual voice: *"Deep in the festering hold thy father lies."* The poet uses these two voices to manipulate the perspective on events that are related to slavery.

The title "Middle Passage" refers to the middle journey of the triangular slave trade that began in the fifteenth century. The first leg of the journey entailed leaving the home port and sailing to the African coast to pick up Africans who would be sold as slaves in the New World. The middle passage is the portion of the journey in which Africans were transported to the New World, particularly the Caribbean, "Hispaniola," or the American South, the "barracoons of Florida." The third part of the trip was the return to the home port.

The major voices in section 1 are from a sailor's diary and a court deposition. The diary conveys the uneasiness, fear, and anxiety of the crew: "misfortune follows in our wake like sharks." It also describes the ways in which captured Africans committed suicide to avoid enslavement: "some try to starve themselves . . . [some] leaped with crazy laughter to the waiting sharks, sang as they went under." The sailor's voice also questions why he and his crewmates are cursed—"Which one of us has killed an albatross?"—referring to Samuel Taylor Coleridge's *The Rime of the Ancient Mariner* (1798).

The voice of the court transcript contrasts a public account of the slave trade—"cargo of five hundred blacks . . . stowed spoon-fashion"—with the previous private account of the middle passage. The deposition describes the nature of the "plague among our blacks"—physical diseases, madness, and thirst arising from "sweltering" conditions—and a shipwreck. The lasciviousness and immorality of the "Crew and Captain" are indirectly introduced as a "curse" upon the captured Africans: "the negroes howling and their chains entangled with the flames," "the comeliest of the savage girls kept naked in the cabins," and the Captain perishing "drunken with the wenches." The slave trade itself may be the albatross. Another voice in this section offers a religious justification for slavery and, indirectly, the inhumane middle passage: to bring "heathen souls unto Thy [God's] chastening." Implicitly, part 1 asks how physical cruelty can be used to bring about spiritual salvation.

The second section is the self-glorifying recollection of an old slave trader, "twenty years a trader," who describes how the vanity and greed of "nigger kings" was used to initiate war "wherein the victor and vanquished/ Were caught as prizes for our barracoons." The old sailor's remembrance indicates that greed among both whites and Africans is the primary justification for the slave trade. He does not regret his inhumane activities, and he would still be involved in the suffering and cruelty described in part 1 "but for the fevers melting down my bones." The "old salt's" voice also provides stereotypical descriptions of Africans as heathens: childlike in their love of cloth and "trinkets," savage in that they drink from cups made out of the "skulls of enemies" and are willing to burn villages and murder "the sick and old" for profit. These negative descriptions, combined with racist epithets, buttress the earlier religious justification for slavery. The attitude underlying the justification of the material exploitation and religious conversion of Africans is that they are beastlike and uncivilized.

Part 3 begins with the voice of the narrative consciousness which was established in section 1. With this voice, the poem moves from a literal and historical re-creation of events to a symbolic re-creation. This voice echoes the implied fate reflected in the image of the shipwreck in part 1—"where the living and the dead, the horribly dying lie interlocked." It also provides a simple but multifaceted assessment of the origins of the middle passage. Further, it clarifies the inherent irony of the previous sections: "the jests of kindness" or "bright ironical names" of the ships. It establishes the middle passage as one of the "shuttles in the rocking loom of history." The image of the loom and the metaphor of weaving are implicit in the interwoven narrative voices that appear throughout the poem.

The second voice, which appears in italicized passages here and in section 1, is that of an invisible spirit. A re-creation of the essence of the angelic spirit Ariel in William Shakespeare's *The Tempest* (1611), this voice symbolizes the irrepressible spirit of humanity: the "deep immortal human wish, the timeless will." It is also the voice of accusation, reflecting the spirit of those "with human eyes whose suffering accuses you, whose hatred reaches you." The essence of this elusive, ethereal, and elemental consciousness is absorbed and is reiterated later in this section by the "narrative consciousness."

The third voice in this part provides an account of a Spanish sailor who was one of the two surviving white slavers on the ship *Amistad* (Friendship). The speech, intended by the Spanish speaker to elicit sympathy for him by detailing the brutalities of the mutineers—"how these apes threw overboard the butchered bodies of our men, true Christians all"—is filled with irony. His tale of "unspeakable misery" contrasts with the earlier descriptions of slaves who "went mad of thirst and tore their flesh and sucked the blood." Unintentionally, he indicates that the "murderous Africans" enacted the timeless will to be free. This voice also explains, indirectly, how slavery can exist in a land in which all men are thought to be created equal and endowed with inalienable rights to life, liberty, and the pursuit of happiness.

The poem ends with the universal spirit of life and "timeless will," which are symbolically linked to the "black gold, black ivory, black seed" of part 1.

Forms and Devices

The poet Michael S. Harper refers to Robert Hayden as a Symbolist poet struggling with the facts of history. "Middle Passage" reflects that view. It is both a historically based dramatic narrative and a Symbolist poem. The narratives, interspersed voices, and names, which are derived from a variety of historical sources, are intended to serve as symbols. Little-known and well-known "objective correlatives," historical and literary rather than personal, are used throughout the poem. For example, the poem begins with "*Jesus, Estrella* [Star], *Esperanza* [Hope], *Mercy,*" which are later referred to as "bright ironical names" of "dark ships." The ship *Jesus* was sailed in 1562 by Captain John Hawkins from England to Guinea. He loaded his ship with Africans, sailed to the islands in Hispaniola, sold his human "cattle stowed spoon-fashion" to planters, and returned with a rich cargo of ginger, hides, and pearls. The large profits Hawkins made encouraged English involvement in the slave trade.

Section 3 refers to a well-known event. In 1839, a group of Africans led by Cinquez mutinied against being transported to Cuba. Gaining control of the ship, they sailed to Montauk, Long Island, and sought freedom. John Quincy Adams defended the fifty-four Africans before the Supreme Court and gained their freedom.

In addition to direct historical references, the poem utilizes literary references. One example is a variation on Ariel's song in Shakespeare's *The Tempest* (act 1, scene 2)— the voice of the invisible consciousness: "Deep in the festering hold [Full fathom five] thy father lies;/ of his bones New England pews [coral] are made/ those are altar lights [pearls] that were his eyes."

Hayden avoids the traditional use of rhyme, meter, and stanza; instead, he uses narrative structure—form and content—to achieve unity of effect. "Middle Passage" also utilizes intertextual verbal complexities, ambiguities, irony, paradox, imagery, metaphor, and symbolism, as advocated by the New Critics. The multiple voices overlap and interweave these devices while the speakers act as participants—and symbols— in the drama. The poet's historical memory and imagination achieve a unity of effect with the whole drama rather than merely a memorable line or phrase.

The intertextual relationships of words—through irony, as with the plague or with slavers as "Christians, all"; paradox, as in "you cannot stare that hatred down or chain the fear that stalks the watches"; ambiguity, as in the multiple meanings of "blindness"; or symbol, as in "bringing home/ black gold, black ivory, black seed"—add unity to the poem. Yet the seemingly disparate elements are unified into a coherent whole by means of structure, voice, and historical theme, and "organic unity"—natural facts corresponding with spiritual facts, in Ralph Waldo Emerson's sense—is achieved. Although some of Robert Hayden's poetry has been regarded as elusive and obscure, an understanding of "Middle Passage" is not dependent upon a knowledge of historical or literary allusions, since the poem's universal symbols and interrelated voices provide the "historical moment and context" from which the reader can understand an event in history.

Themes and Meanings

The central purpose of "Middle Passage" is to record, poetically and objectively, the process of change and the paradox of permanence among all humans: "immortal human wish, the timeless will." The poem does so by using images to illustrate conflicting claims and viewpoints about the slave trade. The nature of exploiters— private, public, religious, and legal—is contrasted with the voices of their victims. "Jests of kindness on a murderer's mouth" assault the concept of moral "human progress" for which the voices are praying.

A protest against man's inhumanity to man and the presence of evil is implicit in the description of the realities of the slave trade. Figuratively, the middle passage can also be regarded as a middle part of the evolving human consciousness—"Shuttles in the rocking loom of history"—a consciousness that requires evolving from a deathlike spiritual condition to a new life, a new beginning.

Another theme, which appears in the symbol of the invisible voice and the image of Cinquez, is the universal and ageless desire for freedom. Ariel, in his angelic whiteness, and Cinquez, in his "murderous" blackness, represent the primeval in the poem. They are also related, historically and metaphorically, to all those who seek justice and liberty. Invisibility caused by various forms of internal and external blindness is a metaphor for African Americans, as in Ralph Ellison's novel *Invisible Man* (1952).

Although the time period of the poem begins in the sixteenth century and its final event occurs in the nineteenth century, "Middle Passage" also reflects a transitory stage in the development of America and African Americans: "weaving toward New World littorals that are mirage and myth and actual shore." The universal quest to arrive safely, in a religious, commercial, private, or public sense, is a recurrent theme in "Middle Passage." By means of this theme, Hayden projects death as an intensification of life. All of humanity is in a middle passage, traveling toward mental, social, physical, and spiritual salvation.

Norris B. Clark

THE MILLER'S TALE

Author: Geoffrey Chaucer (c. 1343-1400)
Type of poem: Narrative
First transcribed: 1387-1400, in in *The Canterbury Tales*

The Poem

"The Miller's Tale" is a comic narrative of lust, deception, and infidelity. The second of Geoffrey Chaucer's *Canterbury Tales*, it follows directly upon the tale of chivalry told by the Knight. Although the Host expects to call upon the Monk to tell an edifying tale, the Miller, by now quite drunk on the "ale of Southwerk," thwarts Harry Bailly's plans, insisting instead on telling his story, much to the irritation of its intended target, the Reeve.

Over the Reeve's objections, the Miller begins his tale of John, a prosperous but gullible carpenter; his young, robust wife Alisoun; and her two admirers—the fastidious clerk Absolon and the clever Nicholas, also a clerk. John and Alisoun have enterprisingly rented their upstairs room to Nicholas, a student of astronomy, who has outfitted the chamber with sweet-smelling herbs, his favorite books, and his "gay sautrye" (a harp-like instrument). Nicholas is understandably attracted to Alisoun, a licorice-eyed lass of considerable charm. Bored with John and feeling trapped by his jealous vigilance, Alisoun soon succumbs to Nicholas's amorous overtures, and the two conspire to find a time when they can be alone.

Their relationship and their plans, however, are complicated by the presence of Absolon, a parish clerk, also in pursuit of Alisoun. Absolon is an accomplished dancer who emulates the refined manners of the court. Like the courtly lovers whom he admires, Absolon woos Alisoun with sweet songs and gifts. However, Alisoun prefers Nicholas.

One Saturday, when John has gone off on business, Alisoun and Nicholas hatch a plan that will provide them the privacy they desire. When John returns, he is surprised to learn that Alisoun has not seen Nicholas all day. By Sunday evening, worried that some accident has befallen the clerk, John and his servant break down the door to Nicholas's chamber and discover Nicholas recovering from a kind of trance in which he reports he has discovered through his astrology that a recurrence of the great flood is due the following Monday. He then advises John on how they might escape drowning. John is to fasten three large tubs—one each for Nicholas, Alisoun, and himself—to the rafters. There they will wait for the rain, ready to cut themselves free and float safely on the flood.

When Monday comes, the three climb up to their tubs and settle in to wait for the rain. John goes quickly to sleep, and Alisoun and Nicholas go just as quickly to the bedroom. That same day, Absolon appears under Alisoun's windowsill, serenading her and begging for a kiss. Annoyed, Alisoun decides to reward him appropriately. Thrusting her naked buttocks out the window, she invites his kiss. Appalled when he discovers her trick, he rubs his lips vigorously. Then, bent on revenge, he secures a newly forged metal blade from his blacksmith friend, and returns to the window. There he requests another kiss, promising Alisoun a ring if she will grant his wish. This time, Nicholas goes to the window, presents his behind, and lets "flee a fart." Ready with the hot iron, Absolon brands Nicholas's bottom. Smarting with pain, Nicholas cries, "'Help! Water!,'" awakening the carpenter who, thinking the flood has come, cuts the rope holding his tub and crashes to the ground. All John's neighbors come running. When John tries to explain what has happened, the lovers drown out his explanation. The tale ends with the laughter of the townspeople, who continue to think that John is mad, despite his oaths to the contrary.

Forms and Devices

For the Miller, Chaucer chooses a fabliau, a form of comic or satiric verse narrative that he composes in iambic pentameter couplets. Bawdy in subject matter, the fabliau was popular in twelfth and thirteenth century France and flourished in England in the fourteenth century. Early examples of this form could be quite obscene, dwelling on the misadventures of lecherous clerics, wayward wives, and jealous husbands. Often the fabliau portrays the cuckolding of a rather stupid husband by a clever wife. This form seems right for the Miller, who is known as a teller of lewd stories. Chaucer would use the form again for the Reeve, Cook, Merchant, and Shipman.

In Chaucer's hands the fabliau rises from a bit of verse to brilliant portraiture. Characters in "The Miller's Tale" are so highly individualized that, as one critic said, the characters seem to motivate the plot, creating a tale bursting with vitality, a far cry from the simple vulgar stories from which it derives. Absolon, the parish clerk, whose name suggests the biblical figure known for his beauty, is notable for his feminine ways. His hair is carefully parted and dressed, his stockings are elegant, and his shoes are elaborately carved. Chaucer adds that he is squeamish of vulgar manners, preparing the way for Alisoun's infamous kiss—the ultimate vulgar act—perfect in its ironic suitability.

Alisoun finds Absolon's fancy city ways unappealing. She is a country girl, portrayed by Chaucer as a healthy young animal—her body as small and gentle as a weasel's, her song as loud and lively as the barn swallow's, and her play like that of a kid or calf. A foil for Absolon, she much prefers the direct country ways of Nicholas to the sophisticated wooing of Absolon. Much of the action involving Alisoun and Absolon is motivated by this country-city contrast.

In Nicholas, Chaucer creates a unique character, individualized by the accoutrements of his apartment and further delineated by the repeated use of the adjective "hende" (handy), a word with several meanings: courteous, clever, near at hand, lecherous—all of them applicable to Nicholas's behavior at various points in the story and capable of moving the plot to its hilarious and inevitable end.

Such careful use of language, especially in the form of the pun or play on words, is a hallmark of Chaucer's fabliaux, many of which hang humorously and meaningfully on one or two of these well-turned phrases. Such is the case when the Miller lectures the enraged Reeve on "good wives" in the prologue to his tale, reminding him that "A husband should not be inquisitive/ About God's secrets or his wife's." In the tale, John's ignominious crash occurs because he has foolishly attempted to penetrate the secrets of the heavens and to restrict his wife to the narrow confines of the house, where ironically he thinks he can watch over her chastity. By using these words even before the tale begins, Chaucer cleverly prepares the way for the two plots—the Carpenter's attempt to avoid the flood and the lovers' tryst interrupted by the misdirected kiss—to intersect at the tale's climax. Upon Nicholas's pained cry for water, John cuts the rope holding his tub and falls to the ground to become the butt of his neighbors' laughter, bringing the two plots together in a master stroke of timing and humor.

Themes and Meanings

"The Miller's Tale" is an outstanding example of medieval humor. In addition, it is a story told to "quyte" or match "The Knight's Tale." Unlike the highly civilized, artificial, formal world of "The Knight's Tale," which is regulated by law and tradition, the world of "The Miller's Tale" is unrestrained, and individuals work out their destinies with little reference to larger patterns of meaning. Deprived of a guide like Theseus in "The Knight's Tale," the characters in "The Miller's Tale" are left to their own devices in a natural state and succeed in bringing chaos down upon all. This naturalness is best seen in the characters of Alisoun and Nicholas, who are most at home in such an atmosphere. Alisoun is described in terms that link her with nature and the senses. Her portrait, with its animal imagery and references to "morning milk," "coal-black silk," "licorice eye," and a mouth sweet as "a hoard of apples," evokes all the senses. She is a perfect match for "handy" Nicholas, responding quickly to his plea for mercy.

Nicholas is what one might call a master of the direct attack. He responds spontaneously to Alisoun's animal magnetism; his behavior is a far cry from the studied, chaste courtship of "The Knight's Tale," or even from the more formal wooing style of Absolon.

In this world Alisoun and Nicholas are free to pursue their own ends, unimpeded by anyone so formidable as Theseus. They have only Alisoun's old husband, John, to contend with, and he is as gullible as Theseus is wise, believing the story of the flood and following Nicholas's instructions to the letter. Adultery and falsehood are not in the lovers' vocabulary. They act on instinct, giving in to every impulse; and it is this which proves to be their undoing, or, at least, Nicholas's undoing. When he offers Absolon the infamous kiss, he has been "handy" just once too often and suffers the consequences.

By placing "The Miller's Tale" in juxtaposition to that of the Knight, Chaucer offers the reader the opportunity to reflect on the values that inform middle-class and aristocratic culture in fourteenth century England. If "The Knight's Tale" is about order, hierarchy, romantic love, and divine providence, "The Miller's Tale" celebrates opportunity, appetite, youth, and cleverness. In this fabliau, Chaucer begins to round out his depiction of the world inhabited by medieval men and women, reminding his readers that these men and women were creatures of flesh and blood who did not always obey the rules set out for them by society.

Carol Breslin

MILTON BY FIRELIGHT

Author: Gary Snyder (1930-   )
Type of poem: Lyric
First published: 1958; collected in *Riprap*, 1959

The Poem

"Milton by Firelight" is a short poem with four stanzas, which vary in length from seven to twelve lines. As its title suggests, the poem reviews the vision of John Milton from the perspective of one who is camping "by firelight." Place and date of composition are provided by the author as "Piute Creek, August 1955." High in the Sierra Nevada, Piute Creek defines an arid, mountainous terrain where during the summer of 1955 Gary Snyder was employed as a laborer. His work was to build "riprap," which, according to his poem "Riprap," is "a cobble of stone laid on steep, slick rock to make a trail for horses in the mountains."

The poem opens with a stanza introduced by a line from Book IV of John Milton's *Paradise Lost* (1667, 1674): "'O hell, what do mine eyes/ with grief behold?'" The well-known and still revered Christian myth "of our lost general parents" is brought into Snyder's poem by this intertextual reference to the great English epic. The line quoted expresses Satan's self-pity and resentment on first viewing Adam and Eve in the Garden of Eden.

The first stanza continues with a statement and a question. The statement, in the form of a long participle phrase, reveals that the speaker of the poem (Snyder himself at age twenty-five) has deep appreciation for "an old/ Singlejack miner" with whom he has been working. The miner is a master at riprapping and is completely at home in the Sierra Nevada: He "can sense . . . the very guts of rock" and can "build/ Switchbacks that last for years" under hard use by both humans and weather. In the face of such wise and skillful interaction with reality, Snyder somewhat testily questions the worth of Milton's "silly story" about humankind's supposed blessed state and subsequent fall from bliss.

The "Indian," or "chainsaw boy," of the second stanza is, like Adam and Eve, an "eater of fruit": He and the mules came down to camp "Hungry for tomatoes and green apples." The Indian, however, like the miner, is not a hero from Christian or Miltonian mythology but a nonfictional contemporary of Snyder who is also a worker. As an American Indian, he has no need to worry about Milton; he has his own indigenous culture, one that goes back thousands of years. The "green apples" for which he hungers are real apples, not symbols of knowledge of good and evil. Like the miner, this boy preserves a certain innocence: He lives with the diurnal cycle of nature, sleeping under night skies and seeing the river by morning, hearing the jays squall and the coffee boil.

Shifting perspective in the third stanza, the speaker flatly states that in ten thousand years "the Sierras" will be "dry and dead," home only to the scorpion. Such is the effect on the mountains caused by "weathering" and the expanses of geologic time.

From this ecological perspective, there seems to be no excuse for human sentimentality; there is "No paradise, no fall." There is only nature and humankind, although the speaker cannot refrain from voicing his frustration with regard to "Man, with his Satan/ Scouring the chaos of the mind." He erupts: "Oh Hell!"

A mood of peaceful acceptance overcomes the speaker in the concluding stanza, as the camp fire fades and reading is no longer possible. "Miles from a road" now, work too is no longer possible; Snyder and the "bell-mare" relax into the promise of a summer's night.

Forms and Devices

To some extent, "Milton by Firelight" is a critique of an outmoded symbolic way of developing a poetic argument. Snyder makes little use of rhetorical or metaphoric flourish, compared with other writers of the late 1950's; instead, he creates by more direct, simple, and "natural" (organic) means. His use of words tends to stress their referentiality (apple as a fruit) rather than their rhetorical effect or symbolism (apple as an emblem of supernatural knowledge). Snyder's poetic stance is both dramatic in its direct presentation of the speaker's total situation and ironic in its treatment of Milton's traditional mythology.

The stanzas may be read as a sequence of dramatic scenes (arranged in a chronological order) that delineates the progression of the speaker's thoughts from his initial disturbed reaction to Milton's myth to his concluding attitude of repose and reconciliation: "Fire down." The dramatic perspective of the poem is centered on the speaker's consciousness and is enhanced by the detailed presentation of the physical setting. The reader seems to know when and why the speaker thinks and feels what he does. The device of omitting the first-person pronoun from the text encourages the reader to enter into the speaker's experience. Mental associations and opinions, as though just then entering the speaker's (and the reader's) consciousness, are encountered with the same immediacy as the jay's squall or the clang of the "bell-mare." In fact, the use of "bell" and "mare" as a single, hyphenated word more accurately names an experience rather than an object: The "clanging" comes from neither the mare nor the bell alone but from both moving together. Thus, the reader encounters a poetry of experience, a meditation rooted in place.

Embedding Milton's myth in Snyder's poem makes possible an ironic framework within which Snyder can evaluate the relevance of Milton's mythology. Snyder is attempting to set up Milton for a fall of his own. In identifying with the miner, the American Indian, and the horse, the speaker of the poem assumes a role analogous to that of the *eiron* in Greek comedy. The *eiron* is a deliberately understated but clever character who typically makes a fool of the self-deceiving and loudmouthed *alazon*. Milton is not really a braggart, but Snyder has necessarily adopted this ironic stance toward this Christian mythology to guard himself (and his reader) from its potentially negative effects.

The stable irony of the speaker's position allows him several times to undercut the authority of Milton's myth, at least for himself in his wilderness situation. The "story/

Of our lost general parents,/ eaters of fruit?" may indeed seem "silly" in the high Sierra, where a miner or an American Indian boy has a real hunger for nonsymbolic "tomatoes and green apples." The Christian myth means nothing to these innocents, who have their own stories by which to live. Eden, with its thornless roses and idealized human nature, is an anthropocentric fiction; it never existed nor will exist—not even when "In ten thousand years the Sierras/ Will be dry and dead, home of the scorpion." As the green apples ironically mock the forbidden fruit of Eden, so the dry and dead Sierra Nevada mountains mock the garden itself and the scorpion image mocks Satan. The reality of the scene seems to send the message that from the ecological perspective, as from the innocent perspective of a primary culture, there is "No paradise, no fall."

Themes and Meanings

"Milton by Firelight" is part of what Snyder was later to call his "de-education." The poem demonstrates the importance of a mythology—that system of inherited stories that shapes a given culture—and the importance of revising it to stay in touch with the total, ever-changing environment. Snyder's stance toward *Paradise Lost* must be skeptically ironic because Milton's system attempts to justify human beings' authority over the natural world, whereas his own beliefs require that humans accept their rootedness—that is, their proper place in the ecological web of life. A false or outmoded mythology not only damages the planet but also gets in the way of fully living one's personal life. The questioning of Milton's story, the narrative of the American Indian boy, the ecological vision of the Sierra Nevada mountains, and the speaker's concluding empathy with the "bell-mare" are all part of Snyder's moral effort to free himself from what he considers the potentially oppressive mythology of American and European culture.

Snyder's wisdom is a complex blend of ecological, Buddhist, and Native American lore. His goal is joyful hard work—with a clear mind—in a healthy wilderness environment; for example, there is the "Singlejack miner, who can sense/ The vein and cleavage/ In the very guts of rock." At one with the land, this miner is in effect married to it. The "rock," no longer apart from the man, is perceived as having "guts," "vein[s]," and "cleavage"—features that, appropriately, are both human and mineral. Both the miner and the American Indian boy are in place, at home, rooted. Their thinking, like the poet's, is concrete—not abstracted from reality. Moreover, the work of the miner in particular is effective: He builds "Switchbacks that last for years." The miner's sensitivity and productivity make him an archetypal embodiment of Snyder's personal vision.

In contrast to the miner's clarity is the self-pitying egotism of Satan, who beholds "with grief" even the idealized Eden. Satan is alienated from the natural world because he selfishly wishes to use it for revenge against God. He is a victim of his own chaotic feelings, "'O hell, what do mine eyes/ with grief behold?'" He projects his inner chaos onto nature, so that chaos is all he can see. He is the archetype of self-conscious humankind: "Man, with his Satan/ Scouring the chaos of the mind." Where "man" and his Satan are, there will be the mental tendency to exploit nature by projecting a heaven or a hell. All too human and sentimental, this tendency clouds the human vision of what is and separates humankind from the world.

Yet, by entering fully into the rhythm of work with the miner, or into the rhythm of nature with the American Indian, one can hope to avoid this tendency to distort reality. As Snyder writes in "Piute Creek," "All the junk that goes with being human/ Drops away," even "Words and books . . . Gone in the dry air." For Snyder, when the self-centeredness drops away, clarity is possible. This sentiment reflects Snyder's respect for the Oriental traditions of meditation.

The final stanza's "Scrambling through loose rocks/ On an old trail" is a phrase that, while overtly referring to the mare, provides the reader with a possible analogue to Snyder's meditative action of reading and reconstructing the "old trails," the mythic life roads of the past. Although Snyder seems to reject the Christian myth of the Fall, he does make use of "Satan" as a metaphor for humankind in its alienated, self-conscious mode, "Scouring the chaos of the mind." Milton's myth was right for his own age, but myths should change as cultural and natural environments change. Snyder's response to his environment has been to help reinvent an adequate mythology for his era.

Gerard Bowers

THE MIND IS AN ENCHANTING THING

Author: Marianne Moore (1887-1972)
Type of poem: Meditation
First published: 1944, in *Nevertheless*

The Poem

"The Mind Is an Enchanting Thing" is a poem of six six-line stanzas. As in most of Marianne Moore's verse, the line length varies in a regular pattern repeated in each stanza. Here the syllable counts vary as follows: 6, 5, 4, 6, 7, 9. That is, the first line of each stanza is six syllables, the second five, and so forth. A subtle rhyme scheme typical of Moore is also repeated in each stanza: *abaccd*. Moore's use of indentation further gives this poem a distinctive shape on the page. Lines 1, 3, and 6 of each stanza appear flush left; line 2 is indented somewhat, and lines 4 and 5 are indented equally but a bit more than line 2. In spite of these typographic variations, the poem is composed of eight complete and grammatical sentences (with Moore using the capital letter only at the beginning of a sentence).

As the title announces, this brief poem is an exploration of the mind, perhaps an attempt at definition. The poem presents a variety of similes and metaphors for the mind and its functions of observation, memory, and emotional balance. Forms of the title word "enchantment" appear three times, revealing different senses in which Moore relates the mind to magical attraction and delight. In the title, the mind itself is "enchanting," that is, capable of enchanting others. In the opening line of the poem, however, the mind has become "an enchanted thing," a subtle shift that indicates the mind's susceptibility to the powers of things outside it that it observes. In the fourth stanza, the mind is described as "a power of strong enchantment," because it is "truly unequivocal." It is clear that we are operating in a difficult and abstract linguistic environment in reading this poetic attempt to fix in words the shifting experiences of consciousness and memory.

Moore's abstractions, however, are almost always combined with closely observed details of the concrete world, and this is true of the metaphors of this poem. The mind is variously compared to the "glaze on a/ katydid-wing," a German pianist performing a work by Domenico Scarlatti, the beak and the feathers of the kiwi (a flightless New Zealand bird), a gyroscope, and the shining of an iridescent dove's neck in the sunlight. None of these are obvious metaphors, to put it mildly. They all point to Moore's penchant for precision: her interest in the details and quirks of specific animals, or the particularities of an individual musician's rendering of a composer's work. That the fall of a gyroscope serves as an image for the abstract quality of being "unequivocal" epitomizes Moore's desire to link the abstract to physical detail.

The various metaphors suggest the mind's power of observation as it notes the minute subdivisions upon the katydid's wing or the shining of a dove's neck feathers in the sunlight. The poem also specifically points to other qualities of the mind. The mind has a certain clumsiness, "feeling its way as though blind,/ [it] walks along with its eyes on the ground." Memory gives mind both hearing and sight, here revealed through the direct metonomies of "ear" and "eye." The mind is capable of correcting for the heart's excessive emotion: "It tears off the veil . . ./ the mist the heart wears." Above all, perhaps, the mind is gloriously inconsistent (a word Moore remarkably works twice into her brief lines). Through all these qualities, Moore celebrates the quirkiness and particularity of the mind engaged in perception, memory, and thought. Unlike the tyrannical Herod, who kept true to his oath and beheaded John the Baptist, the mind can change, and that metamorphic quality is celebrated by Moore in the poem's final lines: "it's/ not a Herod's oath that cannot change."

Forms and Devices

Moore's talent for the unusual but illuminating metaphor is apparent in the metaphoric range of this poem, and the very abstractness of the central subject, the mind, forces the poet into figurative language. "Mind" is as much a process as a concrete entity, but Moore's insistent use of the pronoun "it" (ten times) and the very word "thing" in the title works against this abstraction. The tension of the poem lies in this effort to pin down abstraction with precision.

A consideration of mind is perforce a consideration of language, which shapes thought, memory, and emotion. Moore's poems are always fascinating explorations of sound and diction within her distinctive poetic form. The reference to "Gieseking playing Scarlatti" is probably as appealing to Moore for its sound as for the actual concert she recalls (which, she reports elsewhere, she attended at the Brooklyn Academy in the 1930's). Similarly, Moore uses both "Apteryx" and "kiwi" as synonyms for the same New Zealand bird. The hard *p, t, r,* and *x* sounds of the word resonate nicely with Gieseking and Scarlatti of the previous line, while the exotic "kiwi" is paired with the sounds of *w, f,* and *h* in a stanza including "rain-shawl," "haired feathers," "feeling," "way," "though," "walks," and "with."

Moore's orchestration of sounds is apparent in her often surprising rhymes as well: sun/legion, the/Scarlatti, submits/it's. Some of the rhymes specifically reinforce the poem's themes: most notably, mind/blind, which suggests the limitations of perception, but also heart/apart, which points to the tension between thought and emotion, and unequivocal/fall, which ironically defines trueness and certainty in terms of the inevitable "fall" of the turning gyroscope. Moore's skill in manipulating her strict syllabic line lengths also lends to the subtle brilliance of the poem. One five-syllable line is filled simply by the key word, "inconsistencies," while that word makes up one of three terms in a tongue-twisting nine-syllable line: "it's conscientious inconsistencies." The look of the poem on the page (as well as its syllabic formality) reminds one that this is a work from the age of the typewriter. Like her contemporary William Carlos Williams, Moore composed and revised on a typewriter, and the machine shapes the look of her "manuscripts"—appropriately enough for the machine age in which Moore and Williams grew to adulthood.

The particular surviving manuscript of this poem (part of the Rosenbach collection) is notable for the drawing of a shoe-polish container lid upon it. It is Kiwi brand polish, and the lid reproduces the odd little animal replete with his "rain-shawl/ of haired feathers." This drawing should remind the reader of the care Moore took in gathering her materials from a variety of sources, bestiaries, atlases, anthropological studies, illustrated magazines, accounts of baseball games, and advertisements. As much as Moore's poems are elaborate organizations of words and sounds, they also reveal her fascination with accurately observed particularities. "Apteryx" appeals not only because of its sound, but because of its origin in the Greek word for wing (thus echoing the katydid-wing of the previous stanza). The image of the "apteryx-awl" comments on the kiwi's odd beak—long, narrow, and pointed. Its eyes are on the ground, one suspects, in search of food, but it is important to Moore that that posture should be natural for the bird if the comparison is to work.

Themes and Meanings

"The Mind Is an Enchanting Thing" might well serve as a theme for all Moore's poetry: the celebration of the active intelligence engaged with the things of the world in the complex play of language and meaning. The poem's difficulties are of a piece with what it celebrates, a changeable struggling consciousness. The ability to alter and to grapple with confusion are the mind's strengths, as is its perception of detail, both observed and remembered. The virtues of the mind, Moore suggests, lie not in traditional power but in its ability to complicate and question. Thus the mind pleasurably engages "the inconsistencies of Scarlatti," while it rends the veil of the hyperbolic heart. The mind resists the tyrannical, as the contrast with Herod suggests.

The poem was written and published during World War II, and the sense that the mind is more complex than a bold Herod would countenance is relevant to the time. Gieseking, who enchanted Moore with his brilliant musicianship, was a German pianist whose continued performances in Nazi Germany led to his being banned from the United States for many years. The "inconsistency" that allows the poet to relish the music while deploring the political regime it came to be associated with is appropriately lauded in the poem. It is only when humans cease to be thought of as intricate finely tuned intellects that tyranny and atrocity become possible. The enchantment of the mind works against such dehumanization.

The poem is finally both an example of and a celebration of the mind's activity. The intricate nettings of the insect wing, the fine feathers of the odd bird, the rainbow of colors reflected off the fragile neck of the bird of peace are all images for the almost infinite complexities of human thought in action.

Christopher Ames

THE MIND-READER

Author: Richard Wilbur (1921-   )
Type of poem: Dramatic monologue
First published: 1972; collected in *The Mind-Reader: New Poems*, 1976

The Poem

Richard Wilbur's "The Mind-Reader," a dramatic monologue of 151 lines, unveils the inner world of a fortune-teller. Although Wilbur leaves gender unspecified, out of convention the reader may regard the aged figure as a woman. The reader cannot rely on convention, however, when it comes to judging her psychic talents. While not able to see the future, she can see past appearances. She can read minds and has a special talent for finding lost items by probing people's memories. Nothing put into a mind is ever truly lost: "What can be wiped from memory?" she asks, adding that "Nothing can be forgotten, as I am not/ Permitted to forget."

Unnamed in the poem, the mind-reader begins her monologue by ruminating on loss. Things that no one sees disappear are "truly lost," she says. She imagines a hat that slips over a cliff. "The sun-hat falls,/ With what free flirts and stoops you can imagine,/ Down through that reeling vista or another,/ Unseen by any, even by you or me." She likewise imagines a "pipe-wrench, catapulted/ From the jounced back of a pick-up truck," and a book sliding from beneath the chair of a reader on the deck of a ship, into the "printless sea."

The mind-reader then tells of her childhood, when her talent was used for finding missing objects. She likens exploring a mind to exploring a landscape: "you would come/ At once upon dilapidated cairns,/ Abraded moss, and half-healed blazes leading/ To where, around the turning of a fear,/ The lost thing shone." Her youthful experience led to her lowly profession: "It was not far/ From that to this—this corner café table" where she sits and drinks "at the receipt of custom." She describes the people who come to her, ranging from those who put faith in her talent to those who outwardly scoff but seek her nonetheless. Skeptics arrive, too, "bent on proving me a fraud."

She describes how she performs for customers. She hands them writing materials, turns away, and smokes. Then she touches their hands and engages in the "trumpery" that her audience expects. She recognizes her own showmanship and explains that she obtains the information she needs through her natural ability: It gives her the thoughts of her customers. Within herself, she sees those thoughts unfold "Like paper flowers in a water-glass." She rues that when her talent fails her she is thought a "charlatan." Of actual fortune-telling, she says, "I have no answers." Yet her customers leave satisfied; "It makes no difference that my lies are bald/ And my evasions casual."

The mind-reader concludes with a brief revery, wondering about the existence of a divine level of intelligence: "Is there some huge attention, do you think,/ Which suffers us and is inviolate . . . ?" She then notes that she distracts herself from the burdens of her talent by fleshly concerns. Yet she still yearns for the place where "the wrench beds in mud, the sun-hat hangs/ In densest branches, and the book is drowned." The one who can find lost things wishes, above all, to lose herself.

Forms and Devices

"The Mind-Reader" is in the form of a dramatic monologue, a poetic form in which the poet assumes and speaks through the identity of another. (Nineteenth century poet Robert Browning is known for refining the dramatic monologue into a unique way of examining character and human nature and of producing unexpected or ironic revelations.) Within this framework, Wilbur achieves many of his poetic effects through introducing richly imaginative details that dovetail unexpectedly with metaphor. The reader, by the end of the first stanza, for instance, has vividly seen a sun-hat "plunge down/ Through mica shimmer to a moss of pines/ Amidst which, here or there, a half-seen river/ Lobs up a blink of light," as well as a catapulted pipe-wrench, and the book lost to sea. As concrete and factual as these objects and events seem, by poem's end they have come to represent an unattainable and immaterial goal: oblivion.

Metaphors serve the mind-reader well in describing her own mind and the minds of others. Finding lost objects becomes a search through strange landscapes with their paths and "dried-up stream-beds." She describes a lost thing as someone waiting at a railway platform, where long cars with fogged windows arrive. There is "a young woman standing amidst her luggage,/ Expecting to be met by you, a stranger." Elsewhere she describes her own talent, her "sixth/ And never-resting sense," as "a cheap room/ Black with the anger of insomnia,/ Whose wall-boards vibrate with the mutters, plaints/ And flushings of the race."

Wilbur composed "The Mind-Reader" in blank verse. Although many of the lines fall within a strict pattern of iambic pentameter, Wilbur freely adds syllables, sometimes resulting in hexameter passages. In the lines set in regular pentameter, he frequently employs elision, as in the following example: "See how she turns her head, the eyes engaging." The vowels in "the eyes" elide to make a single syllable, making this line a regular ten-syllable, or five-foot, line.

Themes and Meanings

Speakers and listeners interact on several levels in "The Mind-Reader." As the mind-reader speaks, she makes it clear that she is talking to a privileged listener. In speaking of "truly lost" things, she mentions that such things are "Unseen by any, even by you or me." The "you," the "professore" who is finally addressed directly at poem's end, is not specifically identified. Presumably she addresses the poet, who then transfers the monologue to the reader. Yet the possibility exists that she addresses another poetic persona, who may or may not be the poet. Moreover, her words make clear that, in this poem, speaker and listener are linked in the activity indicated by the title. Both "read" minds.

She refers to this directly only at the end of the poem, in a joking manner. After mentioning that she is "drinking studiously until my thought/ Is a blind lowered almost to the sill," she responds to her listener: "Ah, you have read my mind. One more, perhaps . . ./ A mezzo-litro. Grazie, professore." This ending pair of lines is the only suggestion that the "professore" has said anything at all. He may in fact have said nothing verbally, since he knew he was dealing with a mind-reader. He may have simply conceived the thought of buying her a drink, a thought which she then "read." Earlier she spoke of the "professore" as being understanding of her situation. Presumably, as a mind-reader, she could accurately appraise her listeners. To what kind of person, then, would she entrust her true story? Quite possibly the listener is another mind-reader. "I tell you this/ Because you know that I have the gift, the burden," she says. The listener knows, and the mind-reader knows of the listener's knowledge. If the listener is also a mind-reader, the entire monologue might be unspoken, with speaker and listener reading each other's minds.

On the other hand, since the "professore" may be the poet himself, the reader begins to see that Wilbur may be talking about himself as a poet or about poets in general. In writing a poem such as this, the poet throws herself or himself into the mind of another. The poet divines the truth about another person without words, even though words are the final result. Even the charlatan act may be consistent with the poet: "I lay/ My hand on theirs and go into my frenzy,/ Raising my eyes to heaven, snorting smoke,/ Lolling my head as in the fumes of Delphi,/ And then, with shaken, spirit-guided fingers,/ Set down the oracle." The mind-reader writes fortunes on paper, even as the poet does poems; both feel pressure from their audience, who expect the miraculous on demand.

If both fortune-teller and poet set "mind" down on paper, moreover, what does this suggest of the reader? In reading the monologue, all become, in a sense, the subject of the poem. The reader is reading a mind. The identification of poet with mind-reader allows Wilbur to speak about the poet as the one who gives voice to a silent multitude. The fortune-teller says of her customers, "It contents them/ Not to have spoken, yet to have been heard." Wilbur may well be speaking about readers, who encounter in poetry feelings felt but never expressed and thoughts thought but never spoken.

Mark Rich

MINIATURE

Author: Yannis Ritsos (1909-1990)
Type of poem: Lyric
First published: 1961, as "Mikrographia," in *Parentheses, 1946-47*; English translation collected in *Ritsos in Parentheses*, 1979

The Poem

"Miniature" is a free-verse poem of fourteen lines. The title, especially in Greek, denotes a small-scale drawing of the type that Yannis Ritsos is known to have drawn on hundreds of stones and on the backs of Greek cigarette boxes. While the title self-consciously limits the size of the poem, it is deceptive in that it does not indicate its scope.

The poem captures an awkward moment in which two people who are about to have tea are unable to connect. A woman of indeterminate age stands at a table, slicing lemons. The slices, with sections like spokes, are compared to the wheels of a carriage in a fairy tale. A young officer is sitting nearby, "buried" in his armchair. A tangible distance separates them. Instead of looking at her, he lights a cigarette with a trembling hand.

Time stands still, in the "heartbeat" of a clock. The moment passes, and it is "too late" to act upon the unspecified "something" that has been "postponed." The chance for the two to connect has been lost. Instead of facing each other, they escape into a mundane activity: "Let's drink our tea."

The poem concludes with a series of rhetorical questions. At first glance, these seem unrelated to what has happened, or rather to what has not happened, since the focus of the poem is on the absence of action. "Is it possible, then, for death to come in that kind of carriage?" Evidently, there has been a death, as though life not seized, a desire not acted upon, is not merely the absence of life, but death.

The exact nature of the desire, like the exact relationship between the woman and man, is unspecified. Perhaps she is his mother, wife, sister, or lover. Perhaps he is returning from or going to war. (The date of the poem's composition coincides with a terrible era of Greek history, immediately after the Nazi occupation and during the civil war.) The urgency of life, like the presence of death, stymies them.

In the end, all that remains of the moment is the metaphor of the carriage, created by the woman only to be left behind "for so many years on a side street with unlit lamps." Perhaps the lamps are "unlit" because they missed connecting with the officer's match. Finally, after many years, the moment reappears in "a small song, a little mist, and then nothing." Perhaps the memory of the carriage has inspired the small song of the poem itself, which is followed by an obscure melancholy before it disappears again into the nothingness of forgetfulness or death.

Forms and Devices

Ritsos's strength is in the simplicity of his language, so his work suffers relatively little in translation. He is a prolific and popular poet—his more than ninety volumes have been widely translated, and many of his poems have been successfully put to music—whose work speaks simply to human experience and emotion.

Relatively unconcerned with complexities of form, syntax, or allusion, Ritsos depends on the emotional impact of ordinary objects lovingly observed. In a 1966 poem called "Insignificant Details," Ritsos suggests that common objects are the poet's sacred text: "their secret meaning (beyond gods and myths,/ beyond symbols and concepts) only poets understand." It is the poet's job to cast them in such a light that anyone can be made to understand by feeling their significance.

Ritsos's populist realism is suffused with a magical quality, a result in part of the influence of Surrealism, but his poetry owes its dreamlike effects not to the psychic automatism or the unconscious, but to experiences grounded in the everyday life of the body. In "Miniature," for example, he appeals to the childlike free play of the imagination, in which semblances instantaneously become similes. The thin slices of lemon are "like yellow wheels for a very small carriage/ made for a child's fairy tale," and the clock "holds its heartbeat."

Ritsos's poems are more visual (and visceral) than intellectual. Motifs from sculpture and painting are common. Often, he creates a sort of optical illusion in which metaphor replaces reality. In "Abstracted Painter," a poem that recalls the optical illusions of the artist M. C. Escher, a painter draws a train, and one of the carriages cuts away from the paper to return to the carbarn, with the painter inside. Something similar occurs in "Miniature" when the reader is left not with the human situation, but with the metaphor of the carriage, with death inside. Imaginative symbol replaces experience.

Ritsos gives his poem a dramatic context, as though implying that the magic of metaphor erupts in the midst of the most mundane human activities. The reader is given only a parenthetical scene in a larger drama and is invited to speculate about the nature of the tension of desire and restraint between the woman and the man, the "something . . . postponed" that is unspoken and unenacted. The dramatic conflict is not overtly expressed in their actions; the conflict must be discerned beneath their actions.

Within the two adults are two children who are illuminated by the yellow of lemon slices and match flame. The woman performs her household chores while dreaming of escape, like Cinderella, in a magic carriage (here made of a lemon rather than a pumpkin). The officer is a boy afraid of love, romantic or maternal. His nervous hand holds the match, its warm glow highlighting his "tender chin and the teacup's handle," which connects him with the woman.

It is difficult to say whether "Miniature" is a sonnet or merely a lyric that happens to contain fourteen lines. Ritsos's early work used all the conventions of rhyme and meter, but later he abandoned them for free verse. "Miniature" can, however, be read as an ironic twist on the tradition of the sonnet, with all the trappings of missed connection and imaginative consolation.

Themes and Meanings

"Miniature" appeared in the first of two collections called *Parentheses* (1946-1947 and 1950-1961). In terms of mathematics and symbolic logic, these short poems are "parenthetical" in that they contain unified propositions, symbolic or psychological. In terms of human relationship, writes Edmund Keeley in *Ritsos in Parentheses* (1979), "the two signs of the parenthesis are like cupped hands facing each other across a distance, hands that are straining to come together, to achieve a meeting that would serve to reaffirm human contact between isolated presences."

This is certainly the human theme of "Miniature," but this is also a poem about the dual nature of experience, the ways in which imagination informs and enriches reality. Lemon slices may spice a cup of tea or inspire a fairy tale; both are necessary. It is the poetic moment that connects the real world with the imaginary. In such moments one makes one's meanings. As Ritsos says in another poem, "an endless interchange shaped/ the meaning of things."

The poetic moment also unites time and timelessness. The chatter and business of everyday life, like preparing tea, is ruled by the clock, but the imagination exists between moments, when "The clock/ holds its heartbeat." At these moments, all such sound and fury are suspended, but the stilled "heartbeat" of the clock is also associated with death, which is brought in the fairy tale's carriage.

Yet death and life is another duality that the poetic moment unifies, for it is when one is closest to death that one most appreciates life. One's perception of mortality quickens one's pulse, makes more urgent one's joy in the particulars of life, the smell of lemon peel, for example, and makes one want to live. Lemons always symbolize a desire for life for Ritsos, who, while a political prisoner in 1950, wrote: "[w]e have not come into this world/ simply to die./ Not when at dawn/ there is the smell of lemon peel" ("Chronicle of Exile III," February 15, 1950). Ritsos celebrates poetry's ability to discern the interpenetration of life and death, reality and illusion, for the one always makes one yearn for the other. To alter William Wordsworth's famous claim, in moments of imagination, one sees into the "death" of things.

Ritsos's vision is tragic, not pessimistic or nihilistic. As a Marxist, he sees "nothing" at the end of life to justify existence; as an existentialist, he believes that one makes one's meaning along the way. The nothingness of death is preceded by "a small song, a little mist." The tragic undertone is caught better in the connotations of the Greek: The word for mist also means melancholy, although the homonym for mist (missed) may convey something of what is lost in translation; the word for song (*tragoudi*) echoes its root in Greek tragedy. Thus the little song (*mikro tragoudi*) is only a minor tragedy, resulting in this miniature portrait (*Mikrographia*) of missed connection.

Out of the little tragedies of missed connections, Ritsos suggests, come the consolations of the small songs of memory, those parenthetical miniatures of the imagination called poems. Like the spray of the cut lemon, the song of the poem captures the imaginative moment in a melancholy mist, before the onset of nothingness. It is the smell of lemon peel, however, cut by one's hands and shaped by one's desire, that makes one want to live, and by living create meaning—and connection—in one's life.

Richard Collins

MINIVER CHEEVY

Author: Edwin Arlington Robinson (1869-1935)
Type of poem: Satire
First published: 1910, in *The Town Down the River*

The Poem

"Miniver Cheevy" is a short poem of thirty-two lines satirizing an embittered town drunkard who bemoans the difference between a romantic heroic past and a mundane modernity and yet does nothing to improve his squalid lot in life. The satire is a double-edged blade, undercutting both the illusions of the do-nothing dreamer and his complaints about the triteness of his modern environment. The weight of the ridicule, however, is leveled primarily against the speaker.

Reared in Gardiner, Maine, Edwin Arlington Robinson created a mythical "Tilbury Town" out of his New England birthplace and populated the fictional place with eccentrics, such as Miniver Cheevy, who lead wasted, blighted, or impoverished lives. Robinson's work was an American exemplar of the realism permeating European literature, especially novels and short stories, in the second half of the nineteenth century. Appropriately, "Miniver Cheevy" reads like a revealing and realistic short story in verse, providing readers with a snapshot portrait of a main character whose story is a sad case of inaction and arrested development lost in futile reverie.

The poem opens with Miniver Cheevy so wrapped up in dreams of the past that he loses weight and weeps in self-pity. His frustration stems from idealized visions of medieval glory and classical heroism set in Camelot (King Arthur's legendary castle), Thebes (the realm of Sophocles' Oedipus), and Troy (King Priam's doomed city in the *Iliad*). Sadly, any romance or artistry that once gave rise to epic poetry and grand tragedy seems to him to have dwindled in the present to the stature of a bum on local welfare ("now on the town").

So it is that Miniver daydreams about legendary personages, such as the Medici rulers of Renaissance Florence, whose wickedness would incite him to perform his own evil deeds, if only he could escape into the past and be a member of that infamous family. He would gladly trade his commonplace clothing for medieval armor, although he still holds on to some modern corruptions, such as his love of money, which otherwise he scorns in his escapist imagination.

Poor Miniver, "born too late," wastes his life in intense, useless contemplation that leads to confusion of mind. He blames his futility, not on himself, but on the unlucky timing of his existence, as alcohol fuels his irresponsible dreams.

Forms and Devices

"Miniver Cheevy" is a satire consisting of eight quatrains, each with alternating feminine (weak) end rhymes conveying the futility of the speaker's escapism through sound effects. Assonance and consonance permeate the poem.

The prevailing meter in the first three lines of each quatrain is iambic tetrameter with variations ("Hĕ wépt thăt hé wăs évĕr bórn"). The metrical regularity lends a sing-song effect that seems to lull Miniver into his romantic dreaming, until the illusion evaporates in the ironic dissonance of the short fourth line of every quatrain, with its abrupt two iambic beats and a fluttering unaccented sound of the feminine end rhyme ("Aňd hé hăd réasŏns"). Thus, readers can almost hear the dreams float away into a vapid realm of comic nonsense ("ŏf írŏn clóthĭng") or reality ("Aňd képt ŏn drínkĭng").

The poem is a satire, ridiculing the folly of the speaker for the moral instruction of readers. Instances of burlesque—making what is high appear to be ridiculously low—occur in the descriptions of Priam's heroic compatriots (line 12), romance and art (lines 15-16), the Medicis (lines 17-18), and the wished-for armor (lines 23-24). The medieval and classical allusions to places, figures, and objects create an inappropriate romantic backdrop for modern, mundane Miniver.

The poem is a fine example of ironic compression, with a maximum reduction of the number of words to create a bluntness necessary to annihilate the dreamer's illusions in the minds of readers. The very name "Miniver" suggests, elliptically, both his minimalness and an antiquated medieval knight's name. Moreover, to call Miniver simply "a child of scorn" engenders a double meaning: that he is an object of scorn to others, and that he is the very personification of one who is scornful of his environment. Again, abrupt phrases, such as "And he had reasons" or "And kept on drinking," add to the many ironies reverberating throughout the poem.

Robinson characteristically uses diction that mixes the elegant and the mundane ("He mourned Romance, now on the town,/ And Art, a vagrant"), the abstract and the concrete ("He missed a mediæval grace/ Of iron clothing"), as well as the exotic and the flat ("Miniver loved the Medici,/ Albeit he had never seen one") to achieve the maximum satiric effect, deflating both the dreamer and the dream.

Finally, the repetition of "and thought" in lines 27 and 28, is a brilliant stroke, capturing Miniver's stupid dedication to fantasy. Speaking volumes about Miniver's mental dullness and irresponsibility, the repetition appealed to Robert Frost, Robinson's greater disciple, another twentieth century poet of the New England scene. As Frost noted in his introduction to *King Jasper* (1935), "The first poet I ever sat down with to talk about poetry was Ezra Pound. It was in London in 1913. . . . I remember the pleasure with which Pound and I laughed over the fourth 'thought' in 'Miniver thought, and thought, and thought,/ And thought about it.' . . .[Robinson's] theme was about unhappiness itself, but his skill was as happy as it was playful."

Themes and Meanings

"Miniver Cheevy" is about a small-town drunkard living in the mundane present and wasting his life away in futile fantasies about a medieval and classical antiquity. It is a verse portrait of an irresponsible and idle dreamer who expends his energy in reverie and who will never face up to the truth of himself as a self-created failure.

The poem is built on ironic contrasts between the unheroic Miniver as he is, and his dreams of adventure, romance, and art associated with heroic figures of the legendary

Trojan War in ancient Greece, King Arthur's knights of the Round Table in the Middle Ages, and the dazzling brilliance and corruption of the Medici in the Renaissance. What a great figure he might have been, Miniver reasons, had he been born at the right time. That he has not succeeded is not his fault; he uses the classic excuse that the rest of the world is wrong.

Miniver escapes from the world of reality into a world of dreams induced by alcohol. Each stanza's final short line with its feminine ending provides an appropriately tipsy rhythm. The name Miniver, with its suggestion of the Middle Ages, patchwork royalty, and minuteness, coupled with the diminutive-sounding Cheevy, sums up his failure. The tone of the poem is one of humor, pathos, and sympathetic understanding, but there is a mocking note also, an intimation that Miniver's unfortunate situation is not the result of any cosmic flaw in a nonexistent high tragedy; Miniver is a clown prince of his own tragicomedy of life.

Thomas M. Curley

THE MISSING PERSON

Author: Donald Justice (1925-   )
Type of poem: Narrative
First published: 1967, in *Night Light*

The Poem

Donald Justice's "The Missing Person" is a thirty-five-line free-verse poem composed of seventeen couplets followed by a final single line. The poem narrates the story of a man coming to the police station to report himself as a "missing person," and through this initial paradox the poem examines questions about identity and the relation of individual identity to society.

The poem begins with a person, named only as "He," arriving to report himself as a "missing person." Although the poem does not specifically say where the speaker has arrived, one imagines it to be a police station or other public building where such reporting would be appropriate. In the second stanza the authorities hand him some forms to fill out. The description of the authorities is extended in stanzas 3 and 4, where they are pictured as having "the learned patience of barbers," waiting idly for customers, "Stropping their razors."

Faced with the blank spaces of the forms, the man "does not know how to begin." He does not seem to know who he is, or perhaps who he is will not fit into the spaces that are provided for declaring one's identity. Trying another method to get a fix on his own identity, in stanza 8 he "asks for a mirror." The authorities assure him that he can be nowhere but where he is, "Which, for the moment, is here," as if mere presence were an adequate substitute for identity. The man would like to believe the authorities' easy answer, but he knows there is more to the story.

The image he sees "emerging// Slowly" from the mirror, in stanzas 13 and 14, is intriguing. He finally sees himself, albeit darkly, as an external image. This leads to images of how others see him. He is one who comes out "Only by dark," one who "receives no mail," one whom the landlady knows only for "keeping himself to himself." This trio of visions of himself as others see him, however, hardly adds to the self-knowledge the man desires. Rather, it emphasizes his obscurity and his lack of relations with others, his disconnectedness.

The poem ends with the reflection that it will be years before he can trust to show himself in the light, and even if he does, what he shows will be a disguise, "This last disguise," for who he really is. This ending seems to affirm that the self is essentially unknowable, both to the self and to others. On the other hand, it may be poetry that most closely reveals the self, even as it grapples with the self's disguises.

Forms and Devices

"The Missing Person" looks very simple in its construction, absent of rhyme and meter, with no attempt, indeed, to make the lines come out evenly. The words and punctuation could almost be prose. Justice presents the poem in brief couplets, with anywhere from one to eight words per line, but mostly three- to six-word lines. Laying the poem out this way, with much white space, encourages the reader to take it slowly, meditatively—an appropriate approach for the difficult problem of identity. It is quite interesting and effective that the poem is written in couplets all the way through except for the last line. The poem is about the relationship between a person and his identity, as if the identity could somehow be separated from him, put into words on a form, reflected in a mirror, made into an exterior object such that he could examine and understand himself. The couplets seem to imply a feeling of companionship—each line goes with another—but this only makes the final single line, and solipsism of the "missing person," more poignant.

There are several other images that highlight the possibility of companionship, only to frustrate it. As the man stares at the spaces in the form, into which he will write his identity, the spaces "Stare up at him blankly." There is an implied communion between the man and the spaces as they stare at each other, but nothing comes of it as there is no self in the spaces; they merely stare "blankly." The authorities speak to him, and "he might like to believe them," but he cannot. He is on a mail route, with all the potential for connection with correspondents that that brings, but he "receives no mail." He has a landlady, who could perhaps be a friend, but she only knows him as one who keeps "himself to himself."

In addition, the missing person is nameless; there is no personal handle for others to address him individually. He cannot know himself, and others cannot know him. These are not disconnected phenomena. Part of the reason he cannot know himself is because no one else knows him, and thus he can receive feedback from no one. Just as the mirror reflects a visual image of people, the social network reflects and creates part of people's identity, but for the missing person, the mirror and the social network reflect very little. Although the poem seems simple in style, it grapples effectively with difficult ideas.

Themes and Meanings

The central paradox of "The Missing Person"—one can only report others, not one's own self, as missing—highlights Justice's inquiry into the nature of identity, of one's own ability to know oneself. The difficulty of this undertaking is illustrated through the subject's inability to fill in the blanks in the forms he is given, his request to look in a mirror, and the final image of himself as in a dark house, years away from trusting himself to be out in the light of day.

To a lesser extent, the poem deals with the relationship of the individual and his or her identity to the "authorities." In the second stanza the authorities hand the "missing person" the forms, and in the third and fourth stanzas the authorities are pictured, waiting for him to fill out the forms. They wait "With the learned patience of barbers," idle except for when they are "Stropping their razors." There is nothing especially frightening about their patience until one sees them stropping their razors, and then one need only imagine a little background music from an Alfred Hitchcock film for the image to appear very sinister indeed.

Many of Justice's poems in *Night Light*, the book in which "The Missing Person" first appeared, deal with loners, with isolation. From the boy who imagines a romance with a dressmaker's dummy ("Ode to a Dressmaker's Dummy") to the aging magician, alone on his island ("The Last Days of Prospero"), the book is replete with characters in isolation. Nevertheless, two poems from that collection give an idea as to how Justice finds meaning and connection from within the isolated context. In "To the Unknown Lady Who Wrote the Letters Found in the Hatbox," the speaker addresses a woman who wrote letters of sadness, decline, and implied isolation, which were found in a hatbox after her death. That Justice wrote this "reply poem" suggests that the woman's sufferings and loneliness did have meaning in that they were communicated to a sympathetic listener—Justice—who has taken the time to write a reply.

In "Poem to Be Read at 3 A.M.," the speaker writes while passing in a train a town with a single night light on. The speaker says the poem is addressed "for whoever/ Had the light on." That person can obviously be the original person in Ladora, the town in question, but it is also the reader, whoever is sympathetically reading the poem. In the case of "The Missing Person," even as the subject in that poem searches for his identity and despairs of finding it, he creates a bond with the reader, who has also faced doubts about identity.

Poets are generally excellent at studying subjectivity and identity, and they display their findings in their poems. By giving artistic form to studies of diverse characters, and by examinations of their own musings, poets help readers to better understand the complexity of identity. From that perspective, while the "missing person" may be unsuccessful in discovering his identity, he helps readers to discover their own.

Scott E. Moncrieff

MONT BLANC

Author: Percy Bysshe Shelley (1792-1822)
Type of poem: Meditation
First published: 1817, in *History of a Six Weeks' Tour Through a Part of France, Switzerland, Germany, and Holland*

The Poem

Mont Blanc is a meditative and descriptive poem in five unequal stanzas of irregularly rhymed iambic pentameter. As with several of Percy Bysshe Shelley's poems, scholars still dispute important details regarding its text. An early title specifies that the poem was conceived "at the extremity of the vale of Servoz"; a later subtitle has it "written in the vale of Chamouni," which is a trough-like valley at the base of Mont Blanc. Mont Blanc itself is a stupendous sight as one comes upon it suddenly around a bend of the ravine through which the river Arve (originating in one of the glaciers of Mont Blanc) runs. Shelley probably stood on a bridge (the Pont de Pellisier) crossing the ravine to contemplate the scene. In his day, Mont Blanc was thought to be the highest mountain in Europe. From the bridge, it looms before the observer as one of the most dramatic views anywhere in the Alps; it is noted for its height, its formidably jagged rocks, its unforgettable glaciers, and the eerie whiteness from which it derives its name.

The first stanza of *Mont Blanc* reflects on the human mind itself, comparing it to the ravine of the Arve over which the poet is standing. The Arve flows through the ravine as influences from the material world flow through the mind, like a stream of consciousness. The river and the ravine have shaped each other, but the extent to which each has shaped the other is unclear. The second stanza is a more tangible demonstration of the thought process described in the first. The Arve now is specifically described as Power, meaning not only the material power of matter in motion, but also the power of nature to influence the mind, even to the extent of creating poetry.

In the third stanza, the poet/narrator turns his attention from the ravine below him to the domineering mountain directly ahead and above him. Like everyone else, he is awestruck, almost hypnotized, as he contemplates its impersonal command of the entire scene. Dominating even the lesser mountains by which it is flanked, Mont Blanc appears to transcend all the limits of earthly existence, especially the shortlived mortality of mankind. Despite attempts by the intellectualizing poet to find some kind of beginning for the mountain (through earthquakes or volcanic eruptions), it seems virtually eternal.

Stanza 4 then pointedly contrasts the mortality of man and his works with the timelessness of the material world and its "primeval" (existing from the beginning) mountains. Most of the stanza is devoted to a vivid description of Mont Blanc's glaciers, which are inexorably destructive of anything human placed in their paths to oppose them. The closing lines paradoxically affirm the hydrological cycle, in which snow, ice, glaciers, the Arve (a river derived from the glaciers but bringing fertility to man), the ocean, and the water evaporated from it are all seen to be one.

Finally, stanza 5 sums up Shelley's profound meditation upon Mont Blanc, power, and human existence by first acknowledging the power of nature and then surprisingly but effectively disputing it by championing the primacy of the human mind over any manifestation of the material world.

Forms and Devices

Mont Blanc is a difficult poem, in part because Shelley attempted to capture within it the very rapid workings of his own mind. At several points, the poem seems unfinished, abandoned rather than perfected. For this reason, one's reading of it should probably depend more upon the major images it evokes than upon the precision of its sometimes uncertain language.

The poem abounds with symbolic landforms, some of which cannot be precisely identified or related altogether coherently with others. In stanza 1, for example, lines 6-11 constitute an elaborate simile based upon some landscape not immediately at hand (though perhaps a version of the same scenery that is developed later on). Both the "feeble brook" of line 7 and the "vast river" of line 10 are products of "secret springs" (line 4) and have something to do with human thought; none of this, however, is very clear. The most usual reading is that the "vast river" is the same as the "universe of things" flowing through the mind in lines 1 to 4. If so, then the human mind is dominated by passively received sense impressions (as in the philosophy of John Locke) rather than by its own autonomous creations. Throughout the poem, however, one sees the mind regularly allegorizing the world of nature and thereby giving it a significance that it would not otherwise possess.

In his gripping natural descriptions throughout the poem, Shelley utilizes a category of landscape aesthetics already denominated in the eighteenth century as the sublime. Its complementary opposite is the picturesque, in which (like a modern tourist) one was invited to stand in precisely the right spot so as to see before one a natural scene resembling a landscape painting, with foreground, background, side curtains, and a center of interest all in order, as if arranged by a master artist. Such views commonly celebrated God's creative talent, reaffirmed traditional religious belief, and consequently spared the observer any troublesome awareness that his outlook may have become obsolete. It was different with the sublime, which emphasized the amoral power of nature and its heedlessness of mankind. Far from reassuring and safeguarding the observer, the sublime tended instead to emphasize his helplessness, destabilizing him both physically and intellectually.

One sees the contrast between these two modes of landscape perception most obviously in stanza 3, lines 76 to 83. They too are puzzling, in part because of a major crux (textual difficulty) in line 79, where Shelley wrote "In such a faith" in one version and "But for such faith" in the later and generally accepted one. Do they mean the same thing, or did Shelley change his mind? The kind of faith involved is undoubtedly William Wordsworth's rather than that of Christian orthodoxy; in any case, the stanza's last lines refer to the Mountain's "voice." Shelley apparently wavered here between accepting a benign, Wordsworthian view of nature and the harsher, perhaps more realistic one that he then affirms so impressively in stanza 4.

Themes and Meanings

Shelley's *Mont Blanc* is one of the most philosophical of all landscape poems; it is also among the greatest. It is partly a reply to William Wordsworth's "Lines Composed a Few Miles Above Tintern Abbey" (1798), in which both the type of landscape described and the implications suggested by it are much cozier. Both poems deal with the human mind, but Shelley (unlike Wordsworth) is not concerned with its development through childhood to maturity. Instead, he takes for granted a richly endowed adult mind that simultaneously perceives and abstracts. Unlike Wordsworth, he is not fundamentally concerned with memory. Thus, one not only sees the poet's mind at work, creating the very poem one is reading, but one also sees his mind analyzing itself. It is clear that the mind in question is both rational and creative.

Besides analyzing itself, the poet's mind also analyzes nature, particularly in its relations to humankind. That nature strongly influences human thought is both implied and assumed; for one thing, nature is often beautiful and therefore attracts one's attention. Shelley records no evidence to suggest that natural beauty is in any way purposeful, however; for him, no divine being deliberately created an aesthetically pleasing world for the enjoyment of its human inhabitants. Nor is nature a moral teacher (as Wordsworth held), except in ways that typical nature-lovers had never recognized.

The world of Mont Blanc—which, for Shelley, encompasses the entire earth—is fundamentally indifferent to either the survival or the happiness of humankind. Any benefits it bestows upon humans are therefore not divine favors but mere accidents. The outstanding difference between nature and man, for Shelley, is that nature endures throughout time whereas man does not. This is the real lesson to be learned from nature (lines 92-100).

Yet Shelley does not ultimately concede. In the final stanza, he confronts Mont Blanc straightforwardly, both as a fact and as a symbol. He sees the height, the power, the coldness, and the isolation of Mont Blanc and celebrates them (in lines 139-141). The material universe, already seen to be eternal, is infinite as well (lines 60, 140). Yet in a strikingly abrupt conclusion—three lines that ultimately outweigh all the rest of the poem—a shocking reversal takes place, as Shelley taunts the gigantic mountain by pointing out that its only significance (indeed, nature's only significance) is that given to it by the human mind. In this sense, then, the eternal universe in which humans live is constantly being re-created according to human dictates.

Dennis R. Dean

MONTAGE OF DISASTERS

Author: Amy Gerstler (1956-   )
Type of poem: Narrative
First published: 1997, in *Crown of Weeds*

The Poem

"Montage of Disasters" begins with an italicized query: *"Where's the eloquence in all this?"* The question is followed by, as the title indicates, a montage of disasters—train wrecks, fires, earthquakes, bombs, viruses, biblical plagues, mutant spiders, and sinking ships. The poem is like a series of newsreels spliced together in a random fashion or a collage of cover stories from old newspapers, a few copies of *The Star* and *The National Enquirer* thrown in with *The New York Times.* The narrative begins with the train wreck: "The train lurched, shuddered, and snapped in two." However, the train story is abandoned there, and other disconnected scenes follow: "No one knew for sure how the fire started./ Then the virus got into the milk supply." As cataclysm is piled on cataclysm, the report becomes oddly and blackly humorous as reality merges with fiction and nightmare blends with horror story. After bombs destroy the zoo, setting the animals free, "grinning crocodiles new orphans watched/ slither into fountains by the ruined library."

The poem begins in the third person. However, somewhere around the middle the first-person point of view finds its way into what was hitherto a report by an unidentified narrator: a meteorite is described as crashing through the window and turning "my side/ of the bed to a tidy pile of cinders." Once the first person surfaces it remains until the end of the poem, and the events become continually more bizarre and absurd. Murders and scenes from science fiction horror films are slipped into the mishmash of natural disasters. The dog keeps lunging at the trash barrel until "he tipped it over and out fell/ this manicured hand." Typical film monsters are produced by radiation, which causes "tarantulas in the basin/ to grow hundred of times their normal size." The effect is of fireworks of terror shooting off in rapid succession and then all at once; at the end, "the dead bodies" begin to "glow, bluely" and looters begin to "work the ruins." The final scene changes the "I" to "we" as it invokes the last scene in so many horror movies in which the heroic couple is left over in the debris at the end of the nightmare after the monsters have been killed. The city is still aflame, but the fires are dying:

> . . . We first met
> oh, it seems lifetimes ago, staggering
> through fog banks, dodging columns of oily
> smoke, wandering the city in singed pajamas.

This last scene summarizes the conclusion of all the horrors, real and imagined. At the beginning, the poem asks: What kind of eloquence, what kind of verbal beauty, can appear in such a bizarre sequence? There is no answer, only the strange pileup of odd miseries that suggests the collection of disasters chronicled by Voltaire in *Candide* (1759). The poem has a Voltairean kind of humor throughout. "Montage of Disasters" is similar in tone to Amy Gerstler's other work in her 1997 collection, *Crown of Weeds*. Gerstler's poetry is known for its eccentric jumps, weirdly on-target associations, and oddball personas. Her works tend to begin with startling announcements or scraps of hair-raising action. This poem is another of her thrill-ride narratives. Riding the edge of surrealism, "Montage of Disasters" makes the reader question the smooth surface of the ordinary. It also demonstrates that terror has its own clichés.

Forms and Devices

"Montage of Disasters" is a forty-four-line poem in blank verse. The tone is relaxed and conversational. Most of the lines have three to five accented syllables, or six to eight words, which give a vague uniformity to the poem's slightly ragged rectangular appearance on the page. There is, however, no clear pattern of rhythm, and there is no obvious reason for the positions of the line breaks except to maintain the overall appearance. The enjambed lines are not pulling against an underlying rhythm, and this informality enhances the flat, reporter-style tone of the poem. The flatness of style is also emphasized by the lack of simile and metaphor. Language is simple and direct, with some colloquialisms and some deliberately vague expressions that create the impression of casual understatement: "The women/ caused an awful lot of trouble/ in the lifeboats that night." There is a preponderance of short words, even monosyllables. The sentence structure is intentionally unvaried, with verb predictably following subject. The reader has a sense of being given "just the facts," although the facts themselves are strange and shocking and combine the improbable or mythical with the ordinary: "Nuns poured stiff jolts of whiskey/ into paper cups for sooty rescue crews./ Later, it rained frogs." When the ordinary is consistently and repeatedly combined with the peculiar, the reader tends to blur them after a while, and this blurring contributes to the effectiveness of the poem. Traces of postmodern technique appear in this superficially coherent, though bizarre, narrative. As does much postmodern work, the poem effaces boundaries, allowing material from one world to flow into another. Here the immediately obvious violated boundary is between fact and fiction, but there are others—dream and experience, self and other, night and day, human and animal. The picture is finally something like Pieter Brueghel the Younger's paintings of hell, but this hell is painted with tongue in cheek.

What is most compelling about Gerstler's style is the distinctive voice. The reporter style challenges assumptions about observation and reporting. The reader can almost hear the voice of a newscaster describing horrific events in a determinedly cheery timbre and with a certain standard rhetoric. The mismatch between tone and content becomes even more obvious when the first person enters the story: The speaker exhibits only mild curiosity about the untoward events she is witnessing, and perhaps now and then a certain satisfaction creeps into her own observations, such as when she sees "a tidy pile of cinders."

The way the disasters merge and overlap allows them to lead off in all directions from the central narrative, posing unanswered questions. The montage form itself, in its piecing together of parts of things, has both a limited surface and a wider implication beneath the surface as each piece also implies the rest of the picture. Scraps torn from other complete pictures have been stuck together to create a new shape, the shape of this narrative.

Themes and Meanings

Gerstler's themes in "Montage of Disasters" are similar to those in the other poems of *Crown of Weeds*, which continues strains of thematic concern found in her earlier books. "Montage of Disasters" implies that the conscious and the unconscious are more connected than people think. The surreal narrative, with its clips from nightmares, horror films, and newsreels, may suggest that there is an unconscious, shared script for the disasters people fear and that this script, cribbed from the same sources she uses, is filled with clichés.

In any case, the wild flinging together of disparate images in "Montage of Disasters" asks that readers revise their concept of what is ordinary and expected. In Gerstler's poetry, the unexpected is the expected, and anything may follow from, or cause, anything else. The strange is so close to the surface that it may poke through at any point. Nothing is predictable or reliable, but everything is reported as though it were. "One lesson we learned was this:/ you cannot cut corners when building a dam." Gerstler's poetry often has a social dimension that comes from her emphasis on offbeat characters; although in this poem it is really situations rather than characters that are eccentric, the poem may telegraph a message of egalitarianism through its equivalence of all disaster scenes and all social upheavals. In this surreal landscape of disaster, all are equally victims. The world falls away beneath the feet of humankind.

"Montage of Disasters" is also memorable for its sheer narrative pyrotechnics. Several reviewers have referred to Gerstler's style as "acrobatic," and there is skill in her narrative leaps and loops. As the story jumps from one scene to another, it seems to deconstruct itself. Humor replaces horror. The humor has a sting; the reader is complicit in laughing at all these exaggerated horrors, but what does this say about the reader? The conclusion has a hint of euphoria as the couple wanders through the ruins, having survived and reported upon all these natural and supernatural events. Influenced but not overwhelmed by postmodernism, "Montage of Disasters" is a superficially simple poem, but underneath it is subtle and teasing and defies closure.

Janet McCann

THE MONUMENT

Author: Elizabeth Bishop (1911-1979)
Type of poem: Lyric
First published: 1946, in *North and South*

The Poem

Elizabeth Bishop's poem "The Monument" is written in seventy-eight lines of free verse with a few significant breaks for verse paragraphs. The title is important in that it defines the object that is being described and discussed by the poet. The poem is narrated by a knowledgeable and perceptive speaker who describes the monument and tells the naïve reader, an otherwise undefined "you," how to see it and read it. This speaker asks, "can you see the monument?" with some interest and urgency. It is of prime importance that readers see what is immediately before their eyes, that they understand what it is and what it does.

The word "monument" suggests a memorial or sacred object that holds special significance to a group of people or a nation. The word will acquire other connotations and denotations as the poem proceeds. The monument is made "of wood/ built somewhat like a box." Immediately, there is a clash between readers' expectations about the object and the material of which it is made: One expects a monument to be made of marble rather than wood. The poet-speaker then describes its shape and size. It is not stately but seems to be jerry-built "like several boxes in descending sizes/ one above the other." It does, however, have a form: It has four sides, and four "warped poles" hang from it like "jig-saw work." The speaker then shifts to the monument's context. It is "one-third set against/ a sea; two-thirds against a sky." The perspective is also significant: "we are far away within the view." The sea that it is set against is also a human-made object: It is made of "narrow, horizontal boards."

At this point, the person who is being instructed objects: "Why does that strange sea make no sound?" It is not natural to the naïve reader, who asks if "we're far away." The tone of the poet-speaker changes at this point. She more directly insists on the monument's nature and significance. It is from "an ancient principality" with an "artist-prince" who might have intended it to be a tomb or boundary. The naïve reader is still not satisfied: "It's like a stage-set; it is all so flat!" It does not meet the reader's predetermined and limited expectations of art and nature. The poet-speaker becomes even more insistent. She points to its existential nature: "It is the monument." However, the naïve speaker continues to object and asks, "what can it prove?" Apparently this speaker wants art to be useful and to do something.

The poet-speaker has the final word. She says, "It is an artifact," not a thing of nature. It is organic: "It chose that way to grow and not to move." Its uniqueness "give[s] it away as having life." It is not limited by intention or one meaning; it may be one thing or another. What is inside, perhaps its meaning, "cannot have been intended to be seen." Its existence, rather than any meaning ascribed to it, is what is significant.

The poet finally defines the monument as a work of art: "It is the beginning of a painting,/ a piece of sculpture, or poem, or monument,/ and all of wood. Watch it closely." The poem begins with the demand that readers see the work and ends with it becoming active and alive, something that must be watched closely.

Forms and Devices

Bishop is a poet noted for her use of description, and, in "The Monument," this technique is especially important. Description, in her poetry, tends to replace the use of such traditional poetic methods as metaphor. The poem is a detailed description of an object that acquires significance as the poem develops. It is written in free verse with many run-on lines, very few lines that end with a period or semicolon, and sentences that are long and meandering. This construction mirrors the indirect nature of the argument that Bishop constructs in the poem.

The diction and tone of the poem are especially interesting since it has two very distinct speakers who use very different language. The naïve speaker's sentences are all questions, while the poet-speaker uses direct declarative and imperative sentences. The tone of the naïve speaker is querulous and complaining, while the poet-speaker's tone becomes more insistent, demanding that readers see the monument and see what is significant about it. There are also some important juxtapositions of words in the poem. There is, for example, the clash between "artist" and "prince" in "artist-prince." Furthermore, the monument is always described as an object made of wood while readers and the naïve speaker expect it to be made of marble or granite.

There is a good deal of imagery in the poem, although much of it is set against readers' expectations and the connotations of the monument. There is a lot of wood imagery: "grains," "splintery," and "whittled." In contrast, there are a number of images associated with artifice: The monument is a stage-set and, most important, an artifact. There are also the very different images of light and growth at the end of the poem. There is no specific use of metaphor; however, the monument becomes, through the detailed description, a metaphor or symbol for a work of art. The poet-speaker insists that readers be aware of the nature and existence of that work of art and to see what significance it does and does not contain. To do this, the poet must show readers what a work of art is not: It is not a thing of nature, and it does not prove anything. Bishop's approach is indirect, but the poem begins to grow from mere description into an exemplification and definition of the nature of art.

Themes and Meanings

"The Monument" is about the nature and existence of a work of art. On that theme, Bishop has surprising things to say. For example, the material of the monument is wood rather than the expected granite or marble. This suggests that art is made of everyday material and experience rather than great matter that is wrought into a fixed position. The monument also has an unexpected and irregular shape. For Bishop, one definition of a work of art might be that which defeats expectations and grows out of ordinary material into a shape that is very much its own.

A work of art is also very different from nature. The naïve speaker complains of the artifice of the monument and wants it to be more like nature, to mirror the form of natural elements rather than becoming a thing in itself. One source for Bishop's view is Wallace Stevens's poem "Anecdote of a Jar." Stevens's jar and Bishop's monument are unmoving. They do not ape nature but dominate it, although they are connected to it by analogy. "The Monument" also insists that a work of art does not prove anything or make a statement. Any meanings it may have seem to be accidental or to grow out of its nature. What is inside is not intended to be seen. "The Monument" seems to embody the famous dictum of Archibald MacLeish's "Ars Poetica": "A poem should not mean but be." "The Monument" also suggests that a work of art cannot be limited to one reading or interpretation. The words "might" and "may" recur several times in the poem. To fix the work is exactly what the naïve speaker is trying and failing to do.

The poet-speaker makes clear what the monument stands for at the end of the poem: "It is the beginning of a painting,/ a piece of sculpture, or poem." It represents any work of art. Significantly, it is only the beginning of that work. It cannot come into existence unless a reader becomes aware of its nature and brings it into being. Readers must understand any work of art on its terms rather than on their own. That is why the reader is urged at the end of the poem to "Watch it closely." By giving oneself up to the work of art, the reader can watch it come into being.

James Sullivan

MOONLIGHT

Author: Paul Verlaine (1844-1896)
Type of poem: Narrative
First published: 1867, as "Fêtes galantes"; as "Clair de lune" in *Fêtes galantes*, 1869;
English translation collected in *Paul Verlaine: Selected Verse*, 1970

The Poem
Composed of twelve ten-syllable lines, "Moonlight" is divided into three stanzas, each of which possesses its own regularly alternating rhyme scheme (*abab, cdcd, efef*). The title of the collection in which the poem originally appeared, *Fêtes galantes*, bears considerable importance on a visual level to the interpretation of this piece. Antoine Watteau (1684-1721) was renowned as the painter of "fêtes galantes," jewel-like renderings of men and women dressed in satins, lounging gracefully in nature's lushness. In the same way that Watteau, in *A Pilgrimage to Cythera*, invites the eye to take in the golden splendor of love in paradise, Paul Verlaine invites the reader to discover a world colored by moonlight and enlightened by strolling musicians.

In the first stanza, Verlaine compares the soul of an unknown person—"your soul"—to a landscape, which is personified as being gladdened by masked musicians, who play the flute and dance, dressed in gaudy colors. Contrasting with the happy countryside, the musicians exhibit traits of sadness, scarcely concealed by their colorful disguises.

The second stanza focuses on the musicians, now singing huskily of love that conquers and the fullness of life. Seemingly doubtful of the happiness that they depict in song, they offer music that blends with the softness of the moon's rays. The personification of the landscape in the first stanza continues in the final stanza; the moonlight rays are sad, birds dream, fountains sob in ecstasy. The coldness of marble statues contrasts with the subdued spirituality of personified elements in this concluding stanza.

Through the musicians' "gaudy colours of disguise," Verlaine evokes the timeless opposition between "l'être et le paraître," between reality and illusion. It is ironic that the initial tone of joy and joviality in the first stanza should yield to one of pronounced sadness, permeating nature as well as mankind. The fact that Verlaine chose this poem to be the collection's *pièce luminaire* reveals that, as the introductory poem, it was likely meant to set the stage for further development of similar scenes. Both time and place—night and countryside—lend themselves to a meditative state, one that belies the gaiety conveyed by the strolling musicians.

Verlaine's sensibility is revealed effectively through the painterly aspect of his poetry. The association between the collection's title and Watteau's work is, therefore, all the more fitting, since Verlaine brings into play with precision and wistfulness particular scenes found in eighteenth century French painting. It is, however, the irony in "Moonlight" that goes beyond a simple romanticized landscape, since the main point of this poem is the metaphorical depiction of a person's soul. The development of the poem's focus from the comparison between soul and landscape in the first stanza to the portrayal in the second of the musicians' sadness, and finally to the climax in the third stanza underlining the moon's sad beauty differs markedly from the aesthetics of those plastic arts that evoke a similar scene. Verlaine's skill as a writer enables him, therefore, to illuminate gracefully an aspect of the human condition that is perhaps imperceptible to the casual observer.

Forms and Devices

Verlaine's poetry is extremely mellifluous. It is not surprising that "Moonlight" has been set to music by Claude Debussy (in 1881), Gabriel Fauré (1887), and Gustave Charpentier (1896). The musical qualities of the original text result largely from the resonance of *b*'s, *f*'s and *v*'s combined with the proliferation of *a*'s. Curiously, the smooth flow of the English version is strengthened by the repetition of *s*'s, a some-what dissonant sound that succeeds, nevertheless, in creating an ethereal quality ("soft moonlight rays—so beautiful to see," line 9) that elevates the scene to a dream-like level of existence. Generally speaking, Verlaine utilizes simplicity of form and musicality to encapsulate a commonplace of eighteenth century plastic arts, but at the same time, he offers on a visual level a new dimension to this cliché. By penetrating the façade of the country idyll, he underscores a hidden anguish that seizes the reader's attention in the penultimate line of the final stanza.

The microcosm depicted by the poet serves as an obvious point of comparison with the soul that is mentioned in the first line of the first stanza. At the opening of the text, Verlaine establishes the metaphor evoking "your soul" as a landscape that progres-sively reveals itself to be less than joyous, although it is initially presented as a "cho-sen landscape glad." The irony of this metaphor is that the reader assumes incorrectly from the poem's first line that the remainder of the text will blindly follow a pattern like that of Watteau's paintings, which depict images of pleasure and revelry in a set-ting of natural perfection. The subtlety with which Verlaine visually guides the reader is the key to his use of irony. Given the often romanticized symbolism associated with moonlight, the image of which is present in the title as well as in the second and third stanzas, the reader's expectations that the text will fashion yet another superficial ren-dering of love and tranquillity under the moonlight seem to be confirmed. Gradually, however, there appear indications that "Moonlight" will rebel against romantic con-ventions. The musicians "strum the lute and dance and are half sad" (line 3); "They seem to doubt that they can happy be/ And blend their song with soft rays of the moon" (lines 7 and 8). The minstrels' song tells of the power of love and the fullness of life, and it intermingles with the moonlight, oddly described in line 9 as "sad moon-light rays." This shift from the gladness of the landscape in the first stanza to the sad-ness skillfully rendered in the second and third stanzas culminates in a curious parox-ysm of emotion in the poem's final lines: "And sparkling fountains sob in ecstasy/ Amid the marble statues in the glade." The strangeness of this personification creates an eerie atmosphere, given the odd combination of tears and profound happiness sug-gested by this image. It is to be noted, however, that the marble statues evoke a perma-nent physical state, and that they exist in isolation. This final image completes the metaphor by drawing the reader's eye to the permanence of physical existence, anchored in solitude, and contrasts sharply with the soul mentioned at the beginning of the text. The opposition between the heaviness of physical existence and the ethereal quality of spirituality is, therefore, effectively rendered by means of the ironic development of the text's central metaphor.

Themes and Meanings

Painting a metaphorical picture of a person's soul, "Moonlight" evokes simple desires for beauty, love, and tranquillity. The atmosphere of increasing disillusionment that emanates from the poem lends itself to a meditative and introspective tone. The reader inevitably wonders whether love and happiness can be found in reality. The central metaphor suggests that everyone carries an "interior landscape" within, and in this particular case, the elements that form it are, paradoxically, both beautiful and forlorn. The dichotomy between *l'être* (being) and *le paraître* (appearance) is one of the most important themes of "Moonlight." In addition to this perhaps surprising combination of physical beauty and sadness, Verlaine communicates to the reader the impossibility of attaining complete happiness. In doing so, the poet suggests that in life, as in the afterlife—the latter symbolized by the soul—man's desires for perfection, be it for overly romanticized love or a perfect life, will inevitably remain unfulfilled. In this way, Verlaine guides one through a self-examination that poses various questions concerning one's expectations in life as well as one's appreciation of the ambient world. The true essence of existence is, therefore, not visible on the surface.

There is, however, some ambiguity in the concluding lines of the poem, for although "sparkling fountains sob in ecstasy," "even birds dream in the leafy shade." Sadness is seen not as a stultifying force, but as one that leads to introspection and contemplation. One important aspect of "Moonlight" is Verlaine's obvious love of natural beauty; the poet endeavors to encourage the appreciation of a beauty that is neither gaudy nor artificial. "Moonlight" puts into perspective hopes and desires in order that the individual might have a more balanced conception of existence, one that is unencumbered by the physical, which is symbolized by the marble statues anchored in their own permanence. They are to be admired for what they offer, but one must remember to appreciate them for what they are: objects created by man that render his creativity immortal.

"Moonlight," a deceptively simple narrative poem, addresses philosophical and aesthetic preoccupations that have long fascinated writers and artists. Why does it seem that sad songs are the most beautiful? What special aesthetic attraction does sadness exert? Verlaine does not provide the answers. The poet does, however, endeavor to challenge the reader's beliefs by creating with words a scene that does not conform to the aesthetics of eighteenth century plastic arts. Crossing boundaries and provoking unexpected reactions, Verlaine demonstrates a particular perception of existence through his mastery of irony.

Kenneth W. Meadwell

MOONLIT NIGHT

Author: Du Fu (712-770)
Type of poem: Lyric
First published: wr. 756, as *"Yue ye"*; collected in *Zhuan Tang Shi*, early eighteenth
century; English translation collected in *The Selected Poems of Tu Fu*, 1989

The Poem

"Moonlit Night" is one of Du Fu's most frequently translated short lyrics. Because
love poems are relatively rare in Chinese poetry, "Moonlit Night" is a rather precious
gem.

As the poem opens, the poet imagines that his wife must be by herself in her boudoir, gazing at the moon in Fu-chou (Fuxian county, Shaanxi province). He feels sorrowful because his children, so small and so far away from him, will not understand
why they should remember Ch'ang-an (Xi'an, Shaanxi province). At this point, half
of the poem is already over, and it seems that nothing extraordinary has been said.
Suddenly, however, what could very well be a prosaic poetic idea gathers momentum
and becomes vitalized when the focus shifts back to the wife in the next two lines,
here translated literally:

[In the] fragrant mist, [her] cloud-hair [gets] wet;
[In the] limpid light, [her] jade-arm [gets] cold.

In this couplet, the poet invokes the presence of the absent wife with complex sensory
experiences, suggesting that the wife, losing sleep over the absent husband, must be
pondering deep in the night. Unexpectedly, this suggestion turns around the relationship between the subject and object of the longing, making the separation between the
couple unbearably poignant. In the conclusion, the poet wonders when he and his wife
will be together again, so that, leaning against the open casement, both of them could
have their "trails of tears" dried at the same time by the moonshine.

"Moonlit Night," though apparently a brief and simple poem, was actually composed under circumstances of epic proportions. In 755, a civil war known as the "An-
Shih Rebellion" broke out in China. The revolt was led by the border Commander-
Governor An Lu-shan and his lieutenant Shih Si-ming. An Lu-shan, whose military
and political influence had been accumulating since 742, turned his troops toward the
capital Ch'ang-an, which soon succumbed to the rebel forces. Shortly before the capital fell, the Emperor Hsüan-tsung and his family, as well as Prime Minister Yang Kuo-
chung, had already set out for Ch'eng-tu in flight. On their way, at a place called Ma-
wei-p'o, the imperial guards mutinied and killed the prime minister. Blaming Yang
Kui-fei, the emperor's *femme fatale*, for the insurrection, the guards demanded her
death. The emperor had no choice but to comply. Li Heng, the crown prince, was also
persuaded to leave the emperor and go north; after reaching Ling-wu (in Gansu province), upon the abdication of his father, he succeeded to the throne as Emperor Su-

tsung. Meanwhile, Du Fu, who had been granted a position before the siege of Ch'ang-an, set out from his home in Fu-chou in an attempt to join the new emperor. On his way, he was captured by the rebels and taken to the fallen capital, where he was detained for eight months. The poem "Moonlit Night" was written in these circumstances in the autumn of 766, probably on the occasion of the Mid-Autumn Festival, when family reunion is a general custom.

Forms and Devices

"Moonlit Night" is a poem written in the "recent style," as opposed to the "ancient style." The "recent style," which matured in the T'ang dynasty, requires a poem to follow regular tonal patterns and also to observe the rule of semantic and syntactic parallelism for its couplets. There are two kinds of recent-style poems. One is known as the *lü-shih*, or "regulated verse." It consists of eight lines, usually with two couplets in the middle. The other is known as the *chüeh-chü*, or "truncated verse." A "truncated" poem, which has only four lines, almost seems to be half of a regulated poem. Whether "regulated" or "truncated," a recent-style poem has either five or seven characters per line.

"Moonlit Night" is a regulated poem with five-character lines. Although most regulated poems have two couplets in the middle, "Moonlit Night" has only one. In fact, this poem is rendered extraordinary by its sparing use of a single couplet, which occurs in lines 5 and 6. Because the language of the entire poem is rather plain except for these two skillfully crafted lines, the couplet, which deals with the imagined sleeplessness of the wife, in effect achieves a kind of poetic climax or stasis by arresting the reader's attention.

The beauty of the couplet can be analyzed on two levels. On the rhetorical level, although in fact it is the poet who is saddened by the absence of his spouse, the two lines make the wife grieve over the husband's absence. This is a mimetic or mutual projection in which the interplay between presence and absence is designed to dramatize the separation between the couple. By reversing the subject-object relationship, this couplet allows the poem to elevate itself from prose to poetry. On the semantic-syntactic level, the couplet is also remarkable for its use of two conventional synecdoches— "cloud-hair" and "jade-arm"—to stand for the wife. Furthermore, each of these synecdoches also interacts with the elements of the environment: Just as the "cloud-hair" gets wet in the "fragrant mist," the "jade-arm" also gets cold in the "limpid light." These interactions not only achieve interesting synesthetic effects, but also produce the precise psychological condition that is desired by the poet. Finally, the words "wet" and "cold," which in Chinese can be verbs as well as adjectives, are placed at the strategic endings of the lines in a kind of climatic apposition to the environmental elements and synecdoches, thus suggesting that "wet" could refer to either the "fragrant mist" or the "cloud-hair" (or both), and "cold" to either the "limpid light" or the "jade-arm" (or both). This appositional syntax further reinforces the sensorial synaesthesia as well as the psychological yearning; indeed, the culmination of the couplet in the word "cold" seems to blend the sensory with the psychological by confusing the two levels of feeling.

Themes and Meanings

Family reunion is an important theme in Chinese poetry, and many poems are based upon the "reunion *topos* [topic]." In a poem employing this *topos*, the full moon—especially that of the Mid-Autumn Festival, when the moon is roundest and brightest—takes on symbolic meanings because it reminds the poet of his or a family member's separation from the home. "Moonlit Night" certainly belongs to the genre of poetry built around the "reunion *topos.*"

What sets "Moonlit Night" apart from other poems dealing with separation and re-union, however, is its ingenious treatment of the object of longing. Traditionally, it is usually a man who yearns for a reunion with a friend or a brother. Du Fu has, in fact, written another "Moonlit Night" poem about his brother using the reunion *topos*. The yearning for one's wife in this poem subtly adds to the general theme of separation and reunion the somewhat more novel theme of love. In addition, as far as the tradition of Chinese love poetry is concerned, it is usually the wife who yearns for the return of the traveling husband, whereas here it is the husband who yearns to return to his wife, who he believes is also yearning at the same time for his return. In its layering of yearning upon yearning, "Moonlit Night" may be described as a love poem in which the relationship between subject and object is obscured. The ending of the poem, which must have shocked its readers because of its rather direct proclamation of pas-sionate feelings, in effect inaugurates a new sensibility that Chinese male poets will feel comfortable to exploit thereafter.

From a larger perspective, it can be said that a political theme is also intertwined with the reunion theme and the love theme of the poem. In "Moonlit Night," as lines 1, 2, 5, and 6 make clear, one of the basic situations is that of a woman who is saddened by the absence of her husband. This allows the reader to see the poem from the per-spective of the "boudoir plaint" convention that has been popular since the Han dy-nasty. In a "boudoir plaint" poem, a wife usually laments the absence of her heartless husband, who is traveling as a merchant, fooling around with courtesans in the city, serving in the capital as a bureaucrat, or stationed at the frontier to fight against bar-barians. In a subtle sense, "boudoir plaint" poems are not simply love poems but also, more importantly, allusive critiques of government policies such as war and social evils such as the practice of concubinage that have led to the desolation or desertion of the woman. T'ang poetry is in fact replete with examples of "boudoir plaint" poems that raise serious questions about the tragic dimensions of war. In Du Fu's poem, a po-litical theme along the lines of the "boudoir plaint" tradition thus lurks behind the mention of place names such as Fu-chou and Ch'ang-an. Considering Du Fu's reputa-tion as a patriotic poet, the hardships involving him, his family, the people, and the na-tion as a whole could very well be part of the cause for tears to be shed upon the re-union of husband and wife.

Balance Chow

THE MOOSE

Author: Elizabeth Bishop (1911-1979)
Type of poem: Narrative
First published: 1976, in *Geography III*

The Poem

Elizabeth Bishop's "The Moose" is a narrative poem of 168 lines. Its twenty-eight six-line stanzas are not rigidly structured. Lines vary in length from four to eight syllables, but those of five or six syllables predominate. The pattern of stresses is lax enough almost to blur the distinction between verse and prose; the rhythm is that of a low-keyed speaking voice hovering over the descriptive details. The eyewitness account is meticulous and restrained.

The poem concerns a bus traveling to Boston through the landscape and towns of New Brunswick. While driving through the woods, the bus stops because a moose has wandered onto the road. The appearance of the animal interrupts the peaceful hum of elderly passengers' voices. Their talk—resignedly revolving itself round such topics as recurrent human failure, sickness, and death—is silenced by the unexpected advent of the beast, which redirects their thoughts and imparts a "sweet sensation of joy" to their quite ordinary, provincial lives.

The poem is launched by a protracted introduction during which the speaker indulges in descriptions of landscape and local color, deferring until the fifth stanza the substantive statement regarding what is happening to whom: "a bus journeys west." This initial postponement and the leisurely accumulation of apparently trivial but realistic detail contribute to the atmospheric build-up heralding the unique occurrence of the journey. That event will take place as late as the middle of the twenty-second stanza, in the last third of the text. It is only in retrospect that one realizes the full import of that happening, and it is only with the last line of the final stanza that the reader gains the necessary distance to grasp entirely the functional role of the earlier descriptive parts.

Now the reader will be ready to tackle the poem again in order to notice and drink in its subtle nuances. Bishop's artistry will lie plain, particularly her capacity to impart life to a rather unnerving redundancy of objects and to project a lofty poetic vision from a humble, prosaic incident.

Forms and Devices

Description and narrative are the chief modes of this poem. Nevertheless, at critical moments the actual utterance of the anonymous characters is invited in ("Yes, sir,/ all the way to Boston"). The binder of these varied procedures is the speaker's tone of voice: calm, subdued, concerned with detail and nuance, capable of a quiet humor, in sovereign, though unassuming, control.

The thirty-six-line introduction is the most sustained piece of writing in the poem. It forms a sequence of red-leaved and purple Canadian landscapes through which the blue bus journeys. Then, in smaller units, for another thirty-six lines the bus route is reviewed, main stops mentioned, and further details concerning the passengers, the weather, and the scenic sights duly recorded. Day is replaced by evening, and light gives way to darkness. The eleventh stanza brings in a climactic moment of equilibrium and economy of design. Beginning with the thirteenth stanza, the first quotes are used, as they will again be in the twentieth, twenty-fourth and twenty-fifth, and, finally, in the twenty-seventh stanza. Stanza 14—the moonlight episode—is the very center of the poem. This section is rhymeless, though this is amply compensated for by the triple epithets in the third line, and it marks the transition from the outer, natural world to the inner, human concerns of the second part of the work, which includes lines 85-129. Usually unchronicled and unheroic human tragedy receives an indirect presentation, culminating with the moving and dramatically rendered twentieth stanza. The third part of the poem begins, appropriately, in mid-stanza with line 130. The encounter with the moose—the climax of the entire poem—is allotted two descriptive stanzas (the twenty-fourth and the twenty-sixth). The remaining two stanzas form a kind of a coda, bringing the poem to an end with a powerfully ironical twist obtained by juxtaposing the "dim smell of the moose" to the "acrid smell of gasoline."

The diction of the poem modulates in accordance with the needs of its plot. Thus the first part, devoted to the landscape, is richly descriptive, replete with qualifying epithets that, toward the end (in line 75 and in line 81), come in by threes, like beads on a string. In the second part, dealing with the passengers' plight, learned, latinate words such as "divagation," "auditory," "hallucination," "eternity," and "acceptance" signal the presence of the narrator-commentator. In the third part—the one reserved for the moose—epithets return. In the climactic twenty-fourth stanza, the most distinctly poetic devices—explicit comparisons—are bestowed on the protagonist: "high as a church,/ homely as a house." Moreover, the four additional epithets lavished on the moose contribute to the grandeur of its appearance: "towering, antlerless," and "grand, otherworldly."

By careful calibration and timing of her tropes, Bishop succeeds superbly in achieving her ends. Contrast is attained by her control over all compartments of language, and her austere, restrained tone and strategy of deferral and understatement are dramatically effective.

Themes and Meanings

"The Moose" is ultimately about the human need to be purged and, if possible, cured of selfhood. Self-absorption or narcissism is not only a passing malaise afflicting teenagers. Older people regard themselves in the mirror of their memories; they often run the risk of becoming trapped in despair or self-pity. Hence, the need to forget one's obsessions and delusions is a pressing one.

The moose miraculously appears in Bishop's poem to offer the passengers of the bus, the narrator included, a remedy for their solipsism. Curiosity is stirred in them, and a sweet, joyful sensation supervenes. The author invests her wildlife messenger with an otherworldly or religious awesomeness. The female moose becomes for the nonce Mother Nature—grand, fearless, and unselfconscious. Both like a church and like a house, the moose cow is a prehistoric reminder that humans are not stranded in this world, that there are dignified creatures that seem to be freer and more self-sufficient than humans are, and that human lives are richer because they exist. It is this almost mystical sense of fellowship that pervades the last third of Bishop's poem.

Humans need the moose as a friendly "other" capable of dispelling the anxiety induced by their inability to communicate significantly across the ghetto of the human species. Civilization has ruined nature and has alienated humankind from it. The man-made environment of highways, bridges, and buses cuts across the wildlife habitat in order to reach the Boston of human discontent. At the end of the poem, the clash between the "dim smell" of the moose and the "acrid" smell of gasoline poignantly dramatizes the incompatibility between nature and culture. This disharmony has been foreshadowed in the poem by the subtle overlapping between the reds and purples of sunsets and maple leaves and the "blue, beat up enamel" of the bus, whose hot hood the moose finally gave a welcome sniff. Even though the encounter is brief, its effects will reverberate in the readers' wakened consciousness.

There is a distinguished tradition of poetry writing to which Bishop's "The Moose" belongs. It can be traced back, as poet John Hollander has noted, to William Wordsworth's *The Prelude* (1850), whose so-called episode of the Winander Boy (book V, lines 389-413) deals with the ancestral impulse to talk to nature's creatures. The Winander Boy initiated such a dialogue by mocking the hooting of owls. To his delight, the birds responded in kind. In between the mystic silences, nature's deeper secret motions flooded the boy's heart and soul. For the British Romantic, such a communion with nature could still be available to a few elected spirits whose purity and innocence had already marked them for intense experiences and an early death.

Hollander also noted a connection between Robert Frost's poem "The Most of It" and "The Moose." Frost had his male protagonist proudly call out to nature for something more than the "copy speech" that the Winander Boy had elicited from his owls. His wish for "counter-love, original response" was finally granted by the sheer chance appearance of a powerful buck that, lordlike, tore his way through tarn and wilderness without bothering at all to acknowledge the presence of the human intruder.

By contrast, Bishop's female moose has the curiosity to approach the trespassing bus in order to look it over and assess it in her mute, nonaggressive way. Finally, it is the bus that, pressed for time, leaves the spot—her territory—while the moose remains on the moonlit macadam road without budging.

Stefan Stoenescu

"MORE LIGHT! MORE LIGHT!"

Author: Anthony Hecht (1923-   )
Type of poem: Lyric
First published: 1967, in *The Hard Hours*

The Poem

Anthony Hecht's "'More Light! More Light!'" is a poem of witness, a narration of murders centuries apart: first, the execution, by fire, of a medieval prisoner, and next, the killing of two Jews and a Pole in Germany during World War II. In formal, measured quatrains, Hecht speaks of nearly intolerable atrocities. The poem begins with a painfully detailed account of the death of the first man, who is burned at the stake: "His legs were blistered sticks on which the black sap/ Bubbled and burst as he howled for the Kindly Light." It is part of the poem's irony, and its power, that this horrible death is by far the most humane event in "'More Light! More Light!'" The medieval prisoner is stripped of his life, but not his humanity. He suffers physical torture yet retains the hope of his soul's salvation, as do even his executioners. His is an age of faith; his death is public and ceremonial and not, to himself nor to those who witness it, meaningless.

The twentieth century, in Hecht's poem, is the true age of darkness: a world of "casual death" with no hope of redemption for victims of its random brutality and systematic evil. The only witnesses to the murders of the Jews and the Pole are "Ghosts from the ovens"; the death of a single man at the stake has become a mass burning, a Holocaust both physical and spiritual.

Much happens in this short poem of eight stanzas, and there is an urgency and immediacy in the telling that draws the reader in despite the lack of background. Stanzas 1-3 describe the first death. Hecht does not name the man condemned to die at the stake, nor name his crime—perhaps heresy, the critic Daniel Hoffman suggested—but his description evokes sympathy. Awaiting death, the prisoner writes "moving verses" and calls upon God to witness his innocence. Though little can relieve the cruelty of the means of death, the victim is "Permitted at least his pitiful dignity," and prayers are said for his soul.

With the fourth stanza, the reader enters a different world, a shift made clear by the change in tone. "We move now to outside a German wood," the stanza begins, the poet's voice almost a parody of the narration for a film travelogue. The stark description of events that follows, however, makes clear that any irony here is dark and savage rather than playful. A German soldier, identified only by his uniform and gun—glove, boot, Lüger—orders a Pole and two Jews to dig a grave, then orders the Pole to bury the Jews alive. When the Pole refuses, he is ordered to change places with the Jews. Too drained by war to resist, they begin to bury the Pole; at the last minute, the order is reversed, and the Jews are told to dig him out. This time, when the Pole is ordered to bury the other men alive, he does so, dehumanized by the mocking game of death. The ending of the game is brutal: The German shoots the Pole in the belly and he dies a lonely and anonymous death with "no prayers or incense," no one to comfort or to mourn him.

The final image of the poem places the death of the three victims in the larger context of the millions murdered in the Holocaust, whose ghosts are evoked as "black soot" from the crematory ovens. For such an enormity, Hecht seems to say, there can be no false light of hope, no redemption, and the poem offers none, only the silent witness of the dead.

Forms and Devices

"'More Light! More Light!'" tells its story in eight rhymed pentameter quatrains, or four-line stanzas, in a variation on the traditional ballad form. Like a ballad, the poem tells a story of the past—a story that may or may not be apocryphal, but that feels emotionally true. If the exact incidents described here did not happen, horrors like them certainly did. This blurring of history and myth is heightened by the anonymity of the characters in the poem; neither the victims nor their persecutors are named. The effect is to universalize Hecht's parable of cruelty, denying the reader the luxury of imagining that evil is limited to one person or one time or place. All humanity is implicated in these actions.

Hecht's diction is spare and formal. Like the ghosts from the death camps he evokes, the poet is present in the work as a disembodied spectator, relating the events as they happen. There is no first-person narrator and little attempt to mediate or interpret the action. The details are precise, almost reportorial, viewed as through a lens of time and distance.

In another poem from *The Hard Hours*, "Behold the Lilies of the Field," Hecht speaks in the voice of a disturbed man who relates a dream in which he is forced to watch the torture and death of a fallen Roman emperor; bound and helpless, the watcher is forbidden to close his eyes or look away. In "'More Light! More Light!'," it is the reader who is made to bear witness. Rather than entering into the minds and emotions of the characters, the language works to remind readers of their place as readers, as watchers who, perhaps like the poet himself, can see and know the world's evil but cannot end it. Casting a cold eye on pain that is probably beyond description, the poet elicits emotion from the reader precisely by not demanding it. The starkness of a sentence such as "He was shot in the belly and in three hours bled to death" offers no judgment. Hecht provides the facts and allows the reader to imagine a scene for which ordinary adjectives of sorrow or outrage would seem inadequate.

Synecdoche is a device the poet uses several times, and to great effect. Hecht never describes the Nazi officer in the final scene; his menace is conveyed solely through his gun and glove: "The Lüger hovered lightly in its glove." Appropriately faceless, dehumanized, the soldier represents the institutionalization of evil, opposed to the frail humanity of the Pole, represented by his "quivering chin" and his eyes which, in the poem's final image, are lightless and lifeless. In a sense, too, the events of the poem are themselves synecdoche: miniature scenes of death that represent a larger canvas of

destruction. To read of the death of millions may be more than the mind can comprehend, but by showing one lonely killing "outside a German wood," Hecht takes the
Holocaust out of the realm of statistics and makes it life-sized; like the anguished
watcher of Hecht's other poem, the reader cannot look away.

Themes and Meanings

"'More Light! More Light!'" may be read as a Holocaust poem, a World War II
poem, a historical poem, or simply a modern, quietly anguished asking of an eternal
question: How can God, if God exists, permit the cruelties human beings inflict upon
one another?

Hecht served in Europe in World War II; he saw the concentration camps, spoke
with survivors, viewed the dead. As a Jewish American, Hecht was haunted by what
he saw and heard of the Holocaust; it shadows many of the poems in *The Hard Hours*.
"Rites and Ceremonies," a long poem that is the center of that volume, also views the
Holocaust in the context of humanity's long history of hatred. In it, scenes from the
concentration camps mingle with those of a ritual burning of Jews as scapegoats for
the Black Death; the path from the stake to the ovens is clear. In one of the collection's
most personal poems, "It Out-Herods Herod. Pray You, Avoid It.," the poet, safe in
suburbia, contemplates his children, knowing that he could not have saved them from
the gas chambers.

"'More Light! More Light!'" is rich in ironies, not least of which is its title. Taken
from the dying words of the German poet Johann Wolfgang von Goethe, the phrase
reminds the reader that a culture capable of producing great and enlightened artists
could also produce the architects of the death camps. Light, in the poem, represents
both God and humanity, but in the darkness of the Holocaust both are dimmed: The
"light from the shrine at Weimar" fails to appear, and the "light in the blue Polish eye"
also dies, to be replaced by "a black soot." Hecht is not blind to the hypocrisies of an
earlier age—Christians praying for the soul of a fellow Christian as they burn him or
her alive—but the poem's bleak ending suggests that the Enlightenment, or Age of
Reason, has failed to enlighten humanity. People are no less murderous, only more efficient in their means of killing, able to reduce millions to ashes. "Much casual death
had drained away their souls," Hecht writes of the two Jews in his poem, and this may
describe the world Hecht knew after the war. When death becomes cheap, dispensed
en masse with the flip of a switch or the giving of an order, may not life become cheap
as well?

Hecht is a poet of the modern age who is haunted by history. In "'More Light! More
Light!'," as in other poems, he writes of ancient conflicts and hatreds playing themselves out in new guises. In a poetic era dominated by free verse, Hecht is known for
his virtuosity with formal meter. He writes, with great beauty and control of language,
of savagery and hatred, as if language is the only balm left to salve a wounded world.

Kathryn Kulpa

THE MORNING OF THE POEM

Author: James Schuyler (1923-1991)
Type of poem: Lyric
First published: 1980, in *The Morning of the Poem*

The Poem

"The Morning of the Poem," James Schuyler's longest poem, extends to forty-four pages and is the title poem of the book for which the author won the Pulitzer Prize in literature in 1981. The lines, except those in a few short sections, are long, and the appearance of those lines is nearly uniform, most extending to a second line of indented text. The poem is written mostly in free verse.

The event that has propelled the poem into being is Schuyler's awakening one morning, in July, 1976, at his mother's home in rural East Aurora, New York. Domestic pleasures and comforts abound, nature provides opportunities for reverie and entertainment, and the poet's mother is not overly intrusive: "Then to the kitchen to make coffee and toast with jam and see out/ The window two blue jays ripping something white while from my mother's/ Room the radio purls." Schuyler, however, misses New York City, where his life is centered and where his friends are. The painter Darragh Park, to whom the poem is dedicated, is especially on Schuyler's mind; the "you" addressed in the poem is often Park, whose relationship with Schuyler seems ambiguous. The two appear not to be lovers, exactly, but they are probably more than good friends: "How easily I could be in love with you, who do not like to be touched,/ And yet I do not want to be in love with you, nor you with me," Schuyler writes.

By the conclusion, July has slipped seamlessly into August, and Schuyler is anticipating his return to New York City. There has been very little action, but the reader has learned much about Schuyler. In this poem, which closely resembles a personal journal, Schuyler records quotidian events such as trips to the toilet and petty squabbles with his mother; reminisces about erotic encounters, which occur less frequently as he drifts into later middle age; thinks fondly of his friends, most of whom, such as the painter Fairfield Porter and the poet John Ashbery, were or are closely connected with the New York art world; and delights in both the beneficence and occasional cruelties of the natural world. (It should be noted that Schuyler, Ashbery, Kenneth Koch, and Frank O'Hara constitute the nexus of the "New York School" poets, all of whom have in common, to varying degrees, an involvement with the work of New York-centered artists of the middle of the twentieth century such as Willem de Kooning and Jackson Pollock.)

The structure of the poem is loose. Schuyler's impressions of the physical world, memories from childhood, thoughts of friends, and occasional travel notes ("in New York City you almost cannot buy a bowl/ Of oatmeal: I know, I've tried") do not occur in any clear order but are noted in a stream of consciousness. The poem's beginning and ending, with vivid descriptions of the poet urinating, constitute the most concrete elements of traditional structure. As critic Stephen Yenser notes, "He seems to mock the notion of aesthetic unity by virtually framing the poem with trips to the john." Schuyler is much concerned with the ordinary, the mundane, the flotsam and jetsam of daily life, but he also addresses issues many readers may consider more serious: Deaths of friends, especially of Porter, and more ominously, his own death, which may lie in the not-too-distant future, are a constant refrain.

Forms and Devices

Schuyler laments the dearth of good poets. The problem is that most have "No innate love of/ Words, no sense of/ How the thing said/ Is in the words, how/ The words are themselves/ The thing said . . .// A word, that's the poem./ A blackish-red nasturtium." Schuyler is perhaps echoing the American poet William Carlos Williams, whose dictum "No ideas but in things" influenced later generations of American poets.

"The Morning of the Poem" employs few poetic devices such as simile, metaphor, or symbol. For Schuyler, the "thing said" is interesting enough in itself, and there is little need to obfuscate through abstraction. As *The Diary of James Schuyler* (1997) reveals, Schuyler was drawn to the writings of naturalists and diarists, often from the previous century, whose appeal rests much in their powers of observation. Roses can never be roses for Schuyler. They are, instead, "Bunches of roses on/ The dining table, Georg Arends, big and silver-pink with sharply/ Bent-back petals so the petals make a point . . ./ or Variegata di Bologna, streaked and freaked in raspberries and cream." The poetry is both in the description of the rose and the name of the rose; it is in a similar spirit of collecting and recording that Schuyler reproduces a shopping list or recounts a childhood erotic experience. However, words are not important in simply their power to name or describe. "How the words are themselves/ The thing said" refers as well to the sounds of words. The following lines illustrate:

> . . . the pigs were big and
> to be kept away from: they
> were mean: on the back porch was the separator,
> milk and cream, luxurious
> Ice cream, the best, the very best, and on the
> front porch stood a spinet
> Whose ivory keys had turned pale pink: why? . . .

Schuyler employs a number of poetic sound devices in this selection. The reader notices the internal rhyme in "pigs/big" turning into assonance, or near assonance, and consonance in "milk/spinet/pink." Similarly, the reader may appreciate how the repeated long *e* and *m* sounds in "mean" and "cream" (twice) carry into "ivory," repeating the long *e*, losing the *m*, and picking up "cream's" *r*. There is a certain resolution in "keys," again repeating the long *e* and also the *k* sound established in words such as "kept," "back," "milk," and "luxurious." The plaintive question "why?" is given poignancy by Schuyler's preparing the reader, in terms of sound, by the long *i* assonance in "ice" and "ivory." The passage quoted above is not unique in the poem. The careful reader, noticing Schuyler's complex use of sound devices, may avoid the error of reading the work as a disorganized compendium of sense impressions and memories but may instead appreciate how Schuyler's art, while appearing, upon casual inspection, to lack the kind of linguistic artifice people may associate with poetry, is, in its own subdued way, wrought with great subtlety.

Themes and Meanings

Readers might explore the larger ideas in "The Morning of the Poem" through the prism of Schuyler's homosexuality, which he writes of freely. In this, it is tempting to see Schuyler as an heir of Walt Whitman, whom Schuyler names in the poem and who wrote of homoerotic desire in *Leaves of Grass* (first published in 1855, revised a number of times) in a manner that nineteenth century readers and even some twentieth century readers found shocking. Whitman was compelled to keep his homosexuality under a veil in ways that Schuyler is not. Thus, Schuyler's description of his attempt to pick up a man in the grocery store and not obscuring real curiosity about the man's body ("trying to get a front view of him and see how he was/ Hung and what his face was like") may be read as a sign of poetic kinship with perhaps American poetry's most important figure.

Yet for Schuyler's relative openness about his sexuality, a certain covertness and a certain sadness remain. Schuyler, born in 1923, was fairly entrenched in middle age by the time of the gay liberation movement. Thus Schuyler, with all the importance he places on naming things and people (a love of naming, too, with roots in Whitman), only very rarely names boyfriends or lovers. In this respect, it seems rather sad that Schuyler cannot actually name "the one who mattered most," presumably a lover. Schuyler echoes the experiences of a generation of gay men whose characters were shaped both by the repression of the 1940's and 1950's and the greater freedom of the 1960's and 1970's.

Schuyler's homosexuality might account for many of the poem's tensions. The poet's relationship with his mother, for instance, appears not altogether loveless but remote. Occasional references to the sanitarium, Anabuse (a drug used to aid recovering alcoholics), and psychiatrists remind the reader of the narrator's bouts with substance abuse and schizophrenia, problems associated with societal pressures a homosexual of Schuyler's generation might have faced. Such scattered references, coupled with the fact that "The Morning of the Poem" follows, in its printed form, Schuyler's "The Payne Whitney Poems" (short poems about one of Schuyler's stays in a psychiatric hospital) make the reader wonder whether the visit to East Aurora was planned to aid the poet's recovery. Finally, Schuyler's state of near homelessness underlines a certain deep loneliness the reader senses. Although Schuyler has a mother in East Aurora and friends in New York City, he lacks a true home with a committed, lifelong companion. The reader is left wondering if, when Schuyler returns to his apartment "back to Chelsea, my room that faces south," he will find anything resembling fulfill-ment. The poem's open-endedness ("Tomorrow: New York: in blue, in green, in white, East Aurora goodbye") is liberating insofar as a man weighed down by little may experience life as a series of endless possibilities. However, this sense of freedom is also disquieting: If a man has nothing to weigh him down, what remains?

Douglas Branch

MORNING SONG

Author: Sylvia Plath (1932-1963)
Type of poem: Lyric
First published: 1965, in *Ariel*

The Poem

Sylvia Plath had recently given birth to her daughter Frieda when she wrote "Morning Song" in February, 1961. This eighteen-line lyric is structured in three-line stanzas or tercets. Although the title promises a song, the only song the reader gets is a baby's cry. Plath may be experimenting with a traditional form of love poem called an *aubade* in French or *alba* in Provençal. Both refer to a lyric about dawn or a morning serenade. In such poems, the lover, usually in bed with a beloved, laments the dawn because it signals their inevitable parting. Plath's poem mentions love only in the first line: "Love set you going like a fat gold watch"; that is, the love of the parents gave birth to the baby. The mother love that the speaker is expected to feel is strangely absent in this poem. Instead, the mother-speaker moves from a strange alienation from this new being to a kind of instinctive awakening to the child's presence, her connection to it, and her appreciation for its "handful of notes."

Once the reader grasps the situation of the poem—the birth of a child—the remainder of the poem is reasonably clear. Although the emotional interest of the poem focuses on the new mother, both parents are mentioned: "Our voices echo" and "your nakedness/ Shadows our safety. We stand round." Plath startles the reader with line 7: "I'm no more your mother." Maternal feelings do not automatically occur. Plath is extremely honest to admit such strong feelings of alienation and separation in her poem. In the last three stanzas, the emotional estrangement of the speaker changes. She is compelled to listen to the sound of her child as it sleeps. She seems attuned to that "moth-breath" and says, "I wake to listen." When she hears her baby cry, she gets up to feed it: "cow-heavy and floral/ In my Victorian nightgown." As she breast-feeds her child she observes the coming dawn as the light changes outside the window.

Plath closes with a reference to the sounds the child makes, probably not a cry of need since it has just been fed. The "Morning Song" of the title turns out to be the baby's "handful of notes;/ The clear vowels rise like balloons." Plath makes a definite contrast between the "dull stars" of the morning and the "clear vowels" of the baby. The speaker praises her baby and appears much less alienated than at the poem's beginning.

Forms and Devices

Plath is known for her striking images and her metaphors and similes. In this poem, there is a surreal quality about some of her imagery. In its attempts to express the workings of the subconscious, surreal art employs fantastic imagery and incongruous juxtaposition of subject matter. To compare a child to a "fat gold watch" is surreal.

The child is animate while a watch is inanimate. Love is engaging while winding up a watch is a mechanical act. What the simile suggests is the great distance between the act of love and the fact of the baby. What does this baby—this thing with its own existence—have to do with the emotions that engendered it? By raising this question about what most people consider a most "natural" phenomenon—the birth of a child—Plath helps the reader see something very old (childbirth) as something quite strange, new, and unsettling. The disorienting effect of Plath's style is typical of Surrealism.

Plath emphasizes the child's strangeness—its thingness—by referring to its cry as "bald." Her choice of adjective is odd. The baby's head may be "bald," but by describing its cry this way, Plath seems to emphasize the nonhuman quality of this new being/thing that does not take its place among other humans but "among the elements." Stanza 2 reinforces the nonhuman quality of the baby as perceived by its parents. The child is a "new statue." The parents are pictured as gazing at it "in a drafty museum." In other words, they cannot help staring at the child, but they feel vulnerable and inadequate: "We stand round blankly as walls." With the child as a statue and the parents as walls, not much communication occurs. Plath's surreal images underline the parents' feelings of alienation and strangeness in this new (to them) situation.

Stanza 3 contains not only the most striking line ("I'm no more your mother") but also the most puzzling image: "Than the cloud that distills a mirror to reflect its own slow/ Effacement at the wind's hand." First, clouds do not distill mirrors. The shadow cast by a cloud reflects it; when the wind moves the cloud along, both cloud and shadow disperse. The bond this mother feels to her baby is just as insubstantial and fleeting. Plath's image is convoluted and perhaps deliberately inexact. She suggests the tenuous relationship between mother and child, cloud and mirror. It is as if the birth of the child were external to the mother rather than part of her. Fortunately, the speaker discovers she is wrong. Maternal instincts arise in her.

She is attentive to the breathing sounds her child makes. The imagery animates those sounds: They are like "moth-breath," suggesting how quiet and subtle they are. It is as if she can see the moth as it "flickers among the flat pink roses," suggesting the patterns on wallpaper or fabric. Otherwise, the roses would not be "flat." The contrast signifies the aliveness and motion of the moth-breath versus the less vibrant roses. The new mother, listening to her child's breath-in-sleep, uses the image "A far sea moves in my ear" as if she were holding a shell to her ear and capturing the sounds of the ocean. The child's delicate moth-breath suggests something more ponderous—new life and new possibilities.

The child's mouth is "clean as a cat's," with the emphasis on "clean": This new being is untarnished. Plath uses this word again in "Nick and the Candlestick" to describe her son: "The blood blooms clean/ In you, ruby." It is a word of praise. No longer a statue, the child's presence takes on more spirited animation through the animal imagery. The speaker's lack of feeling for her child gradually transforms into appreciation and wonder, particularly at its sounds—not a "bald cry" any longer but something shaped, "a handful of notes." The child enters the human world when the speaker perceives its attempts at language: "The clear vowels rise like balloons." The poem closes on this image of ascension, a typical Plath strategy. "Morning Song" records how the speaker's perception of her baby changes; her intimacy with her child grants her the vision of its animated being.

Themes and Meanings

The dominant theme in "Morning Song" is alienation and the process by which it is overcome. A woman's poem, it deals with maternal instinct and its awakening. Plath avoids sentimentality in taking up a subject—becoming a mother—that is often treated in a superficial way. A woman—certainly an ambitious poet such as Plath— does not come to motherhood merely by giving birth. New behavior is learned. The being of the mother is as new as the being of the child. Readers can appreciate Plath's honesty in dealing with her subject. It also takes a certain amount of courage to admit to a colossal lack: "I'm no more your mother/ Than the cloud." The alienation in the poem is overcome by such acute delineation of the feelings. Instinct has a role to play as well: The speaker finds herself listening to the child's sounds. This is not self-willed or under her control. She follows her instinct: "One cry, and I stumble from bed." In the end, she is rewarded. Alienation is overcome in her connection to her baby. Her own child serenades her with a "morning song" and a bond is formed through language, the quintessential human act.

The third tercet, with its convoluted imagery, introduces a secondary theme: the speaker's awareness of her child as potentially marking her insignificance, her erasure as a poet: "I'm no more your mother/ Than the cloud that distills a mirror to reflect its own slow/ Effacement at the wind's hand." Can a woman be both mother and famous poet? Plath, writing in 1961, had few predecessors who managed to achieve both. In engaging this theme, she is dealing with one of the major issues that faced women poets in the twentieth century. If mothering absorbed her attention, would she still be the poet-artist she longed to be? This superb poem answers her implied question. Further, the joyous ending proclaims the arrival of both a new singer on the scene and a mother proud of her child's vocal bravura.

Claire Keyes

MORRO ROCK

Author: Garrett Kaoru Hongo (1951-   )
Type of poem: Meditation
First published: 1985; collected in *The River of Heaven*, 1988

The Poem
"Morro Rock" is a long poem in free verse, its eleven stanzas varying in length
from three to twenty-eight lines. The rock of the title is a landmark offshore in Morro
Bay, California; it serves as a focus for memory and meditation as the narrative moves
from various descriptions of the rock to events and images suggested by its form, location, and environs. Ultimately, the rock becomes a symbol for the play and importance of the imagination and for the uncertainty of reality.

Although Garrett Kaoru Hongo's poem is autobiographical, it ultimately moves beyond the personal voice to make a statement about perception and about the act of
writing poetry. In this sense, it can be termed metapoetic.

The poem begins in mid-line with a dash, as if the first description offered of the
rock is simply another in a series of possibilities. In the fog, the rock resembles a fe-
dora; in the sun, it invokes the choppy yet unified movement of a modern sculpture.
No matter how it is described, the rock is perceived as an intrusion, something out of
place and unnatural as it violates the smoothness of the ocean surface and the regularity of the surf. The second stanza is interpretive. The narrator indicates the importance
of the perceiver in giving Morro Rock its identity. He imagines its omnipresence in
various situations, such as a tuna run, the franticness and carnage of which reminds
him of the war. In stanza 3, a day at the beach with one's father encompasses an attempt to capture the perfect photograph, to render the rock as an artistic artifact.
Finally, in stanza 4, the rock plays a part in a love story gone awry.

The last line of stanza 4 offers an important comment on the role of the rock. When
the lovers feel the emptiness of the death of their affair, "The Rock filled the space behind us." Morro Rock is simultaneously an absence and a plenitude, or a fullness of
presence. It offers a hinge for the attachment of meaning, a mass that can occupy the
blank spaces of knowing and reading reality in one's life.

In stanza 5, the "true" affair of the author's teens becomes mythicized, material at
once for sordid retellings at youthful gatherings and archetypal accounts among the
aged for all time, like the biblical narrative of Abraham and Sarah. The love story is
carried forth in stanza 6, the center of the poem. Here are the homely and superficial
details of a typical courtship, its innocuous beginnings. No one can object, just as no
one can truly understand the nature of Morro Rock, until the surface is scratched.
When the lovers merge physically to offer a unit in opposition to or rivalry with the
agreed-on truths and morals of the community, they become scapegoats and martyrs
to their new vision: After "finding the gods/ in each other, . . . the lovers were killed with
stones, . . . and a quick, purging fire of hate." They are the victims of racial prejudice,

but their love becomes generalized with the use of words with mythological resonances: the riders "hooded like hanged men," the women "keening in the night . . . crowlike," the lovers' death "smeared with bruises/ and the beach tar and twigs of ritual."

Stanza 8 restates the indifference of nature and its enduring, cyclical processes, but now the writing is imbued with the magic of human interpretation. The ruined building stands for the rival "religion" established by the lovers, which the society annihilated ritualistically as representing an order that they could not accept. Cranes here can be seen as birds of beauty and sadness, purity of vision, an unattainable ideal, as in Yasunari Kawabata's novel *Sembazuru* (1952; *Thousand Cranes*, 1958). The pair of cranes is real, but they are also symbolic, natural gods that cleanse the area of the sacrifice of the lovers as the amorous birds themselves dance "a curious rite of celebration." The paradoxical images of love and death, of union and destruction, of order and chaos, and of clarity and obscurity merge when the cranes settle on Morro Rock. Their presence of whiteness, naturalness, and fertility contrasts starkly with the "Rock's dark brow." Its status as a proper noun, along with its personification, reveals its somber omnipresence—black, intrusive, and barren—and its paradoxical absence—of color and of meaning.

The parallel three-line stanzas with which the poem ends move away from description, narration, and memory to philosophical reflection about Morro Rock and its agency in this poem. Stanza 9 is a statement reaffirming the merging of opposites in the action witnessed within the poem, which began in love and ended in death but proved them not to be opposites in that process. The poem emphasizes that the truth of the autobiographical experience lies in fact, in memory, and in any similar retelling. Literature and poetry even help to render it more clearly, more true in spirit, like a rock that becomes smoother and more lovely with the erosion of the tide. Finally, one is left with the rock, the initial object of definition in the poem. The entire poem has rotated on its centrality, yet here the narrator releases it to its own independent existence. People fashion reality from the materials at hand, filtered through memory, emotion, sensation, and knowledge of other stories, poems, and myths. The poet captures the truth here, yet Morro Rock remains the enigmatic matter that is only itself, "this chunk of continent equal to nothing."

Forms and Devices

The poem achieves momentum primarily through capturing complex images: moments in time now remembered in their particulars from a distance and therefore crystallized and essentialized. The poet uses the images connected with Morro Rock to show how its meaning and existence change according to the imagination of the perceiver. The rock can be a hat or a horse, but more important it can be a major figure in the formation of art, which symbolizes differing personal realities.

The images ultimately move toward a contrast of opposites, which the poem contrives to merge paradoxically: Two opposing actualities can both be true at once. Morro Rock itself is the principal embodiment of the paradox, for it is the ostensible subject of the poem, present in some form in every vignette, yet it really is not pertinent to the human actions portrayed, except as a pivot for interpreting events. The oppositions are apparent in contrasts of colors (black/white), of textures (fluffiness/hardness), of time (personal/communal past), of emotions (love/hate), of events (sexual union/death), and of diction (specific/mythological).

At the end of each major stanza, the rock has metamorphosed into something symbolic that carries the tenor of the poem. In stanza 1, it is a junked car engine, the churning of its pistons alien to the natural churning of the surf. In stanza 2, it becomes the spokesman for the margin between sea and land, a "black bead . . . eloquent on the horizon." In stanza 3, it is a clipper or messenger ship. In stanza 6, the rock becomes a tacit agent of the murder of the lovers, for they "were killed with stones," perhaps even pieces broken off Morro Rock by the surf.

The poem seems most cryptic in its final three stanzas: The first and last of the trio are philosophical and poetic statements that turn on the metaphor offered in the central tercet. Here, Morro Rock is transformed into a jewel (that is, the artistic rendering of its presence) and a Platonic reality separate from its earthly form, a reality indicated by its starry truth (like a jewel) spelled forth in a human making of meaning (which is art).

Themes and Meanings

"Morro Rock" is dedicated to the poet Mark Jarman. Hongo fashioned the poem in the Chinese tradition of poetic debate. He means to answer Jarman's belief in the necessity of poetic narrative. Hongo's poem reveals the impossibility of certainty in experience and in art. When narrative is attempted, it cannot escape the image and intrusion of the imagination. According to Hongo, "The world exceeds the word" and "Creation itself is the first language." Poems, then, can only be language about a preexistent language, which is the world of experience.

Hongo began the poem while daydreaming about his father, who had recently died, and the particulars of what he enjoyed about the California shore: "how much he loved humble things like a breakfast out, a drive along the coast, a gesture of friendliness between strangers." The memory of his father merged with a yearning for the pier ("the ocean, the gulls screeching, the salty air, the perfumed chill of a winter sea pitching under the pilings") and the repressed memory of his own first sexual experience, a love affair that was deemed interracial and was violently punished. All this description, however, is after the fact. Hongo was not entirely conscious of the poem's genesis as he created it:

> I wrote the poem not knowing I'd fabulize an erotic myth about social outrage and the persecution of sexual splendor. I got something in about violence and love and regret. I got California into it, my father and my mourning for him into it, and I disguised my own memory of a bad time with two big encounters with racism. I remembered the rhythms of those times and caught, for a moment, the scent of a girl's skin under a bronze satin blouse.

Sandra K. Fischer

THE MOST OF IT

Author: Robert Frost (1874-1963)
Type of poem: Lyric
First published: 1942, in *A Witness Tree*

The Poem

"The Most of It" is a lyric poem cast in twenty lines of rhymed iambic pentamer. The title contains a dual meaning that reflects an important contrast between the attitudes of the male character in the poem and of Robert Frost himself.

The man in the poem wants "the most of it": He wants more out of life than it ordinarily provides. Thus he spends time alone in nature, seeking a certain kind of response from "the universe," but he feels disappointed when nature does not provide that kind of response.

On the other hand, the title also ironically alludes to the common phrase "make the most of it." Through this allusion, Frost implies that the man expects the world to do too much for him and that he should participate more energetically in perceiving and creating satisfaction for himself. The poem suggests that the man has not "made the most" of his experience in this sense; Frost, through a powerful display of his poetic prowess, definitely has.

Though Frost does not separate the lines into stanzas, the action of the poem falls into two distinct sections. The first eight lines present the man and his situation, while the last twelve describe his sighting of "a great buck," a large male deer. The first section introduces a man with an exalted—perhaps too exalted—conception of himself: "He thought he kept the universe alone." As another person might think of "keeping" house, this man thinks of himself in a domestic relationship with the "universe," and he seeks a response from nature to reassure him that he does not keep it alone. He is frustrated when all he hears is a "mocking echo" of his own voice, though he is crying out for "counter-love, original response."

In the second section of the poem, the man sights "a great buck," but he seems strangely unmoved by the experience. Disappointed by his quest in nature, the man feels that "nothing ever came of what he cried/ Unless it was the embodiment that" he saw across the lake. He believes that his pleas have produced either no response or perhaps—merely perhaps—one encounter, which is then described in detail. A being, which the man would like to believe is the "embodiment" of the "counter-love" or "original response" that he seeks, crashes through the talus (loose rock below a cliff) on the other side of the lake and swims toward him. As it moves closer, however, the man realizes that it is not another human, but a large male deer. With great power, the buck moves quickly out of the lake, across the rock-strewn beach, and into the underbrush. The poem ends with a curiously abrupt coda: "—and that was all." This flat statement might be taken to mean that neither the buck nor anything like it ever appeared to the man again; more likely, it expresses the man's rueful sense of letdown at this incident and perhaps his entire quest.

Forms and Devices

Through the vivid imagery and powerful form of "The Most of It," Frost draws a vivid contrast between the man's naïvely sentimental expectations of nature and the harsh but awe-inspiring reality that he does encounter but seems to be too narrow-minded to appreciate.

The first section of the poem presents a situation in which the man's sentimental view of nature seems ironically out of synch with the details of the natural world around him. As noted earlier, in his rather domestic scenario, he thinks of himself "[keeping] the universe" as if it were a house. What he wants from nature sounds more like what one would want from another person, perhaps a wife: "counter-love, original response." What he faces in the scene around him, however, is a "tree-hidden cliff across the lake" and a "boulder-broken beach." Frost's images suggest that nature in this situation is too obscure, remote, and harsh to provide the man with the human kind of response that he is convinced he needs to find there.

Similarly, in the second section, Frost's images show how nature provides the man with an experience that is ironically so "original," so "counter" to his own expectations, that it is difficult for him to respond to it. The verbs that Frost chooses for the buck's first appearance clearly associate the animal with the wild and harsh natural scene of the first section: He "crashed" in the talus and "splashed" into the water. On the other hand, by mentioning twice what the man wants to see, Frost emphasizes the way the man's preconceptions obstruct his responsiveness to the buck: "Instead of proving human when it neared/ And someone else additional to him." In contrast to the human response the man had hoped for, the images of the buck's actions present a thrilling spectacle of wild, inhuman nature:

> As a great buck it powerfully appeared,
> Pushing the crumpled water up ahead,
> And landed pouring like a waterfall,
> And stumbled through the rocks with horny tread,
> And forced the underbrush—and that was all.

The abrupt tag-line to this spectacular description, "—and that was all," provides one final indication that the man finds little, if any, satisfaction in the sighting of the powerful deer. Frost, on the other hand, reinforces the impression that as a poet he does "make the most" of the buck's appearance through a virtuoso display of poetic form. He heightens the impact of his narrative by providing a strong underlying rhythm of iambic pentameter. Further, Frost casts his twenty lines into five quatrains with a rhyming pattern of *abab*, and he contrasts the limited perspective of the man with the expansive power of the buck by the way he manages syntax within these quatrains. For example, the two quatrains in the first section are both complete sentences, in consonance with the man's self-enclosed view of his situation. Frost describes the encounter with the buck in one long sentence of twelve lines. It is as if the expansive power of the buck, which gains momentum as Frost adds phrases in an accumulative parallel structure ("And landed," "And stumbled," "And forced"), is trying to burst out of the limited perspective of the man who witnesses it. The beginning and end of the long sentence ("And nothing ever came of what he cried// . . .—and that was all") create a frame that dramatizes the sense that the man cannot let go of his limiting preconceptions.

Themes and Meanings

The central theme in "The Most of It" is the human attempt to commune with nature—to connect with some spirit or presence and lose the sense of isolation and alienation. Frost's poem shares this theme with a long tradition of earlier Western literature, stretching from the classical myth of Narcissus and Echo in Ovid's *Metamorphoses* (c. 8 C.E.) through pastoral, romantic, and transcendentalist literature in the centuries since the Renaissance.

Much of this earlier literature would suggest that the reader might bring to "The Most of It" a sympathetic and supportive view of the man's spiritual quest. In particular, New England Transcendentalists such as Ralph Waldo Emerson and Henry David Thoreau, whose writings Frost admired, posited a pantheistic Oversoul (Emerson's term) that would nourish the spirit of people who sought it in nature. Also, Frost would have been aware of the close correspondence between the man in his poem and a similar character to whom nature's voices do respond in "There was a boy," a famous section in the 1805 version of William Wordsworth's *The Prelude* (Book V, lines 364-388).

On the other hand, Frost's presentation of his character suggests a more ironic sense of the man's similarities to Narcissus, the archetypally self-centered character in the classical myth. Like Narcissus, Frost's man seems to suffer in an echo chamber largely of his own making. He acts on the naïve belief that all he should need to do is call or "cry out" (the phrase conveys passionate desire, but it also connotes a baby crying as if for its bottle), and nature should then respond with some form of "counterlove" or "original response." When nature does provide a startling encounter with a powerful animal, the man seems to consider briefly the possibility that this experience might be significant. Yet the abrupt ending of the poem ("—and that was all") suggests that the man's response is hardly adequate to the spectacle that Frost's powerful imagery and syntax have dramatized.

"The Most of It" indicates that those who would commune with nature would do well not to blind themselves with limiting expectations or preconceptions. Rather, such seekers should be as open, aware, and responsive as they can be to whatever experiences nature provides. Such encounters may not always be warmly reassuring, as Frost's man had hoped; however, to those seekers willing to "make the most" of such experiences through open-minded responsiveness (and perhaps through the work of forming those experiences into art, as Frost and many others have done), the results are often richly satisfying.

Terry L. Andrews

THE MOTHER

Author: Gwendolyn Brooks (1917-2000)
Type of poem: Lyric
First published: 1945, in *A Street in Bronzeville*

The Poem

"The mother" is a short poem in free verse, written mostly in the first person. In her narrator, Gwendolyn Brooks adopts the persona of an impoverished mother. In the tradition of the lyric, this narrator addresses the reader directly and personally to convey her feelings. The poem contains thirty-five lines, which are separated into three stanzas. The title, "the mother," is ironic, for this mother is a woman who has lost her children because of very difficult and painful decisions—decisions that she believes were for the best.

Brooks's "the mother" implicitly explores the impact of abject poverty on the life of a female character. The poem depicts the struggles and regrets of a poor woman who has had many abortions. The mother has continuing anxiety and anguish because of her difficult decisions. The very first line of the first stanza, "Abortions will not let you forget," immediately draws attention to the title, "the mother," and to the importance of the word "love"—what it has meant to the narrator to love her children or, rather, the children she might have had.

The narrator of the poem, the mother of the lost children, ultimately accepts responsibility for her acts, although she seems to alternate between evading and admitting that responsibility. Throughout the poem, the narrator refers to her decisions with concrete adverbs and adjectives.

The brief final stanza is climactic. The narrator confronts her familiarity with her lost children and, despite her decision to abort them, proclaims her love for them. The final line, consisting of only one word, "All," is particularly effective in that it stands in stark contrast to the apparent harshness of both her decision and her own attitude toward that decision.

The city is an important and recurring symbol in Brooks's work. She has created a series of portraits of women inhabiting Bronzeville, a setting for many of her poems, which may be taken symbolically as the African American community. In a way similar to that of Richard Wright, Gwendolyn Brooks's work expresses the tragic and dehumanizing aspects of the ghetto experience. Brooks also ventures deep beneath the surface of the ghetto experience to uncover areas of a poor person's life that frequently go unnoticed and should not necessarily be considered terrible or ugly.

Forms and Devices

A sharp contrast is created in "the mother" between potential—what could have been—and reality, what has been. This contrast establishes a dialectic of dreams versus reality, since, in the mother's imagination, the lost babies still exist and grow even though she knows that the babies are dead. Throughout the poem the mother drifts between the imaginative and the real, finally revealing her need to believe in an existence after death.

In stanza 2, she imagines giving birth, suckling babies at her breast, and hearing them cry and play games; she even thinks of their "loves" and marriages. Yet these thoughts are bluntly followed by the words, "anyhow you are dead."

The speaker cannot quite bear the word "dead," however, and immediately follows it with "Or rather, . . ./ You were never made." The alternation of accepting and evading responsibility, of plainly saying "my dim killed children," then denying that terrible picture, gives the poem its complexity and its deep emotion. The speaker begins, in the first stanza, by using a second-person address—"the children you got that you did not get"—then switches, in the second stanza, to the painfully personal first-person meditation: "I have heard . . . the voices of my dim killed children." Her attempt to keep a distance between herself and the experience she describes fails. In stanza 2, she addresses the children who were never born with a series of clauses beginning with "if," attempting to apologize or explain herself to them: "If I sinned," "If I stole your births." She can conclude these thoughts only with the contradictory statement, "Believe that even in my deliberateness I was not deliberate."

An important unifying device in the poem is memory. Memory is constantly functioning in "the mother." The narrator is in a fluid and changing relationship with the past, and specifically with her decisions that have drastically affected the present. These decisions keep intruding into the present, and her recollections move between her dreams of what might have been and the harshness of her memory of what caused her to decide as she did.

Themes and Meanings

"The mother" mourns the loss of children aborted because of the poverty of the mother. By extension, it also mourns the loss of things that do not reach their potential, such as the loss experienced by a race of people whose growth has been interrupted or altered. One contrast and conflict that emerges in the poem is that between the desire of the mother to do what was best for her children and the finality of her decisions. The depiction of the narrator—honest, reflective, and self-aware—prevents an immediate positive or negative characterization. Instead, like the decisions she has made, the narrator is complicated—full of conflicting emotions regarding both herself and her lost children. Ironically, it was the mother's moving concern for her children as well as her own circumstances which caused her to decide to have the abortions.

Throughout the poem, the narrator examines the fates she knows would have awaited her lost children. Because of the harsh honesty with which she refers to her decisions to have abortions, this reflection upon what the lives of the children would have been like is made more believable. Her reliability as a narrator is established by the time she gets to an accounting for the reasons she made her decisions.

An important difference between Gwendolyn Brooks and contemporary writers Richard Wright and Ralph Ellison, who also use poor urban settings in their writing, is that she devotes much more attention to the experiences of women. Women may not be lacking in Wright's and Ellison's writing, but they are typically in the background and are of secondary importance to the male characters. Like the work of Ann Petry, Brooks's work concentrates on the importance and implications of the poor urban experience on women as well as men.

Brooks's poems offer a realistic view of the diversity of poor urban women. This view is in sharp contrast to the stereotypes which have grown up around such women (whore and matriarch, for example) and have made their way into literature. Brooks intentionally fails to provide some sort of unifying, uniform characterization of poor urban women. The narrator depicted in "the mother" remains one of many possibilities, not the only possibility. There are also women in Brooks's poems who are sexually repressive, ordinary, exploited, protected, despairing, or aggressive. The only common characteristic these women share is a similar environment and heritage; throughout Brooks's poems, women emerge as individuals. The women have different goals, priorities, and values, and have varying levels of misery, tolerance, and talents. This variety points to the recurring theme in Brooks's work of individual identity and individual problems.

David Lawrence Erben

MOTHER IRELAND

Author: Eavan Boland (1944-   )
Type of poem: Dramatic monologue
First published: 1995; collected in *The Lost Land*, 1998

The Poem

"Mother Ireland" is a short poem in free verse in which the speaker is Mother Ireland. The poem repeatedly reminds the reader of the speaker's presence: every sixth word, on average, is a first-person pronoun ("I," "me," "my"). The poem is difficult to classify. It has some qualities of the lyric, with the author speaking through a persona. It sketches the outlines of a story (hence is a narrative), and the story's scale has epic proportions, though the poem (at only thirty-six lines, 142 words) is obviously not an epic. It might be considered a parable, but that term identifies a type of story, not a type of poem.

Mother Ireland tells her story: Once passive, unself-conscious, blind, and voiceless, she became active, self-conscious, sighted, and articulate. At first, she says, she was the land [of Ireland] itself, unable to see, only seen by others. The season early in the poem is winter: "I was a hill/ under freezing stars."

The transformation began because "words fell on me" continually, she says. They were others' words (she calls them by different names: "Seeds. Raindrops./ Chips of frost."), and she was but their passive recipient. From one of these words, in the poem's pivotal lines, she says,

> I learned my name.
>   I rose up. I remembered it.
> Now I could tell my story.
> It was different
>   from the story told about me.

Knowing her own name empowers her, and the change in her is immediately followed by a change of seasons, to spring. Having arisen, Mother Ireland distances herself from and gains perspective on the physical landscape. Once she "was land"; now, having "travelled west," she looks lovingly "at every field// and at the gorse-/ bright distances." However, she "looked with so much love" that those things she gazed upon "misunderstood me./ *Come back to us/* they said/ *Trust me* I whispered. Thus the poem ends with what appear to be Mother Ireland's first words spoken aloud. The reader, trusting Mother Ireland, has faith that the change, though wrenching, is for the good.

Certain puzzles remain in this enigmatic poem. Were the words that fell on passive Mother Ireland those of generations of Irish bards and poets (mostly male)? May one assume that the "wound . . . left/ in the land by [Mother Ireland's] leaving it" is not a physical, but a psychic, wound? Is Mother Ireland's journey west a movement toward roots, toward an older, truer, Irish-speaking (and possibly less patriarchal) Ireland? What, crucially, does the transformation which Mother Ireland undergoes represent? If this is a parable, its lesson seems mysterious.

Forms and Devices

"Mother Ireland" is not divided into stanzas, as most of Boland's poems are; it is, however, broken up on the page, its lines indented irregularly. The lines of no other Boland poem are so scattered across the page, and their scattered appearance reinforces a reader's sense of the disruption caused by Mother Ireland's separation from the land.

The poem has no regular rhyme scheme, yet patterns of consonant and vowel sounds resonate in it. The last syllable in three-fourths of the lines, for example, contains at least one (and often more than one) of the following sounds: *d, r, s,* and *t*. Lines vary in length, unpredictably, between two and nine syllables; meter is irregular, but 80 percent of the poem's metrical feet are anapests or (more often) iambs. If free verse, as Robert Frost said, is like playing tennis with the net down, this is carefully controlled free verse: The ball is as precisely stroked, so to speak, as if the net were still there.

Beginning with inarticulateness and ending with Mother Ireland's first whispered words, the poem also progresses from simple to more complex, verbally and syntactically. The first six lines contain only words of one syllable, twenty-four of them in a row, and almost all words of more than one syllable come after Mother Ireland has learned her name and arisen. Similarly, sentences in the first half of the poem are much shorter, on average, than those in the second. Early sentences tend to be terse ("I did not see./ I was seen."), but the speaker's voice grows relaxed, even faintly eloquent, especially in its second to last sentence, which stretches unhurriedly for one-fourth of the poem's length.

Throughout, the language of the poem tends to be basic, elemental. "Yes," a reader thinks, "this is how the land would sound if it (she) could speak." One of every four words in the poem is a verb or verb form—a high proportion. (In language, nothing is more basic than verbs.) Another one of every four words is a pronoun. There are only the simplest adverbs (now, also, so) and few adjectives, especially in the first half of the poem. In the long sentence toward the end, a phrase such as "the gorse-/ bright distances" stands out by contrast. The elemental quality of the language seems appropriate to the epic scope of the poem's story.

The poem's basic figure of speech is Ireland personified as a woman. The image does not originate with Eavan Boland but has a long history in the literature of Ireland. In her prose book, *Object Lessons: The Life of the Woman and the Poet in Our Time* (1995), Boland is highly critical of what she calls "The nationalization of the feminine, the feminization of the national," by male Irish writers, traditionally. Boland's use of the figure is original in several respects. Her Mother Ireland is not merely a representation of Ireland in female form; she is the land itself, its very topography (Mother Earth/Ireland), as well as the spirit or personality which, acquiring name and self-awareness, emerges from the land. This emergence represents Boland's boldest innovation: the liberation of Mother Ireland.

Themes and Meanings

A 1988 documentary film, also entitled *Mother Ireland* (directed by Anne Crilly, produced by Derry Film and Video), provides background to Boland's poem. The film explores the diverse array of female personifications of Ireland: in literature, in nineteenth century political cartoons, in songs such as "Ireland, Mother Ireland." It demonstrates that, depending upon time and circumstances and the eye of the beholder, Mother Ireland can be a powerful symbol of Irish nationalism or the Sorrowful Mother, either a strong nurturing protector or a pathetic victim of oppression. Eleven Irish women interviewed in the film offer a variety of perceptions of, and a variety of feelings about, the concept and the persona of Mother Ireland. Eavan Boland is not mentioned in the film, and her poem does not allude to it, yet hers could be considered a twelfth voice, extending the film's discourse.

Mother Ireland's progress, over the course of the poem, closely parallels the progress that Boland describes Irish women, especially writers (including herself), undergoing in *Object Lessons*. In the past, she says, the female figure in Irish literature (written by men) "was utterly passive. She was Ireland or Hibernia. . . . She was invoked, addressed, remembered, loved, regretted. . . . And she had no speaking part." She became a "projection of a national idea" and in the process was oversimplified, misrepresented, her true story untold. During Boland's lifetime, however, "women have moved from being the objects of Irish poems to being the authors of them."

The themes of "Mother Ireland" connect with those of earlier Boland poems from the late 1980's and early 1990's—other poems that speak of, for example, "the silences in which are our beginnings" ("The Journey," 1986). From being part of a national mythology, Irish women, in Boland's view, are moving "out of myth into history" ("Outside History," 1989). "[M]yth is the wound we leave/ in the time we have," she writes in "The Making of an Irish Goddess" (1989). Lines 47 to 64 of the poem "Anna Liffey" (1994) provide the most sustained poetic parallel to "Mother Ireland." This section begins, "I came here in a cold winter.// I did not know the name for my own life"; it ends with the poet "Becoming a figure" in her own poem, "Usurping a name and a theme." Mother Ireland also usurps a name, claims a theme, tells her story.

Something of Mother Ireland's own story, "different/ from the story told about me," is suggested by what she looked at lovingly. The "rusted wheel" and the frame of a baby carriage seem to be the domestic debris of a depopulated area. The fields in which they have been discarded are not under cultivation, nor is the land in the distance, though it is beautiful to look at, covered with yellow gorse (a spiky furze). Part of Mother Ireland's story, then, appears to be the ongoing migration, particularly during the nineteenth and twentieth centuries, from the rural west of Ireland to cities (especially Dublin) and abroad, to England, North America, Australia, and so on.

When at the end of the poem the fields entreat Mother Ireland to "*Come back to us,*" her refusal is tacit and gentle, but firm. She will not return to her cold, mute, insensate, helpless former condition. "Mother Ireland," written during the transformative term in office of Mary Robinson, Ireland's first woman president, is a parable about a changing Ireland, changing as—and because—its women and their roles are changing; there is no going back.

Richard Bizot

MOTHER LOVE

Author: Rita Dove (1952-   )
Type of poem: Lyric
First published: 1993; collected in *Mother Love*, 1995

The Poem

The title poem "Mother Love" appears in the second of seven sections of Rita Dove's collection *Mother Love*. Like all the poems in the collection, "Mother Love" examines a dramatic story from Greek mythology, the story of Demeter, goddess of grain and agriculture, and her beautiful daughter Persephone. It is, in Dove's words, "a tale of a violated world," simultaneously ancient and modern.

A summary of the myth is important for this poem. With almost no witnesses and with the permission of her father Zeus, the supreme Olympian deity, Persephone has been abducted and raped by Hades, the ruler of the underworld and her uncle, who subsequently makes her his queen. Unable to find her daughter, an angry and inconsolable Demeter wanders among mortals, disguised as an elderly woman. She comes to Eleusis, where she meets the four lovely daughters of Celeus, king of Eleusis, and his wife Metaneira. Demeter, at Metaneira's urging, becomes nurse to the couple's only son, the infant Demophoön. Determined to make the boy immortal, each night Demeter secretly places him in the fire. One night Metaneira discovers this and screams in terror, thus thwarting Demeter's plans. An angry, radiant goddess reveals herself and disappears, but not before ordering the people of Eleusis to build a temple and altar in her honor and promising to teach them rites that became known as the Eleusinian Mysteries.

It is the episode of Demeter and the young son of Celeus and Metaneira that Dove addresses in the poem "Mother Love" and that precedes the rest of the myth: Still inconsolable, Demeter lets the crops die and refuses solace from the other Olympian gods and goddesses. Eventually Zeus agrees to return Persephone, but because she has eaten pomegranate seeds offered by Hades, she must spend fall and winter with her husband and spring and summer with her mother, thus ensuring the seasons, agriculture, and partial consolations.

Demeter's first-person voice dominates the poem, which is divided into two stanzas of twelve and sixteen lines. These twenty-eight lines suggest a subtle doubling of the traditional fourteen lines of a sonnet, a form that preoccupies Dove throughout the collection. The poem is, in fact, a sort of double mothering and a double mourning. In the three sentences that make up the first stanza, Demeter reflects on maternal instincts that combine deep comforts and fears. Tracing in her mind the nurture and natural maturation of children, she voices parents' universal worries as their children "rise, primed/ for Love or Glory" and as their daughters' youthful myopia blinds them to advancing perils.

The poet then makes a shift between the two stanzas, moving from generalizations to specifics. Demeter recalls "this kind woman" (Metaneira), "her bouquet of daughters," and her young son. Demeter will not stop those daughters from being scattered and taken in marriage, but she decides to save the "noisy and ordinary" boy who, if "cured to perfection," could become immortal. This attempt is not simple. She wants to make Demophoön invulnerable, but Metaneira's terrified screams end all that and force Demeter to remember her own screams and her vulnerable, lost daughter. She thus answers the rhetorical question with which she begins the poem: "Who can forget the attitude of mothering?"

Forms and Devices

In drawing from mythology for this poem's structure and themes, Dove joins a long line of writers, artists, musicians, and choreographers. Her awareness of this shows throughout the collection *Mother Love* in epigraphs taken from works by writers such as H. D. (Hilda Doolittle), Muriel Rukeyser, James Hillman, Jamaica Kincaid, John Milton, Kadia Molodowsky, and even Mother Goose. It shows more deeply in her combined preoccupation with mythology and the sonnet form, a combination she acknowledges as an "homage" and "counterpoint" to *Die Sonette an Orpheus* (1923; *Sonnets to Orpheus*, 1923) by German poet Rainer Maria Rilke.

"Mother Love," like many of the collection's poems, reflects no ordinary approach to traditional sonnet forms with their set meters, rhyme schemes, and stanza lengths. Still, the sonnet form is a stubborn and surprising presence in the poem. For example, unlike the final two rhyming lines (a couplet) with which any Shakespearean or English sonnet ends, Dove begins "Mother Love" with a couplet (rhyming "mothering" with "bothering") that does not create a closure. The second line of the couplet uses enjambment (no end-stop) to continue directly on to subsequent lines and irregular end rhymes throughout the two stanzas. (The second stanza, for instance, is filled with end and internal rhymes of "er" and "ur" syllables.) Furthermore, the poet reverses and doubles the stanza patterns of a Petrarchan or Italian sonnet, which begins with an eight-line stanza (an octet) and concludes with six lines (a sestet). "Mother Love" thus begins with a twelve-line stanza and concludes with sixteen lines. These sonnet cues and reversals are powerful. It is as if, like Demeter's daughter, the revered sonnet forms have been taken underground. Like Demeter's response to Demophoön, the absence of the primary form heightens the reader's awareness of that form and its replacement.

Despite such changes, Dove follows the thematic development scheme of a Petrarchan sonnet. "Mother Love" begins with an exposition of the theme, then elaborates on that theme. The poet then creates the traditional turn between the two stanzas by shifting to a specific example of the theme before moving, in the final two lines, to the theme's conclusion. The reader is certainly more conscious of the poem's voice and language than its nuanced structure. Dove achieves this by giving Demeter highly accessible language and informal, conversational speech rhythms; equally important, each of her six sentences is a natural breath unit. As a result, the reader, drawn effortlessly into Demeter's voice, focuses on the unfolding narrative and the poet's arresting images and diction.

Themes and Meanings

The title of the poem "Mother Love" announces its purpose: to explore Demeter's fierce maternal love and grief. In this exploration, particularly in the poem's second stanza, Dove closely follows one of the episodes included in the ancient Greek "Homeric Hymn to Demeter." However, the poet's complicated treatment of Demeter opens up the larger subjects of the collection *Mother Love:* the complex nature of maternal love and the even more complex nature of relations between mothers and daughters.

The description of Dove's portrayal of Demeter as complex is not based on the poem's horrifying simile: "a baby sizzling on a spit/ as neat as a Virginia ham." It is important to remember (as several critics have not) that the account of the Demeter-Demophoön episode in the "Homeric Hymn to Demeter" does not end with the baby being roasted alive but with an angry Demeter promising that since she was not allowed to make him immortal, the child will, at least, receive "imperishable honor" as a man. The knotty qualities of Dove's Demeter surface in the last three lines of stanza 1: Demeter's pride in her maternal skills and her delight in children give way to an intense denigration of adolescent maturation (girls with their immature "one-way mirrors" of romance and boys as "fledgling heroes") and sexuality ("the smoky battlefield"). That the goddess-mother will not face either this natural cycle or Persephone's sexual awakening becomes clear in the change of subject in stanza 2. By this abrupt shift, the poet underscores the extremity of Demeter's repressive mental state. Her denial and repression of memory are acted out without a single mention of her daughter: Since Persephone was taken from her, she will take another's child—a son rather than a daughter who might remind Demeter of her own; because Persephone was violated by the underworld of death (Hades), she will make sure that this surrogate child is made impervious to death and destruction.

In Demeter's foiled substitution and in the searing understatement of her final sentence, the poet accentuates the open-endedness of Demeter's dilemma: To remember her daughter the child and her daughter the vulnerable, sexual, autonomous adult is to be forced back into an ambiguous, even ruthless circle of love and life. As the poem, young Demophoön, and Demeter demonstrate, this is a place that cannot be "cured to perfection." Nevertheless, this is the charged circle into which the Pulitzer Prize-winning poet Rita Dove places herself and this collection; her dedication in *Mother Love* makes that clear from the start: "FOR *my mother* TO *my daughter.*"

Alma Bennett

THE MOWER, AGAINST GARDENS

Author: Andrew Marvell (1621-1678)
Type of poem: Pastoral
First published: 1681, in *Miscellaneous Poems*

The Poem

In the *Miscellaneous Poems* of Andrew Marvell, published posthumously, "The Mower, Against Gardens" stands first in a set of four pastoral poems centering on the figure of the mower. A significant proportion of Marvell's poetry is pastoral by nature, but, as here, Marvell uses the pastoral convention in a most original way to ask fundamental questions about man's fall, his passions, and the possibility of (re)gaining lost innocence within nature. Traditionally, pastoralism has opposed the innocence of country life (typified by the shepherd) to the corruption of civilization and the culture of the city. Marvell replaces the figure of the shepherd with a more ambiguous one, the mower, and he suggests that country life itself may be invaded by the corruption of the city. In other words, there is a moral and spiritual threat that mere place, or state, by itself, is insufficient to prevent. In the three other "mower" poems, the mower himself is seen losing his peace of mind through his passionate sexual feelings for a shepherdess, Juliana. He "falls" in love and in the ensuing despair and moral confusion thinks of death. As a mower, he sees himself as bringing death to the grass; he, too, has been cut down by passion.

In this poem, however, the mower is much more unambiguously denouncing the corruption typified by the ornate enclosed garden that was coming into vogue in the seventeenth century. The references to horticultural innovations point clearly to this as well as to the enormous prices paid for certain tulip bulbs, and the great effort made to discover new plant species for decorative purposes (lines 15-18; 24-25). The mower believes that this is where man's luxuriousness is most in evidence at the present time (rather than in clothes, jewelry, or houses). "Luxuria" was considered one of the seven deadly sins, covering what is meant by sensuality, hedonism, and excessive appetite. The garden of luxurious man's making is thus the opposite of the original garden, Eden; yet both gardens stand corrupted by man and are prime evidence of his Fall.

The first part of the poem covers evidence of man's ostentatious consumerism, his misapplication of the simplicities of nature. This, by itself, the mower would be willing to forgive. What makes the display insupportable is man's cross-breeding, grafting kind on kind, in a way forbidden biblically (in the books of Leviticus and Deuteronomy). He is thus causing a sort of incest: identity, kind, and species become confused. Even birth becomes unnatural in a new sterility (line 30).

The mower's final figure of this sterility is one of the "fauns and fairies" that exist as spirits in nature but have now become reduced to material ornaments in the garden. His final act of defiance is to suggest the continuing presence of such spiritual forces in that nature which remains.

Forms and Devices

The forty-line poem is written in a non-stanzaic form. Yet there is a hidden stanza structure: The first part of the poem in reality consists of four quatrains and a couplet to round off the first eighteen lines; the second part is similar, leaving a final quatrain as conclusion.

This careful balancing is reflected in the paired rhyming scheme, so that each quatrain is basically two balancing or parallel couplets. Each couplet has as its first line an iambic pentameter line and as its second an iambic tetrameter line—an unusual form for Marvell. The shorter second lines thus avoid the full heroic couplet developed by John Dryden in the next generation of British poets and retain the terseness and epigrammatic quality typical of much of Marvell's poetry. The form also suggests a directness and simplicity that match the poem's opposition to ornateness.

The imagery is also noteworthy, as might be expected of a Metaphysical poet. The recurring train is sexual, manifesting itself in a series of vivid conceits. "Seduce" (line 2) suggests that the vice mentioned in the first line is of sexual appetite and reminds one of Satan's seduction of Adam and Eve—a motif that his contemporary, John Milton, was to weave into the language of *Paradise Lost* (1667, 1674). Sexual fallenness is suggested by the cosmetic conceit (lines 11-14) used of the flowers, with the biblical subtext of Christ's words "Consider the lilies of the field" producing other resonances. "Dealt with" (line 21) suggests sexual traffic; the biblical conceit of "forbidden mixtures" suggests incest and miscegenation. There is sexual immorality in "adult'rate" (line 25), sexual luxury in "Seraglio" and "Eunuchs" (line 27), and unnaturalness in the sexless cherry (lines 29-30)—which has been taken to refer either to the stoneless cherry (with "stones" being a contemporary colloquialism for testicles) or to a cherry fruited through grafting. Sexual purity is suggested only by "pure" (line 4) and "Innocence" (line 34).

Thus the new Fall of Man is still seen in sexual terms. Marvell, however, does fill this out with other striking conceits—the enclosed garden as "a dead and standing pool of Air" (line 6) is particularly forceful, in that water and air both normally connote freedom of spirit and movement. Enclosure thus brings restraint, and the garden becomes a prison where the innocent plants are raped ("enforc'd") and corrupted into double-mindedness (line 9).

Themes and Meanings

Taken by itself, the poem remains fairly unambiguous in its meaning. Humankind, in its economic and cultural development, has generated more wealth than it knows what to do with. In a false sophistication, man has replaced nature with an art that is merely tasteless display. While this is serious enough, what he has really done is to corrupt nature itself. The purity of natural innocence is replaced by a seduced nature, which is then reduced further in its moral and spiritual power by becoming merely a taste, a vogue. Moral and spiritual categories are lost, as is, ultimately, man's identity as a created being. Man's hubris is to take over God's creation, rather than steward it, for his own exploitative pleasures. Such a reading would accord with the Puritan ethos of the seventeenth century as expressed, for example, in Milton's *Comus* (1637); it would also accord with the ecological morality of the late twentieth century.

Such a straightforward reading can be questioned, however, in two ways—first, by linking this poem with the other mower poems, second, by linking it to "The Garden," one of Marvell's best-known poems. If the figure of the mower in all the poems is considered, then he is not, perhaps, the upright Puritan he appears to be here. Ultimately, he is overtaken by passion; he falls himself. Nature's innocence, then, seems either illusory or too fragile for man to hold. Perhaps the mower himself is overly proud or is biased; he may not be the mouthpiece for Marvell that the first reading suggests.

Alternatively, if "The Garden" is placed alongside the poem, the garden there is portrayed as Eden restored, even if not permanently. There the garden retains its luxuriousness—"the luscious clusters of the vine" press themselves on the poet ("The Garden" line 35), for example—but in this luxury the poet is able to meditate imaginatively and enter into a Platonic quietude of spirit. Perhaps Marvell is presenting again to the reader Edmund Spenser's two gardens of *The Faerie Queene* (1590, 1596)—that of Acrasia ("the bowre of Blisse"), which is seductive and dangerous, and that of Adonis, which is the Platonic paradise where souls are regenerated.

If this is so, then juxtaposing these two poems actually brings one back to the original reading. "The Garden" can then represent the rediscovery of the true garden, as against the false garden portrayed in this poem. Even if the figure of the mower is to be seen ambiguously, the point that Marvell is making is still that man, cut off from nature, loses being; any passion, be it lust or luxury, can cause this severance. What must matter for man is spiritual presence, not technical skill or material control.

David Barratt

MR. COGITO LOOKS AT HIS FACE IN THE MIRROR

Author: Zbigniew Herbert (1924-1998)
Type of poem: Meditation
First published: 1974, as "Pan Cogito obserwuje w lustrze swojąá twarz," in *Pan Cogito*; English translation collected in *Mr. Cogito*, 1993

The Poem

The title of this brief six-stanza, twenty-eight-line poem in free verse recalls the seventeenth century Dutch paintings that Zbigniew Herbert greatly admires and strikes a note at once contemplative and pictorial. Narrated in the first person, it takes an unusual approach to a commonplace occurrence: a person looking at himself in the mirror. Instead of remarking how much he has changed over the years, Cogito questions who "wrote" his face. The question suggests that Cogito conceives of himself less in individual terms than in collective or historical terms—which is to say, less as a unique person and more as a cultural product, even a text (the one written rather than the one writing).

Contemplating himself synecdochically in the mirror, Cogito comes to see his face as a mirror reflecting the ways that history, including heredity, has shaped or misshaped him. He begins with the chicken pox, which wrote "its o' with calligraphic pen" upon his skin, and moves on to the ancestors from whom he inherited the protruding ears and close-set eyes that worked to their advantage in the age of mastodons and marauders but that now make Cogito look comical. In the third stanza, this line of thought swerves in a more troubling direction as Cogito contemplates his low forehead filled with "very few thoughts," the result of centuries of subservience to aristocratic rule during which "the prince" did the thinking for Cogito's ancestors.

In the fourth stanza, the poem returns to the trope introduced in the first stanza: Cogito as a failed, or at least an imperfect, work of art. The "powders ointments mixtures" he has purchased "in salons" and applied to improve himself "for nobility" are not unlike the art he has seen, the music he has heard, and the "old books" he has read. Instead of being paths to enlightenment and understanding, Cogito implies that they have been little more than ornaments or mere ointments as he contemplates a face, a self, in ruins. In a startling and characteristically self-deprecating turn of phrase (made all the more effective by its unusualness in a poem of otherwise surprising simplicity), Cogito compares "the inherited face" he observes in the mirror to "old meats fermenting in a bag." Gluttonous ancestors, with their "medieval sins" and "paleolithic hunger and fear," are the ones responsible for his double chin, the outward and visible sign of the thwarted hopes of his soul, which "yearned for asceticism." According to the poem's final line, "this is how [Cogito] lost the tournament with [his] face."

Forms and Devices

The question Herbert and other Polish poets of his generation face is how to find a language and a syntax that can adequately reflect recent experience. Herbert's answer is to strip his poetry of virtually all punctuation ("Mr. Cogito Looks at His Face in the Mirror" contains only one dash and one pair of inverted commas) and all signs of poetic convention and ornamentation. Herbert does not begin new lines with uppercase letters; he eschews rhythm, rhyme, and regular stanzaic structure; and he prefers the synecdoches and metonymies of realist writing to the metaphors upon which poetry, particularly Romantic poetry, usually depends. As Herbert writes in "Mr. Cogito on the Imagination,"

> Mr. Cogito never trusted
> tricks of the imagination
> the piano at the top of the Alps
> played false concerts for him
>
> . . . .
> he loved the flat horizon
> a straight line
> the gravity of the earth.

Cogito prefers "to remain faithful to uncertain clarity" and to use the imagination as an "instrument of compassion." The prosaic quality of Herbert's poetry is deceptive (as are the clean lines stripped of punctuation, which require more, not less, effort and involvement on the reader's part), as is proven by comparison with Herbert's numerous prose poems and essays.

The seeming simplicity of Herbert's Cogito poems (many of his other works are more openly allusive in their treatment of myth and history) contrasts sharply with the more lyrical (and somewhat more conventional) work of Poland's best-known postwar poet, Czesław Miłosz. They also differ from the poems of Wisława Szymborska (like Miłosz, a winner of the Nobel Prize in literature), which, though usually even briefer, are equally modest in appearance but much less ascetic in their pursuit of what Herbert calls "the nonheroic subject." Herbert's terseness, his crystalline and austere style, his modest expression and subdued, level voice play their parts in creating the poetic equivalent of the portraits and still lifes of the seventeenth century Dutch painters, practitioners of a sober, somber art devoid of the tricks of the imagination. Like their paintings, Herbert's poems are both pictorial and narrative, little vignettes to which he adds a wryly ironic and, at times, sardonic note. Equally important, Herbert, like the Dutch painters, also positions his art in public terms rather than narrowly personal terms. As a result, what may prove most startling to American readers of Herbert's poetry is the absence of the highly personal, confessional style of his transatlantic contemporaries such as Robert Lowell and Sylvia Plath.

Themes and Meanings

As the poet and critic A. Alvarez has pointed out, "The tension between the ideal and the real is the backbone on which all [of Herbert's] work depends." This "incurable duality," as Harvard professor Stanisław Barańczak calls it, is especially pronounced in the recurrent figure or persona of Cogito, the title figure of the collection

Pan Cogito (*Mr. Cogito*) who reappears in twelve of the poems in *Raport z oblężonego miasta i inne wiersze* (1983; *Report from the Besieged City and Other Poems*, 1985). Cogito is a tragicomic figure, as comically absurd as Charlie Chaplin's Little Tramp, as attenuated as an Alberto Giacometti sculpture, and as existentially bereft and bewildered as any of Samuel Beckett's tramps and disembodied voices. His name indicates his and modern Western philosophy's origins in René Descartes's famous dictum *Cogito, ergo sum*. However, the synecdochic nature of the name of this strangely representative character also suggests his predicament. He is consciousness cut off from bodily existence, thought cut off from meaningful action, existence in the form of alienated awareness, unless one believes, as Barańczak more optimistically does, that what Cogito represents is the healthy reversal of Descartes, not "I think therefore I am" but "I am therefore I think."

At worst, Cogito evidences a capacity for an unwise and typically Cartesian dualism of mind separated from body ("old meats fermenting in a bag"). There is something ridiculous in Cogito's attempts to improve himself with "powders ointments mixtures" no less than with the art he apes ("I applied the marble greenness of Veronese to my eyes"), the music (synecdochically "Mozart") to which he listens, and the "fragrance" of the "old books" he reads. There is, however, also something sobering, even deeply affecting, in his recognition of "the body linked to the chain of species," which is to say linked genetically, culturally, and historically to something other than oneself, a self considered in the narrowest biological and psychological terms. At the same time, there is also something decidedly comical in Cogito asking who gave him his "double chin" when his soul "yearned for asceticism." However, this is comedy touched by pathos, a combination even more problematically present in the poem's final line (which is also the poem's final stanza): "this is how I lost the tournament with my face." The word "tournament" underscores the possibility of Cogito's ridiculousness, his inflated, romantic notion of himself, unless there is for Cogito, as there certainly is for Herbert, some saving irony (Cogito beating the reader to the punch as it were). Even without the trace of irony, there is certainly the regret of one committed, in his own decidedly nonheroic way, to trying to answer the question that is at the heart of Herbert's poetry: namely, how to live this life. With this regret there is also recognition of the risks run by someone like Cogito: resignation on the one hand and mere romantic yearning on the other. To his credit, Cogito heeds the warning implicit in all of Herbert's poems and most simply stated in the "The Envoy of Mr. Cogito" with which the 1974 collection appropriately concludes: "beware of unnecessary pride/ keep looking at your clown's face in the mirror."

Robert A. Morace

MR. COGITO ON THE NEED FOR PRECISION

Author: Zbigniew Herbert (1924-1998)
Type of poem: Meditation
First published: 1983, as "Pan Cogito o potrzebie scislosci," in *Raport z obleżonego miasta i inne wiersze*; English translation collected in *Report from the Besieged City and Other Poems*, 1985

The Poem

"Mr. Cogito on the Need for Precision" is one of twelve "Cogito" poems published in Zbigniew Herbert's *Report from the Besieged City and Other Poems*. These twelve poems supplement the forty that Herbert collected earlier in *Pan Cogito* (1974; *Mr. Cogito*, 1995). The present poem, one of Herbert's longest, contains 131 lines divided into three parts, which are subdivided into stanzas of from one to eight lines each. Most stanzas contain two to four lines; the shortest, with one line, and the two longest stanzas, of seven and eight lines, appear in the final stanza.

The poem is written in the third person, with Mr. Cogito as a character rather than the narrator of the poem. Herbert uses a stiff, slightly pedantic language to create an aura of pseudo-scientific objectivity. This he deploys ironically to underscore the distance between detached treatment and human subject. The poem begins: "Mr. Cogito/ is alarmed by a problem/ in the domain of applied mathematics/ the difficulties we encounter/ with operations of simple arithmetic."

At one extreme, there is the child's sense of addition and subtraction, "pulsat[ing] with a safe warmth"; at the other, there are physicists who have succeeded in weighing atoms and heavenly bodies with extraordinary accuracy. "[O]nly in human affairs/ inexcusable carelessness reigns supreme." Only here does one find a "lack of precise information."

For the German socialist theorists Karl Marx and Friedrich Engels, the specter haunting Europe in the mid-nineteenth century was communism. For Cogito it is "the specter of indefiniteness," which haunts not merely these horrifically Chaplinesque modern times but "the immensity of history." There follows a brief, illustrative allusion to battles from ancient Troy through Agincourt and Kutno, and of terrors identified only by "colors innocent colors": white, red, and brown. Cogito is alarmed by his own and general ignorance of how many died in each battle and during each reign of terror. He is also alarmed by people's willingness to remain ignorant by accepting "sensible explanations." What "evades numbers," he rightly, and achingly, contends, "loses human dimension." To restore this human dimension necessitates both correcting "a fatal defect in our tools" and atoning for "a sin of memory."

The second part of the poem offers "a few simple examples/ from the accounting of victims." In contrast to history's war, airline passenger lists make accounting for the victims of plane crashes relatively easy. Train accidents are more difficult because they often require reassembly of mangled bodies. Worse still are "elemental catastrophes," such as earthquakes and hurricanes, in which the simple arithmetic of the living and the dead is complicated by a third category, those ambiguously "missing."

In the third part of the poem, "Mr. Cogito/ climbs/ to the highest tottering/ step of indefiniteness." The poem then alludes to the immense difficulty of accounting for, of actually naming, "of all those who perished/ in the struggle with inhuman power." Neither official statistics, nor eyewitness, nor "accidental observers" can be trusted, each for different reasons. Despite the difficulty, Cogito argues, no one must be allowed to disappear "in abysmal cellars/ of huge police buildings" or in "doubtful figures/ accompanied by the shameful/ word about.'" "[A]ccuracy is essential/ we must not be wrong/ even by a single one," he admonishes, because "we are despite everything/ the guardians of our brothers/ ignorance about those who have disappeared/ undermines the realty of the world." Thus is the need to count, to account for, to name, and therefore to know, if one is to be truly human.

Forms and Devices

Herbert was a member of a generation of Polish writers who came of age during and immediately after World War II. Their wartime experiences made them feel it necessary to devise new poetic forms and syntaxes appropriate to life as they had just experienced it. For Herbert this meant stripping away virtually all punctuation. He also avoids what he calls, in another poem, "tricks of the imagination": all merely ornamental language including rhythm and rhyme, even metaphors. Herbert prefers the device of synecdoche—the naming of the part to stand for the whole.

Herbert's vocabulary is generally simple; his tone matter-of-fact, almost prosaic; his lines and stanzas brief, starkly seen against the otherwise blank page. Nevertheless, his poetry is carefully connected to the larger historical, philosophical, and cultural contexts. This he achieves through allusions, either directly presented (Troy, Agincourt, Leipzig, Kutno), or indirectly (the red, white, and brown terrors). His Cogito poems are generally less allusive than his other poems.

For all its cool detachment and prosaic accessibility, Herbert's poetry is surprisingly, and subtly, varied. The formality of the opening stanzas of "Mr. Cogito on the Need for Precision" gives way to colloquialism, which becomes especially evident at the end of the second part. The register changes again in part three, which opens with a cartoonish image, then changes into lines of great moral passion and power, before ending with language more resonant than any before it. The final lines are no less realistic than what precedes, but they are realistic in a different way. Instead of the earlier positivism, Herbert offers up the verbal equivalent of one of the seventeenth century Dutch still-life paintings he so greatly admires: "in a bowl of clay/ millet poppy seeds/ a bone comb/ arrowheads/ and a ring of faithfulness/ amulets."

The poem's subject matter lends itself to the sentimentalism of the film version of *Schindler's List* (1994), but its kitchiness, however well intentioned, is precisely what Herbert's seemingly straightforward but in fact understated, deeply ironic, and blackly humorous poem deftly avoids. The lucidity (or what Herbert elsewhere calls "uncertain clarity") of the writing underscores, by means of contrast, the grimness and horror of Herbert's vision. His, and Cogito's, pose or stance of cool detachment serves as a disguise beneath which the reader can detect the author's barely but brilliantly controlled pain and outrage. It is the immense and purposeful gap separating simple observations, such as "we don't know" or "somewhere there must be an error," and the passion that drove Herbert to write this poem and others like it that gives the poem the extraordinary moral force that enables Herbert to use the imagination as an "instrument of compassion."

Themes and Meanings

"Mr. Cogito on the Need for Precision" is one of the many poems in *Report from the Besieged City* bearing witness to the injustice and inhumanity of life in Poland under the martial law imposed by General Wojciech Jaruzelski in 1981, the year Herbert chose to return to his native land. The government crackdowns, reprisals, arrests, interrogations, torture, and killings that led Herbert to write the poem do not limit it, the fate of so many topical literary works. Even as it gives voice to Herbert's dismay and anger, it reveals his desire to use his poetry "to bestow a broader dimension on the specific, individual, experienced situation" to "show its deeper, general perspective." This broader dimension extends beyond Poland's borders to include the political situation in many other countries during the same period, in Eastern Europe, as well as in Latin America and South Africa. In this sense the poem anticipates the necessity for the many "truth commissions" established in Poland and elsewhere only a few years later.

"Mr. Cogito on the Need for Precision" functions, as does the collection's title poem, as a report from a besieged city where not only is there "a lack of precise information" but where "sensible explanations" are offered and apparently accepted by all but the Cogitos of the world, and where "inexcusable carelessness reigns supreme." The poem's Cogito is like the first-person narrator, the I-, or eye-witness of "Report from the Besieged City" who accepts the part he has been assigned, "the inferior role of chronicler" (or in Cogito's case, the role of accountant, one not so much assigned as chosen). "Keeping a tight rein on my emotions, I write about the facts," Herbert's chronicler reports before ending his litany of betrayals with the words, "and only our dreams have not been humiliated."

To the extent that the title figure of "Mr. Cogito on the Need for Precision" and the eleven other Cogito poems in the collection resemble "Report's" eyewitness, he differs from the central figure of Herbert's earlier *Pan Cogito*. Less comically Chaplinesque, this later Cogito seems closer to Herbert himself in his commitment to this life and how one's life should be lived and measured. In a related poem in the same collection, "Mr. Cogito Thinks About Blood," Herbert sardonically notes that science's discovery of how little blood the human body actually contains does not mean that that blood—and the human life it synechdocically represents—is now seen as precious and is therefore shed any less abundantly than before. In "Mr. Cogito on the Need for Precision," the reader finds a similarly horrific sense of humor and sense of helplessness along with the determination, Cogito's no less than Herbert's, to bear witness to that most absurdly humane of principles "in the struggle with inhuman power," namely, accountability: the fact that "we must not be wrong even by a single one."

Robert A. Morace

MR. COGITO TELLS OF THE TEMPTATION OF SPINOZA

Author: Zbigniew Herbert (1924-1998)
Type of poem: Dramatic monologue
First published: 1974, as "Pan Cogito opowiada o kuszenia Spinozy," in *Pan Cogito*;
English translation collected in *Mr. Cogito*, 1993

The Poem

At sixty-five lines, "Mr. Cogito Tells of the Temptation of Spinoza" is one of the longest of the forty poems of *Pan Cogito* (*Mr. Cogito*). The sense of fullness and completion that such length implies is, however, offset by Zbigniew Herbert's division of the sixty-five lines into twenty-seven stanzas, some just a single line long (and none more than six). All the lines are short, and several are just one word long ("think," "calm," "Great"). At once whole and fragmentary, "Mr. Cogito Tells of the Temptation of Spinoza," with its disconcertingly long and decidedly unpoetic title, seems less a poem in any conventional sense than a vignette with dialogue, a kind of philosophical comedy only loosely tied (and then only by title) to the dramatic monologue form.

The poem's ostensible subject is the seventeenth century Dutch philosopher Baruch Spinoza. Known as "the God-intoxicated man," Spinoza was a fiercely independent person who supported himself by grinding lenses and who frequently moved from one lodging to another in Amsterdam. His dedication to freedom of thought and speech led him to turn down a faculty position at the University of Heidelberg and to refuse a pension from French king Louis XIV because it required him to dedicate a work to the king.

The formal, stilted, and at times clichéd quality of the first three stanzas (nearly one-fifth of the poem) does not so much set the overall tone of the poem (unless the astute reader, familiar with other Herbert poems, detects the carefully controlled irony) as it sets up the reader and Spinoza for what follows. "Seized by a desire to reach God," Spinoza, in his attic, "pierce[s] a curtain" and stands "face to face" with Him. Speaking at length and finding his mind enlarged, Spinoza asks questions "about the nature of man." What follows this rather dramatic opening is a series of one- and two-line stanzas in which readers see Spinoza earnestly inquiring into first and last causes while God acts bored and looks off "into infinity," merely biding his time as he waits his turn to speak.

When God finally does speak, he does not sound like a distant, divine voice coming from a burning bush. Instead, He sounds avuncular, albeit something of a Dutch uncle. He starts by praising Spinoza for his "geometric Latin," "clear syntax," and symmetrical arguments before going on to speak not of first and last causes but of "Things Truly Great." God reproves Spinoza for not taking better care of himself and advises him to settle down, buy a house, be more forgiving and more compromising, and look after his income even if it means dedicating a work to the king ("he won't read it anyway"). Spinoza should, God says, "calm/ the rational fury" and "think/ about the woman/ who will give [him] a child." God's final words prove to be his most self-revealing (another curtain "pierced"), but it is a revelation that, in effect, repudiates Spinoza's intellectual pursuit of God and truth: "I want to be loved," God tells him, "by the uneducated and the violent" because "they are the only ones/ who really hunger for me." The vignette ends much the same way it begins, with a more or less conventional scene. The curtain that was pierced only moments before falls, leaving Spinoza alone in the darkness hearing "the creaking of the stairs/ footsteps going down." He has been tempted, but in what sense, to what end, and by whom?

Forms and Devices

Like virtually all the Cogito poems and many of Herbert's other poems, the simple language and form of "Mr. Cogito Tells of the Temptation of Spinoza" is both inviting and deceptive, a deliberate attempt on the part of Herbert and other Polish poets of his generation to devise a poetry appropriate to their experiences during and immediately after World War II. In Herbert's case, this effort involves stripping away punctuation (the only punctuation in "Mr. Cogito Tells of the Temptation of Spinoza" is a single set of parentheses and a number of dashes to introduce most of the stanzas in which God speaks directly to Spinoza). The dearth of punctuation marks, the absence of uppercase letters at the beginning of lines, and the extreme brevity of lines and stanzas make the words look especially bare, almost vulnerable on the page. Herbert also strips away much of the ornamental language that makes poetry poetic for many readers: not only the rhythm and rhyme jettisoned by earlier practitioners of free verse but also metaphors other than those deployed ironically in order to deflate pretensions (for example, "seized by a desire to reach God," "pierced a curtain," and "his mind enlarged"). Instead of the metaphors so closely associated with the Romantic poets, Herbert prefers synecdoches (parts for wholes, wholes for parts) drawn chiefly from everyday experience.

Herbert also avoids the lyrical impulse and, with it, the intensely and at times self-indulgently personal nature of so much Romantic and contemporary poetry: thus the appeal and the usefulness of a persona such as Cogito who, though usually the focus of Herbert's attention, whether in first or third person, serves here solely as narrator whose presence the reader hardly feels. Refusing both lyrical intensity and epic sweep, Herbert adopts a narrative mode better suited to his simple, austere, almost ascetic style. His "modest expression" and "level voice" provide an anecdotal glimpse, a truncated scene rather than a five-act drama not unlike the pictorial style of Spinoza's contemporaries, the seventeenth century Dutch painters whose portraits and still lifes Herbert so greatly admires for both their style and their choice of nonheroic subjects. The title "Mr. Cogito Tells of the Temptation of Spinoza"—indeed the titles of most of the Cogito poems—strongly suggests Herbert's affinity with these same Dutch painters whose realistic representations of commonplace subjects often possessed a carefully but unobtrusively coded allegorical intent. In Herbert's case, however, both title and Cogito also clearly suggest a truly contemporary perspective rather similar to the skeptical retelling of Christian myths and legends in Ted Hughes's poetry collection *Crow* (1970).

Themes and Meanings

It is precisely this deflating of all that is elevated, poetic language as well as philosophical pretension, that is so noticeable in Herbert's poem. The high-minded diction of the opening lines is put in perspective and in its place by God's colloquial speech, and Spinoza's single-minded pursuit of God is offset, even undermined, by God's unadorned advice on getting ahead and on "Things Truly Great" (though those uppercase letters should give the reader pause). There is something incongruous and therefore comical in someone advising a philosopher of Spinoza's stature to buy a house even if that someone is God, but there is wisdom, not just humor, in reminding Spinoza that pleasure is not in itself a vice and in admonishing him to "forgive the Venetian mirrors/ that they repeat surfaces," for what those mirrors accomplish is rather similar to what the seventeenth century Dutch painters did in so faithfully rendering their commonplace subjects. However, the same title that links Herbert's poem to their paintings also suggests that even if Spinoza is wrong not to heed God's advice, he is right to resist the temptation to abandon or compromise his principles by colluding with those in power (for example, dedicating a treatise to the king who "won't read it anyway").

The poem, with its ambiguous depiction of the nature of both God, who may be the devil, and a temptation that is a reversal of the Faustian bargain and not without its own saving grace, illustrates perfectly "the tension between the ideal and the real" that is, as poet and critic A. Alvarez has astutely noted, "the backbone on which all [of Herbert's] work depends." This "incurable duality," as Harvard professor Stanisław Barañiczak calls it, leads to a "threshold situation," the point where a Spinoza or a Cogito must make a choice, a point Herbert usually takes the reader to but not beyond. Spinoza's choice can be inferred from his career and writings even if not from the poem per se. Spinoza's regret, on the other hand, can only be inferred from the "uncertain clarity" of Herbert's poem, a meditation on the pursuit of the principled life that will take on added ambiguity in Herbert's "Spinoza's Bed" in *Marta natura z wedzidlem* (1993; *Still Life with a Bridle: Essays and Apocryphas*, 1991) and added urgency in his later, more overtly political collection *Raport z obleżonego miasta i inne wiersze* (1983; *Report from the Besieged City and Other Poems*, 1985).

Robert A. Morace

MR. EDWARDS AND THE SPIDER

Author: Robert Lowell (1917-1977)
Type of poem: Meditation
First published: 1946, in *Lord Weary's Castle*

The Poem

Early in his literary career, Robert Lowell researched the life of the eminent eighteenth century American preacher Jonathan Edwards with the aim of writing his biography. He never wrote the life, but two of his best-known poems derive from this purported venture. "Mr. Edwards and the Spider" is a poem of five nine-line stanzas that fuses several experiences of the Northampton, Massachusetts, minister having to do with spiders, either literally or metaphorically. Lowell adopts the voice of Edwards in meditation.

The first stanza summarizes the content of a remarkable letter that Edwards wrote, probably at the age of ten or eleven, to an English correspondent of his father. In it, he recorded his observations of the habits of flying spiders and drew some unusually mature inferences, for example, that since their journeys were always seaward, the spiders were in effect seeking their own death. Written in a decidedly scientific spirit, the letter discloses a gifted naturalist in the making.

In his second stanza, Lowell shifts his attention to Edwards's most famous (though hardly most representative) work, the sermon that he delivered as a guest preacher in Enfield, Connecticut, at the height of the religious revival called "The Great Awakening" in 1741. "Sinners in the Hands of an Angry God" compares the individual members of that congregation to "a loathsome spider" that God dangles over hell. In a dramatic presentation of the intransigent Calvinist version of Original Sin, Edwards assured his listeners that God would be justified in dropping them into hell at any moment. "What are we," Lowell asks, after Edwards, "in the hands of the great God?"

Next, Lowell introduces the black widow, whose bite is poisonous and can be deadly, and reiterates the appropriateness of God's wrath. In the fourth stanza, the poet invents an incident in which Edwards, as a small boy, sees a spider being cast into fire and offering little resistance to it. The final stanza draws in Josiah Hawley, an uncle of Jonathan Edwards, who early in the Great Awakening committed suicide by cutting his own throat. Here and in another poem, "After the Surprising Conversions," Lowell makes use of letters Edwards had written to Benjamin Colman, a fellow minister in Boston, describing Hawley as having fallen into "a deep melancholy, a distemper that the family are very prone to," and attributing his death to the Satanic incursion that the Great Awakening was designed to combat. A few days after the bloody incident, Edwards saw evidence of "a considerable revival of religion," but he later reported to Colman that the temptation to suicide was spreading alarmingly among the townspeople.

Finally, the black widow is death itself, "infinite" and "eternal." To Edwards and no doubt to Hawley, death could be the prelude to an everlasting damnation, although Lowell couches his speaker's concluding words in terms ambiguous enough to accommodate the possibility of different interpretations by successive readers.

Forms and Devices

Lowell works the meditation into an elaborate stanza in an iambic meter ranging from three to six poetic feet long with a demanding rhyme scheme of *abbacccdd*. Having set this restrictive and regularly recurring form for himself, the poet runs the speaking voice across it in such a way as to create felicitous variations of rhythm, pace, and emphasis.

About half the lines as well as the transition between two of the stanzas show enjambment, and half the sentences begin within lines. There is great variety, also, in the length, arrangement, and function of the sentences. The first stanza, for example, is composed of two descriptive sentences of twenty-seven and thirty-five words, while the hexameter line at the end of the second stanza consists of two balanced questions: "How will the hands be strong? How will the heart endure?" Longer, often-periodic sentences combine with abrupt questions such as these and snappy assertions such as the concluding "This is the Black Widow, death" to give the impression of an agile mind at work.

In this and other early poems, Lowell shared the practice of poets such as Dylan Thomas and Marianne Moore, contrivers of intricate patterns who muted the rhymes and disguised the rhythmic schemes, thus artfully concealing art. The sound effects of this poem enhance the movement of the meditating mind without calling attention to themselves—which is why the analysis of such poems must do so.

"Mr. Edwards and the Spider" also illustrates Lowell's penchant for merging seemingly disparate elements into a surprising unity. Edwards's youthful admiration for flying spiders and his heavy-handed appropriation of them twenty-five years later, playing as it does on his congregation's theologically induced loathing of spiders for the sake of frightening them into the straight and narrow path, reveal two totally different aspects of a many-sided man. The modern reader, coming upon these two works of Edwards, are likely to lament the disappearance of the budding naturalist into the fire-and-brimstone preacher, but Lowell teases them imagistically into co-existence in this poem, adding also the poisonous black widow. Edwards's listeners would naturally tend to associate this type of spider with the Devil. In fact, Edwards's fellow Massachusetts minister Edward Taylor (who ended his long pastorate in Westfield about the time Edwards began his in nearby Northampton) had portrayed "Hell's spider" memorably in a poem and had doubtless also done so in his sermons. By amalgamating these spiders, Lowell suggests the complexities and contradictions of Edwards's character in one relatively short poem.

Lowell accomplishes this feat by collapsing time in the consciousness of his speaker. As a result, he could combine several elements, one of which is the early keen interest in nature's ways that surely continued in the preacher. Another is Edwards's painful recollection of an unbalanced parishioner harried by religious emotion into a desperate act. Lowell also infuses his subject's powerful rhetorical gift and, in acknowledgment of Edwards's philosophical bent, his predisposition to meditate on death. The result of Lowell's compression is no doubt a "Lowellized" Edwards but nevertheless a more comprehensive portrait of the man than one is likely to glean from any one of his surviving works.

Themes and Meanings

Lowell is a twentieth century writer whose preoccupation with the dark side of human nature and of modern culture led him to a study of the American colonial mind. No more an apologist for Puritanism than was Nathaniel Hawthorne in the nineteenth century, he could not on the other hand accept the optimistic tradition in American letters that, beginning with Edwards's contemporary Benjamin Franklin and proceeding through the transcendentalists of Lowell's New England and Walt Whitman, discounted or minimized the effects of what Puritans had generally identified as original sin.

Edwards, born only three years before Franklin, exemplifies a religious commitment about to yield to a rationalist, humanist, and increasingly secular outlook. Edwards was a brilliant conservative fighting a rearguard action against irresistible change. Although destined to fail, Edwards unflinchingly faced the reality of powers that defy and belie purely rationalist accounts of human nature. In doing away with an angry God, the generations after Edwards were banishing the most plausible available explanation for many of the afflictions that have since become likely to be summed up in an expression such as "the human condition."

Beginning in his second stanza, Lowell has Edwards address a "you" who remains unspecified until the fifth stanza, when the addressee becomes Hawley, for Edwards as well as for his readers a disturbing example of deviant human behavior. It is easy enough—too easy, in fact—to see Hawley as the victim of ministerial mischief, a precarious temperament driven into psychosis by a kind of religious reign of terror. Such a characterization, however, ignores the fact that the modern world has its Josiah Hawleys, too.

Edwards himself would not have characterized death as "the Black Widow," as Lowell does, but death was nevertheless a terrible prospect to one who could not be sure whether he was destined for heaven or hell. Compounding that dilemma, Lowell's Edwards asks, "How will the heart endure?" and wonders what a life is worth. The poem seems to seek an explanation for the guilt that so many people feel (including rejectors of Calvinism). It questions the disappearance in recent times of the majestic calm that leading intellectuals such as Ralph Waldo Emerson and Henry David Thoreau displayed while upholding self-reliance as an antidote to the mind troubled by a legacy of sin and corruption.

For many readers, "To die and know it" means something different from what it would mean to Edwards. Lowell's black widow has no anger to appease, and no appeal is possible. Lowell has Edwards ask the question "But who can plumb the sinking of that soul?" For Lowell, it is less a moral question than a psychological one. His Edwards continues to be a kindred spirit despite the death of his theology, for even if his answers are not sufficient, at least he knew how to ask the right questions.

Robert P. Ellis

MR. FLOOD'S PARTY

Author: Edwin Arlington Robinson (1869-1935)
Type of poem: Narrative
First published: 1921, in *Avon's Harvest*

The Poem

"Mr. Flood's Party" by Edward Arlington Robinson consists of seven eight-line iambic pentameter stanzas, each rhyming in an *abcbdefe* scheme. The rhythm is steady, natural, and unobtrusive. The rhymes are simple and precise, never forced or ostentatious. Thus, in the first stanza, lines 2, 4, 6, and 8 end, respectively, "below," "know," "near," and "here."

The poem presents an ambivalent verse portrait of an old man named Eben Flood. As he is walking up a hill one night back to his humble little house, he halts in the moonlit road to have a drink or two from the jug he refilled in the village, called Tilbury Town, down below. The first stanza of the poem alerts the reader at once to "Old" Eben's solitary status: He is "climbing alone"; it is dark; and he is returning to his "forsaken upland hermitage," which holds "as much as he should ever know/ On earth again of home." Thus, he has no wife, has no family, is companionless, and undoubtedly has few possessions. The possibility that he is an alcoholic looms quickly—it is said that he "paused warily" to note that there was no "native near." He can safely have a quick drink, not simply for the road but while actually on it.

Instead of lugubriously lamenting that he is close to death, Eben phrases his thoughts aloud in this stoic manner: "The bird is on the wing, the poet says/ And you and I have said it here before." The "I," introduced here, is his other self. Eben begins to think of "the dead," his old friends, salutes them in a wavering voice—to the tune of another welcome slug of whiskey—and grows dim-eyed. Feeling his liquor and apprehensive that he might drop his jug and break it, he sets it down, "as a mother lays her sleeping child/ Down tenderly."

Rather inebriated now, Eben offers to shake hands with "Mr. Flood," his alter ego, and addresses him thus: "many a change has come/ To both of us, I fear, since last it was/ We had a drop together." Welcoming the other Flood "home," he holds "the jug up to the light," perhaps to check the level of what remains, and accepts the implicit invitation. However, this time, "Only a very little, Mr. Flood." Moistened now, his voice is ready for a song, "For auld lang syne." The landscape rings, with only the moon for his uncommunicative companion. Eben "regretfully" inspects the jug again and shakes his head, thus ridding himself of the false notion that he has really been drinking with someone else. Sure enough "again alone," he heads home, well aware that if he had knocked at any of several houses "in the town below," strangers would have shut the doors that many old friends once opened to offer him hospitality "long ago."

Forms and Devices

Although "Mr. Flood's Party" is a short narrative poem of only fifty-six lines, Robinson includes aspects of the dramatic monologue in it. Eben Flood speaks in four of the seven stanzas, for a total of 113 words. His fragmentary snatches of talk thus constitute a soliloquy, during the delivery of which he thinks, or perhaps only pretends to think, that he is addressing his other self, who answers courteously. Moreover, the poem satisfies another requirement of the dramatic monologue: Eben's words reveal his essential character at an epiphanic moment and in the presence of a listener.

Robinson combines generally simple diction and profound meaning. His most complex words here are "acquiescent," "convivially," "harmonious," and "salutation." Similarly, his meter and rhymes are basic and unvaried. For example, the following lines have ten syllables each, which when read aloud are found to be naturally accented on the even-numbered syllables: "Alone, as if enduring to the end" and "And there was nothing in the town below." The words constituting Robinson's rhyme scheme are also precise, with two exceptions, which are sight rather than sound rhymes: "come" and "home," and "done" and "alone."

The point of view in "Mr. Flood's Party" is that of an objective, omniscient, third-person observer. He watches and listens as Eben is returning home, pausing, drinking, and talking to himself. This objectivity is forgotten for a moment, however, when it is said that Eben's boozy rendition of "Auld Lang Syne" is heard by "two moons." The observer is sober enough, but Eben momentarily sees double. This is the poem's only touch of humor.

The most notable technical feature of "Mr. Flood's Party" is a pair of apt figures of speech. Eben is responsible for the first figure, which is a metaphor and occurs when he paraphrases Edward FitzGerald's translation of two lines from *Rubáiyát of Omar Khayyám* (1859, rev. 1868, 1872, 1879): "The Bird of Time has but a little way/ To fly— and Lo! the Bird is on the Wing." Eben's life is obviously hastening toward its close.

The second figure of speech, a simile, comes from the narrator, who describes Eben as virtually helpless but relying briefly on his jug. He stands in the road "as if enduring to the end/ A valiant armor of scarred hopes outworn." Like a knight in a dented breastplate, he resembles "Roland's ghost winding [blowing] a silent horn." The alert reader will visualize Eben shouldering his jug and tilting its aperture to his mouth like a bugle. This is the standard posture of a New Englander sneaking a gulp from his gallon of moonshine in the 1920's.

The brilliant literary reference is to the hero of *Chanson de Roland* (*Song of Roland*, twelfth century). In it, Roland, the legendary knight, sounds his magic horn for help from Charlemagne's army at the battle of Roncesvalles (778), but his appeal is too late. For his part, Eben is merely calling on "the dead," and those old friends can no longer bring him any relief.

Themes and Meanings

This poem is about lonely, old Eben Flood. He was not always a loner, however. Robinson explains that in Tilbury Town "friends of other days had honored him."

However, he has outlived his friends, he might even suffer mockery from new residents, and he now must cope with numbing solitude. He can occasionally do so by leaving his "upland hermitage" and walking to town for a jugful of liquor, which it was illegal to buy if the time of the action is 1921 (the year the poem was published), because Amendment XVIII (national prohibition) had been ratified two years earlier. This bothered neither Flood nor Robinson, who reputedly had a problem with alcohol and who, being a bachelor with dysfunctional brothers (one an alcoholic, the other a probable suicide), often struggled with loneliness and poverty.

Robinson's best poems are often short, tightly structured vignettes about men challenged by hardship, loss or personal deficiency, consequent defeat, and privation. The adverse fate of his numerous titular heroes varies. Some, such as Richard Cory, kill themselves. The title character of "Miniver Cheevy," weaker than Eben Flood, merely "Scratched his head and kept on thinking,/. . . And kept on drinking." Flammonde, protagonist of the poem of the same name, borrows cash to maintain a debonair lifestyle and helps enemies become friends but has a "small satanic . . . kink/. . . in his brain" that keeps him from greatness. The heroine of "Eros Turannos" avoids loneliness by marrying so disastrously that she contemplates drowning herself. All are residents of Robinson's fictional Tilbury Town, which is based on Gardiner, Maine, where the poet grew up and which is the locale of much of his verse.

Robinson regarded "Mr. Flood's Party" as his best poem. There are many reasons for its status as a classic of early modern American literature. It concerns the valiant spirit of an old fellow, an object of admiration, pity, and humor who faces his bleak future with dignity. He is bright; he can quote from *The Rubaiyat*. Robinson perhaps invites his readers to recall, or find out, that the first line of the quatrain that is Eben's source is "Come, fill the Cup." Eben enjoys his swigs.

The Roland image is one of the most brilliant in world literature. When Eben is made to resemble the courageous knight, the old fellow gains dignity, but with it pathos, because, as is true of Roland, his life is almost finished and those he tries to summon are mere phantoms. The best image here, however, because it is bracingly ironic, may be that hornlike jug. Eben treats it like a child; yet whereas his child would have a future, the contents of his jug ignite only memories of his past, as does his singing of "Auld Lang Syne," one line of which concerns "auld acquaintance," never to "be forgot."

Young readers can respond with instant pleasure to the conventional, old-fashioned meter, rhyme scheme, and diction of "Mr. Flood's Party," even as they work through the challenging layers of meaning in it. Young readers ought to welcome being reminded that time is fleeting for everyone, even themselves, and that their parents and grandparents know this better than they do. Therefore, there is a lesson in this poem for everyone, old and young alike.

Robert L. Gale

MR. STRATIS THALASSINOS DESCRIBES A MAN

Author: George Seferis (Giorgos Stylianou Seferiades, 1900–1971)
Type of poem: Narrative
First published: 1940, as "Okh. Stratēs Thalasssinos perigraphei enan anthrōpo," in
Tetradio gymnasmaton; English translation collected *Book of Exercises*, 1967

The Poem

The poem "Mr. Stratis Thalassinos Describes a Man" is a five-part poem in which
the Nobel Prize-winning Greek poet George Seferis describes the stages of the life of
a man: child, adolescent, young man, and man. These stages of life can be seen as the
development of all people, keeping in mind that the poet, writing in June, 1932, was
not cognizant of later, less gender-identified language. Translated from the original
Greek, the poem has a narrative style, does not include rhyme, and features recurring
images of the Greek physical landscape, as well as references to Greek mythology
and the Greek Orthodox Church.

Seferis was born in Smyrna (now İzmir), Asia Minor, which was then inhabited by
Greeks, and was later raised in Athens. He went to law school in France and prepared
for a dual career as poet and diplomat. As a thirty-year-old man on assignment in London, Seferis wrote this poem to describe the dreams and aims of youth as they matured
into adulthood.

Although Seferis was known later as a nationalistic poet, his youthful poems vibrate with a sensuality and awareness of the physical body, of nature and the effects of
natural elements on human life. In this poem the combination of abstract ideas and
concrete images makes his poetry accessible to people of any culture and from any
age. This universality is one of the reasons for which Seferis was awarded the Nobel
Prize in Literature in 1963. In his acceptance speech Seferis described his work: "Poetry has its roots in human breath—and what would we be if our breath were diminished? Poetry is an act of confidence—and who knows whether our unease is not due
to a lack of confidence?" Seferis deserves a place among the great poets of the twentieth century because he read and translated Paul Valéry, Ezra Pound, T. S. Eliot, Henry
Miller, and Lawrence Durrell and added his voice to theirs.

Forms and Devices

Seferis uses the common vernacular language of educated Greeks in his poetry, and
the translation continues this device. With this language he combines his own experiences with images of the Greek landscape and history to bridge the gap between
ancient legends and the present. The first section of the poem sets the scene in which
the poet meets the man whose life he is to describe. Thus the point of view taken
by the poet is outside the main action of the poem; rather, the poet relates the life
story of the fictional character, Stratis Thalassinos, whose life is a symbol of every
man's life.

The man has been watching a flame all day to keep himself alive because a woman has left him. Here one of the main symbols of the poem is introduced, that of a woman: "You know I love a woman who's gone away perhaps to the nether world." Here also is the first mythological reference, which alludes to at least one myth, that of Persephone, who descended to the underworld. Women reappear during successive stages of the man's life.

The second section of the poem is brief and describes the time of youth: learning about the body and nature. The second main symbol of the poem is introduced: trees. "It was the roots of the trees that tormented me when in the warmth of winter they'd come and wind themselves around my body." For the child, thinking about trees deep in the ground protected and comforted him. Trees are an important symbol in Greece, where the weather is quite hot part of the year, and the shade of trees is welcome for travelers. They are a sign of the resurgence of life, of nature's bounty, and fertility. Their absence is a sign of death and decay.

In the third section of the poem the obsession with women is revealed, and Thalassinos relates that he put away his childhood after this time: "the roots of the trees no longer came to me." The man has his first taste of the sea and later falls in love with a girl on a hill. The third major image of the poem is introduced, namely the sea, an eternal image for Greeks, whose lands are surrounded by water. The third section of the poem is vivid in its description of life in a Greek village; the details of the poem highlight the simple rural atmosphere: an old woman, a pot of carnations, a girl, and a cottage. The poet uses color to dramatic advantage by suggesting the color of each person and place mentioned: the white cottage, the girl with red eyes in a black dress. The most telling image in this stanza is the black cock, who could have prevented the death of the old woman. Here the poet also makes an allusion to the superstition and folklore traditions of the island people, and at the end of the stanza a final theme of the poem is introduced, that of grief and death. Once met, both the woman and innocence are left behind. The man returns to the sea and dreams "of a very old olive tree weeping." Here the tree assumes the man's grief.

The life of the young man recalls the voyages of the Greek sailor Odysseus. Yet this is not primarily a poem of sea adventures; these voyages lead the man back to women, this time in the form of prostitutes in Constantinople. The exotic images of Turkey, fruit and nut trees and secret gardens, are combined with descriptions of the luscious women to create a scene of idleness and sex. Although the man indulges himself with the woman, he cannot forget that even at the end of this pleasure, there will be grief and death. He recalls the younger woman he met before his voyages: "the broken pitcher in the cool afternoon" symbolizes once again the insubstantiality of love.

Once man has known woman, known travel and adventure, his life is complete. The last long section of the poem is fully in prose. It provides a dense summary of the voyages of Thalassinos as he travels the world trying to understand the meaning of life. The Christian parable of Lazarus is mentioned, as well as scholarship and the attempt of humanity to know itself and the world. What is life, after all, but all these things: women, travel, adventure, life, and death. Finally, in the end of the poem, the man recalls an encounter with a young couple who could see nothing but each other in each other's eyes, and he envies them their innocence and single pointedness. He says, "they're the only people I've ever seen who didn't have the grasping or hunted look that I've seen in everyone else. That look that classes them either with a pack of wolves or a flock of sheep."

The final lines of the poem find the man, Stratis, and also the poet, longing for an end of life in which all the previous images of the poem come together in an idyllic portrait: a pine tree by the sea, shade, a bit of wind at evening that makes a song. This would be the way to end life and face eternity. This is the greatest hope of Stratis Thalassinos, despite all the torments—to be one with nature at the last. Then one could rise again to a new life. Christian imagery is recalled, though this is not a fervent evangelism. The last lines of the poem, "it doesn't really matter," imply that a man's greatest security is found in the physical world that he knows so well: the sea and especially the trees.

Themes and Meanings

The themes and meanings of the poem are intertwined with the imagery of trees, the sea, and women. Seferis uses graphic visual images combined with common symbols such as flowers, trees, animals, and fish to convey sensuality, nature, and the mystery of unknowable fate. The attempt to learn the meaning of life from all these images yields whatever sense and security is to be found in life. The scope of the poem is philosophical. In order to understand life's meaning many aspects of life are contemplated: Greek mythology is alluded to, along with Christianity, the life of pleasures and the body, the life of travel and adventure, and the life of the mind, or studying. The poet refers to a life of study: "I imagine that he who'll rediscover life, in spite of so much paper, so many emotions, so many debates and so much teaching, will be someone like us, only with a slightly tougher memory." The poet does not desire to present answers to the great questions of life so much as to describe the process of embracing life and trying to find out its secrets.

This is a challenging poem for students, but a worthwhile poem that presents the important questions of life in a common language narrative that is accessible to the diligent student. This poem does not contain the devices of rhyme or rhythm which often occupy poetry studies and may occlude the meaning for some. With persistence, however, most students will be able to understand the meaning of the poem and thereby develop further their own beliefs and philosophies, or be prompted to study Greek or other ancient philosophies more in depth.

Marlene Broemer

MULATTO

Author: Langston Hughes (1902-1967)
Type of poem: Narrative
First published: 1926; collected in *Fine Clothes to the Jew,* 1927

The Poem

Langston Hughes's eleven-stanza narrative poem "Mulatto" explores the impact of a sexual union between unmarried people of different races. The offspring of such a union is a mixed-race or biracial child, sometimes referred to as a mulatto. Biracial people in the twenty-first century are less likely to experience the sense of displacement and rejection Hughes's poem describes. However, the poem has unquestionable historical as well as aesthetic value.

"Mulatto," set in the state of Georgia, relies on the stereotyped situation of sexual exploitation of southern black women by southern white men. The poem has an omniscient narrator who speaks between statements made by a son, a father, and a brother; the opening line is a declaration by a young man who says he is the son of a "white man." After the opening line, the narrative voice changes to that of an omniscient speaker, who explains that as evening approached the pine forests of Georgia, one of the "pillars of the temple fell," a reference to the two pillars that stood outside Solomon's temple (2 Chronicles 3:15-17). The young man's father speaks, saying emphatically that the young man is not his son. In the fourth stanza, the omniscient narrator reminds the poem's readers that the stars that accompany a "Southern night" are yellow, then asks rhetorically, "What's a body but a toy?" In response to the rhetorical question, the poet improvises the rhythm of the stanza so that it contains a six-line reply in blues form about how the bodies of women are indeed toys for entertaining men.

After the blues riff, and within the same stanza, the narrative voice switches to that of the father, who asks his son, *"What's the body of your mother?"* The omniscient narrator, not the son, responds, saying that "Silver moonlight" is "everywhere." The father asks the same question again, and again the reader sees that only the omniscient narrator replies, telling the father that there is a "Sharp pine scent in the evening air." The fifth stanza is spoken by the father's other son, the biracial child's half brother, who, in response to the opening line of the poem, says *"Naw, you ain't my brother."*

The poem's omniscient narrator responds to the brother's statement in another rhythmically improvised stanza, where the poet uses a three-line blues form instead of the six-line form to explain that "Dusk dark bodies/ Give sweet birth." The father orders his biracial son to *"Git on back there in the night"* because he is not white. The son seems to have the last word, declaring again that he is the white man's son; however, the omniscient narrator is the final voice, describing the son in the same way the stars have been described, as "yellow." The final line reminds the reader that the mixed-race child is born of parents who are not married to each other. The child is a "bastard boy."

Forms and Devices

"Mulatto" combines the African American blues form Hughes pioneered with the free-verse form made popular by the modernist American poet Ezra Pound. Originally, musician W. C. Handy identified the blues form as song lyrics sung in three-line rhyme. The first two lines of the rhyme were the same or similar; the third line rhymed with the second line. Hughes adapted the musical form to his poems by extending the three-line rhyme to six lines, meant to be spoken rather than sung.

"Mulatto" contains two blues stanzas set inside two free-verse stanzas. The first blues stanza follows Hughes's six-line structure, beginning with the line "Juicy bodies" and ending with the line "What's a body but a toy?" The second blues stanza, similar to the original design of three-line blues songs, reads: "O, sweet as earth,/ Dusk dark bodies/ Give sweet birth." The poet uses end rhyme irregularly, except in the first blues section, where the rhyme scheme is *abcbdd*, and the second blues section, where the rhyme scheme is *aba*. Hughes alternates trochaic (a stressed syllable followed by a slack syllable) and iambic (a slack syllable followed by a stressed one) feet in lines that vary from dimeter to pentameter to achieve the effect of conversational speech. The poet uses several refrains or repeated lines throughout the poem, such as "*I am your son, white man*," "What's a body but a toy?," "*What's the body of your mother?*" and "Great big yellow stars."

The poet uses slang and informal language with the formal apostrophe (an address or exclamation to an unseen person or a thing). The biracial boy is addressed by Hughes's omniscient narrator who says, "O, you little bastard boy." Later in the poem, the narrator uses an apostrophe to exclaim "O, sweet as earth." This line is also a simile that compares fertile female bodies to the fertile earth.

Aside from the remarkable structure of a stanza form within a stanza form, Hughes's style relies on several voices to narrate the story of a young, biracial man's conception. The voices of the father and the half brothers are italicized, while the omniscient narrator's voice is not. Each voice offers a different perspective. The father and the omniscient narrator imply that the biracial child was conceived in an unholy sexual union, that is, when a married white man turned to a black woman for sexual pleasure. The half brother hints at the bleak future the biracial child will have without his father's heritage when he says "you ain't my brother// Not ever." Yet, the mulatto or biracial child insists on his patrimony. Except for the biracial child's, each voice speaks nonstandard English and uses racial slurs, demonstrating a lack of formal education as well as rampant ignorance.

The poet uses two very strong allusions. The first allusion, found in the fourth line of the poem, is to Solomon's temple. The second allusion is to the abilities of the common solvent turpentine, made from pine trees common to the southern United States. Turpentine is able to dilute color as well as strip the surface color off an object, revealing its essence. The sexual activity that takes place in the "turpentine woods" produces "yellow . . . boys" or boys whose color is diluted, that is, not assessed as black or white.

Themes and Meanings

Influenced by the nineteenth century American poet Walt Whitman and the early twentieth century American poets Vachel Lindsay and Carl Sandburg, Hughes's poetry focuses on the lives and the struggle of African Americans for racial equality. Marked with melancholic passivity, concealed outrage, and finally a transcendence that is repeatedly an assertion of black worth, history, and beauty, Hughes's poetry supports his claim that he is the "poet laureate of the negro race." Unafraid to write about the controversial or the uncomfortable, and passionate about embracing his heritage, Hughes's poetic structure (the blues form) gave voice to those who had never been given the chance to speak. "Mulatto" is an enduring example of Hughes's poetic achievement.

The narrator in the opening line claims he is the son of a "white man." Because the father is identified by race rather than by name, readers know the poem is not just a straightforward presentation of a family drama, but an examination of race relations in the American South, a setting confirmed in the second line, which tells readers of a "Georgia dusk." The omniscient narrator says that "One of the pillars of the temple fell," alluding to the two pillars the ancient Hebrew king Solomon erected as symbols of God's promises of support to the people of Israel. People of faith who passed between the pillars were reminded of the presence and strength of God. When the poet says that one of the pillars has fallen, he is suggesting that either the presence, or the strength, of God is in question, not only in this father-son relationship, but also in the American South.

This allusion is deepened by the omniscient narrator's question "What's a body but a toy?," a refrain that stands in direct contrast to the New Testament passage in I Corinthians 3:16, which says, "Know ye not that your body is the temple of the Holy Spirit?" The deeper message is that the human body is not a toy but a spiritual temple and as such should not be defiled in an unholy union, that is, a union between a married man and an unmarried woman.

The poem's final message is the most poignant and is also illustrative of Hughes's idea of transcendence. The biracial child knows who he is and where he comes from, even though neither the father nor the brother will acknowledge him, their blood relative, as a family member. However, the poet says twice that the "Southern night" is "full of stars/ Great big yellow stars" and repeatedly describes the biracial child as "a little yellow/ Bastard boy," drawing a parallel between the boy and the stars. Hughes implies that the offspring of unsanctified unions, commonly referred to as bastards, are as numerous and widespread as the stars and are able, like the stars, to go "everywhere."

Ginger Jones

MUSÉE DES BEAUX ARTS

Author: W. H. Auden (1907-1973)
Type of poem: Meditation
First published: 1939, as "Palais des Beaux Arts"; collected in *Another Time*, 1940

The Poem
"Musée des Beaux Arts," which is French for "museum of fine arts," is a poem about the universal indifference to human misfortune. Following a series of reflections on how inattentive most people are to the sufferings of others, the poet focuses on a particular rendition of his theme: a sixteenth century painting by the Flemish master Pieter Bruegel, the Elder, called *The Fall of Icarus.*

W. H. Auden spent the winter of 1938 in Brussels, where he visited the Bruegel alcove of the city's Musées Royaux des Beaux-Arts. "Musée des Beaux Arts" was inspired by the poet's fascination with the Icarus painting, as well as by two other canvases by Bruegel: *The Numbering at Bethlehem* and *The Massacre of the Innocents.* It was written in 1939, when Auden was distressed over the defeat of the Loyalists in the Spanish Civil War and the acquiescence of Europeans to the ascendancy of Fascism.

The poem consists of two sections, the first a series of general statements and the second a specific application of those generalizations. Like the great Flemish Renaissance artists, the poet observes how very marginal is individual calamity to the rest of the world. Most others continue with their mundane activities without paying any attention to the kinds of extraordinary events that poets and painters usually dramatize. In particular, instead of highlighting the magnitude of that mythical catastrophe, Bruegel depicts the bizarre disaster of Icarus falling from the sky as if it were peripheral and utterly inconsequential to anything else. Oblivious to what is happening to hapless Icarus, no one and nothing—neither a farmer nor the sun nor a ship—are distracted from proceeding with business as usual.

The second section of "Musée des Beaux Arts" is an abbreviated analysis of the Bruegel work, in which the poet emphasizes how the painter composes his pastoral scene in such a way as to minimalize the significance of a boy's suddenly plopping into the sea. Except for the obscure background detail of individual death, the landscape might seem idyllic. Auden's point is a simple one, and, by expressing it simply, succinctly, and nonchalantly, he intensifies the horror of universal apathy.

Forms and Devices
The first noun in "Musée des Beaux Arts" is "suffering," yet the poem is constructed to demonstrate that it is only in its own first line and nowhere else in the world that human agony receives any emphasis. Elsewhere in his writing, Auden often employs recondite and archaic words, but in this poem he deliberately restricts himself to a very plain vocabulary. The effect of commonplace phrases is to emphasize the banality of suffering. The poet's tone is nonchalant, as if to echo the carefree way in

which most people ignore the tribulations of others. Passion and reverence are out of place in the kingdom of the blasé.

The reader is told that, at the time of "the miraculous birth" (an allusion to the momentous arrival of Jesus), children were most concerned with ice skating and "did not specially want it to happen." The use of "specially" rather than "especially" suggests a child's vocabulary; it projects an air of innocence ominously at odds with the horror the poet feels. Even the reference to ice skating in ancient Palestine is an obvious anachronism, and its flippancy, too, is a deliberate incongruity, designed to call attention to something very wrong: the fact that indeed no one pays attention.

At the end of the first section, the "dreadful martyrdom" of the Crucifixion is undercut by the neighborhood dogs' "doggy life." The adjective "doggy" again suggests a childlike vocabulary, and the deliberately sloppy use of "life" rather than the more grammatically appropriate "lives" embodies the offhanded attitude that repulses the poet. While Jesus is being tortured to death, the executioner's horse calmly scratches his rump; the childish euphemism "behind" reinforces the air of innocence at the same time that it taints it with the reader's knowledge of the utter incongruity of such terminology in the face of blatant evil.

The second stanza reduces the entire catastrophe of Icarus's descent to the ingenuous phrase "a boy falling out of the sky," thereby dismissing it as effectively as the ploughman, the sun, and the ship do. Mockingly, Auden end rhymes "green" and "seen," though those words are less important than others around them and they are not the ends of syntactical units of thought.

"Musée des Beaux Arts" is written as free verse, in lines so irregular and discursive that the poem might seem indistinguishable from prose. It is an appropriate form for a work that deals with the prosaic, with a breezy refusal to recognize drama, so preoccupied are people with unexceptional happenings. The wandering line "While someone else is eating or opening a window or just walking dully along" is a perfect marriage of form and content; a litany of trite activities, the line itself walks dully along the page and seems to end as arbitrarily as a shorter line such as "They never forgot," which appears to break at random. The poem is art disguised as artlessness, depicting a world in which artlessness is a failure of attention and hence of ethics.

The poem is an elaborate exercise in anticlimax, in the effort to undercut any serious, sustained attention to what is significant. Although formal sentences are not supposed to conclude with a preposition, "Musée des Beaux Arts" trails off more than concludes, with the preposition "on." One is left with the specious tranquillity of the foolish half-rhyme "calmly on"—the verbal equivalent of exactly the kind of amoral insouciance that the poem, camouflaging itself as part of the problem, depicts and condemns.

Themes and Meanings

Auden's poem is an example of ekphrasis, the embedding of one kind of art form inside another—in this case, a famous painting summarized in a poem. If art, as traditionally conceived, is the deliberate, labored product of human attentiveness to detail,

"Musée des Beaux Arts" is centrally concerned with the temptations of artlessness. It is itself artful in its own guise of criminal artlessness.

Bruegel's *The Fall of Icarus* captures the final moment of an elaborate and portentous Greek myth. Icarus was imprisoned with his father, Daedalus, the master craftsman, in the labyrinth that the latter had constructed on the island of Crete. In order to escape, Dedalus devises wax wings that will enable father and son to fly free of the island. He cautions Icarus not to soar too close to the sun, lest it melt the wings' wax. With the arrogance of youth, Icarus ignores his father's warning and, after his wings melt, plummets into the sea and drowns. In Bruegel's rendition, as though the event were indeed marginal to the course of human affairs, Icarus's leg is the only part of him still—barely—visible above the water, in the lower right-hand corner of the canvas. The disappearance of the imprudent boy is not the center of the viewer's attention, just as it passes unnoticed by everyone else within the frame. Like Bruegel, Auden would force one to take notice of universal disregard.

James Joyce chose Stephen Dedalus as the name of his aspiring novelist in *A Portrait of the Artist as a Young Man* (1916), and Dedalus, an ingenious architect and inventor, is often appropriated from Greek mythology as a prototype of the artist. Beginning with its title, an elegant French phrase that seems blatantly out of place with the poem's homely style and its rustic landscape, "Musée des Beaux Arts" questions the ability of art to matter in a world of intractable apathy. Not only is Dedalus rendered powerless, but the horrendous death of his son, Icarus, passes unheeded and unmourned. Even the sun, which, by melting the wax wings, is most directly responsible for the catastrophe, shines without pause or compunction.

Written in a conversational, vernacular style, Auden's poem is much more accessible than many of the other major poems of the modern period. Disarmingly direct, it is all the more stunning in its indictment of evasiveness. The "expensive delicate ship" that sails blithely away from an amazing event seems more intent on commercial operations than on concern for an individual human being, as if money mattered more than life. Despite and because of its apparent disingenuousness, "Musée des Beaux Arts" is one of the most haunting English poems to have emerged from the middle of the twentieth century, when millions of human beings were being uprooted, imprisoned, or slaughtered while the rest of the world went calmly about its business. Sociologists have documented the increasing desensitization and alienation of the modern, industrial, urban citizen, but it is probably the museum of fine arts and the anthology of poetry that provide the clearest diagnosis of twentieth century anomie. Readers of poetry are, by definition, attentive. For any reader appalled by widespread failure of attention, "Musée des Beaux Arts" is, like the plop of young Icarus into the green water, indelibly etched in the mind.

Steven G. Kellman

MUTABILITY

Author: William Wordsworth (1770-1850)
Type of poem: Sonnet
First published: 1822, in *Ecclesiastical Sketches*

The Poem

"Mutability," a traditional sonnet of fourteen lines in iambic pentameter, is William Wordsworth's meditation on change and transformation. Something that is mutable is able to shift, alter, and adapt itself, and the poet juxtaposes his reflections on the impermanence of forms to the permanence of Truth. Although grounded in concrete images, the poem addresses the concept of mutability in the abstract and entertains both positive and negative aspects of its manifestation.

In the first two lines, change is described in terms of dissolution, or breakdown. Wordsworth presents change as a kind of corruption that climbs "from low to high" and that correspondingly initiates a descent "from high to low" in that which is being altered. If thought of as a melody, dissolution is a sad or "melancholy chime," and its inevitability is like a scale of notes "whose concord shall not fail."

Yet even a sad tune can be pleasing, and the somber tone of the sonnet changes in the fourth line. Though melancholy, the melody is still "musical," and its harmony is perceived by those who are not motivated by base drives and concerns, such as "crime" and "avarice." This suggests that there is something positive about change that resonates with higher moral values and transcends immediate concerns to which a person might devote "over-anxious care." Wordsworth makes his meaning clear in the seventh line, when he boldly and directly states, "Truth fails not." Though even "outward forms that bear/ The longest date" disappear like frost that melts in the morning sun, the durable essence that they cloak does not. The "tower sublime" will eventually crumble, and the imprint it made will be obliterated. However, that which is known to be true is permanent and impervious to "the unimaginable touch of Time."

In "Mutability," Wordsworth asks the reader look beyond surfaces that are prone to change with time and appreciate the indelible truths behind them. To focus on exteriors is to see only what will decay and drop away; to see through to the core is to locate the eternal. Without denying that it is sad to contemplate the mortality and finality of things, the poet comforts readers with his belief in an intransient essence that endures and transcends and thereby gives meaning to its temporary forms.

Forms and Devices

Though it dwells on the impermanence of the superficial and the transience of forms, "Mutability" is ultimately an optimistic poem. Its reassuring attitude can be attributed in large part to Wordsworth's strategic use of metaphor and simile to express his intentions. Were he concerned solely with the dissolution of surfaces, Wordsworth might have chosen representations of death and decay to make his point. Instead, he carefully deploys images of beauty and grandeur that develop his theme of the enduring substance beneath the surface.

The first of these images is music. The poet perceives the rise from low to high of the forces of dissolution and the corresponding descent from high to low it brings about as an orchestration of notes "along a scale." They are "awful notes," which is to say they are capable of exciting awe in persons attuned to the nuances of their melody. To say, further, that their "concord shall not fail" is to suggest that there is an actual harmony among the notes. The "musical but melancholy chime" that most people hear is but a simple surface overlying a complex structure of counterpoint, craft, and arrangement.

Wordsworth draws his second image from the natural world, likening the changing forms in which Truth is cloaked to "frosty rime" that melts with the morning sun. Wordsworth, like other poets in the Romantic tradition, frequently looked to nature for imagery and symbols to express states of mind and yield instruction applicable to life, and his correlation of the transience of Truth's "outward forms" with the temporarily "whitened hill and plain" of a frosty morning is inspired. It implies that the inevitable dissolution of forms, though regrettable, is natural. What is more, it reminds readers that the frosty covering of the landscape would not have significance but for the durable, permanent substance beneath that gives it shape and contour.

Finally, Wordsworth contrasts the ephemerality of human-made creations with the persistence of a constant value such as Truth. The "tower sublime," which once stood majestically ("royally did wear/ Its crown of weeds"), is no more, having fallen into ruin. It has left no sign of its existence—no trace, even as fleeting as "Some casual shout that broke the silent air." The image invites comparison to a similar symbol used by fellow Romantic poet Percy Bysshe Shelley, in his poem "Ozymandias," in which a monument erected to commemorate a ruler who proclaims himself "King of Kings" has eroded to nothing over time, testifying to the foolishness of human vanity and the shortsightedness of those who attempt to take the measure of the lasting by the immediate. Further, Wordsworth's personification of the edifice as royalty attired in regal garb, capable of shouting to break the surrounding silence, alludes that human beings, like the structures they created, are transient and impermanent.

Whereas Wordsworth develops each of these images over several lines of the sonnet, the principle that they illustrate—"Truth fails not"—takes but a fragment of a line to articulate. Indirectly, then, Wordsworth's poetics elaborate the theme of his sonnet. The similes and metaphors he uses to express the mutable are picturesque and colorful embellishments on Truth. "Truth fails not," even when these embellishments are stripped away or replaced by other forms.

Themes and Meanings

Although "Mutability" stands on its own as an inspiring rumination on change and permanence, it resonates even more powerfully when read in the context of the other *Ecclesiastical Sketches*. Wordsworth wrote these sonnets as an exploration of the history of the Anglican Church and a reflection on how the church had adapted outwardly to changing circumstances of history and cultural evolution. In his examination of numerous aspects of the church, from doctrinal teachings to translation of the Bible, bestowing of sacraments, and even the architecture of chapels, Wordsworth tries to uncover the unchanging foundation of the faith. "Mutability," with its conviction of the persistence of fundamental truths, represents the culmination of his quest.

It is ironic that Wordsworth would write a poem of this kind inspired by observations of an organized religion, since he is traditionally thought of as a revolutionary and poet of the people, who found spirituality and morality not in cathedrals, but in nature and in social relationships with his fellow man. However, "Mutability" is noticeably devoid of religious allusions. Its simple observation that "Truth fails not," even though its outward forms are forever in flux, might just as easily have been inspired by his appreciation of a work of art or his study of human behavior. Wordsworth believed that poetry could be made of "every subject which can interest the human mind," and "Mutability" yields the same universal lesson whether it is read in a religious or a secular context.

Wordsworth wrote "Mutability" comparatively late in his career, when most of the work that distinguished him as a leading poet in the Romantic idiom was already behind him. The poem is considered an example of his enduring visionary brilliance because its themes and devices are consistent with those in the landmark poetry of his youth. As a poet, Wordsworth was renowned for his skill at seeing signs of the eternal in common experiences and relationships. His strongest poems are full of encounters with ordinary people and glimpses of natural scenes that are the catalysts for profound spiritual revelations and moral insights. All of these he described in a language that strove to emulate the thoughts and words of ordinary people. Although "Mutability" is clearly a work of poetic compression and orchestration, its images typify the simplified art that Wordsworth sought to write. A fading melody, a frost-covered landscape in the morning sunlight, and a ruined tower all become symbols of the impermanent and unlasting.

Significantly, Wordsworth never mentions death in his poem. Although the reader is left to infer that human mortality correlates with the dissolution and decline that Wordsworth observes in nature and the landscape, there is something constant that persists even after exterior forms fall away. The optimistic spirit of the poem lies in its suggestion that the transient is merely a patina over the permanent, and that everything in the world—nature, humankind, and humankind's creations—is joined by the eternity of Truth.

Stefan R. Dziemianowicz

MY CAT, JEOFFRY

Author: Christopher Smart (1722-1771)
Type of poem: Meditation
First published: written c. 1759; published in 1939, in *Rejoice in the Lamb: A Song from Bedlam* (William Force Stead, ed.)

The Poem

One of the most delightful and best-known poems in praise of a house cat, Christopher Smart's "My Cat, Jeoffry" is actually one section of a much more complex and difficult work entitled *Jubilate Agno* (Latin for "Rejoice in the Lamb"), composed while the poet was locked in a private madhouse because of religious mania in 1759 or 1760. Despite the bad reputation of eighteenth century hospitals for the insane (which Bedlam, for instance, deserves), Smart's institution was liberal and his time there not totally unpleasant. Already a well-known writer, he was allowed pen and paper, a garden in which to work, privacy, social visits—and the company of his cat. The separate title later given this section comes from its first line, "For I will consider my Cat, Jeoffry." Smart combines naturalistic, careful observation of feline behavior with religious interpretation. The result is that Jeoffry carries the symbolic weight without losing his vivid individuality, and Smart conveys love of his pet without becoming too precious or sentimental. The first image is of Jeoffry, "the servant of the living God," worshipping "in his way," "wreathing his body seven times round with elegant quickness" and then leaping up after "musk" (probably a scented, catniplike plant), "which is the blessing of God upon his prayer." Anyone can see a house cat in these motions, chasing its tail and then leaping up for catnip; Smart's artistry is such that the reader is also able to see it as a kind of worship.

The first third of the poem outlines Jeoffry's daily habits just as Smart had his own habits, which included writing some lines of *Jubilate Agno* every day. After worship, Jeoffry "begins to consider himself." Again the actions are both characteristic and endearing: The cat "looks upon his forepaws to see if they are clean," "sharpens his paws by wood," and "fleas himself, that he may not be interrupted." In this sequence of actions, Jeoffry is both an individual and every cat. The poet also anthropomorphizes Jeoffry, although the human motives attributed to him never clash with his feline nature: "For having considered God and himself he will consider his neighbor./ For if he meets another cat he will kiss her in kindness." Smart artfully combines the image of cats sniffing each other with the idea that it shows courtesy. The other two-thirds of the poem celebrate the many virtues of Jeoffry and cats in general, often with strong religious associations. That "one mouse in seven escapes by his dallying" is a sign of his mercy; to Smart, it also implies biblical uses of seven, such as the seventh day being the Sabbath. Smart writes that the Children of Israel took cats with them when they left Egypt. There is even humor, as when Smart praises the cat as "an instrument for the children to learn benevolence on" or says of his cat's voice, "it has in purity what it wants in music." The last third of the poem describes Jeoffry's activities and "varieties of his movements." Again and again, one can imagine the friskiness of Jeoffry and how much it means to Smart. "For he counteracts the Devil, who is death, by brisking about the life," Smart writes. Jeoffry has learned many tricks that show his "patience" and walks to the rhythm of music. Moreover, his motions form a microcosm of all animals: He swims, creeps, and, "though he cannot fly, he is an excellent clamberer." Interestingly—and in keeping with the scientific interest Smart shows elsewhere in *Jubilate Agno*—the poet has discovered the static electricity from stroking a cat: He sees this "fire" as both protection against "the powers of darkness by his electrical skin" and "the spiritual substance that God sends from heaven to sustain the bodies both of man and beast." Jeoffry's character admirably mixes opposites. As Smart writes, "For there is nothing sweeter than his peace when at rest./ For there is nothing brisker than his life when in motion." Also "he is a mixture of gravity and waggery." At one point, Smart interrupts himself with "Poor Jeoffry! poor Jeoffry! the rat has bit thy throat./ For I bless the name of the Lord that Jeoffry is better." Smart may well have seen himself in the incident, blessed by God but beset by adversity.

Forms and Devices

Jubilate Agno is composed of numerous fragments. Critics debate the relationships among them or even if they form a poem rather than a daybook collection of notes in poetic form. Except for the first two lines, every line in the poem begins with either "Let" or "For" (one view holds that these lines are to be read antiphonally—that is, one "Let" line read with a "For" line read in response). Some fragments do not have sections of both kinds, although the section containing the lines about Jeoffry does. Generally, the "For" sections are more personal; "My Cat, Jeoffry" begins each line with "For." In this structure and counterpoint, Smart was influenced by Anglican liturgy and biblical literature such as the Psalms and the Prophets. Specifically, Smart owes much to Robert Lowth's *De Sacra Poesi Hebraeorum* (1753; *Lectures on the Sacred Poetry of the Hebrews*, 1787). The poem is written without traditional rhyme and meter. Smart relies on similarity of structure and sometimes similar length for unity between lines. Above all, Smart's extreme sensitivity to the sound of words both enriches his work and provides patterns to tie it together. He is especially fond of alliteration, as in Jeoffry "duly and daily" serving God or "at his first glance of the glory of God." Smart also coins new words or adopts old ones, again sensitive to sound, as when he onomatopoeically describes the cat's play as "spraggle upon waggle" (as a noun "sprag" is an archaic term meaning "a lively young fellow"). Humanizing metaphor is basic to the work; Smart's genius is that the religious and anthropomorphic levels do not obscure the literal level. Smart also excels in sharp, visual metaphors as when he writes that Jeoffry "camels his back," an apt description of a cat arching in anger. Elsewhere in *Jubilate Agno*, Smart explains his theory of art in terms of "punching," in which the impact of the words on his readers' eyes convey the visual impression that Smart intended. *Jubilate Agno*, while not composed for publication, is central to Smart's career. Through its experimentation, he went from traditional eighteenth century verse to something much more personal and, in many ways, modern. Some critics believe that it anticipates William Blake's poetry in both the idiosyncratic form and the deeply personal theology conveyed in multiple ways.

Themes and Meanings

According to Smart, *Jubilate Agno* is (and he was aware of the pun) a *magnificat*, a song of praise by all of creation to glorify God. Smart's interest in plants and animals—including unusual or little-valued ones—combines with a theology that finds spiritual significance in everything. This is not pantheism, since creation is decidedly secondary to God, but a vision of all creation as one whole united in God down to its smallest component. The view that nature reveals God in its design spurred Smart's interest in natural history, just as it informed his careful observation of Jeoffry.

Unlike the theory, popular at the time, that human minds are *tabula rasa*—blank pages at birth and written on by experience—Smart's theology adopts the Platonic or Neoplatonic idea that all selves contain knowledge of God, which must be remembered and lived out. In the Jeoffry section, his cat becomes an example of this, not a lesser creature but almost a role model. Jeoffry's natural religion is also reciprocated: As Jeoffry adores God, he is supported by and brought closer to God. Other sections of *Jubilate Agno* explore numerology, semikabbalistic interpretations of the English and Hebrew alphabets, and other hidden sources of understanding. Smart's insight is clearer and stronger when the message is wrought from Jeoffry's life and interpreted through Smart's own. *Jubilate Agno* differs from Smart's other religious poetry (some, such as "The Song of David," is much better as poetry) in its intensely personal nature. Smart interweaves biblical names with those from the newspaper of his day, and conveys—sometimes cryptically and sometimes more clearly—his own adversities and small triumphs. At times, the style approaches that of a modern confessional poem. "I have neither money nor human friends," Smart writes, ever mindful of his feline friend. On another level, the entire poem is an act of Smart's coming to terms with his situation and identity, examining himself in relation to God and those around him. Ultimately, perhaps Smart does not distinguish the personal from the public any more than he divides animals or even plants from people because it is all the same in God's creation.

Bernadette Lynn Bosky

MY DARK MASTER

Author: Nuala Ní Dhomhnaill (1952-   )
Type of poem: Meditation
First published: 1995, as "Mo Mháistir Dorcha/My Dark Master"

The Poem
Written originally in Irish, Nuala Ní Dhomhnaill's "My Dark Master" is a short poem of ten four-line stanzas that loosely follow an *abab* rhyme scheme. Ní Dhomhnaill, a leading voice among Ireland's women writers, was born in Lancashire, England, but grew up in the Dingle Gaeltacht in County Kerry (an area of Ireland that still speaks Irish as its primary language) and in Nenagh, County Tipperary. She has been the recipient of numerous poetry awards, including the Irish American Foundation Award (1988) and the American Ireland Fund Literature Prize (1991).

As the title suggests, "My Dark Master" focuses on the relationship between a dominant figure, the unnamed dark master, and the subordinate speaker. The poem opens with the speaker striking a bargain with "death" to spend time with him. The identity of the dark master is not made clear at first. Instead, the initial stanzas detail the agreement they strike, as the speaker spits in her palm before shaking the dark master's hand (a traditional symbol of a solemn pact) and signs a contract to become "indentured on the spot." In the third stanza, readers learn that the speaker was only nineteen years old at the time, suggesting that her youthfulness contributed to her naiveté about the relationship, which she called "a stroke of luck." However, the optimism underlying Ní Dhomhnaill's initial tone shifts to a more ominous note as she describes falling "into his clutches." The poet makes it clear, however, that she entered into this arrangement willingly and that she was not "meddled with or molested" in any way. Nevertheless, she is clearly subservient to her master, and although she describes their relationship as amicable, it is not a partnership of equals.

In the fifth stanza, Ní Dhomhnaill incorporates traditional pastoral elements into the poem. The movement of "walking out" with her master is extended to herding his cattle across the Irish countryside. Descriptions of the pastures and "hills faraway and green" lend an idyllic air to the poem as she romanticizes her subordinate position as a field hand. The poem's narrator leads the cattle to Lough (lake) Duff, where they find sustenance, but again the poem's tone darkens as the poet's wanderings take her "through the valleys of loneliness." While the cattle appear content in this environment, Ní Dhomhnaill finds no security or comfort from the land. At the top of a hill, she pauses to survey her master's realm and is dizzied by the recognition of how small she is in comparison to it. Her master, she grasps, possesses "riches that are untold," and she can harbor no hopes of rising above the status of shepherdess.

The poem concludes with Ní Dhomhnaill lamenting that she hired herself out to death, and she worries that she will never be able to void that contract. Although earlier she considered herself indentured, suggesting that an ultimate release from her obligation was possible, now she foresees a future filled with the "sough-sighs/ of suffering souls." Despite her efforts to forge an equal partnership, she is not sure what she will gain from her servitude; even having as little as three hot meals a day and a place to sleep seems unlikely. The final line leaves her wondering whether her own autonomy, her voice, will ultimately be subsumed by her master.

Forms and Devices

That "My Dark Master" was originally written in Irish is significant for several reasons. On one level, it serves as a bridge between contemporary poets and Ireland's ancient literary history. Ní Dhomhnaill explains that writing in Irish "is the oldest continuous literary activity in Western Europe, starting in the fifth century and flourishing in a rich and varied manuscript tradition right down through the Middle Ages." She began writing poetry in English as a little girl, but Irish seemed the more natural language to use to express herself. She believes that poetry must come from deep within the individual where native culture lies, so the poet's search for meaning in life mimics an archaeologist seeking to unlock history from layers of cultural sediment. One of the omnipresent themes in Irish literature is the search for a national identity, and to this Ní Dhomhnaill adds the woman poet's search for artistic identity. Working in Irish provides the poet with a stronger connection to the past and thus helps create an artistic genealogy that male writers have enjoyed all along; it also serves as a reminder that Ireland must reestablish an inclusive literature.

In addition to its political implications, composing in Irish allows Ní Dhomhnaill access to "a language of enormous elasticity and emotional sensitivity, of quick hilarious banter, and a welter of references both historical and mythological." Her soul is Irish, so she writes in Irish, not so much as an act of rebellion, but to find the best expression for her art. The popularity of Ní Dhomhnaill's poetry reflects a resurgence of national interest in Irish as a language. Until the late nineteenth century, a majority of citizens used Irish for their daily speech, but the mass emigrations following the Great Famine (1845-1848) and the steady urbanization of the rural western counties where Irish was most frequently spoken has dramatically reduced the number of speakers. In the Irish Republic, an estimated 20,000 to 100,000 people still use Irish as their primary language, and an additional 150,000 are estimated to use it in the six counties of Northern Ireland (although many speakers are bilingual).

Themes and Meanings

Despite Ní Dhomhnaill's statement that death is her master, it is clear that death in this case is a metaphor for the condition of women writers in Ireland. She claims that women have been largely excluded from the Irish literary cannon, so, on one level, the master she serves is Irish literary patriarchy. The females in Irish poetry were, in the words of Irish poet Eavan Boland, "fictive queens and national sibyls." Rather than be allowed to write a literature of their own or to take on roles of substance, women were reduced to playing stereotypical roles such as earth mother, goddess, and hag. In the masculine poetry tradition, Ní Dhomhnaill says that "it has been a long and tedious struggle for us women writing in Irish to get even a precarious toehold in visibility." Accordingly, the poem's narrator wanders about the symbolic Irish countryside without a sense of direction or belonging; it is ironic that she is uncomfortable in a land most often described in feminine language. The theme of the writer in isolation or exile within her own country is common among Irish women poets. By exploring this theme in her poetry, Ní Dhomhnaill is reclaiming a past that was lost in traditional Irish patriarchy, and the poem itself is her poetic search for the voice she cannot seem to find in the final stanza.

While symbolizing the cultural and creative forces repressing her voice, the dark master also represents Ní Dhomhnaill's personal muse or poetic inspiration. Commonly, muses are given feminine personas; however, she believes hers is male and sees herself following in a long history of women writers with masculine muses. She describes her muse as "all or nothing action: killing yourself, walking out of a relationship, black or white, right or wrong . . . [and] he's allied with society against you, against your deeper levels of femininity, because he's male." Instead of struggling against the muse, she surrenders to its control and is led to realizations that she could not have uncovered consciously. Ní Dhomhnaill considers writing poetry a reflective act, so, as with a journey, the poet cannot know what is ahead until the experience has passed and can be reflected upon. In this reflection, the poet matures and must continue to "break through into deeper levels" to discover new creative directions.

With this interpretation of "My Dark Master," the narrator's reaction to the vastness of her master's possessions is not a response to the limited creative space male writers have left her but to the seemingly limitless scope of her muse's artistic vision. He possesses an overwhelming store of subject matter, the "jewels and gems" of life about which she can write. Her anxiety, then, arises from the daunting task of doing justice to what he has shown her. Since for Ní Dhomhnaill writing relies so heavily on the subconscious and meditation, she is unsure of what the final product will eventually turn out to be or whether she will maintain any control over what she writes.

Thomas F. Suggs

MY FATHER IN THE NIGHT COMMANDING NO

Author: Louis Simpson (1923-   )
Type of poem: Meditation
First published: 1963, in *At the End of the Open Road*

The Poem

"My Father in the Night Commanding No" is a meditation on the permanence of childhood experiences and impressions. One of the poet's earliest recollections is of evenings at home when his father would order him to stop whatever he was doing. The father, depicted as silently reading and smoking, is a forbidding figure. Even in the evening he has no time for amusement; he "Has work to do." The phrase "Smoke issues from his lips" suggests something more sinister than the smoking of a cigarette or pipe, something almost demoniacal.

The mother, on the other hand, provides the child with entertainment. She plays a record on the phonograph, perhaps an aria from an opera, which the boy finds jarring. She may also read to him—heroic tales that enable his imagination to stretch to encompass heroic deeds and strange sights. He may even be transported, through these tales, to the mythical island of Thule.

In adulthood the speaker has, in fact, traveled far and seen many things. He lists the cities to which he has gone: Paris, Venice, Rome. He has experienced, he says, "The journey and the danger of the world,/ All that there is/ To bear and to enjoy, endure and do." The language suggests that the journey has not been entirely safe or pleasant, but he has experienced what he had hoped, as a boy, to experience. He is now grown, with children of his own. They play in his presence, not fearing him as he had feared his father: "they were expecting me." Strangely, however, his father is still present in his mind, sitting and reading silently. His mother cries in his memory, presumably for something that happens in an opera or a tale; there is a sense that the past never changes. The speaker has moved beyond them, has avoided the rigidity which marked his father's behavior, but this does not alter their stance.

These figures are fixed and are rigid like puppets. The fact that he cannot change their relationship to him frustrates the speaker. He tries, still, to understand them, to see the reasons his father always seemed to be working, and the cause of his mother's tears, but they are gone and there are no answers. The conclusion of the poem suggests that children, whether his remembered self or his own children, do not realize what role memory will play in their lives.

Forms and Devices

"My Father in the Night Commanding No" consists of eleven four-line stanzas. In each stanza, the first, second, and fourth lines are written in iambic pentameter, and the third line, containing four or five syllables, is in irregular meter. The first and fourth lines rhyme, although the rhyme is not always emphatic or exact. Thus, in the third stanza, "hill" is rhymed with "still," but in the eighth the rhyme words are "move" and "love," in the ninth "sit" and "puppet."

The early part of the poem relies on imagery more than figurative devices for its effects. Some of the images are homely, as when the mother winds the old-fashioned record player (the "gramophone"). Others romantically evoke the stories that aroused the boy's imagination: "a prince, a castle and a dragon." In memory he stands "before the gateposts of the King . . . of Thule, at midnight when the mice are still."

The second part of the poem, dealing with his adult life, finds the speaker moving to more general images and more use of figures of speech: "Landscapes, seascapes" suggest the places he has been but also paintings that depict places he has seen only in works of art. The cities he visited "held out their arms." His imagination lured him on: "A feathered god, seductive, went ahead." When he returns to the memory of his parents, he sees them metaphorically as figures in a puppet show. He speaks of "the stage of terror and of love" on which actors sit, but these actors have wooden heads, and their positions never vary.

The tone of the poem is ironic. The speaker, until the end of the poem, directs the irony at himself rather than at his parents. He is almost sarcastic about what he has done in life and the places he has seen. The flat tone in which he describes the events of his adult life is in sharp contrast to the romantic language about the castle and the prince: "All that there is/ To bear and to enjoy, endure and do." The stronger irony comes when he sees himself in relation to his parents as if they were all mere puppets with no volition of their own. What they felt and why they did what they did is no longer important. Their roles have been fixed by the action of memory. The irony changes in the final stanza; it is made more general, so as to include all memories of childhood and the fact that people do not recognize what is happening while it is going on.

Themes and Meanings

"My Father in the Night Commanding No" is a meditation on the strange role of memory in human life. In Louis Simpson's view, memory establishes permanent images that a person, later in life, does not necessarily understand and cannot change. As an adult, the speaker in the poem wonders about his parents: Why did his father's work make him seem harsh and distant; what was there in the music (which the boy found grating) that made his mother cry? Did the mother have more personal reasons for crying? Why has his adult experience not made him capable of knowing what they felt? The answer to some of these questions may be carried by the wind. The first mention of this conventional symbol of change comes in the pivotal paragraph in which memory brings back the images of the father reading and the mother crying. That stanza ends, "And the dark wind/ Is murmuring that nothing ever happens," a paradoxical notion, given the wind's usual symbolic role.

In the final stanza, the wind is referred to once more: "'*Listen!*' the wind/ Said to the children, and they fell asleep." The wind here seems to be saying that some things, specifically those things of childhood which are held in the memory, are not subject to change. People change, as the speaker's boyhood fantasies have become a kind of adult reality, even though what is recalled from youth remains; but this is adult knowledge. When the memories are being formed, one is unaware of the process that is taking place, ignorant that what one learns then will stay with one for the rest of one's life.

"My Father in the Night Commanding No" is a gentle poem. It contains no images of violence, and other than the early sense of the father as a menacing figure there is little of an overtly sinister nature. There is sorrow in the poem, however, as well as a sense of the mystery of human memory. A dark undercurrent suggests that in some ways people's characters and attitudes are fixed at an early age, without their knowledge. Finally, there is regret that while the speaker's memories will never change, he will never fully understand them.

John M. Muste

MY FATHER MOVED THROUGH DOOMS OF LOVE

Author: E. E. Cummings (1894-1962)
Type of poem: Elegy
First published: 1940, in *Fifty Poems*

The Poem

E. E. Cummings's "my father moved through dooms of love" is an elegy in seventeen four-line stanzas. The poem commemorates Cummings's own father, the Reverend Edward Cummings, a Unitarian minister and Harvard University professor.

The poem is written in the first person. Unlike much of Cummings's love poetry, in which the speaker addresses his beloved while the reader overhears, in this poem the speaker addresses the reader directly. Cummings offers the example of his father's life for the reader to consider and closes the poem with the moral of the story.

The first four stanzas make up the first section of the poem, which introduces the speaker's father as a man with a tremendous capacity for love. His father, Cummings makes clear, understood the complexities and dangers of loving. The repeated pattern "my father moved through *this* of *that*" may be understood to mean "my father experienced *this* before he achieved *that*" or "my father opened himself to the risk of *this* in order finally to achieve *that*." The first stanza gives a picture of a man who realized the danger of being rejected ("dooms"), the risk of losing one's identity in a love relationship ("sames"), and the potential of a lover to become possessive or possessed ("haves"). He faced these dangers squarely and finally emerged as a whole man, capable of loving and being loved. He used this great power to enrich the lives of those close to him. Those wondering "where" found that the answer was "here"; those weeping over "why" were comforted to sleep. No one, "no smallest voice," called to him in vain.

The next section begins with a capital letter (one of only three in the poem), moves through stanzas 5 through 8, and concludes with a period. Here, Cummings celebrates his father's movement through "griefs" into "joy."

The third section, stanzas 9 through 12, again begins with a capital letter and ends with a period. This time, the father moves through "dooms of feel"; that is, he learns to accept and express the full range of human emotion. Stanza 13 speaks briefly of one more quality of Cummings's father: He knew his place in the universe. That is, he knew that the relationship between humans and the natural world was not one of "they" but of "we." The last four stanzas of the poem take a dramatic turn. After the affirmative tone of the description of his father, Cummings now shifts to a harsh description of the society in which his father lived. Now the language is not of joy and singing but of "mud" and "scheming," "fear" and "hate." Stanzas 14 through 16 list the many ways in which people can harm themselves and one another. The language here is simpler; evils exist right at the surface, while goodness may be harder to understand. The final stanza contains the moral: However great or small the evils of the world might be, the fact that one person—Cummings's father—was able to embrace his humanity fully shows that the power of love is greater than the evils of the world. The love that exists as an active force in the world, exerted by individuals, is "more than all."

Forms and Devices

Many of Cummings's most famous poems, including "in Just-" and "r-p-o-p-h-e-s-s-a-g-r," rely on the poet's play with typography and space on the page to convey his message. "My father moved through dooms of love" belongs to the body of Cummings's work that uses more conventional imagery and stanzaic form. Although each of the sections describing his father is self-contained, Cummings unifies them and underscores their common theme of humanity's connectedness to the natural world, by threading through them imagery of the passing of time and the cycle of birth, growth, death, and rebirth.

The imagery in the first section is of awakening and birth, and here Cummings deals with different levels of time. The life cycle is played out with each sunset and sunrise. The father operates at the renewal phase of the cycle in line 3: "singing each morning out of each night." The immediacy of the night-into-day cycle is important to the poem, because Cummings emphasizes the role of the individual within the universe. Stanza 4 reminds the reader that what is at stake is not only tiny roots but also mountains; Cummings is concerned not only with the passing of a day but also with the time it takes for a mountain to grow.

The most important example of the life cycle in this poem is the changing of the seasons. Stanza 3 describes his father's love as an "April touch" that, like spring, awakens "sleeping selves." Stanza 7 picks up the cycle of the year with a reference to midsummer, and the cycle continues in stanza 10 with the "septembering arms of year" and in stanza 11 with "octobering flame." In most poems, the movement from spring through summer into autumn would also be a movement from happiness into sorrow, but in these stanzas the tone is still affirming. The imagery of the changing seasons reinforces the father's role in the natural world, but Cummings is emphatic that the darker seasons are to be embraced, not feared or avoided. Thus, when the poem finally comes to an image of winter, in stanza 12, it is a positive image: "if every friend became his foe/ he'd laugh and build a world with snow." Stanza 13, the last stanza dedicated to the father, is the most explicit, and shows the cycle completed. The imagery here is of spring come again.

There is no imagery of light or darkness, no mention of time, in the description of the evils men can bring. Stanzas 14 through 16 present a list of horrors, but there is no sense here of a cycle—no sense of relief (or re-leaf). There is only "dumb death," with no regeneration to follow. The imagery of the life cycle belongs only to the father, for it is only he who has learned the paradox that in order to escape death one must first encounter and accept it.

Themes and Meanings

"My father moved through dooms of love" is a tribute to Cummings's dead father, but it lacks many of the elements one might expect in an elegy. There is no physical description of the deceased, no mention of mourning or refusal to mourn, and, in fact, no mention of the father's death beyond the use of the past tense. In a very real sense, the poem is not about the poet's father at all, but about a philosophy of love and of life. Cummings raises the poem to this level by avoiding any specific references to his father. There are no details or anecdotes in the poem that point to one particular man, no clues to the identities of those around him. Beginning with his genuine respect for his father, Cummings exaggerates his father's capacities to delineate his own ideals. The poem's father is not a man, but an idealized representation of what an individual could be, of how love can operate in the world.

For Cummings, the individual is of great importance. Love as Cummings believes in it is not an ethereal gift of the spirit world, but a force that exists in the natural world that people inhabit. There is no call to a higher power to solve the world's ills; only the individual, battling evil with the power of love, can redeem the world. Through the example of the life of one person—not a divine savior, but a man as human as the poet's own father—the poem demonstrates the effect that one individual can have on other people. Through his love, he can bring them peace, joy, and nobility. Those who wield this kind of love find it a powerful force, but it does not come easily. Embracing the world means embracing all of it, and there are risks. Love everyone, and some will not love you back. Speak the truth, and some will turn against you. Develop your capacity to feel, and you will feel sorrow as well as happiness. Not many people are willing to try this kind of love, but one individual can give another hope and the courage to try, and then there are two.

"My father moved through dooms of love" is not simply a poem about feeling better. Moving beyond the example of his father, Cummings presents a very specific list of what is wrong with the world. The individual who can confront his own fears and failings can also confront the world's—and must, if the world is to be redeemed. In the last two lines, the poem returns to its key words: "father" and "love." "Father" is the individual person, who has the power to change the world. "Love" is the name of that power.

Cynthia A. Bily

MY GRANDMOTHER'S LOVE LETTERS

Author: Hart Crane (1899-1932)
Type of poem: Lyric
First published: 1926, in *White Buildings*

The Poem

Hart Crane's "My Grandmother's Love Letters" consists of six stanzas, three of which are fairly traditional quatrains, three of which deviate from that established pattern. The "story" of the event that triggered the poem is relatively simple: The speaker discovers his grandmother's letters tucked into a corner of the attic and contemplates reading them. The story of the poem itself, however, is far more complicated. Crane chooses to focus on the process of decision rather than on the act of reading.

"My Grandmother's Love Letters" is one of Crane's most straightforward poems, appearing early in Crane's first book, *White Buildings*. It begins with a simple statement of fact: There are no stars to be seen because it is raining. Yet, even when they are covered with clouds, one knows the stars are there; memory serves as a way to interpret the universe. There is also room for human memory—the letters—which might open doors of human understanding. These letters are old—faded, fragile, friable—and they carry the weight of a personal history. Thus the speaker is acutely aware of the delicacy one needs to enter another person's private terrain: "Over the greatness of such space/ Steps must be gentle."

It is at this point that the reader is made aware that something larger is at stake. The poem suddenly contains a rhymed couplet, each line end-stopped, as though to give the reader time to pause: "It is all hung by an invisible white hair./ It trembles as birch limbs webbing the air."

The speaker is having second thoughts. The letters were not sent to the "grandmother" of the title, nor to his mother's mother, as he has identified her, but to "Elizabeth"—a woman he has never known because she existed before she had taken on the other roles in which he would recognize her. It is significant that her given name occupies a line all by itself in the second stanza.

At the center of the poem a one-line stanza—"And I ask myself:"—is linked by the colon to a complex question set off in quotation marks. The speaker is literally speaking to himself, doubting his ability to read the letters in the spirit in which they were written. He also begins to question his emotional capacity to enter his grandmother's experience.

The final quatrain begins with what also looks like a traditional rhymed couplet, but the second line turns on a semicolon, altering and qualifying the meaning. The speaker would like to lead his grandmother into his own private life but knows there is much she would be unable to comprehend. What makes him think he would be capable of penetrating her private world? And so he "stumble[s]." The caesura stops the reader cold. Will he read the letters or not? The question remains unanswered as "the rain continues on the roof/ With such a sound of gently pitying laughter." The poem ends where it began: rain in the night, the letters with their promise of memory and understanding.

Forms and Devices

"My Grandmother's Love Letters" is a poem that does not become dated. It might as easily have been written at the end of the twentieth century as at its beginning. Part of this is because Crane, along with T. S. Eliot, Ezra Pound, and William Carlos Williams, was experimenting with free verse. The lines have been "freed," so that they resemble a more contemporary poem. From its opening lines with their strong iambic beat, there is a kind of ghost meter that dominates the poem. It comes out strongly in the iambic pentameter of "Through much of what she would not understand" and the broken pentameter of "And back to you again/ As though to her." It is muted in the anapests and trochees of other lines. Nevertheless, the poem plays itself out against the recognized music of traditional English verse.

Aside from the two rhymed pairs ("hair," "air" and "hand," "understand"), there is a series of slant rhymes that thrusts the poem toward its compelling question: "soft," "enough," "mother," "Elizabeth," "roof," "soft," "myself." The word "enough" is echoed twice, further heightening the issue of capacity. "Long enough" and "strong enough" qualify the question and underscore the speaker's growing uncertainty. Their sound reverberates as the poem concludes with the repetition of "roof" and the finality of "laughter."

The poem rings the changes not only with rhyme and meter but also with assonance and consonance. Crane's subtle ear weaves a given sound through several lines: the *l* in "loose," "girdle," "letters," "long," and "liable" and the *o* in "long," "old," "echoes," "strong," "source," "you," and "though." At one point, Crane couples assonance with pacing. The long *a* forces the reader to stretch the quantitative value of the line "Over the greatness of such space," slowing down the pace while the space itself widens, then the poem quickens again with the short *e* of "Steps must be gentle." That same *e* is echoed almost immediately in "trembles" and "webbing," suggesting a web of sound that permeates the poem, culminating in the word "gently." Thus Crane is able to orchestrate the poem and to make of it the "music" that he imagines at the source of the letters.

"My Grandmother's Love Letters" may, in fact, illustrate Crane's break with Imagism. Although the poem unfolds in images, it also contains a syntactical necessity; the lines open with the sound of logic: "There are," "But," "Yet," "Over," "Through," "And so." However, the poem does not add up to its rhetorical moves; instead it relies on the intuition and the nuances that arise from its peculiar combination of image and discourse.

Themes and Meanings.

"My Grandmother's Love Letters" means almost exactly what it says. It does not reach beyond its own experience of the mind's working and reworking a central question: In the silence of time and memory, is it possible to find the original feeling and experience it "as though to her"? The poem works effectively on that level. The reader is left to ponder the same question from the framework of his or her own life. The ambiguities of the poem become part of its meaning. It asks the reader to share the experience through imagery and reflection, not through an identification with the speaker. In fact, the first-person pronoun does not enter until more than halfway through the poem, at which point the speaker rather indirectly raises the issue of privacy. What is it that he thinks she might not understand? The poem demonstrates perfectly what Allen Tate prescribed in his 1926 introduction to *White Buildings:* "The poem does not *convey*; it *presents*; it is not topical, but expressive."

Crane became known as a visionary, almost mystical poet, whose series of complex metaphors taps into an intuitive experience of the world. Crane struggled over the course of his short life to find a subject for his vision and perhaps best succeeded in his long book-length poem *The Bridge* (1930), published shortly before his suicide in 1932. In it, he was able to link an affirmative myth of the United States to one of its most powerful symbols, the Brooklyn Bridge.

In a letter to Harriet Monroe, reprinted in *Poetry* in October, 1926, Crane talked about the "logic of metaphor." In his statement, he said he was "interested in the so-called illogical impingements of the connotations of words on the consciousness." He went on to say that illogic "operates so logically in conjunction with its context in the poem as to establish its claim to another logic. . . ." The letters serve as metaphor, but they take on added meaning in the context of the rain, the image of melting snow, the birch limbs, and the music. The music, in turn, is associated with emotion.

A look into Crane's biography reveals his bisexuality and his several homosexual experiences. It is possible that in his poetry Crane was using his own illogical impingements in order to explore more fully his sexuality. Certainly "My Grandmother's Love Letters" is less concerned with reading actual letters than it is with an identification with the feminine. The speaker not only posits the emotions felt on receiving the letters but also presents the experience with a vocabulary—the loose girdle of rain, the softness of the letters, the invisible white hair, the gently pitying laughter—that fuses the masculine with the feminine. This mixture is mirrored in the fusion of the natural with the human; it is virtually impossible to say whether Crane is imagining his grandmother laughing at, or with, him or simply noting with some irony the anthropomorphized similarities between laughter and the sound of rain.

In a later poem, "Voyages," Crane achieves a complex balance between sexually masculine and sexually feminine imagery that becomes visionary in the best sense of the word. At the end of "My Grandmother's Love Letters," however, it seems likely that none of the internal conflict has been resolved. The figurative stumbling is also a literal hesitation. The enigmatic quality of "what she would not understand" is left unstated—oblique and inexplicit. In the end, the act, or refusal to act, is unimportant; what matters here is the self-evaluative energy generated by the poem's central, all-encompassing question.

Judith Kitchen

MY LAST AFTERNOON WITH
UNCLE DEVEREUX WINSLOW

Author: Robert Lowell (1917-1977)
Type of poem: Narrative
First published: 1959, in *Life Studies*

The Poem

"My Last Afternoon with Uncle Devereux Winslow" is a richly autobiographical poem of 152 lines, divided into four parts. The shortest part is an eleven-line description of the poet at only five-and-a-half, dressed in a sailor blouse; the longest parts (I and IV) are about fifty lines each and narrate an account of Robert Lowell's memory of a young uncle, who was shortly to die of Hodgkin's disease. Lowell's *Life Studies* volume (1959), to which this poem makes a significant contribution, contains many clearly rendered portraits of the poet and his extended, old-moneyed family. These poems mark a turning away from the well-wrought, high modernist poems of Lowell's youth to personal, unguarded, and even "confessional" poems, as they were called by early critics. The later poems came out of Lowell's battles with mental illness, his brief imprisonment as a conscientious objector, his difficulties in love and marriage, and his rich memories of the Bostonian Lowells and Winslows. In this poem, the portrait of three Winslow generations—grandparents, parents, and child—is wonderfully restrained, at times charming, and finally disturbing.

After the title there stands a caption: "1922: the stone porch of my Grandfather's summer house." Part I has several verse paragraphs devoted to this setting. The small child, Robert, is sitting on his grandfather Winslow's porch; nearby, a tenant farmer has placed a pile of earth and lime in preparation for mixing cement for a root-house. This is a working farm, but it is also a Winslow family retreat. The child came here often, and the adult narrator remembers almost every collected item on his grandfather's porch. There is an alley of poplars, a rose garden, a stand of pine beyond the house. Lowell remembers huge sunflowers, as big as pumpkins, and two maids bringing out iced tea and other cold drinks on this particular afternoon.

In part II, Lowell recalls that he was wearing new pearl-gray shorts from the finest children's store in Boston. The poem moves "up" in part III, as a camera might, to show the windows of the billiards room, behind which the child could see his "Great Aunt Sarah" practicing on a keyboard. Lowell's grandmother could barely tolerate Sarah's practicing; she would rather play cards. In the second paragraph of this section, Lowell shares some old family gossip: Aunt Sarah not only tried and failed to become a concert pianist, but she also broke off an important engagement—she "jilted an Astor."

The long last section (part IV) returns briefly to the vantage point of young Robert, now imagining himself taken up high above the farm; he can look down on the small ponds and see his uncle Devereux's duck blind and, beyond that, his hunting cabin, which is already boarded up—either because it is the end of summer or because of the uncle's illness. He describes many of the collected items inside the cabin, which suggest much about the uncle's coming of age before World War I. Lowell, in the long closing paragraph of this section and the poem itself, thinks of how terrified he was to be the child caught between the emotions he felt for both his beloved, overbearing grandfather and his handsome, doomed uncle, who suddenly comes to stand immediately behind the small boy. Devereux, ridiculously overdressed, is reflected in the same mirror used to give the boy an image of himself. Suddenly the young Lowell seems to have a vision of his uncle's bright colors gone. The child has been sitting on the porch with his hands in black dirt and white lime, and the narrative ends abruptly in a portent of death: "Come winter,/ Uncle Devereux would blend to the one color."

Forms and Devices

The most common beat in spoken English is the iamb (a weak syllable followed by a strong syllable). The English language generally alternates its weak-strong stresses with great regularity. For this reason, modern poets such as Lowell can still be highly rhythmic even when they give up the conventions of regular meter. The term free verse, which is not to be mistaken for a total disregard for beats and counts, is fittingly applied to this poem. Free verse allows Lowell a conversational or intimate tone when he wishes and a freedom to make line breaks that group words more or less at will. In lines 24-33, for example, he gives each item on his grandfather's porch its individual line. Then, in drastically shortening his conclusion (lines 34-35), he is able to drive home forcefully four telling adjectives to describe grandfather Winslow. The well-chosen words form a little stack which the eye takes in at once:

> was manly, comfortable,
> overbearing, disproportioned.

Later, Lowell will use the same freedom to create surprises in rhyme and juxtapositioning. The effect is comic:

> tilted her archaic Athenian nose
> and jilted an Astor.

The "archaic" modifies Athenian, but lands on top of the Astors. Much playfulness can come into the decisions that free verse demands and allows. Another example from the poem illustrates the decision-making typical of Lowell's inventive line breaks:

> A fluff of the west wind puffing
> my blouse, kiting me over our seven chimneys,
> troubling the waters. . . .

Lowell could have kept "my blouse" up with the previous line, but he would have lost some of the comic positioning of the fluff/ puff opening and closing of that line. Now "blouse," by its closer proximity to its metaphor (kite), works quite independently of the previous line. Clearly the line about troubled waters, biblical in its nature, gathers strength by standing alone.

This loosely organized poem achieves a formal tightness by establishing early images that reappear in various ways. The child's early reflection in a mirror later gives way to Devereux's; the two images are inextricably tied to each other. The boy ("a stuffed toucan") is overlayed with Devereux (as a brushed "riding horse," "a blue jay," "a ginger snap man," a creamy layer "in the top of the bottle"). Reinforcing this notion of absurd, oppressive clothing are the moments in the poem which glimpse the Victorian poses and hairstyles in Devereux's "almost life-size" posters.

The materials for the poem are mostly generated from the setting, and Lowell uses few allusions. The most important one is the allusion to the dissolution of Rome. Perhaps the fall of empires begins at home: "I was Agrippina/ in the Golden House of Nero. . . ." (The mother of Nero was put to death for her open opposition to her son's personal decisions regarding divorce and remarriage.)

The Lowell family's period pieces, their domestic quirks and habits—their card games, novels, hobbies, souvenirs, and mementos—provide the narrative material and the strong images for much of the poem. Lowell shows much more than he tells, but by so doing he tells much.

Themes and Meanings

This afternoon in 1922 was an important moment for the poet. With him, the reader looks back on such moments and realizes that much of one's personal histories can be compressed into such spots of time. The passing of time is certainly a major theme of the poem.

The stakes do not seem very high in the opening scenes. A petulant child prefers the solid "Norman" (as in architecture) stodginess of his grandfather to the longings of his martini-drinking parents, who wish to escape to yet another family mansion. For a time he delays in letting readers know that the family is coming apart; he takes them safely back to great-aunt Sarah's escapades, for example. No one can see what is coming. The reader is cushioned from it within the pastoral setting. By the time Lowell actually claims that he was terrified and "all-seeing" (as was Agrippina), however, some readers may realize how many hints he has given. Through the untimely death of his uncle, which is something of a portent, this larger family is seen to be standing at the end of the times they have known. The family force is spent; grandfather Winslow and his generation have run their course. An era has passed, and there is a strong suggestion that Lowell's parents, aunts, and uncles are not empowered to bring about the new era. Most telling are the young Devereux's Edwardian trappings. He may have rushed to join the European campaign by volunteering through Canada, but Devereux is a throwback—a romantic who came of age looking at imperial images dating back to the Boer Wars—men bravely dying for country on the African veldt. The horrors of World War I, which caused young men to question the Western world order in poems such as T. S. Eliot's *The Waste Land* (1922), never touched these blue-blooded Brahmins. They will die from lack of change; history will remember them as childish. The grandfather says, with dramatic irony, of his grown son and daughter-in-law, "You are behaving like children."

Much of the poem's meaning is implied in its gradual unfolding not as memoir but an elegy of sorts. Its tones of lament are realized through hindsight on the part of the reader. Details that seemed merely close observation on Lowell's part—the pencil marks on the door proving that Devereux stopped growing in 1911—are not innocent. Time stopped for these people in 1911. A rereading of the poem causes all the autobiographical details to jump out with a resonance that Lowell intends—those "bullrushes" (one now thinks of the baby Moses entering the house of Pharaoh); the "deathlike" silence of Boston's Symphony Hall, where Aunt Sarah used to practice; the hopelessly dated coils like "rooster tails" in the hair of the music-hall belles in the posters; the comic sentimentality in the pastel of Huckleberry Finn, the "fools'-gold nuggets" and reference to silver mines, which in the United States were long defunct by 1922. Winslow had called his silver mine the *Liberty Bell* in his chronic failure to imagine anything beyond his old-world Boston or his virgin pines "forever pioneering."

Beverly Coyle

MY LAST DUCHESS

Author: Robert Browning (1812-1889)
Type of poem: Dramatic monologue
First published: 1842, in *Dramatic Lyrics*

The Poem
   Underneath the title "My Last Duchess" is the name Ferrara, and the poem's sole speaker is the Duke of Ferrara, a character based in part on Alfonso II, Duke of Ferrara (in Italy) in the sixteenth century. Alfonso's wife, a young girl, died in 1561, and Alfonso used an agent to negotiate a second marriage to the niece of the Count of Tyrol.
   In Robert Browning's poem, the Duke of Ferrara speaks to an agent representing the count. The duke begins by referring to "my last Duchess," his first wife, as he draws open a curtain to display a portrait of her which is hanging on the wall. She looks "alive," and the duke attributes this to the skill of the painter, Frà Pandolf. After saying that he alone opens the curtain, the duke promptly begins a catalog of complaints about the way his wife had acted.
   The joyous blush on her cheek that can be seen in the portrait was a result, the duke says, of her reaction to Frà Pandolf's compliments about her beauty. The duke blames his late wife for smiling back at Frà Pandolf, for being courteous to everyone she encountered, for enjoying life too much. She failed to appreciate his name, which can be traced back nine hundred years, and she failed to see him as superior to others. The duke would not condescend to correct her attitude. She should have known better, he says, and "I choose/ Never to stoop."
   The final characterization the duke gives of his former duchess reveals his obsessive possessiveness and jealousy. He acknowledges that she smiled when she saw him, but complains that she gave much the same smile to anyone else she saw. His next statement reveals that he caused her to be killed: "I gave commands;/ Then all smiles stopped together." He does not elaborate further. There is her portrait, he says, looking as if alive. The duke tells the agent that they will next go downstairs to meet others. Then, in not quite five lines, the duke refers directly to the proposed marriage arrangement. In the same suave tones he has used throughout, he suggests that because the count is so wealthy there should be no question about his providing an "ample" dowry for his daughter to bring to the marriage. The duke adds, however, that it is "his fair daughter's self" that he wants.
   As the duke and the count's agent start down the stairs, the duke points out a bronze statue of Neptune taming a seahorse and notes that it was made especially for him by Claus of Innsbruck. Although this appears to be a change in subject, it summarizes the duke's clear message to the agent. In addition to the wealth she must bring, the second wife, like the seahorse, must be "tamed" to her role as his duchess. The clear implication is that if she does not meet his requirements, she may well end up like the last duchess, "alive" only in a portrait.

Forms and Devices

The poem is a dramatic monologue, a form that Browning used and perfected in many of his works. In a monologue, one person is the sole speaker, and often there is a specific listener or listeners; here, the listener is the count's agent, through whom the Duke of Ferrara is arranging the proposed marriage to a second duchess. The reader must work through the words of the speaker to discover his true character and the attitude of the poet toward the character. The poem is "dramatic" in the sense that it is like a drama, a play, in which one character speaks to another, and there is a sense of action and movement as on stage.

The duke claims that he does not have skill in speech, but his monologue is a masterpiece of subtle rhetoric. While supposedly entertaining the count's agent as his guest by showing him the portrait, the duke by implication explains his requirements for his new wife. His last duchess, according to his version of her, had a heart "too soon made glad" by such things as watching a sunset or riding her white mule around the terrace, and she should not have responded with pleasure to anything or anyone but the duke himself. Browning allows the reader to infer what kind of man the duke is by piecing together the past and present situation. A basic device used throughout the poem is irony. Instead of seeing an unfaithful wife as the duke pictures her, the reader sees the jealous and egotistical mind of the duke himself. The duke seems to assume that the agent will follow the logic of why he commanded that his duchess be eliminated, and he lets the agent know how easily it is within the duke's power to issue such commands.

The poem is written in rhymed iambic pentameter lines. A striking aspect of form in the poem is the repeated use of enjambment, in which a line's sense and meaning runs on into the following line, so that the rhymed couplets are "open" rather than closed. This technique, in which the syntactical pauses rarely coincide with line endings, creates a tension in the rhythm and places emphasis on the horrors the duke reveals as the sentences end in mid-line (caesura). The lines thus often appear irregular, an informalizing of a formal pattern, as though the duke is relaxing his proud formality and speaking casually.

The lines are extremely concentrated. Not a single word is wasted. Throughout the poem there is a chilling meiosis, the words imparting much more than they express. The apparent pauses, shown by dashes, purportedly indicate a hesitation as the duke considers what to say, but actually they suggest his consummate arrogance and manipulative control of the situation. Twice the agent starts to question or interrupt, but the duke smoothly deflects the interruptions and continues speaking. He is in total control of the situation, however casual he may pretend to be.

When the duke finally refers to the marriage arrangement directly, he summarizes the situation succinctly. He first mentions the money he will expect, then mentions the count's daughter. At first this seems merely to confirm the duke's emphasis on money. Yet since he had clearly stated his solution for ending his first marriage, the words "his fair daughter's self . . . is my object" become particularly sinister. Unless he can possess his next duchess as he possesses the portrait and the bronze statue, she too may become only an artifact on the wall, as nameless as the first duchess.

The pace of the poem builds toward the revelation that the duke ordered his wife killed, then to the quick summation of his terms for the marriage arrangement. The matter-of-fact tone that he uses throughout the poem shows that the duke considers himself totally justified, and he remains unrepentant and secure in his sense of power over others.

Themes and Meanings

"My Last Duchess" shows the corrupt power of a domestic tyrant. Browning uses this theme again in his longest poem, *The Ring and the Book* (1868-1869), in which the sadistic Count Guido kills his wife after falsely accusing her of adultery.

Spoken monologues often reveal more to the listener (and reader) than the speaker intends, but this arrogant aristocrat has no hesitation. The Duke of Ferrara obviously considers himself superior to others and above laws and morality. He clearly states that he gave the commands that stopped his wife's smiles altogether. After all, he tells the agent, "she liked whate'er/ She looked on, and her looks went everywhere." The duke was irritated by such behavior and had it eliminated. He uses his power to get others to do his will, including, presumably, the agent. As he had others eliminate his wife, and as he had a painter and a sculptor create objects of art to his specifications, he assumes that the agent will provide the kind of duchess he wants. He seems unconcerned about any hesitations a potential second wife might have about how his first marriage ended. He appears confident his demands will be met, both the ample dowry and the subservient wife.

The jealousy and possessiveness that seem to accompany the duke's assertion of power suggest that he will be equally suspicious of any living wife, and indeed the portrait of his last duchess is more satisfactory to him than was the duchess herself. He can open or close the curtain as he pleases; he can exert complete control.

Browning's genius created a character whose own words condemn him and show him as a ruthless, corrupt man who misuses his power. What makes the Duke of Ferrara especially horrifying is that he feels no repentance and no need for repentance. There have been no checks on his abuses of power thus far, and there is nothing to suggest that he will not continue his egotistical and tyrannical ways.

Lois A. Marchino

MY LIFE HAD STOOD—A LOADED GUN—

Author: Emily Dickinson (1830-1886)
Type of poem: Lyric
First published: 1929, in *Further Poems*

The Poem

"My Life had stood—a Loaded Gun—" (the title is not Emily Dickinson's, since she did not title her poems) is a short poem of twenty-four lines divided into six stanzas. The poem is written in the first person from the point of view of a speaker who compares her life to "a Loaded Gun." In fact, the voice of the speaker and the voice of the gun are identical throughout the poem.

In the opening stanza of the poem, the speaker tells how her life—of which she speaks as if it were "a Loaded Gun"—had been full of potential power yet unused and inactive ("a Loaded Gun—/ In Corners") until its "Owner" came by, "identified" it, and carried it away. The speaker (as gun) then contrasts, beginning in the second stanza, what her life is like now that she has been claimed and put into use by her "Owner." Together, the speaker (gun) and her owner are free to wander anywhere they like ("We roam in Sovreign Woods") and have the power and authority to pursue even the prized game of royal reserves ("And now We hunt the Doe").

Halfway through the second stanza, however, the speaker begins to turn away from the power of the royal "We" and to focus instead on her own sense of emerging individual power: "And every time I speak for Him—/ The Mountains straight reply." In these lines, the speaker usurps the owner's right to speak for himself. Moreover, whereas in the past the speaker's life has stood "In corners," unnoticed, like a wallflower, the speaker gleefully reports that now as soon as she speaks, nature immediately takes notice of her ("The Mountains straight reply"). In other words, the gun is fired and the mountains immediately echo the sound.

The third through the fifth stanzas continue to develop—in the voice of the gun—the speaker's growing realization and enjoyment of her own power. The third stanza compares the burst of light when the gun is fired to a "smile" from a volcano ("a Vesuvian face") as it releases its pleasure, and the fourth stanza celebrates the "good Day" that is "shared" by gun and owner. By the fifth stanza, the speaker revels in her power as a "deadly foe," and the speaker's sense of her own volition and power reaches a climax. Her actions are now characterized as completely autonomous, and the poem focuses in detail on delineating the specifics of her power: No one survives "On whom I lay a Yellow Eye—/ Or an emphatic Thumb."

A sharp break occurs, however, between the fifth and the final stanza. As if the speaker—at the height of her power—suddenly realizes that the "Owner" who brought her to life can disappear just as abruptly as he appeared, her ecstatic revel in power halts, and the speaker's voice falters in a frantic attempt to devise some rationale that might enable her to retain her power. For "He longer must

[live] than I," she muses, because "I have but the power to kill" but not "the power to die."

Forms and Devices

The most important poetic device in the poem is the metaphor, a figure of speech used to denote an idea (or an object) by suggesting an analogy or likeness between them. The metaphor of the speaker's life as a gun, in fact, occurs in three stages, structuring the poem in terms of the speaker's past, present, and future life. The speaker first reveals that in the past her life was like a passive "Loaded Gun." She then—for the greater part of the poem (the central four stanzas)—moves into a narration of her life in the present by comparing her life to a gun that is actively engaged in firing. By the final stanza, the speaker contemplates the future of her life as if it were an empty gun, devoid of its bullet, its "emphatic Thumb."

The metaphoric qualities of the poem become increasingly complex as the speaker develops additional metaphors to characterize the primary metaphor, the gun. The gun's fire is spoken of as if it were a "smile," a volcanic ("Vesuvian") eruption, and a "Yellow Eye," and the gun's bullet becomes an "emphatic Thumb." This layering of metaphor upon metaphor functions to underscore—within the language and experience of the poem itself—those qualities of repression and masking that are central to the poem's theme regarding the expression of will and power.

This sense of repression and disguise with respect to power is further enhanced in the poem by the speaker's tone or attitude toward the subject being described. The speaker's simple, matter-of-fact narrative style together with her "cordial" choice of words—"roam," "speak," "smile," "light," "glow," "pleasure," "shared"—to depict the act of erupting, exploding, or killing build into the reader's experience of the poem the work's underlying explosive tensions. The reader is lulled, too, by the perfectly regular, hypnotic metrical rhythm of the language until at the final stanza the reader is jarred by the speaker's desperate rationalization of her existence. This focus in the poem on creating an experience in which the reader participates is one of the qualities that define modern poetry and is a technique that Dickinson characteristically employed in her poems.

Dickinson's effective manipulation of language to construct the poem can be seen in her exploitation of certain grammatical structures. The repetition in the first two lines of the second stanza—"And now," "And now"—conveys the eager, excited, and expectant voice of a newly empowered being. Similarly, the juxtaposition at the end of the poem of repeated grammatical structures containing different words effectively embodies and reveals both the speaker's sense of fragmentation and her desperate attempt to resolve her conflict. The juxtaposed clauses "He—may longer" and "He longer must" followed by the phrases "the power to kill" versus "the power to die" simultaneously contain and convey the speaker's effort to scramble and rearrange the elements of language itself in order to maintain her will and her power.

Themes and Meanings

In this poem, Dickinson begins with a familiar American scene—a gun, a hunter, and a hunting trip in the woods—and transforms it into a poem about a divided self—a self filled with the potential for pleasure and power but without the means to express pleasure and power for herself. The central concerns of the poem are the separation within the speaker of her "Life" from the means to express it autonomously and the consequences for her in the expression of power and pleasure.

The structure of the poem underscores these concerns. The poem's most obvious structure—moving from past to present to future—makes possible the thematic progression of the poem from impotence to power to impotence or, in other terms, from repression to eruption to fear of repression. As the poem develops, the unleashing of the speaker's pleasure and power builds to a climax as the speaker's awareness of her ability to act and enjoy increases. The speaker's interaction with her own autonomous power, in fact, leads her to either the realization or the illusion (the poem never makes clear which one it is) that she can be the author of her own pleasure and power.

At the final stanza, the speaker (as gun) is pulled from her reverie of power by her sudden recollection of her dependence on her "Owner." It is he, after all, who must pull the trigger. Her realization corresponds metaphorically to her emptiness after her powerful bullet has been fired. In response to this threat of static emptiness (reminiscent of her condition at the beginning of the poem), the speaker now makes desperate attempts to puzzle out some rationale that might enable her to perpetuate her ecstasy of autonomous power. The speaker's train of thought proceeds in this way: Although the gun may "live"—in the sense of existing only as an unused object leaning in corners—longer than the "Owner" will, the owner must "live"—in the sense of having the human will and power to lead an autonomous life—longer than the gun will because the gun has only the kind of power that consists of being the means to effect something (death), not the kind that makes it possible to do something on its own, of its own accord (to die).

At this point, one of the most significant questions posed by the poem becomes clear: For whom in the nineteenth century would pleasure and power be problematic should they be expressed? If one asserts that the speaker of the poem is female, another dimension is added to the poem. The poem then depicts not merely the plight of a speaker who is dependent on the actions of another for the release of power but the plight of a female speaker who must—because will and power have traditionally been characterized as masculine qualities—identify extensive portions of her female self as masculine. Thus, to acknowledge and act on those aspects of her self, she must split herself irrevocably. The speaker's own will, pleasure, and power come to be perceived in the poem, therefore, as dangerous forces that give pleasure but that also threaten to destroy the identity and integrity of the female self: In metaphoric terms, for the speaker to express her power is for her to "hunt the Doe." In this way, Dickinson's poem questions society's notions both of power and of the appropriate means for its expression, specifically the way in which ideas concerning power are constructed with respect to males and females.

Angela M. Estes

MY LOST YOUTH

Author: Henry Wadsworth Longfellow (1807-1882)
Type of poem: Lyric
First published: 1858, in *The Courtship of Miles Standish and Other Poems*

The Poem

"My Lost Youth," a lyrical autobiography of the poet's early life, is Henry Wadsworth Longfellow's tribute both to his native city of Portland, Maine, and to the boy who climbed its hilly streets and gazed out over its harbor dreaming faraway dreams. The poem consists of ten nine-line stanzas, the last two lines of each being the famous refrain "A boy's will is the wind's will,/ And the thoughts of youth are long, long thoughts," which, as is made clear in the first stanza, are verses translated from a Lapland song.

Although the refrain is, perhaps, its most memorable component, the lynchpin of the poem is the oft-repeated word "still." Longfellow in "My Lost Youth" is describing memories that still come to him from a city that he still visits. The boy may be lost to him, but the place and the dreams still exist.

The poem opens with the well-known description of Portland found in many tourist pamphlets and travel books of the "beautiful town/ . . . seated by the sea." This setting of place is continued into the second stanza, which emphasizes the city's location on a peninsula surrounded by a sea dotted with islands. These islands fueled the boy Longfellow's romantic dreams as he watched their silhouettes fade into the horizon. This romanticism is echoed in the "black wharves," "Spanish sailors," and "mystery of ships" of the third stanza.

Historical ships and their captains are the subject of the next two memories as the poet remembers the terrifying sound of the guns from the naval battle of 1813 between the American ship *Enterprise* and the British ship *Boxer*, in which both captains were killed and were buried on a hill overlooking the now "tranquil" bay. In this stanza, the "still" of the seventh line is changed, for the first time, into the exciting word "thrill." Although the death and burial of the seamen was "mournful" and the memory is "mournful" now for the grown poet, for a six-year-old boy, himself named after a naval hero who died in battle, the event was a "thrill" in keeping with the guns fired from the fort and the drums and bugles of the War of 1812.

A shift in focus occurs in the next lines as the poet leaves off communal geographical and historical reminiscence to dwell on personal moments and friendships. The tone becomes increasingly introspective until the poet summarily stops his description of the past, declaring that "There are things of which I may not speak." Also, in this eighth stanza, the word "still" changes to the ominous "chill" as the poet confronts memories that he cannot set down on paper.

This fall into sadness is but momentary, however, as the poet utilizes this break in memory to break with time, seemingly leaving the past to return to the present in the final two stanzas. If in the previous lines he could not speak of what has been lost, he goes on to celebrate what still is. He revisits Portland and, even though he does not recognize the passersby, as he walks down the familiar streets the present effortlessly merges into the past, and he and the boy of memory become one again.

Forms and Devices

Although Longfellow is generally not considered a poetic innovator, he continually experimented with different metrical forms. Many of his later poems, such as "My Lost Youth," were in mixed measure or, to use the term made popular by Gerald Manly Hopkins, "sprung rhythm." In this metrical scheme, the rhythm is based only on the number of stressed syllables in a line, the unstressed syllables being discounted. This metrical freedom facilitates the incorporation of the Laplander translation into the text and allows the verse line to lengthen and slow down in accordance with the "long, long thoughts."

Memory is the repetition of words and images, and the core device of this memory poem is the repetition of words and entire verse lines to reinforce the poet's perspective of a past "often" remembered, whose mental pictures float one after another to the surface of his mind. In fact, the first word of the poem is "Often," and, in keeping with this controlled stream of consciousness, the most repeated initial word is "And." Fittingly, the last four lines in each stanza rise in a crescendo of repetition from the always repeated word "song" at the end of the sixth line to the "still," "chill," or final "still" of the seventh to the climactic insistence of the song itself, "A boy's will is the wind's will,/ and the thoughts of youth are long, long thoughts."

Longfellow leads into the refrain's quotation by always repeating the word "song," but, together with the changing perspective of the passages, the objective "Lapland" song of the first stanza immediately transforms itself into a subjective "old," "wayward," "mournful," "sweet," "fitful," "fateful," "beautiful," and "strange" song of the following verses. The cadence of the song also varies with the memory being relived; it can "haunt," "murmur," "whisper," "throb," "flutter," and "sigh." The song, therefore, both personifies and summarizes the emotional hues of remembrance, and, in the last stanza, the "groves" of memory "are repeating it still."

With the exception of the continual repetition, including some use of anaphora— the poetic device used most strikingly with the "There are things," "There are dreams," "There are thoughts" of the beginning three lines of the eighth stanza to introduce the jarring note of the only negative passage of the poem—there is little utilization of poetic conceits or affectation in "My Lost Youth." Longfellow was a Romantic poet, and there is present his familiar sentimentalizing and personification of nature. The sea, the hills, and the woods take on human qualities as they sing the poet's song and echo his moods. In fact, not one friend or acquaintance is mentioned in this poem; the only specific characters are the dead naval heroes, who are not named, and the boy Longfellow, who is the absolute center of the poem.

The poem's progression can be seen as a voyage in which the initial distance between past and present steadily grows narrower until the final merging of present, past, and physical space, but this poetic structure is also a circular one; the ending is/ was also the beginning, the beginning was/is also the past.

Themes and Meanings

In "My Lost Youth," two of Longfellow's overriding interests are strongly emphasized. One is his preoccupation with folk poetry and balladry, an avocation shared with his fellow Romantics. The focal lines of the poem are taken from a translation from the original Lapland by the German Romantic writer Johann Gottfried Herder. The second is Longfellow's insertion into his work of episodes from American history. Longfellow was one of the first American writers to introduce themes from American history and popular story in his writing, a fact of which he was very proud. His Romantic tendencies toward folk literature and indigenous history led him in this direction, and his own family history can be seen as a mini-compendium of early American heroic life—for example, a grandfather who was a general in the Revolution, an uncle who blew up his ship before the walls of Tripoli rather than surrender it to the enemy, another uncle who fought on the USS *Constitution*, and Longfellow himself, who as a boy was eyewitness to history.

For Longfellow, the past is of paramount importance and "still" lives, and it is this historical perspective, both communal and individual, that explains what "My Lost Youth" is and what it is not. Clearly, the "lost" of the poem's title notwithstanding, its explicit meaning is the exact opposite of "lost"; it is time regained or better, time never "lost." Therefore, this poem is not an elegy, it is not a sorrowful lament for a departed time, place, or person, and it is not an *ubi sunt* questioning of "Where are they now?," "Where has the time gone?," or "Why has everything turned to ashes?" The theme of the poem is explicitly the integration of boy, man, time, and place, not its disintegration. Although there are intimations of painful memories in the eighth stanza, this glimpse into a sadder world is not developed, and optimism is the dominant note of the poem, which was written during a contented period in Longfellow's life before the horrific death of his wife and before he became the living archetype of the bearded, graying, morose, sedate poet.

The picture Longfellow paints of himself as a boy is a Romantic/romantic one as he unconsciously lives as one with nature. A self-identification with his surroundings that leads him to a contemplation of more distant places for the sea is the central image of this landscape, the sea carrying the dual significance of familiarity in his native environment as well as serving as a conduit for his dreams of a wider experience. The sea is seen as both natural and strange, but natural and strange are both "beautiful" in the poet's mind's eye.

Everything is equal in this poetic vision; everything is identified with self. In a subjective pantheism, Longfellow dissolves the boundaries between time and space as he literally sees the past as an all-encompassing living entity that is indistinguishable from the present.

Charlene E. Suscavage

MY MOTHER WOULD BE A FALCONRESS

Author: Robert Duncan (1919-1988)
Type of poem: Lyric
First published: 1968, in *Bending the Bow*

The Poem

"My Mother Would Be a Falconress" is a seventy-one-line lyric divided into fourteen verse paragraphs of varying lengths. The poem looks and sounds traditional by Robert Duncan's mid-career (1956-1968) standards. The medium length of the work developed out of its underlying compositional law; the text has been generated concentrically from a core statement that stresses again and again the indestructible relation between the speaker—the poet's alter ego—and his mother's will. There is an unwavering acknowledgment on the speaker's part of his mother's unquestionable authority. Her will to power is expressed by the verbal component of the nominal predicate *"would be* a falconress," which, given the present-tense context of the whole poem, expresses her desire, determination, and single-mindedness of purpose. The complying speaker responds with total submission: "And I . . ./ would fly." An experiment in pedagogy or coaching is taking place. Apparently, it is working smoothly and to the satisfaction of both trainer and trainee.

Imperceptibly, however, two correlative developments gather momentum. With every paragraph, the falconress lets her falcon fly a little farther beyond the circumference or horizon of the previous venture. In this way, she expands the territory of her hunting and at the same time strengthens her falcon's range. A symbiosis of sorts more and more characterizes their relationship, but in spite of that there grows in him a desire to be on his own. Eventually, their antagonism becomes fierce, and the falcon behaves ruthlessly toward his mistress. He never achieves complete autonomy, however, and years after her death the pull of her will still tyrannically restrains and directs him.

The progress through these stages is minutely charted by the poet. The relatively few constitutive elements of the story are permanently reshuffled, reiterated, and only gradually and incrementally modified. With each additional verse paragraph, the reader edges forward toward some dimly guessed resolution. This movement could be described as a slow meandering. Certain statements or phrases are obsessively repeated as in a ballad. The speaker seems to be hypnotized by his own tale. Past, present, and future seem at times indistinguishably blended, and the verbal "would be" becomes a marker of habitual or recurrent action. As in any traditional text, the reader experiences a mixture of linear progression and concentric recurrence with a dramatic sense of impending resolution and closure.

Forms and Devices

In a prose piece entitled "A Lammas Tiding," Duncan gives the following account of the circumstances attending the composition of this poem: "I wakened in the night with the lines '*My mother would be a falconress—And I a falcon at her wrist*' being repeated in my mind. Was the word *falconress* or *falconness?*—the troubled insistence of the lines would not let go of me, and I got up and took my notebook into the kitchen to write it out at the kitchen table. Turning to the calendar to write the date, I saw it was Lammas: 2 AM, August 1, 1964" (*Bending the Bow*, page 51; Lammas commemorates Saint Peter's deliverance from prison).

This extraordinary confession—which is similar to Samuel Taylor Coleridge's famous account of the production of his "Kubla Khan"—goes on to inform the reader about other genetic details. Thus astrologically, Saturn, Duncan's birth planet, was most brilliant between one-thirty and two, the very half-hour during which the poem was put on paper. Then, Duncan muses, William Blake's *Visions of the Daughters of Albion* (1793), which he had been reading for several nights before going to sleep, most likely provided him with the key image of "the ravenous hawk," which in turn triggered a comment from Duncan's life companion, the painter Jess Collins. On and on, the train of associations or dream logic of the poem is disentangled thread by thread.

"Dreams ever betray our minds," Duncan remarks on the same page, thereby suggesting that the remembered dream is a conscious fragment of the unconscious. Hence, as Freud indicated, it is possible to learn much about oneself and one's mind from the verbal accounts of one's own dreams.

This poem was communicated or "received." The poet transcribed it in a state of trancelike wakefulness. There remained very little room for revision or rewriting. The text emerged like Athena from the head of Zeus, helmeted and with breastplate buckled on; or, more accurately perhaps, the poem's body took its shape from the tenebrae of the poet's reservoir of intuitions, archetypes, and recondite knowledge. Duncan was a visionary poet, a great integrator of religious myths and hermetic insights.

The poem was in a way a tribute to his foster mother, Minnehaha Symmes, who had adopted him when he was barely six months old. The affective link between them was so powerful that after Minnie's death Robert continued to write letters and poems to her. It was in his adopted family that the future poet came into contact with esoteric, occult, and theosophical lore, thereby gaining access to the tradition of romantic mystics and mythmakers such as William Blake, Percy Bysshe Shelley, Gérard de Nerval, and William Butler Yeats. As a matter of fact, in spite of his strong ties with experimental postmodern groups such as the Bay Area poets (Jack Spicer, Kenneth Rexroth, Philip Whalen, Michael McClure) and the Black Mountain poets (Charles Olson, Robert Creeley, Denise Levertov), Duncan came to regard his modernity more and more as an offshoot of the nineteenth century mind and sensibility.

"My Mother Would Be a Falconress" is a poem that fits the transcendentalism of this tradition in both rhetoric and sound.

The blood imagery, central to any initiatory myth or rite of passage, lends a lurid coherence to the poem, reinforcing its sense of medieval hierarchy and allegiance with its correlative patterns of obsessively repeated dominance and submission. On a more local scale, the "." sign—larger than an ordinary full stop and placed at some distance from the end of a statement (after the eleventh and the thirteenth sections)—designates, in the poet's own words, "a beat syncopating the time at rest; as if there were a stress. He the artist strives not for a disintegration of syntax but for a complication within syntax, overlapping structures, so that the words are freed, having bounds out of bound" (*Bending the Bow*).

The formal structure of the poem is determined by a moment of inspiration and grace. Both the relationship between the protagonists and the rhythmical phrasing have been communicated to the poem at once. The primary musical feeling about the fittingness of the verbal utterance is, in Duncan's own words, "the criterion of truth in a poem."

The poem's circular restatements and its dialectical progress are compatible, and between them they create the singular complex beauty of the poetic field.

Themes and Meanings

"I am strongly, strongly persuaded that the entire area of poetry is consciousness," Duncan has said. Such a statement offers a reliable vantage point from which to consider Duncan's project as a whole. For beyond rhetoric and incantation, beyond manic insistence, there is a pointed effort to understand the complex give and take of the situation, and there is a genuine striving to grasp, analyze, and discriminate among degrees of involvement, to define the inner tensions and their outcome. There results a clearer picture of the transformations undergone by the original input, or given data, of the remembered dream. What is all this about if not an enhanced state of consciousness?

Now, viewed from a restricted angle, the theme of the poem is the precarious balance between the mutual attraction of dominance and dependency on the one hand, and, in a less conspicuous manner, between the gradual disenchantment and eventual separation on the other. In the words of Duncan's biographer, "Already at the time Robert realized that his mother was to embody the other, restrictive and destructive pole of womanhood in his life and work. . . . According to one account, the difficulties began with Robert's emerging homosexuality" (Ekbert Faas, *Young Robert Duncan*, 1983).

This speculation supports a sexual reading of the poem that undoubtedly has been on Duncan's mind. The symbolism generated by such elements of the text as the treading of the mother's wrist, the bleeding involved, the dreaming within the little hood with many bells, the falling, or such elaborations of these elements as the hooded silence, the muffled dreams, the jangling bells, the tearing with his beak, the curb of his heart, or the still more refined degrees of complication in formulations such as "as if I were her own pride, as if her pride knew no limits" or "it seemed my human soul went down in flames," and, finally, that climactic talking with himself—in addition to its clusters of associations, the symbolism shows also a progression from the merely descriptive to more oblique formulations and thence to the final solipsism of the speaker-narrator. Underlying all this as a common denominator is the ubiquitous blood imagery, a major presence throughout Duncan's poetry, both emblem and binder of his constitutive mysticism.

As the "hood" or sheath image might arguably evoke details of both female and male sexual anatomy, so could it suggest—because of the bells attached to it—the kind of protection, seclusion, and even blindness of the artist who needs remoteness and purity so that his or her imagination can freely spin out its alternative vision of reality. Duncan seemed to have such a possibility in view when, at the very end of his explicatory prose piece "A Lammas Tiding," he pointed out that "there is another curious displacement upward, for the bell which is actually attached to a falcon's leg by a bewit just above the jess, in the dream becomes a set of bells sewn round the hood, a ringing of sound in the childhood of the poet's head."

The punning on "hood" and "childhood" should be read against the eye-injury accident that occurred in Duncan's early childhood, which put his vision out of focus. That kind of protective ringing in his childhood ears would become a compensatory habit of sound or an inner sense of cadence. A poet's discanting is based on that, and Duncan was a poet who relied on the musical possibilities of words.

Another startling disclosure of this quotation is that the whole fabric of the poem, with all its details (one of which at least flies in the face of practical reality; that is, in the sport of falconry the bird is used as killer, never as a retriever), has been a dream. The poem's power and unique attraction are comparable to those of such imagistically related masterpieces as Hopkins's "The Windhover" and Yeats's "The Second Coming."

Duncan's dangerous relationship to his muse, his arduous experimenting to expand the circumference of his domain (an Emersonian and Dickinsonian concern), and his battling against society's distortions, pressures, or demands may equally challenge one's appetite for allegorical readings.

Stefan Stoenescu

MY PAPA'S WALTZ

Author: Theodore Roethke (1908-1963)
Type of poem: Lyric
First published: 1942; collected in *The Lost Son and Other Poems*, 1948

The Poem

In "My Papa's Waltz," Theodore Roethke imaginatively re-creates a childhood encounter with his father but also begins to attempt to understand the meaning of the relationship between them. The poem may be read as a warm memory of happy play, but when one is familiar with the rest of Roethke's work, a darker view of the event emerges. Although the poem is only sixteen short lines, it is one of Roethke's most moving and most frequently anthologized poems.

Theodore Roethke was born and grew up in Saginaw, Michigan, where his father and uncle operated a large and successful greenhouse. Sometimes Roethke's father would stay up late into the night watering and otherwise tending to his plants. After a drink to relax, he would swing his son Theodore around the kitchen in a bearlike dance and then carry him off to bed. Roethke stated in an interview that his father would hook his son's feet through the father's rubber bootstraps and, with Theodore's feet thus trapped, haul the youngster about.

Roethke's poetic description of this scene conveys both the father's love for the son and the son's fear of this overpowering event, a combination which explains why the poem has haunted so many readers. At first the child finds merely the smell of the alcohol on his father's breath overwhelming, but he endures the experience and hangs on to his father's shirt: "Such waltzing was not easy." The "waltz" is so violent that pots and pans begin to fall to the floor, and the audience of this intended hilarity is not amused: "My mother's countenance/ Could not unfrown itself."

This activity comes as a release after the father's hard work in the greenhouse: "The hand that held my wrist/ Was battered on one knuckle;" and "You beat time on my head/ With a palm caked hard by dirt." What is fun for the adult is an ordeal for the child. When his father misses a step in his wild dance, the child's ear scrapes against his father's belt buckle. This detail also indicates that the child is quite small, since, while standing on his father's boots, his head reaches barely past his father's waist; this account must be a recollection of very early childhood.

The entire experience acts as a sort of dramatic lullaby, as it is the last event of the day before bedtime. The child, however, is hardly relaxed and ready for sleep, since to survive the "waltz," he has had to "cling" to his father's shirt; he continues to do so as he is carried away to bed.

Forms and Devices

Roethke uses a number of poetic devices that reinforce the meaning of the poem; the meter, although it is iambic, sometimes adds an extra feminine syllable at the end of the second or fourth lines, such as "Could make a small boy dizzy" and "Such waltzing was not easy." The additional foot produces a stumbling effect that adds to the poem's description of a clumsy waltz.

The poem's short lines also reinforce the fact that this experience is happening to a child. In his later poetry, Roethke uses nursery rhymes, jingles, and playground taunts to suggest the world of children to which he was trying to return in imagination and spirit. In "My Papa's Waltz," however, there is nothing to imagine, since the incident really happened—apparently more than once. Roethke wants the reader to identify with the child, not the adults in the poem, so he not only writes the poem from the viewpoint of a child but also uses the short lines common in poetry written for children (Roethke himself wrote two such volumes) and in the verses that children themselves write. "Papa" is a child's term for a father; nevertheless, the reader is not allowed to forget that this poem is an adult remembrance of an event from childhood. "Countenance," for example, is not a word that a child would be likely to use to describe someone's face.

The diction of the poem also underscores the child's sense of fright at the experience. Although at first reading the poem may seem funny, with utensils falling in slapstick fashion as the father and child bang around the kitchen, it is clearly not amusing to the child who has to hold on tightly to his father to avoid falling like the pots and pans. Dazed by the whiskey on his father's breath, he must hang on "like death." At the end of the dance, he is still "clinging" to his father's shirt, not embracing his father's body with warmth. From the child's perspective, the "waltz" has been something to endure, not to enjoy.

Themes and Meanings

In "My Papa's Waltz," Roethke unites two of his more important themes—his attempt to understand his relationship with his father and his use of the dance as a metaphor for life itself.

Roethke's father, Otto, was a person who enjoyed the outdoors and the pursuits usually associated with masculinity: sports, hunting, and fishing. Like most fathers, he wanted his son to be like him, but it was clear very early in Theodore's life that he could not and would not follow in his father's footsteps. For example, Theodore subscribed to a poetry journal when he was in the seventh grade. In a pattern common in many families, Otto Roethke loved his son but could not approve of his path in life; Theodore loved his father but was unable to demonstrate that love in ways that his father could understand. Worse, Otto died while Theodore was still a teenager, so the father never learned what a leading role in his chosen field the son would play—nor did Theodore have a chance during his father's lifetime to resolve the differences between them.

Much of Roethke's mature work embodies his attempt to sort through this relationship and, ultimately, end it, so that the poet could be free to become not merely the son of his father but himself. "The Lost Son," which many critics regard as Roethke's breakthrough work (in which he first asserts himself most forcefully in his own poetic manner), concerns his attempts to come to grips with the death of his father. Although the father has died, it is the son, unsure of his identity, who is lost. Ironically, in trying to become free of the memory of his judging father, Roethke discovers how much like the older man he is.

The point of connection between the two is the greenhouse and the world of plants that Roethke's father nurtured. Here the tender side of Otto's nature asserted itself, for it takes patience and loving care to raise plants; they will not grow at the point of a gun or as a result of threats. "My Papa's Waltz" significantly occurs after a long day's work at the greenhouse, where the father has developed a "hand . . . battered on one knuckle" and "a palm caked hard by dirt."

The father has fulfilled himself in his work and wants to show his love for his son, but only after taking a drink (or three) to unwind. Like many men, he finds it difficult to express love, even in a physical way, without first becoming someone else through the aid of drink. Men must still be men, so the manner of expression of that love is a roughhouse "romp," not a hug or a kiss. Theodore, who later failed during the hunting and fishing trips in which his father made him participate, does not make a very good dancing partner, either. He is not a willing dancer, but is dragged along; a child, he has no choice but to acquiesce.

The poem also suggests that the "waltz" may be the father's unconscious way of punishing his son, of demonstrating that, even in the feminine and romantic world of the dance, a man must be tough. Is it really necessary to beat time on the boy's head? Does he understand that he may be hurting his child with the scraping buckle? Whatever his intentions, the waltz becomes a seal on the day's activities, a last bit of interaction before the boy is put to bed.

In Roethke's later poetry, he develops the metaphor of the dance as a symbol for life lived to the fullest. To Roethke, a beautiful dance most of all symbolizes love, fulfillment, and union with the rest of life, as in "I Knew a Woman," "The Waking," and "Four for Sir John Davies." The first appearance of a dance in Roethke's poetry is "My Papa's Waltz," and, significantly, because the dance is between the poet and his father, the dance itself is unlovely and, to the child, frightening, and its meaning is ultimately ambiguous. The ambiguity extends to the rest of the poem. Does the child's mother frown because of the father's tipsiness, the destruction wreaked by the dance, the violence of the dance itself, or the fact that it is imposed upon the child? The welter of meanings and associations means that each reader must judge the poem for himself or herself, perhaps drawing on memories of adult expressions of love that were too strong for a child. This confusion also keeps the poem fresh and contributes to its continued life.

Jim Baird

MY SWEETEST LESBIA

Author: Thomas Campion (1567-1620)
Type of poem: Lyric
First published: 1601, in *A Booke of Ayres*

The Poem

"My Sweetest Lesbia" is a song composed of three stanzas, each six lines long, rhymed *aabbcc*. It is the first of Thomas Campion's twenty-one songs in a collection shared equally with lutenist Philip Rosseter. Other songbooks of Campion's era (those by John Dowland, for example) present arrangements for four-part singing, but Campion and Rosseter require a solo voice and a simple accompaniment in their works: a "naked ayre without guide, or prop, or color but his own." As the first song in a group that primarily examines kinds of love (unrequited, bawdy) and contrasts high and low society, strict and loose morals, and age and youth, "My Sweetest Lesbia" stands as an overview, an entryway, an opening statement.

The first stanza is a translation and condensation of the Roman poet Catullus's poem 5 (*Vivamus, me Lesbia, atque amemus*). Addressing Lesbia, which is the *nom à clef* of Catullus's "beloved," Campion's singer makes a proposition that they "live and love," even though wiser people may censure them. (The name, incidentally, does not have any particular lesbian sexual implications.) The reason the singer offers is metaphorical: Sun and moon may set and quickly revive, but as soon as the much weaker light of love sets, he and his lover will sleep "one ever-during night."

Stanza 2 diverges from the Catullus poem. The subject is warfare, and the point of view shifts from the embracing "we" of the first stanza to a distancing "they." If all would live in love, like the singer, war would end and no alarms would disturb peaceful sleep—unless they came from the camp of love. Fools waste their "little light," however, and actively pursue, through pain, their "ever-during night." Love is not merely a consolation for individual lovers; it could be a universal peacemaker, a means of disarmament ("bloody swords and armor should not be"), and a sleep enhancer ("No drum nor trumpet"). Campion seems more disturbed by excess noise than by weaponry, but the languorous "peaceful sleeps" and the "camps of love" are more a matter of aphrodisiacs than of soporifics.

The last stanza switches to "I," then to "you," underscoring the separation to come through death. When I die, the singer declares, I do not want my friends mourning for me, but lovers gracing my "happy" tomb with sweet pastimes. The singer ends by designating Lesbia as his amatory executor: *You* close up my eyes and "crown" with your love my "ever-during night."

Forms and Devices

The poem is written in rhymed couplets of iambic pentameter, the heroic couplets familiar in English from Campion's predecessor Geoffrey Chaucer to his successor

Alexander Pope. In the work of these others, however, the form is used for narrative, expository, or satirical purposes. It is not the usual form for a song, although one other piece in *A Booke of Ayres*, "Follow Thy Saint," is written in heroic couplets and several songs are iambic pentameter. Shorter lines of varying lengths, as in William Shakespeare's "Under the Greenwood Tree," are more likely to be set to music. Most of the songs in this collection employ these shorter lines.

Heroic couplets are certainly not what one would expect from a slightly older Campion, who experimented with quantitative meters, in which the length of syllables, how long or short they are to say aloud, is measured instead of the accents. In his preface, he praises the Greek and Latin poets (such as Catullus) who wrote quantitative verse and were the "first inventors of ayres," while denigrating the "fashion of the time, ear-pleasing rhymes without art." "My Sweetest Lesbia" follows the fashion of 1600 but is extremely artful. Part of Campion's concern with meter is literary, as he looks back admiringly at classical models while sneering at his contemporaries and even at himself, part of his concern is strictly musical. As a composer, he works with quarter notes and the three-quarter time in which most of the song is written.

Campion himself composed the beautiful music for this song, so the question of detaching the words from their setting is more difficult than usual to resolve. Readers can enjoy the poem on the page for its neat three-part structure, its antithetical repetitions ("light" versus "night"), its graceful rhetorical power, and its extension of Catullus's witty, hyperbolic gambit into something profoundly human and moving. The text alone should not, however, be considered as anything more than an excerpt of the work as a whole.

The last two lines of each stanza represent a partial refrain. The first halves of these lines vary, but the second halves are repeated throughout the song and contrast with each other, one's "little light" versus an "ever-during night." The music stipulates that the phrase "ever-during night" be repeated at the end of each stanza. It is the only phrase so singled out, an emphasis intended to deepen the sense of mortality, the dark alternative to the love proposed by the singer. This effect is not present in the text alone. Furthermore, when the song is performed, the last two lines of each stanza are repeated, emphasizing the theme and its urgency.

The rhyming is simple and conventional, making use of thematically important words such as "dive" and "revive." The language is formal but clear, uncluttered and economical, a good illustration of Campion's remark that "What epigrams are in poetry, the same are ayres in music, . . . short and well seasoned." The alliteration of *l* dominates the song's first line, "My sweetest Lesbia, let us live and love," and is used through all three stanzas to emphasize important words: Lesbia, live, love, lamps, "little light," "lead their lives," life, lovers, and the imperative verb "let," which appears four times. The liquid *l* sound is also embedded in several important words: "sleep," "alarm," "fools," "timely." An important function of this alliteration is purely musical: repeated *l* sounds are melodious in themselves.

Themes and Meanings

The most insistent images in the song deal with light and dark. Day and night lengthen into life and death. The "little light" of human beings seems frail, weak, and no match for the "great lamps" of heaven, but if that light is used lovingly, it can be enough to make mortality something to celebrate, rather than something to mourn. By implication, the "sager sort" who disapprove of lovemaking, the lovers' "deeds," ally themselves with the military "fools" who "waste their little light." Those kinds of worldliness deprive men and women of the illumination that might make living worthwhile.

The poem is a declaration of *carpe diem*, "seize the day," a common theme of this period. It takes the rhetorical form of a lover's plea and belongs with the "amorous songs" Campion mentions in his preface. Acting against the passage of time, the warring of nations, and mortality itself, lovers can at least avoid wasting their lives and their light. The modesty is audacious. Love is sufficient in itself to offset the enormities of the world. This love is one that is earthly and enduring, one that makes even the prospect of death almost cheerful, a "triumph." In other words, people love because death looms, but that love makes death an occasion for revelry. Love, the song says, makes living worthwhile.

To what extent is the song really a love poem in the usual sense? Does the reader imagine that the "you" of the poem is a real person, someone being wooed and seduced? Is Campion's mistress more an idea than an individual woman? It may be significant that the song is addressed to Catullus's Lesbia. In another song based on the same original, Ben Jonson changes the name to the more euphonious Celia, a character in his play *Volpone* (1605). At least in dramatic terms, a real woman is represented there.

Campion's beloved, however, seems to live not in his own London but in the Rome of Catullus or out of the mortal world altogether. Her name comes to him secondhand. It is strictly literary and allusive, a means of paying homage to Catullus and thereby to the Greek poet Sappho of Lesbos, who is Catullus's real honoree.

The stately tone and epigrammatic neatness of the song make the love it espouses seem reserved, respectful, and even lofty. This is a hymn to love in the abstract. Campion seems to fret more about impersonal warfare than about personal love, yet his fervor is true and overwhelming. It is tempting to see Lesbia as love itself, or as an earthly goddess who will perform the singer's last rites. She is, in fact, the muse, the generative spirit of poetry and music. As the first piece of a whole collection of songs, "My Sweetest Lesbia" serves as an invocation to the muse. It is a love song to art, to its endurance and enduring beauty.

John Drury

MYRIS: ALEXANDRIA, 340 A.D.

Author: Constantine P. Cavafy (Kōnstantionos Petrou Kabaphēs, 1863-1933)
Type of poem: Dramatic monologue
First published: 1929, as "Myris: Alexandria tou 340 M.X."; in *Poiēmata*, 1935; English translation collected in *The Poems of C. P. Cavafy*, 1951

The Poem

The speaker of this rather long dramatic monologue is a pagan Greek in the city of Alexandria, Egypt, in the year 340 C.E., lamenting the death of his Christian lover. The speaker tells of his visit to the house of the dead man and, of there watching the Christian rites and becoming aware not only that has he lost his lover to death, but that perhaps he never knew him at all. The poem does not quite fit the usual definition of a dramatic monologue, though, in that one cannot be sure whom the speaker is addressing. He may, indeed, be talking half to himself, even as he is reporting what has happened to someone else, someone who may have known the dead man, Myris, but not very well.

The conversational, almost colloquial, intensely felt tone of the poem is expressed in its language, in its lines, and in its word choices. Although the lines have varying numbers of syllables, usually between eleven and fifteen, Constantine P. Cavafy's basic metrical pattern is a deliberately loose iambic. He uses no rhyme, although, since modern Greek has a rather limited vowel pattern and is a relatively inflected language, there are always sound echoes made by the repeated vowels and by those inflections. The poem is divided into stanzas or, rather, verse paragraphs, of varying length; the first three paragraphs are each four lines each, but the next four are ten, eight, twenty-three, and seventeen lines.

The speaker begins by describing how, the moment he learned of the "calamity," he went to Myris's house but did not enter it, since he "avoids" going into Christian houses, especially at times of sorrow or celebrations. The statement itself indicates the distance between the speaker and the beloved. The speaker stands in the hall, outside the room where the dead body lies; he can see a little of the large, rich room, suggesting that this Christian family is well-to-do.

The speaker, saying, "I stood and wept in a corner of the hall," regrets that his and his friends' future parties will no longer be worth much without Myris. Beside him, some old women talk about Myris's pious end, of his holding a cross and having the name of Christ on his lips. Four Christian priests enter, praying "to Jesus/ or to Mary (I don't know their religion very well)."

Here the speaker remarks that he and his friends had known that Myris was a Christian but that Myris had taken a more than active part in their wild parties, although now the speaker remembers a few moments when casual references to religion had been made and the young man had drawn away.

The priests continue to pray, and the speaker becomes aware of how intense they are. At last he begins to realize that he is truly losing, has lost, his love, that Myris has become one with the Christians and is now a stranger or, perhaps, has always been a stranger. Overcome, the speaker runs from their "horrible house" before his memory of Myris can be changed by their Christianity.

Forms and Devices

This is the longest of the poems that Cavafy printed while he was alive. Its very length allows a kind of exploration that shorter poems do not. The gradual lengthening of the stanzas also suggests an intensifying of emotion, a longer explosion of feeling; however, as in most of his later poems, Cavafy makes little use of figures of speech here, no similes, no metaphors, no rhymes except for the partial rhymes given (in the Greek) by the inflected endings of words. Indeed, the first part of this poem seems almost a flat report. As noted above, Cavafy's language, at least in translation, is conversational and colloquial.

It is structure and language then, not figures, which carry the poem's meanings; there is a kind of dialectic at play, a gradual revelation of the speaker's growing awareness. This revelation is given, first, through structure, a shifting between emotional expression and seemingly straight description, and between the past and the present. Second, the revelation is given through language and its "silence," that is, through statement by implication rather than by direct words.

The only word in the first twelve lines that reveals emotion is the word "calamity," in the first line: "When I heard of the calamity, that Myris had died." The next eleven lines are an almost emotionless description of the speaker going to the house and, standing there, observing the displeasure of the relatives of Myris. Although the emotion is there, it is expressed by the silence, the lack of words, rather than by their presence.

Now, however, direct expression of feeling takes over: "I stood and cried," the speaker says. Immediately afterward, he repeats the words "I thought upon" three times in the next seven lines (in Greek this is one word, suggesting "reflecting" upon something). That is, he moves back to the past, remembering aspects of Myris and so attempting to recover the past.

Then he returns once more to description, to the external, presenting the old women and the priests, at the same time emphasizing his alienation from Myris by his admission that he knows very little about Christianity.

Returning to the past, he remarks that he and his friends had known Myris was a Christian, but that Myris had lived as though that fact did not matter, not even speaking of his religion. Still, the speaker begins to reveal how little he had known Myris, since only now does he seem to remember the times that Myris pulled back from their pagan words or acts.

The last section mixes description and emotion. It exists almost entirely in the speaker's present, for the past has been lost. As the priests pray, the speaker is seized with the awareness that Myris has left him, has become one with his own people, the Christians. The speaker, fearing that he has been deluded by his own passion into believing that he knew Myris, flees, hoping to hang onto some positive memory before it is changed by the Christian funeral service. The last line of the poem, with its fear of loss, is a significantly Cavafian line, since loss of love, of home, of culture is a major theme in his work.

Themes and Meanings

Cavafy is a poet of the city, of civilization, of social and personal relations, of humans relating to humans. He is not, at least not directly, concerned with the natural—not even with humankind's relation with the natural. Unlike nature, the individual's life is not cyclic; it does not repeat itself. Loss, losses of all kinds, are therefore inevitable. Moreover, one must note that Cavafy's people are confined within themselves; they live in a world of enclosure with the self as all-consuming, since belief in a greater order than oneself has been lost. Writing about characters in history, as well as about the moments of history that give rise to the characters, allows Cavafy to dramatize all of his themes, but especially that of how one person relates to another.

Alexandria in 340 C.E. was a unique historical moment—a high, dramatic moment. The city was still one of the great centers of Greek civilization, a civilization not yet Christianized. Christianity, although it had been made legal by the Roman emperor Constantine some twenty-five or so years earlier, was still years away from being the prevailing religion of the empire. The sons of Constantine were battling for the throne; there was great conflict over what Christianity itself believed.

If one had eyes, however, the end of the old religion was in sight. There is a willful blindness on the part of the speaker. He is concerned only with his pleasures, with his love for Myris, not with the stir of ideas, the immense changes in civilization going on about him.

Cavafy presents him both affectionately and with some distance. The speaker as egoist, locked within himself, is incapable of seeing others as human beings in themselves. At the same moment, he is a lover who has lost his beloved, a sad figure at any time. At the end he may have learned something, but not in time truly to change. Moreover, he reflects Cavafy's own ambivalence toward Christianity, the religion in which he was reared but into which he never quite fit. The final thematic matters, even teachings, of the poem, then, are that history can and does destroy individuals and individual relationships, that humans live in a world of loss, and that egoism can blind a person.

L. L. Lee

THE MYSTERY OF THE CHARITY OF CHARLES PÉGUY

Author: Geoffrey Hill (1932-   )
Type of poem: Elegy
First published: 1983; collected in *Collected Poems*, 1985

The Poem

   The Mystery of the Charity of Charles Péguy is an elegy in ten parts, consisting of as few as seven and as many as eighteen four-line, irregularly rhymed verses. An elegy—a poetic lament on the death of a person who may or may not be known intimately by the poet—sometimes requires special knowledge of the life of the deceased. Geoffrey Hill has a formidable reputation for being difficult to understand at the best of times, but *The Mystery of the Charity of Charles Péguy* has the added density of reference to the life of this somewhat minor figure in late nineteenth and early twentieth century French intellectual and political circles. Who Charles Péguy was and what he did should be known or the poem may make no sense to the reader.

   Charles-Pierre Péguy, born in France in 1873, was a brilliant scholar who became a journalist, poet, political philosopher, and the founder and editor of *Cahier de la Quinzaine* magazine, which Péguy used to support young writers and to propound his own ideas about French politics, society, and religion. He was a leader in the fight to prove the innocence of Captain Alfred Dreyfus (1859-1935), a French-born Jew who, in 1894, was accused of selling military secrets to the Germans, and whose guilt seemed to be confirmed by the fact that he was Jewish. The Socialists supported the fight to clear the innocent Dreyfus, but during the fight, Péguy became increasingly dissatisfied with the manner in which the Socialists had pursued the matter. He eventually broke with the Socialists in 1900, repudiating his former support of France's Socialist leader, Jean-Joseph-Marie-Auguste Jaurès (1859-1914), and carrying on a running battle in print and in public against what he saw as a debasement of Socialist principles. In 1910, Péguy emerged as a major literary figure with the publication of his book on Joan of Arc, *Le Mystère de la charité de Jeanne d' Arc (The Mystery of the Charity of Joan of Arc*, 1950). The title of his book provides the basis for the title of Hill's poem.

   Péguy eventually returned to the religion he renounced as a young man, Catholicism, and began writing religious poems and developing philosophical ideas. Péguy claimed that he was always a Socialist, despite his return to religion and his repudiation of official French Socialism, but his rigorous refusal to compromise, his moral absolutism, and his support of French military solutions to the growing German problem made him a "man in the middle." He was despised by former friends and colleagues in the Dreyfus and Socialist movement and taken up by and admired by conservatives. He was one of the first to enlist at the outbreak of World War I; he was one of the first to die in the Battle of the Marne.

   In the first section of "The Mystery of the Charity of Charles Péguy," the question of Péguy's responsibility for the untimely death of Socialist leader Jaurès is put in two contexts: the death itself and the more general question of the role of thinkers in moments of history in action. This rhetorical musing leads to an examination of Péguy's character in the second section and his role as a defender of truth in the face of political and social compromise. Unlike his adversary, he is like a child, unaffected by triviality. Near the end of section 2, the place of his death is shown, and it is suggested that in his death his character was confirmed, even if he has become simply one of the innumerable statues in Paris.

In the third section, Péguy is remembered after death in a kind of piling up of the idealities of his life. He had, for example, made two pilgrimages to the cathedral at Chartres on behalf of his children. The other places have either direct or indirect connections with his life or hide allusions to his dreams for France: For example, Domrémy is the birthplace of Joan of Arc, and the Colombey-les-deux-Eglises may be a reference to General Charles de Gaulle (1890-1970), who is buried there and who also had a fearsome reputation for defending France. Saint Cyr is the home of the French military academy.

In the fourth section, the real world of compromise, self-interest, and class interest is examined, and Péguy's failure to win over those forces is expressed in terms of his work as a publisher in his little shop in Paris. In the end of the section, the death of Jaurès is rationalized, seen as inevitable, and juxtaposed against Péguy's own death. That death is explored in section 5 in concert with his love of the land and his connection with the simple people of the land; there is a rightness in the death taking place on the land, in a field of beetroot, where flesh quite properly is absorbed and courage is played out with dignity, as the recondite reference to "English Gordon" implies. (General Charles Gordon, beseiged at Khartoum, Africa, by a Moslem force, was reputed to have walked sedately down a staircase to his death without attempting to avoid the thrust of the spears.)

In section 6, the question of French justice comes up. It is considered in the light of the stripping of Dreyfus of his military trappings, which leads to a suggestion of wider martyrdom, including that of Christ at the hands of societies that have become morally debased and where all are, at the least, time servers or cowards. The seventh section continues listing those betrayed and those who have served and sacrificed themselves for the native lands. Section 8 examines, with a graphic vigor, the soldiers pushing themselves on in thuggish battle to their deaths. There is little suggestion of glamour or glory in this passage, but there is an aura of admiration for the courage and determination of those poilus, ready to give their lives in defense of their native soil.

Section 9 presents an idealized French landscape for which Péguy, in a sense, was always fighting in letters, in politics, and in war, but it ends with somber anticipations of the battle that must be fought and that will be won by men such as Péguy. Section 10 begins on the battlefield, as the dead bodies are collected. The question arises, as in the second verse of the first section, of how humankind is to take such actions—are they tragedy or farce? Whatever the case, there is no question that it is a time both for praise and lament.

The poem is a somewhat rambling, maundering contemplation of Péguy's life, character, and historical importance. As a result, Hill shuffles ideas in and out of the various sections in repetitive waves.

Forms and Devices

The elegy has taken many adjustments through the centuries, but the twentieth century in particular has manipulated it with considerable enthusiasm and not much respect. It has lost much of its romantic oversimplification at the hands of twentieth century poets, and the idea that one should not speak disrespectfully of the dead is often ignored. T. S. Eliot has something to do with the technique of this poem, but W. H. Auden is equally helpful in terms of the way Hill thinks about Péguy's life and death. Auden wrote several elegies, often about famous people, and he was not loath to reveal the weakenesses as well as the strengths of his subjects.

The elegy, as a rule, praised exclusively, although there are intimations of some reservation in how Andrew Marvell contemplates historical figures in his poems of lament. Auden, however, can be frank about flaws in great men; in contemplating the death of the poet William Butler Yeats in his poem "In Memory of W. B. Yeats," Auden openly admits that "You were silly like us." It has something to do with the twentieth century zeal for frankness and suspicion of an idealized version of life; it also may have something to do with an inability to be certain about what is right or wrong, which is an aspect of the twentieth century Western sensibility.

Clearly, frankness is a strong influence on Hill's poem, because Péguy is revealed in an antiromantic way—stubborn, narrow-minded, and sometimes bloody-minded in his attitude toward others, which manifested itself in his attack on Jaurès. So, in a sense, what the poem is, ultimately, is a peculiar mix of admiration and wry reservation that does not resolve itself one way or another, but still allows for an ultimate sadness; it is best described as a kind of antielegy in which excessive admiration is severely curtailed.

The Hill canon, in general, is often the source of critical quarrel because he can be difficult to understand. Often, his lines cannot be turned into prose, a common practice of most poetry readers, although there is a kind of aesthetic "rightness" about them that is unexplainable rationally. This is not a failure on Hill's part, unless it is presumed that poetry must always make intellectual sense. Hill, in fact, is deliberately ambiguous. His debt to Eliot intensifies this problem because he tends to pile up images as Eliot did, without providing the linkages that one expects of ordinary metaphors and similes. Hill's images merely appear, often out of a loose association of ideas.

The last verse in the first section is an example of how this occurs. The problem posed earlier of how to take history, either as tragedy or farce, is now put into the specific context of the troops marching off to battle in World War I. It is seen in the context of early newsreel films, put succinctly in the second-to-last verse as "juddery bombardment of a silent film." What Hill has in mind is the way in which those early films jumped about, made a clanking noise as the film ran through the projector, giving even the military procession a kind of comic inconsequentiality that is reinforced further by his punning on the word "reeling."

This practice of slapping one image on top of another, one thing leading to another without the help of such linking phrases as "as if" or "it was like," can best be understood not as a linguistic device but as a visual one in which one image is often, as in motion pictures, laid on top of another or in which one image melts into another. If the reader thinks of the lines as linguistic attempts to affect visual (or musical) fusions of continual changing images, much of the problem will be solved, as it will be if Eliot or Auden is read in a similar manner.

This inclination to sophisticated imagistic trickery, however, should not be seen as Hill's only strength. He often can be densely lyrical, as in his evocations of the French countryside in sections 5 and 9, and he is much admired for the thick, bruising descriptions of battle that are in many of his poems. For all of his basic tonal seriousness, however, there is a playfulness about his use of blatant clichés, which he often refreshes or, as one critic put it, "rinses and restores." Perhaps the most daring is at the end of section 4, where he joins two clichés to describe the death of Péguy: "So, you have risen/ above all that and fallen flat on your face."

Themes and Meanings

The intention of an elegy is to praise the deceased, provide a kind of solemn listing of the accomplishments of the dead. This poem, given its source in Auden's antielegies and the desire of Hill not simply to idealize Péguy, opens to a wider consideration of Péguy's successes and his failures. In a way, the poem suggests, Péguy's life was a failure, but that does not, ultimately, preclude the poet from admiring his subject. The poem takes a further turn past the antielegy to pick up aspects of the "dramatic monologue" in which a problem is solved, in a sense, in the very act of being discussed poetically. Hill fuses the elegy to the dramatic monologue in which the problem is not the subject's (as it usually is in that form), but the poet's. How is he to praise a man with whose conduct he does not entirely feel easy, particularly if that man's work is so clearly a public failure and that man may have been responsible, even inadvertently, for the death of another man of political and moral importance. How does one praise a person of such mixed accomplishments?

The original *Times Literary Supplement* publication of the poem was preceded by a quotation from Péguy, which has not been reprinted in Hill's *Collected Poems*, but which gives some idea of why Hill admires him. In French, the quotation roughly translates as follows: "We are the last, almost beyond the last. Besides, after us, begins another age, quite a different world, the world of those who don't know anything." In the notes following the poem in *Collected Poems*, Hill has a short biographical note on Péguy that ends, "Péguy's stubborn rancours and mishaps and all, is one of the great souls, one of the great prophetic intelligences, of our century. I offer *The Mystery of the Charity of Charles Péguy* as my homage to the triumph of his 'defeat.'"

The poem is also an indictment of those people, such as the Socialists, who would compromise their principles, even if such compromise was made to further the process of social and political improvement. Even more to the point, the poem is a swinging attack upon the unprincipled, "the lords of limit and of contumely," even if, as is stated in section 4, "This world is different, belongs to them—." The poem does not suggest that the time servers and the incumbents of compromise are defeated, nor that Péguy was always right, but it attempts to bring the spectrum of human endeavor at its worst and at its best into some kind of humane perspective, much in the way that Yeats attempted to deal with the Irish political problem in his poems. Hill concedes in that second-to-last verse of the poem that "Low tragedy, high farce, fight for command," but it still remains that there is room for praise and for mourning ("éloge and elegy") in considering the life of Péguy, a man of such principle that he, in a sense, became a victim of his own character.

Charles Pullen

MYTHISTOREMA

Author: George Seferis (Giorgos Stylianou Seferiades, 1900-1971)
Type of poem: Poetic sequence
First published: 1935, as *Mythistorima*; English translation collected in *Collected Poems, 1924-1955,* 1967

The Poem

Mythistorema is a sequence of twenty-four lyric and dramatic poems in free verse. The title is a colloquial word for "novel" that combines the ideas of myth and history. The author's note states: "MYTHISTOREMA—it is its two components that made me choose the title of this work: MYTHOS, because I have used, clearly enough, a certain mythology; ISTORIA [both "history" and "story"], because I have tried to express, with some coherence, circumstances that are as independent from myself as the characters in a novel."

The poem's narrator, like that of a novel, moves freely among various points of view and identities, yet his voice is always distinctive. This voice, linking past and present in a tone of tragic nostalgia, is the coherent center of the poem.

The sequence begins with a kind of preface to the poems that follow. The narrator and his fellows have been on a journey "to rediscover the first seed," to renew "the ancient drama." They have waited in vain for "the angel" (also translated as "herald" or "messenger") to show them the way. Bodies and spirits broken, they returned with "these carved reliefs of a humble art."

Their "limbs incapable, mouths cracked," they can no longer draw water from the source of inspiration, the "well inside a cave." The seekers are like cave dwellers whose reality is an illusion, as in Plato's myth of the cave. The ropes of the well "have broken; only grooves on the well's lip" remind them of their "past happiness," when it was "easy for us to draw up idols and ornaments." Now, however, "the cave stakes its soul and loses it" in the oppressive "silence, without a drop of water."

The narrator describes waking from a dream with a "marble head in my hands." It has become part of him, though he cannot tell what it is trying to say to him. It has exhausted him and mutilated his hands. Poem 4 begins by quoting Socrates: The way a soul "is to know itself" is to look into a soul. This suggests that the marble head, "stranger and enemy," is to be identified with the narrator. Similarly, the singing and seeking of Jason and his Argonauts are identified with the narrator; all will die unremembered, and in this there is an ironic "Justice."

Poem 5 questions the ability of memory and imagination to give present substance to one's personal (and cultural) past. We try to recall "our friends," but it is only hope that deceives us into thinking "we'd known them since early childhood," before they "took to the ships." In art, one tries to depict the ships, but only in sleep does one approach them and "the breathing wave"; what one actually seeks is "the other life" of imagination wedded to experience that the friends stand for, "beyond the statues."

One who found the ancient "rhythm of the other life" in his art was the "old Friend," French composer Joseph-Maurice Ravel. Far from the Greek landscape, in a room "lit only by the flames from the fireplace" but radiant with the "distant lightning" of imagination, he animated the broken statues and "tragic columns" into "a dance among the oleanders/ beside new quarries." Though the artist will die, hope and light "will spring" from his art.

Modern humanity exists in a parched and stagnant period of alienation and exile, writing letters to fill "the gap of our separation," unable to speak to one another, though bound by a hope that the "Star of dawn" (Venus) offers love, joy, and peace. Feeding on "the bitter bread of exile," the wanderers pay for their "decision to forget" their homeland, as they wonder: "Who will accept our offering, at this close of autumn?"

The exiles ask what their souls seek in wandering "from harbor to harbor." They cannot forget who they are long enough to enjoy earthly or heavenly beauties, flying fish or stars. They find work moving "broken stones," but cannot express their "broken thoughts" in foreign tongues. They breathe the memory of home "with greater difficulty each day" and swim in new seas with no sense of community, alienated from their own bodies. Yet they continue "non-existent pilgrimages unwillingly" to find the beautiful islands "somewhere round about here where we are groping."

A sense of urgency impels the narrator to continue the journey without waiting for his friends to return from known islands or "the open sea." To renew his purpose and power, he strokes rusted cannons and oars "so that my body may revive and decide." Like "Odysseus waiting for the dead among the asphodels," he had hoped to make contact with Adonis and gather his own soul, "shattered on the horizon," but found only enervating silence.

Poems 11 through 14 shed a "little light from our childhood years" in the present darkness before moving to an island one might see in any Greek harbor today, for "the same landscape recurs level after level/ to the horizon." Here Odysseus and his men land to mend their oars, yet they forget that the sea "unfolds a boundless calm" and set out with "broken oars." The sea, "once so bitter," is "now full of colors in the sun." The radiance of the "red pigeons in the light," which are like Homeric birds of omen, inscribes "our fate" in "the colors and gestures of people/ we have loved."

The narrator recalls a lover sleeping, her shadow lost in "the other shadows" of dreams. Living the sensual life the gods "gave us to live," he pities the solipsists who speak to cisterns and wells and drown in the echo of "the voice's circles."

In the voice of Orestes, the exile describes life, this "time of trial," as a chariot race, circling endlessly, observed by "the black, bored Eumenides," who are unforgiving. He longs for the race's end, but goes on because "the gods so will it." He despairs: "there's no point in being strong" because "no one can escape" to the sea. A premonition of battle and death warns that the boy who saw the light must also "study the trees" that bear the wrinkles of the fathers so that he will know all of life.

Poems 18 through 22 bear the heaviness of grief. The speaker is "sinking into the stone"; all he had loved has vanished and collapsed; he laments having let life pass through his fingers "without drinking a single drop." All is uphill, and friends "who no longer know how to die" are "a burden to us" (poem 19). Bound to a rock, a wound in his breast for the vulture and the hawk, he asks how far the stones sinking into time will drag him. He is troubled by death, unlike the trees that breathe "the black serenity of the dead" or the statues with their static smiles (poem 20). Setting out, the travelers saw the broken statues but refused to believe that life could be so "easily lost." Now they are more like statues every day, "brothers in stone," though they have not "escaped the circle" as have the ancient dead, who, risen again, "smile in strange silence" (poem 21). Wandering among the "broken stones" for "three or six thousand years," the travelers try to remember "dates and heroic deeds." What they seek, however, is to know how "to die properly" (poem 22). Unlike the friends who "no longer know how to die," they hunger for a heroic death.

The last two poems offer first a glimmer of hope in the almond blossoms and the gleaming marble, which seem just "a little farther," "a little higher"—then tragic resignation as the travelers admit the failure of their struggle. In death, these "weak souls among the asphodels" cannot offer hope to the future "victims," but they can offer the serenity of death: "We who had nothing will teach them peace."

Forms and Devices

"Mythistorema" was a turning point in modern Greek poetry, largely because of its language. For a hundred years, Greek poets had been divided between the literary (*katharevousa*) idiom and the spoken (*demotiki*) idiom. The purists tended to see ancient Greece through the eyes of post-Renaissance Europe, while the demotic poets concentrated on modern Greece. George Seferis aimed for a vision of ancient Greece as experienced in the contemporary Greek landscape, and this is reflected in his elegant demotic idiom. In *Modern Greek Poetry* (1973), Kimon Friar writes that Seferis "has used only those words in the living demotic tongue which have his own touch and weight and has honed them into what perhaps may be the purest and leanest of modern Greek idioms."

This is reflected in Seferis's use of the mythical method, legendary figures appearing in modern harbors, to show the connection, as well as the distance, between then and now. In the years before writing *Mythistorema*, Seferis was taken with T. S. Eliot's essay on James Joyce's 1922 novel *Ulysses*, which argued that the mythical method could be used instead of narrative to show "a continuous parallel between contemporaneity and antiquity."

The use of metaphor in the poem underscores this parallel between the ancient and the modern. The extended or "epic" metaphor of the odyssey to the beautiful islands, or Orestes' chariot race, combines with the mythical method to form a modern allegory.

As Walter Kaiser writes in his introduction to *Three Secret Poems* (1969), "For Seferis, the Greek sun is this ultimate paradox, both life-giver and death-bringer, desired and feared, 'angelic' and 'black.'" "You stare into the sun," says Seferis in another poem, "then you are lost in the darkness." This use of chiaroscuro (light and dark imagery) is essential to Seferis's poetry, a device that is both metaphorical and thematic.

The controlling tone is a tragic nostalgia (a good Greek word for the "ache to return home"). This tone was what first drew Seferis to Eliot, whose *The Waste Land* (1922) Seferis was translating while writing *Mythistorema*. In *On the Greek Style* (1966), Seferis comments that Eliot's poetry gave him something "inevitably moving to a Greek: the elements of tragedy."

The tragic element, combined with a use of dramatic monologue that is similar to Eliot's, gives Seferis's narrator his distinctive voice, freeing him to move from first to third person or to become Jason, Orestes, or Odysseus as the poetic occasion demands. Yet the voice remains consistent, linking the personal with the universal, the historical with the mythical. As Philip Sherrard has pointed out in *The Marble Threshing Floor: Studies in Modern Greek Poetry* (1956), however, "The human person is the centre of the scene, it is he who as a concrete, living, suffering and perplexed being, speaks. He is not simply a device."

Themes and Meanings

Mythistorema is a poem about the continuity of past and present as it is preserved in personal experience and cultural memory. More specifically, it is about the attempt to discover the heroic past of ancient Greece in the modern landscape. For Seferis, this attempt is a contemporary odyssey, an imaginative journey through the Greek experience, both ancient and modern, which consists of a shared spiritual and historical experience of suffering and disaster. Kimon Friar's translation of the title of this work "The Myth of Our History," suggests that the poem is the story of this shared experience, part myth and part history.

Memory and imagination are the vehicles of this journey, which is really an act of understanding. The narrator's quest in search of the origins of his Greek identity unifies the poem's imagery of the sea, which can be, like life, both embittering and soothing. Seferis has commented that "the bows of ships have a special place in the imagery of our childhood, as perhaps do the shapes of footballs or the photos of deceased relatives for other people." When the narrator tries to recall friends who have sailed away, both memory and imagination fail him; only while sleeping in cellars that smell of tar, like the hold of a ship, does he come close to them and "the breathing wave." His true search, however, is for the life of imagination wedded to experience, which the friends represent: "we search for them because we search for the other life,/ beyond the statues."

The broken stones and statues of Greece, the landscape and cultural artifacts that come down to the present, remind one that one's suffering is neither unique nor uniquely modern, and stir memory and imagination to link one's tragedy with the eternally recurring tragedy of myth and history.

The broken statues that appear throughout the poem—first as an ambiguous inspiration and burden in the form of a marble head found in a dream, and finally as the "brothers in stone" who "smile in strange silence"—communicate with one, though one does not always know what they are saying. Once one has grasped them, however, they become part of one, difficult "to disunite again." Like Ravel's music, they say that it is possible to recapture "a rhythm of the other life, beyond the broken/ statues." They are mirrors of the soul in which it is possible to see "the stranger and enemy"; they break down the barrier between present and past, erasing such illusory oppositions as waking and dreaming, weird and familiar, I and thou. The marble head—the narrator—is a modern Odysseus, Jason, or Orestes. The only difference is that "the ancient dead have escaped the circle and risen again/ and smile in strange silence" to teach serenity. It is this silence that is invoked at the end of the poem, for like them, those who are here will teach "peace" to those who come after.

Water imagery is always associated with the imaginative journey. Modern life is a life of exile. Like refugees caught up in disaster, one is unable to appreciate the beauties along the way, "sorry" to "let a broad river pass through [one's] fingers/ without drinking a single drop." Life itself offers abundance, but in this exile most people are too concerned with searching and suffering to appreciate it. Once, waters "left on the hands/ the memory of great happiness" when human "souls became one with the oars and the oarlocks"; now, one hopes only to be remembered, like Elpenor, by an oar marking one's grave.

The modern landscape is parched; the rivers, wells, and springs of inspiration have dried up: "only a few cisterns—and these empty—that echo, and that we worship." The cistern, a personal and cultural reservoir of faith and inspiration, is an important symbol that Seferis developed in "The Cistern." Modern Greeks, says Seferis, tend to worship echoes of the past instead of creating anew, like Ravel, "a rhythm of the other life." To quench its spiritual thirst, to get rid of "the 'Waste Land' feeling," as Seferis called it, modern humanity journeys in self-imposed exile toward the beautiful islands "somewhere about here where we are groping."

Given modern inertia, the narrator wonders how anyone ever had faith in the future. To marry and to have children now seem "enigmas inexplicable to our souls." Nowadays, going to "the harbors on Sunday to breathe," one sees "the broken planks from voyages that never ended,/ bodies that no longer know how to love." Some know of the cisterns, like the poet, but "drown in the voice's circles" without enjoying the reward of simply living. Only the serenity of death awaits them, and on this tragic note of failure, the poem ends.

It has been said that poetry is the art of delineating the limits of human failure. If the quest for the seed of the ancient drama has failed, the poem has not. For just as the past is inherited in fragments, so the poem passes "the myth of our history" to posterity. Given that all souls are seekers by nature, it is inevitable that the journey will be repeated, but our failure, like that of those who came before us, can be instructive: "We who had nothing will teach them peace."

Richard Collins

NAMES OF HORSES

Author: Donald Hall (1928-　　)
Type of poem: Lyric
First published: 1978, in *Kicking the Leaves*

The Poem

Donald Hall's "Names of Horses" consists of twenty-nine lines of unrhymed free verse, arranged in seven brief stanzas and a final single line. The speaker, who directly addresses the horses and finally provides their names, is clearly Hall himself; the farm on which these horses have worked is called Eagle Pond, and the poem itself is thematically related to essays collected in *String Too Short to Be Saved* (1961). A good deal of Hall's work, both poetry and prose, has focused on that farm in New Hampshire, home for three generations of his ancestors and a retreat for Hall himself.

In the first half of the poem, Hall addresses what seems to be a single horse, praising it for the work it performs season by season. This, readers quickly learn, is not a pet but a draft horse, engaged in crucial activities on an old-fashioned farm. The jobs include hauling firewood, cut this winter for the next; pulling cartloads of manure to spread on the fields; mowing and raking the grass and hauling it to the barn; and pulling the family buggy to church each Sunday.

At about the midpoint of the poem, a shift occurs, and the reader realizes that the single horse is in fact a series of horses, "Generation on generation" taking turns at the work, living and dying on the farm, each horse in turn being put down and buried by "the man, who fed you and kept you." Death comes only when each horse in succession becomes "old and lame," in such constant pain it is unable to graze comfortably.

Over the years, the place where the horses are buried becomes "the pasture of dead horses." Here are the remains of the "old toilers, soil makers," who are finally in the last line addressed by name.

Forms and Devices

"Names of Horses" is quite modern in its rejection of traditional rhyme and metrical patterns, but Hall is nonetheless a careful craftsman who makes every word and sound, the design of each line, and the order of lines and paragraphs contribute to the total impact the poem has on the reader.

The words the poet chooses are concrete and specific. Many of the nouns designate tools and other items that characterize farm life in the days before heavy machinery powered by diesel or gasoline engines replaced horse power, such as sledges, hames, and, most picturesquely, the "leather quartertop buggy." Many of the verbs serve to emphasize the difficulty of the horse's work: "strained," "haul," "culled," "dragged."

Hall uses a long line in "Names of Horses," rather like Walt Whitman's. Most of the lines are enjambed; that is, the sense of the sentence is carried across the line break. When a line is end-stopped, usually at the end of the paragraph, the last word or phrase conveys a vivid image or a significant idea: "as the sea smooths glass" or "shuddering in your skin," for example. A kind of rhythm is frequently supplied within these lines by alliteration, which can make the verse slower and heavier, as in "dragged the wagon," or quicker and lighter, as in "trotted the two miles to church" with a "light load."

The overall arrangement of the poem is seasonal. The first paragraph, four strong lines, begins "All winter your brute shoulders strained against collars" and recounts what is evidently the hardest work the horse does all year: hauling wood to heat the house and to fuel "the simmering range."

"In April," one month that stands for spring, the horse both produces and spreads manure. The work seems lighter. The season of summer takes up six lines and parts of two paragraphs, as well as the most elaborate imagery in the poem. Here the focus is on hay-making and on old-fashioned technology. One hears the "clacketing" of the mowing machine, feels the summer heat, and watches the intricate movement from field to stack to barn and back for another load. These lines—with their internal rhymes of "stack," "rack," and "back"; "drag" and "wagon"; and "hay" and "day"— provide a thematic and musical high point for the poem. Hay-making is as important an activity for Hall as it was for Robert Frost. For both New England poets, it epitomizes the natural life rhythms of the traditional farm.

The next paragraph briefly interrupts this seasonal pattern. The first two lines describe the Sunday trip to church and the horse's opportunity to graze "in the sound of hymns," the horse's lightest work in its happiest circumstances. The phrase "Generation on generation" carries forward the worshipful tone established by the hymns. This passage ends with the attractive image of the horse gazing out the window of its stall.

The next two paragraphs deal with the fall, the last season of the farm year. Horses live for many years, but, come "one October," each horse in succession is taken out to the appropriate "sandy ground above Eagle Pond" and shot. The event is described in detail, from the digging of the hole to the filling of the grave after the horse is "felled" into it—hard work for the farmer, who for once does not have the help of his horse.

The last paragraph focuses on the pasture where the generations of horses are buried. Readers learn that the life cycle of the draft horse has been going on for 150 years at Eagle Pond. Because pine trees are taking root, one can surmise that this ground is no longer being grazed; the cycle has ended. Hall addresses the horses with a pair of powerful epithets (with a haunting internal rhyme) "old toilers, soil makers" and, finally, in the formal apostrophe of the last line, calls them by name.

Themes and Meanings

"Names of Horses" evokes a way of life which had nearly vanished by the 1970's, when the poem was written, painting an attractive picture of the traditional New England farm powered by mighty horses. Hall makes it clear that farm life was not easy. From the very first line, readers see the effort the horse must put into its work. Eventually, it becomes "old and lame" and finds it painful even to bend and graze. One fall then, when most of the year's work is done, the farmer kills and buries the horse. The contribution the horse makes to farm life continues beyond its death, however. Its remains will help build the soil and contribute to new life. Thus the horse has a kind of immortality, rather like the one Walt Whitman evokes in "Leaves of Grass" (1855-1892). In this respect, "Names of Horses" can be read as a conventional celebration of the continuity of life, not just for the horse but also for the farmer.

However, a closer reading suggests that one should not be too quick to accept that interpretation. Something is missing from the poem as it moves toward its flat but powerful ending. There is no colt to take the place of the last horse to be shot; in fact, the only young things in sight are those young pines sprouting in the pasture.

When the horses are finally named, readers may well see some significance in the order in which their names are presented. Roger and Nellie could as well be the names of children born on the farm as of horses. "Mackerel" probably refers to the color of the horse, who may have reminded the owner of the fish itself, or of the pattern of bluish gray and silver that characterizes a "mackerel sky." These names are familiar and friendly, but the last—"Lady Ghost"—strikes a more ominous note; she seems to be the last in a series in more ways than one.

"Names of Horses" has some of the tonal quality of an elegy, a poetic lament for something or, more often, someone dead and gone. The only human being one meets in the poem, however, is the nameless "man" who dispatches each horse when it has outlived its usefulness. Over 150 years, this must be more than a single man, but readers do not know how many or what their names were, making it difficult to lament their passing. One can regret the lost horses, but the poet provides none of the consolation with which most elegies end. There is no sense that what has been lost will be restored.

"Names of Horses" is characteristic of much of Hall's work, especially as represented in *Kicking the Leaves*. Each poem relates some kind of loss, sometimes more than one, and in each the poet attempts to find some way to reconcile himself to the loss. The attempt is always painfully honest, and he is never willing to accept an easy, conventional answer. It may be enough for Walt Whitman that grass grows from graves, but not for Donald Hall.

William T. Hamilton

NAMING OF PARTS

Author: Henry Reed (1914-1986)
Type of poem: Lyric
First published: 1946, in *A Map of Verona: Poems*

The Poem

"Naming of Parts" is a thirty-line lyric poem divided into five stanzas. The poem depicts a group of infantry recruits receiving a familiarization lecture on their rifles. The title reflects the practical, if prosaic, necessity of knowing the proper term for each of the rifle's parts. Readers hear two distinctive voices in the poem—that of the insensitive, boorish drill instructor giving the lecture and that of a sensitive, young recruit whose mind is wandering during this mind-numbing discourse on rifle terminology. The key to understanding the poem is realizing that roughly the first three and one-half lines of each stanza present what the young recruit is literally hearing and enduring while the remaining lines suggest what he is thinking and noticing as his instructor lectures about rifle parts.

The first stanza opens with an overview of the week's training schedule. As the first lines make clear, this day's class will be devoted to learning the names of the rifle's parts. The recruit's mind, however, is elsewhere. He notices the Japonica shrubs blooming in neighboring gardens, a detail that establishes the season as spring. In the second stanza, the instructor is calling the group's attention to the rifle's "swivels," that are fastened to the weapon's wooden frame or "stock." The missing "piling swivel," a part the military deems inessential, inspires the recruit's sudden notice of the branches described in lines 4 and 5. In marked contrast to his present situation, he finds the natural scene to be complete and whole in and of itself. The third stanza concerns the rifle's "safety catch," which functions to prevent unintentional firing. The sudden mention of blossoms at the end of the fourth line once again indicates that the recruit is dividing his attention between the lecture and the springtime scene. He is struck by how the blooms of flowers simply exist. Despite their fragility, they need not learn safety procedures nor must they comply with any arbitrary strictures.

With the next stanza, the instructor has moved on to the principal moving part of the rifle: the bolt. In an effort to demonstrate how the rifle operates, the instructor is mimicking the firing process, using the bolt handle to move the spring-operated bolt back and forth. The military jargon for this procedure is "easing the spring." Witnessing the local bees engaged in the process of pollination, however, inspires the young soldier to reinterpret this phrase in a sexually suggestive sense. As the initial repetition of the phrase "easing the Spring" indicates, the fifth and final stanza functions as a sort of reprise of both the lecture and the recruit's reactions to it. He has obviously seized upon two phrases from the lecture, the "cocking-piece" and the "point of balance." The rifle's "cocking-piece" functions as a fitting symbol of sexual tension, once more suggesting the "release" he and his fellow soldiers are being denied. The rifle's "point of balance" leads the young soldier to reflect on how their present situation has thrown their lives out of balance.

Forms and Devices

Reed divides the poem into five six-line stanzas, each of which follows the alternating pattern already explained. Within the stanzas, the principal poetic devices are imagery and wordplay calculated to evoke connotations at odds with the denotations of the instructor's words and phrases. The effect is to illustrate what Reed sees as the inherent contrast between the world of nature and the world of war. In the first stanza, for instance, the image of Japonica plants glistening "like coral in all of the neighboring gardens" stands in stark opposition to the rifle imagery in the first three and one-half lines. The second stanza turns on the image of the missing "piling swivel"; contrary to this image, the tree branches mentioned in the fourth and fifth lines bespeak a peaceful, harmonious, and integral relation with nature. The phrase "silent, eloquent gestures" sets up a thematic opposition to the third stanza, in which the soldiers are being admonished to release the safety catches of their rifles with their thumbs. This clumsy gesture further contrasts with the serenity of the "fragile and motionless" blossoms, and the corresponding reiteration of the phrase "using their finger" evokes a sexual connotation the instructor hardly intends.

The fourth stanza juxtaposes the image of "easing the [rifle's] spring" with that of bees "assaulting and fumbling the flowers." The imagery and the connotation are again sexual, with the flowers likened to passive victims and bees to sexual predators. The principal play on words is the repetition of the phrase "easing the Spring"— now with an uppercase *s*. The young recruit is thinking of the sexual release symbolized by the bees pollinating flowers. The last stanza serves as a summation: The first few lines are once more devoted to the instructor's phrases, but this time they are taken out of context. As a consequence of what has come before, the phrases and images come home to the reader in the full force of their associated sexual implications. Juxtaposing these once again with the natural images repeated in the fourth and fifth lines heightens the reader's sense of what these young soldiers do and do not have.

Themes and Meanings

"Naming of Parts" addresses an issue philosophers and military historians have long termed "the problem of war." In its simplest terms, this problem is whether war is an aberration or a perennial part of the human condition. Reed's poem posits at least a partial answer. The fact that spring, the season of renewal and rebirth, still unfolds quite heedless of this group's commitment to the mechanistic processes of war and death carries the main weight of the theme. Reed obviously views militarism and war as distinctly unnatural. Reed's choice of the red-flowered Japonica in the first stanza, for instance, is significant. As its name implies, Japonica, or "Japanese quince," is native to Japan—one of the Axis powers against which England and the United States were allied in World War II. (Reed, an Englishman, served in World War II, the ostensible period during which the poem is set.) The effect is to suggest that nature transcends both national borders and human notions of loyalty and enmity.

In the third stanza, the criticism becomes personal and specific. In marked contrast to the instructor's affected anxiety about operating the "safety-catch" correctly, the young soldier is struck by the serenity of the spring blooms all around him. Reed's inspiration may well have been the biblical Sermon on the Mount in which Christ urges his followers to heed the example of the "lilies of the field," that neither toil nor spin (Matthew 6:28). Trapped in the unnatural world of war, this young soldier feels no such confidence about his basic needs being met. By applying the instructor's admonition against using one's finger to floral blossoms, the soldier evokes the sexual connotation of the phrase and betrays his present anxiety. In biological terms, flowers are essentially feminine receptacles and therefore have long been recognized as symbols of female receptiveness. This young man, the reader should realize, is confined to a sexually segregated training camp in the springtime. Sex is clearly on his mind.

The soldier's sexual frustration becomes particularly evident in the fifth and sixth stanzas. The rapid back-and-forth movement of the instructor's rifle bolt calls to mind the corresponding motion of the sexual act, an image this soldier connects to the bees in the process of "assaulting and fumbling the flowers." The connotations and imagery are implicitly sexual, expressing the soldier's frustrated yearning for sexual release. The introduction of two new elements, the phrase "point of balance" and the alluring "almond-blossom" image, is perhaps meant as an ironic evocation of the *carpe diem* tradition that counsels complete surrender to the life-affirming lures of beauty and love. Reed's point seems to be that the enforced segregation of military life precludes striking a wholesome balance between self-indulgence and disciplined abstinence.

In terms of tone, "Naming of Parts" stands in a long line of poetic responses to war ranging from the satiric to the elegiac. It is certainly not a reverent acknowledgment of noble sacrifice in the manner of John McCrae's "In Flanders Fields," nor is it a cavalier endorsement of the traditional martial virtues of courage and honor such as Richard Lovelace's "To Lucasta, Going to the Wars." It is also not an unsentimental depiction of death in the manner of Wilfred Owen's "*Dulce et Decorum Est*" or Randall Jarrell's "The Death of the Ball Turret Gunner." Reed's "Naming of Parts" reflects an earlier modernist mood of "irony and pity," to borrow Hemingway's phrase, and not the bitterness and despair characteristic of the later postmodern movement in literature. A tone of pessimistic resignation rather than a true antiwar sentiment informs the poem. The real problem with war, Reed seems to be suggesting, is that people have long deplored modern mass warfare as dehumanizing and unnatural, as a perverse human superimposition upon the world of nature, yet they find themselves as impotent in the face of this insanity as they would be confronting a force of nature.

Edward F. Palm

NANTUCKET

Author: William Carlos Williams (1883-1963)
Type of poem: Lyric
First published: 1934, in *Collected Poems, 1921-1931*

The Poem

"Nantucket" by William Carlos Williams is a short lyric poem of five two-line stanzas, which vividly describes a room, presumably on the Atlantic island of Nantucket, off the coast of Massachusetts. The poem consists entirely of Imagistic phrases, noting the flowers through the window, the sunshine, a glass tray, a glass pitcher and tumbler, a key, and finally "the/ immaculate white bed." It reads like a verbal still-life, painterly in its precise rendering of things seen and adding to sight another sensual appeal: the "Smell of cleanliness."

Similar to Williams's more famous "The Red Wheelbarrow" in its sharp focus and love for what is ordinary, the poem, within its own small frame, is richly colored and shaped. It creates clean, fresh, airy intimate space, beginning with the enticing and benedictory view from a window and ending, as if inevitably, at a bed, which seems equally luminous and inviting. The poet's palette is limited but lush: lavender and yellow set off by white, the color that sunshine takes on in late afternoon, and the translucent noncolor of glass. This is a vision of pleasure: composed, quiet, secure, anticipatory, reminiscent of some imagined room painted by seventeenth century Dutch painter Jan Vermeer before people have entered it, or an eroticized interior by the modern French painter Henri Matisse. Here is a poem of unswerving objectivity and directness, a poem seemingly without an "I" or any other protagonist, and yet the poem proclaims gladly the subjectivity of the eye, which can glean secret meaning from the very surfaces of objects, from their casual proximity to one another, from their compositional interactions.

The poem showcases Williams's affinity for the modernist school of Imagism, which extolled economical use of language, concentration, rhythmic individuality, and a commitment to presenting "an intellectual and emotional complex in an instant of time," in poet Ezra Pound's memorable phrase. "Nantucket" resists making symbols of the contents of the room it portrays. Yet the poem in its entirety could be said to be a metaphor that suppresses its own tenor, letting the vehicle speak clearly and suggestively. Like the traditional Japanese poetic form, haiku, the poem restricts its subject matter to objective description that nevertheless evokes a definite, albeit unstated, emotional response. Williams was often beguiled by a similar discipline of suggesting a very great deal in the fewest possible words, and he chose ordinary words from spoken American English. In this poem, he declines even the ambiguous commentary of lines such as "So much depends/ upon," or "these things/ astonish me beyond words," which leaven the strict Imagism in two others of his small poems, "The Red Wheelbarrow" and "Pastoral," respectively.

Forms and Devices

Williams's stanza form was not inherited, but finely honed by his intense personal engagement with his subject. Each of the stanzas in "Nantucket" is composed of two lines of almost equal length. Each of these lines contains two or three accented syllables, rendering it light but chiseled, casual-seeming, and yet composed. At first the lines enjamb on nouns and adjectives of solid description, but by line 8, which ends with the pronoun "which," and line 9, ending with the phrase "And the," enjambment on less weighty words causes anticipation of the poem's most emotionally freighted items: the key and the bed.

Three devices contributing to the delicate, brilliant sound and feel of the poem are the four aerated white spaces between stanzas, the reliance solely on dashes for internal punctuation, and the lack of any closing punctuation. This last leaves the impression that there is indeed more to say about "the/ immaculate white bed," which has been so magnificently introduced by a midline, uppercase "And," itself introduced by one of those breathless dashes.

The poem is built of six noun phrases, subjects that promise to lead to verbs and then do not, deferring all action to beyond or after the poem, and thereby riveting the reader's attention on the objects at hand, while increasing the sense that there is more here than meets the eye, and more that could be expressed. The poem relies heavily on prepositions—"through," "by," "of," "on," "by"—which reveal to the reader's visual imagination the compositional integrity of the piece, despite its teasingly incomplete sentences.

Rather than the directness of rhyme, Williams uses smaller, more subtle sound repetitions to weave his poem together, to give it supple form. "Yellow" echoes "window" in the first stanza, as do the *-er* endings of "flowers" and "lavender." Alliteration works its understated way through the poem: "curtains" and "cleanliness"; "tray," "tumbler," and "turned." In a poem devoid, in true Imagist fashion, of superfluous words, the repetition of the word "glass," tying together stanzas 3 and 4, speaks emphatically and reminds the reader of the capacity of glass to catch and reflect light. In a poem built primarily of quiet, forward-moving iambics, the ending spondee of "white bed" impresses the reader's ear with its sudden substance. The insistence on words indicating cleanliness reveals the poet's yearning for a romantic experience both passionate and wholesome, both voluptuous and chaste, purged of guilt and capable of expressing full *joie de vivre.*

Williams resisted symbolism because he felt it too readily and perfunctorily gave up the thing itself for an imposed or imported meaning. However, here the window, the key, the bed, and the glass all declare the beauty and particularity of their physical forms—their ideal reality, their radiant tangibility. This has the paradoxical effect of renewing the symbolic depth and urgency of these objects as potent indicators of intimacy, chosen attributes of a room that will declare its emotional character, if only the reader attends to it as devotedly as does the poet.

Themes and Meanings

"Nantucket" reads as a humble list of things etched out with such care that taken together they add up to a poem spoken by a lover in anticipation of a rendezvous, who savors everything associated with this most significant afternoon. With great delicacy, the poem declines to mention either the beloved or the self, or to speak in what is usually considered the language of emotion. A setting only is described, without the characters, without the action, like a set design revealed for admiration before the action of a play begins. The setting is a bedroom of surpassing beauty and privacy—perhaps in a cottage guesthouse on Nantucket in high summer—as yet untouched, all in readiness, redolent of its own imminent moment of romantic intimacy, passion, and fulfillment.

Like a white page, the white bed awaits its inevitable story. The flowers "changed by white curtains" and the sunshine are all of the wide outdoors that is admitted; the key assures privacy and suggests possession, for a time, of a room's contours and comforts. "For love, all love of other sights controls,/ And makes one little room, an everywhere" as the seventeenth century metaphysical poet John Donne would have it, in his own poem extolling a room set apart for lovemaking, "The Good-Morrow."

Throughout his career, Williams believed in the energies of love and sexual attraction and in the clear presentation of what was in front of his eyes. In this poem, he uses the latter to increase the unspoken power of the former. The poem delights precisely because it does not insist on its own profundity or importance, or on a melodramatic or ideological defense of sexual love; it merely luxuriates in its own present physical surroundings, which are felt to reflect the observer's desire and anticipate its fulfillment.

The poem "Nantucket" serves to demonstrate, within its small compass, many of Williams's characteristic themes, and particularly his conviction that the world is always full of fresh meaning, available by means of close attention and aesthetic imagination. As in so many of his poems, it is charged with eroticism, more startling and wonderful here for being held back, diffused through the entire atmosphere. With its painterly framing, attention to color, arrangement of constituent elements, and emphasis on sight, it declares Williams's appetite for visual art, his careerlong willingness to learn from the techniques and insights of painters.

The poem's preference for beauty and its optimism presses back against the strain of dark pessimism and alienation expressed by other poets of his generation, particularly T. S. Eliot, with whom he had many standing differences in temperament and opinion. It defers to other poems Williams's own tendencies toward disgust and despair and his worry that the United States could sustain no more than a "thin veneer" of culture, apt to corrupt rather than elevate. Yet, to catalog the world as it appears in the here and now, on a particular and particularly American island, in language only slightly elevated from the vernacular, to celebrate sex, love, and beauty, to note the upside-down position of a glass tumbler, to generate delight and anticipation by means of inventive prosody—these are among the tasks that Williams set himself and realized in the poem "Nantucket."

Sara Lundquist

A NARROW FELLOW IN THE GRASS

Author: Emily Dickinson (1830-1886)
Type of poem: Lyric
First published: 1866, as "The Snake"; collected in *Poems: Second Series*, 1891

The Poem

"A narrow Fellow in the Grass" (the title is not Emily Dickinson's, since she did not title her poems) is a short poem of thirty-two lines divided into five stanzas. The poem begins and ends with two balanced stanzas of four lines each, which surround a central stanza of eight lines. Dickinson's poems appear to many readers to be written in free verse; the underlying metrical structure of her poetry, however, incorporates the traditional pattern of English hymnody: alternating lines of eight syllables and six syllables. Although Dickinson employs this traditional metrical pattern as a model in her verse, she frequently violates and strains against its conventions.

The poem is written in the first person from the point of view of an adult male ("Yet when a Boy, and Barefoot—/ I"). The poem thus uses the voice of a persona—a speaker other than the poet—who initiates a cordial relationship with the audience, addressing the reader directly: "You may have met Him—did you not."

The poem is structured to relate the speaker's experience in encountering nature, specifically in the form of a snake. The speaker begins by characterizing the snake in friendly, civilized terms: The snake is a "Fellow" who "rides" in the grass, a familiar presence that even the reader has encountered. Again, in the second stanza, the snake appears to act in a civilized manner as it "divides" the grass "as with a comb." Despite the snake's cultured appearance, the first two stanzas introduce the snake's ability to appear and disappear suddenly.

In the third stanza—the central and longest of the poem—the snake's actions become increasingly unpredictable and inexplicable. The speaker notes the snake's preference for "a Boggy Acre," a place "too cool" even for "Corn," let alone human beings, then recounts a childhood incident in which he bent down and attempted to "secure" a snake but it escaped him: "It wrinkled, and was gone." What first appears to be some tool or toy ("a Whip lash") for the child to use or play with eludes not only human control but also human perception and attainment.

The fourth stanza of the poem finds the speaker abruptly back in the present, asserting—again in the polite language of refined society—his connections with the realm of nature: "Several of Nature's People/ I know, and they know me." The speaker insists that his feelings for these inhabitants of nature are ones characterized by "cordiality." This assertion, however, is contradicted in the final stanza by the speaker's depiction of the effect on him each time he encounters the snake: chilling terror ("a tighter breathing/ And Zero at the Bone"). What begins as a poem ostensibly about a snake becomes, in this way, a poem about the effect of an encounter with a snake—and perhaps by extension with nature itself—on an individual human being.

Forms and Devices

One of the most important poetic devices at work in the poem is the tone: the speaker's attitude toward the subject being described, the snake. The tone is deceptively simple and light, referring to the snake as a "Fellow." As the speaker introduces the reader to the snake in the same way that one might introduce an acquaintance, he constructs a metaphor, a way of talking about the snake as if it were a jaunty "Fellow" who "rides" about, a friendly sort whom one surely has "met" in the course of ordinary, everyday life.

The effect of this light, off-handed tone together with the matter-of-fact narration and the metaphorical construction of the snake as an ordinary, civilized "Fellow" is to lead the reader into a situation in which he or she can be taken off guard just as the speaker is unnerved by his encounter with the snake. Indeed, immediately following the initial three-line, polite introduction to the snake, Dickinson jars the reader with one of her characteristic transformations of language: "You may have met Him—did you not/ His notice sudden is." At first glance, one reads these lines as a question followed by a statement about the snake's abrupt appearance: it gives "sudden notice." Dickinson herself insisted, however, that the third and fourth lines of this first stanza were to be read as one statement. Reading as Dickinson intended, then, the verb "is" becomes transformed into a noun with "sudden" as its adjective, and when the speaker apparently asks the reader, "Did you not notice his sudden is?" he assaults the reader's sense of ease and familiarity with language just as the snake has assaulted his sense of being at home in nature. This wrenching of language from its ordinary functions and the emphasis on the poem as an experience for the reader rather than as a preached message are two important characteristics of Dickinson's poetic technique which make her one of the first modern poets.

The progression of metaphors and images which the speaker constructs to describe the snake reflects the speaker's attempts to deal with his encounters with the snake. Beginning as a civilized "Fellow" who neatly divides the grass "as with a Comb," the snake, by the end of the second stanza and the beginning of the third, has become a "spotted shaft." The speaker relates that this ominously threatening object—far from being a civilized companion—prefers to reside in "a Boggy Acre," a place which resists human cultivation.

The narration in the central stanza of a childhood encounter completes the transformation of the snake from the personified "Fellow" to an object. Now the snake is perceived to be first a "Whip lash" and then some ungraspable "it" which engages in a game of hide-and-seek with the speaker.

At the beginning of the fifth stanza, the speaker retreats to his personification of nature's inhabitants, asserting knowledge of and connections with "Nature's People" and the "cordiality" he feels for them. The sixth and final stanza, however, contrasts his sense of ease in nature with his feelings of terror upon meeting the snake: "tighter breathing/ And Zero at the Bone."

Even as the repeated *s* sounds and the serpentine long and short line lengths in the poem's opening seven lines usher the reader into an encounter with the snake, so the varied *o* sounds of the central stanza—boggy, floor, too, cool, corn, boy, barefoot, noon, gone—give way to the full force of the repeated *o* rhymes which arrive at the end of the poem, blow by blow, with the horror of the snake: fellow, alone, zero, bone.

Themes and Meanings

This is a poem about making a journey into nature, one of the characteristic themes of American literature. According to Ralph Waldo Emerson and Henry David Thoreau—two members of the Transcendental movement in American literature, with whom Dickinson has frequently been compared—such an excursion into nature could put human beings in contact with the higher laws of the universe. Dickinson's poem offers both an exploration and a critique of this view. Hers is a poem about coming into contact with nature—moving from a distance to proximity with nature—but more important, it is a poem which contrasts the perceptions of nature from a distance with the reality of nature experienced at first hand.

Although the poem begins with an Emersonian view of nature as accessible to human understanding, it moves from the perception of the snake as a familiar acquaintance to the snake as something which can freeze the speaker with terror. The poem recounts the dissolution of the speaker's sense of ease and familiarity while in nature. The startling encounter with the snake, in fact, evokes his need to assert and reaffirm a sense of connection to the natural world. His assertion of a knowledge of "Nature's People" indicates his desire for a personified nature that he can know. In short, the speaker needs to believe that nature can still function for him—as it did for other Transcendentalists—as the means for "transport" to some higher yet friendly realm: "I feel for them a transport/ of cordiality."

This statement stands in the poem, however, only as the speaker's attempt to reassure himself because nothing else in the encounter with the snake supports the assertion. On the contrary, the central incident in the poem—the bewildering and frightening meeting with the snake—reaffirms with terrifying certainty nature's true relation to the speaker. Rather than a familiar "Fellow" whose recurrent presence can calm, reassure, and keep one company, nature in some of its manifestations plays an alarming game with human beings, often "Unbraiding" or unraveling their grip on reality. Nature's inhabitants appear and disappear suddenly—leaving the observer both terrified ("tighter breathing") and chillingly empty ("Zero at the Bone") of whatever comforting notions about nature he is able to sustain when nature remains at a distance. By the end of the poem, the implications of the "Whip lash" metaphor become clear: the snake as whiplash represents finally both something in nature capable of violence and pain and the scar left on human consciousness by nature's sudden, violent act.

Angela M. Estes

A NAVAJO BLANKET

Author: May Swenson (1919-1989)
Type of poem: Meditation
First published: 1977; collected in *New and Selected Things Taking Place*, 1978

The Poem

"A Navajo Blanket" is a fourteen-line poem in two stanzas of equal length. In the poem, May Swenson is describing the dazzling colors and distinctive designs of a traditional blanket made by the Navajos of the American Southwest. The colors and shapes of the blanket make her think of what the blanket represents—the Navajo people, their culture, landscape, and ceremonies. In this meditation on the blanket, however, she is also writing about an experience in which the individual undergoes a transformation of consciousness through the experience of a work of art.

The appearance of the two stanzas of the poem on the page suggests the shape and design of the blanket. The lines of words across the page are like the rows of thread in a weaving, and the shape of the whole poem is generally rectangular with a zone of space like a band of white across the center. The words "paths" and "maze" describe what the blanket's design looks like and announce that the poet is going to draw the reader into a complex experience, simply as the pattern and color of the blanket draw the eye into its complex design. The first stanza leads the reader into the maze pattern of the blanket, and the second stanza leads the reader out, a movement that seems to imitate the balanced pattern of the blanket itself. She moves through the various associations and states of mind evoked by the blanket, from being dazzled and disturbed by its brightness, to being calmed at its center, and finally, leaving the blanket and its design with a refreshed mind, described in a striking simile as being like "a white cup." The poem is written in the second person ("you"), which draws the reader into the experience and vision. The poet wants the poem to be more than her own personal response to experience.

When Swenson describes the Blue, Red, and Black lines as paths that pull the reader into the "maze," she seems to be saying that there are different ways by which one can enter into the design, simply as there are different ways to approach a work of art or an experience. She uses the word "field" to describe a flat plane, such as the surface of the geometrically patterned blanket, but she also uses the word to suggest an actual field or open space in a landscape. When she says "Alight," there is a change in what is going on in the poem. No longer is this simply a blanket; it is also a place with "gates" and "a hawk" sitting on "the forearm of a Chief." She asks "you" to undergo a transformation, to become something like a hunting hawk in repose. That the hawk is hooded means that one surrenders to the experience blindly as if going into a trance.

At this point, the poem pauses. Consciousness is suspended between day and night, Sun and Moon; there is no sense of time passing. Then the direction of the poem shifts, and the dreamer in the poem follows "the spirit trail, a faint Green thread," an exit that is part of the traditional design of the weaving, and finds a way out of the maze.

At the end of the poem, the mind is described as a white cup that has been washed like a dish. The white cup makes one think of the skull itself, which is now clean and ready to reuse, as the person in the poem returns refreshed to the everyday world. Thus, looking at the blanket has become a spiritual exercise that restores a sense of balance and calm.

Forms and Devices

May Swenson is well known for her ingenious use of language, giving her the ability to re-create a subject visually and aurally. Here the lines of words, the two blocks of words that make up the two stanzas, and the space between the stanzas imitate the appearance of the blanket. Her use of strong colors re-creates the dazzling effect of the blanket. The colors also may be symbolic, although there is no specific explanation of that symbolism in the poem. Perhaps blue and red suggest the sky and red earth of the Southwest. Black may be death, trance, night, or dry vegetation in summer, among other possibilities. Green leads back to life, like something growing or a life-giving river, and white seems to represent enlightenment, calmness, or emptiness. She capitalizes the colors found in the blanket, as she capitalizes Sun and Moon, which gives these words particular importance, whereas "white" is not capitalized and thus seems to be simply a description of something, not a powerful object in itself.

Besides using the visual effect of the poem on the page and visual images in the language, Swenson makes sound an important part of the poem. Although "A Navajo Blanket" does not have a conventional rhyme scheme, she uses the repetition of various sounds to create mood and meaning throughout. In the second line, she uses the alliterative "paths," "pull," and "pin" to emphasize the connection between these words, and the *i* sound in "Brightness" and "eyes" in the third line similarly helps the reader hear the connection in sense between these two words, both of which have to do with seeing. "Hooded" and "hawk," "fasten" and "forearm," and "sleep" and "center" are other alliterative word pairs that give the poem a musical quality and emphasize important words.

The idea of entering into the design of the blanket and then leaving it is also reinforced by some mirroring in the two stanzas, so that, for example, the first and last lines of the poem both involve color, the second lines from top and bottom have to do with movement from one stage to another, the fourth lines from top and bottom have to do with entering and leaving, and so on.

Metaphor is important in Swenson's poetry, and she often develops a comparison that surprises and delights readers once they recognize it, like a riddle that seems obvious after one knows the answer but that is mysterious until one does. At first, the blanket in the poem is simply an object with a bright, hypnotic design, but words such as "paths" and "field" make the reader begin to see the blanket as a landscape. Looking at the blanket becomes a journey into that landscape.

The poetic devices in the poem are never simply decorations of an idea but are an integral part of the poem itself, creating a concrete experience on the page, in the ear, and in the mind's eye.

Themes and Meanings

May Swenson often writes about things in such a way as to transform common objects and experience into something mysterious and new. She is also interested in states of consciousness—sleep, dreams, meditation, trances, life, and death—awareness and the loss of it. In this poem, she is writing about a transformation in consciousness brought about by a work of art. "A Navajo Blanket" combines several subjects. It is a poem celebrating the beauty of a particular kind of Native American craft. It is also about a mystical experience in which the design of the blanket draws the observer into an altered state of awareness. Finally, the poem is about the experience of art itself, which might include poetry as well as weaving and any other art form. She says that art takes one out of oneself and gives renewal and refreshment.

The nature of art and its effect on human life are subjects that are bound to intrigue an artist, particularly a meditative poet such as Swenson, who often finds her inspiration in common things—an eye blinking, a wave rolling up on the beach, a skunk cabbage, or some other object that is so familiar one has stopped really seeing it. In her poems, Swenson restores a sense of awe to the world. The blink of an eyelid becomes a slow series of monstrous events; the movement of waves becomes a perpetual motion machine. So, too, does "A Navajo Blanket" become a key to past and present, the story of a culture, a mysterious maze into which one is compelled to enter and where one undergoes a strange out-of-time experience, and an allegory about the effects of art on the individual. The poem is also about a blanket, a work of art, that is, artifice, something made by human hand and shaped by human imagination.

Swenson's poems often have a strong sense of closure. This one is no exception. In the last line, the cycle is complete, and, like a chalice or a bone china cup, "your mind/ is rinsed and returned to you." Refreshed, one is free to exit the maze of the blanket and the poem itself.

Barbara Drake

THE NEGRO SPEAKS OF RIVERS

Author: Langston Hughes (1902-1967)
Type of poem: Lyric
First published: 1921; collected in *The Weary Blues*, 1926

The Poem

"The Negro Speaks of Rivers" is Langston Hughes's most anthologized poem. Hughes wrote this brief poem in fifteen minutes in July, 1920, while crossing the Mississippi on a train ride to visit his father in Mexico. It is one of Hughes's earliest poems, and its subject established the emphasis of much of his subsequent poetry. Hughes's poems may be divided into several categories: protest poems, social commentary, Harlem poems, folk poems, poems on African and negritude themes, and miscellaneous poetry on various other nonracial subjects and themes. "The Negro Speaks of Rivers" centers on African and negritude themes. Hughes's writing always shows an identification with Africa, and his later poetry on African subjects and African themes demonstrates his growing sophistication and knowledge of the history and problems of Africa. Along with its emphasis on African themes, this poem so poignantly and dramatically expresses what it means to be a black American that it helps to assure Hughes's continuing fame.

Through the images of the river, Hughes traces the history of the African American from Africa to America. The muddy Mississippi makes Hughes consider the roles that rivers have played in human history. The first three lines introduce the subject of the poem. The primary image of water symbolically represents the history of humanity, acknowledging the fact that rivers are more ancient in the history of the earth:

> I've known rivers:
> I've known rivers ancient as the world and older than the flow of
> human blood in human veins.

The next line connects the poet with the river and acknowledges the influence of waterways on the history of the African American: "My soul has grown deep like the rivers." This line is repeated at the end of the poem, reestablishing the connection between the human essence and the river as well as the river's role in African American life.

The middle section reveals the connections between the history of the African American and four important rivers of the world: the Euphrates, the Congo, the Nile, and the Mississippi. The three African rivers are a part of the ancient history of black people when they were free, living in majestic kingdoms and forming the great civilizations of Africa. The poem more specifically relates to the African American, who is the victim of slavery and discrimination in the New World, where rivers were used to transport black slaves.

The last section of the poem, "I've known rivers:/ Ancient, dusky, rivers// My soul has grown deep like the rivers," re-emphasizes the beginning section by restating the influence of rivers on the soul and life of black people from antiquity to the twentieth century. The final line of the poem repeats the statement that connects the human soul to the rivers of the world.

Forms and Devices

"The Negro Speaks of Rivers" is a lyric poem. Lyric poetry is rooted in song and establishes the ritual of the human condition, in this case the condition of black people. In this poem, Hughes is both teller (poet) and participant (African American) in the drama being described. Through the intense images of this poem, the reader is able to participate in the emotion and poignancy of the history of black people. Since Hughes discusses this history beyond that in America, he transcends localism and projects upon his reader a world experience.

The diction of the poem is simple and unaffected by rhetorical excess. It is eloquent in its simplicity, allowing readers of all ages and levels of sophistication to enjoy a first reading; however, as one reads this poem, the deeper meaning reveals itself.

The primary image of "The Negro Speaks of Rivers" is water; its function as the river of time is to trace the heritage and past of the African American. The flowing, lyrical lines, like water, are charged with meaning, describing what the river has meant to black people in America. Hughes's poetic ability and technical virtuosity are nowhere as evident as in this short poem, which formed the basis for his early acceptance as a brilliant poet. Hughes uses the repeated line "My soul has grown deep like the rivers" to emphasize the way rivers symbolize not only the physical history of the African American but the spiritual history ("my soul") as well. The river is also a symbol of the strength of black people as survivors who move through history. Finally, the rivers reflect the direct path of blacks to America.

The entire poem is based on an extended metaphor comparing the heritage of the African American to the great rivers of the world. The poet reveals the relationship between the river and the lives of black people, starting with a river known to be important during the earliest great civilizations and ending with a river on which slaves were transported, to be bought and sold in the slave markets of America.

Themes and Meanings

Langston Hughes was deeply concerned with the history and social condition of his people. "The Negro Speaks of Rivers" reflects the poet's interest in both topics. This poem also speaks of a mystic union of blacks throughout the world, for it traces their history back to the creation of the world, giving them credit for spanning time and for founding the greatest civilizations that humanity has ever known.

Hughes received the inspiration for this poem as he crossed the Mississippi River by train, feeling melancholy yet drawing pride from thoughts of the rivers that played a part in the history of his race. The images of beauty and death, and of hope and despair, all fused in his adolescent sensibility, causing him to create one of his most beautiful poems. The use of words such as "soul" and "rivers" allows Hughes to touch the deepest feelings and spiritual longings of his own soul and the souls of his people. With the use of the words "deep," "flow," "dusky," and "ancient," Hughes describes the actual rivers that were involved in black history, all the while emphasizing the long and glorious history of his race. With this poem, Hughes, often called "the poet of his people," plunges into the deep well of African American history, uniting it with global African history.

The poem, with its allusions to the setting sun, human blood, and deep, dusky rivers, suffuses the images of death as it speaks of the immortality of the soul. Hughes celebrates the life of black people by acknowledging death, but the images of death presented in the poem are overshadowed by emphasis on the life of the soul—in this case, a racial soul which runs throughout time like a river. As the muddy water of the Mississippi turns golden in the sunset, so does the poet turn the memory of the history and survival of his people into brilliance. With images of water and pyramid, the verse suggests the endurance of the black physical presence and spirit from ancient Egypt to the nineteenth and twentieth centuries. The muddy Mississippi caused Hughes to think about the roles in human history played by the Congo, the Niger, and the Nile, as slaves were passed down these waters to be sold; once sold, these same slaves may have ended up being sold again on the Mississippi. The Mississippi also caused Hughes to think about Abraham Lincoln and the role he played in the abolition of slavery in the United States.

Pride in one's history is a constant theme in the poem. Hughes views the history of black people, even in slavery, with a sense of pride as he points out the ability of his people to survive their harsh and violent treatment in America. Hughes's confidence in the strength of blackness is a major part of his theme of pride; this confidence and pride is his legacy to African Americans. Black culture is still embattled, but Hughes provides a device for countering the argument that black people are without a vital and universal history.

Betty Taylor-Thompson

NEITHER OUT FAR NOR IN DEEP

Author: Robert Frost (1874-1963)
Type of poem: Lyric
First published: 1934; collected in *A Further Range*, 1936

The Poem

"Neither Out Far nor In Deep" is a lyric poem consisting of four four-line stanzas, making use of a regular rhyme scheme (*abab*). The meter is for the most part regular iambic trimeter, although several lines include one or two extra syllables. Only in the second stanza does Robert Frost provide precise imagery; for the most part, he relies on general description.

The setting of the poem is the seaside. The poet's original observation is that the people, out for a day's recreation at the beach, always look toward the water; "They turn their back on the land." What they can see are a ship out on the ocean, passing to an unknown destination, and a gull standing on the wet sand near the water.

This is apparently a puzzle, since there is more variety and presumably more of interest on the land than on the ocean, which does nothing but come to the beach and then retreat. The Line "Wherever the truth may be" in the third stanza suggests that the people are searching for the truth and hope to find it by watching the unchanging ocean, with its endless repetitions of the same movements, rather than on the land, which presumably is more subject to change.

The people being described, like everyone else, have limited vision: "They cannot look out far./ They cannot look in deep." Yet they keep on looking, presumably because there is nothing else for them to do. They cannot help searching for answers, even from such an unlikely source as the inscrutable ocean.

Forms and Devices

The regularity of the form and the abruptness of the lines reinforce the ironic tone of "Neither Out Far nor In Deep." The form implies a rigidity in the minds of the people being described, a lack of imagination which leads them always to look in one direction, however unrewarding their study may be. The poet distances himself from them with the occasional extra syllables which prevent the rhythm of the poem from taking on a sing-song quality.

The language and imagery are unusually generalized for Frost, who preferred to employ specific imagery. The poet does use the word "sand" to represent the entire shoreline, and the second stanza does contain relatively precise visual images of the ship, hull down out at sea, and the "standing gull," but all the other imagery in the poem is deliberately general. Those being described are not individualized in any way; they are simply "The people." That they lack individuality is emphasized by the fact that they turn a singular "back" to the land, instead of individual "backs." They all behave in the same way.

This generalized imagery continues in the third stanza. "The land" is given no specific qualities or dimensions; it only "may vary more." The ocean reaching the shore is not described in terms of breaking waves, foam, or swirling surf; it is only "the water." This seems to suggest that the people in their looking fail to see anything in detail, which can only be one more obstacle to their understanding.

What has seemed to be simple and general description of a common scene has become increasingly ironic through the first three stanzas, and the ironic tone becomes even more forceful in the final stanza, where the poet's scorn for those he describes becomes almost overwhelming. His scorn is not for the question they seem to ask, but for their approach to it. Their vision is extremely limited; they are neither farsighted nor able to look deeply into the questions of existence. They hope that the ocean will give them answers to the ultimate questions, but they are looking at an aspect of the world which is simply there, unchanging in its nature, providing no answers at all. They continue to look, however, since the limitations on their ability to see have never prevented them from continuing their search. The heavy emphasis on the three final words accents the irony. The final irony, available to the reader, is that the poet is no better than they are; he cannot see any deeper or farther than they can.

Themes and Meanings

Frost's poems describing relatively ordinary scenes or events often conclude by raising much larger issues about the meaning of life and death and the nature of reality. Some of these poems, including the popular early poems "The Tuft of Flowers," "Two Look at Two," "The Onset," or the excellent but little-known late lyric, "On the Heart's Beginning to Cloud the Mind," conclude by suggesting a positive answer— that all will somehow be well, and that man's deepest fears are unjustified.

Yet as the critic Lionel Trilling pointed out in a famous speech, given at a dinner celebrating Frost's eighty-fifth birthday, there is another side to Frost's work which belies the easy confidence of those poems in which he assumes the guise of a kindly, reassuring old Yankee. "Neither Out Far nor In Deep," like such other poems as "Design," "Once by the Pacific," "Home Burial," and "Desert Places," evokes the grimness and eventual emptiness of human existence without offering any consolation or grounds for hope. This kind of poem represents an entirely different side of Frost, an entirely different way of responding to those ultimate questions.

"Neither Out Far nor In Deep" was one of the poems cited by Trilling. At first glance its inclusion among the author's grimmer works seems questionable. On the surface, the poem is little more than an amusing observation about an ordinary scene—people at beaches, after all, do always look toward the ocean, and what they see might well include a ship passing out at sea and at least one gull standing where a wave has left water on the sand.

The poem turns around with the second line of stanza 3, "But wherever the truth may be—." Frost here introduces the idea that the people looking toward the ocean are (or ought to be) doing more than casually staring; they hope that the ocean can somehow bring them the truth. As the final line makes clear, their looking is not casual, for they are keeping "watch." This suggests both alertness and danger, since those who keep watch, like soldiers, ordinarily do so because they fear what might be out there.

As the poem clearly suggests, however, their watch is futile. On the one hand, the ocean does not divulge its secrets; nothing happens except that "The water comes ashore" ceaselessly, an endless repetition of wave on wave, the ebb and flow of the tides, reflected in the rhythm of the short, insistent lines. On the other hand, their watch is futile because of the limitations imposed on human vision—these anonymous people are simply not equipped for the task of finding answers to the deeper questions of life.

Frost seems to have been unable to ignore questions of final meaning. Such questions crop up in a high percentage of his poems. The closest he came to resolving them was to say, in "On the Heart's Beginning to Cloud the Mind," "I knew a tale of a better kind" and to choose to believe that tale. In "Neither Out Far nor In Deep," however, he makes no such choice. Rather, he is both observer and participant in a search for meaning in which the searchers fear what they cannot see; the search for meaning is doomed to fail.

John M. Muste

NEUTRAL TONES

Author: Thomas Hardy (1840-1928)
Type of poem: Dramatic monologue
First published: 1898, in *Wessex Poems and Other Verses*

The Poem

Thomas Hardy's poem "Neutral Tones" is a dramatic monologue consisting of four tetrameter quatrains. The speaker addresses an estranged lover and reminisces about a foreseen moment in their past, which anticipated the demise of their relationship. The first three stanzas describe the past incident, and the fourth stanza reflects upon this incident and the nature of love. It is a sad, pessimistic poem that portrays love as painful and doomed.

The first stanza paints the scene. Bleak landscape features set a dismal tone and reflect the bitter mindset of the speaker. The lovers stand by a pond on a winter day. Winter can be a lifeless season, and all the details of the scene contribute to a mood of torpor or constriction. Instead of being bright or even glaring, the sun is "white," as if drained of all its vitality. Dead leaves lie on the ground as a reminder of the end of the natural cycle of life and death. These leaves are "gray" and come from an "ash": Both words reinforce the gloominess of this colorless, inert scene. Other details contribute to a feeling of disappointment and threat. For example, the sun is described "as though chidden of God" and the ground is called the "starving sod."

The next two stanzas, which describe the lover, sustain the dismal mood and increase the feeling of menace. The description of the woman's glance and their conversation suggests that their love had become boring and meaningless to her. Things become even more dire in stanza 3, when the lover's smile is likened—in a metaphor instead of the simile of stanza 2—to "the deadest thing/ Alive," and her bitter grin is compared to "an ominous bird a-wing."

The pain predicted by this bitter grin is confirmed in stanza 4. This moment spelled the death of their relationship, but even more pain and suffering followed in the deceptions and wrongs that ensued. The hurt that the speaker suffered is intensified by the puns on "keen," "wring," and "edge." Used figuratively, the literal or concrete meanings of these words imply physical pain. The vagueness and generalized tone of this last stanza implies that the assertion that "love deceives,/ And wrings with wrongs" is a generalization that applies to all love, not just this particular love.

Forms and Devices

Many prosodic devices contribute to the mood of exhaustion and doom. A tetrameter line is shorter than the English norm, a pentameter. These short lines' feelings of sparseness and constraint underline the feelings created by words such as "starving" and reflect the speaker's impoverished, bitter spirit. Iambic tetrameter lines generally have a quicker pace than iambic pentameters, producing a sense of energy. However, many monosyllabic words and an abundance of anapests retard the pace of these lines. In the first stanza, for example, line 1 has one anapest, line 2 has three anapests, line 3 has two anapests, and line 4 has two anapests. The poem has twenty-three anapests or dactyls. The many unaccented syllables in anapests or dactyls weaken a line and contribute to a sense of fatigue and alienation. There are also quite a few trochaic feet. Trochees and dactyls, which consist of an accented syllable followed by unaccented syllables, are "downbeat" and suggest disappointment or diminishment.

Alliteration, assonance, and rhyme also reinforce many words' negative connotations. "Day," in line 1, is not inherently negative, but its rhyming associations with "gray" and "lay" infect the "winter's day" with bleak fatigue. The alliteration in "leaves," "lay," and "fallen" underline their torpor. The assonance of the long *e* in "keen" and "deceives" taints the bare "tree" in the first and last stanzas with peril. The assonance of many low-frequency vowel sounds, such as *oo* ("stood"), *aw* ("God"), and *ah* ("fallen"), brings down the mood of the poem.

The diction is simple, with almost entirely one- or two-syllable words. In such a context the threatening archaic word "chidden" attracts attention. The only three-syllable words in the poem—"tedious," "bitterness," and "ominous"—also stand out and mark the defining features of the couple's love.

The poem's syntax is, for the most part, also simple. Therefore, when the syntax is awkward, it calls attention to itself. The syntax that describes the landscape in the first stanza is straightforward. Four simple clauses, with one long prepositional phrase, are joined by the word "and." All four lines are end-stopped at predictable syntactic pauses.

As the speaker describes his lover in the next two stanzas, however, the syntax begins to contort. It is as if the memory of the lover has crippled the speaker's language and imagination. The farther he progresses into the description, the more awkward the syntax becomes. Enjambed lines that no longer pause with the syntax betray his mental perturbation. The last line in the second stanza, which describes the meaninglessness of their conversation, is all but unintelligible: "On which lost the more by our love." The next stanza's inverted word order, enjambment, and semantic as well as syntactic confusion in the descriptions of deadness and aliveness also reveal the speaker's failing powers. The speaker is so injured by love that his fraught mind is at a loss for words as he tries to relate his experience. This poem is about the failure of spirit and imagination as well as love.

Themes and Meanings

One of Hardy's earliest poems, "Neutral Tones" was written in 1867 but not published until 1898. A prolific fiction writer, Hardy did not start publishing his poems until he was fifty-eight years old and had finished his career as a novelist. Although this poem was written in the middle of the Victorian era (1837-1901), it reflects the *fin de siècle* consciousness of its publication date. *Fin de siècle* works often evoke feelings of exhaustion and disillusionment.

Hardy's Victorian sensibility was forced reluctantly into the modern world. He was nostalgic for the security and optimism of the Victorian era, but he stoically and uncompromisingly faced the harsh realities of modernity. This often led to pessimistic works. His career straddles the Victorian and modern periods. Scholars often treat his novels *Tess of the D'Urbervilles* (1891) and *Jude the Obscure* (1895) and his poetry as modern and his earlier novels as Victorian. In spite of its traditional verse, "Neutral Tones" has many qualities that would come to be seen as modern.

One of the hallmarks of modern literature is irony. The disparity between what things seem to be or what things pretend to be and what they really are resonates with the modern consciousness. Many of Hardy's poems are ironic; he even has a volume of poems called *Satires of Circumstance*. The title of this poem, "Neutral Tones," is ironic. The colors of the landscape are "neutral," but the mood (or "tone") these colors create is dismal, not neutral. The lover's features, such as her eyes and her smile, may seem neutral or indifferent, but they are in actuality bitter and hurtful.

The poem's attention to the mundane details of a seemingly trivial moment is also modern. The scale, scope, and ambitions of modern poetry are considerably reduced; its typical mode is understatement. Romantic poets soared to reveal the wonders of the imagination and aspired to be the "legislators of the world." Victorian poetry preached the truths of science, philosophy, religion, and politics unabashedly. Modern poets, who had lost confidence in their own authority and also the authority of institutions, focused much more narrowly. Virginia Woolf's "moments of being," James Joyce's "epiphanies," and Ezra Pound's Imagism all result from this circumscribed scope. The attention to a particular moment also grows out of realism's emphasis on the everyday. Realism held that seemingly unimportant people could be important, and seemingly insignificant details or moments could hold significance.

In "Neutral Tones" the speaker's imaginative failure comments on a failure of the modern imagination in general. Hardy's poems frequently ask whether or not the circumstances of modernity can foster a vital imagination. The speaker's mention of "an ominous bird a-wing" alludes to and contrasts with the many exultant birds in Romantic poetry, especially the nightingales. In nineteenth century British Romantic poetry, nightingales stimulate the imaginations of their eloquent, inspired speakers.

"Neutral Tones" has the form of a conversation poem, or greater Romantic lyric, which was commonly adopted by Romantic poets William Wordsworth, Samuel Coleridge, Percy Bysshe Shelley, and John Keats. These poems begin in a particular landscape, soar to an imaginative vision, and then return to reflect upon the landscape and vision that have transformed the speaker. This poem recalls this form, except that the speaker fails to have an imaginative vision and is not transformed. Hardy seems to imply that the modern world stymies the spirits of its poets and its people.

Laura Cowan

NEW YEAR LETTER

Author: W. H. Auden (1907-1973)
Type of poem: Epistle/letter in verse
First published: 1941, as "Letter to Elizabeth Mayer"; collected in *The Double Man,* 1941

The Poem

"New Year Letter" is an occasional poem written to commemorate the beginning of 1940. Although it is a letter to W. H. Auden's friend Elizabeth Mayer, its scope greatly exceeds the parameters of most personal letters, as it reflects upon an incredible range of subjects. It can be considered primarily a meditation on World War II and a tribute to Auden's friend. The poem's three parts develop by association rather than by logic.

Part 1 focuses on the disorder of the world in 1940, the human desire for order, and the order that art creates. It begins with a depiction of Americans filing along the streets on January 1, 1940. Auden captures the mixed atmosphere of "singing," "sighing," "doubt," and anticipation in the United States; which had not yet entered the war but was acutely aware of it. The Americans' preoccupation with "Retrenchment, Sacrifice, Reform" reminds Auden of the atmosphere of anticipation and fear in Brussels "twelve months ago"—before the war had begun.

Vague about the cause of contemporary social problems, Auden describes Europe as a "haunted house" threatened by "the presence of The Thing." His concluding statements compare the worldwide dilemma to a crime in a conventional mystery novel: "The situation of our time/ Surrounds us like a baffling crime./ There lies the body half-undressed// And under lock and key the cause/ That makes a nonsense of our laws." The poet wants to warn against too easily blaming or accusing others. All are responsible for the crises of 1940: "our equipment all the time/ Extends the area of the crime/ Until the guilt is everywhere." The principles that underlie civilization have failed.

A discussion of art and a catalog of "great masters" of literature follow. Auden celebrates art because of its harmonious order, which can enlighten and inspire: "For art had set in order sense/ And feeling and intelligence,/ And from its ideal order grew/ Our local understanding." This tribute to art and artists, however, ranging from Dante through Rainer Maria Rilke, is confused by constant disclaimers. The impulse to impose art's order upon life willfully results in fascism. In this poem, he "would disown,/ The preacher's loose inmodest tone." "No words men write," Auden claims at the end of part 1, "can stop the war." Yet, art—the "greatest of vocations"—can give order to be imitated and general parables that can be applied to the particulars of human lives: Just as it is necessary to search in order to understand the parables behind art, one must search to understand one's personal and political lives.

The danger inherent in art's order and the too fervent desire for order or "preacherly" truths is developed in part 2's discussion of the preference for absolutes, for "*idées fixes* to be/ True of a fixed Reality." Part 2 examines evil but always returns to the heresy of the search for absolutes. It begins with a portrait of an Inferno-like landscape, the world of World War II. The entire section maintains an allegorical atmosphere by personifying evil as the devil.

The fear of change and the desire for personal and social perfection lead to the monism that Auden decries in his criticisms of "vague idealistic art" and the "Simon-pure Utopian." Good and bad people alike have been guilty of fixed commitments to inflexible ideals. Auden demonstrates the inevitable error of such a devotion in his description of characters as disparate as the devil ("Prince of Lies"), Sarah Whitehead, William Wordsworth, and Karl Marx.

Although Auden believes in an eternity which transcends the imperfect human condition, he does not believe that humans can apprehend this perfection. The devil is the "Prince of Lies" because he pretends to be the "Spirit-that-denies" this imperfection. Ironically, Original Sin underlies the duality that the devil would disprove. Change is inevitable and, because of humanity's fallen nature, the truth cannot be known. Auden's discussions of Marx, Christ, and Charles Darwin praise them for the falsehoods that they betrayed. The inevitable duality of human beings and the impossibility of absolutes lead Auden to the paradox of the essential human condition. The ability to live with this paradox and to accept the multiplicity of human lives results in the "gift of double focus."

Part 3 develops the poem's recurring topics and specifically blames industrialism and the Enlightenment for World War II. It begins with a description of the disorder of New Year debauches in New York City, which Auden juxtaposes to the order and harmony of Mayer's house a week earlier. This order created by art and love is a model of the "real republic" for which all should strive. Yet, such order cannot be imposed. Humans live in an imperfect world of "Becoming" rather than a perfect world of "Being," which results in choice and freedom. Freely accepting the inevitable imperfection of the world can allow for moments of "perfect Being."

Auden next turns to the chaos and anxiety around him and contrasts the catastrophes of 1940 with the fall of Roman civilization. Whereas "Rome's hugger-mugger unity" was destroyed by the animal forces of barbarians, modern civilization has been destroyed by the intellectual powers of industry. Hitler—whom he describes as a "theologian" and a self-created "choice"—is a direct result of the selfishness that drives modern culture.

Auden insists that humans recognize that they live in both private and public worlds, explains the importance of history in the formation of human character, and reminisces about his childhood in England. England differs from the United States, which as a "fully alienated land" epitomizes the modern condition. These reflections on alienation lead to a description of the war in Europe, which he explicitly blames on the Renaissance and the Enlightment. The religious (Martin Luther, Councils, translations), philosophical (Michel de Montaigne, scholars), political ("Prince" Niccolo Machiavelli, cavalry), and scientific (navigation) changes of the Renaissance resulted in "Empiric Economic Man." The rationality, selfishness, and free will of this new culture were responsible for isolation and loss of community.

Auden admits that the material conditions of human existence have improved and that this cultural revolution has never completely dominated: Jean-Jacques Rousseau, Søren Kierkegaard, William Blake, and Charles Baudelaire all protested its philosophy. The freedom that humans have given themselves has turned on them. They blame politicians and governments for failures, but a harmonic community necessitates an acceptance of personal responsibility for contemporary crises.

The rest of the poem indicts the selfishness, materialism, free will, and isolation of Empiric Economic Man, especially as realized in American culture. New York's skyscrapers are condemned as "secular cathedrals," and machines are blamed for revealing that "aloneness is man's real condition." Auden argues that the only way to create a unified community is to recognize failings and to accept others' weaknesses and differences: "true democracy begins/ With free confessions of our sins" and "all real unity commences/ In consciousness of differences."

The poet invokes a series of beneficent and loving powers (Unicorn, white childhood, Dove, Ichthus, Wind, Clock). He then addresses his "dear friend Elizabeth," whose loving kindness brings peace and "a warmth throughout the universe." He ends by admitting human imperfections and thanking Mayer for "forgiving, helping," and illuminating the world with love.

Forms and Devices

"New Year Letter" is a verse epistle in rhyming tetrameter couplets. It was the second poem in Auden's collection of poems entitled *The Double Man* (1941; entitled *New Year Letter* in England). Its fifty-six pages of rhymed couplets were followed by eighty-seven pages of notes to the poem. These notes include citations that explain particular lines, sections from works whose meanings bear on the poem, and additional poems by Auden. The poem is most fully understood with its explanatory notes and in the context of this volume.

Long and carefully contoured verse epistles and verse essays reached their height during the Augustan Period of English Literature with Alexander Pope and Jonathan Swift. Auden reverts to a decorous and social poetic form used by poets who lived in a more socially coherent time. His verse is formal; its rhythm and rhymes are exact. He uses this conventional, traditional verse to suggest the unity and coherence to which lives and art, and the world, should aspire.

Although he observes such traditional conventions, Auden uses many technical devices that call this order into question. Auden's shorter line gives his epistle a momentum and urgency that iambic pentameter couplets lack. His heavy use of enjambment also pressures the pace of his lines and prevents his couplets from becoming predictable or monotonous.

One of Auden's main arguments is the impossibility of absolute or "preacherly" truths. It is a great feat, however, to use a metaphysical and rational discourse while denying the validity of such a discourse. Auden undoes his primary discourse in several ways, especially in his notes to the text. Beneath the apparently smooth surface of tetrameter couplets lies an array of fragmented poems, notes, and excerpts which constantly suggests chaos. Auden's description of the "snarl of the abyss/ That always lies just underneath/ Our jolly picnic on the heath" could apply to the relationship between the poem and its notes.

The self-consciousness of Auden's use of traditional form, apparent in the omnipresent comedy and humor, destabilizes the text. Comic rhymes—such as "links and thinks"—present specific examples of the humor that pervades this text: The devil knows "that he's lost if someone ask him/ To come the hell in off the links/ And say exactly what he thinks." Comic rhyme and diction constantly undermine the authority of the poem, even as it speaks wisdom. Humorous and irreverent diction, such as "through the Janus of a joke/ The candid psychopompos spoke," seems to trivialize Auden's insights. They exist, however, in order to avoid the egotism and self-importance that he deplores.

Another prominent formal device is the use of periphrasis or euphemism. Auden rarely names his subjects: He does not say, "We are at war," but rather mentions "the situation of our time." His description of war or fascism as "the presence of The Thing" that hangs over Europe is vague and unspecific. He does not name Rousseau, Marx, Christ, or Darwin, but rather refers elliptically to "a liberal fellow-traveler," "the German who,/ Obscure in gaslit London," "the ascetic farmer's son," and the "naturalist, who fought/ Pituitary headaches." The United States is "that other world" in which I stand/ Of fully alienated land." Auden's refusal to name is a denial of authority and is a way of involving the reader in his text. The poem insists that literature be used as parables to help unravel the mystery novels of history. Auden's evasion compels the reader to probe and search his poem as he would have one probe and search the world for understanding.

Themes and Meanings

Auden surveys the world around him in 1940 and finds isolated individuals at war with one another. He wants a plural, loving community which he describes at various points in the poem: "The seamless live continuum/ Of supple and coherent stuff,/ Whose form is truth, whose content love,/ Its pluralistic interstices/ The homes of happiness and peace,/ Where in a unity of praise/ The largest publicum's a res,/ And the least *res* a *publicum*. The importance of a genuine, unselfish love touches almost every aspect of Auden's discussion. Great art, for example, is praised because of its ability to engender "charity, delight, increase." The tribunal of former artists who oversees contemporary artists does not judge them, but rather "love[s]" them. Marx is praised because of his charity and because of his discovery that "none shall receive unless they give;/ All must co-operate to live."

In order to undo the isolating and alienating tendencies of civilization, Auden suggests humble acceptance of one's own limitations and living a life which contributes to others. Auden's letter itself acts out many of the aspects central to his message. As both a letter and a tribute to his friend Elizabeth Mayer, it is a loving and unselfish act which gestures outside himself and ends in humble recognition of his own inadequacies. It is also important to Auden's themes that both he and Mayer are exiles—aliens in the most alienated of countries—and that she is German. Auden cautions against too quickly casting blame for "the situation of our time" on one nation, people, or political party. Adolf Hitler is a product of a civilization for which all are responsible. By hating or dismissing all Germans, the Allies would be no better than he.

The description of Auden's loving community—"the seamless live continuum"— ends with *res* and *publicum* united. Personal responsibility for civilization's founderings means that a thing cannot be separated meaningfully from its society. Part 3 explains the fallacy of presuming that public and private lives can be separated. "New Year Letter," however, highlights the importance of the private life by continually referring to the little worlds of order that Mayer creates. Preoccupations with political problems were causing Auden's contemporaries to shun the private life and to disdain the personal as a subject of poetry. "New Year Letter" makes clear that personal gardens must be cultivated if the public situation is to be salvaged. The poet's frequent turning from general description to personal address highlights this fact.

The importance of both public and private lives is implicated in the title of this volume, *The Double Man.* The title embraces the multiple aspects of human beings and underlines the most important operative principle in the poem: paradox. This paradox resulted from the Fall and has governed the human existence of mixed uncertainty and faith ever since. The inevitability of human imperfections accounts for the mixed tone that describes life as a "reverent frivolity" and that underlies the confusing, tortured play with words and contradictions. The omnipresence of paradox discredits linear, rational thought.

Laura Cowan

NEW YEAR LETTER

Author: Marina Tsvetayeva (1892-1941)
Type of poem: Epistle/letter in verse
First published: 1928, as "Novogodnee" in *Versty III*; English translation collected in
   Selected Poems, 1987

The Poem

One of the greatest friendships in the life of the Russian poet Marina Tsvetayeva
was conducted wholly by letter during a few months of 1926 with the Austrian writer
Rainer Maria Rilke. Rilke, one of the most important German-language poets of the
twentieth century, represented for Tsvetayeva the ideal poet. After Rilke died unexpectedly on December 29, 1926, Tsvetayeva's shock and grief took the form of several works in prose and verse that reacted to his death. "New Year Letter," written in
February, 1927, is an attempt to come to terms with Rilke's death. It also represents
one side of a companionable conversation between two poets about their craft and
constitutes a statement about Tsvetayeva's philosophy of poetry.

The poem, written in the first person and addressed to Rilke, opens with the traditional Russian New Year's greeting, *S novym godom*, "Happy New Year." Tsvetayeva
calls the poem "my first epistle to you in your new/ . . . place"—that is, in the after-
world—thus implying that the poem is a continuation of their previous correspondence and denying the power of death. The poem then describes how Tsvetayeva
learned of Rilke's death when an acquaintance dropped by to ask if she would write a
memorial piece about him for a newspaper. Tsvetayeva, who cannot conceive that the
great poet is dead, and who regards an acknowledgment of his death as a kind of betrayal, refuses; most of the remaining part of the poem is concerned with her ideas
about writing as an act of immortality, and about the life of the poet as both eternal and
full of sacrifice. It is couched in the form of a letter to Rilke, who, as a newcomer in
heaven, is still getting accustomed to the working conditions there.

The poem alludes to a number of things that appear in the two poets' letters to each
another (such as Rilke's questions about specific Russian words) or in Rilke's poetry
(such as the famous Orlov trotting horses, which appear in his poem "Nächtliche
Fahrt. St. Petersburg" [1908, Night Ride, St. Petersburg]). Throughout the poem,
Tsvetayeva asks Rilke questions about his new state of being, assuming almost the
role of an interviewer. She wants to know what the journey was like, and asks about
his first impressions of the universe and his last ones of the planet Earth. Tsvetayeva
implicitly compares the human world to a sad farce when she portrays Rilke leaning
over the "scarlet rim" of his theater box and looking down on humanity from his position beyond death.

In the next section, the focus shifts from Rilke's new situation to Tsvetayeva's, as
she recalls that New Year's Eve is almost upon her, and wonders with whom and to
what she can drink a toast. Rilke's death has made her pensive, and she does not wish

to celebrate in the usual boisterous fashion. Instead, she says, she will drink a quiet toast with Rilke to his new, third state of being, which is neither life nor death, but, she implies, a kind of place outside time where poetry is created. Tsvetayeva ponders the many obstacles that life throws in the path of a poet and concludes that Rilke has achieved this new state, where he will create with a "new sound," "new echo," "new hand-position."

The last section presents Tsvetayeva's wishful vision of the afterlife: a succession of Heavens ascending like terraces; a succession of growing, mutable Gods (referring to a central image in Rilke's works); and finally, a ladder rising into the sky above Rarogne, the Swiss village where Rilke is buried. The poem ends with the poet's hopes of someday meeting Rilke after all, and with the image of Tsvetayeva herself climbing up the ladder, her hands filled with gifts for him—the gifts of her poems.

Forms and Devices

"New Year Letter" is a poem of some 195 lines of varying length that uses a variety of metrical patterns. Rather than being organized into regular stanzas, the poem is divided into sections, ranging from four to thirty-two lines long, according to subject matter and to the rhythm of the poet's thought processes. Sections sometimes contrast with the sections that precede them in tone or lexical level, as, for example, when an emotionally charged passage is followed by a laconic, colloquial one. One device that serves as a kind of structural leitmotif is the formula "Happy . . .," which is used in the first line to wish Rilke a happy New Year. This phrase, with other objects substituted for "New Year"—such as "Happy break of day," "Happy whole me," "Happy new world"—appears throughout the poem. The phrase underscores the sense of new beginnings associated both with the day and with Tsvetayeva's conception of the "third state" in which Rilke now finds himself. It also bears with it the theme of generosity and giving, which was important to both poets and figured in their correspondence.

It is difficult to explain the linguistic innovations of a poem written in one language to an audience who will read it in another. This is especially true of Tsvetayeva, whose uniqueness lies at least in part in her bold, fresh treatment of Russian. Her poetry is technically challenging even for a Russian reader. She is known for her strong, rapidly changing rhythms, which can resemble anything from jazz to a religious chant.

Equally characteristic is her unusual approach to rhyme. "New Year Letter" is a good example of this, and the David McDuff translation does a good job of reproducing the effect, though the specific rhymes cannot be carried over. Except for one short section, the poem is written in rhymed couplets. Tsvetayeva uses a variety of rhyme types, from true rhyme, sometimes several syllables deep, to mere assonance (repetition of vowel sounds) or consonance (repetition of consonant sounds). The fact that many of these rhymes are only approximate makes the overall effect subtle and unobtrusive. It is only on second reading that one realizes the unusual juxtapositions. The pattern of rhymed couplets is sustained except for a four-line section in which Tsvetayeva, realizing that Rilke has been freed by death to devote himself totally to poetry, reverts to the formula of the New Year's greeting and wishes him a "Happy new sound," a "Happy new echo." Here Tsvetayeva uses an alternating rhyme in an *abab* pattern, and rhymes the words *drug* and *zvuk* (friend and sound). In life, she says, everything was a hindrance to Rilke's work, even passion and friendship. Now he will be able to work unhindered, and his words will harmonize with his world, as *sound* and *friend* are now allowed to harmonize in rhyme.

Another peculiarity of Tsvetayeva is her habit of inserting foreign words into the Russian line, even in the rhyming position. There are several examples of macaronic (multilingual) rhyming in this poem, such as *krajnyj* (extreme) and *Rainer*, Rilke's first name, or *ladon'ju* (with my palm) with *Rarogn'a*, the site of Rilke's grave. Tsvetayeva was fluent in German and French, and as she made clear in numerous poems, essays, and letters, she felt a profound kinship with Germanic culture. Acutely aware of language, she apologizes to her friend for writing to him in her native Russian instead of German, the tongue in which she had written to him in life. She seems to feel that using Russian creates a greater distance between them than has Rilke's death itself. Then, however, Tsvetayeva makes a point that she had already made in her letters to Rilke and elsewhere: The specific language in which one writes is immaterial, since all poets write in the same "angelic" language that transcends nationality. Her mixing of languages is a symbol of her belief that the boundaries between languages, between nations, are evanescent.

Themes and Meanings

It has been suggested that any poem written as a lament for the dead has a strong autobiographical component. In other words, the poem tells the reader as much about the living poet as it does about the dead person. This is true on several levels in "New Year Letter," and each level illustrates a major theme of the poem. Tsvetayeva is the first-person heroine of her own poem, addressing Rilke from a number of points of view. First, she writes as a person deprived of a friend whom she never met. She and her fellow Russian poet Boris Pasternak had planned to visit Rilke in Switzerland, but the latter's sudden death destroyed those plans. In the poem, Tsvetayeva muses on what it would have been like to have had a rendezvous and a chat with Rilke in a poor Paris suburb like the one in which she lives.

Second, "New Year Letter" is a kind of love poem. Always impulsive, Tsvetayeva in her letters to Rilke had quickly assumed the personal *du* form of address, and her tone of intimacy and longing had nearly frightened Rilke away. Now, with no chance that a relationship can ever develop between them, Tsvetayeva laments as if for a dead lover, while at the same time admitting poignantly but accurately that "nothing has worked out for us at all." They were never lovers—indeed, they never even met—but Tsvetayeva feels she knows Rilke so well through his words, and through the things they have in common, that she claims the right to address him as if they had been.

Finally, Tsvetayeva writes as a poet whose main concern is her craft, and who regards Rilke as an inspiration, a symbol, and her own ideal audience—for who but a master poet can fully understand another? In their correspondence and in the poems he wrote for her, Rilke had helped Tsvetayeva through a crisis of insecurity about her work. Living in poverty in Parisian exile, she was often faced with problems of literal survival for herself and her family. Her poetry was constantly threatened by lack of time, energy, solitude, and even an audience, since the Russian political situation had virtually deprived her of readers. Rilke himself had been forced to make difficult decisions concerning the role of poetry in his life; painfully but firmly, he had chosen his art, to the exclusion of family and a life as a normal social being. By his friendship, his example, and the literary fruits of his sacrifice, Rilke had encouraged Tsvetayeva to go on.

For Tsvetayeva, Rilke was also a symbol of all poets. Elsewhere she refers to him as Orpheus, the greatest singer in Greek mythology, and in "New Year Letter" she says of the heaven she imagines for him, "If you're there, so is verse, in any case," thus equating him with poetry itself! By writing this "letter" to Rilke, engaging him in a dialogue about his writing and hers, it must have seemed to Tsvetayeva that she was somehow keeping him alive, postponing the time when she must admit his physical death, and therefore both the possibility of mortality and the death of poetry. Throughout the poem, Tsvetayeva echoes themes and images that play a central role in Rilke's writing: death, love, the angels, God, childhood, poetry. In "New Year Letter," she has created both a tribute to a loved fellow poet and a promise to go on writing herself, in the face of all obstacles.

Patricia Pollock Brodsky

NEXT, PLEASE

Author: Philip Larkin (1922-1985)
Type of poem: Lyric
First published: 1951, in *XX Poems*

The Poem

Philip Larkin's "Next, Please" is made up of six four-line stanzas. The first three lines of each (with several exceptions) are in iambic pentameter, while the last line of each is noticeably shorter (either four or six syllables). The rhyme scheme of each of the stanzas is *aabb.* The poem examines the common desire many people have to focus their attention on the future instead of living in the present. Many spend their entire lives waiting for the good things the future will supposedly bring to those who faithfully wait for them. However, the poem warns its readers that such hopes will always end in disappointment, for the only thing that is certain to arrive is death. The first stanza begins by pointing out disapprovingly that "we" are "Always too eager for the future" and, as a result, "Pick up bad habits of expectancy," living life in the hope that the future will surely make life better than it is in the present.

The next four stanzas explore this "expectancy" through the ironic development of the old maxim about waiting for one's ship to come in. From a cliff, people watch the sea, waiting for the sight of a "Sparkling armada of promises" to approach. However, the expected ships are, annoyingly, in no hurry to arrive. In addition, as the third and fourth stanzas explain, even after a ship arrives, it leaves those who waited for it "holding wretched stalks/ Of disappointment." Although the watchers' hopes are not vague dreams and they are able to see every detail of an approaching ship clearly, "it never anchors; it's/ No sooner present than it turns to past." Time is in constant flux, and to live in the hope that it will somehow stop and deliver "All good into our lives" is to be constantly disappointed. Still, the watchers continue to wait expectantly, believing that, surely, they will be rewarded "For waiting so devoutly and so long."

The last line of the fifth stanza states emphatically that "we are wrong," however. Those rewards will never come. Instead, the only ship that will drop anchor is the ship of death, which will be totally unexpected and will bring an end to all hopes of what the future will bring—and to the future as well.

Forms and Devices

"Next, Please" proves to be a fairly typical work by a poet generally regarded as a member of what came to be called the Movement, a group of nine university-educated English poets who, in the 1950's, were in rebellion against the political and artistic preoccupations of the poetry of the 1930's and 1940's. They regarded themselves as part of an alternate tradition of twentieth century English poetry, one opposed to the complex and confusing modernism of T. S. Eliot, William Butler Yeats, Ezra Pound, and their followers. This tradition was closely associated with Thomas Hardy; like

Hardy, Larkin and his fellows regarded the use of rhyme, regular meter, and stanza forms as a necessity of English poetry, not as a choice.

The poetry of the Movement also conveyed the dominant tone of postwar England in the 1950's, a time of diminished expectations. The poet was no Romantic hero, celebrating the powers of poetry and the imagination. Instead, he had to be a realist, carefully recording the grimy reality of an empire on the decline in straightforward, simple language. Thus, Larkin's use of the old cliché about one's ship coming in reflects the clichéd, moribund life he knew in the 1950's. This mood is reinforced by the description of one of the ships about to arrive. It is a "promise" seen clearly and in detail, but the overall effect is tawdry. The ship's "brasswork" is highly polished, but Larkin uses the word "prinked" to describe it—a word related to "preen" and "primp." The suggestive image of the ship's "figurehead with golden tits/ Arching our way" is obviously intended to undermine any idea the reader may have developed of a proper and stately sailing vessel.

The primary poetic device used in the poem is the conceit, an extended metaphor whose working out provides the structure of the poem. People wait for their ships— their expectations—to come in, building up "bad habits of expectancy." The detailed description of one ship allows Larkin to reveal how artificial and even seedy people's expectations may be. The last ship (death) brings an end to everything. As Hardy does in poems such as "The Convergence of the Twain" (1912), Larkin uses irony of situation—in particular, the mistaken expectation of something other than death— forcefully. The ships of promises never dock, yet people still wait for them and for their deserved rewards. "But," Larkin informs readers, "we are wrong." Ironically, only Death will ever come to anchor. That ship, in fact, provides the only allusion in the poem, one that suggests the medieval "ship of fools." It may also allude to D. H. Lawrence's poem "The Ship of Death" (1932), which urges its readers to create, through the poetic imagination, their own ships to enable them to sail the sea of oblivion. However, for Larkin, one is powerless before oblivion's "huge and birdless silence."

"Next, Please" makes use of both enjambment and end-stopped lines, with the former being more prevalent. The enjambment (or the run-on line) is used to reinforce the poem's meaning. In the first stanza, for example, the opening line ends with the subject of a sentence that is completed in the second line: "Always too eager for the future, we/ Pick up bad habits of expectancy." The "we" at the end of the line creates a sense of "expectancy" itself, as the reader anticipates the predicate to come.

Enjambment is most effectively employed at the end of the poem, where the ship of death makes its appearance. Larkin is able to place stronger emphasis on the hyphenated modifier "black-/ Sailed" by splitting it so that the first line ends with "black-." The second line is also enjambed: "towing at her back/ A huge and birdless silence." The third line concludes with an opening prepositional phrase, and the rest of the sentence follows in the final line: "In her wake/ No waters breed or break." While enjambment is usually employed in poetry to create a quick "flow" from line to line, often, for narrative purposes, "Next, Please" creates instead pauses at the ends of the lines in which enjambment occurs.

Another device Larkin uses is the shortened fourth line at the end of each stanza. Where the first three lines of a quatrain establish one metrical pattern (in this case, an iambic pentameter line), the last, because it is considerably shorter, surprises readers and has the tendency to draw the line out in their minds to the length it would be expected to have. Thus, each word of each last line acquires more emphasis than it would if it were part of an iambic pentameter line.

Themes and Meaning

Larkin's decision to reprint "Next, Please" in his 1955 collection *The Less Deceived* illustrates how central the poem is to one of his primary themes: the need to see things as they really are. (The volume's title is an oblique allusion to Ophelia's response to Hamlet—"I was the more deceiv'd"—after his telling her that he did not love her.) Larkin is determined not to have deception make the world appear in any way other than what it actually is, and expecting future happiness to make everything right is, possibly, the ultimate deception. In "Next, Please" the reader is encouraged to see life for the limited, diminished thing it is.

The main impetus of the poem is Larkin's fear of death. This fear pervades his poetry from the beginning of his career to its end and is most fully revealed in the 1977 poem "Aubade" (Larkin's ironic morning song), which shows his obsession with "the total emptiness for ever,/ The sure extinction that we travel to/ And shall be lost in always." That which only finds direct expression in the last stanza of "Next, Please" is dealt with in detail throughout "Aubade." Larkin's sinister title for "Next, Please" came, according to his sister, from the poet's childhood dread of reaching the head of a line, where the words "Next, please" meant that this shy boy with a stammer would be forced to speak. Further, the ship of death is common in Larkin's poetry. For example, it appears in the early poem "Ultimatum" (1940), in "The North Ship" (1944), and in "How Distant" (1965).

"Next, Please" illustrates Larkin's finding his poetic voice, breaking from the influence of the poetry of the 1930's and 1940's, and making effective use of such traditional poetic devices as regular meter, stanza form, rhyme, conceit, and irony to produce a distinctive, powerful twentieth century poem. In addition to its importance as an illustration of the poet's concerns and methodology, it is a well-crafted work dealing with a universal theme that has become central to much of modern and postmodern literature.

George F. Horneker

NICODEMUS

Author: Howard Nemerov (1920-1991)
Type of poem: Dramatic monologue
First published: 1950, in *Guide to the Ruins*

The Poem

"Nicodemus" is a fifty-five-line poem divided into six stanzas and three parts. The dramatic monologue is an imaginative rendition of the New Testament Nicodemus's response to Jesus's statement that no man sees the kingdom of God without being born of water and spirit (in John 3). "Nicodemus" is the priest's account to an unknown audience of his and Jesus's encounter. Written in the persona of Nicodemus, the poem depicts the spiritual seeker as a lonely, bitter man who, although he seeks the company of Jesus, cannot or will not understand his words.

Part 1 of the poem follows the biblical account closely. John 3:1 states that Nicodemus was a Pharisee who visited Jesus at night—undoubtedly to avoid controversy, although this is not stated in the gospel. The poem opens with Nicodemus's admission that he went down back alleys, not because he was ashamed, but from a "natural discretion." As the Pharisee made his way to Jesus, he saw a couple embracing against a white wall and hastened to turn his eyes away, no doubt to follow the pharisaic tradition of avoiding "impure" thoughts. Although he quickly averted his eyes, he confesses to whomever he is speaking that at the sight of the lovers he was shaken. He tries to analyze whether his agitation was from the aridity of his mind or from the lovers' hot blood. Nicodemus recalls the howling of a dog in a stone corner right after seeing the lovers—a parallel to his solitary state.

Part 2 also begins by paraphrasing John 3, "How is a man born, being old?" and then shifts to Nicodemus's central philosophical stance, that life is miserable and empty and that nothing can ever be known. He argues against the concept that a man can be reborn, then says that even if he could, he himself would not be born again. Nicodemus views life as being forced on humankind and implies that it is a blessing that it can be forced only once. He recounts the illnesses, sadnesses, and indignities of childhood, especially that of being forced to study despite eyestrain. He cites as particularly distasteful the obedience demanded despite a child's lack of understanding. The next stanza expresses bitterness at having trusted to the learning and conforming process so as to establish a suitable adult identity. Despite his long study, he finds that he has achieved no real knowledge or enlightenment. Nicodemus is puzzled that even though he has earned enough accolades to be called a master, he is still as ignorant as a child.

Part 3 continues in this pessimistic vein. Nicodemus argues with Jesus, saying that although the rest of nature "flowers again," a man does not. From intellectual debate, Nicodemus shifts to an encapsulization of his life as a profound disappointment. His parents have been sorrow and humiliation, he says, and he has never been swept up in fleshly or spiritual concerns, no doubt a response to Jesus's declaration that "What is born of the flesh is flesh, and what is born of the spirit is spirit" (John 3:6). After his confession that he has been engrossed in neither realm, Nicodemus again expresses bewilderment that he is "exalted in Israel" for "all I do not know." He has no answer to Jesus' question, "Are you a teacher of Israel, and yet you do not understand these things?" (John 3:10).

The next stanza intensifies Nicodemus's despair as he states that "the end of [his] desire is death." His life contrasts sharply with that of his foremother Sarah, who laughed during her life and just before her death—first with a mocking laughter at God's promise to cure her barrenness, then with a delighted laughter at God's fulfillment of that promise. Nicodemus proclaims that not only will he not laugh but that he will produce no new word because of "the dryness" of his mouth.

The final stanza moves from unmitigated gloom into asking Jesus to let him go to the ancient burial ground and cave of Abraham and Sarah. In this wish, the old priest echoes Genesis 23, which recounts how Abraham struck the first land claim of Israel when he bought a field which contained a cave in which he buried Sarah.

Forms and Devices

"Nicodemus" has a conversational tone yet also contains the stately, formal rhythms befitting a prestigious old man. The metrics are lavishly iambic but are so varied that the poem must be classified as free verse. Its slow, long lines support the often slowed speech of age and the deliberate manner in which Nicodemus tells his story. The heavy use of vowels in internal rhyme creates a mournful tone: "howled," "once," "stone" (line 23); "forced," "only," "one" (line 46); and "nor," "not," "born" (line 46). Juxtaposed against the dirgelike internal rhymes are sharp consonant alliterations which not only quicken the tempo but also support Nicodemus's negative statements: "dryness," "driving," (line 9); "book," "burning," (line 20), "bitter," "bewilderment" (line 30), "cold," "cave" (line 55). Nemerov alternates harsh alliteration with soft *s* sounds when he mentions positive aspects of life, such as lilacs, honey, and the laughter of Sarah.

The poem makes use of images to heighten the contrast between life and Nicodemus's spiritual death. Images of dryness—Nicodemus's mind, mouth, and burning eyes—support the portrayal of Nicodemus as a dried-up intellectual who is bitter because his earnest studies have not brought him definite knowledge or understanding. Nicodemus's death-thrust is also illustrated by images of cold. He wants to end in a "cold cave" where even Abraham's seed is "cold." The dog's howl in a stone corner as Nicodemus travels to visit Jesus prefigures his lost, lonely wish to be buried in a cold cave. Other striking parallels are Nicodemus's declaring sorrow and humiliation to be his parents but wishing to return to the parents of Judaism, Abraham and Sarah—once vital but now cold and dead. A subtle device is that the first two-thirds of the poem "answer" Jesus, although Jesus is never directly quoted. The effect of leaving out Jesus's comments is powerful, for it suggests that Nicodemus assumes his audience knows the details of the encounter or that he is too troubled to fill in missing parts.

This omission also adds to Nicodemus's self-justification, possibly to his colleagues, who would approve of his desire to go back to his Old Testament roots.

Themes and Meanings

"Nicodemus" is about an old man who will not take chances on a new way of living or on anything he cannot understand. His modus operandi of understanding is intellectual, and he will not brook the possibility of any other knowledge. Like many old people, he looks backward instead of forward—to the glorious foundation of Israel, which even Nicodemus himself knows is now "cold."

It is not simply age which causes Nicodemus to reject the possibility of rebirth or perhaps even rebirth itself, but Nicodemus's assessment of life as essentially suffering and disillusionment. His intellectual attainment produced respect from the people but emptiness in himself. He trusted that study would produce answers, but it failed him, and he admits to knowing nothing. In answer to Jesus' declaration about life in the flesh or life in the spirit, Nicodemus states that he has attached himself to neither, thereby revealing another reason for his emptiness. His bitterness is enhanced by what he implies is his community's stupidity for exalting him. To Nicodemus, life is a bad joke. Therefore, he clings to his belief that a "man may not flower again," principally because he himself does not want to flower again.

In a painful summing up, Nicodemus states that he has had nothing to laugh over and that unlike Sarah, who produced an heir in her old age, he will produce no new word of truth or knowledge. Instead he is confounded by Jesus' words and wants to return to the source of his roots, however cold and dead. Ironically, if Nicodemus had immersed himself in aspects beside the intellectual, he might not have become dry and might have found life worthwhile enough at least to delight in some of its incongruities. Although Nicodemus is honest in his admission that study has taught him nothing, he remains convinced that he is right rather than admit that his lifelong perceptions might be wrong. Nicodemus visits Jesus because he has a hunger for knowledge, but when he is presented with something he does not understand, he rejects further learning. In the last analysis, he will not again be the child who must endure the "malady of being always ruled to ends he does not see or understand" (lines 22-23). Despite Nicodemus's rejection of Jesus' teaching, he treats Jesus as an authority. He asks permission not to enter the kingdom of God but to go back to his cold "home" to die. Although Nicodemus ends his story on a proper political note, his reverence for Jesus reveals the subversiveness that first brought him to visit under "cover of night."

Mary Hanford Bruce

NIGHT

Author: Robert Bly (1926-   )
Type of poem: Lyric
First published: 1962, in *Silence in the Snowy Fields*

The Poem

"Night," written in free verse, is a short poem divided into four sections, each of which is four lines long. Like many of Robert Bly's titles, "Night" appears to be a title without pretense or philosophical complexity; the poem is, however, richer in meaning than the title indicates. Night is a time for dreamlike thought, unmoored from the world of daylight's reason and logic. Bly's four sections offer four visions of night's mysteries.

The poem is written in the first person, but it moves from a particular first-person-singular speaker—Bly himself—to a more generalized first-person plural. By writing in the first-person plural—"we"—the poet takes an enormous risk, because he appears to be speaking for all humanity. When a poet says "I," the reader must believe the speaker. When a poet says "we," thereby including the reader in his or her pronouncement, the reader may object to the statement or worldview.

The poem begins with what appears to be an extremely logical "if/then" proposition: "If I think of a horse," then "I feel a joy." Bly complicates the logic, however, by appending what appears to be an odd metaphor: If he thinks of a horse he feels joyful, as if he had thought of a pirate ship. The circular movement from thought to joy and then back to thought again is counteracted by the centrifugal force in the logic of the poem that jumps from the horse in a field to a pirate ship surrounded by flowers. The mood of the poem is immediately set by the dreamlike logic of the metaphors and the poem's eccentric movement.

The second section is typical of Bly's work: He anthropomorphizes the natural world. The happiness Bly felt in section I becomes so contagious that even the box elder trees "are full of joy." The magic of night leads to the melting together of normally separate objects: The horse becomes like a ship, and the joy passes from Bly the observer to the observed trees. Because it is night, Bly tries to convince the reader that the lilacs and the plants are sleeping, once again blurring the boundaries between things by anthropomorphizing. The final image is loaded: "Even the wood made into a casket is asleep." The wood still participates in the natural order, being able to sleep as well as the lilacs, even though it has undergone the transformation from nature's tree to humans' wood. The casket is also the final resting place for someone lodging in the realm of eternal sleep.

The third stanza once again melds disparate realms. The butterfly joins earth with air by carrying "loam on his wings," while the amphibian toad—the bridge between two worlds—joins earth with water by "bearing tiny bits of granite in his skin." The zone of sleep in section 2 is revisited in the final image of section 3, in which the tree leaves and "bits of earth at its root" are asleep.

The concluding section wakes up the poem with copious movement. If the trees and plants can sleep like humans, why cannot a person be like a "sleek black water beetle./ Skating across still water"? In a "night poem," the possible metamorphoses are endless. The final change in the poem is perhaps the most startling. In a poem that has been silent, devoid of voices and animal sounds, the final image of a mouth opening, not to speak but to swallow, is arresting. The poem is stopped by death.

Forms and Devices

"Night" is so deceptively simple that a reader might miss the careful structuring in the poem. Generally, there is a falling away or a downward movement in each of the four sections. The first three prepare the reader for the jolt of the final macabre image of death swallowing its victim.

In the first stanza, a scene filled only with moonlight is transformed when Bly imagines a horse "wandering about sleeplessly." The thought of this horse is immediately replaced by that of the pirate ship, and the horse's sleeplessness gives way to the sleep-coated trees and plants and flowers in the rest of the poem. The poet proffers one thing, then takes it away. The second stanza drops from the heights of the box elder tree to the lilacs and plants and, finally, into the casket, which might already be in the ground. The third stanza recapitulates this downward movement twice: It begins with a loamy butterfly on the wing and moves downward to a granite-infested toad; it observes the crown of a tree and ends with the "earth at its root."

This downward movement echoes the thematic transformation from joy to the eeriness of death. The concluding death of the beetle is everyone's death, which should not come as a complete surprise. Each section tries to warn the reader by establishing this pattern of presence and disappearance, of flight and a final resting place in the earth. Each person is like the beetle skating across the water in seemingly perfect freedom, only to discover that will means nothing in the end. Each person moves from life to death as easily as this night poem shifts from the crowns of trees to the earth around their roots.

Each section of the poem enacts the death of the beetle. The poet's imagination apparently skates along in any direction it wills, but the form of the poem belies this haphazardness. Each time the poet tries a flight of fancy, the world of death pulls him down. Night is a time when the imagination runs wild, but finally, at least in this poem, the imagination runs back to the ultimate form of night, which is death.

Themes and Meanings

The form of the poem, as discussed earlier, leads the reader to its meaning. The poem suggests the obvious truth that human beings often want to ignore: Life leads to death as inevitably as day leads to night. Despite the downward movement within each stanza, however, Bly also seems to suggest that joy need not be forgotten simply because decline is inevitable.

Bly risks using the pathetic fallacy—providing nature with human traits—in order to remove the boundaries that normally exist between the natural world and the human one. The risk lies in the believability of the image: Do plants really sleep? Can trees feel joy? Do trees actually obey anything, since obedience implies will? Bly would like to remove this world of reason because he sees in it the basis for human alienation from the environment. In Bly's world, one enters a mythic landscape before the fall, in which the human and the natural elements are one.

The poem resists a totally depressing reading as a result of this use of the pathetic fallacy. If the trees and plants are like humans, why cannot humans be like them? The trees are full of joy, at least in Bly's eyes, even though their death is inevitable. The earth that gives them life is also the earth that will accept them in death. The butterflies, emblematic of the spirit world, contain bits of earth or loam in their wings; their flight joins spirit and flesh, life and death. If the poem suggests that death is contained in life, the other side of the argument is also put forth: Life is contained in death. In another poem in *Silence in the Snowy Fields*, "Summer, 1960, Minnesota," Bly creates an image that is very similar to the closing one in "Night":

> Yet, we are falling,
> Falling into the open mouths of darkness,
> Into the Congo as into a river,
> Or as wheat into open mills.

The image of falling into a dark mouth is bleaker in "Night" only because one is not given a clear picture of what happens on the other side. In "Summer, 1960, Minnesota," the transformation of wheat into bread in the open mouths of the mill suggests that there is no such thing as death; in "Night," the final image of the skating beetle being sucked under can have positive resonances only if one remembers previous poems in the collection or the hints of metamorphosis given earlier in the poem. If things are constantly changing places inside a poem, then there can be no final, gruesome image: Death must lead to something else, even if that something else is present only in the white space at the end of the poem.

In Bly's world, tragedy comes from a willful struggle to deny what is inevitable; comedy, or true joy, derives, as in the case of the box elders, from "obeying what is beneath them." Death is always lying beneath one, no matter how easily or comfortably one is skating along. In order to achieve the type of joy that Bly thinks is possible, one has to become one with the animals and all created things and say yes to life, a life that has death as its final word. The trick seems to be that, in order to become like leaves or loam, one must dispense with the kind of self-consciousness that makes art possible. Bly, by writing in unrhymed free verse that is extremely associative in its organization, seems to suggest that an unfettered imagination can be the key to a healthy mind and soul. The very care with which he organizes his poem's structure, however, points to the paradox at the center of his poem: Death is in life, and life is in death; pain is in joy, and joy is in pain.

Kevin Boyle

NIGHT AND MORNING

Author: Austin Clarke (1896-1974)
Type of poem: Lyric
First published: 1938, in *Night and Morning*

The Poem

"Night and Morning" is a short poem of thirty-six lines, divided into four stanzas with nine lines each. The title indicates the direction the poem moves—from night to morning—but also the division of feeling expressed by the speaker, who has thoughts at night that subvert his feelings in the morning.

The first stanza opens with a statement of certain knowledge, as the speaker expresses his personal identification with those who have suffered misery for hundreds of years. As in a dream, in his sleep he feels the injury of pride, the shame of mockery, and the humiliation of insult. These are elements of the suffering narrated in the Passion of Christ, as suggested by the reference to "the house of Caesar." This identification is only partial, however, since the speaker's thoughts are divided by doubts. The result is that he is tormented into a despair that must borrow clothing to disguise his doubts.

When morning comes, in the second stanza, the speaker goes to Mass, where he arrives with others at the appointed hour. He observes the celebration of Holy Eucharist (Holy Communion) as a ritual of mere appearances: There is no awesome transformation of the wafer and wine into the body and blood of Christ. The priest turns his back on his congregation when he adores his God. The speaker still feels his spiritual torment, even after Mass, even after the saints have all been celebrated.

In his continuing torment, the speaker recalls in the third stanza how humble acts of faith in the past have annihilated the complications of thought and deliberation. He recalls that many have labored, in great intellectual discourses, from rostrums, in early morning hours of composition, to lift simple life into heights of significance. All those labors, however, are now as forgotten as are the many intellectual martyrs who sought to restore truths of dead languages (including Latin) into living ideas.

Finally, in the last stanza, the speaker celebrates the time when, long ago, Europe was alive with intellectual debate and followed the lead of logic. Then the reality of heaven united with the reality of earth; human beings felt whole, proud, and united in their communion with one another. In that time, faith was a product of intellectual commitment, as divinity shared its being with humanity: "God was made man once more."

Forms and Devices

"Night and Morning" is both a form of confession and an internal debate. It uses metaphors and allusion within a framework of irony to make its meaning rich and complex. As a confession, it may be spoken to a priest, or a psychoanalyst, but it is confessional mainly in an ironic sense: What ought to be confessed, loss of faith, cannot be confessed to those with faith. It can only be expressed, or confessed, to one's self. In this respect, the poem has the form of a debate between body and soul, with a translation of the disputants into "thought" and "belief."

Biblical and church (Roman Catholic) allusions give the poem context and orientation. "The house of Caesar" of stanza 1 is countered by "the nave," "the altar," "adoring priest," and "the congregation" of the second stanza. Kneeling and Holy Communion (Eucharist) allude to church ritual in the third stanza, continued into the final stanza with its "choir" and making of God into man. The poem alludes to specific biblical events from the New Testament and the church calendar, beginning with the Passion of Christ in the first stanza, All Saints' Day in the second, "cock-rise" and "miracle that raised . . . the dead" in the third (as references to the Resurrection and the raising of Lazarus). Historical allusions are broadened in the third stanza, with "councils and decrees" (such as the Council of Trent) and scholastic debates of the Middle Ages and Renaissance in the last stanza's "learned controversy" and "holy rage of argument."

Metaphors join abstractions with concrete images to dramatize the pain of intellectual doubt: "the tormented soul . . . must wear a borrowed robe," "minds that bled," and "logic led the choir." Metaphors also unite logical contraries in conceits of paradox: "every moment that can hold . . . the miserable act/ Of centuries," and "God was made man." When these are expressed from within a framework of irony, they acquire an additional feeling of pain. Their very expression becomes subject to doubt, as if to say, it is not church figures who have bled in body for humankind—rather, it is the intellectual skeptics, the doubters themselves, who have bled and sacrificed to make possible a religious history of doubtful substance.

Irony unfolds at the center of the poem, when the speaker observes that the priest turns "his back/ Of gold upon the congregation." Literally, this occurs in the celebration of the Mass; figuratively, it exposes the sterile and hypocritical relationship of priests (church/religion/faith) to people. Irony here develops from the device of punning, continued into the final couplet of the second stanza: "All saints have had their day at last,/ But thought still lives in pain." Besides echoing the expression "Every dog has its day," this couplet turns upon the celebration of "All Saints' Day" to show how ineffective it is in relieving the speaker's spiritual pain.

Themes and Meanings

"Night and Morning" has three main themes. Modern individuals of thought and education find it difficult to hold on to traditional religious beliefs; moreover, the modern Church has failed to keep alive the faith of the past, because the modern Church does not foster intellectual inquiry. Finally, modern individuals suffer from internal conflicts of self-division, hidden under the same cloak of hypocrisy that afflicts the institution of the Church itself.

These themes are developed in ironic and self-critical ways. Intellect should be laid to rest during the sleep of night, but instead it asserts itself to challenge faith.

Ironically, at night the speaker can most fully identify with the suffering Christ, because the speaker suffers most at night from his pain of doubt. The Church, like the priest, turns its back not only on the people of the congregation, but also on its own history; its "many councils and decrees/ Have perished," partly because they did not address individual needs, partly because they did not educate simple minds, and partly because they were merely abstractions without force to survive uncomprehending persons who submitted without thought—"gave obedience to the knee." Instead of keeping Europe "astir/ With echo of learned controversy," the Church has acquiesced to a passive authoritarianism.

The consequence of that acquiescence, for a person of thought, is unbearable agony. Unable to believe in miracles and mysteries entirely, yet unable to refuse belief entirely, the speaker resigns himself to sharp self-division: He goes through the motions, like other "appointed shadows," gives "obedience to the knee," and observes "the miracle" in which "God was made man once more." At night, however, after the "dreadful candle" is snuffed, he will know once again "the injured pride of sleep."

The meaning produced by this mixture of themes is that the modern mind suffers beneath the appearance of conformity to public ritual. It goes on with the appearance, wearing "a borrowed robe," because it does not have a more certain answer to spiritual questions. It yearns for the vitality of a past when thought and belief were one, but in the present that yearning is felt as a burden, not a relief, of history. Read again after one has finished the final stanza, "Night and Morning" grows in power and complication. The first stanza reads with more pain, more even than the pain of the suffering body of Christ, because the speaker cannot be relieved by the Passion and sacrifice— he can only be tormented, like Christ himself. Night brings more suffering, with confession of unbelief, to the morning, with its confession of belief. Darkness of night produces enlightenment within the speaker; light of morning conceals an interior darkness of soul.

These themes are elaborated with variations by the ten lyrics that follow "Night and Morning" in Austin Clarke's *Night and Morning* collection of 1938: from the ironies of celebrating Holy Week as the shadows of "Tenebrae," through the thoughtless, almost inhuman ritual observances of "Martha Blake," to the unholy madness exhibited when the "heavens opened" to reveal deep darkness in "Summer Lightning." Such themes and such poems represented a significant turn in the career of Clarke; he pressed more of his painful emotions more often into such bitter and ironic lyrics as those introduced by "Night and Morning."

Richard D. McGhee

THE NIGHT-BLOOMING JASMINE

Author: Audre Lorde (1934-1992)
Type of poem: Meditation
First published: 1993, in *The Marvelous Arithmetics of Distance: Poems, 1987-1992*

The Poem

Audre Lorde's poem "The Night-Blooming Jasmine" expresses its author's meditation on the "Lady of the Night," a fragrant, night-flowering jasmine plant native to the tropics, whose white, five-cleft blooms resemble stars. The poem is made up of a series of reflections on a night-blooming jasmine the speaker encounters "along the searoad" between her "house" and "tasks" that lie before her. In five stanzas of five to twelve lines of free verse, the speaker describes how the sight of the flowers opening at night triggers or "calls down" the desire to create a song about the "star-breathed" or five-cleft blooms of jasmine. She imagines this song played on "a flute/ carved from the legbone of a gull," an instrument appropriate to the nature of the flower.

In the second stanza of the poem, the speaker begins to find points of comparison between herself and the night-blooming flower. She describes herself as a being strung together with wire "upon which pain will not falter/ nor predict." The speaker admits she has not been a stranger to the "arena" of pain, suggesting she has fought this adversary before at "high noon" much like a gladiator or bullfighter or gunfighter. She finds this pain is not "an enemy/ to be avoided" but rather a "challenge." From the challenge of her pain, the speaker's "neck [grows] strong." The metal at the core of her being, once "struck" by the challenge of pain, rings out "like fire in the sun."

In the third stanza, the speaker draws upon a different set of images to explain what happens when she confronts her pain. She thinks of the scar that runs down the center of her body as a line on a battlefield separating enemy forces, a line she "patrols" with "sword drawn." She thinks of the scar line as a series of "red-glazed candles of petition," or prayers. She also thinks of the scar line as a "fractured border," like a boundary between countries, running through "the center of my days."

These images of the body as a battleground give way in the fourth stanza to a comparison between the speaker and bees drawn by their need for the honey of flowers to fly "beyond the limit of their wings." This natural image, accurately rendered from the life history of worker bees, celebrates the coming death of the speaker, who is like the bees who will drop where they fly, laden with baskets of pollen, "the sweet work done."

The fifth stanza contrasts the speaker with the bees, who will never "know" the "Lady of the Night," the jasmine blossoms that open only at night while bees sleep "between my house and the searoad." The speaker suggests she may remain similarly unknown, for she herself by this point in the poem can be considered a "Lady of the Night," a being similar in situation to the night-blooming flower in that she has found that her soul also blooms only as the shadow of death nears. The fifth stanza returns to the song of the "flute/ carved from the legbone of a gull," the poem that will remain after the speaker is gone. The final two lines of the poem, "your rich voice/ riding the shadows of conquering air," appear to refer to the song of the flute—the poem—whose presence as a reader's voice will be carried on the breath in "shadow" and so manage to outlive the night that is death.

Forms and Devices

In "The Night-Blooming Jasmine," Lorde uses the central image of a night-blooming flower to present an intellectual and emotional complex of thoughts associated with death by disease. The first stanza, comprising the first five lines of the poem, is echoed in the final seven lines of the poem, the last stanza, which bring closure to the poem and suggest the arc of its content. The "tasks" that lay before the speaker in the first stanza disappear in the final stanza, reinforcing the thought that the speaker's "sweet work" is done. The song of the "flute/ carved from the legbone of a gull" remains from the first to last stanza. However, the final stanza contains two lines which do not appear in the first stanza: "your rich voice/ riding the shadows of conquering air." This addition suggests that a certain amount of control, together with the material of the poem itself (which exists as an entity of the sound of the voice carried on the air), has been gained by the speaker over the course of the the movement of mind that constitutes the poem.

The poem opens with an invocation of the "Lady of the Night," an entreaty that calls to mind the image of not only the night-blooming jasmine but also the nocturnal streetwalker and the color of the speaker's African American skin. "Metal" and "wire" are the first images the speaker uses to describe herself; however, as the poem progresses, these metallic images give way to organic ones associated with bees and the flowers they frequent during the day. Bees cannot visit those who are "night-blooming," a mental representation the speaker uses to describe herself as she approaches the time of her death. Yet she does point out the similarity between herself and bees laden with pollen, which die in flight fulfilling their "need" for "sweet work."

Themes and Meanings

In addition to her poetry, Lorde wrote *The Cancer Journals* (1980), a courageous account of her struggle to overcome breast cancer and mastectomy. Themes of "The Night-Blooming Jasmine," written between November, 1990, and May, 1992, the year of Lorde's death from liver cancer, take on specificity when read in the context of the *Journals*. In the *Journals*, begun six months after her mastectomy in 1979, Lorde discussed her feelings about facing the possibility of death. Beyond death, she feared dying without having said the things she "needed" to say as a woman, an artist, an African American, and a lesbian.

Lorde saw her battle with cancer as part of her work as a woman to reclaim power on this earth. After her breast was removed, she refused to wear a prosthesis, seeing in it hypocrisies of the medical profession and an empty comfort. Instead, she wished to share with other women the strength she had found in her battle with breast cancer, so that they could be empowered in their own struggles. She felt that the social and economic discrimination practiced against women who had breast cancer was not diminished by pretending that mastectomies do not exist.

Lorde's poem "The Night-Blooming Jasmine" works off the same perceptions of cancer that characterize *The Cancer Journals*, images that suggest that women with breast cancer are warriors whose feelings need voice in order to be recognized, respected, and of use. The poem places the scar of mastectomy at the "center of my days." She did not want her anger, pain, and fear about cancer to fossilize into silence or rob her of whatever strength might lie at the core of the experience if it were openly acknowledged and examined. In this, she followed the observation of French feminist Simone de Beauvoir that "it is in the recognition of the genuine conditions of our lives that we gain strength to act and our motivation for change."

Lorde also felt that if one were to be strong, it was important to find some particular thing the soul craves for nourishment and satisfy it. Her journey home to St. Croix to die, a journey into the tropics where night-flowering jasmine might be encountered, was such a nourishment. Her poem suggests that before the end, her identity had matured and "blossomed" like the jasmine, which blooms only after night has fallen. Her "sweet work" complete, she left behind the poem from which others may draw their own strength and consolation.

Elaine Laura Kleiner

NIGHTMARE BEGINS RESPONSIBILITY

Author: Michael S. Harper (1938-   )
Type of poem: Lyric
First published: 1974, in *Nightmare Begins Responsibility*

The Poem

Michael S. Harper's "Nightmare Begins Responsibility" traces the feelings and re-flections of a father witnessing, through a glass partition, a team of medical personnel trying to save the life of his newborn son. The setting is a hospital, but the poem's drama unfolds in the father's mind as he reports what he sees and the distrust he feels toward the technicians, a distrust that is ultimately muted by understanding and resolution.

At the poem's outset, the father feels imprisoned by the glass, shut off from his son, and helpless. The infant, is in a "tube-kept/ prison," completely at the mercy of the medical team, as is the father. The poem's first line focuses on the father's anguish, connecting it to his external environment with a pun on "pane": "I place these numbed wrists to the pane." Able only to watch, the father is gripped by fear and distrust throughout the poem—Harper uses the words "distrusting" four times and "distrust" once to reinforce the father's primary emotion. The father distrusts the hospital staff, fearing "what they will do in experiment"; he distrusts them because they are white, clad in white hospital garb and clad in the whiteness of their race, which contrasts with his own dark skin and that of his child.

The father's anguish stems in part from conflicting feelings, the poem's principal focus. Seeing the white technicians struggle to save his child, the father is intensely aware that, in a historic sense, white people have tried to snuff out the lives of his peo-ple. His ethnic roots continue to tug at him as he watches "*distrusting-white-hands-picking-baboon-light/* on this son." The music from his past runs through his mind like a moving train; the poem's rhythms and language reflect the stream of his thoughts, "hymns of *night-train*, train done gone." The image of the train creates a vi-sual counterpart to the poem's sounds and rhythms, the lines lengthening, snaking along without pause as memories from his childhood mingle with the details of his son's struggle beyond the glass partition.

His distrust of the medical staff entwines with memories of his home, his mother, and, finally, his other son who has died, and he realizes that he is responsible for this son's death and the death of his other son. This night is a nightmare for everyone involved in it, but most of all for the father, who must go on living with the knowledge that two of his sons have died in infancy. The poem is about loss, the loss of one child and then another, the loss of control over what happens to his children, and the loss of freedom.

Forms and Devices

The poem is divided into one stanza of twenty-three lines and a second one of six lines. The lines range in length from one word to eight to ten words—some of the longer lines contain several words fused together. The poem's rhythms arise often from the expansion and contraction of word lengths. To quicken the pace and highlight meaning, Harper connects words with hyphens: "*distrusting-white-hands-picking-baboon-light*," putting them in italics as if to increase their intensity. The fused words in the twentieth line,

> *gonedowntown*   into   *researchtestingwarehousebatteryacid*

reflect the rhythms of the father's thoughts and the intensity of his emotion, suggesting that his disparate memories form a single experience and perception. The fusion of words into complex units of thought and feeling is a visual counterpart to the father's sense of connectedness, of moving forward, of being fused with his past, his son, and himself. Their sinuous shape and unbroken rhythm suggest the train that is one of the poem's major symbols, representing the ongoing motion of the father's life, the repetitive rhythms of the heartbeat, and the haunting thought of arrival and departure. His infant's arrival and imminent departure remind the father of the "*nighttrain*," both the song and the train that is "done gone." The train, its rhythmic sound and linked units, forms an apt metaphor of the father's life as well as a metaphor of the poem itself: words forming lines linked by sound as they carry the poet's meaning to its conclusion.

In addition to rhythm and word fusions, Harper uses sounds to emphasize the symbolic significance of the poem's three major elements, the color white, light, and night, which form contrasting ideas even as they rhyme, thus giving the poem one of several ironic twists. Each of these words stirs great emotion in the father, and each is associated with other elements in his life. At the beginning of the poem, he is "watching white uniforms whisk"—Harper suggests motion with a deft use of alliteration—a few lines later, "white-pink mending" appears, then "*white-hands picking*," and near the end, "*white-doctor*." The father has discovered that white represents an inversion of the purity for which it traditionally stands.

The word "light" is used only once in the poem, linked with the word "baboon," which suggests its opposite. Nevertheless, light is implicit in the hospital's setting, which imprisons the father with its punishing glare. Of this trio of words, "night" offers the richest meaning and resonance with the father, who associates it with the departing train, with the soul music of his past, and with this night, the night of his ordeal, which turns into an unending nightmare.

Harper further complicates his meaning by shifting points of view. At the beginning, it is not clear who is imprisoned—the father by the glass partition, by his fear, even by his genetic history; his infant son by his disease; or the technicians by their professional duty and white skin. The father's ambivalence is further registered by the play on the word "pane," which evokes his pain even as it refers to the glass partition. Harper continues to underscore the father's ambivalence in his use of the words "distrust" and "distrusting," whose repetition links many of the lines in a chain of shifting emotions and perspectives. The meaning of lines 7-9, for example, changes according to how "distrusting" functions. The "infirmary tubes," the child's shaven head, or the father's "gasolined hands" may be "distrusting." When the father speaks of his "infinite distrust of them," he voices the poem's complex treatment of certainty and conflict, for the father's distrust is emphatic, but whom he distrusts is blurred into an unspecified "them."

Themes and Meanings

Whatever he may feel about the white hospital staff, about whites generally— "them"—the father is at the center of an ongoing nightmare. He feels responsible for not being able to help his infant son. The reference to his "asthmatic/ hymns" hints at a genetic responsibility. The father also feels responsible for the future, which begins with this child's death and begins at the close of this poem, his song of sorrow and confession. The poem moves from the father's sense of imprisonment to his final breaking out of that prison. The penultimate line marks the climax of his struggle to gain an understanding of his ordeal. His journey to this point has been through his past, has been a painful train ride from fear and helplessness to an understanding of his responsibility and of his ability to endure the nightmare. His recollections of his own childhood have helped him gain an understanding of his responsibility to his dying son and living family.

The poem's ending has the sound of triumph: He has gained insight, which empowers him. The train that has given him rhythms and connectedness with his roots has also carried him to this moment of understanding and resolution. In the middle of the poem, Harper says that the father, or the son, or both, "has flown/ up into essential calm unseen corridor." Somewhere at the center of the father's vision is a stoic peace. The nightmare, the train ride, can be endured from this calm center.

The father's understanding also brings an acceptance. The nightmare includes having to live with "them." He must join with the white establishment, represented by the hospital staff, if he is to endure. However reluctant he is to accept them, this night has shown him that some whites at least can cross racial lines, for whatever reasons.

The final stanza voices the father's understanding that he distrusts even himself and that the "*white-doctor-who-breathed-for-him-all-night*" has done all he can to save his child, has done more than he himself has done or could do. On this note of acceptance, he bids the doctor—and the reader—to join him in his pained outcry that voices his triumphant insight: "say nightmare, say it loud/ panebreaking heartmadness:/ nightmare begins responsibility." The pane and the pain that separate white and black are at last broken, and those on both sides must accept the responsibility that their shared nightmare has brought.

Bernard E. Morris

NIKKI-ROSA

Author: Nikki Giovanni (1943-   )
Type of poem: Lyric
First published: 1968, in *Black Judgement*

The Poem

"Nikki-Rosa," a short, introspective poem of thirty lines, dispenses with the conventional marks of written poetry—punctuation and capitalization—creating the effect of the narrator speaking directly to her audience. The title, "Nikki-Rosa," suggests the merging of the personal life with the public or political one and indicates the evolution of a radical, from the girl Nikki to the militant Rosa, the name alluding to Rosa Parks, a Civil Rights activist.

In the poem, a black narrator addresses a black audience, assuming a store of shared experiences, experiences that would be foreign to a white middle-class audience. The narrator—a woman, as indicated by the title—realizes that her childhood contained a mixture of good and bad events. Nevertheless, the negative memories, caused by poverty, are outweighed by the positive, provided by a strong, close family. Unfortunately, "they," the critics and biographers, will record the lack of an "inside toilet" but will fail to mention the warm baths given in "one of those/ big tubs that folk in Chicago barbecue in." The critics will "never talk about how happy you were to have your mother/ all to yourself." The narrator fears that the simple pleasures of her childhood will be overlooked.

The poem juxtaposes the events of the narrator's youth with future biographers' misreading or misinterpretation. The biographers will mention her father's drinking and her parents' fighting but miss the closeness of the extended family. They will not see "that everybody is together and you/ and your sister have happy birthdays and very good christmasses." The biographers will notice the poverty but not the richness of the strong, supportive family. They will not understand that "Black love is Black wealth." Because of this blindness, the narrator hopes that "no white person ever has cause to write about me." The white critics would note the hardships but miss the love: "they'll/ probably talk about my hard childhood and never understand that/ all the while I was quite happy."

Forms and Devices

The poem "Nikki-Rosa," void of any punctuation, appears as one long thought. The memories of childhood are jumbled together, much the way someone would remember his or her youth. This seemingly formless nature of the poem thus mimics the thought processes of the narrator. The particular events merge, leaving the feel of a happy childhood that presumably would elude the biographer or critic.

Nikki Giovanni's poems, including "Nikki-Rosa," are accessible to a wide and diverse audience primarily because the images are drawn from everyday life and the language is simple and direct. This accessibility has made her a very popular poet; her public readings have large audiences and her books and sound recordings enjoy good sales. In "Nikki-Rosa," as well as in many other of Giovanni's poems, the commonplace images are taken specifically from a working-class setting. The narrator describes family meetings, birthdays, and a large tub used for bathing. Thus the poem presents a realistic portrayal of day-to-day family life.

Rooted in an oral tradition, Giovanni in "Nikki-Rosa" combines ordinary language with the natural rhythms of speech. She avoids dense vocabulary and obscure symbols and allusions, relying instead on simple words, a conversational tone, and the clarity of the lines to convey her meaning.

Themes and Meanings

"Nikki-Rosa" introduces several themes that are important to the poem, to Giovanni's other poems, and to her development as a poet. "Nikki-Rosa" first appeared in *Black Judgement* (1968), which contains both revolutionary poems and brief, introspective lyrics. The political poems from the volume received the most critical attention and earned for Giovanni the reputation of a radical militant. Her work was discussed as part of the "new Black poetry of hate." These poems were the result of anger caused by the continued oppression of blacks, and the poems urged violence, black assertiveness, aggression, and black pride. Nevertheless, the lyrics, with their emphasis on the individual and on relationships, prefigure her later work.

"Nikki-Rosa" contains both elements and therefore bridges the gap between the two styles. The poem, written on April 12, 1968, a few days after the funeral of Martin Luther King, Jr., hints at the division between whites and blacks: "I really hope no white person ever has cause to write about me." Whites cannot understand the black experience. In addition, because of the power structure in America, whites should be held accountable for the poverty that is experienced by many blacks, poverty caused by an inferior education, lack of social services, and discrimination.

"Nikki-Rosa" presents the childhood of a girl from an impoverished family who later will become a black activist. Nikki, the young girl, will grow up to be the radical Rosa. The name Rosa recalls Rosa Parks, who, in 1955, refused to give up her bus seat to a white rider, precipitating the year-long Montgomery, Alabama, bus boycott that brought national recognition to Martin Luther King, Jr.

While it is tempting to see the Nikki of the poem as Nikki Giovanni, it is best not to. Giovanni, from a middle-class family, did not experience directly the poverty of the narrator, although as a child she learned about urban poverty from her parents, who were social workers. As a college freshman, she considered herself a Goldwater Republican. Nevertheless, through the example of her outspoken, militant grandmother and because of the events of the 1960's—the antiwar demonstrations; the Civil Rights Movement; the assassinations of Malcolm X, John F. Kennedy, Martin Luther King, Jr., and Robert Kennedy; and the riots in various urban centers throughout the nation—she became radicalized. Thus, while the poem is not strictly autobiographical, it does suggest the development of a radical consciousness that parallels the development of Giovanni's.

The poem hints at the anger that is found in the other poems in the volume and in *Black Feeling, Black Talk* (1968), but primarily "Nikki-Rosa" emphasizes the importance of the love and support that is often found in the black family, a theme that becomes important in her later volumes, such as *The Women and the Men* (1975). As seen in "Nikki-Rosa," the love of the immediate and extended family can overcome the problems that poverty engenders. It is the family that will enable its members to survive the racism that is prevalent in the society. A strong black family will lead to a strong black community, which in turn leads to a strong black nation. This evolution is Giovanni's hope: As she writes in the autobiographical work *Gemini* (1971), "I really like to think a Black, beautiful, loving world is possible." The wealth of the black community is not measured in stocks, savings accounts, and possessions but in something more intangible, love. Outside the black community, however, "they never understand Black love is Black wealth."

"Nikki-Rosa" hints at the radical nature of Giovanni's early poems. Yet, more importantly, it points to the direction that her later poems would take, a shift to a more humanistic view which encompasses all races.

Barbara Wiedemann

THE NINE MONSTERS

Author: César Vallejo (1892-1938)
Type of poem: Meditation
First published: 1939, as "Los neuve monstruos," in *Poemas humanos*; English translation collected in *The Complete Posthumous Poetry*, 1978

The Poem

"The Nine Monsters" is a seventy-line poem, divided into four stanzas of varying lengths. The poem is written loosely in the form of an address, perhaps a speech, in which the poet discourses on the subjects of pain and misfortune to an audience of "human men" and "brother men." It would appear that the poem begins somewhere in the middle of the speech, since the opening line of the poem implies continued speech.

After the outbreak of the Spanish Civil War in 1936, César Vallejo was active as a vocal defender of the Spanish Republic. In Paris, where he had lived since 1923, he attended meetings and assemblies and helped in the effort to raise money for the Republican cause. While autobiographical information is not necessary to study "The Nine Monsters," it is helpful to know that at the time Vallejo wrote the poem (it is dated November 3, 1937), he was out canvassing the streets and speaking to crowds about the war. The speechlike nature of the poem is more apparent in this context.

In the first stanza, the poet or speaker notes the rapid and ceaseless spread of pain in the world. Pain has become the dominant fact of life, so much so that those who suffer are virtually martyrs to it. Pain is so great that it constantly redoubles itself.

The speaker then turns his attention, in the second stanza, to the historical moment. It is the age of pain, he says. There has never been a time more vulnerable to its debilitating attack. Even affection has been marred by pain. Health, paradoxically, means death. Everything conceals pain, and the speaker wishes to draw everyone's attention to the fact—even the government (the secretary of health) must hear his appeal.

The third stanza shifts attention to pain's cousins: misfortune, evil, and suffering; they, too, are spreading rapidly, flooding the world and overturning the established order. At this point, the speaker elaborates on the "nine monsters" of the title. Six times in six lines he repeats the number nine, each time using it to enumerate another aspect of what, presumably, constitutes the monsters mentioned in the title. One thing is sure: The "monsters" are closely connected to sound, primarily apocalyptic sound.

The fourth stanza is the poem's longest. Whereas in the previous stanzas the speaker has commented on the extent of pain in the world and on the places where it is active, in stanza 4, the reader's attention is directed to the activity of pain. Pain is seen as an active force. It grabs people, drives them wild, nails them, denails them. In effect, pain is personified; it comes alive and stalks human beings. It is associated with creative and destructive principles: Life and death occur "as a result/ of the pain."

The poem ends with the speaker's personal agony, the sadness he feels at witnessing this enormous suffering. It is all too much for him; there is nothing to be done about it; the extent of the suffering is too vast.

Forms and Devices

The distinguishing characteristic of Vallejo's poetic technique is his extraordinary ability to shatter language—the very thing poetry depends on—and through its deconstruction, to create a new (albeit esoteric and unnatural) medium to communicate the chaos he sees all around. In essence, Vallejo conveys his message by destroying the traditional means by which a message can be communicated. Syntax, grammar, and even vocabulary come apart in his poetry. From the rubble, he re-creates the text, in completely new combinations, so that meaning is reconstituted in a way never before possible. Vallejo uses words the way a Cubist such as Pablo Picasso or Georges Braque uses shape. Cubism forces one to view an image simultaneously from a multiplicity of new angles, so that "normal" perception of that image is no longer valid. Similarly, Vallejo requires language to be read in an entirely new way: The traditional logic of grammar is discarded, and readers are forced to reconstruct it themselves so that the "normal" interpretation of the words is no longer valid. As the syntax is wrenched apart in a Vallejo poem, so, too, is meaning wrenched apart. Readers are often left with irrational, private, and ultimately ambiguous images that parallel the ambiguous nature of contemporary experience.

The first stanza of "The Nine Monsters" is a good example of this technique. The stanza appears to be a single, medium-length sentence—at least it is punctuated that way—however, this sentence has no beginning and no conclusion. Although a subject and a verb are provided ("pain grows"), the sentence soon loses all grammatical sense. The phrase "the pain twice" is repeated several times as though the speaker has lost the train of thought and must return to what he has already said. The broken syntax of the first stanza is reminiscent of other modernist poems, such as T. S. Eliot's "The Hollow Men," in which a sequence of fragments is spliced together. The resulting jumble falls short of effective communication. This device may baffle the reader, but there is a point to the confusion: Many of Vallejo's poems are meditations on the modern human's inability to discover meaning in his or her experiences. In "The Nine Monsters," moreover, the broken phrasing gives the impression that someone in excruciating pain is trying to speak. The manner of the speech thus reflects the theme of the speech. The poet finds the pain of life so unbearable that his ability to deliver coherent discourse is impaired.

Vallejo is also a great poet of swift association, a device that allows the poet to leap from one image to another, thus bringing together ideas and images that superficially seem to have little in common. He is willing to take risks in these associations. For example, few other poets would dare to associate cabinet drawers with the heart and wall lizards. Such seemingly implausible connections are jarring and disturbing. The reader is forced to account for the contradictions in these connections. Perhaps in doing so, the reader can glimpse deeper, hidden realities.

Themes and Meanings

The greatest difficulty in discussing the meaning of this poem lies in deciding what to do with the title. The title appears to be significant. There is, therefore, a temptation with a title such as this—a title that names something—to determine its symbolic intention. Vallejo refers to "nine monsters." The reader's job, it would seem, is to figure out what those monsters represent. There is, however, a danger in approaching the imagery of a poem as a set of hieroglyphics that must be deciphered. It is not always the case that symbolism can be neatly solved, as though it were a code. In poetry, the ideational bias is especially problematic. This bias overemphasizes the interpretation of meaning in a work of art, when in fact a complete system of aesthetics focuses on numerous aspects of that work in order to discover its effectiveness. Meaning, then, is not something hidden to be solved like a riddle. Rather, meaning is derived from the total aesthetic experience.

In lines 33 through 37, Vallejo repeats the number "nine" several times, clearly echoing the title. Although the monsters are not named, it is apparent that these monsters have something to do with sounds heard in the inner ear. This ear creates the sounds itself; and it creates them in response to moments of suffering and pain—"the hour of crying," or "the hour of hunger," for example. So the monsters might be related to the intensification of pain at certain moments, such as throbs or jolts or anything that aggravates maladies. Beyond that, their significance is esoteric.

One thing is clear in the poem: Pain itself is monstrous; it grows phenomenally; it attacks humans; it causes upheaval in the world. In several instances, the speaker makes some curious assertions about pain. There has never been so much pain, he says in the second stanza, but why does the speaker locate pain in the lapel or in arithmetic? Through swift associations, the poet connects some rather mundane items, thereby drawing attention to the extent of pain's infiltration into daily life. Everything, he wants to say, contributes in some measure to our suffering. He particularly associates pain with modern gadgetry and entertainment. Even those things normally thought of as comforts or diversions, such as movies and music, are in fact sources of pain.

The poem ends with a question for the secretary of health: What can be done about this rampant pain? This is a rhetorical question, not a demand. The speaker knows all too well that political or governmental solutions to the problem are ineffectual or nonexistent. Anything humankind attempts will be overwhelmed by suffering.

Stephen Benz

MCMXIV

Author: Philip Larkin (1922-1985)
Type of poem: Meditation
First published: 1964, in *The Whitsun Weddings*

The Poem

"MCMXIV," like many of Philip Larkin's poems, is a meditation. This poetic form, modeled on John Donne's prose *Meditations*, begins with a description of an object, a place, or an event. The description leads directly into a response or a consideration of the issues, problems, and complexities suggested by the object; this consideration then leads to a conclusion or resolution. In "MCMXIV" the object is a 1914 photograph of British volunteers lined up in front of an army recruiting office after England entered World War I. By extension the poem considers the prewar British society that those men represent. The poem itself does not overtly indicate that the photograph is the object of meditation; rather, the title (Roman numerals for 1914) and the description provide that context. While readers can not know whether Larkin was contemplating a particular photograph, there are examples of this type of picture in most illustrated histories of World War I.

The first three stanzas of the four-stanza poem offer an interpretive description of the scene in the photograph. The men stand patiently in line, as they might wait to gain admission to a sporting event or an "August Bank Holiday lark." (In England a bank holiday is a legal holiday when the banks are ordered closed.) This holiday is in August, since August 4, 1914, was the date England declared war on the Central Powers. The scene Larkin describes is holiday-like: The shops are closed, but the pubs are open. Children are playing; the men in line are grinning. No one yet suspects the horrors that World War I will bring.

Stanza 3 moves beyond the photo of the men in line at the recruiting office to include the countryside. In the poetry, novels, and memoirs of World War I, idyllic, pastoral prewar England is often contrasted with the horrors of European trench warfare. Therefore Larkin's meditation on innocence includes such pastoral references. Significantly, the grass and wheat fields cover place names and property lines, much as they would later cover the graves and names of the five million Allied casualties of the war.

Also recalled as background to the photograph and the war experience is the orderly class structure of prewar England: "The differently-dressed servants/ With tiny rooms in huge houses." Many authors, such as Ford Madox Ford in his *Parade's End* novels (1924-1928), wrote about men from all social classes, content in their separation before the war, who suddenly found themselves fighting side by side in the trenches. The belief in the inevitability and morality of the class structure was part of the "innocence" lost during the war.

"Never such innocence" is the poet's interpretative conclusion. The prewar world "changed itself to past" and could never be recaptured. The photograph shows a large crowd of men willingly, happily volunteering for the war. They were doing their duty as well as heading off for an adventure, never imagining the misery and destruction ahead of them. While the poem does not describe the battlefields, the idea of lost innocence brings into the poem World War I as described by those who experienced it. The trenches, mud, rats, barbed wire, tanks, snipers, poison gas, grenades, and air attacks (vividly described, for example, in Wilfred Owen's poetry) were yet unimagined horrors. The war destroyed all fantasies of war as a glorious, heroic adventure played out on orderly battlefields by gentlemen: "Never such innocence again."

Forms and Devices

"MCMXIV," like all of Larkin's poems, is characterized by clear, straightforward, unadorned language. Larkin is the best-known and most successful of a group of British poets from the 1950's known as "The Movement" (other Movement poets include Robert Conquest, Kingsley Amis, and Donald Davie). All these poets used direct, plain language, which was deliberately chosen in rejection of the rich, melodic, metaphoric language of Dylan Thomas and the dense, allusive, intellectual language of T. S. Eliot. It was an appropriate language for the skeptical, unsentimental, sometimes hopeless worldview of their poems. Larkin, like other Movement authors, worked within a narrow emotional range, ironically noting the pain and dreariness of everyday experience that must be accepted.

When Larkin departs from his usual plain language, the effect is striking. In stanza 3, describing rural fields, he refers to "Domesday lines": These are the boundaries between property first defined in 1086 by William the Conqueror and recorded in the *Domesday Book*. The historical reference is a jarring pun, since the *Domesday Book* is also known as the *Doomsday Book*. The men in Larkin's photograph were taking their first step toward their doom.

That Larkin's language is generally plain does not mean that he eschews metaphor entirely. The lines of men waiting to enlist in the British army are like lines waiting to see a cricket match at the Oval in London. The atmosphere on the day war was declared was like that of a bank holiday. The rural fields are, in their description at least, like the war cemeteries of Europe. Most significantly, the men, in their eagerness to go to war and with their belief that nothing will be changed when they come back, are a metaphor and a symbol for innocence that would be lost.

The images of the poem, like the language, are clear and straightforward. They move in an ever-expanding pattern. The first stanza limits itself to the actual content of the photograph: the appearance of the men standing in line. Stanza 2 moves just outside the picture itself to provide details about the neighborhood of the recruiting office. One sees the advertisements in shop windows, the children playing, the pubs. Next one moves outside the city to the fields and the manor houses. All of England is drawn into the picture. Finally, in the last stanza, the larger significance of the scene is stated; at the same time, the poem returns to the individual men in the photograph, each with his own tidy garden and marriage.

Themes and Meanings

World War I was a highly literary war—it was unusual in the number of soldiers who wrote poems, novels, and memoirs about their experience. Wilfred Owen, Siegfried Sassoon, Rupert Brooke, Ford Madox Ford, Robert Graves, and David Jones are but a few of the authors to write major works about the war experience. So important is World War I as a subject in modern British literature that it is in no way unusual to see Larkin returning to it nearly fifty years after the event. With "MCMXIV" he places himself in a significant literary tradition.

He also restates for his time the major literary interpretation of the war. His conclusion that innocence was lost as a result of the horrors of war is consistent with the reading of the experience given by his predecessors. In fact, this reading has reached the status of myth or master narrative—a coherent story which claims to explain a major social phenomenon. In this myth, prewar England is seen as idyllic. The social order was fixed and secure: Each class knew its role and strove only to succeed in that role. The country shared adherence to the Church of England. Science assured an unbroken path of progress, promising that life would continue to get better and better. All was orderly, civil, and decorous. In fact, in an ironic contrast, the summer of 1914, the months immediately before the war, were warm and sunny, the most beautiful summer anyone could remember.

The decorous and orderly men who lined up patiently to enlist in August of 1914 were to have their faith in order (even their faith in God) seriously shaken in the trenches of Europe. Those who were not killed by bombs or snipers might face excruciatingly painful deaths from poison gas or entrapment in barbed wire. Those who survived had to live in dirt trenches containing a foot or two of collected rainwater, sharing the space with rats. They were changed, according to the story, by the experience; when the war was over, nothing could be the same. Their world had changed, and romanticism gave way to cynicism and despair. The lower classes were no longer content; the Church of England lost its influence; those who had seen the bestiality of the war could no longer believe in progress: "Never such innocence again."

The myth of World War I has resonance beyond twentieth century experience. It has literary parallels in John Milton's *Paradise Lost* (1667) and William Blake's *Songs of Innocence and Experience* (1794). Through them it repeats one of the fundamental narratives of Christianity, the fall from innocence in the Garden of Eden, and a basic psychological pattern of maturing from naïve childhood to disillusioned adulthood. From his meditation on an old photograph of men waiting to enlist in World War I, Larkin recapitulates one of the most enduring stories of Western culture, the story of the inevitable movement from idyllic naïveté to disappointed experience.

Bruce H. Leland

NINETEEN HUNDRED AND NINETEEN

Author: William Butler Yeats (1865-1939)
Type of poem: Meditation
First published: 1921; collected in *The Tower*, 1928

The Poem

William Butler Yeats's "Nineteen Hundred and Nineteen," from the 1928 collection *The Tower*, is not the most accessible of his poems, but it encompasses many of the themes, motifs, and techniques of his mature poetry. It is probably best understood and best enjoyed in the greater context of his work. Written in six parts of unequal length, the poem uses, as its focal point, the bloody retribution of British soldiers against the Irish citizenry during the time of the Sinn Féin rebellion (1919-1921). Although rooted in the Irish Home Rule struggle, it is more than a political poem, examining the fluctuating relationship between time and understanding, reality and illusion, and nature and artifice. What seems clear at one point in time can easily be thrown into flux by the events of a later time, perpetuating an ascending series—a metaphysical "tower"—of transformation and reappraisal. Woven together with the poet's private pantheon of symbols are allusions to contemporary, historical, and classical events, challenging the reader to follow the byways of Yeats's visionary landscape.

The first section introduces all the threads that will appear, in ways reminiscent of a fugue, throughout the poem. In the first two stanzas, Yeats takes pains to emphasize the difference between appearance and reality. "Things" that seemed miraculous and "protected" have vanished; laws and opinions—presumably immutable—have changed; most tragically, the assumption that the "worst rogues and rascals had died out" has been proven wrong.

Readers familiar with Yeats's frequently anthologized poem "Sailing to Byzantium" (1928) will recognize the same world of artifice in the "famous ivories" and "golden grasshoppers" of the first stanza. By stanza 4, however, Yeats plunges back into the writhing physical world of Ireland in 1919: "Now days are dragon-ridden." Here is the kernel of the poem, the events that inspire this reflection. Here, as well, are the poem's most vivid and most horrific images: the slain mother in her blood juxtaposed against the murdering, drunken soldiers who escape. The visual impact of these verses is all the greater given the contrast with the philosophical musings that have preceded them.

By the sixth stanza, the last in the first section, Yeats poses the question that is preeminent in his work: "Man is in love and loves what vanishes,/ What more is there to say?" Love and loss are the twins who inhabit every cranny of Yeats's poetic territory. His strongest work, poems such as "Crazy Jane Talks with the Bishop" (1933) and "The Circus Animals' Desertion" (1939), affirm the necessity and, indeed, the inevitability of love, even in the face of change and disintegration. In this context, it is significant that it is a mother, not simply a woman, who is killed, since motherhood is emblematic of both love and renewal.

The second section amplifies the theme of the recurrence of change, while at the same time emphasizing its ultimate superficiality. The poem mentions Loie Fuller, a dancer who was a contemporary of Yates and who specialized in dramatic spectacle and illusion; the grisly image of the dragon in the first section has been transformed—and tamed—into an artificial "dragon of air" in the hands of a dance troupe. In a reversal of the anticipated, the Platonic Year brings in nothing new but rather what is old. Nothing has been learned from history, no real or lasting achievements have been made. Over the course of time, humankind still participates in the same "dance," but, ominously, the gong that sounds the music is "barbarous."

In the third section, Yeats concentrates on classical allusions, returning to the philosophizing of the early part of the poem. The dominant image is that of the swan, or the soul, as conceived by some earlier voice. Yeats is deliberately vague about whom this might be, a "moralist or mythological poet." History has tricked him out of any personal fame. This swan later comes to life, as it were, leaping into "the desolate heaven." The theme continues to be one of loss.

In the fourth and shortest section, the swan has disappeared, and Yeats takes up an earlier image, that of the weasel. The cynical fifth section invites the reader to "mock at" the great, the good, and the wise for their inefficacies, and finally to mock the mockers. Both poet and reader are implicated in all those who "Traffic in mockery."

In the final section, Yeats unleashes a whirlwind of visual scenes, hurling pell-mell on one another, a veritable "tumult of images." Confusion reigns; "all are blind," the poet affirms. In this maelstrom of bleakness, the final image is of misguided love bestowed on an object unworthy and "stupid."

Forms and Devices

For effect, "Nineteen Hundred and Nineteen" relies heavily on allusion: classical (Platonism, the Athenian sculptor Phidias), biblical (Herodias), historical (the fourteenth century Robert Artisson), and contemporary (Loie Fuller). It is not as important to identify each and every reference, however, as it is to understand that the poet's disillusionment over any real human progress dates from earliest history and permeates subsequent ages of time. The range of allusions serves to emphasize the essential sameness of history and to connect the present with the past.

These connections are reinforced by the language and the structure of the poem. Each section has its own regular rhyme scheme, but Yeats intensifies the internal pattern by frequent repetitions. Commonly, he will use a word several times in quick succession: "thought" three times in two lines in the second stanza, "dancers" three times in the second section. The fifth section turns on the word "mock" and its cognates. In addition, sections are joined by such repetitions: The short fourth section appears to exist solely to reintroduce the weasel image from the first. In the last section, none of the symbols are as important as the sheer accumulation of the language of despair: "violence" (twice in one line), "evil," "crazy," "angry," "blind," "stupid," "insolent," "fiend."

Themes and Meanings

"Nineteen Hundred and Nineteen" is a poem that explores the contradictions of the human condition. In a world filled with change, where the things most precious are irretrievably lost, what remains constant is a propensity toward violence and the inevitable loss that follows in its wake. The loss is twofold, at least: the loss of confidence in one's understanding—whereby the accomplishments of humans (art, philosophy, laws) are reduced to "pretty toys"—and the actual loss of those "toys." Time alters everything, not the least of which is perception. Additionally, the weight of the poem suggests these illusions are also delusions and diminishments, the "great army" unveiled as a "showy thing," the towering statue by Phidias eroded to "that stump on the Acropolis." The best that humankind can do is seen as paltry if it cannot rid the world of the "worst rogues" who slay mothers.

For all the universality of Yeats's poetry, he remains very much an Irish bard, and it would be a mistake to overlook the Irish heart of this poem. Like "Easter 1916" (1916) and "The Second Coming" (1920), "Nineteen Hundred and Nineteen" is political, and it is a memorial to the troubles of Ireland immediately following World War I. Irish patriots, many of whom were connected intimately with Yeats, had hoped that, with England's attention focused on Europe, the time would be propitious for freeing their country from the English yoke. Should any reader be tempted to overlook the specific and particular historical events that infuse this poem, Yeats keeps them in strong focus with his title. All Irish readers (presumably) would understand the context; all others would be expected to discover it.

"Nineteen Hundred and Nineteen" is a dense and tightly connected poem, but it also contains verses of great simplicity, such as "Violence upon the roads: violence of horses." Herein is Yeats's "natural world"—the world of real people and their real pain. Within the intricate structure of his many symbols and allusions, Yeats maintains the balance between direct and ornate language and keeps the poem from sliding into purely idiosyncratic or private images. It is no accident that the most spare and simple language is usually reserved for contemporary events, the ones with most urgency.

The verses more laden with symbols belong either to the world of the mind or the world of history (usually the ancient kingdoms of Greece, Rome, or Byzantium). These historical references often function as other manifestations of the creative domain. The "ingenious lovely things" of the first stanza are exemplified by "Phidias' famous ivories" and an "ancient image made of olive wood." When, in the second stanza, he speaks of "habits that made old wrong/ Melt down, as it were wax in the sun's rays," one hears echoes of the fall of Icarus, flying too close to the sun. In the bitter vision of this poem, all the golden ingenuity of humankind lies naked to the ravages of the weasel.

Linda Turzynski

1929

Author: W. H. Auden (1907-1973)
Type of poem: Narrative
First published: 1930, in *Poems*

The Poem

W. H. Auden spent part of the year 1929 in Berlin, hoping to get away from the stultifying atmosphere of the more socially conservative London. Thus began his most political period, when he got caught up in antifascist movements and, eventually, went to Spain during their civil war. In the late 1920's, Berlin was becoming a battleground between conflicting political factions. Auden and his English contemporaries often blamed older generations for the destruction of World War I, concluded only ten years earlier. They also saw, or thought they saw, the early indications of the next war. Political demonstrations often turned violent. Clashes between the police and demonstrators were common, as were brawls between communists and fascists. This political situation, which Adolf Hitler used to his advantage when he came to power in 1933, eventually led to World War II, the outbreak of which Auden marked with the poem "September 1, 1939."

The poem known as "1929" was included in Auden's first book of poetry, *Poems* (1930). The poem is often printed without a title, but Auden also published it in a slightly revised version in his *Collected Shorter Poems, 1927-1957* (1966), giving the year of its composition as its title. It is a composite of four segments—dated April 1929, May 1929, August 1929, and October 1929—taken from four separate poems. It has a fractured autobiographical narrative to match its fractured syntax. Some of the fragments were written while the poet was living in Germany (the public garden in which the poet walks is the *Tiergarten* in Berlin), and the whole thing was most likely compiled in England in late 1929 or 1930.

The first and last sections are narratively connected but separated by the poet's meditations, very personal and somewhat obscure, about his development as an intellectual in a time of social unrest. The poem starts with seasonal imagery but departs sharply at the beginning of the second stanza, when the poet's attention turns to thoughts of death and failure. Describing his own personal situation and that of his friends, Auden shifts to a more general description of life in Berlin.

Section 2 describes his engagement with friends discussing political events. The poet appears to be both engaged in the situation and observing it, saying that he is pleased, while he is really feeling angry at both sides. As an observer, the poet considers the development of people as individuals in whom he can see "fear of other" and a basic inability to forgive. The poet, however, can see the goodness in life and feel peace.

Part 3 describes Auden's return to England and to his mother's house. The poet shifts from his own development to a general process of growth and individuation experienced by young people who take their first steps away from home, falter, and eventually come to appreciate home. Although this section is dated August, there is a growing awareness of winter. Here, winter is an earthly indication of death, arranged so that one will be familiar with death when it comes. In both sections 2 and 3, Auden shifts from the personal to the general, indicating that the development of the individual parallels the development of a culture. As the individual grows to fear others, so too do societies; as the individual grows through an awareness of death, so too do nations.

The final segment returns to the idea of error with a strong statement: "It is time for the destruction of error." This section describes autumn in England, when furniture is brought in from the garden, and makes the analogy between the end of an era in England, the dawn of a new age in Europe, and the hope for a more honest life in the new decade (eventually termed, by Auden, a "low dishonest" one). In a poem so infused with the idea of death, the last stanza offers hope. The poet and his companion are aware of the needs of love, "more than the admiring excitement of union," and they know of the necessity of death for rebirth.

Forms and Devices

The poem mixes observation and meditation. As the line "Tiny observer of enormous world" indicates, the poet is interested in describing what he sees as well as the effect his observations have on himself. The world tends to make him feel insignificant, like a cog in a machine. In fact, the monuments of modern life, machinery, factories, and industry, figure prominently in the political landscape of "Auden country," as scholar Samuel Hynes dubbed it in the 1970's. With his contemporary Stephen Spender, Auden brought the reality of contemporary England and Europe into English poetry. The poem "1929" is rife with images of ordinary life and the materials of that life, such as buses, bicycles, and the "strict beauty of locomotive."

In a similar move, Auden adds intensity to the poem by using a specialized kind of language, that of the postcard or telegram written with an urgency that may sacrifice clarity. The poem is noticeably lacking in definite and indefinite articles; that is, Auden leaves out "the" and "a" ("solitary man" rather than "a solitary man," for example). In his preface to *Collected Shorter Poems, 1927-57*, Auden attributes this style to "some very slovenly verbal habits. The definite article is always a headache to any poet writing in English, but my addiction to German usages became a disease."

Aside from the issue of articles, however, the diction in this poem has a quality that a reader might see as similar to that of American writer Gertrude Stein. Employing repetition and variation, the poet gives the impression that he enjoys his words. For example, section 2 opens with the lines, "Coming out of me living is always thinking,/ Thinking changing and changing living,/ Am feeling as it was seeing—." Like other writers in the early half of the twentieth century, Auden was also very interested in psychoanalysis, especially the work of Sigmund Freud and his followers, and so the idea that "thinking is always living" becomes the basis for the deliberate archaism of the poem and the imitation of the language of the "primitive man" in the fourth stanza of section 2: "Is first baby, warm in mother."

Another, perhaps stronger, influence is Irish writer James Joyce, whose *Portrait of the Artist as a Young Man* (1915) is written from the perspective of Stephen Daedalus. The famous first chapter begins when Stephen is a young boy: "Once upon a time and a very good time it was there was a moocow coming down along the road." Writing in the voice of the very young, Auden uses a similar technique in the line, "Is first baby, warm in mother." It is Auden's attempt to write not only in a prebirth voice but also from a preverbal state, as if from the point of view of an uncivilized man. He does this to describe what he sees as the primeval fears and drives of humankind.

Themes and Meanings

Perhaps the first idea the reader notices in this poem is that of death, which seems to permeate it from beginning to end. The opening line identifies Easter as the day on which the poet takes his walk, and Auden immediately signals the dual themes of death and rebirth. Easter is, after all, the celebration of Christ's resurrection, his death a "necessary condition" of his rebirth into something greater than his earthly being. Yet, for a poem that starts out sounding so hopeful, with its "emphasis on new names, on the arm/ A fresh hand," the shift to a discussion of death can be disconcerting.

The subject of death, however, is constantly mingled with images of natural life, such as the colony of ducks, and with the poet's appreciation of the human life he sees around him (the hymns he hears in the village square, for example). So it is the combination of death and life that intrigues him and that he sees as necessary. In order to fully love life, one needs a knowledge of death.

The truly strong man, as he calls his friend Gerhardt Meyer, recognizes this idea and acts accordingly. For Auden and his friend Christopher Isherwood (the novelist to whom Auden dedicated his *Poems* of 1930), the truly strong man is the antiheroic hero. Unlike traditional ideas of male strength—a glorious, risk-taking hero—Auden and Isherwood see the truly strong man as one who possesses inner security and self-confidence, who does not need to prove himself to anyone, and whose actions are, consequently, pure in heart. The truly strong man is able to resolve traditional dichotomies, such as public/private, inner/outer, and, as in this poem, life/death, to achieve peace within himself. Auden develops this idea in "The Orators" (1931) as does Isherwood in *Lions and Shadows* (1938).

The final image of the "lolling bridegroom, beautiful, there" may leave the reader a bit perplexed. It is a variation on the Lady of the Lake of Arthurian legend, who gives the sword, Excalibur, to Arthur. The mysticism implicit in the image connects back to the image of the risen Christ, for the figure in the lake will eventually rise, be reborn, and bring a new power of good to the world.

James J. Berg

NINETIETH BIRTHDAY

Author: R. S. Thomas (1913-   )
Type of poem: Meditation
First published: 1961, in *Tares*

The Poem

R. S. Thomas's "Ninetieth Birthday" is a poem of two stanzas of unequal length written in free verse. The second stanza is further divided for emphasis, the seventh line beginning immediately below the end of the sixth line rather than at the left margin as do the other lines. The poem is written in the second person; though the speaker seems to be addressing another person, it is possible to read the poem as the speaker's own memories or thoughts about an event. The poem describes a person going to visit an old woman, perhaps a mother or grandmother, on the occasion of her ninetieth birthday. The first stanza describes a walk up a steep hill on a midsummer day and does not indicate where the person is going or why the person is going up the hill. Instead, the stanza portrays the landscape: a road, probably dirt, on which it is better to walk than drive, a rocky hillside where trees give way to bracken, a distant view of the sea, and a small stream. The description is similar to those in other poems by Thomas set in the mountainous areas of Wales.

The second stanza moves from a description of the landscape to the description of an old woman waiting for her visitor at the top of the hill. The old woman "Waits for the news of the lost village/ She thinks she knows, a place that exists/ In her memory only," which indicates that she rarely, if ever, leaves her farm and that the world has changed in ways of which she has no knowledge. This point is emphasized later in the second half of the stanza: "Yet no bridge joins her own/ World with yours." The poem concludes with a description of the visitor listening to the old woman but with the sense that what she has to say has no relevance to the present.

The movement from the first stanza to the second is a movement from the external to the internal; although the second stanza contains descriptive elements as well, it makes judgments about the characters and their worlds while the first stanza sets the place. The poem does not contain a description of the visitor's world; the first stanza's precise images bring the reader into the poem and provide the sense that the visitor is familiar with but not part of the landscape. The second stanza reinforces this, implying not only that the visitor is removed enough from the landscape to notice it but also that the visitor can never become part of that landscape. Even the landscape does not serve as a bridge between the two worlds.

Forms and Devices

"Ninetieth Birthday" is written in very plain language with sentences that are long but not syntactically difficult. It uses neither rhyme nor formal meter, and there are very few metaphors or other figures of speech. Thomas does not usually dress up his poems, particularly the earlier ones, with many adjectives or long words, and this poem is typical in its plainness. In the first stanza, the only word of more than two syllables is "history," and his few adjectives are simple and ordinary: "green," "warm," and "far," for example. Such simple language is particularly effective in describing the landscape; it is precise enough for the reader to visualize it clearly, and it gives the poem a quiet and thoughtful tone.

The second stanza differs from the first in that it contains more metaphors, and the metaphors are used more to create a complex emotion than to clarify an image. For example, the first stanza uses the metaphor of lichen "That writes history on the page/ Of the grey rock," which strengthens the mental picture of lichen on a stone, covering it like words on a page or hieroglyphs on a clay tablet. It also creates a sense of the mountain's age. In the second stanza, however, the metaphor of "time's knife shaving the bone" does not provide a useful visual image if one tries to picture it literally. While it does function as a description of the physical diminution that comes with aging, it is more effective when read as an account of the old woman's life. Each year there is a little less. She is slowly dying. The stanza's other metaphors, "bridge" and "abyss," both function on a conceptual rather than visual level. There is no physical abyss between the old woman's world and the visitor's world, but there is a vast cultural and social difference.

Formally, one of the more interesting aspects of the poem is the use of the second person. While the second person is not unusual for poetry, there is often a clear sense that the speaker is addressing another person. In "Ninetieth Birthday," however, the quiet and sad tone as well as the privacy of the moment—only the visitor and the old woman are present—imply that the poem could well be the speaker's own thoughts or memories. While it is certainly possible that the speaker is addressing a close friend, the speaker might also be using the second person to feel more detached when describing a painful experience. The phrase "all you can do" near the end of the poem expresses feelings of futility and helplessness, emotions from which the speaker might well want to be somewhat distant. The visitor is glad that the old woman is still alive, but her old age and solitude are deeply sorrowful to the visitor. In using the second person, the speaker lessens some of the immediacy of the sad feeling. Yet, powerfully, the distance increases the reader's sense of the depth of the sadness. The distance between the speaker or reader and the visitor gives a greater idea of the distance between the visitor and the old woman.

Themes and Meanings

"Ninetieth Birthday" is not a particularly complex poem thematically; it reveals the cultural difference between people of earlier and later generations. Such a difference is not stated; rather, it is implied by the phrases such as "lost village," "a place that exists/ In her memory only," and "words that were once wise." When one steps outside the poem to look at its author and the time of its writing, however, other related meanings emerge. Thomas is Welsh, and many of his poems are about the changes in Welsh culture, language, and history. Thomas's poem "Welsh History" presents an image of

Wales trapped in the past, the people, having lost their language, confined by their own history of poverty and violence. In the poem "Expatriates," Thomas describes Welsh people leaving the mountains for the city and leaving their language behind. When one reads "Ninetieth Birthday" with an awareness of the changes in Welsh culture, the old woman's separation from the visitor is even stronger.

"Ninetieth Birthday" was published in the volume *Tares* in 1961. If the poem is supposed to be taking place at the time of publication, the old woman would have been born in 1871. In 1871, many Welsh people did not speak English, a condition that had changed by 1961; furthermore, the number of people who spoke Welsh decreased substantially over the same period. With increases in technology, cars replaced horses, and tractors replaced the old horse-drawn ploughs. The old woman's farm seems to be a farm caught in the nineteenth century, her words of wisdom applying to a time that is long gone. The second line of the poem describes the track as one "That will take a car, but is best walked"; the modern world and the old woman's farm do not connect. The visitor's sadness is not only about the old woman's aging but also about how the world has changed so that the old woman no longer fits in with it. What has been lost is a culture, a way of living, perhaps even a language. The "history" in the first stanza becomes, in the second, a history that encompasses loss and alienation: Time cannot be reversed to counter aging, and it cannot be reversed to alter changes in a culture.

Elisabeth Anne Leonard

NO SECOND TROY

Author: William Butler Yeats (1865-1939)
Type of poem: Lyric
First published: 1910, in *The Green Helmet and Other Poems*

The Poem

William Butler Yeats's poem "No Second Troy" is composed of four sentences, each of them a question, and is shaped into twelve lines of iambic pentameter. The poem is a typical lyric in that it expresses the poet's personal feelings about his love, and it remains focused on a single issue. The poet suggests through his questions that he should not blame his love for filling his life with misery because she is unable to find a proper outlet for her talents in the Ireland of her day.

The first question Yeats asks is actually made up of three parts, one entirely personal, the others more political. He asks why he should blame this woman for filling his life with misery, teaching violence to the ignorant, or encouraging class conflict. By linking these three, Yeats equates to some degree his own personal misery with what he considers to be social misery: political violence, especially when it is involved in pitting one class (the working class in this case) against another (the aristocratic class).

Once the poet establishes the harm this woman has done and exonerates her for that, he describes the woman herself and contrasts her with her milieu. He clearly states that she could not be peaceful, that she had to do violence to him or encourage violence in others, because her mind, her body, and her soul were not in harmony with her world. Her mind is noble; Yeats suggests that others in the society are not. Her beauty is not something common or ordinary or crass; instead, it is "high and solitary and most stern," a type of beauty and character that is "not natural in an age like this." Thus Yeats, while refusing to place blame on this woman, clearly places blame on the times and the culture that would not allow a woman of this type to find a proper release for her capabilities.

The third and fourth questions are tied together. The third seems to merely reiterate what has already been said, asking what she could have done differently, "being what she is" and given the culture of the times, but the fourth question, and final line of the poem, brings a whole other dimension to the poem by mentioning the burning of Troy. Certainly this comparison between Helen of Troy and the woman spoken of in this poem is expressed in the title, but this final image of the burning of Troy strengthens the allusion and explains, to some degree, the images used earlier in the poem.

Forms and Devices

Knowledge of Greek myth and Yeats's biography is essential for an understanding of this poem. Yeats loved and proposed marriage many times to Maud Gonne, an Irish revolutionary patriot, but she rejected him each time. In 1903, five years before this poem was written, Gonne married John MacBride, then separated from him in 1905. Gonne is the woman spoken about in this poem and many other poems by Yeats. Here she is compared to Helen of Troy, the woman whose abduction by Paris led to the Trojan War and the final burning of that city by the Greeks. This allusion to classical myth is the literary device that drives the poem forward and gives it the unity of design that is a central facet of this poem.

Yeats is essentially asking how he could blame Maud Gonne for making his own life miserable because she is like Helen, the daughter of Zeus. Gonne, according to Yeats, could not find a proper role in a society, unless she lived in the mythic world of ancient Greece.

The metaphorical language used in the second sentence of the poem only makes sense in this context of Greek myth. The comparison between the nobility of her mind and the simplicity of a fire is not an arbitrary comparison: That fire is linked with the destruction of Troy. Similarly, the comparison between her beauty and a tightened bow refers to the violence of the Trojan War. The tightened bow of her beauty and the fire of her mind must find outlets, but because she lives in Ireland, not Greek myth, she can only bring pain and misery, not glory and victory.

Another unifying force in this poem is the rhetorical device of using the four questions to structure the poem. Less obvious is the repetition of the interrogatory pronouns that start the questions. The third question begins, "Why, what could she have done," and this line of iambic pentameter has an extra syllable in the line; instead of a line made up of ten syllables, it has eleven. It seems clear that the first "why" could have easily been dropped; for metrical and syntactical purposes there is no reason to write "why, what"; "what" could suffice. Yet Yeats is drawing the poem tightly together, not only by using allusions to Greek myth in his title, his imagery, and his metaphors, but also by unifying his three questions asked. The first begins, "Why should I blame her"; the second begins, "What could have made her"; and the third ties these two together by asking, "Why, what could she have done."

Themes and Meanings

This poem's vitality comes partially from its joining together of the personal, the political, and the historical or mythical worlds. Yeats was a poet who was deeply involved in his country's movement to cultural, if not political, independence from Great Britain, and his work is strengthened by this involvement. He, as is evidenced in this poem, managed to include his own love life in his poetry, without excluding the larger social and mythic realms. Perhaps he is offering a recipe for great poetry in this poem: Create a unified whole by mixing personal obsessions with the power of contemporary events, but do not forget the timeless world of myth.

Although this is, on one level, a love poem, it also contains many of Yeats's political views, partially because his love—Maude Gonne—was a very active, political person. Even though Yeats was in love with Gonne, he was not in love with her political activism. Given the opportunity, Gonne "would of late/ Have taught to ignorant men most violent ways,/ Or hurled the little streets upon the great." Yeats, as is clear from his word choice, opposes such action; it is equivalent to filling his "days/ With misery." Yeats was troubled by Gonne's involvement in nationalist and working-class organizations that espoused violence as a method to achieve political ends. Yeats shows his hand very clearly by calling those involved in these organizations "ignorant men." He questions not only their intelligence or learning but also their courage by saying they could have "hurled the little streets upon the great,/ Had they but courage equal to desire." The "little streets" is a figure of speech representing the poor, or working class, and the "great" refers to the aristocracy that Yeats respected. He does not question the desire of the poor to wrest power from the rich, but he does question their courage.

Yeats makes his poem about his love different from others not only by blending the political with the personal but also by creating a different kind of heroine. Too often male poets writing about women whom they love use stereotypical language or imagery to talk about the them. Often the women are merely objects, inactive beauties whose bodies are the focus of the work. Yeats, writing at a time when the women's suffrage movement was sweeping through Europe and the United States, conjures up a different portrait, one that emphasizes not beauty as object, but beauty as something active, powerful, "like a tightened bow." The portrait is extended to include "a mind/ That nobleness made simple as a fire." Both the bow and the fire suggest power, vehemence, and action, and they are not images normally associated with women in traditional poetry.

In addition, in the Greek myth Helen is merely a beautiful victim, someone who is stolen by Paris and used as a pawn in the dispute between the Trojans and the Greeks. In this poem, even though Gonne is compared to Helen, she is not a victim, but rather an active force; Helen may have caused others to burn Troy, but Gonne in this poem is imagined burning Troy herself. This type of presentation of a woman in poetry could be considered revolutionary. Unfortunately, Yeats's poem does not really allow Gonne any option in the real world of modern Ireland. He may acknowledge her power, but he does not imagine a world in which that power can be used productively. Instead, her power, which is frustrated, turns into a destructive force; her power leads to violence without just cause or positive result.

Kevin Boyle

A NOCTURNAL UPON ST. LUCY'S DAY

Author: John Donne (1572-1631)
Type of poem: Lyric
First published: 1633, as "A nocturnall upon S. *Lucies* day,/ Being the shortest day,"
in *Poems, by J. D.: With Elegies on the Authors Death*

The Poem

"A Nocturnal upon St. Lucy's Day" is characteristic of John Donne's art: It is compressed verse full of tightly woven images and concepts, it is rapid, and its metrics and shape are atypical of traditional verse. The rhythmic diversity suggests speech and debate. The act of reading the poem is rather like that of deciphering a cryptogram or solving a puzzle while riding over a bumpy road. In sum, it is difficult to imagine anyone but Donne writing this poem.

It begins with a time reference, namely to the shortest day of the year—the winter solstice (December 12 in the Julian calendar)—and more specifically to the dying moments of the year. The speaker contemplates this day while (fictionally) writing the poem on the previous evening. He deploys this strategy as a way to explain by comparison that his condition is more dire than is the death of the earthly year: "yet all these seem to laugh/ Compar'd with me." The reader is left to wonder what has brought him to this calamitous, exaggerated grief.

In the second stanza, the speaker enjoins the readers (who are lovers, or will be lovers in the next spring) to study him in order to learn how love transformed him. In this arrangement, love is a personified being who miraculously produces a restorative substance ("quintessence," and later "elixir") from the speaker's destruction. Thus the lovers are offered a cautionary story of the transitory nature of humankind, but a story that also hints at potential good as a result.

The third stanza continues the regenerative concept by contrasting love's treatment of him with how good is normally produced. He again emphasizes that he has been reduced to nothing. In the middle of the stanza the subject shifts. The speaker considers how he and an implied lover have produced cataclysmic effects: floods, chaos, and zombies, or carcasses without souls. The effects of their love have been great, superhuman if not supernatural, suggesting a power consistent with that which might affect time.

The occasion for the grief expressed in the poem is presented at the outset of the fourth stanza. Here readers learn that the speaker's lover has died. Her death has resulted in his return to a primordial nothingness, and it troubles him that he loses his identity in the process. He realizes that her death has transformed him into a being that is no longer easily classified.

He begins the last stanza by arguing that he is none of the possibilities listed in the previous stanza—man, beast, or ordinary body. He invites the lovers to enjoy their time together, including an implied reference to sexual activity ("the Goat is run/ To fetch new lust"). While they are thus occupied, he asks to be allowed to offer devotion to his dead as both tribute and means to a kind of resurrection. The poem then ends with the recurrent image of the death of the year.

"A Nocturnal upon St. Lucy's Day" is said by many critics to be one of Donne's most complex poems. Some believe that Donne is too obscure most of the time and conclude that this poem in particular is impenetrable. Another objection that has been voiced concerns the extreme expression of grief, especially in the first stanza, with some critics considering it overblown bombast.

Forms and Devices

"A Nocturnal upon St. Lucy's Day" consists of five nine-line stanzas following the unusual rhyme pattern *abbacccdd* over a total of forty-five lines. The rhymed units cohere to form an initial discursive block of four lines, followed by a recursive or appositive group of three lines, followed by a concluding couplet. This pattern encourages a narrowing or a distilling of thought. It also reflects some of the characteristics of both the rime royal and Spenserian stanzaic forms, most notably in the sense of completion caused by the comparatively longer last line.

The metering and rhythm are irregular, somewhat echoing patterns of speech. In general, the lines of each stanza initially tend to favor a tetrameter length (in mixed iambic and anapestic feet), leading up to the stanza's iambic trimeter fifth line. This pattern produces a necessary pause and a heightened emphasis on that fifth line. The halting cadences of the sixth through eighth lines lead to a greater balance in the stanzas' concluding pentameter lines. Donne adds to this scheme an inventive use of the caesura to create more frequent pauses and shifting emphases. Though Donne's habit of engaging in metric irregularity occasioned Ben Jonson's remark that Donne "should be hung for not keeping accent" (meter), in this poem the effect is consistent with the wracking grief the persona expresses throughout his song.

Most compelling as evidence of Donne's artistic control is the poem's symmetrical structure. The poem offers a precise midpoint, the middle of the middle line of the middle stanza (line 22 in stanza 3). This line consists of four syncopated feet. The second foot is broken. This is the only line in all the stanzas that engages an end-stop caesura in the middle of a line—in this case, a period—and the beginning of a new sentence after that second foot. This occurs immediately after the word "nothing," which in Donne's time would most probably have been pronounced as two separate words: "no thing." It is clear that this is a thematically significant division, for it further emphasizes both the speaker's devastation and the potential generative ambiguity.

The question of resulting substance, positive or negative, depends upon this pattern of alchemical and generative imagery. Donne's word choice suggests careful arrangement, especially in how the liver's death produces an elixir that is related to images of growth and continuation. The images simultaneously occupy spiritual and material domains, suggesting a tension often noted in Donne's writing.

Themes and Meanings

Donne intertwines the sacred and profane in this poem. At once readers have the physical death and subsequent mourning, and the spiritual celebration and rebirth of the year. Readers can sense Donne pondering the paradox of these as simultaneous events, forcing them to ask how they could coexist.

Though few of Donne's *Songs and Sonnets* are datable with any precision, ample evidence supports the claim that Donne contrived "A Nocturnal upon St. Lucy's Day" after the death of his wife, Ann, in 1617. Some scholars find such biographical implications to be distractions and prey to fallacious interpretative logic. Others attempt to blend historical material into various interpretive stances. It is certainly hard to deny the power of the poem if one imagines the poet's personal grief. It is even more fitting when one considers that Ann died after an ill-advised twelfth childbirth. It has been suggested that her sacrifice in marital fruition was similar to Saint Lucy's martyrdom—both died unswerving in their manifest faith.

Interpretation of this poem often takes one of two positions: that the poem is an anguished expression of grief and ends in despair, or that it encourages faith in restoration and ends in hope. Either camp must clarify how one should interpret the nulls, zeroes, absences, and no-things that pervade the work. One interpretation involves accepting a sexual representation of the word "thing" as standing for the penis, apparently a common slang usage in Donne's time. This approach presents readers with the implication of emasculation or, in a bawdier sense, a lack of erection: The speaker is reduced to "no thing." Some critics reject such physical punning as inconsistent with the decorum necessitated by the mourning expressed in the poem; others find the correlation between sex and death, consistent with Freudian concepts, to be psychologically appealing.

Further irony may be found in the contrast between the lack of light emphasized in the long-night, short-day positioning, and the fact that celebrations of Saint Lucy often involved emphasis on light and vision. The name "Lucy" is itself cognate with the Latin *lux*. Much of the poem plays off this loss of light, Donne's loss of his wife as loss of the sun (or son). Such verbal punning is regularly found in Donne's writing, and his sermons often focused on the emanations and explications of key scriptural words.

Beyond these themes is the fact—the existence—of the poem itself. It is something produced from a death, and in several instances the poem calls attention to itself. Further, the speaker enjoins the reader to "study me then," which must refer as much to the study of the poem as to the study of the speaker. Since the speaker has indicated that he has become the couple's epitaph, reading the poem is tantamount to reading or studying the speaker. To read the poem is thus both to see the folly of temporal love and to see the restoration that is possible if one has sufficient eternal faith (in the beloved, in God, and perhaps in the poem).

Scott D. Vander Ploeg

NOCTURNE

Author: Tomas Tranströmer (1931-   )
Type of poem: Lyric
First published: 1962, as "Nocturne," in *Den halvfärdiga himlen*; English translation collected in *Twenty Poems of Tomas Tranströmer*, 1970

The Poem

"Nocturne" is a short poem in free verse, its sixteen lines divided into four stanzas. The title, suggesting a musical composition, establishes the mood of the poem. The night, in one of its traditional aspects, is a time for reverie, permitting the free play of thought and emotion expressed, for example, in the nocturnes of Frédéric Chopin. The poem is written in the first person. Sometimes poets use the first person to speak through a persona, whose outlook and experience may be quite different from their own. Here, however, no distinction is implied between Tomas Tranströmer the poet and the speaker of the poem. In the classic tradition of lyric poetry, the poet addresses the reader directly, with the authority of personal experience.

"Nocturne" takes as its point of departure an experience that will be familiar to most readers. When one is driving at night, objects that are caught in the beam of the headlights loom out of the darkness, almost as if they were moving forward. Instead of ignoring this trick of perception as one normally does, Tranströmer accepts it at face value. The scene is transformed, as in a folktale or dream. There is a childlike quality to this vision, too; the magically animate houses, which "step out/ into the headlights" as deer or cattle might, "want a drink."

When the poet turns his attention to sleeping humanity, there is an important shift in perspective. In the second stanza, instead of speaking from immediate personal experience, the poet adopts the generalizing manner of the sage. The last two lines of the stanza in particular recall the voice of the Preacher in Ecclesiastes. (In Swedish, the quasi-biblical parallelism of these lines is even more pronounced.) Like the Preacher, but more gently, he records human folly.

In the third stanza, there is a shift back to immediate personal experience as the nighttime drive described in stanza 1 continues. Again the lyric vision is triggered by precise observation of familiar details: the "melodramatic color" of the trees caught in the headlights and the uncanny clarity of leaves illumined against the night. The metaphorical transformation enacted in stanza 1 continues here as well: The trees are granted sentience and mobility.

The fourth stanza concludes the poem yet leaves it open-ended. In stanzas 1 and 3, the poet has been seeing in the dark, thanks to the headlights of his car; now, in bed and on the verge of sleep, he is seeing in the dark in another sense. Tranströmer notes how the images one sometimes "sees" immediately before sleep seem to come from outside one's consciousness, of their own volition.

Something from outside wants to get in—not to force entry, but to give a message. The poem concludes with another image that is rooted in a familiar sensation: the tantalizing experience of a revelation that cannot quite be grasped before sleep takes over.

Forms and Devices

References to music abound in Tranströmer's poems. (By profession a psychologist, he is said to be an accomplished pianist as well.) Readers who know his work in Swedish lament the loss in translation of the music of his verse. A recording of Tranströmer reading his poems (*The Blue House*, Watershed C-214) is very helpful in this respect; "Nocturne" is one of several poems that he reads in Swedish as well as in English. Inevitably much is lost in transit between languages. Still, if it is true, as Robert Hass writes in his introduction to *Tomas Tranströmer: Selected Poems, 1954-1986* (1987), that Tranströmer "has been translated into English more regularly than any European poet of the postwar generation," much in his poetry must survive and even flourish in translation.

One reason that Tranströmer translates so well is that he is above all a poet of metaphor. "My poems are meeting places," he has said. "Their intent is to make a sudden connection between aspects of reality that conventional languages and outlooks ordinarily keep apart." What is particularly interesting about this credo is that it could serve equally well as a definition of metaphor.

"Nocturne" consists of a series of images in which one thing is seen in terms of something else. Most of the metaphors are implicit at least to some degree; the comparisons are not completely spelled out. For example, the poet never explicitly compares the houses that "step out" to animals, but his description unmistakably suggests the comparison. Some of the metaphors require a bold leap (it is surprising to think of houses transformed into living creatures), while others delight by their simple rightness (the flickering light on the trees from the passing car resembles firelight).

In "Nocturne," many of the metaphors follow a common pattern, reinforcing one another. The pattern is established in the first stanza with the "Houses, barns, nameposts, deserted trailers" that "take on life." In stanza 1, inanimate objects come alive; in stanza 3, trees are described in terms normally reserved for the animal kingdom: They are said to be "silent in a pact with each other," as if they could talk if they wished, and they follow the poet home. In stanza 4, "unknown images and signs," instead of being drawn by the poet, sketch themselves.

This pattern of transformation, which suggests a magical spell cast by the night, culminates in the image that concludes the poem: "In the slot between waking and sleep/ a large letter tries to get in without quite succeeding." A letter is normally a passive object, but here the poet attributes will, intention, purpose to it. Not every metaphor in the poem, however, fits the pattern of passive-into-active. The "slot between waking and sleep," for example, is a marvelous metaphor in which a unit of time—the brief interval of heightened receptivity before sleep—is described in terms of a unit of space.

It is characteristic of Tranströmer to end a poem with an enigmatic image which, like the last line of a haiku, requires the reader to make a connection with what has gone before. "After a Death," "Out in the Open," and "Going with the Current" are other good examples of Tranströmer poems with this kind of ending.

Themes and Meanings

"Nocturne" is a poem about vision. What makes a poet a poet? In one of their guises, poets are visionaries or seers; they see things that many people do not see, or they see familiar things in an unfamiliar way. Countless lyric poems since the Romantic period have centered on this visionary faculty; to a greater or lesser degree, they are poems about the very power of vision that they exemplify.

Addressing this theme, many poets have employed a paradox: Darkness, normally a time when vision is limited at best, heightens their perception. For Octavio Paz, for example, in poems such as "Same Time," "Clear Night," and "San Ildefonso Nocturne," night is the realm of interior vision, yielding poetic revelation. This is a favorite motif of Tranströmer as well; one of his books of poems published after "Nocturne" is entitled *Mörkerseende* (1970), variously translated as *Night Vision* (1971) and *Seeing in the Dark* (1970).

Why should night be conducive to poetic vision? By day, people are preoccupied with their jobs, families, and all the business of everyday life. (For the purposes of the poem, one must ignore the fact that many people in modern societies have to work at night. "Nocturne" implies not a literal contrast between day and night but a contrast between attitudes.) Even while they sleep, they remain in the grip of those preoccupations; meanwhile, "the mystery rolls past." The poem's primary focus, however, is not negative (the lack of vision); rather, the poem shows how a contrasting attitude—receptiveness to mystery—opens one to unsuspected wonders.

There are two ways in which "Nocturne" differs from many poems on the same theme. The first is the modesty of its claims. The poem ends with a failure: The revelation that seems to be right at the edge of the poet's consciousness, within reach, is not after all vouchsafed to him. Moreover, this whimsical, domesticated image invites the reader to identify with the poet ("I too have had such intimations") rather than regard him as one possessing special powers. Nevertheless—here is the second distinction—it is important to note that the poet's visionary power entails receptiveness to something that is trying to get through to him. He is not essentially alone in the universe; he is not arbitrarily imposing meaning on a meaningless world.

Beyond that, to drag the poem into a philosophical debate would be silly; it does not pretend to bear that kind of weight. One version of the poet-seer is the poet-as-child. "Nocturne" resembles one of those children's stories in which, after everyone is thought to be asleep, the dolls and the stuffed animals and the toy soldiers begin to frolic, unaware of the spellbound child who is watching them through the not-quite-shut nursery door.

John Wilson

A NOISELESS PATIENT SPIDER

Author: Walt Whitman (1819-1892)
Type of poem: Lyric
First published: 1868; collected in *Leaves of Grass*, 1871

The Poem

"A Noiseless Patient Spider" is a short poem, its ten uneven lines divided into two stanzas of five lines each. The initial focus of the poem is a spider that is being observed by the speaker. The use of the indefinite article "a" in the title and the first line individualizes this arachnid, separating it from the representative mass and emphasizing the personal nature of its efforts. The adjectives "noiseless" and "patient" anticipate the poem's tone of pathos.

This poem is written in the first person, which is typical of lyric poetry; less common, however, is that the speaker directly addresses and converses with his own soul, which occurs in the second stanza. The reader observes the one observing (the speaker), the one observed (the spider), and the one addressed (the soul).

"A Noiseless Patient Spider" begins with a description of a common and relatively insignificant incident: A spider, all alone on a little promontory, quietly and tirelessly casts out web-threads from its spinnerets into an illimitable, inestimable emptiness that is all it can see; quickly, untiringly, continuously, it attempts to examine and define this significant, palpable unknown that binds it. In this first stanza, the speaker, a seemingly dispassionate viewer of this scene in nature, is almost indiscernible, the only reference to his presence being the words "I marked."

The designation that the spider "stood isolated" makes clear that its continued launching of filaments is a personal endeavor, its location on a promontory, as opposed to the plain, adding a dimension of precariousness. The description of the filaments emanating "out of" the spider "itself" makes clear that the process is innately creative; the metaphor of the web intensifies the action by conveying ambiguity concerning success.

In the second stanza, the poet transfers his focus from nature to humanity: In the pantheistic tradition, the experience of the spider becomes a metaphor symbolizing the soul's quest for the unification of earthly and heavenly existence. Directly addressing his own soul, the persona visualizes in the spider's action a reflection of the pathetic yet heroic struggle he is waging to find immortality. The sense of human insignificance is monstrous. The speaker is imprisoned, "surrounded" by the barrenness, yet alienated, "detached." The unknown vastness is palpable: "oceans of space." Intimidated by the gulf between life and what follows, the soul stands "Ceaselessly musing, venturing, throwing, seeking the spheres to connect them."

The instability of the situation is confirmed by the soul's attempts to "anchor," and the improbability of success is made explicit with the confessed ignorance of the destination, which is identified only as "somewhere." The means available to effect a connection is also less than encouraging: A silken thread seems much too fragile to form an eternal bridge. The poem concludes without resolution, leaving only the lingering image of the soul casting forth its gossamer threads, with the persona's final "O my soul" sounding like a cry.

Forms and Devices

In another poem, "Had I the Choice," Walt Whitman expresses a special preference for the ability to convey the "undulation of one wave" and asks the sea to "breathe one breath . . . upon my verse,/ And leave its odor there." "A Noiseless Patient Spider" (like numerous other poems) communicates indirectly this sound and sense of the sea. In the lines "And you O my soul where you stand,/ Surrounded, detached, in measureless oceans of space," the poet simulates the flux and reflux of the ocean, simultaneously communicating the motion of the action that is occurring: the soul perpetually casting forth, anticipating a connection with heaven.

In this instance, much of this sensation of waves laving the shore is achieved by the poet's use of alliteration of the sibilant *s*, making up 28 of the total 140 syllable sounds in the poem. This marriage of sense and sound occurs often in Whitman; equally effective in this poem is his simulation of casting: "Forth filament, filament, filament."

In a letter to Ralph Waldo Emerson (August, 1856), Whitman spoke of poets "walking freely out from the old traditions"; he became the forerunner of such innovation through his rejection of conventional subjects, language, rhythm, and rhyme. Yet his preference for open verse, although unorthodox, provides, surprisingly, plentiful evidence of his frequent reliance on traditional uses of repetition.

One such reiterative device is epanaphora (initial repetition), which is used effectively in the conclusion of "A Noiseless Patient Spider": "Till the bridge you will need be form'd, till the ductile anchor hold,/ Till the gossamer thread you fling catch somewhere, O my soul."

Epanalepsis (internal repetition), however, contributes more than epanaphora to this particular work. For example, the word "marked" refers first to the persona—"I marked"—then to the spider, who "mark'd how to explore," providing an essential transitional link between the two. Other examples of the use of internal reiteration of words (or their variant forms) to provide coherence in this short, ten-line poem follow: "you," "stood and stand," "surrounding" and "surrounded," "them," and "ever." Whitman's use of the interjection "O" affords yet another example of epanalepsis, and the sense of awe imparted by the usage is sustained indirectly by means of assonance in "Soul," "oceans," "form'd," and "anchor hold."

In his 1876 preface to *Leaves of Grass*, the poet referred to his verses as his "recitatives" (the recitative is a musical style in which the text is presented rhetorically in the rhythm of natural speech with some melodic variations), and Whitman's poetry exudes a sense of music throughout, not in the traditional manner, but in a new vein, much of it emanating from his expertise in using the repetition of sounds, words, and phrases to create expressive rhythms.

Whitman's handling of the centrifugal metaphor of the spider affords an excellent example of the Romantic concept of nature as wayseer for human truth; as he wrote in

"Song of Myself," "The nearest gnat is an explanation, and a drop or motion of waves a key." The spider throwing out webs and the soul thrusting toward eternity afford a singular analogy that can be extended logically even beyond the poem. If the actions are successful, the processes will end with a miracle in the beautiful symmetry of an intricate web for the spider, and the achievement of the fusion of the carnal and the spirit for the soul.

Themes and Meanings

"A Noiseless Patient Spider" is a poem about loneliness, a common theme in verse. This loneliness, however, cannot be relieved by a pensive memory as in William Wordsworth's "I Wandered Lonely as a Cloud," nor is it an emotion emanating from a lost relationship as in Robert Frost's "Reluctance." This is a loneliness that grows out of an inherent tendency of the body and soul to attempt to unite with an elusive divine entity in order to gain immortality.

It is significant that loneliness arising from separation from one's kind is self-generated and voluntary—the spider "stood isolated." Ironically, "detachment," which is related to the soul, connotes instead a severing of ties by some force on a higher level; such an unnatural separation generates a compelling inner urgency to re-attach and thereby restore access to the immortal circuit. The absence of color in the poetic description intensifies the pathos of the plight of the soul, infusing a feeling that is almost despair.

The sense of skewed proportion is frightening. A minuscule spider, attempting to chart a boundless vacuity with grossly inadequate equipment, becomes a living symbol of the pathetic plight of mortal humanity. The human soul, too, must deal with the unknown. Unlike the spider's day-by-day spinning, however, the soul's reaching out is not part of the daily routine: It is an essential, extraordinary phenomenon. The impending premonition of a continued moral crisis is disturbingly inherent in the effort: Everything (immortality) is hanging on a silken thread, which is being tossed tentatively and figuratively into an unidentified, undefined "somewhere."

In "Song of Myself" (stanza 50), Whitman affirmed: "There is in me—I do not know what it is . . ./ It is not chaos or death—it is form, union, plan—it is eternal life— it is Happiness." In "A Noiseless Patient Spider," the poet focuses on this conundrum of death and immortality. Neither the persona nor his soul realizes the euphoria suggested by the title of the group of poems in which they first took breath, "Whispers of Heavenly Death," for the poem ends without closure. In keeping with his concept of life and death as ongoing and evolutionary, Whitman chose neither to present the beauty of the symmetry of the finished web nor to record the necessary order imposed upon earthly chaos. Instead, he paused to expose the trauma of the soul's desperate search for meaning, and in the untiring throwing out of gossamer threads, he revealed the infinite beauty of the heroic dignity of the human soul.

Phyllis J. Scherle

THE NORTH SEA

Author: Heinrich Heine (1797-1856)
Type of poem: Poetic sequence
First published: 1826-1827, as *Die Nordsee*, in *Reisebilder*; English translation collected in *Heine's Poem, The North Sea*, 1916

The Poem

The North Sea is the last section of the collected poems in Heinrich Heine's *Buch der Lieder* (1827; *Book of Songs*, 1856) and consists of two cycles of poems in free verse. In the final version, authorized by Heine, the first, optimistic cycle contains twelve poems and the second, less cheerful one has ten.

The title indicates how important the sea is for Heine as a setting. Despite predecessors such as Johann Wolfgang von Goethe and Rahel Varnhagen von Ense, Heine is credited with having established the sea as a topic in German literature and with being the foremost poet of the sea.

The poems of *The North Sea* are among Heine's most important works. They are unique among his works: Only in 1825 and 1826, when he wrote these poems, did he use free verse. In his mastery of the new form, Heine achieves a beauty of style in verses with well-chosen words, striking contrasts, and mythical imagery. *The North Sea* proves Heine's strength and independence as a poet.

Heine's own love for the sea enters directly into the poems. Visits to the North Sea in the summers of 1825 and 1826 supplied motivation and material for the first and second cycles, respectively. Heine felt the sea was invigorating and good for his health. His personal experience is subtly reflected in the poems and in the cycles' moods. Since he felt less relaxed in 1826, the second cycle is less cheerful.

The first person in the poems is largely Heine himself. He took his impressions of the sea and transformed them into great poetry about nature, which in turn is the point of departure for philosophical and mythological reflections. With such a combination of nature and reflection, he adds new energy and new irony to the Romantic tradition that influences his sensitivity. These poems were perceived as turbulent and restless by the contemporary audience, explaining why their reception was initially slow. Nevertheless *The North Sea* was, in Heine's lifetime, translated into many languages and contributed to his world fame.

Each individual poem of *The North Sea* can stand by itself. The "Evening Twilight" at sea brings back pleasant childhood memories, while in "Sunset" the poet feels comfort only compared to Heine's own myth of the sun's and moon's eternal separation. In "A Night by the Sea," the love encounter between a woman and the godlike poet undergoes an ironic reversal because he is afraid of an "undying cough." In yet another reversal, the poet is told in "Poseidon" that he is not worth divine wrath.

"The Avowal" is a key poem of the first cycle because the poet expresses an optimistic view of love in the grandiose metaphor of writing his proclamation of love in the sky with a burning tree. This poem is as much about love as about poetry itself.

"Night in the Cabin" consists of six songs professing love to woman, while in "Storm," the poet imagines a faraway woman's loving thoughts reaching out to him. "Peace at Sea" is contrasted with the ship's boy stealing and with a seagull catching fish. The following two poems reflect one another directly: in "A Wraith in the Sea," the underwater apparition of a city and the poet's love invite him to leap into the sea. In "Purification," the poet understands this apparition as his own madness and wishes to ban it.

"Peace" praises Jesus Christ, who walks "over the land and the sea," bringing peace to the world. Heine had converted from Judaism to Lutheranism in June of 1825, and the version of the poem in *Book of Songs* does not contain earlier satirical elements. Some critics contend it is a weak ending for the first cycle.

The less cheerful second cycle begins with "Ocean Greeting," which celebrates the sea's liberating force. The next poems evoke threatening forces, with Greek gods as forces behind the "Tempest," and also mourn the loss of love with the imagery of being "Shipwrecked."

"The Setting of the Sun" varies Heine's myth of the unhappy marriage of gods. As the second cycle's key poem, "The Song of the Okeanides" reveals the reality of separation hidden behind the poet's illusion of love. The next poems vary the theme and then give way to more optimistic ones.

Even "The Gods of Greece" are dead and replaced by Christianity. Only a fool waits for the answer to the "Questions" about the meaning of life. Changing the thematic flow, "The Phoenix" asserts new hope for love. The poet's increasing intoxification in "In Haven" ultimately extends to the whole drunken world, and is thus both pessimistic and humorous.

"Epilog" ends the collection of *Book of Songs*. It gently asserts love in a comparison that alludes to the powerful Romantic image for yearning: the blue flower.

Forms and Devices

Heine paid close attention to questions of form, so the interpretation of form is particularly important in regard to the author's intentions. Three major formal devices shape the structure of the poems in *The North Sea*: free verse, compound adjectives, and ironic reversal.

Heine wrote free verse only during the years he worked on *The North Sea*. The verses are without rhyme, fixed meter, or set length; they are flexible according to the poet's needs. Free verse was introduced to German poetry by Friedrich Gottlieb Klopstock and was used by major poets such as Johann Wolfgang von Goethe, Friedrich Schiller, and Novalis. Heine is a master of the form and uses it to create various effects—for example, the motion of the waves: "more wild than wind and waters."

This example uses alliteration to help echo the rhythmic and musical effect of the sea. Alliteration is often lost in translation, just as is the second major formal device, compound adjectives. Heine invents words, such as "happiness-blinded" and "Olympus-shaking," to describe persons or events in a new and precise way. Depending on the translations, sometimes only one out of five compound adjectives in German is translated by an English compound adjective. Yet, since such word formations are even more extraordinary in English, the effect of the translation is comparable to that of the German original.

Heine's rhetoric and, in particular, his compound adjectives make his poems sound like epics by Homer. In fact, part of Heine's experience of the North Sea was the reading of Homer, whose German translation is reflected in Heine's poems. Especially in those poems with Greek themes, it becomes obvious that Heine is both part of a long-standing tradition and independent because of his awareness of history. The latter enables Heine to use traditional elements for his own purposes—for example, to express the theme of love and separation.

A third major device in Heine's poetry affects the structure of the poems. It is the ironic reversal for which Heine is famous. Typically, this device takes the mood of a poem and turns it around: Suddenly and unexpectedly, the sentimental tone shifts to bitterness, as in "The Song of the Okeanides," or to mockery, as in "A Wraith in the Sea" with its abrupt ending, and as in the first poem of *The North Sea*, in which celebration of his new love surprisingly ends in the poet relinquishing his reason. This aspect of structure leads to questions of themes and meanings.

Themes and Meanings

Although the sea is ever-present as the setting of the poems, the three major themes in *The North Sea* are mythology, love and separation, and poetry itself. Heine's use of mythology is threefold. First, he uses myth as a form of expression; second, Heine creates his own myths; and finally, he mocks antique myths.

In Heine's day it was common to use mythological references to talk about something else. In Heine's case, myths expressed his existential theme: love and separation. In the "Song of the Okeanides," the poet first indulges in reveries of love and is then interrupted by the "compassionate water-maids" who, calling him a fool, show him the reality of separation and desperation.

The myths that Heine invents about the unhappy marriages of gods have this same function in "Sunset" and "The Setting of the Sun." On one hand, both poems intensify the feeling of separation by showing that the gods suffer eternally. On the other hand, this adds a humorous tone when the poet feels blessed because he is mortal and, thus, will not suffer forever.

Heine extends the humorous tone to mockery when, in "A Night by the Sea," the godlike poet is afraid of catching colds that are as eternal as divine existence. Particularly in "The Gods of Greece," Heine shows his irreverence: The poet confesses that he has never liked the Greek and Roman gods, who have degenerated and now merely "drift slowly like monstrous ghosts" in the night sky.

This poem demonstrates a considerable distance from the serious role Greek mythology played for German classicists such as Johann Wolfgang von Goethe and Friedrich Schiller. Schiller mourns the death of the old gods in one poem; Heine borrows its title and writes a new poem mocking the gods. Heine embeds his ideas about

Greek mythology in description of nature and understands the gods' decline as part of the eternal struggle of being.

"The Gods of Greece" have been replaced by Christianity. The latter, however, appears to be both positive ("Wonder-worker") and negative ("doleful"). In connection with the poem's description of Venus Libitina, the "corpse-like goddess," Heine seems to attack the tendencies in Christianity that deny sensual pleasures. It is important here that the old (sensual) gods have only been pushed aside and are still present. Like most of his other poems, this one varies Heine's basic assumption of the world's incoherence, which is the source of his second major theme: love and separation. Even in the positive poems, the poet is typically away from his love, either preparing to meet her or simply thinking about her. These situations are very delicate. In "Coronation" the poet states that love robs him of his reason, and in "The Song of the Okeanides" his positive feelings are transformed into depression.

"The Avowal," probably the most positive poem of *The North Sea*, can be understood as strangely removed from real love. It presents Heine's third major theme: poetry about itself. The poet professes his love, but the poem is more about his power to do so than about a woman. He uses a tree that he dipped into a volcano as his "colossal flame-soaked pen" in order to make his words stay in the sky forever. Thus Heine celebrates both the power of poetry and his own stature.

Ingo Roland Stoehr

NOTES TOWARD A SUPREME FICTION

Author: Wallace Stevens (1879-1955)
Type of poem: Meditation
First published: 1942

The Poem

   Notes Toward a Supreme Fiction, considered by many to be Wallace Stevens's most important poem, did not receive much critical attention until the 1980's. Regarded as long and unwieldy, the poem was overlooked in favor of shorter and more easily accessible poems until critics became aware that much current theory has its parallel in Stevens's *Notes Toward a Supreme Fiction*. Contemporary notions of historicity, aesthetics, and even chaos theory can be read from this work.

   The notion of the "supreme fiction" was a major preoccupation of Stevens, who, in the early 1940's when this poem was written, was attempting to find a stronger justification for poetry in times of war and social disintegration. Poetry was not to be accused of escapism or irrelevance. Rather, the poet was to assume a heroic role in attempting to find meaning in chaos and to articulate the human myth. Indeed, this long, philosophical poem gives a relatively complete discussion of Stevens's later aesthetic and can be used to gloss his other work. *Notes Toward a Supreme Fiction* was first published in 1942 and then collected in the 1947 book *Transport to Summer*. It is prefaced by a dedication and an eight-line introduction that addresses the fiction itself. The poem is organized formally, with three sections of ten sets of seven three-line stanzas, each developing a subtopic (or a single "note") of the main theme, and a concluding set of seven tercets. The three subtopics are "It Must Be Abstract," "It Must Change," and "It Must Give Pleasure" ("It" in each case refers to the supreme fiction). The last group of tercets does not have a title, but it is an address to a soldier that attempts to make poetry and poetry writing relevant to war. When the poem was first published in 1942, Stevens wished to have the "soldier" lines emphasized. He claimed at one point to have planned a fourth section titled "It Must Be Human"; although this fourth part was never written, the humanity of the supreme fiction is assumed or asserted throughout the poem. The dedication ("To Henry Church") is confusing; the reader is likely to connect it with the introduction to the poem, which begins, "And for what, except for you, do I feel love?" However, the dedication was a last-minute addition, and the opening lines are actually addressed not to his friend Church but to the fiction, an entity that seems as much creator as created. It is the fiction that is the ultimate object of desire.

   The first section of the poem considers the process and nature of abstraction, one of the three essentials of Stevens's supreme fiction. Abstraction is equated with seeing in "the first idea"—the poet must strip perception of accumulated interpretations in order to restore the freshness of the first-time vision. The speaker addresses an "ephebe," or pupil/apprentice, whom he instructs in the art of abstraction. The goal of such rigorous stripping is to get back to the uninterpreted base of reality. The sun, to be seen in the first idea, must "bear no name . . . but be/ In the difficulty of what it is to be." "Do not use the rotted names," Stevens says elsewhere, and this instruction is at the bottom of his concept of abstraction. The supreme fiction cannot be another perfunctory statement of what has been previously thought and said—it must be fresh, and the revitalization of reality calls for stripping it. Abstraction is not easy, as the rest of this section explains. Reality is not merely a human thing: "There was a myth before the myth began" in the "muddy centre" of prehuman history. The world humans know is not theirs, and its foreignness both causes and complicates poetry. However, the creators of present fictions are human, although they have a superhuman task. After describing the meaning and process of abstraction, the poem turns to the figure of the poet. Who is the poet, and what is the result of this attempt to abstract not only the indifferent world but also humankind itself? A series of images is proposed, and the final and lasting one is an old clown, a Charlie Chaplin type, who will create and who will be the subject of the ultimate poem.

The second essential characteristic of the supreme fiction is explored in "It Must Change." This part of the poem is filled with images of fruition and change, creating a picture reminiscent of the bountiful earth described in Stevens's more famous poem "Sunday Morning." These nature images are contrasted with a statue of the General Du Puy that does not change and therefore belies nature. (This poem is really about the process of creation rather than about the product, but it is clear that the speaker, here indistinguishable from the poet, believes following his directions for creation would provide the best art.) The speaker describes the meeting of opposites and the resulting births and speaks of the pleasure brought by change and the delight that comes from the natural cycle of birth, ripeness, and decline. The cycles of nature allow for renewal and refreshment, whereas art that turns flesh to bronze is deadening.

"It Must Change" is closely linked to the third part, "It Must Give Pleasure." In the second section, the poet establishes that change produces delight, while in the third he examines the relationship between pleasure and art. It contains a long parable of the Canon Aspirin and his sister, that explores the differences in their perceptions of the world. She is more of a bare minimalist while he is a creator of order; neither one is able to create ideal art because neither strikes the right chord of the relationship between reality and the imagination. In the most difficult sections of this poem, the speaker tries to define what this relationship might be. The Canon imposes order, but the true poet must be able to discover rather than impose. It must be possible, the speaker muses, "To find the real,/ To be stripped of every fiction except one,/ The fiction of an absolute." This point, at which invention becomes discovery, would be the locus of the supreme fiction. The speaker then retreats from his assertion that the poet can find this point of conjunction. (Stevens often retreats from positions he explores, as though unwilling to make any absolute statement.) However, the poem concludes with the possibility of a conjunction between mind and world that encompasses all his essentials: abstraction, change, and delight. The last group of tercets is addressed to a soldier and shows the connection between poetry and war, which is seen in the perspective of the human myth: "The soldier is poor without the poet's lines." Poetry gives meaning to the soldier's life and sacrifice.

Forms and Devices

The three-line stanzas are appropriate for a long, meditative poem and may evoke the spirit of Italian poet Dante Alighieri, who seems to be a ghostly presence in the poem (Stevens saw Dante as the creator of a powerful but now historical fiction that continues to haunt today's would-be fiction maker). Stevens's late work frequently uses the tercet together with a relaxed blank verse in extended explorations of poetics. The result is a kind of essay in verse enhanced by poetic devices such as alliteration, consonance, metaphor, and a variety of rhetorical devices.

The images and metaphors, mostly from art, nature, or art and nature combined, attempt to demonstrate the facets of the supreme fiction: abstraction, changeability, and capacity to delight. Each section is very different in tone and metaphor because the three characteristics differ, although the second and third sections are more closely allied than is the first with either of the others. Images of nature and art in the first section tend to serve as illustrations of abstraction or as analogies that demonstrate how the poet sees. Images of animals show the process of mythologizing, while art is wedded to nature in passages illustrative of how perception turns to art: "Weather by Franz Hals,/ Brushed up by brushy winds in brushy clouds." The interpretation has been welded to the perception so that metaphor becomes equivalence, with art and nature mirroring each other. At the end of part 1, a sustained metaphor illustrates the notion that "The major abstraction is the idea of man." This concept is further defined: "The major abstraction is the commonal,/ The inanimate, difficult visage. Who is it?" The figure that emerges is the old clown, the Charlie Chaplin type in "slouching pantaloons" seen "Looking for what was, where it used to be." This is the basis for the image that must serve as the "final elegance."

Images crowd together and change rapidly in "It Must Change." The sequence of images of nature in flux (bees, apples, and pigeons, among others) is in stark contrast to the "great statue of General Du Puy" that is not subject to change and therefore not reflective of reality. There follow images of mystic marriages that represent the thesis, antithesis, and synthesis that constantly create new versions of reality. Part 2 also contains what may be an appealing reprise of one of Stevens's early poems, "The Comedian as the Letter C," which details the adventures of Crispin as he tries and discards different types of art only to completely succumb to the life of the world at last, becoming a cabin-dwelling farmer instead of a poet. In *Notes Toward a Supreme Fiction*, the "planter," by yielding to reality rather than attempting to impose order on it, has not lost out on anything.

"It Must Give Pleasure" uses images of music, a beautiful woman, and angels in its argument that pleasure is an essential ingredient of the supreme fiction. The complex concluding image of this poem is teasing and inconclusive. It is another scene of sexual attraction. The speaker addresses a woman who is identified with the earth, with the real: "Fat girl, terrestrial, my summer, my night/ How is it I find you in difference . . . ?" He is compelled by her, just as the imagination is compelled by the real; what he wants to do because of her attractiveness is to name her. This naming is the act of poetry and the act of love: "this unprovoked sensation requires/ That I should name you flatly, waste no words." He concludes that the supreme fiction is "the more than rational distortion,/ The fiction that results from feeling." Thus, images of mind and world merge with the male and female lovers: "I call you by name, my green, my fluent mundo./ You will have stopped revolving except in crystal." The mind's embrace of the world is the same as a lovers' embrace. As in a lovers' embrace, both mind and world are participants.

The last section, the seven-tercet address to the soldier, uses images of the soldier's life in a comparison between the real war and the poet's war in an attempt to justify the ways of poetry to the war-torn present. This section was not a part of Stevens's original project. For many readers, the triumphant meeting of poet and world at the end of "It Must Give Pleasure" is the high point of the poem and its true conclusion.

Themes and Meanings

Stevens expressed in letters his desire to define a role for the poet similar to the role of the priest. This poem is an effort to exalt poetry and to explore its possibilities as a replacement for religion or perhaps as a religion in itself. In one letter, Stevens commented, "In principle there appear to be certain characteristics of a supreme fiction *and the NOTES is confined to a statement of a few of those characteristics. . . .* In trying to create something as valid as the idea of God has been, and for that matter remains, the first necessity seems to be breadth." The varied themes of *Notes Toward a Supreme Fiction* bind into one strand leading toward such an exalted definition of the supreme fiction. Interestingly, Stevens said to one correspondent that the supreme fiction was poetry, but to another correspondent, after he had immersed himself fully in the project, he claimed that he did not want to be so limiting. The concept had begun to widen and to transcend itself.

Stevens was preoccupied throughout his life with the way art becomes dated so quickly, and, in "The Noble Rider and the Sound of Words" (a paper first given at Princeton in 1942 and later published, in his essay collection *The Necessary Angel*, in 1951), he described how some well-known statues reflected their culture and were incomprehensible if divorced by time or space from that culture. His long poem looks at the possibility of setting poetry or art or even the creative act itself free from the limits of time and circumstance. He suggests that this be done by altering the way the artist looks at the world. Creative perception requires all of the perceiver's resources. It involves stripping away the accretions of the past to look at the real world as if through Adam's eyes, accepting change as the basis for all art, and opening art itself to change. It also involves being aware of the pleasure that comes from both the world and the artistic act, thus allowing the work, in a sense, to celebrate itself. Thus the ideal fiction as described in this poem is not time-bound because it is abstract, changeable, and pleasurable. It is the one love object worthy of the poet's desire. It is both subject and object, creator and created. To be abstract, the reality on which the fiction rests must be stripped of the perceptions of others and the fictions of previous perceivers. It must be of both humankind and the alien world. The poet and his human subject are to be realistic rather than aggrandized or presented as caricatures. To be changeable, the fiction must be based on nature's cycles, not a prison for nature. Statues of generals or anything "set in stone" cannot be the truest form of art. To produce delight, the poem must be an energetic search for the real, in which the mind approaches the world like a lover. This poem is Stevens's sustained effort to create, as a poem, a poetics that demonstrates itself in the lines that describe it.

Janet McCann

NOW SLEEPS THE CRIMSON PETAL

Author: Alfred, Lord Tennyson (1809-1892)
Type of poem: Lyric
First published: 1847, in *The Princess*

The Poem

"Now Sleeps the Crimson Petal" is a short lyric of fourteen lines. It begins with two stanzas of four lines each. Next comes a couplet, and the poem concludes with another four-line stanza. The reader of the poem will at once note that it has no title but is known by its first line. The reason for this is that the lyric forms part of a large epic, *The Princess*. The epic includes several famous lyrics, including "Tears, Idle tears" and "Come Down, O Maid."

"Now Sleeps the Crimson Petal" is read by Princess Ida to the prince, who is recovering from wounds incurred in battle. The prince loves Ida; she, although well-disposed to him, has yet to reveal her own feelings. In the lyric, she at last does so; its content makes it clear that she reciprocates his love.

Alfred, Lord Tennyson faced a difficult problem in writing about love. The Victorians held extremely strong views about what might properly be discussed in public. Sexual love was definitely not on the acceptable list: Much that might appear in a modern motion picture rated acceptable for family audiences would by the Victorians have been classed as beyond the pale.

Tennyson fully shared the values of his time. The task that thus faced him in "Now Sleeps the Crimson Petal" was to suggest the circumstances of a romantic encounter while shunning any direct description that violated propriety. Tennyson accomplished this feat through the use of appeals to nature and references to mythology.

Although the poem is read by the princess, the speaker in it is a man appealing to a woman. The scene is a palace garden at night. The flowers personify sleep, and the trees are quiet: "Nor waves the cypress in the palace walk." In a striking image, a fish is represented as sleeping: "Nor winks the gold fin in the porphyry font" (porphyry is an igneous rock, often used in Persian palaces). The speaker invites the lady he addresses to wake up.

The purpose for which he wishes her to do so becomes quickly apparent in the next stanza. He refers to the Greek myth in which Zeus, disguised as a shower of meteors, ravished the maiden Danaë. He suggests that the lady is willing to receive him: "And all thy heart lies open unto me." The couplet, which now follows, suggests that the encounter has ended. The speaker, continuing to identify himself with Zeus, departs: "Now slides the silent meteor on." As the woman bears physical evidence of the encounter, so does he have her thoughts imprinted in him.

The intermingling of thoughts implies that the encounter has been of deep significance. This is confirmed in the concluding stanza, in which it transpires that the speaker and the lady have by no means finished their romance. Drawing an analogy with the lily, which folds itself up and "slips into the bosom of the lake," he invites the lady to follow suit: "So fold thyself, my dearest, thou, and slip/ Into my bosom and be lost in me." The poem then concludes with an image of the total unity of lover and beloved.

Forms and Devices

The lyric is written in an unusual form. It is a ghazal, a Persian love poem, in which a single word or phrase is repeated at short intervals. Each stanza ends with "me": "with me," "to me," "unto me," "in me," and again "in me." The repeated phrase acts as a substitute for rhyme. A number of images in the lyric are standard in the Persian love poem: roses, lilies, peacocks, cypresses, and stars.

By using this exotic form, Tennyson suggests a situation and a mood out of the ordinary. The normal conventions are suspended for the duration of the romantic encounter.

To speak of a romantic encounter is often to suggest a difficulty: How can the man overcome the woman's resistance? The speaker solves the problem by avoiding it altogether. The result of the encounter between him and the lady is, in his mind, inevitable. Tennyson's choice of words, along with the extraordinary circumstances suggested by the poem's strange form, aids in creating the illusion of inevitability. Each stanza begins with "Now," suggesting a continuous movement. The effect is enhanced in the first stanza, in which the second and third lines begin with "Nor." This word is so similar to "now" that the reader must pay close attention to avoid a misreading. Given the progression of "Nows," resistance on the woman's part becomes next to impossible.

Tennyson also uses words that suggest peace and drowsiness rather than violence. The poem scrupulously avoids the slightest hint of struggle. The flowers sleep: The activities from which the cypresses and goldfish rest are waving and winking, both rather mild affairs. The humorous "winks" suggest a lighthearted mood. A similar effect occurs in each stanza. The peacock "droops" and "glimmers." The "silent" meteor "slides"; the lily "folds" and "slips." All these verbs hint at peace and repose.

Tennyson's most serious problem in conveying a mood of peace stems from his use of the legend of Danaë, in Greek mythology a story of rape. He solves the difficulty with characteristic ingenuity. He turns the name Danaë into an adjective: "Now lies the earth all Danaë to the stars." The separate existence of the woman is thus elided: She fails to resist because she cannot. She has been emptied of her substance and transformed into a modifier.

The poem also reverses standard male and female attributes, adding even further to the motif of unity. Traditionally, males are active and females are passive. Thus, the feminine peacock "droops," and the lady's heart "lies open." The male, personified as a meteor, "slides on" and "leaves." The final stanza, however, executes a *volte-face*. Now it is the feminine lily that "folds" and "slips" into the lake. It is the lady whom the speaker calls upon to take the initiative by "folding herself." The poem's careful combination of figures is unified to achieve a common effect—the two lovers cannot be parted.

Themes and Meanings

"Now Sleeps the Crimson Petal" exemplifies a peculiar feature of the Victorian attitude toward love. Although by convention writers were supposed to exercise extreme reticence, in fact they did not do so. Tennyson cannot give a direct description of physical love, but his suggestions make his meaning unmistakable. When the speaker says, "And all thy heart lies open unto me," the reader cannot help but wonder what really "lies open."

The use of indirect allusion rather than direct description enhances the erotic effect. The reader cannot take in the scene passively but must use imagination in order to grasp the poem's meaning. Because of the beauty of the words, the reader is in danger of missing the fundamental occurrence represented by the lyric's appearance in *The Princess*. A woman reads an erotic poem in the presence of a man who has earlier professed his love for her. Nothing could be more alien to the notion of feminine modesty, but unless the reader portrays the scene in his own mind, the radical challenge to customary behavior will be missed.

The analysis just given might appear to fit a conventional picture of Victorian hypocrisy. In this view, the Victorians avoided certain words and aspired to a high-minded righteousness. In fact, they failed to practice what they preached: So long as the correct forms were observed, behavior was much less restricted than might appear. Many were reluctant to use the phrase "breast of chicken"; yet, at the same time, prostitution flourished.

There is no reason to accuse Tennyson of hypocrisy, whatever may be true of others among his contemporaries. He believed that love was a spiritual experience of great value. A romantic couple in their behavior reflect the movement of nature toward unity. The key to Tennyson's attitude to love lies in the final stanza, in which the lily slips into the lake. If the lady follows the behest of the speaker and, imitating the lily that is self-absorbed into the lake, becomes lost in the lover, an advance toward the unity of nature has taken place.

One can thus see why Tennyson is the reverse of hypocritical in the poem. He does not use poetic conventions in order to suggest pruriently what law and custom will not permit him to state directly. Instead, he sincerely believes in a philosophy of unity that nature and human loves illustrate. The theme of organic unity in nature was a near constant in Tennyson's work. A famous line of *In Memoriam* (1850) states: "I doubt not thro' the ages, one increasing purpose runs." The theme was common to many of Tennyson's contemporaries, including Thomas Carlyle and Francis Thompson.

Bill Delaney

THE NUN'S PRIEST'S TALE

Author: Geoffrey Chaucer (c. 1343-1400)
Type of poem: Mock epic
First transcribed: 1387-1400, in *The Canterbury Tales*

The Poem

Geoffrey Chaucer's *The Canterbury Tales* circulated in manuscripts from shortly after his death in 1400 but did not reach print until several decades after the invention of the printing press. The work is an unfinished, but more or less unified, collection of tales as related by the characters of a fictionalized April pilgrimage from Southwark, a borough south of London, to Canterbury Cathedral, where Saint Thomas Becket was martyred in 1170. "The Nun's Priest's Tale" is found in a part of the work usually designated as "Fragment VII."

The teller of this tale is a priest who serves the prioress of a Benedictine convent and another nun as chaplain on the pilgrimage. He is a man who takes his vocation seriously. Although he displays a wry sense of humor and a relish in describing the action of a barnyard chase, there is no reason to doubt his assertion that his tale exists to support "our doctrine." The tale is a fable of a type often used by medieval preachers to exemplify the topic of a homily, but because of the way the tale is framed, it is also a mock epic incorporating various satirical thrusts.

The pilgrims have just listened to "The Monk's Tale," actually a series of short *de casibus* tragedies, which medieval critical theory defined simply as the accounts of the fall of persons from high places. Harry Bailly, the self-appointed host of the pilgrimage, then asks the priest, Sir John, for a change of pace, a "merry" tale. The priest obliges, but in a way that comically echoes the monk's tale, for Chanticleer is a proud rooster who falls from dignity and barely escapes becoming a fox's meal. The first character in the tale, however, is a "poor widow," a plain working woman who with the help of two daughters and a dog, maintains a modest farm.

On the farm lives Chanticleer, with seven hens as consorts. His favorite is Pertelote, whom the rooster describes in a manner that imitates the descriptions of fair ladies in the courtly verse of the day. Chanticleer tells her of a bad dream in which he was menaced by "a beast like a hound." When he insists that this is an omen of danger, Pertelote claims that something he ate caused the dream and that he should "take some laxative." Both defend their positions by the standard medieval method of citing the texts of literary experts.

Later, as Chanticleer struts proudly around the little barnyard, a black fox named Russell intrudes, but instead of attacking, he flatters the rooster by praising his singing. Russell even claims to have known Chanticleer's father, who had once been "in my house to my great ease," adding that the father had a way of closing his eyes that made his crowing particularly effective. Chanticleer does the same, at which point the fox seizes him by the neck and runs off. Alerted, the widow, along with the daughters and the dog, chases after the fox, but just as it appears that he will escape, Chanticleer urges the fox to turn and taunt the pursuers. When he loosens his grip on the rooster to do so, the latter flies safely up into a tree. Thus, the priest implies, humans are beguiled and will fall victim to the evil forces unless they eschew sin and make appropriate use of their God-given faculties.

Forms and Devices

Considered as a reflection of its teller—one popular way of reading *The Canterbury Tales*—"The Nun's Priest's Tale" exemplifies a pattern of medieval homiletics. Although the poem is not arranged like a sermon, the teller's insistence on its moral significance places it in a tradition of popular preaching that strove to emphasize a moral message by means of fable. As such it reflects medieval Christianity's genius for appropriating and adapting secular subject material for instructional purposes. In its most common form, the ancient "beast fable," animals speak and act like human beings and thus call attention to human failings, such as destructive pride. Although Chanticleer is foolishly vain, his pride runs much deeper and is more serious. He is "puffed up" to an extent that endangers his very life. The priest does not feel the need to discourse on pride as the first and foremost of the seven deadly sins (something that another pilgrim, the parson, or parish priest, does at excruciating length later in *The Canterbury Tales*), but his audience knows that in the tale's most general allegorical reference, Chanticleer represents humankind and Russell the devil.

The "cock and fox" story is much older than Chaucer, but he characteristically reshapes his source material in a highly original way. By setting his fable into the frame of a widow's small farm he fashions it also into the literary form that has come to be called the mock epic. Chanticleer regards himself as preeminent in various ways, but the setting and the opposition prove his smallness and insignificance. He is a mighty ruler, but his rule extends only over seven hens in a small barnyard. He is a scholar who can cite a host of learned authorities on the subject of dreams, but it is all he can do to best Pertelote, a mere chattel, in argument. He regards himself as a great singer and a physical force to be reckoned with (a "grim lion"), but Russell proves him only a vain crooner like his father and no match at all for his foxy opponent.

Like all of Chaucer's most successful works, "The Nun's Priest's Tale" is a poem composed, like the majority of his tales, in iambic pentameter couplets. The effect of his couplets is far different from that of the "heroic" couplets that became the fashion in the seventeenth and eighteenth centuries. Understanding the importance of swift movement in narrative, Chaucer produced an effective blend of end-stopped lines, partial stops, and enjambments.

The tale is 313 couplets, or 626 lines long, but the fox does not appear until line 395, and Chaucer devotes only about a quarter of these lines to the action of the tale. The first three quarters of the poem are given over mainly to the description of the setting and the establishment of the characters, primarily Chanticleer. The rooster himself expends sixty-six lines telling a story designed to justify his conviction that his dream portends coming danger—but then becomes so entranced by a subsidiary theme—"Murder will out!"—that he almost forgets to conclude with the proper emphasis on his main point. Chaucer loved to both explore and exploit rhetoric. Not only does he tangle Chanticleer in his own rhetoric, but he also has his priest, Sir John, slip into similar rhetorical excesses, including at one point a diatribe against "women's counsels" of the sort that "made Adam from Paradise to go."

Themes and Meanings

The Canterbury Tales and Chaucer's long narrative poem *Troilus and Criseyde* (1382) are his two most important works by far, and the individual tales of the former, although often read separately, are best understood as part of an intricately planned, though incomplete, whole—indeed one of the most ambitious poetic works in Western literature. In the central fiction of the pilgrimage, the tales are meant to provide both instruction and pleasure to the pilgrims on their journey to Canterbury. The host has promised the teller of the best tale a free supper after their return. Some of the tales, such as the relentlessly doctrinal "Parson's Tale," are mainly instructive but of limited entertainment value, while others, like the bawdy "Miller's Tale" of the violation of a carpenter's marriage by a parish clerk and an all-too-willing wife, provide much robust entertainment but not a great deal of improving message.

Had the pilgrims completed their round trip, "The Nun's Priest's Tale" no doubt would have contended strongly for the prize, for it is one of the tales combining a pleasing proportion of both entertaining and instructive elements and has justly become a favorite among Chaucer's readers. From its initial description of the plain-living, hardworking woman farmer whose values contrast so sharply with the aristocratic, self-indulgent prioress whom the priest serves as spiritual adviser, the humor is good-naturedly, sometimes slyly, satirical. Among its other targets are the rhetorical excesses of writers of Chaucer's time, exemplified by Chanticleer and the narrator; the genre of *de casibus* tragedy, much overworked by the immediately preceding teller; and the medieval habit of frequent and lengthy citations from authoritative ancient texts, in this instance two sets embodying wildly contradictory theories of the significance of dreams.

Above all, Chaucer's mock-epic characterization of Chanticleer exemplifies a familiar biblical text, which is probably more honored in the breach than the observance: Proverbs 16:18, "Pride goeth before destruction, and a haughty spirit before a fall." It was by pride that Chanticleer fell into captivity, and it was by the fox's fall into pride that the rooster was able to escape. It was this type of fall, emblematic of the Fall of Adam and Eve in Eden, rather than the often unmotivated falls of *de casibus* tragedy, against which the priest is warning the pilgrims and, by extension, Chaucer is cautioning his readers.

Robert P. Ellis

NUTTING

Author: William Wordsworth (1770-1850)
Type of poem: Narrative/pastoral
First published: 1800, in *Lyrical Ballads, with Other Poems*

The Poem

"Nutting" is a short autobiographical poem of fifty-six lines. It describes a youthful encounter with nature that helped to chasten William Wordsworth's moral sense and heighten his poetic sensitivity to the life shared between himself and the outer world. In remarks dictated to Isabella Fenwick in 1843, Wordsworth said that the verses, written in Germany in 1798, started out as part of his great autobiographical poem on the growth of the poet's mind, *The Prelude* (1850), but were "struck out as not being wanted there. . . . These verses arose out of the remembrance of feelings I had often had when a boy, and particularly in the extensive woods that still stretch from the side of Esthwaite Lake towards Graythwaite."

The geography of the poem is the magnificent English Lake District, through which Wordsworth's life and art as a poet of nature have become famous. Wordsworth was born in Cockermouth, West Cumberland. After his mother's death, the eight-year-old Wordsworth went to Hawkshead Grammar School, near the scene of "Nutting," in the remote rural region that he and collaborator Samuel Taylor Coleridge made the poetic center of a literary revolution in England. Wordsworth and his three brothers boarded in the cottage of Ann Tyson, "the frugal Dame" rearing the boy of "Nutting," who gave to young Wordsworth simple comfort, ample affection, and freedom to roam the countryside on free days and some nights. These wanderings produced the traumatic experiences of poetic development amid nature documented in this poem and throughout *The Prelude*.

"Nutting" opens by noting a double consciousness: a speaker's mature mind discovering the "heavenly" impact on his youthful mind (lines 1-4) of an early encounter with nature. It begins very abruptly to narrate one of those watershed experiences in Wordsworth's poetic growth. He set out to gather hazelnuts, suitably attired with pack, stick, and secondhand clothes that he had saved at the bidding of Ann Tyson for protection against nature on the way (lines 5-15).

His walk into the woods ends at a solitary bower, the scene of his impending spiritual revelation in nature, where the hazel trees symbolize a sexual and unspoiled life force in their resemblance to male genitals: "Tall and erect, with tempting clusters hung,/ A virgin scene" (lines 16-21). The boy gazes at the hazel trees with a gluttonous, self-satisfied appetite of hunger and sex, as if he were an explorer who had at last discovered an exotic treasure all for himself (lines 21-29).

Refusing to rush into the actual nut-gathering in order to savor his conquest, he rests his cheek against a fleecelike mossy stone. He hears a murmuring stream and seems to begin achieving a joyous communication with nature that is, however, undercut by the mature speaker's harsh comment on his remembrance of his youthful heart's response to mere "stock and stones/ And . . . vacant air" (lines 30-43). The harshness is perhaps explained by an intervening memory in the mature speaker's mind about the boy's subsequent cruelty to a virginal nature. The boy proceeds to unleash rape and riot ("merciless ravage") on the "mutilated bower" of hazel trees and to violate the innocent sexuality of the universal life force that inheres in nature (lines 43-51). As a consequence, guilt rushes into his youthful mind to teach him at that moment and in later years (in the company of his "dearest Maiden") that "there is a spirit in the woods" at one with individuals who have gentle, sensitive souls (lines 52-56).

Forms and Devices

The apparent simplicity of "Nutting" should not blind readers to the subtleties of its rhetoric and meaning. The poem might be designated a pastoral narrative, because it is a seemingly straightforward story of a rural protagonist in a country setting, pursuing pastoral pleasures that touch on love and sex, despite the absence of conventional items such as shepherds, lutes, and love laments found in ancient bucolic poetry.

Yet "Nutting" is new, revolutionary poetry in form and meaning, created by Wordsworth as a conscious challenge to classical norms of literature. For example, it is an autobiography of unprecedented intimacy and such deceptive simplicity that traditionalists might have considered its unpretentious tale about a boy's walk into the woods too commonplace to be dignified enough for elevated poetry. Such a detailed narration of an ordinary person's spiritual crisis struck a daringly confessional note. Wordsworth spearheaded the innovations that would help to democratize modern poetry with an unrestricted range of subject matter and with a vernacular speaking voice.

Wordsworth's mastery of an elegant yet flexible blank verse is part of the remarkable intimacy of "Nutting." Blank verse is unrhymed iambic pentameter that Wordsworth inherited from John Milton's much more solemn *Paradise Lost* (1667, 1674) and transformed into a supple sound system capturing the speaking voice of a common man who is sensitive, simple, and yet cultivated enough to reflect on the larger meaning of his unthinking youthful adventures in nature.

Although "Nutting" seems straightforward and ordinary, it is a mythic narrative of everyman's pilgrimage of life elevated beyond an uneventful walk into the woods by two interrelated metaphors of a knight's quest and an explorer's journey of discovery. As M. H. Abrams remarked in *Natural Supernaturalism* (second edition, 1973), the pilgrimage motif was central to Wordsworth's poetry: "It is time to notice that Wordsworth's account of unity achieved, lost, and regained is held together . . . by the recurrent image of a journey: . . . Wordsworth's 'poem on my own poetical education' converts the wayfaring Christian of the Augustinian spiritual journey into the self-formative traveler of the Romantic educational journey."

So it is in "Nutting." The little boy is first depicted as an overdressed and raggedy knight-errant of yore "sallying forth" with a "motley" armament for nut-gathering that ominously distances him from nature and, even worse, will be used to destroy nature in the bower of pristine sexual bliss (lines 5-21). Allied with this motif of a knight's dubious quest is the complementary motif of an explorer's exploitative journey of discovery on which, like cruel conquistadores in the New World, the boy invades the *terra incognita* of unspoiled nature and guiltily pillages the new-found treasures of the primitive environment (lines 22-53).

Themes and Meanings

"Nutting" is a poem about the possibilities and problems of communion between humans and nature; it involves the irony that the boy's revelation of communication between himself and nature occurs by means of his violation of nature. Wordsworth's *The Prelude*, arguably the greatest nineteenth century poem in the Western world, terms such revelations of nature's presence "spots of time" and narrates similar moments of the poet's spiritual development through youthful violations of nature in episodes of boat stealing and woodcock snaring. "Nutting" was originally designed to be part of these traumatic experiences of poetic growth in Book I of *The Prelude*.

Excerpted from the longer poem, "Nutting" is a beautifully complete poem in its own right that was published in the 1800 edition of the groundbreaking *Lyrical Ballads*, which contains an influential literary manifesto in the preface authored by Wordsworth under Coleridge's inspiration. The poetic principles of the preface find embodiment in "Nutting." The typically Wordsworthian theme of the poem focuses on a semimystical experience of a young man's joyous, if fitful, apprehension of the spirit of life in the universe, the meaning of which is probed in the mature mind of the narrator remembering an early time of mindless pleasure in nature. The poem shows that moments of spiritual apprehension are not easy to come by, to preserve with the same initial pleasure, or to interpret clearly. At the outset, the mature narrator has to point out the special significance of his boyhood adventure in nature ("One of those heavenly days that cannot die"), because the ensuing narrative begins stressing a contrary message of civilized resistance to, rather than communion with, the countryside. The boy's overdressing and weapon-wielding are a defensive posture, almost a gesture of belligerence against the pristine bower of hazel trees that in his insensitive mind represents only a feast to devour and, implicitly, a male sex organ to rape and mutilate.

Not until line 33, where he pauses from undertaking the nut gathering, does he first hear the sounds of nature and let his imagination transform surface reality into deeper fantastic insights of oneness with the woods ("fairy" water-breaks of a flowing stream murmuring to the boy; mossy stones that are not simply rocks but, through simile in the creative imagination, become "like a flock of sheep"). These insights cause momentary "pleasure" and "joy" within the communing heart of the boy and create later recollection and spiritual solace in the mind of the mature narrator, who must combat the inevitable disillusionments of life springing from the aging process. An intervening memory of the boy's ensuing rape of the bower, however, sullies the remembrance of those joyous insights for the mature narrator (lines 41-48). The narrator ends by recollecting the boy's second communication with nature, which is no longer a heartfelt enjoyment of the rural scene but becomes the guilt-ridden recognition of being discovered in wrongdoing under "the intruding sky" for having devastated the now "silent" hazel trees (lines 48-53).

In the company of an unspecified "dearest Maiden," the mature narrator affirms the lesson he has learned—that, despite all human devastation, there is an unconquerable spirit in the woods ready to be in sympathy with a humanity of humble and open hearts. So ends a poem that is beautifully representative of the Romantic movement in European literature.

Thomas M. Curley

O CARIB ISLE!

Author: Hart Crane (1899-1932)
Type of poem: Lyric
First published: 1927; collected in *The Collected Poems of Hart Crane*, 1933

The Poem

"O Carib Isle!" is a lyric poem of thirty-four lines divided into seven irregular stanzas with intermittent rhyme. The stanzas are further grouped into two sections followed by a concluding four-line stanza. The poem presents a beach scene in which a Caribbean island teeming with nonhuman life is associated with death in the mind of the speaker, the poet Hart Crane himself rather than an imaginary persona. In the first stanza, the poem describes the foot end of a grave in white sand where lilies have been laid and a tarantula rustles among the dry flower stalks. Crabs scuttling sideways seem to rearrange the letters of the name of the dead written in the sand. However, nothing in nature seems to mourn except a partly withered eucalyptus plant.

In the second and third stanzas, the speaker sees the seashells littering the sand as mother-of-pearl "frames of tropic death." Empty of the bodies that once gave them life, the shells themselves are reminders of death. The shells also seem to the speaker to mark off graves in squared patterns in the sand. If the speaker can count these shells, then he may "speak a name" that the names of the living and dying trees and flowers near the beach contradict. The name may be death, or it may be God. The "brittle crypt" suggests shells and bones in which the dead are encrypted. A wind mounting toward hurricane force also suggests the poet's withdrawn breath. The breathless silence evokes the atmosphere before a storm begins and represents the speaker's emotional and creative deadness.

The second major section, subdivided into two parts, asks who is in charge of this deserted island where a pirate captain may have buried gold doubloons. The island is "Without a turnstile" such as one might find at an airport or a train station because no one wants to be there, and there is no obvious escape. Only the crabs occupy the land, patrolling the infertile underbrush. The absent captain or commissioner has created the complexity of what the speaker sees through sun-baked eyes. Called into question, this captain stands for a God whose "Carib mathematics" reminds readers of the shell count in the first stanza. The second subdivision of the second part of the poem represents a prayer to let the speaker's ghost be "Sieved upward" until it meets the "comedian" who "hosts" the blue sky. This ascension is preferable to being left on earth where he can look around on the beach and see the "slow evisceration" of his body, dying like terrapins turned on their backs and helpless to return to their element, the sea. The final stanza is a four-line coda. Left in the wake of the hurricane hinted at earlier, the speaker admits that he has only the dry fragments of shell rather than the soul he hoped for, his own mortal body the "carbonic amulet" on the necklace of shells littering the beach.

Forms and Devices

"O Carib Isle!" comprises two groupings of fifteen lines, each ending with a rhymed couplet. (Metrically, the seventh line is a single line that is divided to indicate a paragraph break.) These two groupings are followed by a four-line concluding stanza. Crane uses rhyme sparingly to define the poem's overall structure and to emphasize key points. In spite of the loose and, at first glance, haphazard placement of rhyme, a careful reading reveals that the poem actually falls neatly into three parts with its major division marked by rhymed couplets as well as spaces on the page.

"O Carib Isle!" is characterized by complex meter rather than free verse. Iambic pentameter and end rhyme provide a foundation for the lines that depart from the regular pattern. For example, the divided line "In wrinkled shadows—mourns./ And yet suppose" is perfectly even metrically: ten syllables with stresses on the second, fourth, sixth, eighth, and tenth syllables. The opening line further illustrates the poem's metrical complexity. The first line has twelve syllables rather than the ten expected in a perfect iambic pentameter line. After the definite article, an unstressed syllable, Crane begins boldly with a four-syllable word ("tarantula"), which is two iambs, then finishes the line with four iambs starting with the accented first syllable of "rattling." The effect of the very word "tarantula" is to make the line heavy with syllables like the big spider's legs moving slowly at the stalk of the lily. The line is at once busy and slow moving, very much the effect a tarantula might have on an observer.

Throughout the poem, Crane plays longer and shorter lines against the basic five-stress line. For example, line 20 ("Is Commissioner of mildew throughout the ambushed senses") has fifteen syllables but only five strong accents (on the third, tenth, twelfth, and fourteenth syllables). That long line comes right after a line of only four syllables ("What man, or What") that has two strong accents (on "man" and on the second "What"). The fact that this is the shortest line in the poem calls attention to it. Inside the line, the repetition of "What" further focuses the reader's attention on that syllable. The first "What" does not receive a stress; the second does. The repetition and the end stress arguably make the second "What" the central note of the poem—the unknown force that created the grim scene the speaker surveys.

Crane tries to force his inspiration with a visual rhyme: "senses" and "lenses." However, the sound is not quite right. Should readers trust their eyes or their ears, their "ambushed senses" or the "baked lenses" of their eyes? The end couplet of the second grouping of fifteen lines again offers a visual rhyme, "strain" and "again," which may or may not be a sound rhyme depending on how one pronounces "again." At the end of the first fifteen-line section of the poem, "Death" and "breath" is an easy and tired rhyme, at first glance surprisingly amateurish in the work of a poet as skillful as Crane. "Death" also ends line 8. However, the technically lazy rhyme suggests the very thing the poet is describing: a failure of inspiration and a spiritual weariness. A lack of inspiration is both a lack of breath and a lack of spirit.

Themes and Meanings

As is often the case in Crane's poetry, "O Carib Isle!" relies on images and word associations to release its emotional energy. Sensuous description of a hot, dry Caribbean island stands as an extended metaphor for the dry, desolate state of the speaker's consciousness. Ironically, it is a beautifully realized poem about the failure of poetic inspiration. The poem expresses the poet's exhausted sensibility and spiritual pessimism but creates in the poem itself a belief in something beyond himself, if only in Satan. Actually, Satan is no more present in the poem than the absent "Captain" (God). However, the depressed and weary speaker is more inclined to believe in the hot, desolate landscape of the island as hell rather than paradise.

Poetry also begins with the process of naming. However, although "name" or "names" appears four times in the first section, these appearances are in the context of generalities ("tree," "flower," "a name") rather than the specific eucalyptus of poinciana named elsewhere in the poem. Furthermore, Crane chooses his specific names carefully: For example, the poinciana, a red-flowered plant, was named for a former governor of the French West Indies, M. de Poinci. The landscape is torpid, dead, or inhuman, and in some cases all three. The scuttling crabs "anagrammatize" an unstated name, thereby obliterating a specific identity and reminding the poet that any naming of the mystery of life is conditional and temporary—written in sand, to use the familiar cliché. (It has been observed that "crab" is a rearranging of the letters of "carib" with the *I*, or identity, deleted.) Counting shells is a way of giving order to a mind at least temporarily incapable of the richer possibilities of naming that are the beginnings of poetry. In a later and more hopeful poem, Crane seeks a transcendent "name for all."

Although the speaker seems depressed and doubtful of transcendence, he retains some faith in his poetic powers. Many of Crane's poems are written in four-line stanzas. "O Carib Isle!" has only one clearly delineated quatrain, whose position at the end of the poem oddly suggests a return to confidence and to a sense of himself. The richly alliterative last line, "Sere of the sun exploded in the sea," which describes a sunless world in which human life is either nonexistent or powerless, is, perhaps ironically, a tour-de-force conclusion. Offering such triumph as sound and verbal grandeur can provide, it reads against the grim description in the rest of the poem.

Thomas Lisk

O TASTE AND SEE

Author: Denise Levertov (1923-1997)
Type of poem: Lyric
First published: 1964, in *O Taste and See: New Poems*

The Poem

"O Taste and See," the title poem from Denise Levertov's sixth collection of poems, urges readers to experience life fully and sacramentally. Reading the poem one can imagine Levertov riding a subway train in New York, where she lived at the time of the writing, looking up at the advertising signs, and reading or imagining the words "O Taste and See," then, as she often did, making a connection between her experience and the possibilities of that phrase in order to form a constellation of perceptions (to use her term) intense enough to suggest the opening lines of the poem: "The world is/ not with us enough./ O taste and see."

These lines contain two reversals. The first is a curious reversal of William Wordsworth's title "The World Is Too Much with Us." For Wordsworth the "world" is commerce and exploitation, while for Levertov it is nature and the potential for satisfying experience. The second reversal is the counterintuitive order of "taste and see." The natural and logical order would seem to be seeing something first and then deciding to taste it. Yet the implication of the title, and the poem, is that tasting or experiencing enables one to see or understand. Such is the obvious intent of the biblical origin of the phrase "O taste and see that the Lord is good" (Psalms 34:8). In other words, only by experiencing God or life can one truly know or appreciate God.

The poem tells readers to taste and see "all that lives/ to the imagination's tongue." Then there follows a litany of pleasures that are concrete, abstract, emotional, spiritual, physical, aesthetic, and richly sensuous: "grief, mercy, language,/ tangerine, weather, to/ breathe them, bite/ savor, chew, swallow, transform// into our flesh our/ deaths, crossing the street, plum, quince." All seem equal, such as grieving and savoring; all seem equally ordinary, as when death is as ordinary as crossing the street; and all, from their ordinariness, evoke mystery and meaning.

"O Taste and See" concludes with one more surprising twist: an image of one's present existence as paradisiacal or edenic. "[L]iving in the orchard and being// hungry, and plucking/ the fruit." This image is not the Eden of the Fall of Man on one hand or an unattainable utopia on the other, but a description of life as it could be if lived fully.

Forms and Devices

"O Taste and See" is structured in five stanzas. The first and fourth stanzas consist of three lines each; the second and third, four lines each; and the last, two. The lines of the first and last stanzas are shorter than the rest, so that, visually, the poem appears rather symmetrical. However, one's lingering impression, after closing the book, is that the words and phrases of the poem scampered down the page in an improvised dance.

Because "O Taste and See" is an unrhymed poem without a regular metrical pattern, giving the impression of free form, one might categorize it as free verse. Levertov, however, would have objected, preferring to describe it, instead, as an "organic poem." By organic form she meant that content determines form. In other words, if the poet is attentive to the sense and sound of the content, those will suggest the form the poem should take: the length of the lines, the line breaks, the look of the poem on the page. By breaking the first line of the poem after "The world is," for example, she creates a moment of wondering what the world is before the slight surprise of the next line: "not with us enough." By including "O taste and see" in the first stanza, she invites readers to test her thesis that the world is not with us enough before they connect "O taste and see" to "the subway Bible poster said" in the following line (and stanza). In a similar way, the break between line 12, "into our flesh our," and line 13, "deaths," creates a moment of slight suspense.

Levertov's stanza breaks are as deliberate as her line breaks. The last line of each stanza runs on into the following stanza, and the pull of the run-on is especially effective in the last two stanza breaks. Between the third and fourth stanzas, the line "savor, chew, swallow, transform" is the closest to a natural and logical sequence in the list of pleasures, and it sets up the natural, but surprising, continuation in the fourth stanza: "into our flesh our/ deaths." At the end of the fourth stanza, the line "living in the orchard and being" seems complete in itself and consistent with the existential theme of the poem. The first line of the last stanza draws attention down to "hungry, and plucking/ the fruit," thus modifying and enlarging one's understanding.

Another device that Levertov employs in her poems is the use of different typefaces, and in "O Taste and See" she uses boldface for the phrases "O taste and see" and "The Lord," implying that these are borrowed or quoted lines. The boldface also highlights and emphasizes them. Although the poems of *O Taste and See* were written during what Levertov called her agnostic period, they echo both the language and the precepts of the Bible, which cannot be ignored in the interpretation.

Themes and Meanings

Levertov's poetry is grounded in experience but is not a direct description of experiences. "O Taste and See" grew from an experience on a New York subway train, but it is not about the subway or its passengers or the city. Yet the theme of the poem is not an abstraction, nor is it spiritualized—though it was suggested by a biblical text. It is expressed concretely. Here Levertov is true to the creed of William Carlos Williams: no ideas but in things. Those things are fleshly and frankly Epicurean. She invites readers to savor, chew, and swallow tangerines, plums, and quinces. Fruits are staples of her poems, beautiful for their color, shape, texture, scent, and taste. Fruits are also nourishing: They feed one literally as well as aesthetically.

The poem does not suggest that the life experienced fully is an escape from reality. It includes, among its pleasures, transforming the fruits of life "into our flesh our/

deaths." The truth that death not only is a reality but also enriches life is clarified in another poem in the collection, "Another Spring," in which Levertov writes, "Death in us goes on/ testing the wild/ chance of living/ as Adam chanced it." Then, so that her meaning will not be mistaken, she adds, "I am speaking of living,/ of moving from one moment into/ the next."

Full engagement with life led Levertov into social protest. *O Taste and See* was published before her anti-Vietnam War demonstrations of the late 1960's and early 1970's, but her involvement in these causes—chronicled in *To Stay Alive* (1971)—is consistent with, and an application of, the theme of full engagement.

"O Taste and See" is not only about experiencing life fully but also about living life sacramentally. These pleasures that live "to the imagination's tongue" are gifts from God—grace. "O taste and see," she writes, "meaning The Lord," implying that acceptance of this grace is at least part of experiencing life fully. That the fruits of the earth are divine graces is implied in other biblical passages with which Levertov, the daughter of an Anglican priest, would have been acquainted: "God . . . giveth us richly all things to enjoy" (I Timothy 6:17), and, most certainly, the words of Jesus to his disciples at the Lord's Supper: "Take and eat" (Matthew 26:26).

Readers who appreciate "O Taste and See" will enjoy other poems from the collection that reinforce its theme. Her poem "To the Muse" echoes the possibilities of abundant pleasure for those who welcome the muse. "Who shares/ even water and dry bread with you [the muse]/ will not eat without joy," Levertov writes, echoing Matthew 10:42.

Other poems in the collection provide negative examples or foils to the theme. "The Old Adam"—a common euphemism for the sinful or carnal nature of fallen humanity—describes a lost old man who has lived a "life/ unlived" and asks in the last line of the poem, "What have I done with my life?" His life was empty, and, as implied by the title, his refusal to live life fully was sinful.

Gaymon L. Bennett

O THE CHIMNEYS

Author: Nelly Sachs (1891-1970)
Type of poem: Meditation
First published: 1946, as "O die Schornsteine," in *In den Wohnungen des Todes*; English translation collected in *O the Chimneys*, 1967

The Poem

A free-verse poem of twenty lines originally in German and divided into four stanzas, "O the Chimneys" is a meditation on the Nazi death machine that destroyed six million Jewish people in the Holocaust. The chimneys of the title refer to those ovens built to incinerate the bodies of concentration camp victims killed in gas chambers.

Throughout the poem, the Nazi death camps are called "abodes of death" that are "devised." That is, they are technologically planned and scientifically administered for destruction. This statement conveys with chilling horror the clinical efficiency, the numbing methodicalness and appearance of business-as-usual that filmmakers such as Claude Lanzmann and philosophers such as Hannah Arendt have associated with the implementation of the Final Solution.

The smoke of the furnaces in which the Jewish people are burned, in the first stanza, becomes dust, which the poet associates with Jeremiah and Job, both martyrs to stubborn, defiant faithfulness to God. In the Hebrew Scriptures, Jeremiah becomes a political outcast, Job a social one, as each resists easy presumptions about God's justice.

Similarly, the poet raises questions about her people's suffering: Who or what receives it? Who devised it? These questions hang in the air with their tangible evidence: ashes, dust, smoke. Such suspension freezes the event, in history and consciousness. The event is moreover a cosmic one, blackening stars or sunbeams. The poet—and the reader, both now witnesses to the crime—find themselves on the border, the "threshold," between life and death.

Quoted beneath the poem's title is a verse from Job (19:26): "And when this my skin has been destroyed, from my flesh shall I see God," which some interpreters have understood as an affirmation of resurrection. Rather than a sense of discontinuity, however, the poet's revelation conveys a sense of metamorphosis, in which Israel's body and the smoke rising through the air are "dissolved" into each other, ever present in the atmosphere.

Forms and Devices

With its emphasis on imagery—on metaphor, juxtaposition, and ellipsis—rather than on complex rhythmic texture or intricate rhyme scheme, Nelly Sachs's poetry can be readily appreciated in translation.

The poem images the Jewish victims of the Holocaust as a single human body; thus particularized, their suffering is made more concrete, more immediate, more identifiable. Unlike the Nazi administration of the Final Solution, the fate of the victims cannot be abstracted into numbers, into statistics. The poet further concretizes the Holocaust by embodying the Nazi genocide in its death camps. The controlling image of the camps resonates in specific references to "chimneys," "abodes," "stone upon stone," "house," and "threshold."

The dynamic imagery of transmutation is evident throughout the poem, as flesh is dissolved in smoke and roads materialize from dust. As in Sachs's other work, biblical imagery submerges the poem in the depths of myth. The casualties of the Holocaust are associated with Jeremiah and Job, linking their suffering with that of the prophets and wise men. The simultaneity of Jewish existence, transcending time and space, confounding life and death, is thereby grasped in the poet's vision.

The poet asks rhetorical questions regarding the sufferings of the Holocaust, conscious of the inadequacy of any conventional explanation. Such questions echo the series of rhetorical questions with which God reveals himself to Job out of the whirlwind. The reader is thus drawn into the eternal dialogue engaging God and humanity.

Themes and Meanings

By alluding to Job in the poem, Sachs connects the Holocaust to the thorny question of innocent suffering, so scandalous to moral certitude. Her conjuring of natural and cosmic imagery, her parable of smoke and dust and air, suggests that the scandal of the Holocaust can best be comprehended by metaphysical or mystical insight. Such comprehension is not explanation; rather, it is an encounter with the mystery of existence. This encounter occurs at the nexus of flesh and dust, spirit and matter, life and death. Thus, on the verge of extinction, the enduring presence of the Jewish people is revealed.

Sachs herself was a survivor of Nazi Germany, emigrating to Sweden in 1940. Her major work, which established a reputation that eventually led to a Nobel Prize in Literature in 1966, was written during and after World War II. Her body of poetry forms a witness to the Holocaust. This witness, like that of other Holocaust writers, especially Elie Wiesel, is unflinching and resistant to moralizing. The spirit of Job, who affirmed his integrity in the face of doubt and suffering, informs the work of these authors.

Sachs, in addition, demonstrates sympathy with the Jewish mystics, the Kabbalists, who relentlessly pursued *tikkun*, or the reconciliation of a shattered creation. Her poetic vision unites body and spirit, nature and the cosmos, death and life, in a ceremony of metamorphosis.

Amy Adelstein

THE OCCIDENT

Author: Georg Trakl (1887-1914)
Type of poem: Lyric
First published: 1914, as "Abendland," in *Sebastian im Traum*; English translation
   collected in *Selected Poems*, 1968

The Poem

The poem's German title, "Abendland," usually translated as "The Occident,"
names the West as the land of evening (*Abend*), the land where the sun sets. In Georg
Trakl's time, the word referred primarily to the Western European nations. In haunting imagery of evening and approaching night, the poet found a perfect metaphor for
what he saw as the late hour in the decline of Western culture, a powerful tool for expressing his sense of foreboding about the depth of night to which that decline might
lead. The poem was written in the last months before the outbreak of World War I. The
very name the Occident (*Abendland*) invoked for Trakl this imagery of evening and
this sense of lateness.

"The Occident" is divided into three sections. In the first, the central tension of the
poem is established in the contrast between two stanzas. The first contains remarkable
images of death and decline, and the second centers on the image of Elis, a boy who
seems to be unaffected by decline and to await a time of rebirth or springtime. Elis, a
subject of two other poems by Trakl in the same volume, represents the original world
from which the real world has declined, as well as the rebirth that will come after decline reaches its nadir.

The second section of the poem evokes a quiet tone of lament for the heartbreaking
beauty and peace of late evening. The world of evening is lovely and restful, but it is
fragile and is only a distant echo of its pure source and beginnings. Its beauty is always about to be lost in night. Uneasiness about what will come surfaces as singers
wander with hesitant steps near thorns and people are said to have wept in their sleep.
The peace seems to be an ominous quiet before the storm.

The final section turns to the cities on the plain, above which angry clouds are forming. By the end of the section, and the poem, the apocalyptic storm is breaking, and
even the stars are falling from the sky. This last image echoes the book of Revelation,
in which the world at the end of time descends into increasing darkness until the stars
themselves fall before the resurrection. (Trakl used this allusion and the theme of a decline to absolute darkness earlier in his poem "Helian.")

When one considers the title again after reading the poem, "Abendland" or "The
Occident" seems a land filled with portentous evening light, about to lose itself in the
depths of darkness, with lightning bursting in the sky above its dying people. The
poem seems to invest decline with an uncanny force, as if the West, the land of evening, were being carried to its fate by the irresistible forces of spiritual history.

Forms and Devices

Trakl, like Else Lasker-Schüler, to whom this poem is dedicated, is a poet of the German expressionist movement. The expressionists, who viewed the image as the basic unit of poetry, sought to intensify the vividness and expressive power of their images. They composed their poems of intense images much as one might compose music of notes or musical phrases. The coherence of a sequence of images is thus often thematic or emotional instead of logical, temporal, or spatial.

In "The Occident," Trakl's images are not connected with spatial transitions, as one might expect in the realistic description of a landscape, and one cannot piece together a story that the poem might tell. His sentence structures are also often incomplete or interrupted, so the images do not fall into a logical pattern of explanation. The first word of the poem, for example, the noun "Moon," appears in isolation, and serves no identifiable grammatical function in a sentence. A dependent clause compares the moon to something indefinite but pale, a "dead thing" as it would look if it were to step from a blue cave, but here the sentence breaks off and is never completed. As a result, the moon seems to loom symbolically. The reader can see this moon, with a patch of the sky lit up to a shade of blue around it, and has a sense of its eerie, deathlike presence. It stays before the mind, and a strong tone is established. Rather than subduing the image by means of description or a logical context, Trakl instead presents the reader with a series of other images, of petals falling across a stone path, a "sick thing" that is silver weeping by the "evening pond," and lovers who "died over" on a black boat.

In most poems by Trakl, one can reconnect the isolated images in a stanza by imagining them to be fragments of a landscape, but not without first sensing a strong undercurrent, a unity of tone and theme that makes the images and the landscape seem symbolic. Here the tone is uncanny and eerie, as if the strange moon were inscrutably related to the petals falling and the sick thing weeping. Thematically, the images all seem connected to decay, decline, and death.

Similarly, in each of the remaining stanzas, a symbolic landscape must be pieced together out of fragmentary images and the discovery of the unifying sense of tone and theme. In the second stanza of the first section, Elis walks in a grove full of hyacinths, seemingly free of the decline of the first stanza. In the second section, a quiet evening landscape is troubled by uneasiness and seems to be only a reprieve before a storm. In the last, cities on a plain are surrounded by a storm and dying peoples fall into apocalyptic darkness.

Trakl's apparently disjointed images present a series of symbolic landscapes that are not necessarily related spatially, or in the context of a narrative, or in a framework of logical development of ideas. Once one observes how these landscapes change color and tone and mood, however, one begins to grasp the feelings of lamentation and foreboding that Trakl sought to express. One accepts his vision of things to the extent that one finds his tone and imagery emotionally compelling.

Trakl also often reuses elements of images that he has developed in other poems. The moon, the pond, the cave, and the boat of the first stanza, for example, and later the grove, the footsteps, the hillside, the thunder, the wall, the hedge, and the thunder-clouds, are all elements used in other poems in the same volume. Trakl constantly shifts color words in combinations with these elements, so that there is a red pond in another poem, a black hill in another, and a golden boat in a third.

Trakl also reuses symbolic figures he has created and developed elsewhere. The boy Elis and the lovers who may be spared decline by early death appear in several poems. The wanderer in the third section is the figure of the alienated artist that is familiar in Trakl's work.

For the reader of Trakl's poetry, these recurring figures and elements of imagery seem familiar, even though they appear in new contexts and combinations and their meanings change. Trakl seems to work with a basic set of symbolic elements and a kind of underlying grammar for their combinations in the symbolic landscapes of his poetry. The shifting combinations and variations make the vocabulary and grammar he has created seem flexible enough to express powerfully the truth of different types of spiritual climates.

Themes and Meanings

Trakl's poem was completed in June, 1914, a few months before the outbreak of World War I. In August, 1914, Trakl was drafted into the Austrian army as a pharmacist-lieutenant, and after three months of service in which he witnessed scenes of horrible carnage, resulting in his being placed under observation for psychological trauma, Trakl died of a cocaine overdose in November, 1914. As a result, the tone and subject of the poem seem eerily prophetic, and the disjointed syntactical arrangement of images is often thought to reflect the pressure of the time and the unraveling of logic in a world on its last legs, about to collapse into war.

"The Occident," then, is a marvelous expressionistic portrait of an era in which a civilization was carried irresistibly toward destruction. In his search for the expressive potential of the image, Trakl managed to reach a level of expression that is beyond the expression of personal feelings. He captured the anxiety of a period of history. In a language that is, in its repetition of elements and its portentous symbolic tone, so reminiscent of the language of prophecy, Trakl managed to anticipate the calamity in which the entire world would be involved.

The poem, however, is not concerned solely with decline. Trakl's poetry, prior to his last military assignments, is never a poetry of ultimate pessimism. The wanderer, the figure of the poet, turns aside from the materialistic current of the times to seek, uncertainly, a new idealism. The boy Elis, developed in several poems in Trakl's last volume, does not undergo the prevailing decline but awaits a time that will come after the decline has reached its lowest point. Such figures in Georg Trakl's poetry represent hope for the reawakening of spiritual values after the magnificent and terrifying sunset of the first decades of the new century, and after the night that would follow. They represent the hope of a new dawn.

Von E. Underwood

AN OCTOPUS

Author: Marianne Moore (1887-1972)
Type of poem: Meditation
First published: 1924; collected in *Selected Poems*, 1935

The Poem

"An Octopus" is a long, meditative, free-verse poem of 193 lines of varying length. Though meditative, it is not a reflective poem but one of active processes. Like many of Marianne Moore's poems, the title runs immediately into the first line of the poem, thereby limiting any sense of positioning the poem or preparing the reader. The reader confronts a series of shifting possibilities as suggested by the first sentence: "An Octopus/ of ice." This incomplete opening sentence establishes a metaphoric comparison that will be explored—but not fully or completely—in the poem.

The poem is a continuous shifting of perspectives, not on a single subject, but on the movement of analogies. Thus, after the poem's description of Mount Rainier and its surrounding ice fields as an octopus and its tentacles, it quickly compounds the activity of description with questions of travel, of perception, the difficulty of art, and the appropriation of nature as an aesthetic object.

"An Octopus" resists division into component parts of a whole argument; however, there are implicit shifts of focus. These shifts may be briefly outlined in the following manner: The first thirteen lines displace the reader because the metaphoric comparison of the mountain to the octopus is suspended. Lines 14 to 22 counterbalance the first section, for they become increasingly descriptive. At line 23, Moore self-reflexively shifts, stating: "Completing a circle,/ you have been deceived into thinking that you have progressed." The poem offers both descriptions and challenges to making the mountain, nature, or the other familiar and thus reduced to merely the scenic and clichéd.

The poem continues in this long section offering descriptions and suggesting that such descriptions are inadequate in various ways—grottoes that "make you wonder why you came" (line 62) or a beauty never fully spoken of "at home/ for fear of being stoned as an impostor" (lines 73-74). At line 75, the poem shifts from these questions of travel—that is, descriptions of the mountain in relation to a "you"—to a larger human presence among the various wild creatures, who themselves have become anthropomorphized. It is at line 75 that Moore names the site of this meditation, Big Snow Mountain; this is Mount Rainier, which she visited in 1922. Thus far, the poem's focus has been the mountain, with varying layers of particularized description. The poem nevertheless poses the paradoxical condition of knowing the other that is always difficult to apprehend: "conspicuously spotted little horses are peculiar;/ hard to discern among the birch-trees, ferns, and lily-pads" (lines 117-118).

The poem's single break follows line 127, which marks the poem's shift from the descriptive to the conceptual. Moore derides any pastoralism or appropriation of the landscape for moral purposes in the opening lines of this section. The Aristotelian ideals of attaining knowledge and propriety are contrasted to the "odd oracles of cool official sarcasm" (line 154); Moore shares with the Greeks the desire for accuracy and the understanding that knowledge will never be complete. This meditation continues with her linking Henry James's writing to the mountain, in that both have a "Neatness of finish! Neatness of finish!" (line 172). The Greeks' love of "smoothness, distrusting what was back/ of what could not be clearly seen" (lines 140-141), serves to draw Moore's sensibility into agreement with James and the Greeks.

The poem, however, closes with a long meditation on the ability of a word to signify an object: "Is 'tree' the word for these things" (line 180). The full understanding or perceiving of the mountain, or anything, can never be concluded. Moore's "Relentless accuracy" (line 173), like that of the Greeks or James, prohibits full closure.

Forms and Devices

"An Octopus" can be viewed as a collage; it contains citations from various sources, as indicated in the notes Moore provided to accompany the poem. These citations, set apart by quotation marks, introduce a sense of an assemblage of multiple perspectives or multiple voices other than the conventional lyrical "I." The quotation marks also create a tension between the apparent author and the cited words. Nevertheless, the various citations are seamlessly incorporated into the flow of the poem's descriptions. As a collage, the poem fits into a modernist aesthetic that sought to both create poems that were objects and to draw into poetry the daily and mundane and transform it into art.

"An Octopus" contains numerous examples of various tropes. Paradox is perhaps the striking trope outside of Moore's use of images. Again, the opening line provides an example of what is prevalent throughout the poem: The octopus is of ice—though significantly Moore omits the verb "is" so as to draw the juxtaposition of living creature and a lifeless elemental into a new thing. What she views—or how she views the mountain—is highly mutable, for "its clearly defined pseudo-podia/ [are] made of glass that will bend—a much needed invention" (line 4). The metaphor of the glacier as an octopus is further complicated by the metaphoric comparison of it as having the "crushing rigor of the python" and then further shifting the comparison to "'spider fashion/ on its arms' misleadingly like lace" (lines 9-11).

The poem celebrates the mountain through extraordinary images. Moore accumulates images through the use of catalogs, including catalogs of colors, "indigo, pea-green, blue-green, and turquoise" (line 34), of animals, "bears, elk, deer, wolves, goats, and ducks" (line 40), of gems, "calcium gems and alabaster pillars,/ topaz, tourmaline crystals and amethyst quartz" (lines 49-50). Her use of images often fuses with the paradoxical, as in "cliffs the color of the clouds, of petrified white vapor" (line 64). Here, as throughout the poem, the paradox is alchemical in that it transforms and fuses the opposing elements of stone and vapor. Indeed, she points to this idea of drawing together disparate elements: "moisture works its alchemy,/ transmuting verdure into onyx" (lines 126-127). The full landscape is always in the process of transformation.

It is also characteristic of this poem, and of many of Moore's works, that the syntax cannot be simplified. Sentences are often complex, compound structures that depend upon momentum and the moment. Their form and logic is associative and accumulative, often carrying the reader away from the subject. Though Moore also includes short, direct sentences, none are statements of truth. The unfolding structure of Moore's sentences is thus also an aspect of the verbal collage's juxtapositions and the transformative processes of metaphor and image. Moore's sentences, however, do not lead to obscurity, rather they attempt a precision of observation and a desire for fact. The weaving of various citations with the observer's voice reinforces the drive for "Relentless accuracy."

Themes and Meanings

Among Moore's concerns in "An Octopus" is the view that writing is a phenomenon or an otherness analogous to the mountain. The reader's approach to the poem would entail similar dilemmas to that of viewing the mountain. Moore explores to what extent one can avoid objectifying an object—that is, turning away from its complexities and changing it into something identifiable. The demand for identity must be resisted, Moore implies through the poem's use of paradox, shifting perspectives, citations, and other devices. To resist identity, however, is not to give up "Relentless accuracy." The unresolved and incomplete quality of the poem suggests that neither the mountain nor the poem can be seen fully. Moore does not consider this as failure, but rather a sign of the necessity for a relentless pursuit of accuracy as well as a demand for active curiosity.

"An Octopus" exemplifies Moore's genius as an observer and a collector of observations. The naturalist's desire for details is demonstrated with her use of citations about the environment of the mountain. Yet, importantly, Moore does not settle for simply a descriptive poem. Like her protégé, the poet Elizabeth Bishop, Moore was concerned with such metaphysical and aesthetic issues as uncertainty, provisionality, voice, the definition of self, and the processes of seeing. "An Octopus" explores each of these concerns while offering a meditation on writing. Moore offers a continually shifting range of emotions in her descriptions of the mountain; the poem suggests the capacity writing has to contain these emotions while simultaneously not limiting them or fusing them into a unity. The analogy of the octopus never becomes symbolic, an identity, or a solitary truth. Moore, instead, assembles possibilities, all of which accumulate but never reach a summation.

The resistance to completion occurs in various ways. It should be noted that the poem underwent several substantial revisions after its original publication in *The Dial* magazine. In Moore's view, the poem as object was never a static piece, but always a process. And certainly a poem such as "An Octopus," concerned as it is with observation and description, questions the possibility of a full vision of an object. Perception hinges upon the position of the observer; in "An Octopus" the observer is essentially a tourist and not a native of the place. Notably about America's western landscape, "An Octopus" questions the definition of self and of an American or native self. Like the painter Georgia O'Keeffe or the poet William Carlos Williams, Moore was not an expatriate. Like Williams or O'Keeffe, Moore develops an idiosyncratic vision and reveals peculiarly American idioms. The self, construed as both personal and social, is portrayed as always in process, always appropriating perspectives and shedding them. Neither the self nor the object perceived can be captured in completeness or static essence.

James McCorkle

ODE FOR THE AMERICAN DEAD IN ASIA

Author: Thomas McGrath (1916-   )
Type of poem: Ode
First published: 1957, as "Ode for the American Dead in Korea," in *New Poets of England and America*; collected in *The Movie at the End of the World*, 1973

The Poem

Thomas McGrath's "Ode for the American Dead in Asia" is poem composed of three numbered stanzas of fourteen, fifteen, and fourteen lines, respectively. The subject of the poem, indicated by the title, is taken up with an extremely somber tone. Each of the stanzas, at least in significant part, is addressed to a "you"—the dead American solider in Korea. Too, in each stanza it is clear that many of the lines are addressed to a plural "you." This, however, does not provide the poem with confusion and ambiguity; rather, it provokes in readers a realization that these deaths—so pointless and futile—are also so numerous.

McGrath begins his poem with the lines "God love you now, if no one else will ever,/ Corpse in the paddy, or dead on a high hill." He goes on to describe the circumstances of this singular dead soldier, in actuality referring to all such dead American soldiers. The words "your false flags were/ Of bravery and ignorance" indicate a certain disdain for the youths who have given their lives for some reason which is not discernibly good or necessary, but "false." He records that the "safe commanders sent/ You into your future" with words that display both irony and sardonic terror, for that future is death. In the last lines of the stanza he calls the dead youth a "changeling," truly a curious word choice that can be explained only when one realizes that the "safe commanders" have exchanged this soldier's life for his death.

The poet continues in the second stanza by speaking of a "bee that spins his metal from the sun" and a "shy mole drifting like a miner ghost/ Through midnight earth." These, he explains, are "happy creatures" that run on "Blind instinct." He then, again, directly addresses the dead soldier and mentions both church and state, which provided "elders to confirm you in your ignorance." They have given him a "tennis racket" as an "Ark against the flood." In other words, the guns with which he was equipped failed miserably, for the "blind mole dies,/ And you on your hill, who did not know the rules [also die]."

Recalling wasteland imagery from T. S. Eliot and others, McGrath begins the last stanza with references to a crow, swallows, and a scarecrow. He turns from the war fields of Asia to his home state of North Dakota, where, presumably, this youth is either buried or remembered, but dead in either case. In the last two lines ("The limestone histories: brave: ignorant: amazed:/ Dead in the rice paddies, dead on the nameless hills"), bravery and ignorance are once again equated. Moreover, while the rice paddies of Southeast Asia are not comparable to the slag heaps of North Dakota, the "dead on the nameless hills" are the same in either geography.

Forms and Devices

In writing this ode, McGrath followed many of the usual conventions for this poetic form. It is organized into three stanzas, identifiable as the strophe, epode, and antistrophe, in that order. Consistently, lines contain ten to twelve syllables with no discernibly repetitive meter. In a few instances, the poet uses end rhymes, but there is no pattern ("see" and "eternity"; "kill" and "hill"). Also, he also includes a few examples of half rhymes: "ever" and "war"; "gaze" and "gone." Most of the lines have at least one instance of alliteration, such as "And God (whose sparrows fall aslant his gaze)."

It is in matters of subject and style that this work is most demonstrably defined as an ode. The serious, exalted subject of death—enhanced by the fact of its senselessness and futility—is even more compounded because of its mass occurrence; some fifty-four thousand Americans died in Korea. The poet manifests supreme pensiveness bordering on depression as he mourns the deaths of these soldiers throughout the poem, but especially in the last lines: "We will mourn you, whose fossil courage fills/ The limestone histories: brave: ignorant: amazed:/ Dead in the rice paddies, dead on the nameless hills." Also apparent in this last sentence is that the syntax itself of such expressions is often formal and convoluted. McGrath saves the punch for the end of his lines. Some of the lines are disjointed, with half stops or full stops that readily qualify them as caesuras: "the dead commanders sent/ You into your future. Oh, dead on a hill,/ Dead in a paddy."

As the poet speaks to the dead soldiers, he uses several different words: "corpse," "changeling," and "scarecrow." However, his most frequent form of address is the simple pronoun "you." This conveys a sense of intimacy, as if the poet is in the presence of the corpses themselves, rather than merely thinking of them in Korea from the distance provided from North Dakota, the home of the poet and identified as the contemplative setting in the antistrophe. In other places his word choice is formal, though not dauntlessly so. The poet alludes to God twice—in the opening line where he calls on God's love for the dead corpse in the rice paddy, and at the beginning of the last stanza, when he claims that God "blinks" and the crow (here, a vulture-like creature) is gone. A single biblical reference is given in the second stanza when McGrath refers to Noah's ark: "The rulers stuck a tennis racket in your hand,/ An Ark against the flood." It is puzzling to intermingle a tennis racket with the ark; yet the poet does not mean a tennis racket at all, but rather the soldier's rifle. The incongruency succeeds as readers realize that his intention is to emphasize the soldiers' ignorance and the manner in which their leaders had ill-prepared them, not merely for fighting, but for death itself.

Themes and Meanings

"Ode for the American Dead in Asia" succeeds as both a pacifist statement about all wars and an antiwar poem about a particular war, the Korean War. Except for the references to rice paddies, the poem in its entirety is general. McGrath's most important theme is the connection of "bravery" and "ignorance," which he makes in all three stanzas and which he focuses upon in the last lines. Clearly, McGrath, himself a vet-

eran of World War II and a person who had been on the battlefield, believes that bravery, in war at least, is a product of ignorance:

> You mined a culture that was mined for war:
> The state to mold you, church to bless, and always
> The elders to confirm you in your ignorance.

A cliché of Western civilization going back to the Greeks is revisited here in thought if
not in words: "Old men legislate wars that young men fight." However, in this work
bravery is to be lamented, not celebrated.

Perhaps of more importance than the connection between bravery and ignorance is
the connection between bravery and death. Ignorance accounts for bravery, and bravery, in turn, accounts for death. The poet seeks recognition of this, but there is no call
to action—no sense that readers (mourners) should do anything more than realize the
futility of deaths in these faraway countries. In the early 1970's, the title of this poem
was changed from "Ode to the American Dead in Korea" to "Ode for the American
Dead in Asia." McGrath's reasons were all too tragically true. The United States government, having not learned any lessons about bravery and deaths of soldiers in Korea
in the 1950's, became involved militarily in Vietnam in the 1960's, which resulted in
exactly the same consequences. American youths lay dead in rice paddies in Asian
jungles in "scarecrow valor" to be returned to places such as North Dakota, where
their courage would count for nothing, and would continue to exist only in the form of
"fossil . . . [that] fills/ The limestone histories." The "nameless hills" are in Asia where
American youth were killed, and they are in the United States where these brave one
are buried.

Carl Singleton

ODE, INSCRIBED TO W. H. CHANNING

Author: Ralph Waldo Emerson (1803-1882)
Type of poem: Ode
First published: 1847, in *Poems*

The Poem

"Ode, Inscribed to W. H. Channing" alludes frequently to historical people and events. The William Henry Channing to whom the ode is inscribed was a nineteenth century author and Unitarian minister, like his more famous uncle, William Ellery Channing. The younger Channing, a vigorous opponent of slavery, apparently occasioned this ode by urging his friend Ralph Waldo Emerson to join the cause in some formal or active way. The abolition issue was dividing increasing numbers of people. Daniel Webster, whom Emerson once greatly admired and probably had in mind all the while he wrote the ode, had turned against the Abolitionists in an effort to preserve the Union. Also, the Mexican War had just begun. This ode is Emerson's explanation of his reasons for remaining aloof and a proclamation of his strong feelings regarding the issues.

Addressing Channing as the "evil time's sole patriot," the poet begins with an explanation of why he cannot leave his "honied thought" and study: "The angry Muse/ Puts confusion in my brain (lines 10 through 11). The "evil time" is riven by "the priest's cant" and "statesman's rant" and by politics ("politique") that are at best fraudulent. Anyone who chatters ("prates") about improved "arts and life" (line 14) should behold his country's raids into Mexico. Anyone who praises the "freedom-loving mountaineer" of the North should know that the poet has found, by the banks and in the valleys of its rivers, the agents ("jackals") of the slave owners (in search of fugitive slaves).

The fifth stanza cites New Hampshire as an example (or source) of the "evil," for it is "taunted" by little men—"bat" and "wren." The list of ills is long: If the disturbed earth should "bury the folk,/ the southern crocodile would grieve" (lines 30-31). "Virtue" babbles or equivocates ("palters"), and "Right" has disappeared; "Freedom" is hidden, and funeral eloquence disturbs those buried heroes it purports to put to rest; these two lines, and the earlier reference to "little men" (line 26), may allude to Daniel Webster, a native of New Hampshire, and to his funeral oration at Bunker Hill, which Emerson heard.

Stanza 6 addresses Channing again ("O glowing friend"), alluding to his apparent support of dividing the North from the South over the slavery issue. The poet asks rhetorically what good separation would do, since commerce and other affairs (represented by Boston Bay and Bunker Hill) would continue as the evil is everywhere ("Things are of the snake"). Further examples (stanza 7) show how affairs are topsyturvy: They serve who should be served. Deference to things rules the day (line 48), and the consequence is that mankind is ridden like a beast of burden by the very things it worships.

Stanza 8 returns to the causes of this travesty: People have confused the laws governing man and thing (line 55). Men should not be governed by physical law, which is good for building "town and fleet," but runs wild and destroys man's supremacy ("doth the man unking"). The next two stanzas develop the idea that different laws apply to different spheres. Physical laws fittingly fell trees, build, grade, till, and so on. Humans should make laws themselves for friendship and love, to benefit truth and harmony. The state should adjust to these laws "how it may" (line 69), as Olympus is ruled by Jove.

The longest stanza, 11, continues the idea that a proper order should obtain in human affairs. People have their fit realms of activity (line 75); when one is forced out of one's proper sphere, things go awry. The poet implies that man should trust the "overgod," who rules human affairs with a knowledge and power beyond man's, for he "Knows to bring honey/ Out of the lion" (lines 86-87). The final stanza turns again to conditions as they are—in Europe, aggression has reduced Poland—but the ode ends with a promise: The victors divide into two camps, half fighting for freedom, and the "astonished" Muse finds thousands defending her.

Forms and Devices

The poem is an irregular ode composed of twelve stanzas of unequal length, ranging from five to nineteen lines each, totalling ninety-seven in all. The lines have a range of two to five stresses (only lines 20, 21, 74, and the last line of the poem have five stresses). No consistent pattern is apparent in the use of stresses, though the seven lines in the third stanza all have three stresses each, and often lines with an equal number of stresses are grouped together. Most of the metric feet are iambs, and most of the lines end on a stressed syllable.

Freedom of form is also evident in the use of rhyme, which displays no consistent pattern from stanza to stanza. Most of the stanzas have only four rhymes, many of them paired (*aa* or *bb*, for example) and many alternated (*abab*). Though structurally diverse, the poem is also unified by a number of structural features. The individual stanzas are knitted together by the rhymes, which are usually metrically stressed; by grouping together lines of equal number of stresses; and, often, by repetition. In stanza 7, for example, the first four lines repeat the same structure and verb: "The horseman serves . . ./ The neatherd serves . . ./ The merchant serves," and so on. Stanza 9 repeats the same sentence structure through a series of seven lines, each with two stresses.

The poet uses other means to unify the ode and elevate its tone. The apostrophe is used ("O rushing Contoocook!") along with personification ("Virtue palters; Right is hence") and allusions to classical figures, using the "Muse" at the beginning and end to represent the arts in general and poetry in particular, and citing classical mythology: "As Olympus follows Jove." These "learned" reminders of the formal nature of the ode are interwoven with indigenous material, place names (Boston Bay, Bunker Hill), and local topography (forest, mountain, orchard, glebe) to demonstrate the breadth and nature of the poet's vision, and to give much of the poem considerable symbolic power. The odic structure itself and references to classical figures place the poem in one tradition, while place names would be expected to arouse powerful associations in the minds of readers all too familiar with the importance of geography.

Themes and Meanings

The principal argument of the poem is that the times are clearly out of joint. Its strongest sentiments relate to the failure of men (such as Webster) to stand on the side of freedom and humanity, and against slavery and military aggression, whether in Mexico or in Poland. Though the poem is not a call to arms, its lofty stanzas accuse the "little men" who have betrayed Virtue and Right and give only lip service to Freedom. Instead, men force things and people out of their proper spheres and thereby "mix and mar," confusing things with human values. This idea is expressed sardonically in the use of "chattel" (line 48)—placed appropriately at the center of the ode— which means "movable possessions"; here, it refers to both livestock and slaves. In their passion to aggrandize themselves, men have reduced humanity to a thing and elevated things to a place of eminence. The poet suggests a remedy: One should live for "friendship," for "love," and for "truth's and harmony's behoof" (lines 67-68). One must not be too zealous and get taken in by the "priest's cant" and "statesman's rant" or drawn into their "politique."

The poet is centrally concerned with the arena in which the issues are bruited and the battle waged. He depicts this concern by using geographical references (New Hampshire, Boston Bay, and the "southern crocodile," for example) and by instancing local figures and activities (the horseman, neatherd, merchant, and so on). In this way, the poem asserts that though one must be cognizant of the revered past, the present has a place and importance equal to the other, if not superior to it, and the issues addressed are endemic to the setting.

A strong faith permeates the ode and explains in part the poet's attack on the "little men" and those who have lost sight of Virtue and Freedom; it is a faith in order ("Every one to his chosen work"), in the issues, in the "over-god," and in man himself. Despite the destructive nature of man, the "over-god" will find "thousands" who will defend freedom and the arts. Meanwhile, the poet does not turn away from the evils—he is no "blindworm," for he has beheld the transgressions of "the famous States" (line 16) and has himself found, by the rivers of the North, the "jackals of the negro-holder." Perhaps the poet's "honied thoughts" are akin to the "honey" that the over-god "Knows to bring . . ./ Out of the lion" (lines 86-87). If so, the lion remains for the moment in his den ("My study"), naming the evils and their causes and cautioning his countrymen to proceed with a clear understanding of the distinction between men and things. The poet is optimistic that freedom and poetry will be defended even when a state is devastated, and the soldiers shall come from the ranks of the invaders themselves.

Bernard E. Morris

ODE: INTIMATIONS OF IMMORTALITY

Author: William Wordsworth (1770-1850)
Type of poem: Ode
First published: 1807, in *Poems in Two Vols.*

The Poem

In "Ode: Intimations of Immortality" William Wordsworth writes in the compli-cated stanza forms and irregular rhythms that are typical of the ode form. The 205 lines are divided into eleven stanzas of varying lengths and rhyme schemes. In the ti-tle, Wordsworth attempts to summarize and simplify the rich philosophical content of the poem.

The poem begins with an epigraph taken from an earlier poem by Wordsworth: "The Child is father of the Man;/ And I could wish my days to be/ Bound each to each by natural piety." In this section of "My Heart Leaps Up," the speaker hopes that, in his maturity, he can maintain an intimate connection to the world, similar to the bond that he had in his own childhood. Since the "Child is father of the Man," people should respect the child in them as much as they are bound to their own fathers.

The first two stanzas of the poem quickly establish the problem that Wordsworth, the first-person speaker, faces: "There was a time" when the earth was charged with magnificence in the poet's eyes, when every common element "did seem/ Appareled in celestial light," but that time has gone. The ode begins in elegiac fashion, with the poet mourning because "there hath passed away a glory from the earth."

Oddly enough, this problem seems almost resolved in stanza 3 when Wordsworth announces that "a timely utterance" (which is never revealed) relieves his grief. Critics have never decided definitively what that "timely utterance" could be, but all agree that Wordsworth seems tremendously healed by it. He boldly predicts that "No more shall grief of mine the season wrong." The poem, which began in generaliza-tions, becomes focused on a particular day in May, the heart of which makes "every Beast keep holiday." Stanza 4 continues this celebratory mode for another fifteen lines. The formerly sullen Wordsworth now senses "the fullness of [the] bliss" of the "blessèd Creatures" and the joy of the "happy Shepherd-boy," the children culling flowers, or the infant "on his Mother's arm."

The poem shifts suddenly, however, with the simple connective "But" in line 52. Despite the spring revelry of which Wordsworth says, "I hear, I hear, with joy I hear!" the poem shifts into a melancholy mode: "—But there's a Tree, of many, one/ A single Field which I have looked upon,/ Both of them speak of something that is gone." Wordsworth returns to the elegiac tone of the first two stanzas when he asks, "Whither is fled the visionary gleam?" The poem leaves the joyful sounds of May and tries to answer this question by turning to philosophical issues. Stanzas 5 through 9 track the complex musings of Wordsworth as he tries to explain what happens in adulthood to "the glory and the dream" of youth.

Stanzas 10 and 11 return to the natural world and the "gladness of the May," but in them the reader can see that Wordsworth has been changed by his meditation. He acknowledges that "nothing can bring back the hour/ Of splendor in the grass, of glory in the flower" which belongs to the young only. Yet he suggests stoically that "We will grieve not, rather find/ Strength in what remains behind." Wordsworth finally salutes the power of the human heart, "its tenderness, its joys, and fears," and the poem ends not with the giddy and transient happiness of stanza 3 but with a mature, chastened poet accepting both the pleasures and the pains of "man's mortality."

Forms and Devices

Although, in some senses, "Ode: Intimations of Immortality" is an extremely abstract, difficult poem, Wordsworth does aid the reader by providing visual images for his philosophical ideas. Figurative language functions in the same way as a parable in the Bible: Concrete images help the reader *see* the point.

The fifth stanza, which begins the highly abstract and philosophical section of the poem, presents three metaphors that are repeated in later stanzas: God "is our home," heaven is filled with light, and as an individual grows up "shades of the prison-house begin to close" upon the child. The celestial light, which represents the spiritual realm, eventually fades and dies away as the "Youth . . . farther from the east/ Must travel." Literally, the youth, as he grows older, does not travel westward or move into a shady prison-house; Wordsworth uses metaphorical language to help the reader see the change from the liberty of pure spirituality to the gradual imprisonment by matter or the flesh.

In stanzas 6 and 7, Wordsworth adds to the philosophical picture. Nature, or the material world, "with something of a Mother's mind," makes "her foster child, her Inmate Man/ Forget . . . that imperial palace whence he came." Nature is figuratively represented as a foster mother, in opposition to God as the true father. The "imperial palace," or celestial home, is gradually forgotten by the "Inmate Man," who is Everyman, as he grows accustomed to the "prison-house" of earth.

Another attempt is made in stanza 8 to explain, through figurative language, the journey of the soul. The "heaven-born freedom" that is the infant's birthright becomes, in time, the "inevitable yoke" of mortal life, an "earthly freight," or "a weight,/ Heavy as frost."

This poem does not offer a sustained conceit or extended metaphor but moves somewhat quickly from one image to the next. The relationship between the foster mother and God the Father is pursued for two stanzas and then dropped. The image of the youth moving from east to west appears only once. The contrast between the "prison-house" that holds the "Inmate Man" and the "imperial palace" that lodges the soul, although it is central to the poem, is stated explicitly in only three lines. The home of the soul becomes the "immortal sea" in stanza 9, and what was formerly described as westward movement or a prison-house is visualized as distance from the sea: "Though inland far we be,/ Our Souls have sight of that immortal sea/ Which brought us hither." One of the joys of the poem lies in this constant shifting as the poet,

in a meditative mode, tries to approximate in physical terms the complexity of his philosophy. With its rhythmical irregularities and stanza variations, the ode is particularly well suited to this discursive, expansive style.

Themes and Meanings

Between the third and the ninth stanza, "Ode: Intimations of Immortality" seems
extremely bleak. Wordsworth suggests that human growth leads downward from the
splendor of youth to the emptiness and grief of "palsied Age." He accepts Plato's notion that souls exist before as well as after they are joined with bodies. Unlike Plato,
however, Wordsworth believes that little children and infants inhabit a world which is
full of "visionary gleam" because they have only recently left the "imperial palace" in
the spiritual realm and, "trailing clouds of glory," have entered the fallen world of
matter. In childhood, according to Wordsworth, one's own immortality is intuited and
so young people are perpetually joyful; they have a "heart of May" not because their
bodies are strong and capable but because of their spiritual health. The bleakness
comes when the "years . . . bring the inevitable yoke" of customary actions and "endless imitation." When the "celestial light,/ The glory and the freshness" of youth disappear, what is left?

The final three stanzas answer this question in a hopeful fashion. Memory serves
as an important key for a kind of hard-earned happiness, "all that is at enmity with
joy" cannot "utterly abolish or destroy" as long as one can recall the "delight and liberty" of childhood when God's light was all around. As the title explicitly states, in
maturity, one garners "intimations of immortality from recollections of early childhood."

Wordsworth finds strength not only in memory but also in "the philosophic mind"
that develops over time. In his poem "Lines: Composed a Few Miles Above Tintern
Abbey," he claims that he need not mourn the loss of youth because he has received
"abundant recompense" in his more mature vision of the world and his appreciation of
the "still, sad music of humanity." The same idea is reshaped in "Ode: Intimations of
Immortality." Speaking for all of humanity, Wordsworth admits that "nothing can
bring back the hour/ Of splendor in the grass, of glory in the flower," but he insists that
"We will grieve not, rather find/ Strength in what remains behind." What remains are
not only those memories of early childhood but also the "primal sympathy . . . the
soothing thoughts that spring/ Out of human suffering." Wordsworth powerfully suggests that it is sensitivity to others' suffering and compassion that distinguish the mature person from the youthful one and that provide a "recompense" for falling into the
"prison-house" of consciousness. He finally suggests that the mature mind develops,
over time, a "faith that looks through death."

The poet is able to conclude, in stanza 11, that he loves the "Brooks which down
their channels fret,/ Even more than when I tripped lightly as they." There is a sense of
reconciliation in these final lines; time is no longer the enemy because Wordsworth
recognizes that the "philosophic mind" can develop only as one moves toward death.
He loves nature even more than in youth because he has earned a sober appreciation of

the human heart, "its tenderness, its joys, and fears." The false, transient euphoria of stanzas 3 and 4 is gone. Instead, the poem ends with a powerful, if somewhat muted, joy. Through suffering, a "philosophic mind" develops which allows one to endure and keep "watch o'er man's mortality."

Kevin Boyle

ODE ON A DISTANT PROSPECT OF ETON COLLEGE

Author: Thomas Gray (1716-1771)
Type of poem: Ode
First published: 1747; collected in *Six Poems by Mr. T. Gray,* 1753

The Poem

The three elements of the title prepare the reader to understand the poem. First, it is an ode, a lyric poem on a serious subject conveyed in dignified language. Second, it focuses on "a distant prospect." This distance is both in place—Thomas Gray's view of Eton, his old school, from across the Thames River—and in time—the years since the poet's graduation from Eton. Furthermore, the prospect is a literal view of the campus as well as an imaginative vision of what the future will hold for the boys now on the campus. Third, Eton College refers not only to Gray's school but also to one of England's oldest and greatest preparatory schools for boys, the alma mater of many of England's leaders and writers.

The epigraph "I am a man, reason enough for being miserable," a quotation from the Greek playwright Menander, crisply states the poem's theme: the ultimate trouble and unhappiness of human life. Gray's use of an ancient quotation also suggests the timelessness of the theme.

The Eton College ode represents, for Gray, a homecoming to his old school as he reflects on his time there as a boy and on what the future will bring to the present students.

In the opening stanza, Gray, standing alone, describes the campus—its spires and towers, Windsor Castle in the background, the surrounding groves, lawns, and meadows, and the shade trees and flowers along the winding Thames River. His references to Henry (King Henry VI, founder of the school in 1440), whose "shade" (or spirit) presides, and to the "shade" of the old trees affirm the harmony of history and nature at the school—and they hint at the "shade" of death that awaits everyone.

Stanza 2 conveys a refreshing wistfulness as Gray remembers the playing fields, "beloved in vain," on which he showed little athletic promise and observes "careless childhood" now at play. His memories of youth are "gales" that bring a fleeting joy, a "momentary bliss" to him.

The third and fourth stanzas show Gray apostrophizing (directly addressing) Father Thames, spirit of the river and rural nature, who has seen centuries of boys ("a sprightly race") at the school. Poetic diction (language that seems either artificial or archaic) marks these stanzas as Gray depicts the boys' activities: "Disporting on thy margent green" (playing on the green riverbanks), cleaving "thy glassy wave" (swimming in the river), chasing "the rolling circle's speed" (chasing a hoop), and urging "the flying ball" (playing cricket). All of the boys find their playtime more sweet because school rules and study are the "graver hours" that limit their fun. Other boys explore the campus and even wander, against the rules, off school grounds. Aware of their disobedience, they imagine that the wind reprimands them, tempering their forbidden joy with fear.

In stanza 5, Gray reflects that hope is driven only by unrealistic imagination: "Gay hope is theirs by fancy fed." Because he sees typical childhood as a blend of brief disappointments, enthusiasm, health, wit and invention, and vigor, its days are carefree, its nights restful, its mornings bright. Gray thinks that children imagine, unrealistically, that their good times will last forever.

However, in line 51 of the sixth stanza, the very middle of the poem, the ode's tone and direction change. The nostalgic tone of the first part becomes melancholy; the childlike hope of the fifth stanza now becomes doom: "Alas, regardless of their doom,/ The little victims play!" Now, instead of describing the boys' joyful present, Gray foresees their fateful future. Because they are "regardless of their doom," he wishes to "tell them they are men," that is, that they are subject to all the troubles and mortality of human beings.

Stanzas 7 through 9 are a catalog of the troubles of adult life. Furthermore, because Gray thinks them to be typical, he personifies (depicts an abstraction as human) them. Stanzas 7 and 8 reveal these "fury Passions" that accompany adulthood, including "Shame that skulks," "pining Love," "Grim-visaged comfortless Despair," "The stings of Falsehood," and "moody Madness laughing wild."

The ninth stanza presents "A grisly troop . . ./ The painful family of Death" whose "hideous . . . queen" is Persephone, Greek goddess of death and the underworld. This "death" group consists of racking pain, numbing poverty, and degenerative aging, all personifications of human mortality.

Gray's conclusion in the final stanza is that while suffering is the human lot, there is no point in preaching that lesson to children, for such a "Thought would destroy their paradise." Rather, "where ignorance is bliss,/ Tis folly to be wise."

The paradox of "foolish wisdom" shows both Gray's insight and virtue, for if he knows that happiness is fleeting and cannot be realized, then letting the boys enjoy their brief "paradise" is, indeed, the virtue of kindness.

Forms and Devices

The poem's ten stanzas, each consisting of ten alternating iambic tetrameter and trimeter lines, is a fine version of the Horatian ode, developed by the Roman poet Horace, which is noted for its restraint and the regular similarity of its stanzas in length, meter, and rhyme.

Gray's Eton College ode is constructed in a perfect symmetry with an exact balance between the first fifty lines and the last fifty lines. This symmetry is seen in the contrasts between each part that, together, unify the poem: the joys of youth versus the ills of age, childlike innocence versus adult experience, hope versus despair, the Thames valley versus the "vale of years," wit versus madness, health versus sickness, Gray's past (and the boys' present) versus Gray's present (and the boys' future), a tone of wistfulness versus one of melancholy doom, boys at play versus a man in reflection. A further symmetry is evident in the end rhymes of the fifth and sixth verses that link the two parts of each stanza.

Assonance (repeated vowel sounds) is a device that enhances the ode's tone, particularly the number of long, low "o" and "a" vowels that echo the nostalgia of the poem's first half and the melancholy of the second.

Two other devices, thought to be old-fashioned, are explainable. The first, poetic diction, was, in Gray's time, considered proper for the ode, which demanded elevated, traditional words. According to eighteenth century reasoning, since a poem is artificial—a work of art and not of nature—its proper diction should likewise be artificial. Thus, phrases such as "margent green," "enthrall," and "the rolling circle's speed" are the proper materials with which to build a well-constructed ode. Another device, personification, also seems dated, but, in the eighteenth century, it was valued as a way to express a universal truth. Gray's personifications are not flat; rather, he brings them to life with telling verbs or modifiers: "Shame that skulks," "grinning Infamy," and "moody Madness laughing wild." These and others grant a vividness to his generalizations.

Themes and Meanings

Two themes play through Gray's "Ode on a Distant Prospect of Eton College." The major theme is the inevitability of suffering, death, and unhappiness for humankind. Sad though the theme is, Gray tempers it with his own fatherlike concern in keeping this knowledge from the children. Because he knows that the "paradise" of their youth is brief, he tenderly allows them to enjoy it.

Related to this theme is a minor biblical one, the key to which is again paradise: the state of happiness before the Fall. As Gray watches the boys at Eton, he notes their health, hope, and joy. However, he reveals neither a desire to return to youth nor a disgust with adulthood. To Gray, the children are happy but deluded, and their delusions keep them happy until their growth to knowledge unveils the hardships and sadness of life. Both themes evolve from Gray's philosophy of stoicism: that all life must be endured with fortitude, self-control, and restraint of feelings.

Gray's concern with children, rural description, reflective imagination, and melancholy are tendencies that made him a forerunner of the English Romantic movement. Writing in the mid-eighteenth century, however, Gray was also one of the last English Augustan or neoclassic poets who used balanced poetic architecture, poetic diction and personification, and classical poetic types, and who tended toward the ethical and the didactic. Along with his great *Elegy Written in a Country Churchyard* (1751), the Eton College ode reveals Thomas Gray's poetry as an important, strong, and beautiful bridge between two very different periods of English literature.

H. George Hahn

ODE ON A GRECIAN URN

Author: John Keats (1795-1821)
Type of poem: Ode
First published: 1820, in *Lamia, Isabella, The Eve of St. Agnes, and Other Poems*

The Poem

It is important to apprehend the dramatic situation in "Ode on a Grecian Urn" both to understand the poem on a literal level and to glean any larger meaning from it. A narrator looks at the pictures that decorate the outside of an urn; between the "leaf-fringed legend[s]" (line 5)—literally, the decorated borders on top and beneath the painted figures on the vase—the narrator sees two distinct scenes, consisting primarily of figures engaged in two activities common to Greek life: raucous sexual play and religious celebration.

The speaker in the poem addresses the urn directly, as if it were a living object. Viewing the first scene, which consists of a collection of young people engaging in some form of revelry, the narrator asks about the identity of the people and about their motives: Are the women escaping from the men, or is this a courting match? Why is there music (represented by a figure on the urn who is playing an instrument)? The scene makes the narrator realize that he can only imagine his own answers—but in a sense, the "unheard" melodies that he imagines are "sweeter" than those he might actually hear (lines 11-12). Gazing at what he believes to be two lovers about to embrace, he observes that, though they can never consummate their relationship, they will never change, either; instead, they will be forever in that heightened state of anticipation that precedes the climax of a love affair.

At the beginning of the fourth stanza, the narrator shifts his gaze to the second scene on the urn; in it, some townspeople are leading a calf to an altar for sacrifice. Once more the narrator asks questions: Who are these people? Where do they come from? Again he realizes that he cannot get the answers from viewing the urn; the questions will be forever unanswered, because the urn is not capable of providing such information. Rather, it sits silently, provoking his curiosity.

In the final stanza, the narrator recognizes the futility of his questioning and acknowledges that the urn is simply capable of teasing him "out of thought" (line 44)—leaving him unable to come to some logical conclusion about the stories depicted on the urn, and hence about the value of the urn itself. The narrator concludes by calling it a "Cold Pastoral" (line 45) whose ultimate worth lies in its beauty, not in its message.

Forms and Devices

John Keats's meditation on the significance of the pictures on this piece of classical pottery shares many of the characteristics of the Horatian ode. It consists of five stanzas of equal length (ten lines), with a consistent rhyme scheme in each: The first four lines are rhymed *abab*, and the final six lines contain three rhymes, arranged in various patterns (*cdecde* or *cdeced*). The limited number of rhymes, coupled with the many end-stopped lines, give the poem a restrained quality; readers are forced to pause often and are constantly, if subtly, brought back to previous lines by the rhymes. As with any rhymed composition, the reader comes to develop a sense of expectation at the end of a line; that expectation is fulfilled when the rhyming pattern is fulfilled. The regularity of stanzaic pattern and rhyme scheme is further reinforced by the poet's use of iambic pentameter as his basic meter. The slow cadence of this conversation-like line gives the poem a quality of meditation and seriousness. All these techniques work together to achieve Keats's aim: to get readers to pause, as his narrator does, to contemplate the significance of the two scenes on the urn.

The regularity of these formal devices is undercut, however, by Keats's use of ambiguity in his language. He makes extensive use of double entendre and paradox in describing both the urn itself and the scenes displayed upon it. For example, in the opening line, the narrator refers to the urn as a "still unravished bride." The word "still" can be read as an adjective meaning "unmoving" or "at rest," or it can be an adverb modifying "unravished," in which case it means "not yet." The urn is the "bride of quietness" and the foster-child of "silence" and "slow time," yet the narrator calls it a "Sylvan historian"—suggesting that it has a story to tell. Certainly such ambiguities create a tension within the poem; the reader is not really sure what kind of story can emerge from such a storyteller. That tension is reinforced by the pictures themselves, in which people seem to be arrested in the midst of activity. In the first one, the narrator sees a figure playing an instrument; no sound comes forth, however, and the only melody possible is that which the narrator imagines. Similarly, in the same scene two lovers are about to kiss, yet they remain as if in suspended animation. That situation is seen as both good and bad—"never, never canst thou kiss" (line 17), the narrator observes sadly to the young man pictured on the urn, but he immediately follows with the admonition, "yet, do not grieve," because the youth's beloved "cannot fade, though thou hast not thy bliss." These lovers are "For ever panting and for ever young" (line 27); they will never suffer the tribulations of real passion, which leave "A burning forehead, and a parching tongue" (line 30). This may be true, but the possibility lingers that they will never feel the joy of consummated passion either.

Similar tensions are present in the narrator's discussion of the second scene. Though the group taking the heifer to sacrifice appears happy, the narrator realizes that the "little town" from which these people have come will "forever" be "silent" and "desolate" (lines 38, 40). The implication is that, despite the joy depicted in the scene, there will remain an unexplained loss to counterbalance the apparent euphoria this work of art exhibits.

Themes and Meanings

The central theme of "Ode on a Grecian Urn" is the complex nature of art. The dramatic situation—the narrator's puzzling one-way exchange with the urn as he views the scenes painted upon it—is intended to provoke in the reader an awareness of the paradoxes inherent in all art, but especially visual art. The central question raised by the narrator is: What good is art? What purpose does it serve? The urn is beautiful, to be sure, but as a vehicle for conveying information it is woefully inadequate. No story on the urn is ever finished and communicated; all action is arrested at a single instant. Only through imagination is the narrator able to come to some human understanding of the "message" on the urn; hence, the work of art does not really have a message for its viewers at all, but only serves as a stimulus for engaging the imaginations of those who look upon it.

Perhaps Keats is suggesting that the "message" of art is always achieved through a participatory act. If there is a "truth" to be gleaned from the appreciation of art, it is a truth found only when the viewer serves as a co-creator with the artist in developing meaning. Such an interpretation helps to make sense of the final enigmatic lines of the poem: "Beauty is Truth, Truth Beauty—That is all/ Ye know of earth, and all ye need to know" (lines 49-50). Even that interpretation is subject to question, however, since readers cannot be certain exactly what the urn actually "says" to the narrator. In most publications, some or all of the words in the final lines are placed in quotation marks; in Keats's manuscripts, no quotation marks are used. The shift from "thou" (used by the narrator to address the urn) to "ye" (used in the final lines only) suggests that the entire sentence in the final lines are to be read as the urn's "message" to viewers. If that is the case, then the lesson of the poem is that one can never arrive at logical truth through an apprehension of art, since art does not work in the same way that logical thought does. The narrator's observation that the urn seems to "tease us out of thought" (line 44) supports such an interpretation. Nevertheless, art—here personified by the urn—has great value to serve as a form of pleasure and solace; it "remain[s]" a "friend to man" in the "midst of other woe" (lines 47-48). Keats is making a case for art on its own terms; he wants readers to see that appreciation of art for its own sake is as valuable as—perhaps even more valuable than—the extraction of meaning from works intended primarily to uplift the spirit of man simply by conveying a sense of the beautiful.

Laurence W. Mazzeno

ODE ON MELANCHOLY

Author: John Keats (1795-1821)
Type of poem: Ode
First published: 1820, in *Lamia, Isabella, The Eve of St. Agnes, and Other Poems*

The Poem

"Ode on Melancholy" is a three-stanza poem addressed to people who are suscepti-ble to fits of melancholy, and it offers a prescription for coping with "the blues." John Keats says that the melancholy mood is full of beauty and potential spiritual instruc-tion. Therefore, instead of seeking escape through intoxication or even suicide, the melancholy individual should savor the mood because it has divine properties. Lethe, referred to in the opening line, was one of the rivers of Hades in Greek and Roman mythology; drinking from it was supposed to cause forgetfulness. Proserpine was the goddess of Hades. Psyche was a nymph who represented the human soul. Wolfsbane, nightshade, and yew are all plants which have poisonous properties, and yew trees are commonly planted around cemeteries.

In the second stanza, the words "glut thy sorrow" encapsulate the poet's prescrip-tion. Do not be afraid of melancholy: enjoy it. Look at all the beauty of nature, includ-ing the beauty in a beautiful woman's eyes, and reflect upon the sad truth that none of it can last. Similar thoughts are expressed in Keats's "Ode on a Grecian Urn" and "Ode to a Nightingale." The fragility and perishability of beauty evoke melancholy but make the beautiful object more precious.

Pleasure and pain, joy and sorrow, delight and melancholy are opposite sides of the same coin: It is impossible to have one without the other. Anyone who is particularly sensible to beauty and pleasure is bound to be painfully susceptible to melancholy. Only the aesthetically sensitive person can appreciate the beauty of melancholy; mel-ancholy adds dignity and spiritual significance to beauty. Vulgar, insensitive people will be afraid of it as of some threatening aberration and will try to escape from it with drugs or in extreme cases even in suicide.

Keats suggests throughout the poem that the way things look depends upon the emotional state of the observer. When one is in a melancholy state, things can look particularly vivid and beautiful. This impressionistic approach to artistic subjects be-came an enormously important movement throughout Europe and America later in the nineteenth century, and Keats may be regarded as one of its forerunners. It is not until almost the end of the poem that Keats uses the word Melancholy, with a capital "M," personifying or reifying melancholy and turning it into a goddess. There was no goddess of melancholy in Greek or Roman mythology; Keats is creating his own my-thology. By doing this, he is suggesting that melancholy can be more than an aesthetic experience—it is actually akin to a religious experience—and implying that the nu-minous quality of the experience frightens unworthy people into seeking escape through oblivion.

Forms and Devices

One of the most striking devices of this poem is the use of *o* sounds to evoke a mood of melancholy. The first five words of the poem all contain the letter *o* and, in contrast to the dominant iambic rhythm of the remaining lines, these first five words, "No, no, go not to," are all heavily stressed. As well as setting the overall mood, the stress on the first five vowels serves notice that the poem is intended to be read slowly. What is being done here is similar to what a composer does with a musical composition when he marks his score *largo*: The performer is advised that the piece is to be played in a slow and solemn manner.

The *o* sounds are so densely crowded into the first two stanzas that scarcely a line does not contain at least one. The word "nor" is used four times in the first stanza, echoed by the word "or" which is used three times in the second stanza. In one line in the first stanza, there are five *o* sounds: "Your mournful Psyche, nor the downy owl." These sounds mimic the moans and groans of a person suffering from acute melancholy and help produce a mood of sorrow and despair.

A poet can convey feelings through the manipulation of the sounds of words just as a composer can with musical notes; modern poets, beginning notably with the French in the time of Charles Baudelaire, Prosper Mérimée, Arthur Rimbaud, and Paul Verlaine, experimented extensively with the use of such purely mechanical devices to create emotional effects. It is impossible to say who invented the idea, because it goes back at least as far as ancient Greece, when poets accompanied their recitations by strumming on musical instruments. William Shakespeare was certainly well aware of the power of the mere sounds of words to create moods, and Keats revered Shakespeare to the point of idolatry. Keats also seems to have been influenced in this area (as well as in his interest in the subject of melancholy) by the senior Romantic poet, Samuel Taylor Coleridge, who was a bold experimenter with the technical aspects of poetic composition, as demonstrated in his strange and wonderful fragment "Kubla Khan."

In "Ode on Melancholy," the *o* sounds are so densely crowded into the first two stanzas that scarcely a line does not contain at least one. The word "nor" is used four times in the first stanza, echoed by the word "or" which is used three times in the second stanza. In one line in the first stanza, there are five *o* sounds: "Your mournful Psyche, nor the downy owl." These sounds mimic the moans and groans of a person suffering from acute melancholy and help produce a mood of sorrow and despair.

As in all of Keats's best poetry, there is extensive employment of visual imagery in "Ode on Melancholy." The many references to drugs and poisons reflect Keats's early training as an apothecary. He was developing a dangerous fondness for alcohol, and some of his poems, including "Ode to a Nightingale," suggest that he may have done some experimenting with drugs as well. The unusual images are what admirers of Keats admire most about him. Some examples in "Ode on Melancholy" are the twisting of wolfsbane until the roots are tightly wound around each other like the strands of a rope; making a rosary from poisonous yew berries; the downy owl; the weeping cloud; the bee-mouth sipping nectar from flowers. All these images demonstrate

Keats's unusually vivid visual imagination, the faculty he exploited to write his greatest poems. An image worthy of Shakespeare himself, and reminiscent of his play *The Tempest* (1611), is "the rainbow of the salt sand-wave": that is, the rainbows that can be seen hovering just above the crests of breaking waves on bright, sunny days. This is the kind of natural beauty that people see but are not usually aware of seeing until an artist takes the image out of nature and uses it in a painting or a poem.

Themes and Meanings

It was because Keats took such intense delight in all the visual beauty of nature that he was also subject to melancholy. He had to reflect that he was going have to leave all this beauty when he died, and he was already suffering from premonitions of death at the time he wrote his "Ode on Melancholy" and the other great odes of his *annus mirabilis*, 1819. His brother had recently died of tuberculosis, and Keats had apparently become infected with the disease while nursing him. Keats was only twenty-five years old when he died in 1821. During his short career as a poet, he managed to secure a permanent place among the foremost English poets; however, one of the great tragedies of literary history is the loss of all the works this genius might have produced if he had been permitted to live out a normal lifespan.

Since Keats was subject to fits of melancholy, he took a strong interest in it. He lived long before the days of Sigmund Freud, or he would have been fascinated by psychoanalysis. One of Keats's favorite books was Robert Burton's *The Anatomy of Melancholy* (1621), which might be described as a primitive study of psychoneurosis. Like Burton, Keats realized that melancholy was a complex state that could be the source of intellectual as well as artistic inspiration, and that it was an ailment to which artists were particularly susceptible. As another great Romantic poet, Percy Bysshe Shelley, expressed it: "Our sweetest songs are those that tell of saddest thought."

What Keats is doing in "Ode on Melancholy" is exactly what twentieth century musical artists such as "Blind Lemon" Jefferson, Huddie ("Leadbelly") Ledbetter, Louis Armstrong, Charlie Parker, Eleanor ("Billie") Holiday, and other jazz greats did with the blues. Melancholy can be defined as "the blues," and the word "melancholy" is invariably used in defining the blues.

In his "Ode on Melancholy," which by definition is a piece written in praise of melancholy, Keats is saying that the mood is something to be relished rather than something from which a sensitive person should seek to escape. His thesis is summed up in the following lines of the concluding stanza: "Ay, in the very temple of Delight/ Veil'd Melancholy has her sovran shrine." The fact that he was able to use his melancholy moods to create this masterpiece is proof in itself of his thesis.

Bill Delaney

ODE ON THE DEATH OF A FAVOURITE CAT, DROWNED IN A TUB OF GOLD FISHES

Author: Thomas Gray (1716-1771)
Type of poem: Satire/elegy/ode
First published: 1748; collected in *Odes, by Mr. Gray,* 1757

The Poem

The title of Thomas Gray's "Ode on the Death of a Favourite Cat, Drowned in a Tub of Gold Fishes" signals that the poem is to be read as a light satire. Because an ode is a serious lyric poem on a dignified subject in elevated language, and death is the subject of an elegy or a meditative poem of mourning, the very linking in the title of two high poetic types and a lowly animal signifies humorous intent.

Set in an elegant drawing room, the poem traces the demise of the pampered cat Selima. Reclining on the edge of the fishbowl, she stares admiringly at her reflection on the water's surface. The "joy" of her waving tail and the "applause" of her purring indicate her vanity.

Selima's self-admiration is interrupted when two goldfish glide through her reflection and call attention to themselves as tempting food. Stretching too far with her paw, Selima loses balance and tumbles headlong into the water. She rises eight times, each time meowing for help, which comes neither from mythical saviors such as dolphins and Nereids (sea nymphs) nor from the servants, Tom and Susan, who no doubt are jealous of the better treatment their master gives to the "favorite" cat. The closing of the poem is a satiric moral directed to ladies about the dire consequences that follow vanity and temptation.

Forms and Devices

Gray's use of classical tradition is a primary device in the poem. First, it is a polished example of Horatian satire. Named for the Roman poet Horace, this type of satire is gentle, more sprightly than angry, and is aimed at general traits of human nature, in this case vanity and sentimentality. Second, the poem is indebted to the specific classical models of Ovid's mock mourning for a parrot in *Amores* (c. 20 B.C.E.; English trans., 1597) and Catullus's grieving for a sparrow in "Lugete Veneres."

Following in this satiric tradition, the poem is a masterpiece of eighteenth century poetic form. It is a parody, a mock imitation of another style, in this case of the high styles of the ode, or poem of praise, and the solemn pastoral elegy, or funeral poem. Because cats generally do nothing praiseworthy and have no solemn funerals, let alone poems commemorating their lives and deaths, the poem's style and subject are at humorous odds. Gray's joke is to overdress a simple beast fable as an ode and an elegy.

The poem is divided into seven stanzas, on the cat's vanity (1 and 2), the cat's temptation and greed (3 and 4), the cat's fall (5 and 6), and Gray's didactic moralizing (7).

Each stanza is a sestet (six lines) of *rime couée*, another hint of the poem's humorous intention. This type of stanza incorporates two couplets of any single length and two shorter lines. One short line follows each couplet in a rhyme scheme of *aabccb*.

Versified mainly in iambic tetrameter, the poem is more faithful to the syllabic system at the time favored over the accentual system. The syllables of the succeeding lines in each stanza number 8-8-6-8-8-6 to correspond with the rhyme scheme. The syllabic system also accounts for the contractions called aphaeresis ("'Twas") and syncope ("dy'd," "gaz'd," "Fav'rite"), which preserve the syllable count. The long assonance, or repeated long vowel sounds, especially those in every end-rhymed word, carries the mock funereal tone throughout the poem. The anastrophe (inversion of normal syntax), especially in stanzas 2 and 4, approximates the tense behavior of a cat in eager anticipation—the gaze, the twitching whiskers, the waving tail. Finally, the imagery of richness—"lofty vase," "China's gayest art," "velvet," "jet," "emerald," "Tyrian hue," "richest purple," "golden gleam," "glisters," "gold"—conveys an elegant atmosphere of class, wealth, and taste.

A classicist, Gray uses Latin etymologies (word origins) for a scholarly humor. Selima is "pensive" (from the Latin stem "pend-," meaning to hang or weigh) as she hangs over the bowl's side. When she sees the goldfish, her "conscious tail" (from "con-," meaning "with," and "sci-," meaning "know") knows. Selima is "Presumptious" ("pre-," meaning "before"; "sumpt-," meaning "consume"): She consumes the fish mentally before catching them.

Within this exacting formal fence, Gray uses satiric irony with words, conventions, and tones incongruous with the subject. One type of irony is the mock heroic, inflating or exaggerating the insignificant. Gray's voice in describing such a trivial event is an example of bathos, a ludicrous tone that grossly overstates emotion. His use of the flower design on the vase and the water in it are a burlesque (a mocking imitation) of two conventions of the pastoral elegy, the strewing of flowers and the passage of the dead by sea or river. Other burlesqued features of the elegy are the grief-stricken poet and epigrams such as "What female heart can gold despise?/ What cat's averse to fish?" and "Nor all, that glisters, gold."

Gray uses auxesis (magnifying something's importance) in such words as "lake," "tide," and "flood" for describing the fish tub and "Genii" and "angel forms" for goldfish. Gray exaggerates as well with his mock sadness of a dolphin not coming to save Selima. To think of a dolphin in a fishbowl or a cat on a dolphin's back in a fishbowl suggests the humorously grotesque. Gray's second type of irony is travesty, or deflating the dignified. He reduces ladies to cats and brings the supernatural—"Malignant Fate," "wat'ry god," and "Nereid"—down into a subhuman situation over a fishbowl. All these ironies either inflate the trivial or deflate the significant to render them ridiculous.

Another of Gray's devices is allusion. Besides the general mock allusions to the ode and elegy, the poem echoes specific works known to every cultivated reader of the time. Selima's staring at her reflection in the fishbowl recalls at once the mythological Narcissus of Ovid's *Metamorphoses* (c. 8 C.E.; Eng. trans., 1567), the biblical Eve of

John Milton's *Paradise Lost* (1667, 1674), and the coquette of Alexander Pope's *The Rape of the Lock* (1712, 1714), all vain characters who admire their reflections before their falls. Likewise, Selima's eight frightened surfacings allude to the proverbial nine lives of a cat and thus prefigure her death.

Themes and Meanings

Death is central in Gray's major poems. "The Bard" laments the death of Welsh poets, "The Fatal Sisters" presents death in battle, "Ode on a Distant Prospect of Eton College" regrets the end of carefree youth, "Elegy Written in a Country Churchyard" is both a dirge for Gray's best friend, Richard West, and a memento mori (reminder of mortality) for the human race. "Ode on the Death of a Favourite Cat, Drowned in a Tub of Gold Fishes" likewise treats the subject but in less a melancholy than a mocking way, which touches recurring themes in eighteenth century English literature.

First, Gray laughs at the human traits of vanity and greed, staple themes of Horatian satire of the 1700's. That he associates a pampered cat with privileged coquettes is neither sexist nor misogynistic, for to show the baseness of these traits Gray needed an animal—and the animal that occasioned the poem was Selima, a dead female cat.

Gray also ridicules another human trait, sentimentality. In this case it is that of a man, Gray's close friend since his school days, Horace Walpole. Gray wrote the poem after Walpole's cat Selima drowned in a goldfish bowl. Gray's intent was no doubt to make his friend laugh to cheer him out of his excessive grief for an animal, something only a good friend would attempt. The effect is that of a smile and a wink between cultured gentlemen, one of whom now sees that his maudlin emotion has marred the cool, urbane, and ironic demeanor prized by Augustan gentlemen.

A minor theme satirizes the folly of violating hierarchy or the order of things. Although only a cat, Selima is the "Fav'rite," more privileged than either of the servants, Tom and Susan. Her grooming and leisure, especially contrasted with the lives of the servants, show clearly that order, degree, and common sense are out of joint.

A final theme is delicately sexual, based on the poem's close association between cat and coquette. With her romantic name, Selima is demure and sleek, her face fair, her coat elegant, her ears beautiful, and her emerald eyes captivating. Personified, she is a nymph and a maid gazing at her reflection. After Milton, the word "gaz'd" began to carry a sexual connotation. Thus this vain cat's slip, caused by unrestrained desire, becomes a fall and parodies the "slip" and "fall" of Milton's Eve and Pope's Belinda with their sexual connotations. Gray's satiric target here is not women, but vain and foolish ladies, leisured flirts with "wand'ring eyes." (Susan, a woman but not a lady, is not satirized.) Thus Gray's little animal fable plays out the proverb that Pride goeth before a fall. Its mock moral to those leisured ladies—"From hence, ye Beauties. . . ./ Know"—is that from this story of a drowned cat, they should avoid temptation "with caution bold," a fitting oxymoron to close a highly ironic "ode."

H. George Hahn

ODE RECITED AT THE HARVARD
COMMEMORATION, JULY 21, 1865

Author: James Russell Lowell (1819-1891)
Type of poem: Ode
First published: 1865 (including stanza 6, which was written after the recitation;
stanza 9 added for printing in *Under the Willows and Other Poems*, 1868)

The Poem

James Russell Lowell's *Ode Recited at the Harvard Commemoration, July 21,
1865* consists of 426 irregularly rhyming lines of six to twelve syllables (the first line
has four syllables) divided into twelve stanzas of varying length. The Civil War ended
on April 9, 1865, and President Abraham Lincoln was assassinated on April 14.
Lowell's ode was commissioned to be read at a service to commemorate Harvard men
who died fighting for the Union. The poem praises the dedication of the fallen to a
high ideal, and a lengthy stanza pays tribute to Lincoln. The poet and his audience,
taking inspiration from the dead, vow renewed devotion to the "rescued Nation."

The first stanza concedes that poetry seems too weak to honor the valor of the slain,
yet it may preserve their memory. Science and the arts cannot raise humans above
death, but truth can "entice" people to courageous deeds. Those who seek truth in intellectual labors or contemplative faith rank below those who seek truth through action. Life is fleeting and wasted in material ambition and trivial pursuits, but something higher beckons people to claim a heavenly birthright. The path to a higher fate is
steep and difficult. Peace has its value, but when conflict erupts, the Ideal and Truth
claim stalwart, heroic action in their defense. The manly, drawing on inner strength,
respond. Such was "our Martyr-Chief" Lincoln. Formed by nature of clay from "the
unexhausted West," he shepherded his people with wisdom. He is thus a new kind of
hero, "the first American," with "nothing of Europe."

Returning to the theme, humanity's hope points to something beyond the self, faith
in "some ideal Good," whether called "Freedom, Law, [or] Country." Those who meet
this challenge deserve and will always win "man's praise and woman's love." The
thought of the fallen again plunges the poet into sorrow. Yet, compared to their faith
and courage, survivors seem to be the dead. Can their remembrance escape change
and oblivion, which rule everything?

Manhood is larger than a single man. The soldiers' courageous deeds will raise
up "a new imperial race." Europe's dynasties are outworn, but these men bequeath
high honor to a democratic nation. The nation's song must end in exultant gratitude.
The achievement of these men, the "pith and marrow of a Nation," strengthens all
people. Church bells and beacon fires spread the news across the continent that the
country is saved. The twelfth and final stanza exhorts the very land to bow down
in prayer and praise to God. The poet speaks for all people in expressing deep love of

his beautiful country and vowing readiness to dare whatever the land may ask of people.

Forms and Devices

The poem's form is that of the Pindaric or "irregular" ode. Its lofty style and irregular meter are suited to deep thought and intense emotion in response to an important public occasion. The language is consistently elevated, dignified, and general; the diction is archaic and literary. Phrases such as "feathered words" and "slender life" echo Greek poetry. The diction is appropriate to the formality and dignity of the occasion and theme; to the Harvard audience, which included distinguished scholars; and to the poet's own academic position. Various phrases echo Miltonic ("that clear fame") or Shakespearean style ("we poor puppets, jerked by unseen wires,/ After our little hour of strut and rave"; "That is best blood that hath most iron in 't/ To edge resolve with"). Many images are conventional and ancient: The dead are crowned with laurel, the poet sweeps the strings of his lyre, mortals are like leaves that fall, the path to fame is steep and harsh.

While responding to its occasion, the ode aims at a generality that transcends the particular. Neither Harvard nor Lincoln is actually named. By praising the soldiers' dedication to truth, Lowell alludes to Harvard's motto, "Veritas" (Latin for "truth"). Readers are not told how or why the "Martyr-Chief" (Lincoln) has fallen. The issues in the Civil War are only allusions; for example, the poet says that now even the poorest within America's borders can lift "an enfranchised brow" (meaning they were "set free"; emancipated slaves were not guaranteed the vote until 1870). Personified ideas serve as agents of action: Ideal, Nation, Land, Truth, Danger, Soul. Thus the style directs the reader away from specific historical facts toward deeper and enduring meanings.

Another side of the poem's generality is its deliberate effect of vigorous, spontaneous, unrevised thought under the pressure of the occasion. Energetic condensation, even at the cost of some violence to diction or syntax, engages the reader's active effort to decipher the meaning. Lincoln's mind, for example, was not a lonely mountain peak, sometimes hidden in vapors; it was like the prairie (where he grew up), genial, level, yet near the stars. Similarly, in a visionary moment, the poet sees the "aureoled presence" of the dead and says, "We feel the orient of their spirit glow." The light of a brighter morning shines on the young heroes, but they are themselves a source of light to those left behind. "Orient" captures this double sense.

Paradoxes and thoughts contrary to the conventional reinforce the effect of strenuous thought. Thus, those who died for truth achieved so intense a life that those who are left behind seem dead. Elaborate and surprising metaphors contribute as well: The soldiers write poems in their blood by their deeds; Peace has its value until "the sharp, decisive word/ Light the black lips of cannon."

The varying line lengths and rhyme patterns also support the impression of intense and sharply changing emotion. More than once, the mood of a stanza reverses at the midpoint, marked by a phrase such as "But stay!" or "Say not so!" Meter is used most effectively to create incantatory rhythms. In the climactic stanza 11, where the poet finds consolation for fallen individuals in the legacy they leave their country, the first half of the stanza consists mostly of seven-syllable lines with the rhythm of a magic charm. In the second half, the meter reverts to mostly ten-syllable lines, suggesting the achieved stability of mood and thought as the poet praises the nation. Similarly, the poem ends with a rhythmically compact group of six-syllable lines with feminine rhymes as the poet and his audience rededicate themselves to their country.

Themes and Meanings

Lowell's ode seeks consolation through a meaning based on the motives and purposes of the fallen soldiers; he does not propose Christian immortality or Greco-Roman enduring fame. At first, the contrast between the active life achieved by the soldiers and the merely intellectual or ordinary lives of those who did not participate in the war is sufficient to argue that their sacrifice was worthwhile. They have mastered fate and stand as a beacon to the future, showing what true manhood is. Yet, the poet is forced to concede, everything passes; no one man's fame endures. Their devotion to a higher cause is worthy of "man's praise and woman's love," and they have found the "better way."

However, praise and celebration are undermined by the irremovable fact of death: The poet's paean continually turns into a dirge. This tension is resolved as the poet reflects that the dead may be lost as individuals, but they have left a legacy to their fellow and future citizens that raises them into "a new imperial race." As a result, the "rescued Nation" has attained a nobility beyond any aristocratic European models. Rather than isolated individuals, the "pith and marrow of a Nation" have accomplished this great victory. The nation, restored to peace, can be confident in the face of any challenge. All can join together to dedicate themselves to the nation and its distinctive merit: freedom, truth, openness to all.

This theme underwrites the elegy to Lincoln in stanza 6. He too has fallen but has shown a new model of leadership and heroism. Out of the West has come a traditional shepherd of the people, yet with something new: great not by birth but by sincerity, humility, and equality, in contrast to European aristocrats. He is "New birth of our new soil, the first American."

A counterpoint to these themes is that of the poet's relation to the heroes and to the nation. At first, the poet depreciates the value of mere poetry in comparison to the deeds of the fallen. Yet his reflection and feeling turn as he grasps the legacy of courage and devotion to the country's cause and ideals that moved these young men. He takes inspiration from them and finds the point of view and the tone suited to celebration. The poet's "passions, hopes, and fears," his "triumphs and his tears," keep "measure with his people." He can then legitimately join in the gratitude of the nation restored and—confident that he is expressing the feelings of his audience—vow that whatever the nation asks, "we will dare."

Donald G. Marshall

ODE TO A NIGHTINGALE

Author: John Keats (1795-1821)
Type of poem: Ode
First published: 1819; collected in *Lamia, Isabella, The Eve of St. Agnes, and Other Poems,* 1820

The Poem

"Ode to a Nightingale" is a poem in eight numbered stanzas; as the title suggests, it takes the form of a direct address to a nightingale. The speaker, evidently the poet John Keats himself, hears a nightingale singing. This beautiful but melancholy sound, which has inspired legends since the time of ancient Greece, fills him with complex and conflicting emotions. It makes him happy because he can empathize with the bird's zest for living and procreating at the height of the spring season; at the same time, it makes him sad because he is alone and has been preoccupied with morbid thoughts.

In stanza 2, Keats wishes he had a whole "beaker full" of wine so that he could get intoxicated and lose consciousness. He describes the red wine in loving detail, then goes on to specify the mortal woes from which he would like to escape—primarily those associated with old age, sickness, and death. "Where youth grows pale and spectre-thin and dies" refers to his brother Tom, who had recently died of tuberculosis, the disease which was to claim Keats's own life in less than three years.

Since Keats has no wine, in stanza 4 he decides to escape by creating poetry. He makes his poem engrossing by seeming to take the reader along with him in the process of creating it. He will become a wild bird in his imagination and share in the nightingale's view of the world. This notion represents the essence of the Romantic spirit: the attempt to achieve what is known to be impossible.

Nightingales are rather small, retiring birds that live in forests, thickets, and hedgerows. Consequently, in stanza 5 Keats imagines the nightingale's world as being dark and mysterious but at that time of year full of the scents of blossoming plants. This is the high point of the poem, but he is unable to sustain his illusion. Thoughts of death intrude. In stanza 6, he confesses sometimes to "have been half in love with easeful Death." He feels comforted by his experience of sharing in the nightingale's immortal consciousness, however; he realizes that life goes on, and his own death is a small matter in the overall scheme of things. The idea of death even seems "rich." In line 1 of the seventh stanza, Keats addresses the nightingale as "immortal Bird" and traces the nightingale's song through historical and magical settings.

Then his near-religious experience comes to an end. He is inexorably drawn back into the world of reality, with all its mortal concerns. The bird's plaintive song fades into the distance, and the poet is left wondering about the validity and nature of his experience.

Forms and Devices

This entire poem is based on a single poetic conceit that is so matter-of-factly taken for granted that it is easy to overlook: The poem tacitly assumes that the bird to whom Keats is addressing his ode is immortal—that in fact only one nightingale exists and has ever existed. It looks exactly the same and sounds exactly the same as birds of that species have looked and sounded for countless centuries. Furthermore, the nightingale is immortal because it has no conception of death. Only human beings suffer from the fear of death and the feeling of futility with which death taints all human endeavor. Finally, the bird can be considered immortal because of the familiar Greek legend that the nightingale is the metamorphized soul of the ravished princess Philomela.

The bird that Keats hears singing can be only a few years old at most, yet the subtle assumption of its immortality is perfectly natural because the nightingale looks the same and sounds the same as its ancestors, which were heard "in ancient days by emperor and clown" and even further back by Ruth, whose story is told in the Book of Ruth in the Old Testament. Keats was an ardent admirer of William Shakespeare, and the naturalness of the poetic conceit in "Ode to a Nightingale" shows that Keats appreciated and understood the essence of Shakespeare's greatness, which lay in his use of simple, natural imagery—rather than imagery employed by some of his better-educated contemporaries that was pretentious, bookish, and artificial.

Keats's outstanding poetic gift was his ability to evoke vivid images in the mind of his reader. "Ode to a Nightingale" is full of such vivid images, the most famous of which is his "magic casements, opening on the foam/ Of perilous seas, in faery lands forlorn." Because of the spell that Keats has created up to this point, the sensitive reader is given a glimpse of those bright, blue, foam-crested seas through those magic casements—but only a glimpse of that magical world is ever allowed to any mortal, and then both Keats and his reader must return to reality, with its troubles, fears, and disappointments.

Another example of Keats's inspired imagery is contained in the lines, "The coming musk-rose, full of dewy wine,/ The murmurous haunt of flies on summer eves." With one stroke, Keats creates a large half-open flower glowing with soft interior lighting like a comfortable pub where the flies like to gather with their elbows on the tables to sip wine and talk about whatever flies might talk about on long summer eves.

Other striking images in "Ode to a Nightingale" are the beaker "full of the warm South" that has "beaded bubbles winking at the brim," the syncopated effect of "fast fading violets covered up in leaves," and poor Ruth standing in tears in a land so alien and unsympathetic that even the very grain in the fields looks strange and unappetizing.

Keats soon discovered that his forte lay in his vivid visual imagination, and his greatest poems are so crowded with visual imagery that they seem like beautiful murals.

Themes and Meanings

In "Ode to a Nightingale," Keats is really only talking about the beauty of nature and how painful it is to think of dying and having to leave it. These are thoughts with which every reader can identify. What makes Keats a great poet is that the feelings he expresses are common to all humanity. This feature, found in all of his greatest poetry, is called universality, and it is generally regarded as the distinguishing feature of all great art. An aspiring writer can learn from Keats that the secret of creating important work is to deal with basic human emotions.

Keats was going through considerable mental anguish when he wrote this poem. His brother Tom had just died of tuberculosis. He himself had premonitions of his own death from the same disease, which turned out to be true. He was in love with young Fanny Brawne but found it impossible to marry her because he had rejected the career in medicine for which he had been trained; he was finding it impossible to make a living as a writer. Like many present-day poets, he was tortured by the fact that he had chosen an impractical vocation; yet, it was the vocation for which he believed he was born, and it was the only thing he wanted to do.

The ode has a piquant, bittersweet flavor, not unlike the flavor of a good red wine, because it deliberately blends thoughts of beauty and decay, joy and suffering, love and death. Keats had rejected the teachings of the established church, as can be seen in his posthumously published sonnet entitled "Written in Disgust of Vulgar Superstition," in which he describes Christian church dogma as a "black spell." This left him in the position of having to find his own answers to questions that the church had automatically answered for centuries. Keats thought that all religions consisted of stories made up by imaginative individuals to mask the real truth about life. Borrowing from Greek mythology and other sources, he tried to create new stories; however, as a modern man with a modern scientific education, he knew that his stories were inventions, whereas the poets and prophets of the past really believed in the gods about which they talked; they were not using them as mere poetic metaphors. This is why Keats cannot stay with his nightingale. The elusive bird might even be seen as a metaphor for the alienated condition of modern man.

Bill Delaney

ODE TO AN ARTICHOKE

Author: Pablo Neruda (Neftalí Ricardo Reyes Basoalto, 1904-1973)
Type of poem: Ode
First published: 1954, as "Oda a una alcachofa," in *Odas elementales*; English translation collected in *The Elemental Odes*, 1961

The Poem

"Ode to an Artichoke" (it has also been translated under the title "Artichoke") is a short poem consisting of thirty-three lines of free verse. The poem establishes the poet's connection to the elemental or basic qualities of objects that surround everyone in daily life—here, common food items or vegetables. Pablo Neruda imagines the relationship that an artichoke may have to the rest of the members of the vegetable kingdom and, in the broadest terms, to reality itself. The artichoke is described as being "of delicate heart" yet dressed for battle inside its small "cupola" (a rounded vault that forms a roof). It keeps itself isolated and protected under its scales. This humble member of the food chain is surrounded by less prudent inhabitants of nature's botanical kingdom. Wild, even crazy, vegetables bristle, raising their backs as if to engage in battle. At the same time, the carrot sleeps under the soil and the cabbage busies itself trying on a skirt. The spicy oregano perfumes the rest of the world while the artichoke, armed for a battle, stays quietly in its garden plot, burnished and proud like a pomegranate.

The poem presents a vision of the natural world, of grapevines and common vegetables come to life, conscious of their place in the scheme of nature and able to make choices about the ways in which they live their lives. Like humans, they can be either calm or belligerent; they can be showy and pretentious or stoic and independent. In the poem Neruda takes an approach quite different from that of many Latin American modernists, such as Rubén Darío, who express a vision of human life in terms of a so-called "poetical" reality. Rather, Neruda utilizes mundane objects as a springboard for his divagations on the nature of human life and the role of the poet in the midst of the flux of history.

Forms and Devices

The poem's references to plant life establish a basic and obvious metaphor for the various modalities of human life. The poem's style is spare and abrupt; the ode begins with a direct naming of Neruda's center of interest, the artichoke, without any fanfare. Neruda's personification of the vegetables does not stop with the artichoke itself but continues throughout the work. The poem has an effect something like a Disneyized cartoon in which the plants and flowers suddenly come to life to adopt human emotions and act in human relationships.

The artichoke protects itself within its "cupola," Neruda's way of describing the green fibers that protect the central part of this plant. Rather than indulging in myriad adjectives to describe a humanized scale of emotions, the poet uses simple action verbs such as " perfume," "try on," "bristle," and "sleeps." He consciously refrains from interjecting personal reactions or emotions into the goings-on of the various members of the botanical kingdom.

The short, even terse, lines of the poem—sometimes limited to only two syllables—contribute to the starkly direct effect that this work has. The ideas are generated by broken syntax in lines of poetry which are most often incomplete in themselves. They must be read in groups of two or three to understand their basic meaning. The result is a choppy, brusque, poetic expression that may be seen as a linguistic corollary to the prosaic and "antipoetic" nature of the subject itself.

Certainly Neruda's choice of the artichoke to be his vehicle for an allegory on certain aspects of human life is original and deceptively simple. Casual readers may read this as just one more poetic description of a garden as can be seen in traditional ballads or in the more saccharine productions of late Romantic and Victorian poetry. The depiction is mundane to the point of being prosaic. It clearly avoids the pitfalls of clichés that often spring up around the poetry of gardens. It is simplistic to the degree that it would be easy to find this a one-dimensional poem in which the author indulges his well-known affinity for the sights and sounds of immediate reality without engaging a deeper level of literary meaning.

Themes and Meanings

Neruda refers to the artichoke as having a tender heart, and he extends the metaphor of the poet—a tender-hearted artichoke—to himself. The poet must find ways of accommodating his sensitivity to his life and to the world in order to survive. Here the artichoke-poet is stoic in his courageous defiance of the madness that surrounds him. He digs deep into his own cupola, the ecclesiastical connotations of this domelike structure suggesting that this protectionism becomes his religion. It is his way of reaching transcendence or is at least his path to survival as he readies himself to do battle with the forces of reality that surround him.

Somehow he manages to keep calm, "impermeable bajo sus escamas" (untouchable under his scales). Other plants, such as the carrot, prefer simply to stay asleep, while the vines in the orchard expose themselves to the dangers of the strong rays of sunlight and wither and die. The cabbage is pretentious and aspires to physical beauty, while the oregano seeks sublimity through the piquant aroma that it gives off. Through all this the humble artichoke, dour and prosaic, does not aspire either to sublime beauty or to the popularity that a spicy oregano enjoys because of its aroma. It remains quiet and calm, always ready to do battle but stoically unmoved by the pretention of the other plants. It is sure in its own identity and proud of its ability to give pleasure in and on its own terms.

Clearly Pablo Neruda is alluding to his own existence—to the poet's place in the world and to his willingness to acknowledge his gifts as well as his limitations in the vast panorama of human life. He is sure that he will have to do battle, like the Romantics and the modernists before him, against the crassness of the profane modern world, but he is also sure that his art and the strength of his poetic gift can shield him to a certain degree from the blight of that reality.

The poet appears to be content to be himself, to adopt a stoic and slightly bemused view of the contours of the society in which he finds himself. Yet Neruda's vision is also one of praise. The poem is an ode to the beauty that he finds in the commonplace, in the sensuous world, full of its own secret poetic meaning and special beauty.

Arthur A. Natella, Jr.

ODE TO EVENING

Author: William Collins (1721-1759)

Type of poem: Ode

First published: 1746, in *Odes on Several Descriptive and Allegoric Subjects*

The Poem

"Ode to Evening," a single stanza of fifty-two lines, is addressed to a goddess figure representing the time of day in the title. This "nymph," or "maid," who personifies dusk, is "chaste," "reserv'd," and meek, in contrast to the "bright-hair'd sun," a male figure who withdraws into his tent, making way for night. Thus "Eve," or evening, is presented as the transition between light and darkness.

William Collins further stresses a female identity in his appellation "calm vot'ress." With this feminine form of "votary" he designates a nun, or one who vows to follow the religious life. This combination of modesty, devotion, and "pensive Pleasures" alludes to the dominating figure of John Milton's "Il Penseroso."

The poem has three parts: the opening salutation, locating Eve in sequence and in the countryside; the center, a plea for guidance in achieving a calm stoicism, with a qualification, showing the reason for the request, and a shift to a personal viewpoint; and a grand finale with a roll call of the seasons and a return to a universal dimension.

Throughout most of the poem, Collins acknowledges Eve's authority and twilight's pleasures, combining pastoral imagery with classical allusions. These give the poem a Miltonic overtone, familiar to readers of Collins's day, and a close connection to his contemporaries, such as James Thomson and Joseph Warton.

After the opening apostrophe to Eve, nature takes over the first section (lines 3-14), with images of water in references to "solemn springs" plus the sun's "cloudy skirts" and "wavy bed." The wind plays a small part in setting the scene with only the one reference to "dying gales" subsiding to the point where "air is hush'd." An allusion to John Milton's "Lycidas" appears in the auditory image which invades the stillness in these lines: "Now air is hush'd, save where the weak-ey'd bat,/ With short, shrill shriek flits by on leathern wing" (lines 9-10). Other noises, less ominous, come from the beetle and the bee, a "pilgrim born in heedless hum."

The second part of the poem starts with a request to the "maid compos'd," who is worthy of emulation. "Now teach me," Collins says, to write lines in keeping with the atmosphere Eve creates. The term "numbers" here stands not only for versification and metrics but also for poetry in general. This section splits into the prayer itself, the details of evening's "genial, lov'd return," and an ominous dimension that makes the depiction more realistic than the classical allusions do. The signal for return is the appearance of Hesperus, the evening star. At this point, place deities, termed "Hours," "elves," and nymphs, become servants preparing evening's chariot for her entrance.

The poet takes center stage here, injecting a view of nature with "chill blustering winds" and "driving rain" that make him reluctant to follow Eve. A scene reminiscent of William Shakespeare's King Lear being exposed to violent weather on the heath is softened with the sound of a church bell.

Finally, the poem presents the cyclical pageant of nature. Starting with a series of images befitting "meekest Eve" and sharply summarizing each season, the ending brings together the benefits possibly resulting from devotion to the goddess.

Forms and Devices

Written in imitation of the Roman poet Horace, this poem is considered a Horatian rather than a pastoral ode, although it contains rural imagery and some conventions associated with pastoral poetry. The verse is unrhymed, with a metrical pattern developing as follows: alternating sets of two iambic pentameter lines and two shorter lines of iambic trimeter.

The sequence of longer and shorter couplets is more important for purposes of unity here than it would have been had the lines been rhyming couplets. Collins's use of couplets follows the neoclassical tradition, but his introduction of the short trimeter lines is viewed, in that context, as an aberration. His balancing of long and short couplets helps to structure a poem considered too short for the verse paragraphs of blank verse and too long for one stanza. If each four-line set is viewed as a unit, the poem could be divided into thirteen stanzas. Ultimately, the metrical balance reflects the alternation of day and night, although only a transitional part of this cycle is the focus of the content and the imagery.

Collins uses conventional neoclassical poetic diction without resorting to extreme or ridiculous phraseology. One possible exception is the "pilgrim born in heedless hum," a metaphor for a bee. Primarily, however, Collins's metaphors stand on their own merits, sometimes coming close to clichés but not overcome by them. Language depicting pastoral images, such as "oaten stop," "yon western tent" of the sun, the "folding star" of Hesperus, and the mountain and valley landscapes, establish the general tone of the poem and reflect Collins's neoclassicism. The Miltonic overlay created by these images, by the imitations of Miltonic style, and by lines alluding to others by Milton cannot be ignored.

Nature imagery serves to depict how darkness begins to take over the atmosphere without fanfare and develops a personality for Eve. The combination of these details and the adjectives used to describe Eve, such as modest, chaste, and meek, creates a comfortable feeling.

The comforts of tone and quiet devotion are driven off, however, by personal references to the poet, who, in spite of "willing feet," is hiding inside the "hut,/ That, from the mountain's side,/ Views wilds, and swelling floods" (lines 34-36) because of the cold and rainy winds on a suggestively Shakespearean heath. The image of spring would be overpowered by this picture, despite the sound of the church bell, were it not for the compelling pictures created for the other seasons in the ending.

Themes and Meanings

Ostensibly, "Ode to Evening" is a nature poem, one of those often considered a prelude to the Romantic movement or a deliberate and intentional antidote to the heroic genres most prominent in the earlier part of the Augustan age. The poem looks forward to the Age of Sensibility, a label which poems such as Thomson's *The Seasons* (1730) and Warton's *The Enthusiast: Or, The Love of Nature* (1744) helped to create. Collins's ode promotes scenic nature, as do these poems, in contrast to the neoclassical emphasis upon human nature. Similarly, it even hints at the sublime in the section describing the mountain storm and the view from the hut as well as in the images of winter at the end. Nevertheless, just as evening is neither day nor night, this poem is neither fully pre-Romantic nor conventionally neoclassical. It is transitional, subtle, and generally quiet, like its subject.

Even though Collins follows convention in imagery, diction, and verse form, he demonstrates that he is not a slave to it. The ode exerts the "gentlest" of influences, as its subject does. Even the superlatives Collins uses are not exaggerations, but the superlative forms of adjectives such as "gentle" and "meek."

The striking passages are, first, those depicting the prospect of a violent mountain storm as well as attack by winter on Eve's entourage and her flowing garments; and second, the images which are more sharply focused in the pageant of seasons which ends the poem. These seem to establish the grounds for the earlier prayer in hopes of adopting evening's calm demeanor and reserved behavior. Especially poignant are the lines describing how the wind and rain of the storm keep the poet's "willing feet" from obeying their desire to follow Eve. These lines seem highly personal in light of Samuel Johnson's famous phrase describing the poet, "poor dear Collins." Contemporaries' accounts of Collins's life, including those by his friends, record mental breakdowns which are entirely relevant if one notes the poet's own signals in this and other poems. The allusion to Lear on the heath is not the poet's personal equation of himself with Shakespeare's egotistical king; other characters who join the scene in the hut would be more suitable for comparison with Collins's presentation of himself. This passage is a faint echo of feelings expressed in the "Ode to Fear" from the same volume (1746). Although "Ode to Fear" is generated by Aristotle's discussion of pity and fear in his concept of catharsis, the personal element is a noticeable dimension and reinforces a biographical interpretation for both poems.

The final section ventures into a more vivid style of natural depiction. The fragrances of spring, the length of summer days, the effect engendered by autumn colors and temperatures are just as compelling as the violence of winter and are not overpowered by it. The apparent timidity of the earliest passages and the passion tapped in the heath scene have a purpose within the poem itself: a careful buildup to a final celebration. Collins's skillful manipulation of imagery and versification, along with the consequent modulations in tone and atmosphere, have created a poem representative of both the era and the inventive genius of the individual poet.

Emma Coburn Norris

ODE TO PSYCHE

Author: John Keats (1795-1821)
Type of poem: Ode
First published: 1820, in *Lamia, Isabella, The Eve of St. Agnes, and Other Poems*

The Poem

"Ode to Psyche," made up of sixty-seven lines, is divided into four stanzas of vary-ing lengths. Although iambic pentameter is the dominant meter of the poem, John Keats often includes lines of iambic trimeter as well. The rhyme scheme is generally in a quatrain form of *abab*, but rhyming couplets are also employed. This technical complexity is typical of the ode form.

The poem begins with a direct address to the goddess Psyche, the personification of the human soul, and this one-sided conversation continues thoughout the poem. Keats himself is the first-person speaker, and "thou" is always the silent Psyche.

The first stanza, the longest in the poem, describes a vision or a dream Keats has of Psyche and her lover Eros lying "In deepest grass, beneath the whisp'ring roof/ Of leaves and trembled blossoms," beside a brook and "cool-rooted flowers": The soul—Psyche—and the body—Eros—lie together in the heart of nature. Keats imagines them not in a passionate embrace, but in a static, restful pose, as if he has come upon them after their lovemaking has ended. In another poem, "Ode on a Grecian Urn," he witnesses an eternal moment before any physical activity takes place between lovers and examines the difficulty in this position: Although "the maiden" will always re-main beautiful and the man's love will last forever, the couple, frozen in the marble of the urn, will never share a kiss. "Ode to Psyche," in its peaceful description of Eros and Psyche, offers no such disquieting picture of love or art.

In the second stanza, the shortest in the poem, Keats disturbs the idyllic setting. He once again begins with an address to Psyche, describing her as the "loveliest vision far" of all Olympus's goddesses, more beautiful than Phoebe or Vesper, the moon or the evening star. The difficulty enters the poem, however, in Keats's description of the Greek gods as "Olympus' faded hierarchy!" He acknowledges their displacement in the West by Christianity and mourns it. Psyche, the "latest born" of all the Greek gods, was not embodied as a goddess until the second century C.E., so she was never prop-erly worshiped, in Keats's mind. Although she is "fairer than" all the other goddesses, she has no temple in her honor, "nor altar heap'd with flowers;/ Nor virgin-choir to make delicious moan." In his poem, Keats attempts to remedy Psyche's abandonment. She may have "no shrine, no grove, no oracle" or prophet associated with her, but the poet, through the power of the human imagination, offers her recompense.

Keats admits in the third stanza that Psyche was born "too late for antique vows," and he realizes that the blessed time has passed when "the haunted forest boughs" were holy, when "the air, the water, and fire" were holy; reason and science have dis-placed the power of myth. The poem, however, does not give in to despair. The poet, once again addressing Psyche directly, asks permission to serve her: Let me be "Thy voice, thy lute, thy pipe . . . Thy shrine, thy grove, thy oracle."

Stanza 4 resolves the problem wonderfully. Keats will build a fane, or temple, "in some untrodden region of [his] mind." The poet will become the soul's priest, using his "working brain" to create a world filled with "soft delight" for the goddess. The mind of the poet will re-create the scene pictured in the first stanza; after the goddess is pleasantly seated in his brain, Keats will leave a "casement ope at night,/ To let the warm Love in!" Eros and Psyche will be reunited.

Forms and Devices

Part of Keats's reputation as a great poet derives from the appeal of his sensual, opulent phrasing. In "Ode to Psyche," however, the lush language is perhaps over-shadowed by an atypical technique: Keats risks a monotonous sound in the poem by repeating certain key words. In order to make a point about the mind's ability to compensate for loss, Keats first describes what has been lost and then, by using the same wording, replaces it completely. For example, in stanza 2, Keats despairs because Psyche never had a "virgin-choir to make delicious moan/ Upon the midnight hours." In stanza 3, he offers himself to Psyche, saying "let me be thy choir, and make a moan/ Upon the midnight hours." In stanza 2, he mourns because Psyche, in the classical world, had

> No voice, no lute, no pipe, no incense sweet
> From chain-swung censer teeming;
> No shrine, no grove, no oracle, no heat
> Of pale-mouth'd prophet dreaming.

In stanza 3, he once again speaks to Psyche, saying, let me be

> Thy voice, thy lute, thy pipe, thy incense sweet
> From swinged censer teeming;
> Thy shrine, thy grove, thy oracle, thy heat
> Of pale-mouth'd prophet dreaming.

In the same way that the abundance of stanza 3 contradicts the emptiness of stanza 2, the fourth stanza contradicts the first. Keats concludes the poem by returning to the opening site, that forest in which he came upon the two lovers. Stanza 4 re-creates that pristine scene, but the new location is changed into a "fane," or temple, inside the poet's mind. Whereas the first stanza talks about a natural scene with fragrant flowers in blossom and the wind in the trees, the fourth stanza has a gardener named Fancy, or imagination, "breeding flowers" that are never the same and the "branched thoughts" of the poet's mind, "instead of pines," murmuring "in the wind." The original forest and its wildness are transmuted by Keats into a "rosy sanctuary" dressed "With the wreath'd trellis of a working brain." This extended metaphor, or conceit, of the final stanza concludes by joining the two lovers, or at least allowing Eros an entranceway into the sacred fane: "a casement ope at night" is an odd and metaphorical window in the brain through which Eros can pass to be with his love.

This dialogue between the stanzas, in which the first is joined with the last and the second with the third, is balanced by another device: The poem moves forward powerfully from start to finish simply because it is driven by the initial phrases of each stanza. The first three stanzas all begin with a similar technique. The goddess is invoked or praised in an exclamatory phrase that begins with an interjection: "O Goddess!" "O latest born and loveliest vision far/ Of all Olympus' faded hierarchy!" "O brightest!" The reader must wait until the final stanza to find an alteration of the form; after the first three stanzas address the goddess, the fourth stanza records the poet's resolve: "Yes, I will be thy priest!" Keats creates tension in the poem by combining these two techniques, which forces the reader to look at the relationships between stanzas in two different ways.

Themes and Meanings

One of the chief concerns of "Ode to Psyche" is the poet's role in a modern society. Like the other major poets of the early part of the nineteenth century, Keats found himself in a world that was beginning to be denuded of myth and ritual, a world in which reason and progress had started to strip "the air, the water, and the fire" of their holiness. The Christian ceremonies and rituals did not seem to have the same power, according to Keats, that the ancient, classical rites of worship had. In "Ode to Psyche," Keats attempts to reopen the door to mystery and holiness using the human imagination.

Keats's cure for the problem, however, is extremely self-absorbed. It is as if the poet can have an effect only on the level of the individual. The poem does not offer a recipe for a great awakening among the people of England or the world; instead, the poem traces a single poet's attempts to save a portion of the ancient mysteries for himself.

Apparently, this type of spiritual rebirth was not available to the "average" man or woman; Keats accentuates his special gift when he announces that "even in these days so far retir'd/ From happy pieties" of the past, he is able to see Psyche and sing about her "by [his] own eyes inspired." The poet is in no way a lowly creature; he creates his own inspiration, and his mind serves as the sacred temple in which the goddess will find her "soft delight." This ode has never been regarded by most readers as equal to "Ode on a Grecian Urn" or "Ode to a Nightingale," perhaps because of this poetic self-assuredness. Keats triumphs too easily in the poem; he rectifies the problem of a desacralized world by retreating into the mind of the poet alone.

The strengths of the poem, however, lie in the sheer power of Keats's imagination, his attempt to conjoin Eros and Psyche, the body and the spirit, in one being. He wants his mind, his own imagination, to be the place where the lovemaking takes place. The priest has become a poet who encourages the dalliances between the sexes. Although the reader never actually sees Eros and Psyche enter the "untrodden regions" of Keats's mind, the poem suggests that the union is possible. It ends with tremendous hopefulness, since it is in fact a hymn of praise not only to the goddess Psyche but also to the human soul and imagination, unaided by divine intervention.

Kevin Boyle

ODE TO THE CONFEDERATE DEAD

Author: Allen Tate (1899-1979)
Type of poem: Ode
First published: 1928, in *Mr. Pope and Other Poems*

The Poem

This ninety-two-line stream-of-consciousness meditation contrasts modern man with the heroes of the Civil War. Originally called an elegy, the poem's form suggests John Milton's "Lycidas" (1637), which is at once a lament for the dead Edward King and an examination of life in the 1630's. Similarly, Allan Tate both eulogizes the fallen Confederate soldiers and analyzes the plight of those living in the twentieth century. Written largely in iambic pentameter, the poem also employs hexameter, tetrameter, and trimeter. The poem oscillates between the regularity and formality associated with the sections portraying antique heroism and irregular rhythms reflecting the collapse of that world. Like the rhythm, the rhyme scheme varies. The second stanza, for example, begins with a quatrain, and the third with a couplet; rhymes recur at unpredictable intervals. Thus, "tomorrow" in the third stanza echoes "grow," "row," and "below" in the second.

In his essay "Narcissus as Narcissus" (1938), Tate remarks of the poem, "Figure to yourself a man stopping at the gate of a Confederate graveyard on a late autumn afternoon." Standing outside the cemetery, he sees the ordered rows of tombstones being worn away by time; the regular iambs of the first line break down before the elements in the second. The wind blows leaves about the neglected graveyard, and the fallen foliage impresses the onlooker with "the rumor of mortality." As he thinks about the soldiers who fell like leaves, he tries to derive consolation from the thought that the memory of those men endures, but he can summon only the cycle of nature. Tate describes the stanzas as "a baroque meditation on the ravages of time."

In the third stanza, the spectator addresses the soldiers directly as "you." Those men understood heroism; theirs was the complete vision of the Greek philosophers who could distinguish reality from illusion. Wanting to fuse himself with that world, the onlooker momentarily imagines that the leaves are soldiers, but he cannot sustain the illusion. Historical evocation of Confederate general "Stonewall" Jackson and of notable battles also fails to remove him from his own time; he is left with only the wind and death.

The image of the dying hound ends the first part of the ode, the strophe. The antistrophe begins in midline, posing the question of what remains for the spectator, representative of modern man, to do. How can he even speak of the dead, let alone become part of the past? The penultimate stanza suggests that he cannot, that creativity is impossible. All that remains is silent speculation culminating in self-destruction. The last lines offer another, only slightly more promising alternative—the worship of death—setting "up the grave/ In the house," implying a backward-looking poetic that imitates antebellum literature. "The ravenous grave" suggests not only death but also Edgar Allan Poe's "The Raven," representative of older versification and, because of its refrain, of doom.

The question of creativity remains unresolved. The spectator departs, and in his place Tate leaves "the gentle serpent" to guard the graves. Even here the ambiguity endures. The green color and the mulberry bush implying the silkworm (as Tate himself noted) suggest life, especially since the snake reminds the reader of Tate's "Mr. Pope," also published in 1928. In that poem Pope is likened to a snake, a symbol of creativity. Yet, as Tate remarks, the serpent "is the ancient symbol of time, and . . . time is also death."

Forms and Devices

The poem abounds in animal imagery that comments on the spectator. The first animal, "the blind crab," appears at the end of the second stanza. Again Tate's gloss clarifies the symbol: The crab "has mobility but no direction, energy but from the human point of view, no purposeful world to use it in." Moreover, with its hard exoskeleton, the crab is walled within itself. The Confederate soldiers also lie within a wall, but one that unites them in a common frame. The spectator, like the crab, is trapped in his own world. The crab also lacks vision, being blind, just as the spectator is cut off from the heroic image of the past.

The onlooker also resembles the hound bitch waiting for death. He has lost his vigor and his purpose. The hunt, like battle, is deadly but ritualistic, unifying and purposeful. The hound, a hunting dog, no longer engages in the activity for which it was born; instead, it lies motionless, as the onlooker remains stationary at the cemetery gate.

Tate next introduces the spider and owl, both associated with death. The former suggests as well the thin Confederate soldiers in their gray uniforms, and their heroic if doomed struggle resembles that of Arachne, who challenged Athena to a fatal spinning contest. The spider is like the onlooker, too, for like the crab it has an exoskeleton, and it lives within its own web. The jaguar and serpent conclude the catalog of animals. The jaguar that leaps into the pool represents Narcissus, yet another figure locked within himself. Like the crab, this jaguar has energy that lacks proper direction and so destroys itself.

The myths of Narcissus and Arachne are the most obvious classical allusions in the poem but not the only ones. Twice Tate suggests the paralyzing gaze of Medusa. The first reference appears in the second stanza when the stare of the stone angels on the tombstones petrifies the viewer. This image recurs in the penultimate stanza; Tate writes of "mute speculation, the patient curse/ That stones the eyes." This latter allusion links Narcissus and Medusa, for in the root of speculation is the Latin *speculum*, mirror. The means of slaying the Gorgon becomes the instrument of self-destruction as the inward searching of modern man deprives him of feeling and isolates him from the heroism of a Perseus.

Yet another series of references derives from Christianity. The cemetery is a walled garden with a serpent, suggesting that the old world of the Confederacy is an Eden, but a decaying one because no one tends it in this fallen world. Even the angels charged with guarding paradise are crumbling. The word "election" in the first stanza carries religious weight: The soldiers, unlike the observer, were among the chosen, the blessed, who have been absolved through the "shrift of death." Whereas those men had vision, for the spectator night (darkness) rather than the divine (light) "is the beginning and the end," the alpha and the omega. Hence the wind, the spirit, fails to move him and is outside him, not within.

Themes and Meanings

Tate's own comments provide a good place to begin to understand his intent. The poem, he writes in "Narcissus as Narcissus," deals with solipsism—with modernity's lack of cohesion and the isolation of the individual. The world of the Confederate dead was unified. The soldiers knew "midnight restitutions," rage, heroism, the entire range of emotions that the spectator unsuccessfully attempts to evoke; the older society understood and believed what the twentieth century can only analyze. The soldiers acted, but moderns are merely onlookers. In the third stanza, the man at the gate assumes the guise of a sociologist, and later he becomes a historian recalling the old battles, but the tradition he seeks is dead. He can mummify it and so preserve the memory, but he cannot revitalize the heritage. Just as modernity has lost the unified vision of Parmenides and Zeno, so it has lost their heroism. Zeno's voice is muted in the present, but Tate also alludes to the philosopher's biting off his tongue so that he could give no information to his captors.

Tate's confrontation with modernity is at once universal and personal. Everyone living in the twentieth century, Tate says in the poem, is a Narcissus, but for the Southerner this problem is particularly acute. Shortly after Tate completed the first version of this poem, he sent copies to various other writers for comments. His fellow Fugitive writer Donald Davidson wrote back,

> The Confederate dead become a peg on which you hang an argument whose lines, however sonorous and beautiful in a strict proud way, leave me wondering why you wrote a poem on the subject at all, since in effect you say . . . that no poem can be written on such a subject.

Divorced from his past, Tate was asking how the Southerner, how Tate himself, could continue to create. The Fugitives rejected modernity, but Davidson sensed that Tate was abandoning the effort to link himself with the agrarian world of the Old South. However desirable that fusion, Tate believed that it no longer was possible.

The poem is an elegy not only for the Confederate dead but also for the unusable past and for Tate's former belief in the viability of the Confederate tradition. Tate wrestled with the poem for a decade, and his ability to complete it marks a triumph. The Southerner could write about his heritage, could draw on the past, but he had to do so as a person of his own time. Tate proved Davidson wrong: A poem could be written on the subject, but it could not be a nineteenth century poem. Tate had come to recognize that by living in the past one creates rhetoric; by wrestling with it in the present, one produces poetry.

Joseph Rosenblum

ODE TO THE MOST HOLY EUCHARIST
Exposition and World

Author: Federico García Lorca (1898-1936)
Type of poem: Ode
First published: 1928, as "Oda al Santísimo Sacrament o del Altar"; in *Obras completas*, 1938; English translation collected in *Collected Works*, 1991

The Poem

"Ode to the Most Holy Eucharist: Exposition and World," a relatively short poem in classic hexameters, is divided into three overall sections of four-line stanzas ("Exposition," "World," and "The Devil"), which are thirty-six, forty, and sixteen lines long. The title indicates the serious nature of the poem, but also suggests the possibility of an ironic reading by emphasizing the superlative degree in "Most Holy." This blending of high seriousness and ironic detachment is one of the hallmarks of the poem. When its first two sections were published in 1928, the poem carried the subtitle "Fragment" above the dedication, indicating that Federico García Lorca intended to add to the poem. The poem was completed during García Lorca's visit to the United States in 1929.

The poem's original dedication to the Spanish composer Manuel de Falla (1876-1946), a devout Catholic and friend of García Lorca, irritated de Falla; the composer agreed to accept García Lorca's friendly homage only because he hoped that the unfinished sections of the poem would reverse the evidently sacrilegious direction of the first two. De Falla's reaction has been typical of many readers of the poem in predominantly Catholic Spain; the poem is infrequently translated into English and is rarely included in anthologies of García Lorca's work.

The poem is written in the first person, and the speaker might easily be seen as García Lorca himself. In 1928, following the critical success of his "Gypsy Ballads," García Lorca experienced extreme emotional difficulty in adapting to sudden fame and the possibility that his homosexuality might become widely known. In a letter to Jorge Zalamea in the autumn of 1928, García Lorca noted: "By sheer will power, I've *resolved* these past few days, one of the most painful periods I've experienced in my life." Many critics have argued that "Ode to the Most Holy Eucharist" marks a brief return to the security of his Catholic upbringing in an effort to combat the emotional turmoil brought upon him by the increased scrutiny of the public. In essence, García Lorca was searching here for a way to come to terms with a *Dios anclado* (a God "anchored" in human terms). While he is clearly longing for the security of such a God, he cannot conceive of such a God in other than somewhat shocking human terms.

In the letter to Zalamea mentioned above, García Lorca referred to the composition of the rigorous hexameters of "Ode to the Most Holy Eucharist" as an exercise: "for discipline, I'm doing these precise *academic* things now and opening my soul before the symbol of the Sacrament." García Lorca's longing for control over the fragments of his life is reflected in the last line of the "World" section: "Immutable Sacrament of love and discipline." García Lorca also referred to "Ode to the Most Holy Eucharist" as "probably the greatest poem I've done."

The three sections of the poem might best be considered as three panels of a stained-glass window viewed in a large cathedral. "Exposition" focuses on the moment during the Catholic Mass when the wafer of bread is transformed into the body of Christ. "World" contrasts the nature of the divine with the nature of man and offers images of mankind's tawdry existence. The final section, "The Devil," presents a sensuous incarnation of evil in a manifestation of beauty. In order to understand García Lorca's method here, however, it might help to imagine that the stained-glass window had at one time been broken; what one sees now in the poem is a reconstruction, an assembling of fragments. In other words, much of the difficulty in reading this poem stems from the fact that there is no real narrative pattern or story to follow; García Lorca chooses to present an array of compelling images for contemplation rather than a series of methodical points for understanding. In this respect, the use of regular hexameters (frequently employed for heroic subjects, and therefore appropriate to the "Most Holy Sacrament") contrasts with the decidedly nonheroic images that the hexameters convey. The final effect is one of unease, of not knowing whether García Lorca is celebrating or mocking the "Most Holy Sacrament" of the Eucharist.

Forms and Devices

"Exposition" uses the setting of the Catholic Mass as its basic motif and specifically focuses upon the elevation of the wafer at the moment of consecration. As the elevation of the wafer within the monstrance (*ostensorio*, display frame) is accomplished, the speaker marks its comparison to, of all things, a frog's heart: "Live there, my God, inside the monstrance./ Pierced by your Father with a ray of light./ Trembling like the poor heart of the frog/ that the doctors put in a glass bottle." García Lorca is emphasizing a double transformation. The first transformation, depicted in the symbology of the mass itself, is devout, reflecting the transubstantiation of God into man: the mass commemorates the moment when God became man. The second, in the construction of the poem, is ironic and appears to devalue divinity by comparing the beating of the divine heart with that of a frog in a dissecting bottle. García Lorca also indicates, however, that the God in the monstrance is "trembling," having been pierced by a ray of light from his Father. Several traditions are blending here. First, García Lorca alludes to the Catholic belief that Jesus Christ was the son of God the Father. Second, he identifies that Father as a source of light (of enlightenment, or salvation to medieval Catholics). Finally, however, he emphasizes that God the Son, inside the monstrance, is trembling like the heart of a dissected frog. This last comparison emphasizes the contamination that the Son of God encountered as a result of his connection with humanity, and perhaps suggests that the Son of God made the transformation into the human with some fear. In any case, García Lorca's God here is a "God in infant's dress, diminutive, eternal Christ,/ a thousand times pronounced dead, crucified/ by the impure word of sweaty man."

In "World," García Lorca focuses on the human environment that divinity has chosen to enter. He presents this environment with a type of fragmented-image technique that is closely akin to T. S. Eliot's style in *The Waste Land* (1922). Most of the images are taken from the seamier side of life: "The razorblades lay on the dressing tables/ waiting impatiently to sever the heads"; "Clerks asleep on the fourteenth floor./ Prostitute with breasts of scratched glass"; "To assassinate the nightingale came three thousand men armed with shining knives." In each of these clusters of images, the meaning depends more upon the compelling quality of the image itself than upon its reference to a known story. In other words, unlike Eliot's *The Waste Land*, which ultimately rewards the reader who examines the sources used in the poem's composition, "Ode to the Most Holy Eucharist" relies solely on the arresting power of the images themselves to convey a picture of the dangerous nature of the world that the incarnating (recall that the poem focuses on the moment that God enters the flesh of man) God will inhabit. The entrance of God into such a world provides the antidote, or relief, for such danger, but García Lorca is aware that such relief requires a nonrational standard of belief. In two of his favorite lines, "The unicorn seeks what the rose forgets/ and the bird attempts what the waters impede," García Lorca emphasizes that belief in the impossible (the unicorn or the incarnation of Christ) makes possible what was hitherto thought to be out of the question (roses remembering or birds flying, or the salvation of man). Only the sacrament of the Eucharist is capable of soothing the heart of the frog in the glass bottle and the hearts of twentieth century humankind: "Only your balanced Sacrament of light/ soothes the anguish of unloosed love./ Only you, Sacrament, manometer that saves/ hearts flung at five hundred per hour." Finally, the sacrament is compared to a measuring device that would recognize an excessive speed and warn the operator against exceeding his own limitations.

Themes and Meanings

"Ode to the Most Holy Eucharist" is a poem about the nature of divine-human transformation. In it, García Lorca wonders whether humankind can be redeemed from essentially squalorous surroundings by faith in a deity that has entered into the form of man. García Lorca is challenging the notion that gods need to be resplendent in their divine powers—superhuman, larger than life, elevated in a monstrance for all to see. He wonders if the reverse is not more true: Instead of emphasizing the grandiose nature of the divine transformation, he instead emphasizes the "love and discipline" required for salvation. That is, "Ode to the Most Holy Eucharist" commemorates a ritual that is the enactment of a discipline; García Lorca's choice of regular hexameters echoes that discipline.

At the heart of that discipline lies simple love, a love that defies understanding, in the way that García Lorca's images of tawdry street scenes defy rational understanding but readily enable and reward contemplation. The last line of the "World" section captures this paradox beautifully: "Immutable Sacrament of love and discipline!" In "Ode to the Most Holy Eucharist," García Lorca strove to discover a way out of his own increasing agitation with the world around him, feeling the condemnation of his society and his childhood religion for his homosexuality, but yearning for the peace of that "God in infant's dress, diminutive, eternal Christ." "Ode to the Most Holy Eucharist" is a demonstration of García Lorca's own dedication to love and discipline.

Peter D. Olson

ODE TO THE WEST WIND

Author: Percy Bysshe Shelley (1792-1882)
Type of poem: Ode
First published: 1820, in *Prometheus Unbound: A Lyrical Drama in Four Acts*

The Poem

Like many of Percy Bysshe Shelley's poems, "Ode to the West Wind" was inspired by a natural phenomenon, an autumn storm that prompted the poet to contemplate the links between the outer world of nature and the realm of the intellect. In five stanzas directly addressed to the powerful wind that Shelley paradoxically calls both "destroyer" and "preserver" (line 14), the poet explores the impact of the regenerative process that he sees occurring in the world around him and compares it to the impact of his own poetry, which he believes can have similar influence in regenerating mankind.

In each stanza, Shelley speaks to the West Wind as if it is an animate power. The first three stanzas form a logical unit; in them the poet looks at how the wind influences the natural terrain over which it moves. The opening lines describe the way the wind sweeps away the autumn leaves and carries off seeds of vegetation, which will lie dormant through winter until the spring comes to give them new life as plants. In the second stanza, the poet describes the clouds that whisk across the autumn sky, driven by the same fierce wind and twisted into shapes that remind him of Maenads, Greek maidens known for their wild behavior. Shelley calls the wind the harbinger of the dying year, a visible sign that a cycle of nature's life is coming to a close. The poet uses the third stanza to describe the impact of the wind on the Mediterranean coast line and the Atlantic ocean; the wind, Shelley says, moves the waters and the undersea vegetation in much the same way it shifts the landscape.

In the final two stanzas, the speaker muses about the possibilities that his transformation by the wind would have on his ability as a poet. If he could be a leaf, a cloud, or a wave, he would be able to participate directly in the regenerative process he sees taking place in the natural world. His words—that is, his poetry—would become like these natural objects, which are scattered about the world and which serve as elements to help bring about new life. He wishes that, much like the seeds he has seen scattered about, his "leaves" (line 58), his "dead thoughts" (line 63)—his poems—could be carried across the world by the West Wind so that they could "quicken to a new birth" (line 64) at a later time, when others might take heed of their message. The final question with which the poet ends this poem is actually a note of hope: The "death" that occurs in winter is habitually followed by a "new life" every spring. The cycle of the seasons that he sees occurring around him gives Shelley hope that his works might share the fate of other objects in nature; they may be unheeded for a time, but one day they will have great impact on humankind.

Forms and Devices

The structure of "Ode to the West Wind" is exceptionally complex. Each of the five stanzas is itself a terza rima sonnet, consisting of fourteen lines divided into four triplets and a concluding couplet. Through the complex, interlocking rhyme scheme of terza rima, Shelley gives the poem a strong sense of rhythm. The form also gives emphasis to the concluding couplet in each stanza, thereby focusing the reader's attention on the final line or lines. The effect Shelley achieves is important, for he wishes to emphasize, in the first three stanzas, the speaker's plea that the West Wind heed his call, and in the final stanza he wants to highlight the significant rhetorical question with which the poem ends.

The primary literary trope in the poem is personification. Shelley repeatedly addresses the West Wind as if it were an animate, intelligent being; one might be reminded of the way elements of nature are represented in classical Greek or Latin literature, or in American Indian writings. Shelley wants readers to consider the Wind a living force that helps shape the landscape—literally, the physical landscape, and metaphorically, the landscape of human minds and attitudes.

Shelley uses three major images of the poem—the wave, the leaf, and the cloud—to demonstrate the ways in which the West Wind treats elements of the physical landscape. The poet's scene-painting is especially noteworthy; in a few short lines in each of the first three stanzas he depicts the effects of the fierce autumn wind on the ocean, the earth, and the sky. In the fourth stanza, he applies these descriptions to himself, calling on the West Wind to work its magic on him in the same way it has on the natural world, so he too will "die" only to rise again and give life—intellectual life.

One of the most striking images in the poem is used in the fourth stanza to describe the poet's present plight: "I fall upon the thorns of life! I bleed!" (line 54) he cries out to the West Wind. In that single line, following his plea that he be made like the wave, the leaf, or the cloud so he can be transformed by the powers of the wind, Shelley expresses the problem of the Romantic poet: He would soar to new heights of understanding and deliver insight into life to all humanity if he could, but his human nature keeps him affixed to the earth, with all its troubles and stumbling blocks. Life itself is seen as a painful rosebush whose thorns afflict one who wishes to rise above the day-to-day humdrum of human existence. Shelley realizes that he cannot do so. Nevertheless, he has hopes that his works may be like those natural objects that seem to die in winter only to rise to new life in spring. He compares his verse to "ashes and sparks" from an unextinguished fire (line 67), which he hopes the wind will scatter so they may flare up in other places, thereby widening his impact on others.

Themes and Meanings

In "Ode to the West Wind," Shelley examines and compares two phenomena that are particularly potent: the power of nature and the power of poetry. Like most Romantic poets, he sees a clear link between these two, believing that the poet's power arises from nature, inspired by it and akin to it in many respects. Many similes in this poem, and in others by Shelley, focus readers' attention on the comparisons. Donald

Reiman has described the themes of this poem as "the Poet's personal despair and his hopes for social renewal" expressed "in images drawn from the seasonal cycle" (*Percy Bysshe Shelley*, 1969). Hence, the destructive power of the West Wind parallels Shelley's fear that the beauty of the natural world, and metaphorically the beauty of his own works, is doomed to oblivion by a hostile and insensitive force. At the same time, however, he recognizes that the destructive power of the West Wind is but a part of a larger cycle in which what seems like death is merely a necessary stage in the process of regeneration that perpetuates life itself. In the final stanzas of the poem he offers some hope that, despite his being constricted by his humanity and possibly being ignored by those whom he wishes to enlighten, he may one day be able to speak to others. Like the new life that comes inevitably every spring, his works may be "reborn" when people (perhaps those other than his contemporaries) discover them and listen to Shelley's calls for social and moral reform.

The specifics of Shelley's plan for reforming the world do not appear in "Ode to the West Wind." Rather, this poem focuses on the process by which his other works may one day achieve their purpose in the world. Those familar with classical or Renaissance poetry may notice a similarity between this poem and those by Horace or by Ben Jonson, whose "Go, Little Book" verses appeal in a similar way for the continued life of their poetry. Like those poets who preceded him, Shelley hopes that his work will one day be read and appreciated by an audience that can understand his deep concern for the improvement of humankind, one that will be willing to listen to his plan for bringing about such improvement.

Laurence W. Mazzeno

ODE TO WALT WHITMAN

Author: Federico García Lorca (1898-1936)
Type of poem: Ode
First published: 1940, as "Oda a Walt Whitman," in *Poeta en Nueva York*, 1940; English translation collected in *Poet in New York*, 1955

The Poem

The Spanish poet and dramatist Federico García Lorca wrote his famous "Oda a Walt Whitman" ("Ode to Walt Whitman") in 1930 while completing a year of study at Columbia University. The poem did not appear in its entirety, however, until it was collected in the first two editions of *Poeta en Nueva York* in 1940, more than three years after the poet was executed by Generalissimo Francisco Franco's fascist troops during the Spanish Civil War. From the outset this emotionally charged piece, translated by Ben Belitt in *Poet in New York* (1955), subsumes the confusing onslaught of city images that bombarded the non-English-speaking García Lorca during his first ever trip abroad in the wake of the disastrous stock market crash of 1929. The irregular stanzas and varying lengths of the poem's 137 free-verse lines accurately reflect the bustling, chaotic character of this major metropolitan center. In addition, the poem implicitly contrasts the city's arduous striving for economic recovery through local industry with the splendors of its half-concealed natural beauty. Thus the poem's speaker can address "filthy New York" as the city of "cables and death" while musing in the very next line, "What angel do you carry, concealed in your cheek?"

García Lorca uses the ode, a celebratory lyric form, to praise the charitable nature of the influential American poet Walt Whitman (1812-1892), a writer closely associated with New York City, where Whitman published his landmark collection of verse, *Leaves of Grass*, in 1855. Some see in the style and structure of "Ode to Walt Whitman" García Lorca's attempt to emulate the lilting cadences of Whitman's long, rhythmic lines, his spontaneous, lush diction, sincere outpouring of feeling, and fluid, highly personal voice. García Lorca undoubtedly admired Whitman's verse for embodying America's democratic ideals and elevating the genuine decency of the common man to a more exalted plane. Yet in all likelihood García Lorca harbored a more immediate reason for choosing Whitman as the subject of his poetic paean.

Both García Lorca and Whitman were homosexual, and both deplored their societies' moralistic intolerance of same-sex love. "Ode to Walt Whitman" repeatedly distinguishes the (assumed) purity and sincerity of Whitman's sexual predilections from its own cold-eyed depiction of the largely self-gratifying, sometimes violent, even depraved aspects of urban homosexual relations. To the poem's speaker, Whitman is nothing less than a "blood-brother," a "lone man in a sea," a "comely old man" who is an "old friend," while the "perverts" around him are "so much meat for the whiplash,/ for the boot or the bite of the animal-tamers." Whitman's easy relation to what little of nature remains visible amid the hardscrabble cityscape of New York may be viewed in stanzas such as this one:

> You looked for a nude that could be like a river,
> the bull and the dream that could merge, like seaweed and wheel,
> sire of your agony, your mortality's camellia,
> to cry in the flames of your secret equator.

Clearly, the speaker of the ode finds the scenario of two people sharing a love akin to transcendent bonding infinitely preferable to seeking fleeting and sordid sexual encounters, "looking for the scar on the eye,/ or the overcast swamp where the boys are submerged."

Forms and Devices

Throughout "Ode to Walt Whitman," García Lorca uses the richly evocative, highly figurative, and elusively metaphorical language that is a hallmark of both his lyric and dramatic work. In writing a poem about male love during the early part of the twentieth century, García Lorca would have felt compelled to approach his subject with linguistic indirection. So, while the ode opens with the obviously homoerotic image of young men "singing, baring their waists,/ with the wheel and the leather, the hammer, the oil," it phrases an ensuing (imagined) sexual fantasy of Whitman's obliquely as "your dream/ where the playfellow munches your apple." Similarly, one of the first images describing Whitman refers to him suggestively as a "bird/ whose sex is transfixed by a needle."

In making allusions to both classical and biblical antiquity, the poem reminds the reader of the grandeur of times past, to which the "fallen" present of New York City (as well as other European and Latin American cities) compares unfavorably. The ode mentions, for example, the "faun of the river"; Whitman is conceived as having "chaste, Apollonian thighs" and as being the "satyr's antagonist," an "Adam" whose authenticity in seeking a communion in love will prepare the way for greater sincerity between sexual partners in the future. Both the hopeful evocation of natural images and capitalization in the following lines attest this possibility: "Tomorrow our passion is rock, and Time,/ a wind come to sleep in the branches." As it stands in the poem's present, though, "life is not noble, or wholesome, or holy."

The greatest tension in the ode concerns the opposition of human-made reality (often mechanical) and the marginalized realm of nature that survives on the outskirts of the city in animal life and, more important, in the East River mentioned in the very first line. What should be a beautiful, pristine "moon-rise" in the fifth stanza is marred: "the block and the tackle will veer and startle the sky." The figure of Whitman, introduced in the twenty-ninth line after a lengthy preamble, promises a return to nature and the natural love lacking in grimy, industrial New York, as García Lorca's speaker declares: "Not for one moment . . ./ have I ceased to envision your beard full of butterflies." Throughout the poem, Whitman is associated with the natural world, especially with the eternal, purifying force of the river. The speaker wonders, using still more natural imagery, "What ineffable voice will speak the truths of the wheat?"

Themes and Meanings

The vituperative stance of the poem's speaker regarding urban homosexuals, called "perverts of the cities" and "mothers of filthiness," implies a certain distance between the speaker and García Lorca himself. These wanton carriers of disease who "bestow upon boys/ the foul drop of death with wormwood of venom" disgust the speaker with their base disregard for the feelings of their sexual partners and the studied artifice of their appearance.

Midway through the ode, these "toadies of women" and "dressing-room bitches" improbably try to claim Whitman as one of their own, pointing him out publicly with the "taint of their fingernails." Their obvious antagonism to the natural world, though, precludes this possibility. Indeed, even when described in natural terms as animals, these raffish urban homosexuals appear in a negative light as "catlike and serpentine" and are later pronounced "dove-killers." After all, sexual desire need not manifest itself so vilely; in contrast to the primarily physical and self-indulgent encounters of the city, the speaker reminds men that "we might, if we would, lead our appetite on/ through the vein of the coral or the heaven-sent nude."

Having suitably praised Whitman for the sincerity of his motivations, the speaker unhesitatingly goes on to group his poetic forebear with those homosexuals whose honest embracing of their identity is reason for admiration. Addressing Whitman directly, as he does throughout much of the ode, the speaker explains that he does not denounce all urban homosexuals, such as "the boy who inscribes/ a girl's name on his pillow," or "the young man who dresses himself like a bride/ in the dark of the clothes-closet," or "the stags of the dance-hall/ who drink at the waters of whoredom and sicken." These men suffer unjustly because of who they are, and they harm no one (except, in some cases, themselves) as they poignantly attempt to come to grips with their confusing sexual stirrings. The speaker sympathizes with their plight and hopes that "the pure, the bewildered,/ the illustrious, classic, and suppliant/ shut the festival doors" in the face of their less genuine and more selfish counterparts.

In dire contrast to the "perverts," then, Whitman, the poet so in tune with nature that he is dubbed a "patriarch, comely as mist," emerges as the only figure in the ode to exist in spiritual harmony with New York City's East River. "Nobody slept/ or wished to be: river," the ode recounts of the single-minded workers in the first stanza. Of Whitman, again addressed directly by the speaker, the reader learns: "you dreamed yourself river, and slept like a river." While "America drowns under engines and tears," the poem closes with Whitman "on the shores of the Hudson . . . asleep," García Lorca's ode having again reiterated the poet's enduring promise of love as peaceful, supernal coupling:

> It is fitting that no man should seek
> in another day's thickets of blood for his pleasure.
> Heaven has shores for our flights out of life,
> and the corpse need not make itself over at dawn.

The poem's final striking image takes another step toward this ideal union of men by heralding the arrival of a phallic reign of nature in which "a black boy declares to the gold-getting white/ kingdom come in a tassel of corn."

Gregary J. Racz

OF MODERN POETRY

Author: Wallace Stevens (1879-1955)
Type of poem: Lyric
First published: 1940; collected in *Parts of a World*, 1942

The Poem

"Of Modern Poetry" attempts to redefine poetry for a world with no stable structures or values. Its form approaches blank verse, but it is not close enough to that form to be so labeled. The form is flexible, with five stresses in most lines but six or four in others. The loose form is appropriate for this poem, as a part of its argument is that modern poetry refuses labels, designations, and categories of all kinds.

The poem begins with its basic definition: Modern poetry is "The poem of the mind in the act of finding/ What will suffice." Contemporary poetry must be self-descriptive; it must look at itself searching and must observe its own invention. Thus, poetry is not so much a product as an act or activity. In the past, the speaker continues, the "scene was set": Poetry was formerly a matter of following the conventions. Everyone knew what was considered poetic material and what the acceptable forms of poetry were. This is no longer the case. The new poetry must be written in today's language, and it must reflect changing times and shifting concerns. It must include a consideration of war, for example. (The poem was published during World War II.) It must make use of the materials that are currently available to create a representation of those who will read it.

The poem then compares the poet with other types of artist for whom performance is a major part of their artistry. These comparisons help communicate the point that poetry must be activity if it is to speak to the present. The poet becomes an actor, a musician, and a "metaphysician in the dark" in his attempt to portray the time period as it is, for those who live in it. Elements of other arts and disciplines are attributed to poetry.

The concluding lines add to the previous definition, stating that poetry must be "the finding of a satisfaction." The earlier quest is identified as a search for "what would suffice." These two words, "suffice" and "satisfaction," suggest that poetry has as its goal a kind of consolation. The suggestion looks forward to Wallace Stevens's major statement of his poetic theory, "Notes Toward a Supreme Fiction," in which he develops a substantial argument concerning poetry: "It Must Give Pleasure." In the conclusion to "Of Modern Poetry" he also offers possible subjects for poetry—"a man skating, a woman dancing, a woman/ Combing." His subjects are all actions, activities which might be considered celebrations of the present by those who feel enough at home in it to move with its movements. Flux and flow are a necessary part of "the poem of the act of the mind."

Forms and Devices

The form of the poem as a whole reflects its insistence that form not be prescribed for modern poetry. The twenty-eight lines are arranged according to no set pattern, but the suggestion of blank verse underlies the poem and gives a feeling of coherence to it. The poem is broken into sections which provide its major propositions. It is not a syllogism or formal argument, but it makes three main points. It begins by introducing the issue of modern poetry and the difference between past and present poetry. In its most extended section, it then describes the new demands made on poetry by a complicated and skeptical age. Finally, it comments on possible subjects for poetry.

The metaphors in this poem all point in the same direction; they are all attempts to describe modern poetry in such a way as to make "Of Modern Poetry" both explanation and example. Traditional poetry is described as a theater in which "the scene was set." Past poets could repeat "what was in the script": Their powers of invention were not taxed in the same way that those of poets now are. To introduce the new poetry, the poem personifies or animates poetry itself, saying that it has to "learn the speech of the place" and "think about war." Poetry is then compared with an actor who is speaking into "the delicatest ear of the mind." In turn, the actor is compared with yet another figure, a metaphysician, who is then presented as a musician. All these shifting comparisons are confusing if analyzed logically, but they serve to characterize a poetry that is itself shifting, grounded on uncertainty, and reflective of lived life rather than tradition or convention. That drama, metaphysics, music, and poetry are in some ways equivalent and that they can flow from and into one another is a part of the theme of the poem. The metaphors demonstrate what the poem explains.

That action is a necessary part of contemporary poetry is suggested by the flowing run-on lines and by the number of present participles and gerunds that appear throughout the poem, such as "passing," "twanging," "skating," and "dancing." The modern poetry that is the "poem of the act of the mind" reflects the particular actions which are contemporary life.

Themes and Meanings

"Of Modern Poetry" is one of Stevens's most frequently anthologized poems, and it may be the most commonly encountered poem from the collection that contains it, *Parts of a World*. Its popularity may be attributable in part to the relative clarity with which it presents its themes. The quest for "what will suffice" appears in other Stevens poems as well, including "Man and Bottle." The search for a fiction that will be sustaining or nourishing to human beings in their uncertain lives is Stevens's major theme. In this poem, the theme is not hidden or presented indirectly.

The poem explores what characteristics poetry must have if it is to "suffice"—that is, to be enough or to satisfy. It is the uncertainty of the time that places so many demands on poetry, because poetry, to satisfy, must not violate reality. Therefore, wartime demands poetry which confronts war issues rather than hides from them. As each age speaks its own language, so the speech of the poem must reflect and partake of the discourse of the time. Otherwise it will not satisfy. It is axiomatic in Stevens that building a romantic world which can serve as a shelter from the unpleasantness of reality is not the function of poetry. Some of Stevens's early critics thought of him as an escapist, an ivory-tower poet who had little contact with the real world and little interest in it. He fought such dismissal vigorously in both poetry and essay, claiming that the poet must confront reality. The work of the imagination lies in its interactions with the real, not in disguises or evasions of reality.

The presentation of what modern poetry is actually like or should be like is more complex, presented as it is in a series of metaphors of actors, musicians, and metaphysicians. The substance of poetry is its sounds; these sounds ideally have all the dimensions that they could be given by those other art forms and disciplines.

Still more subtle is the description of the response to this ideal poetry. The audience is really listening "not to the play, but to itself." If the reality of the present is adequately represented in sound, the reader will find himself or herself in the poem. There will be an identification, described in the poem in terms of music that is somehow metaphysical: "The actor is/ A metaphysician in the dark, twanging/ An instrument." Poetry is thus presented as a metaphysical music that helps the mind define itself and learn of its own limits and possibilities. The identity of mind and music is a positive pleasure, consisting of "Sounds passing through sudden rightnesses, wholly/ Containing the mind."

The conclusion of the poem retreats from the intensity of the middle section as it presents some of the materials of poetry. The subject matter of poetry is far less significant than the creative act itself, suggests the poem, and only as an afterthought should poetic subjects even be mentioned. Nevertheless, the images of the three people, two women and a man, caught in their acts of living, provide appropriate closure. It may be true that all of Stevens's poetry is about writing poetry, but that does not make it— or this poem—narrow or exclusive. Stevens describes the creative drive as a basic force that is part of what it is to be human.

Janet McCann

THE OLD AND THE NEW MASTERS

Author: Randall Jarrell (1914-1965)
Type of poem: Lyric
First published: 1965, in *The Lost World*

The Poem

In order to understand Randall Jarrell's "The Old and the New Masters," one must look first to English poet W. H. Auden's "Musée de Beaux Arts," which begins: "About suffering they were never wrong,/ The Old Masters." Auden's poem claims that the master painters—his primary exemplar is mid-sixteenth century Dutch painter Pieter Brueghel—recognized and depicted humankind's callous indifference to the suffering of others. Their depictions are endorsed by Auden, not as the way things should be but as the way they are, and the title implies that art at its best presents this view. In "The Old and the New Masters," Jarrell initially challenges this assertion by means of example, a series of paintings elaborately and lovingly described. As readers move through his argument, they see that in order to dispute Auden's glib characterization of the old masters, Jarrell has created a gallery of his own, made up of other artists for whom the suffering in the world is the single most important fact of human existence.

Jarrell has little interest in formalistic constraints on his poetry. He intends for the subject and the dramatic occasion to determine the shape of the verse. This sixty-one-line poem is constructed of three parts. The first section sounds the Auden echo and posits Jarrell's own poem as response. It goes on to describe French Renaissance painter George de La Tour's *Saint Sebastian Mourned by Saint Irene* in such a way that the martyr's pain and the witnesses' responses to it are connected to the agony of Christ. The second part moves chronologically backward in art history to Belgian Renaissance painter Hugo van der Goes's *Nativity* from the "Portinari Altarpiece." Jarrell notes the way in which the painting manipulates time so that "everything/ That was or will be in the world is fixed/ On its small, helpless, human center." The brief third section advances to the "new masters" who "paint a subject as they please." These artists are contrasted with Italian Renaissance painter Paolo Veronese and a description of his *Feast in the House of Levi*. The poet reminds readers of how the Inquisition challenged the painter's overly realistic depiction of Christ sitting at the feast with dogs playing about his feet. Jarrell bemoans the "abstract understanding" of the "new masters," how they diminish the human element. The final image of the poem becomes both a jab at Auden and a lament for art in which Earth itself is that "small radioactive planet" off in the corner of the canvas.

One of Jarrell's foremost critics, Suzanne Ferguson, has described him not as a born poet but as a born teacher, and in a poem such as "The Old and the New Masters" that desire to instruct comes through forcefully. Just as strong as the desire to instruct is the desire to correct: Jarrell sees a mistake with dire consequences in Auden's assumptions about art, and he sets about putting it right.

Forms and Devices

This poem is fueled by allusion, and to grasp the full import of this device readers should remember that an allusion does not merely force another text into their consciousness; rather, it borrows a mood, announces a debt, calls up another context that no longer exists, reminds the reader of an absence, and interjects a tone of pity for the reader's loss. Another term for this effect is "intertextuality," the acknowledgment that no text can be read outside its relations to other, already existing texts. In this case, the poem begins by calling to mind another poem (therefore another poet) that, by its title, declares as its subject the whole realm of fine arts. Jarrell then follows Auden's lead in calling forth the exemplary works that will make his case. His careful choice of examples—religious subjects, emphatically Christian—brings into his poem the very elements that Jarrell fears are disappearing from more contemporary art: respect for the human being and for human suffering. Through such depictions of an art with a "human center," Jarrell points beyond the poetry and beyond the painting to the world of spiritual and moral value.

In Jarrell's poetry, the sentence is often more important than the line, and the sentences in this poem are built upon simple declaratives that are then embellished and extended by additional details, all connected by semicolons. By means of such sentences, the poet focuses the readers' attention on a central point of the examined canvas and then, in what seem like concentric circles, moves their eyes to a wider and wider comprehension of the total picture. To some degree that comprehension is vital. Jarrell tries not to call attention to himself or to his language by the showy employment of metaphors and other tropes (figures of speech). His similes, when he uses them, are functional rather than exploratory, as when he speaks of all the elements in a painting being pointed "like the needle of a compass." For his poem, like the paintings he so admires, the human center is the crux.

However, even though he spurns a densely figurative idiom, Jarrell's voice might be considered the other dominant device in the poem; at times its tone is that of a guide or instructor, loving, passionate, and, in the words of author Joseph Conrad, determined "to make you see." Just as the paintings are themselves focused on the perception of suffering, on attention being paid, Jarrell's carefully modulated descriptions of the painters' visions direct and sharpen readers' recognition of what is important. To this purpose, the voice is itself a rhetorical strategy, foregrounding the poet's awareness of his audience: "far off in the rocks/ You can see Mary and Joseph and their donkey/ coming to Bethlehem." By speaking to the readers directly, Jarrell involves them in the dynamic that these paintings establish: "everything/ That was or will be in the world is fixed/ On its small, helpless, human center."

Themes and Meanings

In "The Old and the New Masters," Jarrell declares that art is meant to confront and acknowledge human suffering. Through all his poems depicting the victimization of soldiers, women, and children by the great forces of what he calls "Necessity," he has staked out an aesthetic based upon the perception of suffering as a defining act for the human being. It is a kind of adoration, the kind that can be seen in versions of the Nativity. To attend to the hurt and the helpless is a human's finest expression of a godlike capacity. The alternatives to such attention become evident in the curious final stanza. Jarrell is not lamenting the disappearance of an overtly religious perspective in modern art; rather, he pleads for a humanistic, overarching sympathy and projects dire consequences in the final passage of the poem:

> Later Christ disappears, the dogs disappear: in abstract
> Understanding, without adoration, the last master puts
> Colors on canvas, a picture of the universe
> In which a bright spot somewhere in the corner
> Is the small radioactive planet men called Earth.

With the telescopic power of art to bring past, present, and future into synchronous alignment, the poem itself composes this picture with which it ends, a "painting" that seems the logical extreme of the art Auden depicts in "Musée de Beaux Arts":

> In Brueghel's *Icarus*, for instance: how everything turns away
> Quite leisurely from the disaster; the ploughman may
> Have heard the splash, the forsaken cry,
> But for him it was not an important failure . . .

It is likely that Jarrell has seen Auden's position as posturing, as a grimly stoic pose. He mockingly calls up the older poet's interpretation and shows how such an attitude makes possible far greater disaster. Auden's "Old Masters" are Jarrell's new ones. The Cold War, an imminent threat when "The Old and the New Masters" was composed, looms over the meticulous re-creations of Renaissance painting within the poem, upping the stakes. At risk here, Jarrell implies, is not a point of aesthetic interpretation but humankind's very survival. It does not seem too outlandish to read that "abstract understanding" as a version of what Jarrell sees around him in the daily discourse of print journalism and television news: Civilian deaths become "collateral damage," millions of lives cindered in seconds become "acceptable losses," and the escalation of nuclear arms development and deployment becomes a policy of "deterrence." All this abstraction threatens to displace the "human center"; the result is a small radioactive planet off in the corner of the canvas. The "last master," according to the terms of the poem, is no longer an artist at all but a dictatorial ego far gone into the realms of power for its own sake, and Jarrell subtly juxtaposes the master with a "subject" to reinforce this notion.

Nelson Hathcock

OLD HEROINES

Author: Julia Alvarez (1950-   )
Type of poem: Narrative/verse essay
First published: 1984, in *Homecoming: Poems*

The Poem

In "Old Heroines" and in the other poems in her first collection, published when she was thirty-four, Julia Alvarez tests, develops, and polishes the incipient feminist voice that emerged clearly in her subsequent novels, *How the García Girls Lost Their Accents* (1991), *In the Time of the Butterflies* (1994), *¡Yo!* (1997), and, most particularly, *In the Name of Salome* (2000). In her afterword to the 1996 edition of *Homecoming*, Alvarez claimed, "The only models I had been given by my mother and aunts and the heroines of novels were the homemaking model and the romantic model, both of which I had miserably failed at by age thirty-four."

In "Lost Heroines," Alvarez combines the homemaking model and the model provided by the romantic novels mentioned in her afterword. The poem begins with the simple question "Where do heroines go when their novels are over?" In the first ten-line stanza, Alvarez outlines the possibilities: Marry or board a train that will take the lost heroine to an old lover. These are the alternatives open to the heroines of novels. These were the two alternatives long available to women in a male-dominated society.

Alvarez's heroine boards a train that races through a countryside, perhaps Russia, perhaps Iowa. Place does not matter. Women everywhere face the same kinds of problems. The old heroine "looks out the window, the dark fields rolling by,/ or maybe the night sky grainy with stars. . . ." Seeing her face reflected in the window, she muses about her future, wondering, "how long must I still play this part?" She questions whether women are submissive pawns in a game controlled by men.

The second ten-line stanza transports the reader from the train to what lies outside its windows in the dark night. The tracks carry the train past "farmhouses bathed in pale porchlight." Alvarez ruminates on what lies behind the facades and on "the unstoried women who formed the mere backdrop/ to her beauty." These are not the heroines of novels. These are house-cleaning, bread-baking, child-tending women, the kinds of women of whom Alvarez speaks in her afterword.

Who are these women, and what are their inmost hopes and dreams? As they "drift off to sleep/ in the arms of their husbands," they become the heroines of novels, bedecked in beautiful furs, being whisked off to the excitement and sophistication of Chicago or Moscow or some other fabled city. Momentarily, they are queens—or at least princesses—in their own right. Yet the dream abruptly ends: "They wake with a start/ turning on lights to make sure of their status," and the lost heroine on the train sees the brief lights in their windows,

> from her jailhouse train
> as she rides on forever in the haze of bright dreams
> which her sorrows inspire in these happier women.

The poem, while it poses many questions about the identity of women and about their status in society, also, in twenty succinct lines, explores some of the sources of that status.

Forms and Devices

In the first stanza of "Old Heroines," Alvarez presents a generalized portrait of an old heroine, a woman who was the centerpiece of a novel that has run its course and that has probably been remaindered. In the second stanza the poet juxtaposes this portrait with that of more conventional women, farm wives whose lives are filled with domestic chores, women who dream briefly in the night that they are glamorous and lead exciting lives. They waken from their dreams jarred by the realities of their own mundane lives. As the old heroine looks from the train window to their lighted windows, however, it is she who is confined and isolated. The dichotomy of these two stanzas heightens the contrasts between the two types of women.

This poem has no consistent meter. It begins with iambs, many of them containing eleven or twelve syllables to the line. As the poem progresses, however, some of the lines, such as "though it's clear from the ending he has broken things off," are hypermetric and some deviate from iambic to anapestic lines. Only two of the poem's twenty lines rhyme, and even then the rhyme is not sufficiently close to call it exact. Line 1 ends with the word "over" and line 3 with the word "lover," which gives the suggestion of rhyme, although the *o* in each word is pronounced differently so that the rhyme is inexact.

Although Alvarez seldom depends upon such poetic devices as rhyme and alliteration—only infrequently are words in the poem alliterative, such as "She sees," "pale porchlight," "beauty, betrayals," and "wake with"—she engages her readers through strong, vivid visual imagery such as a "night sky grainy with stars" and through her use of unique diction, as "in that afterward light." The author uses effects of this sort sparingly, electing to write simply and straightforwardly, often choosing generalities over specifics to reinforce what she is saying. Certainly the center of the poem, the lost heroine, remains a generality, never emerging in detail because she represents a general type. As such she delivers a significant impact. This sort of presentation also permits and encourages readers to shape the old heroine within their own minds into whatever form they wish.

The first stanza is one of motion. The train rolls through the countryside. Images flash by, and impressions pile up in rapid succession. The second, contrasting stanza is static. It is about simple people inhabiting simple houses in rural settings. The women in Alvarez's farmhouses dream of a life they cannot experience, then wake to "make sure of their status." Alvarez uses this sharp contrast as an effective device for enhancing the impact of her poem.

Themes and Meanings

In the afterword to the 1996 edition of *Homecoming*, Alvarez, looking back on this collection a dozen years after its initial publication, claims

> In writing *Homecoming*, I can see now how fiercely I was claiming my woman's voice. As I followed my mother cleaning house, washing and ironing clothes, rolling dough, I was using the material of my housebound girl life to claim my woman's legacy.

The poet's models in life were the domestic models of the women around her as she was growing up and the romantic models provided by the heroines she encountered in the novels she read. She was personally incapable of becoming what either of these models represented.

In this poem, Alvarez, as a modern woman and an emerging feminist, deals with the theme of women resisting prevailing sentiments about what women should be. The only men in the poem are the "he" in the first stanza, the old lover who "has broken things off," and the husbands in whose arms the wives in the second stanza fall asleep. The women in the poem are passive creatures whose lives seemingly revolve around men.

The old heroine has had her day. She now rides in isolation toward some unstated end. She sees her face reflected in the train window, "a face still dramatic,/ pale and young in that afterward light." Life has passed her by, as it does all old heroines, both those drawn from the pages of novels and those in real life.

There are, on the other hand, the real women, the wives, the mothers, the women who, although they treasure their dreams, are realistic enough to know that they will never fulfill them. They can, in their sleep, concoct for themselves other, more exciting lives, but in the end, they waken and turn on the lights "to make sure of their status." This is perhaps the most controlling line in the poem because it suggests not only that women cannot move beyond where they now find themselves but also that they really do not wish to.

One might expect Alvarez, as a feminist, to rant and rave about this unequal situation, but instead she seems to accept it. A dominant theme in the poem seems to be one that has to do with dreams. Just as Alvarez derived her early self-image from women who represented domesticity and from the women she encountered in the novels she read, she has in this poem constructed two worlds, one of dreams, the other of realities.

The two kinds of women presented in this poem—the lost heroine and the ordinary housewives—do not meet and never interact within the poem. The ideal is indeed eclipsed by the real. The old heroine "rides on forever in the haze of bright dreams/ which her sorrows inspire in these happier women." Alvarez, for any feminism she might profess, in this poem casts her lot with the ordinary housewives, whom she calls the happier women.

R. Baird Shuman

OLD IRONSIDES

Author: Oliver Wendell Holmes (1809-1894)
Type of poem: Dramatic monologue
First published: 1830; collected in *Poems*, 1836

The Poem

Oliver Wendell Holmes wrote "Old Ironsides" in ironic agreement with the news that the famous frigate USS *Constitution*—nicknamed "Old Ironsides" because of its formidable strength—would soon be demolished. The poem exalts the ship to elegiac status in three octaves (stanzas of eight lines), written in alternating tetrameter and trimeter syllabic accents. Holmes composed the now-famous poem immediately upon reading of the planned demolition in the *Boston Daily Advertiser.* The report he read, drawn from the *New York Journal of Commerce*, called for the preservation of the ship.

"Old Ironsides" begins with the word "Ay," an echo of the traditional "Aye-aye, sir" used by sailors to acknowledge orders from a superior officer. By using "Ay" rather than a simple "Yes," Holmes sets the tone of the poem, allowing the speaker to appear knowledgeable of sailing matters as well as willing to obey the authority demanding the demolition of the ship. The "Ay" also involves the reader in tacit agreement with the planned demolition. The rest of the line calls upon the destroyers of the ship to tear her "tattered ensign" down. The ensign, or flag, symbolized the power of the United States Navy, especially after "Old Ironsides" defeated the British ship *Guerrière* in the war of 1812. Holmes also recognizes the length of service the ship had given when he writes of the flag that it had long "waved on high."

Holmes goes on to describe the joy the ship has created over the years, with "many an eye" dancing to see the ensign waving as a "banner in the sky." The ensign has overseen battles fought amid shouts and the roar of cannon. Holmes refers respectfully to the ship as a "meteor of the ocean air," noting that it will no longer "sweep the clouds." The comparison of the ship with a meteor may have come from Holmes's own fascination with meteors. In 1830 almost any weather phenomenon or light in the sky would be described as a "meteor," but Holmes was particularly enamored of comets, writing another poem that same year describing the devastation a comet could bring to earth.

Holmes continues to celebrate the ship's history of service by portraying the blood of heroes turning the ship's decks red—amid which the defeated enemy has been forced to kneel. He then enlarges the reader's view of the ship, placing it among the "hurrying" wind and white waves, a stormy sea that will no longer feel the "tread" of its victory. Holmes uses a reference from classical mythology to describe those who would demolish the ship, calling them "harpies of the shore." These execrable half-human birds of prey are vile creatures that desire to "pluck" the frigate he characterizes as an ennobled "eagle of the sea."

Holmes suggests in the last stanza that it would have been better if "Old Ironsides" could have met a more fitting end by being shattered and sunk in the open sea, where she might have a grave in the "mighty deep." In an extravagant scene he imagines her "holy flag" being nailed to the mast and her worn sails set so that she could sail out into a storm and be given to the lightning and wind, the "god of storms."

Forms and Devices

Without doubt "Old Ironsides" was composed as a protest, somewhat comparable to a letter to the editor. It is written as a dramatic monologue in which one speaker conveys a persuasive message to all. The poem is also an example of "occasional" poetry—a form in which the poem celebrates or discusses a specific event. Holmes had already established himself as a writer of occasional poems, reading his entertaining verses before audiences at school and publishing them in the Harvard student magazine. In "Old Ironsides" the occasion is the plan to scrap the ship. Holmes wrote to point out the gallant service of the ship to its country and to scorn plans to end her career in an ignoble way.

The meter of the poem is established through alternating lines of four and then three stresses. Holmes, who was a physician as well as a writer and teacher, later suggested that verse stresses may well be in keeping with the individual body's pulse and respiration, thus accounting for the differences in rhythms and line length used by different poets. "Old Ironsides" is written in a steady rhythm, an appealing quality as illustrated by the popularity of lullabies, rhythmic games, and modern musical forms such as rock and roll and rap. Rhythmic verse is also very much a part of the oral tradition in which long passages of poetry are memorized for recitation.

Rhyme is another appealing poetic element that Holmes uses, in this case adapting a pattern of end-rhyme: *ababcdcd*. Nonrhyming words also appear in order to maintain meaning and avoid inverted structures. In the first stanza the second and fourth lines end in "sky" and "high" respectively, while the sixth and eighth lines end with "roar" and "more." Six of the eight lines in the second stanza end in rhyming words: "blood" and "flood," "foe" and "below," and "knee" and "sea." The last stanza is similar to the first, rhyming "wave" with "grave" as well as "sail" and "gale."

Critics have disparaged "Old Ironsides" for its common imagery—"battle shout," "cannon's roar," and so on. Additional criticism of the poem has labeled it a rhetorical exercise or a work of propaganda. In later collections of his work, Holmes himself relegated "Old Ironsides" to a section he called "Earlier Poems," in which he explained that its composition had been an "impromptu outburst of feeling." However, readers still enjoy the imagery of "Old Ironsides," especially such vivid phrases as "conquered knee" and "red with heroes' blood." Readers also respond to the deeply inspiring tone of the poem, especially inasmuch as Holmes never overtly argues for restoring and preserving the ship, the ultimate result he inspired.

Themes and Meanings

The overall theme of "Old Ironsides" is implied rather than stated because of the ironic structure Holmes used. Thus, his meaning results from the emotional experience readers feel as Holmes recounts the ship's history. Many readers in Boston would have been quite familiar with the USS *Constitution*, one of the first three frigates built for the United States Navy, as it had been constructed in Boston Harbor by local workmen. Launched in 1797, it had outmaneuvered and sailed faster than enemy ships, earning new respect for its country. The nickname "Old Ironsides" referred to the ship's strong oak sides that had proven nearly impenetrable to enemy cannonballs; the actual use of iron as a material for strengthening the sides of ships would not be achieved for many years to come.

In 1830, when Holmes read of the planned demolition, the ship had seen heavy service and was considered old and outdated. After quickly composing his poem during a single morning, Holmes sent it to the newspaper in which he had read the demolition notice. It was soon published by the paper and rapidly attracted support from patriotic Americans anxious to save the ship, first in Boston and subsequently in other locales as newspapers up and down the East Coast reprinted the poem. Holmes was only twenty-one years old at the time.

The stature of the poem derives largely from the manner in which it celebrates the dead who had manned the ship and fought on its decks for the honor and preservation of the United States. The brilliant defeat of the *Guerrière* in 1812 had come at a time when national morale was at a low ebb, and the win was followed by another victory, the destruction of HMS *Java*. The performance of "Old Ironsides" in the War of 1812 clearly helped to ensure that the United States would remain independent of British hegemony. The poem thus venerates the history of the entire country and appeals to its readers' patriotism. In a Romantic vein, the poem also celebrates the glory of victory in war.

"Old Ironsides" became a familiar declamation piece as students in nineteenth century schoolrooms recited the poem from memory, often with one arm raised as a gesture of patriotic reverence. In his conclusion, Holmes suggests that it would be better if the ship had shattered and sunk rather than be destroyed at harbor. This vision of a more fitting ending for the famous ship fired the imaginations and hearts of readers and listeners whose sentiment ultimately prevailed. Repeated restorations to maintain the ship have been performed over the more than two hundred years since its launch. The USS *Constitution* has been permanently moored at the Charlestown Navy Yard in Boston Harbor since 1934, a part of a National Historic Site at the end of the Freedom Trail.

Margaret A. Dodson

OLD MASTERS

Author: Zbigniew Herbert (1924-1998)
Type of poem: Lyric
First published: 1983, as "Dawni mistrzowie," in *Raport z oblężonego miasta i inne wiersze*; English translation collected in *Report from the Besieged City and Other Poems*, 1985

The Poem

"Old Masters" consists of thirty-five lines of free verse, divided into short verse paragraphs of two or four lines which, though irregular, often resemble stanzas. The poem is broken into two main sections, demarcated by a shift in the left margin; the first section is descriptive, while the second verges on invocation or prayer.

The title refers to the anonymous master-painters of the early Renaissance in Italy, in the eleventh or twelfth century. These artists painted scenes of religious importance and were employed by the Roman Catholic Church to depict events in the life of Christ, the miracles of saints, and well-known figures from the Bible. Many of them were themselves monks or were closely affiliated with religious orders.

The poem begins by emphasizing the anonymity of those Old Masters; they were not concerned, Zbigniew Herbert says, with signing their names to their work in order to achieve fame or notoriety in years to come. Rather, they suppressed their artistic egos, preferring to "dissolve" into the religious wonders they were depicting. As artists, they strove not for personal glory, but to portray the glory of God.

Herbert uses the Old Masters' native Italian language when he describes their paintings in order to draw himself and the reader closer, linguistically, to the textures and visions that they would have experienced. The reader hears the actual words the painters used. The pink towers "di citta sue mare," meaning "of the city above the sea," may refer either to Venice—where many of these painters lived—or to the celestial city—the New Jerusalem of Revelation—which was often depicted floating above the earth's surface. The life "della Beata Umilta" refers to Saint Humility, or Rosana, a pious abbess of the thirteenth century. That "they dissolved/ in sogno/ miracolo/ crocifissione"—into dream, miracle, and crucifixion—suggests the emerging oneness of artist and religious subject matter.

Herbert asserts that the Old Masters discovered "paradise" in their art. Their paintings are "mirrors," he suggests, in which to view the divinity in the self, but they are not "for us" in the present spiritual state of alienation, disaffectation, and what he elsewhere calls "disinheritance." They can have meaning only for those who have somehow been "chosen" or sanctified.

The second section of the poem is a prayer for this sanctity, which calls upon the Old Masters as intercessors. Herbert pleads with them, as his brother artists, to help him defeat the satanic temptations of fame and pride and to rediscover the holy "Visitation" that has passed him by. This plea seems rather strange coming from the mouth of an avowed doubter and apparent agnostic, but nevertheless carries a large amount of spiritual and poetic energy.

Forms and Devices

Herbert's streamlined Polish translates extremely well into other languages, and the English here captures his clipped, telegraphic style, as well as the poetic dynamism of his finely crafted imagery. Herbert's poetry is not pretty or opulent, but strives on the whole for both visual clarity and structural balance. His work has sometimes been characterized as "antithetical"—concerned with holding opposite worldviews or contrary figures in tension in the same poem—but here one finds only a hint of such opposition, when he contrasts the perfection of the Old Masters' paintings with the present-day fallen state; rather than exploit the ironies of, or discontinuities between, past and present, Herbert chooses to try to immerse himself in the art and technology of his masters, to turn away from the present and rediscover a lost "paradise."

The tone of the poem is not antithetical, ironic, or argumentative, but pietistic; it recalls the supplications and prayers of a catholic liturgy. Herbert merely substitutes artist for saint as his divine instructor and intercessor. Accordingly, the text is characterized by anaphora, an incantatory repetition of the same words or grammatical forms at the beginning of a syntactic unit, as in "they dissolved . . . they found . . . they drowned" or "I call on you . . . I call upon you. . . ." The last four lines of the poem repeat an invocation, attempting to name the nameless, godlike painters through their various works. Indeed, the original Polish of this section further emphasizes the sense of a writer calling out in desperation to his lost gods, when the poet employs a rarely used vocative case: "Malarzu. . . ." (*Malarz* means "painter"). Herbert's anaphoric style creates an aura of beatification and divine wisdom around the subjects of the poem; one senses, through the tone of the poetry, the spiritual qualities of their paintings.

"Old Masters," as with most of Herbert's other poems, uses little or no punctuation. Herbert demarcates the ends of sentences or of grammatical units either with line breaks or with separate verse paragraphs. His lack of periods or commas does not impair the clarity of his writing. On the contrary, by eliminating unnecessary typographical clutter from his pages, he gives the reader a sense of transparency and simplicity, which, though sometimes deceptive, nevertheless invites one to participate closely in his work, just as he would "melt" into the work of the Old Masters. The reader feels no offensive rhetoric or grandiloquence in his poem.

Furthermore, when combined with his sparing use of initial capitals, this lack of punctuation gives Herbert's verse a fluidity across the frequent line breaks, and a sense of motion that plays against the innate tendency of a syntax to close off into discrete sentences, implanting a type of musical tension into his poetry. The reader hears the pull, in Herbert's work, of a pure, musical continuum against the logical order of proper grammar.

Themes and Meanings

Like many of Herbert's earlier poems, "Old Masters" expresses a profound dissatisfaction with the present state of the world and a longing for a better, more meaningful way of life. This poem, however, differs substantially from most of its companion poems in *Report from the Besieged City* in two important ways. First, "Old Masters" is more deliberately nostalgic than the other pieces in the volume. The contrast between past and present is implied more than actualized, and Herbert dwells at length on the sweetness and beauty of the Old Masters' art, into which he longs to escape. The present state of the world holds almost no interest for him, except as something to be radically changed. Second, Herbert's usual ironic complexity is almost entirely absent here; gone are the antithetical twists and layered juxtapositions that characterize the "Mr. Cogito" poems of this volume. Instead, Herbert offers the reader a surprisingly candid and direct appeal for an imaginative, sentimental return to bygone days of spiritual unity and artistic selflessness and longs for a recapitulation for a Renaissance that had run its course over six hundred years ago.

It is peculiar, as well, that the theological center of the Old Masters' work—God—goes unmentioned in the text, as if Herbert, while crying out for the values of a lost mastery, cannot bring himself to pronounce the deity's name without violating his own post-Nietzschean sense of bathos and overt sentimentality. To say "God" would be to go too far in a world where God has been declared dead. Herbert finds himself, in the poem, performing a difficult balancing act, faced, on the one hand, with a great need to combat his "hard moments of doubt" with some sort of stable value system and, on the other hand, with an inherently modern, ironic sensibility that does not trust itself enough to utter the name of God without calling its motives and position into question. As well as of a longing for the spirituality of the Old Masters, then, Herbert's prayer reminds the reader of his irreconcilable differences from them.

Kevin McNeilly

OLGA POEMS

Author: Denise Levertov (1923-1997)
Type of poem: Elegy
First published: 1966, in *The Sorrow Dance*

The Poem

The 182 lines of this poem (its subtitle identifies its subject—"Olga Levertoff, 1914-1964") are divided into six major sections that range in length from fourteen to forty-seven lines. The two longest sections are further divided; section 3 has three numbered parts and section 5 has two. The poem begins with a recollection of the poet and her sister in an early domestic scene: The older sister kneels before a gas fire, undressing while her seven-year-old sister watches from her bed. The memory of Olga's physical maturity is followed by an image of Olga now: "bones and tatters of flesh in earth."

Section 2 shifts to a vision of Olga active in a political cause, wanting "to shout the world to its senses . . . to browbeat" as she reacted to the slum conditions she had seen as a child. The memory ends with Denise Levertov addressing Olga as the "Black one," a (dark-complected?) political activist whose heart was alight with the white candle of her political commitment.

The third section is divided into three glimpses of the politically committed Olga. The first returns to a time when Olga, muttering *"Everything flows,"* attacks "human puppets." The poet, a child still, felt "alien" to her sister's muttered words but also felt a link between them and lines from a hymnal they both loved. Next, Olga is with her sister "in the garden . . . we thought sometimes too small for our grand destinies." Even then Olga's passion for reform was active, aroused by her "dread" of "the rolling dark/ oncoming river." Olga's "bulwarks" against it were to perform trivial chores, write verses, pick "endless arguments," and press on to "change the course of the river." Olga's "rage for order" disordered her "pilgrimage" and drove her to "hide among strangers," still determined to "rearrange all mysteries in a new light." In the third image, Olga is again the "Black one," an evil spirit, still anguished, riding fiercely ("as Tartars ride mares") through bad years. In a dream, Levertov sees Olga, "haggard and rouged," standing in a slum street. During these "pilgrim years," Levertov lost "all sense, almost" of what Olga was experiencing.

The fourth section opens in a hospital room where Olga lies ill and in pain, her "hatreds . . . burned out." Seeing her sister "afloat on a sea/ of love and pain," Levertov remembers one of Olga's favorite cadences and sees the past (Olga's, the world's) reduced to a "sick bone" except for her sister's passionate belief and political ambition.

The fifth section begins with a quotation from an old poem about lusty youth. Olga once put it to a music that pervades the poet's own life, as Olga's life has. This thought recalls the grassy place of their childhood, where Olga spun a magical tale about a tree root leading them into a nether world. Other lines from the old poem follow as she recalls their entering the world of "silent mid-Essex churches" adorned with effigies of medieval figures. The reminiscence evokes more lines from the same poem with which the section begins.

The second part of the fifth section follows Olga the year she was "most alone," revisiting "the old roads" and sights she and the poet had explored together as children. Now, Olga finds changes, still anguished. The winter's "damp still air" and frost, her poverty, the loss of her children—all reflect Olga's depressed circumstances and hint of political failure, the stage lights gone out, the "theater" empty and locked. The vision ends with an image of Olga in her room, reading books "that winter," and outdoors among the furrows and strange cries of birds, which the poet herself had once longed to embrace, only Olga was then "trudging after" her own "anguish."

The final section recalls Olga's "brown gold" eyes, which the poet has always seen while crossing the bridge over the river Roding and "by other streams in other countries." The thought brings back another moment in their childhood when Olga's passion drives her through the Ludwig van Beethoven sonatas "savagely." The poet recalls "the fear" in Olga's eyes in a photograph and wonders where the fear went as Olga passed through troubled years, what kept the "candle" lit as she journeyed. Lines suggest that Olga is last seen in an "obscure wood" with a house; from its open door, a hand beckons to Olga "in welcome."

Turning toward her own life, Levertov has seen in the "many brooks in the world . . . many questions" her own eyes want to ask of Olga's. In those eyes, the poet glimpses "some vision/ of festive goodness" behind a gaze that is "hard, or veiled, or shining" but ultimately "unknowable."

Forms and Devices

The open structure of the poem is evident in both line and stanza. Stanzaic lengths range from one to thirty-six (in section 6) lines, the most common lengths being two and three lines. Only section 2 contains stanzas of equal length—all triads—though stanzas of equal length are often grouped together throughout the first five sections, and a pattern of diminishing lengths is evident in sections 1, 3, and 4. Stanzaic patterning and length subtly pace the reader through the poet's recollections and experience, diminishing in section 1, advancing regularly through section 2, diminishing again in part 1 of section 3, and so on. The pauses within the stanzas and lines themselves counterpoint or modulate—or refine—the structure that is developing on the more general level. Clearly, the poet has shaped the lines and stanzas to keep time with her experience of her subject, to shape and ultimately to understand it.

Line length is the immediate expression of Levertov's mood as the ideas and recollections surface and form, as it were, pools of meaning, threads of understanding, and strings on which the poet plays her revelations about Olga and explores her present relationship to past lives. No predetermined pattern could accommodate this shaping force, and no other rhythms but those discovered in the making of the poem could express Levertov's experience. Even the spaces between stanzas represent more than pauses or shifts; they are leaps in Levertov's experience from one perception to another. Within the grasp of her own search for understanding, the poet lets the lines fall as they must, stopping on a natural pause—"To change,/ to change the course of the river!"—or continuing across the "abyss" created by spaces between stanzas. The result is a naturalness of rhythm and voice only occasionally intruded upon by such "poetic" devices as enjambment: "setting herself/ to sift cinders."

The more characteristic use of line ending may be seen in lines 37-38: "there was a white/ candle in your heart." There, the pause on "white" does more than rhyme would to emphasize both attitude and meaning. The poet needs fidelity to tell the truth—Olga's candle was white—but knows that a flash of color expresses a higher truth, her sister's purity of heart, set against the background of the previous line: "Black one, black one." In this way, the poet discovers the image, the placement of a word, and line rhythm that reveal her understanding. At the same time, these three lines conclude another understanding—begun at line 15, "The high pitch of/ nagging insistence," and continued through the psychological counterpointing of Olga's strident political "rage" and her younger sister's teasing—which concludes with the taunting rhythm of "Black one, black one."

Music, which was at the heart of Levertov's relationship with her sister, now helps render the poet's experience of that relationship. One element of the poem's imagery is its shape, and certainly its rhythms create more than a felt experience. If a symphony can inspire images in the minds of the audience, this poem's modulations bring to the surface of the reader's mind images that "rhyme" with, or correspond to, the ones Levertov actually provides. The very rightness of the poet's images is established by the very rightness of the poem's rhythms.

Themes and Meanings

An attempt to resolve the poet's conflicts regarding her sister informs the entire poem, perhaps is its *raison d'etre*, and certainly determines its rises and falls, its ongoing insistence, its tabulations of Olga's activities, its discords and harmonies. The poem's many breaks, stops and starts, and shifts in rhythm and mood suggest a similar array within the poet's own feelings about Olga. Without being fitful, the poet displays conflicting attitudes toward her sister. The poem opens with the poet as a child eyeing her sister undressed and already well developed. How did the child feel: suspicious—"beady-eyed in the bed"—unconcerned—"or drowsy was I? My head/ a camera"—or envious—"Her breasts/ round, round, and/ dark-nippled"?

Olga's political activities also stir conflicting feelings in the poet. As a child, she mocked Olga's social consciousness, and she has felt the sting of Olga's passionate nature, felt the alienation that came from Olga's superior knowledge and "rage for order," all the while feeling a close bond between herself and her sister—"but linked to words we loved." Pity follows Olga through her "bad years," her "pilgrim years," her hospitalization, to the end. These images of a harried, driven, "burned out" Olga are interrupted by a recollection of the sisters as they played in the sylvan setting of their childhood. This magical tour is the closest the sisters get in the poet's journey toward a synthesis of feeling and understanding, for in this brief interlude, the poet confesses, "your life winds in me."

Levertov's vision is fluid from beginning to end, as is evident in the water imagery and the many references to water, music, and cadence. Structurally, this theme is expressed in the unendingness of many of the lines—the dashes point the reader onward as the current of a river carries one toward the sea. The cascading lines and stanzas are evidence that the poet is composing her own feelings and shaping her own acknowledgment of her sister's life and influence on her. The statement *"Everything flows"* might stand as an epigraph of this elegy and an epitaph to Olga's life. The sisters were musical, the poem is saying—one was, one is. Olga's life, played out with the same passion that informed her playing Beethoven "savagely," was an endurance "in the falls and rapids of the music." The events of her life were the "arpeggios" that rang out, that were absorbed into the younger sister's poetics and played like a psychic keyboard. They compose themselves into the images—tree roots, rivers, streams, lines from poems and songs—that run through the poet's own self: "you set the words to a tune so plaintive/ it plucks its way through my life as through a wood . . . your life winds in me."

The poem seems to ask whether the myriad notes, however fluidly shaped and thematically harmonized, can coalesce in the poet's understanding. In the final section, the dominant images—water, music, lyrical consonance—are brought together in a crowd of lines that review the poet's main subject, Olga's passionate and apparently sterile politicism, and call up Olga's "brown gold" eyes and the candle. Earlier, the candle symbolizes Olga's purity and political rage; here, it is "compassion's candle." Acceptance marks the final mood—"'a hand beckons/ in welcome.'" Yet whether Olga herself ever took the hand remains unknown. The "rolling dark/ oncoming river" flows onward, becomes the "'selva oscura.'" Did the river engulf Olga? Did the dark wood envelop her and extinguish the candle? The answer is as mysterious as the final vision of Olga herself, her eyes hinting of "festive goodness" but hard, veiled, shining, unknowable. The final ellipsis symbolizes Levertov's failure to arrive at a conclusive understanding of her relationship to her sister—and a triumph of the two sisters' belief in the eternal flow, in which the poet has discovered an unending confluence.

Bernard E. Morris

OMEROS

Author: Derek Walcott (1930-   )
Type of poem: Epic
First published: 1990

The Poem

Omeros is a searching, evocative 325-page modern epic poem. It is searching in the sense that it has a mission: to right the wrongs of history by illuminating shadowed chapters of events in the lives of ignored or victimized races and individuals. It is evocative in the sense that it is sophisticated, multilayered, complexly symbolic, and artfully musical. It is also vigorous human drama. Largely on the basis of its publication—but also in recognition of earlier published poetry and drama—its mixed-race author, born on the Caribbean island of St. Lucia and teaching at Boston University, was awarded the Nobel Prize in Literature on December 10, 1992.

Literally, *Omeros* gives the impression of being loosely chronological, set on St. Lucia and spanning one day—from sunrise, when fishermen are felling laurel trees to fashion into canoes, to sunset and then a full moon on the sea after a successful day of mackerel fishing. Figuratively, however, the poem is far more complicated, spanning as much as three hundred years in its many time-warp flashbacks. Walcott tells several different stories, parts of which are embedded in other stories, so that to begin to make sense of the poem the reader must attend carefully to the identity of the narrator, or rather, narrators, who are often unidentified.

The cast of characters in *Omeros* is one of simple Caribbean fishing people with derivative Greek names—Hector, Achille, Helen, Philoctete—who swill white rum, swear in French patois, bounce to Bob Marley reggae in a blockorama dance, and play out their lusts and feuds in the hot sun. There are also a pair of long-married, decent colonialist settlers, Irish homebody Maud Plunkett and former British soldier Dennis Plunkett, who have moved to St. Lucia to retire. Maud dies and is buried during the course of the poem. For a time the seductive black beauty Helen is employed in the Plunkett household, though she is dismissed for her arrogance and for stealing clothing items. Though Maud gives Helen some money out of pity for her unborn child, she refuses to reinstate her. Helen is the object of jealousy between brawny fishermen Achille and Hector, and she is uncertain which man has impregnated her. Hector gives up the sea to drive tourists around the island in his transport van. After he dies in a crash, Helen moves in with Achille to raise her baby, though the couple cannot agree on what the child should be named.

One of the poem's few non-Caribbean episodes takes place at the Standing Rock Indian Reservation right before the massacre at Wounded Knee, focusing on a minor but intriguing historical figure. Catherine Weldon, a well-heeled East Coast widow, in 1889 decided to travel west with her adolescent son under the auspices of the National Indian Defense Association. She worked for a time in Buffalo Bill Cody's touring

Wild West Show, actively protested the government mistreatment of the Sioux, and served as personal helpmeet to Chief Sitting Bull. Her story, occupying fewer than twenty pages of the poem, culminates with her pitiable, solitary death on a winter night in her rocking chair, her finances depleted, her son having died of tetanus, the Sioux bent on ignoring her pleas to keep peace with the government by refusing to participate in the Ghost Dance.

The most intriguing and elusive character in the poem is the shape-shifting narrator, who suffers many things and spellbinds the reader with his protean nature. The poem is named for this figure, which is also place, sound, and object:

> *O* was the conch-shell's invocation, *mer* was
> both mother and sea in our Antillean patois,
> *os*, a grey bone, and the white surf as it crashes
> and spreads its sibilant collar on a lace shore.
> Omeros was the crunch of dry leaves, and the washes
> that echoed from a cave-mouth when the tide has ebbed.

This chameleon figure becomes, by turns of page, the ancient Greek poet Homer, an inanimate carved white marble bust, a blind old man named Seven Seas who keeps a khaki dog, Omeros the salt-sea life-force and inspiration, and Walcott the poet, who visits his mother in a nursing home, who is jilted by a promiscuous Greek lover named Antigone (whom he fruitlessly pursues throughout Boston), and who experiences a profoundly liberating sea-change that ends his midlife crisis. This transformation in poet Walcott is brought about when he follows another character, named Dante, through the St. Lucian sulfur pits known as Maleboge, a difficult, purgative journey that liberates him to own, to verbalize, and to celebrate the history and identity of his native people. They come to symbolize the dispossessed, displaced, and discriminated against peoples of all time.

Forms and Devices

Omeros is divided into seven books and sixty-four chapters, each with three parts or movements. The first book is the longest, having thirteen chapters, and the fourth book, with four chapters, is the shortest. There is an identifiable theme to each book, which is introduced near the end of the previous book. The first book, appropriately, introduces all the important characters and hints at all the major themes. Near the end of book 2, Achille is on a fishing trip and follows a sea-swift, an action that provides a segue into an important dream vision and reunion with his now-dead father in Africa in book 3. The poet narrator visits his elderly mother at the end of book 3, which sets the course for book 4, with its angst-filled present-day wanderings of the poet and the historical tragedy of the Sioux Indians right before the Battle of Wounded Knee. Book 5, even as it continues the anguished tale of the Sioux and the Ghost Dance, widens the voyages to Portugal, Spain, England, and Ireland, glimpsing black slaves, Greek slaves, and a Polish waitress in Canada, all shadows of diaspora and exodus.

Book 6 brings the narrator and the focus of the story back "home," to the island and characters of St. Lucia. It ends in an African ritual dance in the capital city of Castries. This location sets the stage for the purgation and catharsis of the final book, in which Dennis Plunkett sees a loving vision of his dead wife in a seance, the poet reaches his inner vision and peace through a trial by fire, the sea-swift figuratively stitches up wounds in the soul of the world by joining two hemispheres together (the old world and the new), and the supremacy and eternity of the sea is affirmed and celebrated. The poem ends with the phrase "the sea was still going on," and the past progressive verb suggests that past hopes, dreams, fears, and realities will continue intentionally into the present and the future. Now and ever, the salt sea, the origin of life, offers blessing and renewed and invigorated life for those who intuit and accept it. The source of all salves for the wounds of all of the characters is, directly or indirectly, the sea.

Omeros is written in eight thousand lines of terza rima stanzas. Its meter is irregular. The rhyme scheme is often unpredictable, unlike that of traditional epics, which tend to maintain a very strict rhyme scheme and meter. Walcott's poem is full of exquisite and uncommon versification. It is an ambitious enterprise and a technical masterpiece, with rhymes varying from *rime riche* (rhyming words with identical sounds but different meanings, such as "stair" and "stare") to assonance and eye-rhyme. Walcott seems to be showing off his artistry, giving readers a catalog of all the varieties of rhyming possibilities. Yet nowhere is the language strained: It is fluid, musical, and even simple, and where appropriate it follows rhythms of conversation or evokes sounds of ocean waves.

Walcott's lines are visually, though not metrically, the same length, and the number of lines in a stanza (three) seems to be fixed, with one notable exception—an anguished passage of thirty-four lines of tetrameter couplets at the very center of the poem, where the loveless poet narrator contemplates his empty house. The form uses couplets, but the poet himself is sadly solitary. The section begins, "House of umbrage, house of fear,/ house of multiplying air/ House of memories that grow/ like shadows out of Allan Poe." This section details the heartbreak of a failed marriage and the pangs of loneliness. The poet feels trapped and cursed, his house is "unlucky," and he would "uncurse" it "by rites of genuflecting verse." He wishes that he could "unhouse" his house because it is such a hard, cold place, and the only guests are "fears." The placement of this section in the heart of the poem reveals the tragedy within the poet's heart, his anguish and angst. It is fall, a time of dying things, and the section follows episodes of various losses, abandonments, disappearances, "castaways," and "dead-end[s] of love." Following this section the poet expresses a more general nostalgia for transitory things, which is preparatory to the Catherine Weldon and Sioux Indians section.

Omeros is an epic poem that, in many significant aspects, reverses epic convention. The very writing of an epic in the late twentieth century is unusual; the long narrative form flourished with Homer, Vergil, Dante, and Johann Wolfgang von Goethe. While traditional epics begin with an invocation, *Omeros* ends with one that is both a salutation and a leave-taking:

I sang of quiet Achille, Afolabe's son,

. . . .

who had no passport, since the horizon needs none,

. . . .

whose end, when it comes, will be a death by water

. . . .

. . . I sang the only slaughter
that brought him delight, and that from necessity—
of fish, sang the channels of his back in the sun.

I sang our wide country, the Caribbean Sea.

The passage continues, "but now the idyll dies . . . // . . . let the deep hymn/ of the Caribbean continue my epilogue."

While epics usually chronicle a journey or a quest, *Omeros* is fabricated of many diverse voyages—some highly charged, others slight—that are means to a more important end: gaining meaningful insight into what matters the most—first for self, then for the world. Walcott explores why traditional historical accounts are problematic and seeks to flesh out incompleteness and inaccuracies. This is, finally, the poet-narrator's means of coming to terms with himself, of owning up to his mixed identity.

Themes and Meanings

Omeros is about memory, history, and identity, and these issues are explored from both a personal and a global perspective. An intriguing aspect of Walcott's art is his merging of elements of personal biography with global history. For example, the invalid mother whom the poem's narrator visits refers to "Roddy" and "Pam" (Walcott's siblings in real life) in speaking with him and calls him "Warwick's son" (Warwick is the actual name of Walcott's father). An important thread in the poem is the poet's trying to solve a midlife crisis that is rooted both in living in an empty house and in experiencing writer's block. *Omeros* celebrates the hard-won discovery of the subject best suited to the poet's individual expression: his own island people of St. Lucia. The affirmation of parental and ancestral ties is connected with this personal and ethnic exploration. It is explored, for example, in the beginning of book 3, where Achille figuratively goes back to Africa and spends time with his father, Afolabe. Their anguished discussion of naming and identity resonates hauntingly with the experiences of black slaves enduring the Middle Passage. A slave was customarily renamed by his owner at the time of purchase.

The narrator-poet tells readers that he has "stitched" wounds into his characters because "affliction is one theme/ of this work." The biggest wound of all is the most obvious: a weeping, starfish-shaped sore on Philoctetes's shin that he incurred from a rusty anchor and that he moans about throughout the entire poem. For a dollar he will display it to tourists so they can photograph it. In despair, he drinks himself into daily oblivion at the No Pain Cafe and tears out tender white yams from his own garden by the roots in frustration. Finally, blessedly, he is healed by a voodoo woman named Ma Kilman, owner of the No Pain Cafe, who bathes his leg with tincture of an elusive ill-smelling herb that she has gleaned in the forest, having followed a line of ants in her search. Significantly, the seed of the healing herb originated in Africa and was carried to St. Lucia in the beak of a sea-swift.

Bird imagery is very important in the poem: flight, crossings and criss-crossings, building bridges and connections between hemispheres, races, and generations. Maud Plunkett, who is homesick for Ireland, stitches an elaborate quilt that displays the rich variety of birds that inhabit St. Lucia, many of which have immigrated just as she has:

> The African swallow, the finch from India
> now spoke the white language of a tea-sipping tern
> with the Chinese nightingales on a shantung screen,
>
> while the Persian falcon, whose cry leaves a scar
> on the sky till it closes, saw the sand turn green,
> the dunes to sea, understudying the man-o'-war,
>
> talking the marine dialect of the Caribbean
> with nightjars, finches, and swallows, each origin
> enriching the islands to which their cries were sewn.

Maud's quilt, symbol of cultural diversity and harmony, becomes her shroud in death.

Cultural blending and melding is a central theme that infuses almost every aspect of *Omeros*. The simple Caribbean fishermen's names connect them with Greek gods. Black Helen is as beautiful and desired as her Greek counterpart who ignited a war; the poem compares them—"one marble, one ebony"—and seems to prefer the one who is "here and alive." Helen's identity as a woman is also merged with the island of St. Lucia; Walcott finds connections in the entomology of their names: "the island was once/ named Helen." Helen's promiscuous vacillation between Hector and Achille is compared with the island's having changed hands fourteen times between the French and the English before it gained its independence in 1979. The narrator-poet, of mixed racial heritage, seeks to re-enter his "reversible world," aware that his "disembodied trunk [is] split/ along the same line of reflection that halved Achille." Connecting essential halves is both method and message of the poem.

Jill B. Gidmark

ON A BOARD OF RASPBERRY AND PURE GOLD

Author: Osip Mandelstam (1891-1938)
Type of poem: Lyric
First published: 1964, as "Na doske malinovoi, chervonnoi," in *Sobranie sochinenii*;
   English translation collected in *Poems*, 1973

The Poem

"On a Board of Raspberry and Pure Gold," written by Osip Mandelstam in 1937, is a poem of sixteen lines. The Russian original, written in rhymed trochaic lines of five to seven feet and organized in a single stanza, has been translated by Clarence Brown and W. S. Merwin as a lyric of four stanzas in free blank verse, which, however, preserves a trochaic tendency. The poem offers the reader a winter landscape and the poet's reflections upon it. In fact, there is abundant testimony, from the poet's widow, Nadezhda Mandelstam, and others, that the poem presents a view of the old city of Voronezh, seen from the vicinity of 40 Kaliaev Street, the home of Natasha Shtempel', a young teacher who was virtually Mandelstam's sole confidante during much of the Mandelstams' exile to her town in 1934-1937. Situated on hills above a high river-bank, old Voronezh (much of which would be burned down under the Nazi occupation) was very picturesque; the neighborhood portrayed in the poem was one of single-story houses descending down the hillsides to the Don River—"half town half river-bank," as the poem puts it.

The poem's opening line (which is also used in lieu of a title, since Mandelstam did not provide one) presents an art medium, a board whose surface holds a painting with two dominant tones, raspberry and gold. Although the adjective translated as "pure gold" more often means "dark red," a subsequent allusion to yellow supports the translator's choice. This allusion comes as part of a catalog of the motifs of the painting, which occupies the next seven lines. Two somewhat more concrete images, "red coals" and "yellow resin" (in a more literal translation, "yellow mastic"), reinforce the initial color impressions. The yellow shade probably refers to the yellow paint so traditional for Russian exterior walls, while the "red coals" might refer either to outdoor fires, to the glow of sunlight on red tin roofs, or to the light issuing from the windows of the houses.

The next four lines are a warning to the reader, which simultaneously raises and rejects a comparison between this provincial Russian landscape and a Flemish genre scene in the manner of Pieter Bruegel's skaters. In the final four lines, the reader is further told to "cut off" the poet's "drawing," as he now calls his picture in verse. The English preserves the ambiguous meaning of the requested action: The Russian verb has the primary meaning of "to separate," but also has the idiomatic sense of "to cut off someone's speech rudely." This ambiguity is echoed in a closing simile, likening the poet's picture to a maple bough consigned to the fire. Thus, the poet's direct address to the reader may express his own will, or it may imply his gloomy prediction of how a hostile reader will react to the poem.

Forms and Devices

"On a Board of Raspberry and Pure Gold" is a highly metaphoric poem, using juxtaposition for the purpose of giving presence to what is not there in the physical scene. The first such metaphor is the scene as painting, the two-dimensional board onto whose surface the city is transposed. Next, there is a submerged but nevertheless demonstrable metaphor, picturing the cluster of houses as a horse-drawn caravan advancing to the river shore. In another animal metaphor, the children skating and sledding become a flock of cawing birds. Finally, there are the poem as drawing and the comparison to a maple branch.

On another plane of juxtaposition, Voronezh is being implicitly likened to the Low Countries (the setting of Bruegel's landscape). Mandelstam makes this association, however, by a means that closely resembles what folklorists call negative comparison (when one is told, for example, that Vseslav the Magician, a personage in the Russian national epic, does *not* take on the form of a gray wolf, one immediately visualizes him as a shape-shifter who becomes a wolf at will). Thus, negative comparison is a technique of simultaneous denial and assertion. Once they are invoked, the Bruegelian overtones of the Voronezh scene or the (absent) children absorbed in their winter games become quite vivid.

In the Russian, the sense of the poem is reinforced by a range of versification techniques, several of which find counterparts in the Brown-Merwin translation. The original consists of two sentences of eight lines apiece. The translators preserve the first, but break up the second into three shorter sentences, each set off as a stanza, apparently to set off the logical movement and to let the variety of sentence structures substitute for the variety of rhythmic structures within a strict, binary meter in the Russian.

In the first sentence, Mandelstam uses rhythmic effects, in conjunction with rhyme and sound play, to suggest the action implied by the idea rendered as "sleigh-tracked" in the English. The entire eight lines are bound by an identical feminine rhyme, with the final unstressed vowel preceded by two n's in a row. In five of the first eight lines, the final stressed syllable is preceded by a three-syllable, unstressed interval. This lets the verse line mimic the effect of a steep, slow climb up the hill, a moment's pause at the top—which Mandelstam would emphasize by pronouncing each *n* in the rhyme separately—and the rapid onset of the descent, signaled by the single, unstressed syllable at the end of the line.

The English, while it does preserve several *n* sounds, gets a similar effect by purely syntactic means. The first seven lines, all of which belong to the grammatical subject, never allow intonational or cognitive closure. We travel uphill until we finally arrive at the rapid cadence of the predicate ("was carried away") in the eighth line—a predicate that also suggests the appropriate semantic overtones of the children's sleds rushing down the hill.

Themes and Meanings

"On a Board of Raspberry and Pure Gold" is both the opening poem in the "Third Voronezh Notebook" and the last in the long series of meditations on the Voronezh landscape that are scattered through the first two "Voronezh Notebooks." Mandelstam considered the notebooks as the three divisions of a single book—"Natasha's Book," as the Mandelstams called it, since the poems were arranged in sequence and written out in the notebooks for Natasha Shtempel', into whose safekeeping they were put. In this lyric diary, one of the unifying themes is the poet's changing relationship to his place of exile.

Selected Poems contains a good sampling of these lyrics. Some poems treat only the despair of exile; in "Let Me Go, Release Me, Voronezh," for example, the poet creates his own etymology for the place-name, breaking it down into *voron*, "raven," the bird of evil omen, and *nozh*, "knife." More often, however, he finds positive inspiration in the fecund black earth of the region, the broad plains and wide vistas emblematic of the potential spiritual freedom Mandelstam found so lacking in Moscow.

The poetry of exile is an important mode in Russia, whose poet-exiles see their archetype in the Latin poet Ovid, banished to what is now southern Russia. One of the commonplaces of this tradition has the poet looking back from the barbarian fringes upon the metropolitan culture. In several poems written before "On a Board of Raspberry and Pure Gold," Mandelstam wills to see the Voronezh landscape within the framework of his broader cultural loyalties. The April sky, for example, becomes the region's Michelangelo; its hills and dales are said to be worthy of van Ruisdael.

At a reading in 1937, Mandelstam responded to a provocateur by redefining Acmeism—the current to which he had given his allegiance as a young poet—as a yearning for world culture. This anecdote points out the dilemma to which he is responding in "On a Board of Raspberry and Pure Gold." There are two dimensions to the problem: Must one turn one's back on a more universal cultural legacy in order to come to terms with Voronezh, that is, with perhaps the least worst chance for survival for a poet in disgrace with the regime? Even more generally, do art (here, painting and drawing) and life have any guidance to offer each other, or is art completely sundered from life, like the drawing/branch at the end of the poem? On the surface, Mandelstam's poem answers these questions in the negative, but all its energies are bent on performing the truth of the affirmative.

Charles Isenberg

ON A VIEW OF PASADENA FROM THE HILLS

Author: Yvor Winters (1900-1968)
Type of poem: Lyric
First published: 1931, in *The Journey*

The Poem

"On a View of Pasadena from the Hills" is made up of seven stanzas of varying length written in heroic couplets (units of two lines of rhymed iambic pentameter that are self-contained in meaning and terminate in a full stop). The physical setting is the home of the poet's father, a man in late middle age. The speaker may be identified as a version of the poet, a man in his early thirties. As the poem begins, the poet notes the subtlety of the transition from night to day at dawn: "No light appears, though dark has mostly gone." There are no sharp distinctions between one stage and the other, yet there are boundaries and divisions. The garden is arranged in terraces supported by concrete. The poet's mind shifts to the past as he notices what is not there. The palms of his childhood have disappeared, and this observation gives rise to a vivid memory of walking in this area before the changes. However, images of "powdered ash, the sift of age" suggest that impermanence and mortality had their place in the design of things even then.

In the fifth stanza, the place is specifically identified and the poet's father is situated in that place, his home, his "phantasy of Paradise." He is also situated in time. He is approaching the last stages of a life that has included some success but has been ultimately unfulfilling, each "step . . . gained" matched by a "loss of heart," at least in the eyes of his grown son. The poet's father is also situated within his generation, his friends who "With tired ironic faces wait for death." Even at home, the father is held within limits: He is "Forbidden . . . to climb." For his part, the poet holds himself, at least to some extent, apart from the scene, knowing as he does that he will never live here. This is his father's home, not his.

In the sixth stanza, Pasadena, the California city named in the title, finally appears. Or does it? It is concealed by mist. Yet the poet senses its presence at dawn on the edge of sleep—that is, on the edge of waking. The poet also notes in the neighboring hills the evidence of the automobile culture that for some passes for progress and others revile as decline. Of such issues he has nothing to say. The poem ends neither in celebration of progress nor in nostalgia for an irretrievable past; rather, the closing lines include the marks of modernity in the larger setting, as much natural as it is anything else. The poet sees not a war between nature and civilization but a whole containing both.

The reader senses the poet's willingness to be poised on the edge between sleep and waking, night and day, past and present, nature and civilization, father and son, and life and death. His position allows him to hold these opposites in a delicate balance, acknowledging both difference and continuity. He feels no need to move to a higher level where all opposites can be reconciled and the many can finally be perceived as one. In both his poetry and his criticism, Yvor Winters has turned away from the Romantic tradition in poetry. In the resolution of this poem, he rejects a strategy of transcendence characteristic of that tradition.

Forms and Devices

The heroic couplet, the verse form adopted by Winters for "On a View of Pasadena from the Hills," dominated English poetry in the late seventeenth and eighteenth centuries, the period often referred to as the neoclassical age in English literature. It largely fell out of favor in the course of the nineteenth century, although it was still occasionally and effectively employed. By the 1930's, when Winters wrote this poem, the form had been largely abandoned as tied inextricably to the ideologies of earlier eras. Thus Winters went against the grain of contemporary poetic practice, a move he was never unwilling to make. In its days of dominance, the heroic couplet was often put to satirical or didactic use by poets such as John Dryden and Alexander Pope, its most revered masters. Winters's application of the form, however, is more reminiscent of the practice of George Crabbe, who emphasized the form's descriptive and expository possibilities. Robert Bridges, one of the few poets of the nineteenth century who excelled in couplets and a poet Winters greatly admired, may also have served as a model.

One of the attractions the heroic couplet may have for a poet is the discipline it imposes on the expression of feeling. Another is the possibility it affords for subtlety. Because the rules are so rigorous, the slightest variation can assume expressive power. For Winters, the poet must match emotion precisely to motive, to the event or occasion that gives rise to the emotion. Rhythm is an essential component of that precision, and working with and against the restraints imposed by the couplet's conventions can create the finest of rhythmic nuances. To take just one example, note the force in the first stanza of one of the poet's few deviations from the practice of ending each couplet with a full stop: "The hills/ Lie naked but not light. The darkness spills/ Down the remoter gulleys." Rhythm and darkness spill together. Furthermore, as Winters knew from the examples provided by poets who had gone before him, the closed couplet allows a cadence not dissimilar to that of the speaking voice while at the same time imposing the formality of artifice. In turning to what others might have regarded as an obsolete form, Winters escaped the vernacular of a particular time and place without abandoning the sense of actual speech.

Of the many critical utterances of Winters, perhaps none has been quoted more often, whether in agreement or disagreement, than his observation that a poem is a statement about a human experience. His adversaries have zeroed in especially on the word "statement," suggesting that it is scarcely adequate to the intensity and variety of poetry. It should be noted, therefore, that "On a View of Pasadena from the Hills," while it contains statements, is in no sense the poetry of statement. Rather, it resolutely evades any final summarizing statement, finding its resolution in a rich and ultimately ambiguous image.

Themes and Meanings

In acknowledging the artifice of terraces as "bastions of our pastorals," Winters affirms a tension. In one sense, the pastoral is readily associated with the natural, and bastions, the work of human hands, are restraints. To a certain kind of Romantic temperament, the imposition of restraints on nature is unnatural, and "unnatural" is the strongest possible term of condemnation. For Winters's classical temperament, no such issue arises. The cultivation of nature, inevitably involving some measure of restraint, is simply one of the things that human beings do. The gardener arranges the garden in terraces supported by concrete, and the poet organizes the stuff of human emotion into the twenty syllables, regular stresses, and recurrent rhymes of the couplet. Moreover, in these activities poet and gardener imitate a quality of nature that Romantic temperaments sometimes overlook: the regularity suggested in the "metronomic" pulsing of fish's mouths. This, says the poet, uttering what may be his strongest term of approbation, is "true."

Winters, then, refuses to perceive life in the sentimental terms of a corrupt Romanticism. If what lies before the poet is not a vernal wood but a mowed lawn, the poet's work is to observe that lawn so closely that he finds the life in it as Winters does here. "On a View of Pasadena from the Hills" implies a deep recognition and acceptance of limits as a part of life. The ultimately defining limit is death, awaited by the poet's father and his friends and, after all, by the rest of humanity as well. This implies that even the closest human relationships, between parent and child for example, do not and should not exclude boundaries. Winters is exquisitely aware that he shares with his father all that belongs to the human condition, but he recognizes as well that he is not his father. In the light of that knowledge, he views his father's circumstances with a sympathy that is not less honest or authentic because it is disillusioned.

As for Pasadena, the poet finally does not view it because it is concealed by mist. Yet it is nonetheless there, and a view of Pasadena concealed remains at some level a view of Pasadena. This is, the reader may feel, very much a poem about boundaries, limits, the edge, and the place between. It is not, however, a poem about uncertainty. To recognize the individual reality of whatever is on either side of the boundary is not, for this poet, to surrender to relativism. If this poem is listened to properly, it is possible to hear in it the affirmation of a man so little a slave to fashion that he was proud, in the middle of the twentieth century, to declare himself an absolutist.

W. P. Kenney

ON ALL THAT GLIDES IN THE AIR

Author: Lars Gustafsson (1936-   )
Type of poem: Lyric
First published: 1984, as "Om allt som ännu svävar," in *Fåglarna, och andra dikter*;
English translation collected in *The Stillness of the World Before Bach*, 1988

The Poem

"On All That Glides in the Air" is a short lyric poem of forty-two lines divided into three unequal stanzas originally written in Swedish. The title of the poem suggests a casual meditation on the joys of floating through the air. When a bird in flight appears to be resting, it is considered to be "gliding," an apparently effortless motion. However, a closer examination of the poem's three stanzas suggests that "gliding" has multiple meanings, many of which are not as benign as they appear on the surface.

The first line in the first stanza implies that the narrator is expecting to die soon because he says, "My grave is still nowhere to be seen." With no clear resting place, the narrator is forced to continue searching and gliding. He is joined in the latter activity by other beings: companion gliders, companions at rest, and even those who are already dead. The image is of a vast landscape in which all beings, both dead and alive, join together in one continuous motion. Although the speaker admits that there is no word to express the image that he sees in his mind's eye, he compares this gliding to the sailing of a balloonist through the sky in an "ocean of air." The speaker abruptly shifts to the second-person point of view in a warning to the reader: "this ocean of air is yourself." In one quick turn of phrase, the speaker moves from a dreamy, peaceful image of a hot air balloon floating through exterior space to a chilling reference to the loneliness of interior space.

In the second stanza, the narrator contemplates the precarious border between life and death as he recalls an early-morning experience in a diving pool. The view from the high dive is both exhilarating and terrifying. Looking at the deep, clear water gives the sensation of floating through the air, but there is also an awareness that an uncontrolled fall so far from the water would mean almost certain death. In this context, the speaker thinks of gliding as a multilayered experience whereby one falls and glides at the same time, the fall turning into a glide that is somehow aided by an unknown force. However, there is no assurance that the fall will be broken, so exhilaration becomes inseparably mixed with fear. The recollection of the view through the swimmer's goggles reminds the speaker of another way of seeing, the way that observers see a two-dimensional Renaissance canvas. Because of the technique of linear perspective, the canvas appears to create a three-dimensional world. Not surprisingly, it is the depiction of birds in flight that most interests the speaker. He says that the birds come alive precisely because they are placed in a kind of in-between state, "between earth and air, between light and shade,/ between water and land." The birds, looking "like reckless punctuation marks," are not unlike human beings struggling to discover their interior existence that they can never see or completely understand.

In the last stanza, the narrator continues contrasting images of positive and negative with "signs" gliding over "white pages" and "rooks" (black birds of prey) gliding over "snow." However, at issue is more than just a comparison of good and evil. The narrator returns to the landscape image where "everything" is both gliding and standing "as the angels stand/ in an unthinkable motion," just as the world itself, although it appears to be immobile, is actually in continual rotation.

Forms and Devices

In "On All That Glides in the Air," Lars Gustafsson's most obvious technique is the repetition of words and phrases. For example, the word "glide" is used six times, "glides" is used twice, and "gliding" is used four times. Another repetition is the phrase "ocean of air," which is used three times. These are important images that lead to the poem's central concept. Another device is counterpoint, which, in music, refers to the combination of two or more independent melodies into a single harmonic texture. Gustafsson uses words and word variations to create a kind of rhythm. For example, "swimming becomes gliding" and "living with all that lives" are variations of sound that contribute to the poem's central paradox that humans are all parts of one whole. Another poetic technique is the use of simile, which the speaker uses to compare his movement through the air to the motion of a hot air balloon through the sky. In still another image, Gustafsson likens the apparent flight of birds in a Renaissance painting to "reckless punctuation marks." Finally, the motion of all humanity is compared to the nameless "flight of the world."

What makes the poem intriguing and gives it tension is the use of irony or the contrast between expectation and fulfillment. The first stanza begins with a familiar description—the soaring motion of birds as they move through the sky—and ends with a suggestion that the great expanse is actually interior rather than exterior. In the second stanza, the narrator suggests that the *trompe l'oeil* (trick of the eye) that painters use to create linear perspective is also a trick that humans use to fool themselves about the true nature of existence. The third stanza, which begins with yet another gliding image, ends with a haunting pun on "flight" to suggest that the world both glides and escapes humans in the same motion.

Themes and Meanings

"On All That Glides in the Air" is a poem in the Romantic tradition that considers the immediate, emotional impact of an experience to be closer to a real understanding of truth than the logical, reasoned reaction to the same experience. For a Romantic writer, the images of floating, gliding, and soaring represent a release from the natural, pragmatic world and are therefore closer to nature, to God, or to previously unknowable truths. The Romantic sensibility is further reinforced by Gustafsson's reference to the super-analytical Renaissance painters' re-creation of the visual world not as a work of beauty but as a "childish trick." However, "All That Glides in the Air" is far from a Romantic poem because the predominant images are not positive and optimistic but neutral and unsettling, particularly at the end of stanzas 1 and 2 where the physical freedom of open spaces turns inward to subjugate the human psyche.

In the passage comparing swimming and gliding, the feeling of uncertainty is reinforced by the recognition of the close relationship between life and death. One false step on the diving board could cause a fatal fall, but even that free fall might change to a glide "by something invisible." The suggestion that free-falling and gliding are intertwined is strengthened by the image of the painted birds that are frozen in their landscapes between the juxtaposed "earth and air," "light and shade," and "water and land." Just as perspective in a painting is more than the technique of drawing straight-edge lines directly to a single vanishing point, the truth of existence is more than simply living and dying or motion and stasis. It is in the passage on art that the narrator shifts from the first person "I" to the more inclusive "we," which suggests that the contrasting experiences are universal; at the same time, however, it is up to all humans to discover "the interior/ of their own picture." Unfortunately, there are no clear rules or maps for such an exploration.

The most problematic passage occurs in the last stanza in which the narrator comments that "signs glide over the white pages." At first glance, the word "signs" appears to refer to symbols or letters on a piece of paper. However, "sign" can also mean "emblem," "mark," or "omen." The latter seems to fit best in the light of the next image in which birds of prey glide over white snow. Next, the birds of prey are juxtaposed with another type of flying being: angels. The paradoxical comment that all beings both glide and stand "as the angels stand/ in an unthinkable motion" suggests that all motion, like existence itself, is both contradictory and indescribable. There is "no name" for either mortal existence or for the existence of the world. Gustafsson, then, uses varied images of gliding to suggest the complex, paradoxical nature of existence not only for humankind but also for all living things.

Sandra Hanby Harris

ON BEING BROUGHT FROM AFRICA TO AMERICA

Author: Phillis Wheatley (1753?-1784)
Type of poem: Meditation
First published: 1773, in *Poems on Various Subjects, Religious and Moral*

The Poem

The four heroic couplets that constitute Phillis Wheatley's "On Being Brought from Africa to America" delve deeply into the psyche of the young African American slave narrator who attempts to come to terms with her being torn from her native African soil and being forcibly relocated to colonial America. The poem's original title, "Thoughts on being brought from Africa to America," when written in 1768, clearly indicates that the work was intended to represent the speaker's pondering her situation rather than serving as a mere statement, which is often misread for various reasons.

The first quatrain sets the tone for most readings of the poem by seeming to parallel spiritual and physical rescue. The speaker's "mercy" was the underlying factor that took her from her home, her "Pagan land," and brought her to a world centered upon "redemption [which she] neither fought nor knew." The result of her resettlement, the narrator says, was her becoming aware "That there's a God, that there's a *Saviour* too." This resulting understanding, no doubt, echoes the rationalization that many who brought slaves to the new world used to vindicate their actions.

The second and concluding quatrain moves Wheatley's meditation to a new realm, in which the narrator places herself and her race into context with the views of those who eventually enslaved them. Regardless of intention, the takers of slaves held the blacks in low esteem. To illustrate her point, Wheatley uses such terms as "our sable race," "diabolic die," and "black as Cain" as descriptors for those thrust into slavery. The perceptions depicted in the second quatrain seemingly intensify the significance of the situation presented in the first.

Taken together, these two quatrains set up a rhetorical paradigm by which many readers confront Wheatley and this poem and come away with the perception that Wheatley is writing a poem of gratitude, much in the vein of her many elegies that address important individuals who have passed from the scene but whose influence continues. In "On Being Brought from Africa to America," Wheatley mourns the passing of freedom in spite of the superficial thanks expressed by the narrator.

"On Being Brought from Africa to America," as well as the other works collected in *Poems on Various Subjects, Religious and Moral*, has brought Wheatley both admirers and detractors. For her work, Wheatley is now known as the first published African American writer. Because of the superficial complacency of the narrator's statements, many have criticized the poem for denying Wheatley's real situation and voicing the sentiments of her enslavers and for her not speaking out more clearly for her race.

Forms and Devices

Much of Wheatley's acclaim has come from her elegies that celebrated the lives of great men such as George Washington and the Reverend George Whitefield. However, many of her most complex and delving poems are her meditations, which investigate such abstract concepts as fancy and imagination. For what has become her most famous work, "On Being Brought from Africa to America," Wheatley chose to use the meditation as the form for her contemplation of her enslavement, because the narrator (Wheatley) meditates on the institution of slavery as it applies to her instead of making a more vocal condemnation or acceptance.

The first-person meditation makes the message of the poem more personal than if it had been presented in another pedantic pronouncement. "On Being Brought from Africa to America" is clearly an internal monologue through which the narrator bares her soul and voices her conclusion that even "*Negroes*, black as *Cain,*/ May be refin'd, and join th' angelic train" in spite of their captors' strong belief that the dark race is hopeless and greatly inferior.

Wheatley utilizes a white/dark contrast to demonstrate the narrator's movement from a life of misunderstanding and ignorance in a "*Pagan* land" to a life of deliverance and revelation in her new home. Up until the last line of the poem, Wheatley inserts such dark language as "benighted soul," "sable race," "diabolic die," and "black as Cain" to depict both her and her race's real and perceived place in the psychological world of their new homes. Although the last line contains no definite reference to light, Wheatley creates a light tone when she says, "refin'd, and join th' angelic train." Thus, the possibility of a darkened soul's moving into a spiritual light under the most adverse of conditions becomes evident.

Wheatley even utilizes semiotics, although the term may have been unknown to her, when she creates a title which illustrates the underlying concept of her poem. Wheatley draws attention to her being forced to leave her home instead of to her being taken to a better place by titling her poem "On Being Brought from Africa to America." By placing Africa first, Wheatley intimates that her past holds as much if not more importance than her future.

However, the strongest but often missed device to be found in "On Being Brought from Africa to America" is Wheatley's subtle irony which she presents through limited use of italicized words. This irony allows Wheatley to placate her white reading public by permitting them to hear what makes them feel good while, in fact, she is saying exactly how wrong her captors' perceptions are. For instance, her readers no doubt understood her reference to "my *Pagan* land" as a condemnation of the place from which they had freed her. Rather, when one accepts Wheatley's irony, "*Pagan* land" illuminates the concept that the most ungodly of actions came when the rescuers forced Wheatley and others into enslavement. This same ironic approach should be considered when pondering the word "*Saviour.*" Although one immediately thinks of a religious salvation, the italics draw attention to the specific word and to the distinct possibility that the speaker did not completely want to be saved from the life she knew.

It is in line seven, however, that the significance of italics becomes evident with the inclusion of the proper nouns "*Christians*," "*Negroes*," and "*Cain*." Again, a superficial reading of these words leads to the conclusion that the speaker is offering a statement of gratitude for having been delivered from her previously spiritually dark life. One must look closely at the pronouncement that "Remember, *Christians*, *Negroes*, black as *Cain,*/ May be refin'd, and join th' angelic train" and appreciate Wheatley's placement of her race on an even playing field with her captors through the possibility that the black race's shortcomings can be just as completely forgiven as those of the white race and that the white race is the one destroying its brothers as Cain did Abel.

The poem's two quatrains of heroic couplets serve the same artistic and philosophical purpose as do the octave and sestet of a traditional sonnet. The first section lays the foundation for the speaker's argument, while the second section presents the speaker's conclusion or resolution. For instance, in the first quatrain, the narrator tells, in a relatively positive voice, of her removal from a world of darkness into one of light. The second quatrain then provides a sounding board for the narrator's more complex conclusion, that blacks as well as whites, the enslaved as well as the enslavers, have the same potential for salvation and becoming a member of the "angelic train," thus negating the egocentric attitude of whites. This message is often misread by careless readers.

Themes and Meanings

In her meditation, Wheatley attempts to come to terms with artistic and personal abstractions such as what art is and when fancy becomes imagination. However, one of the most significant abstractions with which she contends is where the African American slave fits into the grand scheme of things. Much of her need to understand comes from the refusal of many in the white reading community to take her seriously as an artist because she was both black and a woman. In "To S. M.," Wheatley articulates the reality of blacks' ability to create art in spite of the whites' refusal to accept this "inferior" group of people as able to create anything of significance or be anything more than second-class individuals at best.

The conflict between racial reality and perception is most vividly and artistically presented in Wheatley's "On Being Brought from Africa to America" when she uses such poetic devices as irony, italics, and first-person narration to express her unwillingness to be cast into a second-fiddle role. In order to magnify the discrepancy between the whites' perception of blacks and the reality of the situation, Wheatley guardedly speaks of the good the whites have done in bringing blacks into the Christian world. It is not until the second half of the poem, however, that Wheatley brings into play an understanding that runs counter to the careless reader's impressions. In the concluding four lines of the poem, Wheatley argues that blacks and whites are made from the same spiritual cloth and that both can "be refin'd, and join th' angelic train" of salvation.

In most meditations, poets move from the physical to the metaphysical or to a philosophical or spiritual foundation for existence. This is what Wheatley does in "On

Being Brought from Africa to America." First, she shows how life is perceived by white enslavers and many of the enslaved. Then she moves on to argue that in the final analysis both races have the same potential and are one in their relationship with the same supreme being who, as her subtext discloses, is color-blind when granting salvation.

Tom Frazier

ON FIRST LOOKING INTO CHAPMAN'S HOMER

Author: John Keats (1795-1821)
Type of poem: Sonnet
First published: 1816; collected in *Poems*, 1817

The Poem

"On First Looking into Chapman's Homer" is a sonnet describing the excitement experienced by the narrator upon reading a translation of Homer's *Iliad* (c. 800 B.C.E.) by the sixteenth century poet George Chapman. Though it is often unwise to equate the narrator of a poem with the author, in this instance it seems appropriate to assume that John Keats himself is speaking of his own sense of amazement and delight in discovering the joys of reading Homer in such a vibrant English rendition.

The focus throughout the poem is on the feelings engendered in a person when a discovery is made. The narrator expresses himself directly to the reader, attempting to find parallels to explain what it feels like to make a great discovery for oneself. To make that feeling clear, the narrator speaks of himself as a traveler who has set out to explore uncharted lands—at least, uncharted by him. He portrays himself as someone experienced in visiting exotic places ("realms of gold," in line 1) and as having seen "many goodly states and kingdoms" (line 2) among the "western islands" (line 3) that are inhabited by "bards" who pay homage to the god "Apollo" (line 4). The conscious reference to poets and to the Greek patron of poetry should suggest to readers that this is not a literal journey; instead, it is intended to represent the mental travel one undergoes when one enters the imaginative world of literature.

The narrator describes his journey around those imaginary islands, noting finally that, though he is quite a veteran of such traveling, he had never set foot on the land ruled by the revered Homer until introduced there by Chapman, who serves as a kind of herald into the epic bard's court. Through Chapman's introduction, the narrator is able to breathe in the "pure serene" (line 8)—literally, the stimulating quality of the air in that favored land, but metaphorically, the exhilarating atmosphere that Homer's poetry creates.

The results of the narrator's arrival in the land of Homer are almost overwhelming. He feels himself like a scientist who discovers a new planet or like an explorer setting foot in the new world of America and seeing the hitherto unknown sights there. He compares himself specifically to Hernando Cortés, the conqueror of Mexico: The experience of being enveloped in the land of Homer (the environment created by Homer within his epic poem) is much like that felt by Cortés and his men when they first saw the Pacific Ocean; it leaves the traveler speechless.

Forms and Devices

Keats uses the form of the Italian sonnet to express his joy at discovering the wonders of the Homeric epic as Chapman presented it in his seventeenth century English translation. Invented by the Italian poet Petrarch (1304-1374) and first made popular in English by the sixteenth century lyricists Sir Thomas Wyatt (1503-1542) and Henry Howard, Earl of Surrey (1517-1547), the Italian sonnet is divided into two parts: An eight-line quatrain usually sets forth a problem or a dilemma, and the six-line sestet offers some resolution. Keats follows this rhetorical pattern in "On First Looking into Chapman's Homer." Using the first eight lines to describe his experiences in reading poetry by comparing them to the wanderings of a traveler to many small islands, he then follows in the sestet with an analysis of the joy he felt in discovering Homer's poetry by comparing it to the feelings of elation a scientist or explorer might feel upon first encountering a strange phenomenon. Keats follows the strict rhyme scheme of the Italian sonnet, using only four rhymes for the entire poem: *abba, abba, cdcdcd*.

The dominant literary device in this poem is metaphor. Keats plays with the notion of comparison on many levels. The entire composition can be seen as an extended metaphor, in which the narrator—a reader of books—is compared to an explorer whose voyage is rewarded with a great discovery. Individual comparisons follow the lead of that general parallel. The experience of reading is described as traveling "in the realms of gold." Individual works are compared to "many western islands" which "bards in fealty to Apollo hold"—a suggestion that writers are like so many landholders who owe allegiance to a great lord (in this case, the Greek god who was the patron of the arts). Epic poetry, one form of the literary art, is described in terms of a great tract of land, "one wide expanse" (line 5), and the Greek poet Homer, whose two epics serve as models for subsequent works in the genre, is lord of that realm. Two specific comparisons are used to describe the reader's excitement at discovering Homer through Chapman's translation. First, the narrator compares himself to an astronomer ("some watcher of the skies," line 9) who notices a new planet through his telescope. Then he likens his excitement to that which must have been felt by the Europeans who traveled to the new world and first looked upon the Pacific Ocean (lines 11-14). In both cases, the poet wishes to evoke a feeling of awe at the discovery of such a magnificent natural phenomenon. Keats suggests that those same feelings are experienced by the reader who picks up a copy of Chapman's translation of Homer and begins to read.

Themes and Meanings

"On First Looking into Chapman's Homer" is intended primarily to give readers a sense of the excitement that comes from discovering for themselves the works of a great author. Concurrently—and this is a point not often stressed—Keats suggests that the delight in this discovery is often an experience dependent on circumstances beyond those over which the author himself or herself has had direct control; in this case, the narrator's experience comes from reading the Homeric epic in translation. It is important, then, to recall that it is "Chapman's Homer" that excites the narrator; the translator has had a major role in creating the experience by serving as a bridge in communicating the story through language the reader understands. The impact of the reading experience, which Keats describes metaphorically as "breath[ing] the pure serene" air in a beautiful land, comes not directly from Homer's Greek, but from Chapman's rendition of that Greek into polished English verse.

Keats wants readers to realize the impact that a great work of literature can have. There is a clear sense that the narrator has come to his reading of Homer with some anticipation—"Oft," he says, "had I been told" of the greatness of the Greek epic (line 5). Nevertheless, the experience itself far surpasses any second-hand account; hearing of something is no substitute for experiencing it oneself. The two examples in the poem's sestet are intended to convey the sense of wonderment that can come only from direct experience. Keats wants readers to understand that reading great literature can bring the same kind of excitement to them that scientific discovery and travel can engender.

On a larger scale, the poem deals with the process of discovery itself, a human activity that has excited men since the dawn of recorded history (and before, no doubt). It is important to note that "On First Looking into Chapman's Homer" is about the process of discovery that every individual goes through when having any kind of experience for the first time—no matter how many people have had the experience before. This distinction is important, for it explains what many critics have considered the great "mistake" in the final lines of the poem: the apparent misidentification of Cortés as the first European to "discover" the Pacific Ocean. Because historians usually attribute the "discovery" of the Pacific to Vasco Núñez de Balboa, some scholars have accused Keats of not knowing his history. That may be true, but it would have no bearing on the meaning of this poem. There is no suggestion in the poem that Cortés or his men (both mentioned in lines 11-12) are the first to see the Pacific; rather, the implication is that they are viewing it for the first time in their lives. Similarly, Keats is suggesting, the reader who comes upon great works of literature for the first time will experience a sense of awe and wonder at the power of literature to excite them and to make a difference in their lives.

Laurence W. Mazzeno

ON HIS MISTRESS

Author: John Donne (1572-1631)
Type of poem: Elegy
First published: 1635, in *Poems, by J. D.: With Elegies on the Authors Death*

The Poem

"On His Mistress" (sometimes called simply Elegy 18) is an elegy of fifty-six lines in twenty-eight rhyming couplets. The poem's title discloses its contemplative nature, a characteristic mandated by the elegiac form. The poem is written in the first person; this highlights the personal nature of the poem, conceived by a man before he departs on a long journey to the European continent. He seems to lament leaving his love behind as he meditates on their relationship, yet the poem's intent is ultimately ambiguous.

"On His Mistress" takes as its point of departure a stressing of the seeming futility of the lovers' efforts to stay together. The narrator discloses his love's intended scheme—she would like to dress like a man and accompany him on his journey to the Continent. Surprisingly, given the poem's elegiac form and its elevated rhetoric, the narrator chides this notion; she would be easily identified because "Richly clothed apes, are called apes" (line 31). This does not seem to be the tone a lover normally adopts when writing about and to his beloved. When the narrator adds to this notion by turning to the vulgarities of the peoples of other nations, the poem shifts in tone. Gone is the elevated rhetoric of lovers; instead, the narrator and the poem adopt an aura of superiority and absurdity: The men of France are diseased, the Italians are bisexual, and the Dutch are slovenly drunks. These clichés are meant to rationalize the narrator's reasons for dissuading his love from joining him, yet they are also serious insults aimed at those from the Continent.

By the poem's conclusion, the narrator has shifted back to the sentimental mode more typical of the elegiac genre. He instructs his beloved to remember him during his absence, but this conventional plea is then usurped by the poem's strange final lines. The narrator asks his mistress to dream happiness for him (nowhere is it mentioned that she should dream happily of the two as a couple). This demonstrates the connection between lovers even while they are separated by hundreds of miles, yet it also shows the self-centered nature of the narrator. Perhaps this could be justified by the notion that their love has been a covert affair, an idea forwarded by his hope that she will tell nobody of their feelings; however, this does not excuse the apparent one-sidedness of his plea.

The poem concludes with further irony: The narrator pleads that his mistress not have any nightmares or fear for his safety. While it is human nature to comfort one's love before departing on a long journey, the "comforting" done here is presented with an odd twist. The very mention of the possibility that he may be slain, presented in the graphic terms of line 54 ("Assailed, fight, taken, stabbed, bleed, fall, and die"), can only reinforce the fears of his lover. This expression of peril is compounded in its written form, for speech may be forgotten, while written words may be forever preserved. Thus, the attempt to calm and reassure has become, instead, a seed of doubt, a worry that could grow every day while he is gone.

Forms and Devices

"On His Mistress" is an elegy, a poem which sets forth the poet's contemplations. Elegies are usually about death, but they may be concerned with another solemn or elevated theme, such as love. The elegy form, dating back to classical literature, originally signified almost any type of serious meditation by the narrator and his concerns with love, death, hostilities, or even the presentation of information. In the Renaissance, Elizabethans such as John Donne used the form for love poems; they often were composed as complaints. While the classical authors composed their works in a distinct pattern called the "elegiac stanza," the Elizabethans strayed from this rigid technique.

Donne also varies from the traditional Elizabethan structure and subject matter in his "On His Mistress"; the elegy begins typically as the narrator laments impending departure, yet this lamentation comes in ironic terms: The lovers' meeting was a "strange and fatal interview." This introduces the first idea that this will be a non-standard love poem, a point stressed by the narrator's description of the covert nature of the lovers' affair. These lovers have obviously run the gamut of emotions during their relationship in their attempts to keep their affair secret. Yet the narrator relies upon his "masculine pervasive force" (line 4) to take the matter of their departure into account. Therefore, it is not surprising that he "calmly begs" (line 7), since the manly aspect of the elegy has already been established.

Donne also relies upon the use of anaphora to distinguish the three distinct stages of Elegy 18. The repetition of "by" in the first part of the poem serves as a precursor to the inevitable departure of the two lovers, as it hints at the lovers saying good-bye. The narrator explains or rationalizes the lovers' stormy history: They met, desired, hoped, and regretted their love. This caused the pain from which the narrator is now purposefully departing. The tone then changes as the poem shifts from a revelation of their love to the external problems of their affair. Her father certainly would not approve of their relationship, so they must keep it secret. Now they must part; only they know the truth of their affair. The language in this section is powerful and elevated; their covert affair was obviously a strain on both of them. His departure will both add to this problem and reduce it; the two will not have to worry about being detected while he is away.

The second section of the poem moves to the narrator's rationale for leaving her behind—because of the vulgarities that she would face—and examines the impractical notion that she dress as a man and accompany him on the trip. The nationalistic digression disrupts the tone of the first section and lowers it; the poem's final section will again move to a loftier level.

In the final section, Donne returns to anaphora to push a point forward. The repetition of "nor" overburdens the love images suggested by the conclusion with a negative tone. By suggesting that she should dream about him (not "us") and his happiness, he has broken the union they had created. He then asks her not to worry that he be cursed and not to have a nightmare that he has been injured or killed; all this does is plant images in her mind which will cause worry after he is gone.

Themes and Meanings

While Donne's "On His Mistress" is seemingly straightforward in its meanings, there are several aspects of Donne's life that may provide more background and add to the understanding of the poem. The elegiac conventions, here somewhat altered, are usually used as a form to express the poet's love. This is accomplished in "On His Mistress" in a backhanded way. Further, the poem contains a distinct nationalistic attack on the Continent on the part of the narrator.

Donne, while in the employ of Sir Thomas Egerton, the Lord Keeper of the Great Seal, became enamored of Egerton's young niece, Ann More. In 1601, Donne and More were secretly married, much to the dismay of Egerton, who had Donne dismissed from his estate and briefly imprisoned. For the next fourteen years, Donne was somewhat blacklisted and had a terrible time finding permanent employment. He ended up living off the good graces of his friends and patrons. This incident suggests the possibility that when Donne writes of covert affairs and their implications, he does so from experience. It may also help explain the manly tone and attitude that becomes a major theme in "On His Mistress."

The poem also is notable for its prominent disconcerting attacks on other nationalities, attacks which show the increased nationalism among Englishmen in the wake of the English defeat of the Spanish Armada in 1588. Donne himself sailed with the Earl of Essex in 1596 to sack the Spanish coastal city of Cadiz; he also accompanied Sir Walter Raleigh in 1597 on an expedition to hunt Spanish treasure ships off the Azores. Given the success of these ventures, it is evident that Donne is again speaking from personal experience as he degrades the men of continental Europe; his manliness, in a sense, has been earned.

What is surprising, however, is the seemingly indignant nature with which the narrator seems to treat his beloved. He comments on the difficult nature of their relationship, scoffs at her proposal to join him on the journey, and then plants seeds of fear in her concerning his departure and the potential perils that await him. This may be explained, at least partly, by remembering the audience to which Donne directed many of his poems. He would commonly write them to be shared with his friends in the inns and alehouses of England; the men would share camaraderie while reading one another's literary works. It is not too farfetched to suggest that this may be the reason for both the nationalism and the ironic degradation of his mistress that occur in Elegy 18. Part of the enjoyment of gathering to read one another's works, or to hear them read aloud, may simply have involved the reiteration of the writers' and listeners' masculinity.

R. T. Lambdin

ON INHABITING AN ORANGE

Author: Josephine Miles (1911-1985)
Type of poem: Meditation
First published: 1935; collected in *Lines at Intersection*, 1939

The Poem

"On Inhabiting an Orange" is a short, low-key poem about the discrepancy between hopes and actuality. It briefly, dryly, and precisely notes that travelers never arrive anywhere near their exalted destinations but rather follow the route defined by the shape of the globe on which they walk. Like other poems in Josephine Miles's first major collection, *Lines at Intersection*, "On Inhabiting an Orange" makes use of geometrical imagery. In this poem, Miles makes an extended metaphor of a geometrical puzzle. Miles's early work is preoccupied with shapes and figures and sometimes plays with multiple meanings of geometrical terms. This approach led some of her early critics to criticize her work for lack of passion; because the emotion in a Miles poem is never on the surface, they claim that her poetry is more interesting than moving. However, this philosophical poem does have feeling that is not expressed directly but is carefully confined within the imagery.

"On Inhabiting an Orange" takes as its basis the paradox that one cannot walk straight (in a theoretical sense) upon a sphere. The curved surface of the earth disrupts the projected straight line, drawing the walker's path toward its origin. Because the earth is a sphere, humans "inhabit an orange." At first glance, the title might suggest living within a sphere, but this is not what is intended. The earth dwellers live on the surface of the orange, forced by its shape to travel paths unimagined by the walker. The poem speaks in the first person plural, using a casual editorial "we" that includes the whole human race: "All our roads go nowhere." Because humans are on the surface of the sphere, their roads do not, in fact, go anywhere beyond that surface—maps are "curled" like a piece of paper around an orange to make the streets conform to the curved surface. The demands of this geography make all trips intended to go somewhere simply fall back against the roundness. Instead of the "metric advance" people intend and expect from forward motion, their footsteps "lapse into arcs." The circumstances of gravity and geography prevent advance. Journeys forward toward space cannot be undertaken—the physical conditions simply prohibit their progress: "All our journeys nearing Space/ Skirt it with care,/ Shying at the distances/ Present in air."

Travelers intend to follow the imaginary lines their minds envision, and they thus set forth "blithely" with the goal of some kind of exalted arrival; they do not learn from their experiences. Although they are "travel-stained and worn," they remain "Erect and sure," their attitudes untouched by the reality they experience. They do not ever realize that they cannot follow their hearts out into the distances and that they are constantly forced to make "down the roads of Earth/ Endless detour." That the lines in their heads do not correspond with their footpaths does not faze or discourage them.

The contrast between ideal and real, straight and curved, what is expected and what happens, creates the central irony of the poem.

Forms and Devices

"On Inhabiting an Orange" is a seventeen-line poem with an idiosyncratic form: The second and fourth lines of the first three four-line stanzas are rhymed, while the last stanza has five lines and rhymes *abccb*. The first and third lines of each stanza are longer, while the second and last lines of each, the rhyming lines, contain only two stressed syllables. There are many trochaic feet (single syllables followed by un-stressed syllables); this falling rhythm seems particularly appropriate to the content. The last stanza contains the extra longer line but otherwise follows the pattern.

This is a straightforward poem consisting of an extended metaphor announced in the title and developed throughout the poem. It is similar to the Metaphysical poetry of John Donne, George Herbert, and others in the use of the extended metaphor or conceit, although Miles's conceits are much simpler. Miles, who was greatly influ-enced by the poetry of Donne, liked her poetry to have the fine-tuned precision that the Metaphysical poets found in the detailed comparison of apparently dissimilar ob-jects and thoughts. Indeed, the comparison in "On Inhabiting an Orange" recalls the drawing compass image that concludes Donne's "A Valediction Forbidding Mourning," in which the central pole of the woman's love perfects the path of the speaker, who is joined to her as the two halves of the compass are joined. However, the circle of the in-habitants of the orange is not a happy circle; their deflection from their hoped path is made by circumstance, not love. Even the bumpy figure of the orange contrasts with Donne's perfect circle.

The rhythms tend to suggest falling short of high hopes or noble goals. The lines tend to curve back like the footsteps of the frustrated travelers who really wish to leave where they are and arrive somewhere else but cannot because their roads go "no-where." The short lines seem to fall short, to be pulled back from a high enterprise. The additional line in the last stanza adds a meditative tone and adds to the sense of closure ironically provided by the final deliberately inconclusive image of "endless detour." Though some critics scoff at the notion of imitative form, the poem may be seen to reflect the progress of someone attempting to travel in a straight line, con-stantly pulled by gravity away from this goal.

Themes and Meanings

"On Inhabiting an Orange" is a playfully ironic poem. It uses common terms and concepts of geometry in an attempt to describe human disappointment in its failure to attain goals. While this poem is not very passionate in tone, it does neatly describe the irony of the human failure to recognize limitations (in the metaphor, the inability of straight walkers to see the curves that control their direction and prevent them from making any real progress). Thus the walkers always have high hopes, and, even though they should know better, their minds follow the stars while their feet follow the curve of the earth. The attitude expressed in the poem is of resignation and regret. The realization that the environment is not made for human aspirations has been treated by many other writers and poets. One of the most vocal of these was Stephen Crane, whose poetry and prose on the subject ("The Open Boat" and "A man said to the universe") is widely known, but Miles's attitude is less bitter. She presents the problem as universal. The failure of the world to conform to human desires is simply accepted as how things are.

The poem also invites the reader to play with its meanings and explore its implications. To be earthbound means to always walk in circles, to make endless detours away from a goal that is not earthbound. The figure of Donne and his ideal circle lurks in the background, providing a subtle, ironic contrast to the tired and unproductive circles walked in this poem. Other geometrical issues arise: What happens to parallel lines if they are traced on a sphere? What is the poem's concept of dimensionality? What is angularity if there are no straight lines? What is the true difference between the two-dimensional map and the three-dimensional world?

The image of the earth as an orange is also provocative. An orange is a fruit meant to be eaten, its peel discarded. Is the outside shape of the orange the only factor to be considered in this metaphor? Besides being perishable, the orange is an imperfect sphere, and it sometimes has shades and shadows on its skin that resemble those on a globe. Is this relevant? The simplicity of the poem invites examination of its terms. The pleasure of this poem is in how it engages the reader. The easily grasped and appropriate geometric metaphor attracts the reader's attention, and then the delight of the intellectual game takes over as the reader attempts to push the comparison into other areas besides those specifically noted. The spareness of the poem contributes to its effect as a puzzle designed to entertain as well as present a well-known perspective on the human situation. In "On Inhabiting an Orange," Miles provides an extended metaphor not unlike those of the Metaphysical poets but without the difficulty of Donne and the others and with more room for individual interpretation and intellectual play.

Janet McCann

ON LOOKING INTO SYLVIA PLATH'S COPY OF GOETHE'S *FAUST*

Author: Diane Ackerman (1948-   )
Type of poem: Elegy
First published: 1985; collected in *Jaguar of Sweet Laughter: New and Selected Poems*, 1991

The Poem

"On Looking into Sylvia Plath's Copy of Goethe's *Faust*" is a short poem in free verse with one stanza of nineteen lines and a second stanza with fourteen lines. The title of the poem makes two allusions that are expanded and explored throughout the rest of the poem. In the title, Diane Ackerman refers to Sylvia Plath, the promising young American poet who committed suicide in 1963 at age thirty. She also refers to Johann Wolfgang von Goethe's play *Faust: Eine Tragödie* (1808; *The Tragedy of Faust*, 1823).

The first stanza is a direct address by the poet to Plath: "You underlined the jugglery of flame'/ with ink sinewy and black as an ocelot." Ackerman identifies Plath with Faust, a medieval alchemist whose story has been retold most notably by the English playwright Christopher Marlowe and later by Goethe. Faust's tragic flaw was his insatiable desire to know the unmediated truth of the universe. Like Faust, Plath explored the natural world for authentic experience. In the first stanza, Ackerman portrays Plath as "keen for Faust's appetite, not Helen's beauty." Plath looked to the natural world for answers, dissecting each part of life with words. Ackerman details Plath's transformation into "the doll of insight . . ./ to whom nearly all lady poets write." According to Ackerman, Plath was alternately angry and wistful. Within the characterization of Plath, however, are chilling references to her own self-destructiveness: "You wanted to unlock the weather system/ in your cells, and one day you did."

The second stanza shifts focus to the speaker. Whereas the first stanza has four lines beginning with the word "you," the second stanza has three lines beginning with the word "I." In shifting the focus, Ackerman connects herself to Plath as naturalist and poet. Ackerman, whose writings include several long prose works on natural science, seems to identify with Plath's "nomad curiosity." What Ackerman admires most about Plath is not her pain but her ability to see and report on the world with "cautionless ease." In line 25, Ackerman reveals her mistaken thoughts about Plath: She had thought that Plath had come to terms with her existence. Line 31, however, returns to Faustian imagery in order to correct Ackerman's mistaken assumptions: "But you were your own demonology,/ balancing terror's knife on one finger,/ until you numbed, and the edge fell free."

Forms and Devices

An elegy is a meditation, often one that mourns the death of another individual. Although Ackerman does not follow the rules of meter and rhyme common to classic elegy, she does employ a number of devices to give her poem a decidedly elegiac tone. Through the use of apostrophe, Ackerman turns away from her audience and addresses the dead poet directly, speaking to her as "you." She uses images from the natural world to draw her picture of Plath: The ink Plath uses to underline the text is "sinewy and black as an ocelot," and her cells contain "a weather system." Furthermore, Ackerman describes the pleasures Plath took in life, including collecting bees, cooking, and dressing simply. She also identifies Plath's talents and her tragic flaws. Finally, Ackerman reveals that she does not mourn Plath for the pain she "wore as a shroud" but for her "keen naturalist's eye." It is Plath's talent as a poet, not her tragic life, that ranks highest in Ackerman's estimation, a stance that differentiates Ackerman from other "lady poets."

Another device that Ackerman uses effectively in this poem is the pairing of oppositions; by doing so, she emphasizes the paradoxes of Plath's life and helps explain Plath's inevitable suicide. For example, early in the poem she opposes "Faust's appetite" and "Helen's beauty," suggesting the mind/body split with which Plath struggled. Immediately after describing Plath as "armed and dangerous," she describes her as "the doll of insight." Dolls are without passion and without power; they are the creation of someone else and are certainly not armed and dangerous. In addition, Ackerman uses the strange image of "a morbid Santa Claus who could die on cue." It would seem that the gift Plath gives to "lady poets" is her death; that is, it is her suicide, not her poetry, that offers inspiration to would-be poets. In the second stanza, Ackerman continues the use of oppositions. In lines 23 and 24, Ackerman opposes mind and body by portraying Plath's mind as something like a knife sliding "into the soft flesh of an idea." Finally, Ackerman opposes "a hot image" with "cool words." This opposition is at the heart of Ackerman's notion of poetics: Authentic experience must be rendered intelligible to a reader through words.

Themes and Meanings

"On Looking Into Sylvia Plath's Copy of Goethe's *Faust*" is more than an elegy for Plath. It is also an exploration of two poets, Plath and Ackerman, and their notions of poetry. Through the use of allusion, Ackerman expands and widens the scope of her poem; however, in order for readers to understand the poem, they must know something about Plath's life, work, and death, and about Goethe's *The Tragedy of Faust*. Plath, a graduate of Smith College in Massachusetts, had her first poem published when she was a child. After that, she wrote hundreds of poems. She married the English poet Ted Hughes and the couple had two children. In the semiautobiographical novel *The Bell Jar* (1963), she chronicles her own struggle with depression and attempted suicide. On February 11, 1963, alone and ill in a London flat, her marriage in ruins, Plath killed herself by sticking her head into the oven and turning on the gas.

The recognition of Plath's talent as a poet has grown in the years since her death, and Ackerman's careful characterization of Plath reveals close attention to her poetry. For example, Ackerman writes that Plath "undressed the flesh/ in word mirrors." This line alludes to the poem "Mirror," in which Plath, speaking as the mirror, writes, "A woman bends over me/ Searching my reaches for what she really is." This line suggests that words can somehow mirror reality in such a way that a reader can find truth in poetry. Likewise, Ackerman writes that Plath "wanted/ to be a word on the lips of the abyss," a reference to the creation story according to the Gospel of John: "In the beginning was the Word." This reference speaks the belief that words can create worlds *ex nihilo* just as God created the world out of the abyss.

In the most important allusion in the poem, Ackerman links Plath with *The Tragedy of Faust*, a play about a medieval scholar who makes a pact with the devil in order to obtain knowledge, wealth, and power. Faust's deal requires Mephistopheles to give him whatever he wants of earthly pleasures, but Faust will forfeit his life and soul if he ever stops striving to experience more, if he ever becomes satisfied with what he has. In the poem, "Faust's appetite" refers to his longing to know the world directly, something Ackerman also attributes to Plath.

It would be a mistake, however, to suggest that this poem is only about Plath. Ackerman is known for her intense curiosity and her sensory appetite. She longs to explore the natural world and lay its secrets bare. Consequently, some of the same images and allusions she associates with Plath appear in other poems Ackerman has written. For example, the ocelot image from line 2 surfaces in another poem from *Jaguar of Sweet Laughter:* In "Dinner at the Waldorf," Ackerman writes, "Unleash me and I am an ocelot/ all appetite and fur." Even more telling, Ackerman's earlier collection of poems is called *Lady Faustus* (1983). In the title poem she writes, "I rage to know/ what beings like me, stymied by death/ and leached by wonder, hug those campfires night allows,/ aching to know the fate of us all." This is the theme of much of her work: the desire to know the natural world directly and to learn the truth of existence. Thus when Ackerman writes that she thought Plath had "found serenity in the plunge/ of a hot image into cool words" and that she thought that Plath had taken "the pledge/ that sunlight makes to living things," it seems likely that she is writing to herself, for this certainly describes how Ackerman has come to terms with her overwhelming desire to know. For Ackerman, the tragedy of Plath's life is not her suicide but rather her numbness, her growing inability to experience life's terror and joy.

Diane Andrews Henningfeld

ON MR. MILTON'S "PARADISE LOST"

Author: Andrew Marvell (1621-1678)
Type of poem: Lyric
First published: 1674, in the second edition of *Paradise Lost*

The Poem

Andrew Marvell's poem chronicles his reactions to the artistic merit of John Milton's *Paradise Lost* (1667) in seven verse paragraphs of fifty-four rhymed iambic pentameter lines. The opening sentence forms a grammatical unit of ten lines. The remaining lines, marked with a grammatical pause at the end of each couplet, follow the poetic practice of end-stopped couplets.

Initially, Marvell contrasts Milton's "slender Book" with its "vast Design," its Christian topic of salvation history and its cosmic scope of infinite time and space. He fears that Milton will mar or disfigure "sacred Truths" by expressing them through, or by confining them within, the devices of an epic poem, a pagan or nonbiblical art form. Also, Marvell deals bluntly with Milton's blindness, mentioning it in the first line as well as in lines 9-10 and lines 43-44. Milton had become blind at least fourteen years prior to the first publication of *Paradise Lost* in 1667. Marvell assumes that Milton's blindness may have had something to do with his choice of a biblical "Argument" or subject. Tentatively, he questions Milton's "Intent," comparing Milton's motives in writing the poem to those of the biblical Samson, who sought "to revenge his sight."

As Marvell then begins to reflect upon his experience of reading, he grows "less severe." He favors the poet's "Project," but he fears that Milton will not succeed, given the inherent difficulty of the subject matter. Milton's poem concerns truths beyond physical nature and beyond human comprehension. He might, for example, leave his readers "perplex'd" with matters of thought and faith, doctrines involving paradoxes and simplicities. In addition, Marvell associates Milton's epic with the contemporary literary scene. He imagines that someone less skillful will imitate Milton's poem by writing a play based upon it. He seems to refer to John Dryden, who had recently written a dramatic version of *Paradise Lost* in rhymed verse entitled *The State of Innocence, and Fall of Man* (1677).

In his next paragraph, Marvell unexpectedly addresses Milton directly, speaking with deep respect and sympathy. He now realizes that a view of the poem as a whole demonstrates its artistic perfection. Consequently, he apologizes to Milton for his "causeless" doubts or speculations. He believes that Milton's artistic achievement is so great that other writers will have to work within the frame of reference Milton has laid down, even though *Paradise Lost* will demonstrate "their Ignorance or Theft." Also, Marvell praises the "Majesty" of Milton's poem, which "Draws the Devout, deterring the Profane." He believes that Milton's handling of religious truths within the medium of a pagan epic leaves those truths as well as Milton himself "inviolate."

Moreover, Milton's sustained elevation of style and his ability to handle large and fearsome truths leave his readers awed and delighted because he sings "with so much gravity and ease."

Marvell specifically commends Milton's powers of mind and determination. Earlier in the poem, he had called Milton "blind, yet bold," as well as "strong." Blindness had not diminished Milton's poetic ambition, daring, or capability. In the sixth paragraph, Marvell asserts that "Heav'n" must have offset Milton's loss of physical sight with the power of prophecy. In the last paragraph, Marvell defends Milton's decision to reject rhyme at a time when the popular taste called for it. Other poets, such as Marvell himself, have used rhyme as ornament or fashion. Rhyme, however, seems trivial next to the unrhymed grandeur of *Paradise Lost*. Milton's blank verse is as sublime as his theme; it does not need the support of rhyme.

Forms and Devices

As Marvell recounts the way *Paradise Lost* unfolded itself to him, his thoughts evolve dramatically from doubt to resolution. He begins by addressing readers and ends by addressing Milton himself. Although a personal friend of Milton and a professional colleague in the Cromwellian government, Marvell takes a detached, agile, skeptical, and reflective stance toward Milton's poem. As a critic seeking to illuminate Milton's epic for himself and for other readers, he maintains his integrity and a sense of perspective. He reads the poem carefully, assimilates the overall meaning, and describes, analyzes, and evaluates both substance and style. He candidly expresses his fears regarding the main features of *Paradise Lost* and Milton's own motivation in writing it.

In addition, Marvell maintains his independence as a poet. For example, he knows that Milton virtually created a new poetic medium of narrative blank verse and acknowledges its superiority to rhyme. Nevertheless, he does not abandon rhyme in praising Milton's unrhymed verse. Instead, with gentle irony, he asks Milton to overlook his rhyme. Once he has grasped the poem as a whole, Marvell realizes that his doubts, though well intended, are "causeless." He does not, however, explain the exact reasons for his change of mind. He conveys his conclusions through assertion and through a change of attitude or tone. He demonstrates the assurance that grows out of wide literary knowledge and a principled, independent stance. His praise of Milton communicates itself as accurate and sincere, rendered by someone qualified to give it.

Marvell uses blind heroic figures of the past to convey his transition from doubt to certainty. For example, when Marvell compares Milton's poetic strength to Samson's physical strength, he suggests that Milton might have misused his abilities, perhaps to bring down and not build up the "sacred Truths" of Christianity. Marvell's mention of Samson is of biographical, political, and literary significance. Milton had published *Samson Agonistes* in 1671. In this lyrical drama, Milton's Samson becomes a heroic deliverer who brings God great glory. Marvell's reference to Samson may not be entirely negative. In lines 44 and 45, Marvell follows Milton's own comparison of himself to Tiresias in *Paradise Lost*. Tiresias, a blind man from Greek mythology, was rewarded with prophecy. Marvell suggests that Milton is similar to Samson but is perhaps more similar to Tiresias (even though Tiresias was not a biblical figure) because he exemplifies heroic achievement in the service of heaven. *Paradise Lost* results from divine influence working through an extraordinary individual. Marvell has no doubts about the purity of Milton's motives or his intent.

Themes and Meanings

Marvell's poem concerns fundamental questions of whether or not Milton can artistically combine the "sacred Truths" of Christianity with the devices of a pagan epic. Marvell recognizes Milton's imaginative, intellectual, and moral challenges, which stagger the mind. For example, as with all his major poems, Milton's epic is a form of biblical explanation. It involves *"Messiah* Crown'd, God's Reconcil'd Decree,/ Rebelling Angels, the Forbidden Tree." Milton cannot redefine biblical meanings, put strains upon the text of scripture, or inject personal, unwarranted, or offensive elements. He must impress Christian beliefs into the mind and memory of his readers without violating the letter or spirit of scripture. Faith, however, guides the apprehension of religious truths. Marvell fears that a presentation of Christian mysteries in poetic terms may confuse matters of thought and faith or that the attempt to do so may be vain. In addition, the restrictions of the ancient epic form might lower "sacred Truths" to the level of a "Fable and an old Song," an amusement or curiosity in which the moral content is not well integrated into the work itself. Furthermore, Milton outdoes all previous epic poets in the cosmic setting of his poem. The poem develops against a background of "Heav'n, Hell, Earth, Chaos, All"—all the regions and all the time known to human imagination and experience as well as regions and time beyond human conceptual range. Milton must describe both natural and supernatural environments and the characters who inhabit them or who are shaped by them. Marvell has good reason to question Milton's intent; too many factors must combine to make the poem successful. Milton could easily lose artistic control of his material.

Nevertheless, after considering the imaginative challenges Milton faced and his response to them, Marvell fully approves of Milton's artistry: "Thou hast not miss'd one thought that could be fit,/ And all that was improper dost omit." The "Majesty" that reigns through Milton's poem indicates that Milton had maintained the decorum required by his subject matter and the epic genre. Marvell wonders how Milton could have stretched his mind sufficiently to express truths and situations beyond direct human experience. He uses the word "sublime" to describe the elevated nature of Milton's poem and its grand subject matter, a term critics have associated with it ever since. Marvell's poem is one of the first responses to *Paradise Lost* and one of the first critical recognitions of an individual English literary work.

Timothy C. Miller

ON MY FIRST SON

Author: Ben Jonson (1573-1637)
Type of poem: Elegy
First published: 1616, in *Epigrams*

The Poem

Written around 1603, Ben Jonson's deceptively plain elegy, "On My First Son," consists of one twelve-line stanza of iambic pentameter rhyming couplets. Taking the form of a "classical" *consolatio* expressing the Christian-Platonic-Stoic reasons to celebrate the child's release from the pains of human life, the poem poignantly stages the tension between the "poet's" wish for this intellectual consolation and his emotional expressions of paternal grief. By seeking reasons for the death of his "loved boy," the father reveals his own religious doubts, which test and contradict both the Christian teachings of acceptance and the literary decorum of the elegiac form.

The "poet" ends by incorporating into the poem a formal epitaph, narrated by the boy himself, which punningly equates the boy with the father's other "creative" work, his poetry. However, rather than finding closure, the poet's final moral lesson or "turn" masterfully expresses the complexity of his response and the painful coexistence of bitterness alongside Christian wisdom.

The opening line's apostrophe to the dead son ironically both acknowledges his passing while calling him back into existence for this final paternal address, a circular structure completed by the boy's speaking his own epitaph at the poem's end. The remainder of the first quatrain then contains the father's attempted explanation for the boy's early death and his assumption of blame (Jonson was absent when his son died of the plague), believing perhaps that, rather than loving the son in the present according to the teachings of Saint Augustine and others, he instead invested too much in "hope of thee" for the future. The commonplace theological imagery of monetarism, in which the child is lent by a "just" God and must be paid back on the "just day," is combined with the Christian doctrine of children being born innocent and gaining sin through bodily existence as they "age," another traditional elegiac trope that is expanded in the next quatrain.

However, the second quatrain begins with an emotional outburst, in which the opaque syntax reveals the tension between control and grief. To "lose all father" could mean either to "lose" or relinquish willingly all feelings of fatherhood and thus freely give up the child, but it could also mean that the "poet" might unleash or "loose" (Jonson's original spelling) the manly control of being the adult and instead become an emotional child by expressing his wild grief. Such connotations show the poet's ambivalence, and his emotional subtext also disrupts the verse form, displacing the caesura and providing the first dramatically enjambed line in the poem.

After this outburst, though, the rhetorical questions of the second quatrain argue for acceptance of death, and the final quatrain begins with an easeful transliteration of the

Latin epitaphs *Requiescat in pace* and *hic iacet*. This apparent acceptance introduces both the poet's punning tribute to his son, "his best piece of poetry," in which he equates procreation with poetic creation, and a moral lesson, which counsels the reader (and the poet) not to invest emotionally in these worldly possessions, and which is translated from the Roman poet Martial, Jonson's chief model in his *Epigrams*.

Yet even in this closure the linguistic instability of the "quibbles" or puns may not only highlight Jonson's distinction between paternal "love" and the nonmaterial, Christian "like" in the final line, but also undermine the consolation that the poem offers as a whole. Through the "natural" pun of the shared name, Jonson the poet apparently buries not only his son in the grave but also himself, as well as his future hopes for his other "creations"—his poems, such as this one.

Forms and Devices

Jonson's neoclassical aesthetic is possibly shown at its height in his varied *Epigrams*, which he terms "the ripest of my studies" in his dedication to the Earl of Pembroke. The poems' range of subject, feeling, and style displays Jonson's skilled imitation and adaptation both of the Roman poets, notably Martial and Horace, and of classical Augustan ideals of balance, stoic self-sufficiency, urbanity, and, most crucial, decorum. Stylistically, these ideals translate into a mastery of versification and an economy of expression, which became known as the English "manly" or "plain" style. Each poem must be an organic unity, with form carefully integrating with meaning. In terms of his epigrams, Jonson's neoclassicism appears in his witty conciseness, his subtle use of irony and implication, and his occasionally elliptical density.

These qualities are readily apparent in this elegy in both the sincere, conversational mode produced by the precisely selected iambic couplets (typical of classical epigrams and the Horatian style—the classical elegy's alternating lines of hexameter and pentameter are here anglicized into the indented second pentameter lines) and in the intricate multilingual puns and allusions, which belie the surface simplicity. The first line offers examples of both these devices in Jonson's appositive construction "child of my right hand," which quibbles on his son's name. "Benjamin" means "fortunate" or "dexterous" in Hebrew. Through a trilingual pun on the Latin "dexter," meaning "right," Jonson simultaneously displays his learning and explores the connotations of the phrase, both as the English idiom "right-hand man," suggesting comfort and support, and as the biblical son sitting "on the right hand" in heaven. Furthermore, the nostalgic addition "and joy" offers an ironic subtextual biblical allusion to Rachel's name for her son Benjamin, which was Ben-oni, or "child of sorrow."

A similarly dense etymological pun appears in line 10 in "poetry," which depends upon the classical Greek derivation of *poet* meaning "creator" or "maker," the latter also being the Middle English term for poet. Jonson is "maker" both of poetry and of his son, both children "of my right hand." Buried within this wordplay is also the pervasive early modern pun on the word "pen" as "penis," which further aligns Jonson's different creations. His somewhat surprising humor here seems to express the beginnings of stoic acceptance in the face of death.

This semantic play, produced by puns, classical allusions, and occasionally elliptical syntax, threads throughout the poem, disrupting the surface calmness and the closure that the couplet form seems to suggest and conventional Christian doctrine advises. Instead, the multiple significations and allusive meanings stage, and parallel, the thematic struggle between the "poet's" feelings of grief and the wish for consolation or emotional balance.

Themes and Meanings

Jonson's brief but touching poem not only offers clear examples of his classical learning and his decorous mastery of form and emotion but also, when placed within the context of the *Epigrams* collection and Jonson's other poetry, reveals the poet's preoccupation with themes of identity, particularly his own self-fashioned identity as a public poet who must both represent and personify certain classical ideals of ethical behavior, ideals signaled in the poetry's style and structure and described by Jonson in his prose works, notably *Timber* (1641). In addition, the moral importance of poetry, and the role of the poet himself as a secular priest that Jonson constructs throughout his writing, further underline here the father's great tribute to his son as "his best piece of poetry."

This elegy was published by Jonson next to a contrasting epigram about poor fatherhood, so Jonson seems here to be placing or staging himself as a model parent, who acknowledges his real feelings but balances them with stoic resilience and tough humor. However, this emphasis on control also betrays the need for such control. Jonson's son was "seven years" old, a very important liminal point not only in the development of the boy's own identity but also in his relationship with his father in a society based on laws of paternal authority and primogeniture. In early modern child development it was at this age that boys were "breeched," differentiated from female children in dress for the first time by wearing breeches. Furthermore, the responsibility for their formal education would now transfer from the female household to the male. This symbolic transition may help to explain both the elegy's delicate tonal modulation and Jonson's apparent guilt and obsession with fatherhood, since he seems so concerned with confirming his relationship with his son that the mother is totally elided from the poem, which is not the case in his comparable epigram "On My First Daughter."

Perhaps the most important of the Augustan social and ethical ideals is the one sought for here by the poet-father, which is the notion of "balance," of the controlled fusion of form and meaning, of sense and emotion, of passion and equanimity, in order to create the *integer vitae*, the whole life of moral integrity that is necessary for "the good poet" who must also be a "good man." Jonson's elegy seems to be almost an exercise in this practical and aesthetic principle in the face of personal loss, the measured couplets balancing the complex disruptive allusions and emotions. Yet Jonson was fully aware of both the need to strive for this ideal and the impossibility of reaching it—his *impresa*, or personal emblem, was a broken compass. This poem apparently stages that never-ending human search for consolation and for completion, for what Jonson termed his "Center."

Nicolas Pullin